Lawrence Russell

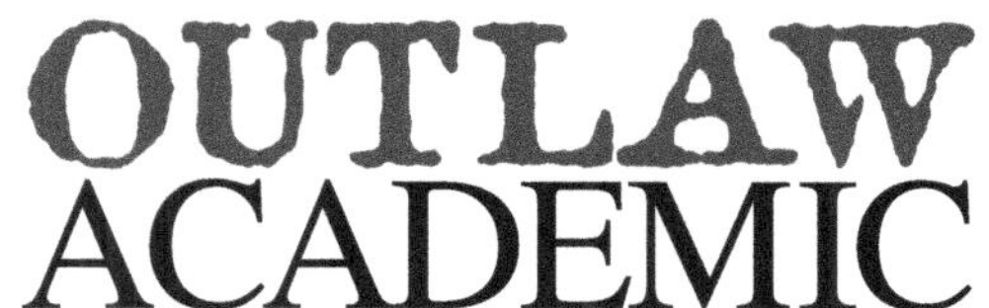

Selected Non-Fiction
Film • Literature • Music & Media

TERMINAL PRESS
TP

First Edition

ISBN: 978-0-9940982-4-5

Published By
The Terminal Press
135 MacPherson Avenue
Toronto, ON
M5R 1W9
Canada

Visit us: www.facebook.com/theterminalpress

Back Cover photo by Diana Russell

Contents

Section I: Film

Section II: Literature

Section III: Music & Media

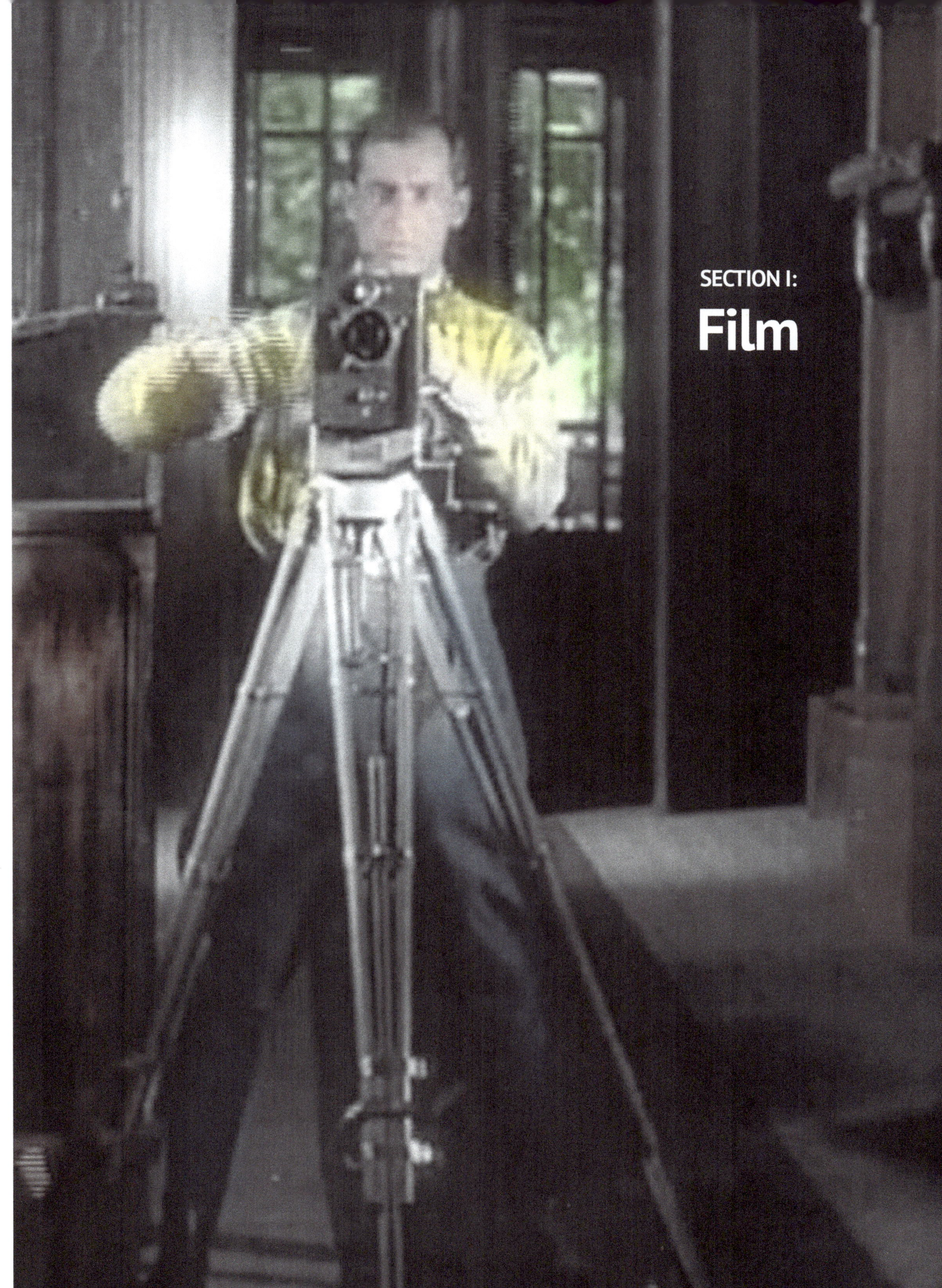

SECTION I:

Film

PART ONE:

The Movies And Me

First movie I saw, I didn't see. It was during the Second World War and I went to the theatre with my parents, the balcony, really high up. Must have been three at the time, and grew very fearful when a man came out from behind the curtain and started speaking to the audience, probably an introduction. He was very small, way down there on the apron of the stage, like a doll, some miniature in a nightmare, and I was having plenty of nightmares in those days as we lived close to an aerodrome where my father was a test pilot and the fields were littered with crashed Lancasters and Spitfires and other aircraft gutted for parts. Sometimes there was a bombing raid, the Germans trying to take out the field... thunder and lightning my mother always said when a flash passed through the room and the bungalow shook from an explosion.

Later in life I learned there was a decoy runway on the beach beyond the dunes and they'd flash the lights just to confuse the enemy.

This little man on the stage, though, frightened me. It was the scale that unnerved me—he couldn't be real, he wasn't like anything I'd ever seen. When I cried out, he stopped speaking. My mother tried to calm me, but it was no good, I just continued to panic, emit anguished cries. So we had to leave.

Don't remember anything more about it, what was said or what the movie was. My parents separated soon after that, 1945 or 46... wonder if my fit had anything to do with it, don't know, never will, I guess.

The Village Hall

I was in love with the projector as much as I was with the picture it threw on the screen. Magic. The chatter of the film as it spooled through the gate, the sound of the cooling fan, the lamp, the smoky beam... magic.

A man would carry it into the village hall, open the box and set it up on a small table. The screen might be a sheet or a white wall or sometimes a proper portable screen. Three Stooges, short documentaries, and westerns. Horses and gunfights were everything, accept no substitutes. The Old West was a long way from Broughshane but somehow those grizzled men were us, men and boys alike. They spoke through their teeth, rode fast, had no fear even when they were doomed, cut down in a hail of bullets, or launched, rider and horse, over a cliff or got swept away, rider and horse, down some fast flooding river, they were doomed.

We all practiced dying, based on the movies, the more theatrical the better. We fell and twitched, perhaps uttered a scream or a curse, fell and rolled, staggered and fell, the spasm and the stillness, we fell.

So, when we engage with others, are we always acting? When I think back on it, growing up was just an apprenticeship in acting. Inspiration could come from many places, although film was stronger than religion. We didn't want sermons, we wanted action... the way film drama could engage fantasy and come back as reality was unbeatable. Defeat was just as sweet as victory, and there were no Sunday School taboos... or fewer, at least.

All you needed was some attitude and a weapon.

Rifles? Some of us had rifles. Anyone with a farm had one or two around, a shotgun certainly, maybe an old service revolver. Hunting rabbits and pigeons had nothing to do with it... or mad dogs, sheep worriers... or rats... nothing to do with it really although sometimes they got shot. It was the IRA—the Irish Republican Army—always active in our romantic imaginations, even if it was mostly in abeyance in the 1950s. You had to be ready. You just never knew when the "Fenians" would show up some night with a Thompson sub-machine gun and a couple of bombs, start some mischief.

Of course I never saw James Mason in *Odd Man Out* (1947) where he plays a wounded IRA man on the run in grimy old bombed-out Belfast, as such a sympathetic portrait of a "papish rebel" would not have gone down well here in Protestant Orangeman country, even if the village was in the shadow of Slemish, the mountain where the young Saint Patrick was a swineherd.

Yet I was in that film, even if I didn't know it. The drunken artist Lukey who takes the wounded Mason back to his garret, makes him sit while he paints the IRA fugitive's portrait as if he's Jesus Christ escaped from the Cross, although it was the Crown Bar he escaped, a famous ancient pub in old Belfast, it's still there, an Ulster Heritage site. I was like an apprentice Lukey, a sort of artist who came to love the bar, any bar, considered it a source of material, a place of pretences and no pretences, a place where life in the raw could be experienced for the price of one or two drinks.

Directed by Carol Reed, the English director with a chick's name, although no one thinks of it that way now, as people make up their own names, stylize their own spellings, demand exotic pronunciations. Great director, had that German shadow and light expressionism down, captured the grim post-war wreckage of the European trauma, as much a state-of-mind as it was topographical. *The Third Man* (1949), that's his, hits it best. The theme tune was a huge hit in Britain, the powerful zither of Anton Karas, although I thought it was Les Paul or somebody at the time, some gypsy on an electric guitar maybe.

Probably heard the radio play version first. The idea of Harry Lime (Orson Welles) living in a sewer was very attractive. Who knew? Who knew such things were possible?

But these clever movies were later.

When I was about ten, I got a small silver metal projector for Christmas, something I'd seen in the back pages of a *Boy's Adventure Magazine*, where they put the cheap ads (this is also where/how I acquired a Luger pellet pistol, although that's another story) and I'd circled it, sent it to my father who was still living near the aerodrome where he served in the War, said this is what I want. It projected 35 mm stills, so it was really a slide projector but I didn't care, as it came with some sci-fi strips, black and white, and I could project them on the white plaster wall of the shoe closet just off the kitchen. No windows, no light, just me and the spacemen on the moon or some planet, their cool rocket pointing at the stars.

Later I pointed the projector across the big back yard where we killed the pigs and serviced the farm equipment, shone it off the stone walls of the pig houses and the old horse harness room. I tried it out front on the trees as well, where the spacemen became huge and ghostly, part of a dreadful invading force.

And this wasn't all that fantastic, as I remember the night the German bombers passed over, in a low thundering roar, three or four, banking over the Braid Valley as they headed for Belfast to unload... or maybe Dublin, as they made a mistake once. Dublin was the only city between New York and Moscow to run its lights. Planes were always getting lost over Ireland, missing targets in England, Scotland and Wales... some crashed, and the crew would spend the rest of the war interned in the Republic. Germans, some Allied. I was maybe four, just old enough for the memory, experienced enough for the fear.

Maybe I dreamt some of this, stuff picked up from adult talk during and after, fragments destined for the movies of the mind. There were some Americans stationed in the forest near the house, a few Nissan huts in the beech tree plantation that covered parts of the estate, camouflage for the landed gentry once upon a time, camouflage for these Americans now. After D-Day they vanished, leaving nothing but the concrete pads the huts stood on and a few trenches scattered through the plantation.

The family estate, 200 acres, half mile driveway, and an old stone mansion with fifty rooms, half of which were sealed off, no longer needed, unsafe and creaking with ghosts. That's Ireland, always in the past, seldom in the future, a nightmare hammering at the door. When I was at Ballymena Technical, the teacher showed us David Lean's *Great Expectations*, as this was the novel we were studying in English, easier than reading it, although I read it, did o.k. on the exam. Black and white, Victorian Gothic, easily recognizable to me, the orphan Pip being raised by relatives, hanging out at Miss Haversham's rotting mansion with the candlelight and rats and the cruel, beautiful Estella as the only possible salvation. What a plot, what a story, what a novel, what a movie. Yes, easily recognizable to me, ditched to live with my grandmother at the family farm, a de facto orphan, the moan of the wind in the trees, the scream of the pigs as the axe fell. I knew these characters, these people, I knew this situation, trapped between the plebs and the gentry, the carriage and the grave. I knew these people... the brutish escaped convict Magwitch, ill fortune in the graveyard, good fortune in the gentleman's club, the irony of it, the ugly truth behind it all... I knew it, even knew Estella... that bourgeois ghost, a town girl, not a country girl, bourgeois and fragile, like the Presbyterian minister's daughter or the merchant's daughter, these girls in Rovers or riding Raleighs.

Ballymena

When I was still an adolescent, the movies were a place for hooliganism, a Saturday matinee in the "scratchies", the cheap seats down front below the screen, where we could jeer and catcall with no provocation at all in the darkness, eyes like feral cats. String of licorice hanging from the mouth as Mantovani's plush strings play *Charmaine* over the theatre system, chewing like animals as we wait for the curtains to open, thick whispers and crude repartee, bring on the Hopalong Cassidy or the Gene Autry... well, what's this? Someone has a catapult, might be me, fires a steel fence steeple as an Indian gallops across the screen.

The screen flinches, depresses, maybe a small tear develops. Does anyone notice? An usher shines her torch across the stalls, threatens someone at the end of the row. Further back a patron shouts in outrage—some inconsiderate in the balcony has tipped his ice cream over the balustrade, let it drop, bombs away.

They say live theatre shows in the Georgian and Victorian eras were just as bad, even worse. The Pit. Standing only, just like Shakespeare back in the day. Bad behaviour was a professional qualification. These days they talk about interactive media and all, but there's always been interactive theatre. The idea of alienation—the "glass" wall between the players and the audience—is an ideological thing, a pre-film style meant to create a state of awe between the subject and the object, like the silent protocol of art gallery contemplation. Institutional. Keep your trap shut or get thrown out.

There were two cinemas in Ballymena—the town where I was born—one near the railway station, The Tower, and the more glamorous State, closer to the centre. The State was modern, was what later became known as Art Deco, had a red neon sign and classy thick pattern carpet in the foyer. This is where I saw my first serious films... or should I say I first saw seriously. *The Sound Barrier* (1952), saw that there. David Lean directed it and the Ulster actor Joseph Tomelty was in it, small part... he was also in the IRA flick *Odd Man Out* and Huston's *Moby Dick*, small parts, but he was famous in Ulster as an actor and playwright, even wrote a couple of novels.

Once, when I was returning from England, I saw Tomelty on the airport bus that was transporting passengers from the plane into Belfast. He was sitting just across from me, two seats to himself, relaxed and very bohemian, long white hair, chatting with a couple of women who also recognized him. I thought, so that's Joseph Tomelty, I've heard him on the radio, sort of remember him from *Moby*, and they say he's a playwright. Never thought one day I'd be a playwright too, even though I was already writing short stories for my English teacher at the Tech, yet somehow the image of Tomelty remained in my head, the careless self-assuredness of the somewhat famous.

Read somewhere that Sting's first wife was Joseph's daughter, the actress Frances Tomelty. Seen her? She's done some TV drama, like *Midsomer Murders, Inspector Morse... Cracker,* the sort of stuff you see on Public Television in North America.

Some Movies

Brando, now there was an imprinting influence. Saw *On the Waterfront* (1954) at the State with my pal Natch, the guy who alerted me to Brando in the first place. New York, a miserable hole down by the docks, especially in black and white, yet not all that different from Belfast. And Brando, the mumbling hipster with the pigeons who let his hands do the talking, Brando, coulda been a contenda, great smile, the patsy who set Joey up for the knockoff, Brando, his hoodlum brother Rod Steiger gets bumped off and left to hang in an alley, dangling from a longshoreman's bale hook like a piece of meat in the butcher's,

Brando, man, he breaks down the door to get at the virginal blonde beauty Eva Marie Saint, Brando, so cool, so masculine, cannot be denied, the animal with a conscience, the animal who slugs it out with the corrupt union boss Lee J. Cobb, bells ringing in his head, punching it out down on the wharf as the longshoremen watch, the union hoods watch, the priest guy Karl Malden and maybe the babe, the desperate brutality of it... man, that's the movies! Bigger than life, bigger than live theatre, bigger than anything, no boundaries, as unpredictable as a REM dream on Midsummer's Eve.

When you're a teenager, you're looking for a way, a hero to show it, and some of these movie stars like Brando could show it. Saw *Moby Dick* at the State; Peck as Captain Ahab, shot off the west coast of Ireland, as we all knew, great to look at, but not somewhere we wanted to be. *Dick* was like something they'd show at school, serious stuff, but not hep.

Lust For Life, Kirk Douglas as Vincent van Gogh, the mad artist, now this was more like it, even if it wasn't set in the here and now. I was doing a bit of art myself at the Tech, wasn't bad at it, and was wondering just how mad you had to be to get good, maybe famous. Kirk was something. *Spartacus*—saw that. Kirk... clenched teeth, aggression pouring through the nose, the cheek bones, the eyes. He was another anti-hero, even when he was playing good guy hero. Kirk was dangerous, Brando definitely dangerous... Mitchum? Yeah, he was dangerous bad too. *Thunder Road* (1958), those Ulster hillbillies in Tennessee running the bootleg whiskey through the back road ambushes... living in the Braid Valley, Country Antrim, this was something you could understand.

Trapeze (1956)... Burt Lancaster, Gina Lollobrigida, Tony Curtis... outstanding then and still is today. *Night of the Hunter* (1955)... Mitchum as the 'ole Love-Hate' preacher, crazy as free market religion can be. They call it noir now but for me it was the switchblade popping through Mitchum's pants as he watches the burlesque dancer that made my eyes bug. Mitchum was so subversive, so anti-institutional, so bad, how could you take the old folks seriously anymore? While it was supposed to be fiction, this stuff just showed us life in the raw, the big world without the shepherds telling you where to lie down and close your eyes.

Hell Drivers (1957), with the great Stanley Baker as the desperado truck driver—he had the intensity and the anger, was bucking the system no matter what movie, what role. Welsh, like Burton, his pal. You might remember him from *The Guns of Navarone* (1961) or *Zulu* (1964) that he and Michael Caine made brilliant. He was also pretty good in *Robbery* (1967), which was based loosely on the infamous "Great Train Robbery", and got the director Peter Yates a Hollywood gig directing Steve McQueen in *Bullitt* the following year. Baker had the look, the voice, the urgency... and he was smart, as he produced many of his own films.

These films, these darkened theatres, were like Night School, where you got some advanced education outside the loop. Movies were off the book, another curriculum, like sleep immersion and dream therapy.

And the re-education just kept coming.

By the time I was 15 I was already hopping the train, going south to Belfast, walking up Royal Avenue, having a look around, checking the Opera House, maybe baby, see a flick or a show, maybe baby. Three things I remember watching there: a live Christmas pantomime, Bill Haley & the Comets, and the last movie I saw before leaving Ulster, *The Curse of Dracula*, with Peter Cushing. But Bill Haley was by far and away the most influential of the three.

In many areas, Belfast in the fifties was still a mess from the German bombing of WW 2, like other UK cities... and I saw lots of them, travelling back and forth through England by rail, the hypnotic clip of the carriage wheels on the tracks as we passed ruined buildings, piles of rubble, overgrown lots, craters, blackened walls and empty windows, staggered orphan chimney flues, and the endless litter of the welfare state on the polluted embankments, discarded cigarette packets, chocolate bar wrappers, newspapers, booze bottles, frenchies, sanitary napkins... bits of just about everything, so the mess was just as much an industrial stain as Blitz damage.

In Belfast, the walls of the wrecked buildings were vandalized with sectarian graffiti... No Pope Here, No Surrender, Remember 1690... Up the IRA, Provos etc... the Tricolor, the Union Jack, the odd swastika, Chad Wus Here, weird esoteric symbolisms and love notes, the usual guerrilla advertising... the Orangeman hero King Billy on his horse Stor... Victorian tenements, now slums... bitter little plebeian "hards" in sectarian gangs chucking bricks at the buses or bullying lone pedestrians... whole blocks of asbestos pre-fabs, fast solutions to the housing problem.

And of course the gantries of the shipyards looming above the slate roofs and warehouses of tough and rough East Belfast and, looking west, the Cave Hill, three caves, hard to get at, and Belfast Castle just below.

The resort area for Co. Antrim is a town on the north coast called Portrush, set on a promontory above the Atlantic, great air, great beach—if a bit risky for swimming—sandunes and a castle ruin. Not far from the Giant's Causeway. Full of hotels and guest houses and amusement arcades. Fun fun fun... almost as decadent as Las Vegas if you're a teenager. Shot my first pretend movie there in 1960 during a trip back home, pistol grip Yashica cine 8 bought in New York. Was in 'rush for a couple of days with some old pals who were at Queen's University, and they were happy to clown around for the camera. Amazing how exhibitionist people can get for a camera, so cleverly crude. Never developed the film, never used the camera after that. Lay around for years, still loaded, like a taboo memory... and then disappeared. Typical, eh... and these days I collect cameras and projectors as *objets d'art*. Who knows? One day I might come across that Yashica in the Sally Anne, still loaded, ready for blackmail. Well, if you don't have a fantasy life, you don't have a life.

Fantasy drives the future.

Dragon Rapide

My uncle dropped me off at the airport in Dublin and I flew over to Wales to see my father, whom I hadn't seen in years. Was fifteen, fresh into Elvis, and dressing like him, or as close to that style as I could. It was an interesting flight, as it was on an Aer Lingus De Havilland Dragon Rapide bi-plane, a twin engine beauty from the late 30's, streamlined like a stunt plane, eight passengers... flew low over the Irish Sea, then followed the Welsh coastline south, then east. Nice weather, great views and I remember banking towards the runway which came to the edge of a huge black cliff, the engines throttling back and us swooping in like a big gull for an easy landing.

My best flight? Probably. The Dragon belonged to the days when short distance flight was just as scenic and comfortable as taking the train, and when planes could still land in a farmer's field if they had to. Not sure where this airport was but it wasn't far from the location of my earliest memories, somewhere not far from Tenby. Cliffs, sea caves and sea arches, long sandy beaches and saw grass dunes, idyllic Bristol Channel setting, pirates Westward Ho!

I relate this because I saw a movie during this visit that I didn't give a damn about, although the theme stuck in my head: Charlie Chaplin's auteur production *Limelight* (1952) which was finally showing in town (1955) and my father and his crippled wife wanted to see it. What I didn't know was that Chaplin had been branded as a commie and refused re-entry into the US, much to the indignation of the British intelligentsia, left-leaning as it was in the post-war period. Would this knowledge have made any difference to me? Probably not. Clowns weren't my thing, Chaplin left me cold. There was an old world misery about *Limelight* that didn't appeal in the Age of the Actor's Studio and the existential hipster.

Well, we're all dumb some of the time, politics or not. I'm still not wild about Chaplin or Keaton or panto, but I now recognize that *Limelight* was/is an important movie... and not only just because of how it fits into Chaplin's personal life story. The whole business of the pantomime comes from the Italian "harliquinade" and the comedy routines introduced by this *Commedia dell'arte* improvisation genre. The most famous harlequin clown before Chaplin in British theatre was Joseph Grimaldi (1778-1837) whose career straddled the Georgian and Victorian periods, when live theatre went from candlelight to gaslight. Read Grimaldi's autobiography (edited by the novelist Charles Dickens) and you'll see some Thespian similarities to *Limelight*. Grimaldi experienced the vagaries of fame and fortune, saved an actress or two, had a prodigal son, became a has-been and tried to get it all back, kept failing and then, near the end, did, sort of.

You know Fellini liked it.

The Liner

To this day I remember this bloke, this old guy, even though I only spoke to him once or maybe twice when I was taking the view of the big Atlantic swells through the long promenade deck windows. A gimp, no more than five five and looked like Andy Capp, the wee man from the weekend UK newspaper comic strip. Glaswegian, had worked in the coal mines all his life, was wracked with arthritis. Showed me his right hand, which had a hole in the palm, and his fingers were bent back like a claw.

"When I wake up, me finger is in that hole," he said. "By lunchtime it might be straight enough to hold a fork. Aye, going down the mine did that to me. Forty years! Can you comprehend forty years, laddie?"

Of course I couldn't, nor did I want to. I could forget the days as fast as they arrived if they didn't suit my fantasy, and my days on this ocean liner were great, the food, the booze, the crazy women... the dancing, the ping pong, the swimming pool... and the pitching in the heavy seas never made me sick and I never fell to the floor during a big sideways roll. I had arrived at my destination. It was here, on this boat, it was here in the plush little movie theatre where I saw Hitchcock's *Vertigo*, new release, great color, powerful romance, Kim Novak, babe of blonde babes, and James Stewart as the traumatized detective, crazy with vertigo, crazy with love and a big enough sap that you felt you could push him aside, get Kim, as you felt no fear, no vertigo in the middle of the Atlantic.

This is how I arrived in Montreal in 1958, 17 years old, living in a complete fantasy. Everything was so big, so new, so like the movies, so free, so beautiful, so like the movies. Hey, I could act, be anyone I wanted. New life? Hey, that's what they advertised.

Took a taxi to Dorval Airport, was sitting in the back wearing my Elvis jacket, steel gray or blue, depending how the light hit it, with long lapels and patch pockets, some silver sparkle in the fabric, so hep, so rock & roll cool. It was dark, heading towards midnight, streetlights flickering past. Heard a roar to the right, looked out, saw a huge shadowy building.

"What's that?" I said.

The cabbie chuckled, said, "Zat? Zat is the hockey game, monsieur."

Ice hockey. Boots with skates. Hmm—real men play rugby, don't they?

When I landed in Calgary, there was a Chinook going on, so it was quite warm and there was next to no snow. Checked into the Palliser Hotel, then went to see a movie, *The River of No Return*, starring Marilyn Monroe and somebody else. Filmed near Jasper in the Rockies, very Canadian, but I wouldn't remember it if I'd seen it anywhere else. When I came out of the theatre, the temperature had dropped and it was snowing lightly. Went into a Men's shop, bought myself a fedora and a pair of gloves. Some men were still wearing fedoras in 1958, not many, some. I just wanted to get into the Hollywood spirit. I also bought one of those tartan lumberjack shirts, as that was what they were wearing in the *River of No Return*. Mitchum. He was in it, but y'know, it's not one of his best. A Western... somehow the Rockies aren't my idea of a Western.

I Married A Monster from Outer Space (1958) was the first flick I saw in Kitimat... well actually it was at the drive-in theatre in Terrace, 40 miles up the highway, where I went in my '48 Chevrolet Fleetline, a torpedo back two door I bought for a hundred bucks, put a fur muff on the steering wheel and sprayed the ceiling fabric red. You had to have wheels to get around in the wilderness... and I had a fedora, didn't I? Black, pure film noir before the term existed. *I Married a Monster* was something else, a B movie masterpiece of American Cold War paranoia and Freudian malfeasance. Thinking about it now, it has a plot similar to the later film *The Stepford Wives* (1979) in that the men are alien zombies and the Stepford women are pharmaceutical zombies. Both films are social gestalts of their respective eras. What was beautiful about *Monster* was that it was performed dead-pan, the characters right out of small town USA, groomed and dressed and driving cars such as I could see around me here in Kitimat. The alien invasion notion was popular discount paranoia then, and the commies could subvert a culture with the silent ease of a virus. The guy with the ducktail and the '57 Monarch with the hot blonde from the drugstore—who was he really? Commie or extra-terrestial?

There were a lot of movies about a nuclear apocalypse

coming out in those days—*The World, The Flesh & The Devil* (1959), *On The Beach* (1959)... couple of older ones, *Split Second* (1953), *Invasion U.S.A.* (1952), *Five* (1951]—but the counterpoint, the one that summed up the glittering optimism of the late fifties was Hitchcock's *North By Northwest* (1959), a spy thriller that showcased the North American landscape and techno affluence beautifully. Although I looked nothing like Cary Grant and thought he was too vanilla compared to the new boys like Brando and James Dean, his gallivant across the New World landscape in pursuit of Eva Marie Saint and the always villainously cool James Mason was H.I.T. (High Identification Targeting) all the way. Hadn't I just crossed the continent in a gleaming silver train, stayed in the best hotels, flirted with travelling beauties and carried on like a secret agent?

The romance of it all was incredible, and the use of American topographical wonders outstanding. Sure, Hitch used the plane attack before in *The 39 Steps*, and sure, he used the fight on the face of an American monument before in *Saboteur*... but I didn't know this then. The cornfield attack was seminal, the Mount Rushmore fight for survival seminal, the stuff of nightmares and pulp fiction. *North By Northwest* made you long for the smell, shape, and warmth of a beautiful woman... even if she was a double-agent and a heartbreak.

The femme fatale—O love me once, kill me later.

When I was living in Kitimat I had a dream, a strange meta-realist vision of deadly simplicity. A brilliant blue sky, and an unknown white swept-wing bomber approaching silently. I knew it was carrying a nuclear bomb and I knew escape was impossible. It was as if I was in the snowy mountains (as I was in a way)... was it heading south for continental America or was it going to unload here in the wilderness? I felt ill and powerless, as if chained.

The clarity of it was disturbing. Of course all the young people I knew and befriended here were carrying this trauma, were cynical almost beyond hope. Person after person I spoke with expected and accepted the inevitability of nuclear destruction. It had to happen. The bombers and missiles would be flying over the Canadian North, a lot of WW 3 would be fought over Canada. Kitimat was fairly isolated, almost like a United Nations lunar base or something experimental, a gulag for studying racism maybe. A "company town". Big Alcan aluminum mill, lots of "DPs" from the war, immigrants, hustlers, wild cat construction hombres... and the native Canadian-born who were forced into colonies at the Rod & Gun Club and the Firehall. The dream repeated. Then I met a girl and I was o.k. Told her about the dream... no big deal, she said. She had it too... now and then. Get used to it.

But here's the the thing—did I dream her too?

University & The Cuban Missile Crisis

When I was at university in Victoria, I saw a few movies, needless to say... although books went better with the monastic life and there were better movies in the bar. Still, there were some landmarks to be sneered at: *Lawrence of Arabia* (1962) which, as History was one of my majors, should've fitted nicely, but y'know, O'Toole wasn't my kind of guy... and then there was the first James Bond, *Dr. No* (1962) which was just flippin' ridiculous, how could any thinking fella take it seriously?

Yet it was influential, subversive even, perhaps the only antidote to the Cuban Missile Crisis. And I remember the Crisis, the collective fear that burned a hole in the mind like a solar flare. One day you're driving into the city, look towards Esquimalt Harbour, the Canadian navy ships are there; next day you're passing, and they're gone, all of them. Radio says "Hawaii", a friendly visit. At the campus parking lot you get out, hear jet engines in the sky, concealed in the overcast. TV is black and white, the picture curved at the corners. Most don't realize it, but Berlin is the checkmate.

Invasion or embargo? Embargo. Kennedy issues an ultimatum: the Soviet warships carrying the nuclear missiles into Cuba must turn back. They do.

It was like a long-growing fever that breaks. The Cold War was never the same thereafter.

Well, there was Kennedy's assassination a year later, and many people felt Castro and the Soviets were behind it. Oswald had emigrated to Russia for a while, had a Russian wife, didn't he? In a significant way, the Kennedy assassination in Dallas in late 1963 established the preeminence of television over cinema. We saw the President get shot, we saw Lee Harvey Oswald get shot, both in real time. We saw the infamous Zapruder 8 mm film replayed on TV, saw Zapruder interviewed on TV. Television was now the medium of real-time drama, where art and political semiotics merge, and big screen film now quarantined as dream therapy.

By the mid-sixties, I was moving away from film as a source of inspiration and aesthetic advice. Literature... books, where the movies were inside the head. In writing, there was the adage, the less you reveal, the more you see.

Inner Space

But there was one movie that both unsettled and inspired me: Sidney Lumet's *The Pawnbroker* (1964) about a Jewish concentration camp survivor played with maximum realism by Rod Steiger. Remembered Steiger from *On The Waterfront*, of course, and also *Across The Bridge* (1957) which was starting to show up on late night TV. *Bridge* was based on a novel by Graham Greene, and was clearly Steiger's apprenticeship for the more haunted persona he used in *Pawnbroker*. I was now paying attention to narrative, to how the story was told, and Lumet used some killer montage to reveal Sol Nazerman's—what a name—state of mind. First time I saw it, the black and white flashframe of the Nazi guard unnerved me, thought, am I hallucinating or is there something wrong with this movie... then gradually the flash inserts become longer... three, four, five frames or however many, until Nazerman's flashback memory reveals itself, delineating the horror of his past, the rape of his wife and the death of his children. Brilliant... and brilliantly acted by Rod Steiger, seemingly the unsympathetic and heartless money lender.

Deep stuff... the "heart of darkness" now in East Harlem.

It was/is a damning portrait of human behaviour, nothing false here. Yet there was no way you could use this subliminal flash narrative approach in fiction writing. It was something that only film could do, a stroboscopic awakening of the bicameral mind.

Late fifities, early sixties there was a bit of a renaissance in UK film, a generational thing, portraits of angry young men which started with Burton's Jimmy Porter in *Look Back In Anger*

(1958), extended through Laurence Harvey in *Room At The Top* and Albert Finney in *Saturday Night & Sunday Morning*. These stories started as literature, ended as anthems, revolts against the industrial and psychological wastelands created and perpetuated by Britain's elites. It was all part of the love-hate relationship with the class system, and right then the culture was in the hate mode. These characters, these young men, driven by hormones and bad attitude, were sick of being conscript patsies and hard labour mules, wanted degrees, good jobs, and runway models.

The revolt was picked up by rock and roll, where all the formal art channels were bypassed in a loud, spontaneous expression that spread globally like a virus and established a new idea of "cool" well beyond the classical channels controlled by church and state. You didn't need a degree, you didn't even need to know music anymore than you needed to know how to shoot to use a machine gun. This revolt went clear through the entire English-speaking world, and you saw it in all the arts, this exponential move from public service to the cult of "Me".

These "Angry" movies were all black and white—for the same reason Italian neo-realist movies were black and white—because monochrome was cheaper than color, and monochrome was considered "art" by the *cognizanti*. Even to this day, many photogs consider colour to be the medium of amateurs. Black and white was an urban medium, in many ways the best suited for expressing the polluted industrial light created by fossil fuel factories and over-crowded living spaces. Space was a mysterious thing, full of darkness and hidden atrocity. The sun was veiled, the public driven underground in an Orwellian group-think that suited the Masters. Lang had touched on this in *Metropolis*.

Seminal among these "kitchen sink" dramas was Tom Courtney in *The Loneliness of the Long Distance Runner* (1962) and Richard Harris in *This Sporting Life* (1963). I certainly could identify with both these films, especially *Sporting Life*, as I'd played a bit of rugby while at Ballymena Academy and was well acquainted with the brutish behaviour that went with this cult of masculinity. Harris was Irish and I looked a bit like him too, could pass for a Beatnik or a monk. Harris played Frank Machin, a beast of darkness from the deepest of coal mines in the industrial north. Who could forget his angry sexual hump of the coal seam with the big drill? I wrote later:

> 'The players scrum down in the mud, struggle like two giant crabs locked in combat. Scrum-half Machin sticks his head into the scrum, expecting to receive the ball, but gets an anonymous fist in the mouth, smashing his teeth. The nicotine crowd roars in hatred and satisfaction, a rough blend of opposing desires. Machin lies stunned and bleeding on the ground. The montage cuts to Machin drilling into a coal seam, his mouth rolling rapidly as he chews gum. He leans into the heavy drill like an animal in the throes of sexual congress. He's tough, he's confident, he's a man heading for the top, cutting through anyone and anything that stands in his way.'

Harris had established his creds playing Sebastion Dangerfield in the stage version of J.P. Donleavy's *The Ginger Man*, one of those taboo novels originally published by Maurice Girodias in Paris (Olympia Press 1955). *The Ginger Man* was a generational refit of James Joyce's *Ulysses* and became the bible for bad behaviour for more than one undergraduate. While Donleavy went on to write in a more stylized and narcissist fashion and never recaptured the genital power of *The Ginger Man*—Girodias viewed it as porno—this book stands as part of the pivot from "they" to "me" in the fight for freedom of expression in the English language arts.

The last rugby I ever played was against the Coleraine Inst Under Fourteen Squad. It was a cool sunny day on a pitch that bordered the Bann River and it wasn't long before we lost one of our best players, the Hooker, the forward who's supposed to win possession of the ball during the scrum and hook it back to the Scrum-half, who's then supposed to pass the ball to the line of running backs. I was playing Wing, as always, as I was fast and devious at full throttle, scored lots of points.

Heard a scream as the Hooker went down. Dislocated shoulder and a couple of fractures, although we didn't know that at the time, only that he was out of the game and in those days you weren't allowed any substitutions. So Coleraine ran all over us, just about pushed our forwards into the river and we never got the ball. I was angry, cursed without regard, switched positions so that I could get closer to the scrum, maybe get the ball. I ended up as Scrum-half, all for naught as our forwards had given up, and Coleraine scored at will. It was embarrassing... well, it was humiliating, but by the end of it I didn't give a shite. That was it for me and rugby. It was all a con anyway, just a system of control, something to keep you in a state of adolescence. Movies and girls were far more interesting than this bollox. Waste of a Saturday. And who watched rugby anyway? No one. As sports went, it was low on the pole. The hell with it.

Fantastic Voyage

It was an evening in April 1967 when I pulled into Berkeley and parked outside an old house, one of those "Arts & Crafts" shingle jobs you see all over the west coast from Frisco to Vancouver, with wide front steps and a shady veranda. This was a couple of blocks back from Telegraph Avenue, the main drag. Knocked on the door. No answer. Door was unlocked, so I went inside, called out... but there was still no answer. What a zoo! I'd seen some psychedelic makeovers around and about the Bay area—there was one in Sausalito that had a beautiful blue mandala painted on the ceiling, a sort of teleportation channel for those lying on the Indian rug contemplating Nirvana—but this was creepy. There was a large fir branch nailed to the ceiling, sagging like it was about to drop, the needles turning brown. The walls were painted with crude, garish abstractions, demonic and unfriendly. There were a few weird idols parked here and there, sculptures or something. I thought immediately of the Zodiac Killer who was in the news, still uncaptured. This wasn't Love and Peace, this was psycho shit, very unhealthy.

Had a message from a man in San Diego to deliver, had been down there for a few days, taking a break from my studies. Tore a piece of paper from my notebook, wrote, "The eagle has landed, call Orlock collect," followed by the telephone number, stuck it on the fridge.

Orlock—not his real name, of course—was doing a bit of import-export down in Diego even though he was supposed to be in graduate studies at UC La Jolla trying to improve himself.

He looked like Oliver Reid, the British actor—black hair, big baby eyes, and face that could go from dawn to dusk in a psychopathic flash.

"Do me a favour," he says. "Get this fellow in Berkeley to give me a call...."

Seems simple, right? So I hustled up Highway 99 in my wife's '52 LowBoy Studebaker, the Raymond Loewy Champion model. Took me all day... slow through the usual L.A. gridlock, overheating a bit on the Grapevine, right up top before you drop down into Bakersfield, then highway hypnosis all the way up to Stockton and west into the East Bay. Stopped to pick up the wife at the Cherry Blossom Motel—kitchenette, living room, bathroom, bedroom, and a David Hockney swimming pool—then up the Nimitz freeway to the "Maze" (the MacArthur interchange) and into Berkeley. Why the details? The traffic was—and still is—pure Russian roulette, and pretty scary for a chump Canadian, longtime Irish. Listen, a fellow grad student had failed to show up at class recently and it was a week before they found him in his '59 Valiant upside down in some bushes in the Nimitz meridian. Six lanes each direction, nobody saw him flip and roll, and if they did, hey, not my problem, *senor*.

Tragic, you say, but what's this got to do with the movies? The sci-fi film *Fantastic Voyage* (1966) was showing at a theatre in Berkeley and we went to see it right after I dropped off the message. This film had been showing non-stop for nearly a year, was on an unbelievable run, fueled by the local LSD and pot-head crowd who just loved the psychedelic cine and the atonal music score. It was like a light show at the Fillmore West, a stoner's paradise for half the price. The Belfast actor Stephen Boyd, famous as Messala, the nasty Roman charioteer in *Ben-Hur* (1959), and Racquel Welch, famous as Loana the Fair One, the sexy fisherwoman with a spear and a bikini in *One Million Years B.C.* (1966) were the pretty faces. I was always curious about Boyd—from Co. Antrim, 10 years older than me, and had the good luck to get it on with Brigitte Bardot *In The Night Heaven Fell* (1958).

How did this Bogman do it? The women were coming at him like mosquitoes.

The plot is quite good—a miniaturized submarine injected into the blood stream of a stricken scientist with the mission of destroying a blood clot in his brain... and this scientist is an expert in the technology of sub-atomic miniaturization. A-list cast, including Donald Pleasence, UK theatre, and Edmund O'Brien, US film noir. In one way it's just a psychedelic refit of Jules Verne's *Twenty Thousand Leagues Under the Sea*, but in another, it's a mainstream retinal adventure using the cinematic expressionism that the critic Gene Youngblood called "expanded cinema".

At the time, I thought it was cheap. But then, I thought *2001* was cheap, a bunch of special effects to cover up an inarticulate story.

We were driving back to our groovy California motel, second level of the rectangle, overlooking the groovy aquamarine pool that neither of us ever used, when I stopped at a corner store for a jug of groovy rotgut red when I discovered the tail-light, driver's side, was detached, just hanging by the wires. The hell was this? Well, Orlock had given me a nice bag of Acapulco Gold as a token of his appreciation, and I'd hidden it behind the tail-light for the drive back... then I'd carefully stashed it in the power cord cavity of my reel-to-reel tape recorder at the motel before we set out for the Zodiac's. Guess I hadn't put the screws back in properly.

But I knew I had... and I got real paranoid just thinking about it. Had Orlock stuck a key of weed in the wheel well unbeknowst to me? Had the Zodiac been watching me in the freak den, then followed us to the movies, liberated the stash?

Or what if, God forbid, the cops had been tailing me? Me, the patsy, the unwitting mule? I was in a cold sweat for a few hours... but then, as time passed and nothing happened, I relaxed. San Francisco was a counter-culture zoo, people did whatever the hell they liked. No injury, no crime.

A few weeks later Orlock came for a visit, see his man in Berkeley. Apparently they took in a show, *Fantastic Voyage*, *de rigueur*, man, so cool. Seems business was good, and his studies put to one side for the time being.

He laughed when I wondered if he'd hidden a couple of kilos in the rear fender of the Studebaker, said the "Zodiac" (he liked the name) was into bigger merchandise, like a whole truckload, hey, stuff was moving.

I drove him to a couple of prospects in Frisco, one guy who claimed to be a friend of the Zen Anglican philosopher Alan Watts... maybe so, he looked the part, somewhere between a priest and a pimp, but then in those days everybody claimed to be a friend of some New Age genius, like Timothy Leary or Oswald Mosely. I'd seen and listened to Watts a few months earlier when he came up to Victoria, talked about expanded consciousness and eternal life. Quite pragmatic, actually. Talked about his houseboat in Sausalito and the absurdity of wanting to live forever, that your memory just didn't have the storage capacity for a voyage to infinity. He was an old school transcendentalist with a mandala around his neck, a bit more formalist than Aldous Huxley, and probably more gregarious.

Watts was on the edge of the Beats, so I liked him, bought a couple of his books. He was quintessential San Francisco psychedelia, combining freedom, spirituality and artistic minimalism to find a way forward, return religion to its roots in Nature. A Romantic, like the old poets, Byron going East. Too bad he died so young. Booze, some say. Hypocrisy, others.

Orlock was definitely on the New Age path to Hell. He didn't wear a robe, he didn't wear a mandela... and he didn't go psycho the way he did in earlier times. Stocky, like a rugby forward, always smiling, like a guru. He got all my fellow grad students stoned and then returned to La Jolla for some body surfing in the mornings, some phone calls and networking with the Mexicans later. Was it two years, or three years afterwards when he was busted by the FBI? Sting operation, phone tap.

Crime? What the hell was crime? Forever stoned and magnanimous, Orlock was easy, as he never thought he was involved in crime. He was an apostle of dope and the Big Mind. The pigs? They were for traffic violations and bad vibes at the anti-war demonstrations. Anyway, they got him, the Feds, conspiracy to sell chemical Enlightenment or something, put him in the slammer, Lompoc, the Penitentiary 300 klicks north of L.A., just beside Vandenburg AFB where they test those ICBMs and the sharks cruise the hidden beaches looking for dozy surfers.

He did a couple of years, then they drove him up the Interstate chained and handcuffed, dumped him at the Canadian border near White Rock, deported, free to continue his post-graduate studies in some other jurisdiction.

Bergman

The university crowd thought the Swedish auteur Ingmar Bergman was the cat's ass. TV was still black and white in the late sixties and Bergman's early great films were black and white, so made good broadcast programming for Public Television. The PBS station in Seattle had a low watt transmitter, so the reception could be dodgy in Victoria if you were using rabbit ears for an antenna, but you could get the Bergman, and if there was a bit of channel drift, some noise, what the hell, just goes with the gloomy surrealism of the maestro.

Bergman. He came out of the theatre and you can see it in his first films, see it in the ensemble casting and the symbolist narratives. What is *The Seventh Seal* (1957) but a medieval morality play jived with a bit of Italian neo-realism? The opening scene remains famous to this day—the Knight, just back in Sweden from the Crusades, his horse standing in the gentle surf, encounters Death, robed and hooded, who engages him in a chess match on the beach. The Black Plague rampant, people dropping dead regardless of age, sex or piety. Not for kids, the devout or young families. Bergman at his most reactionary, with the low-light manic depression that made him famous.

The Virgin Spring (1960) is even more brutal, if possible. The apostasy is relentless. Christian faith is delusional, its rituals mere cosmetics compared to the old pagan religions which better understood the primitive power of Nature. No wonder the new class of secular intellectuals in the West liked Bergman—as an institution, the Church had failed, and he was telling it like it was. He'd picked up where Bertolt Brecht had left off—less ideological, more psychological, less expressionist, more surrealist. *Through A Glass Darkly* (1961) with its Strindbergian narrative blew everyone away... the way it was photographed, the stasis and the shimmer, it was its own metaphor. And these middle class characters with their insular, Nordic madness—catharsis denied, as if staying out of WW 2 made it worse instead of better—lost on islands of their own accelerating disbelief and corroding guilt. *Winter Light... Wild Strawberries... The Magician...* the existential dread and the false promise of occult inventions... it was all wild stuff, these dramas where normal people go nuts in unexpected incidents of symbolic intensity.

By the time he made *Persona* (1966), he was making home movies, albeit with professional equipment. More existential than ever, he channeled the horror of the Vietnam War and modern life through the persona of Liv Ullmann, another guinea pig in the hands of the auteur. The doctor and her patient, the director and his actress—again, another drama that is a metaphor of itself, a post-modern circularity of being and nothingness.

I always thought this film was uneven, lost in its own noise. Bergman made subtitling hip, the signature of the intellectually legit. In this sense a Bergman flick and other foreign films became more poetic by accident, modernist "silents" in which the montage becomes a poetic voyeurism subject to a multiplicity of interpretations. For the secular intellectual, Bergman replaced the Bible.

Anyone who has read his autobiography *The Magic Lantern* will know his personal life was a mess, of course. Four marriages, nine kids, many liaisons... he was a sort of Swedish Nanny State experiment. Look around—you see him all over the place these days, except these auteurs of the penis and pussy don't even bother with a script, go straight to TV.

Bergman was one of the first film makers to be taken seriously by university academics. He was worthy, Hollywood wasn't. It was the theatre connection, of course, the literary sensibility, the sense that he was serious business, not cheap sensation. Yet he was sensational... madness, murder and suicide were Bergman staples, and sex impossible to ignore. He opened the door for the Italians, even though he owed something to Italian neo-realism. Fellini became legit... Antonioni, Pasolini, Visconti... and Vittorio de Sica, the quintessential neo-realist, was rediscovered.

More Movies & Teaching

Fellini's *La Dolce Vita* (1962) was another trigger film in the gaining of academic acceptance. Like Bergman, Fellini was also making film drama a more personal expression. Fellini went completely auteur with his follow up, *Otto e Mezzo* (*Eight and a Half*), making himself the protagonist, albeit dressed as fiction. Fellini was using the camera as a writer would use a pen or a typewriter, rather than working as one hired hand in a team of hired hands slaving for the Man, i.e the Studio and its assembly line. This move into "personalism" had already happened in the novel, in painting, and had been in poetry forever.

A generation raised on talking film and the newer medium of TV was now at university and more interested in how they reflected culture. Print was a police medium, something they were told to do, had no pop culture mojo.

So you had to go back to the beginnings, to Eisenstein, montage, the silents, narrative as a metric rhythm akin to music and poetry. The tonal dematerialization was just beginning. Others, of course, went further back, wanted to understand the magic of motion photography, back to Edward Muybridge and how he captured the motion of the Governor of California's race horse to prove that all four hooves actually left the ground.

Deep Throat. 1972, when things were right out of control and anything went. Porno chic. The birth control pill had just kicked the jams out from under sexual restraint and the public was hungry for more explicit sex, and Gerard Damiano's film brought artistic recognition to porn if not actually making it art. It fit in with the art gallery conceptual movement, where the action itself is the art, not the object. The dismantling of the old taboos was fun, the consequences unclear. I didn't see it until much later when it was showing up on late night TV, but the student film society at UVic brought in a 16 mm print for a packed house viewing. It was university film societies that made *Deep Throat* and other movies like it an underground success. Cinema had always been voyeuristic, and now the act of viewing became just as important as the cultural propaganda. All you had to do was put movies like this and *Emmanuelle* (1974) and *The Story of O* (1975) on the curriculum and the course was packed... well, you might want to throw in *Hiroshima Mon Amour* (1959) to give some counter-balance, some interracial guilt and radiation sex to cool the marijuana crowd, let the Board of Governors know you were serious, not an academic pimp.

You have to understand that film was not considered an academic subject until the 1970s. Before, a film might be used to illustrate a novel on a literature course, but never worthy as a discipline unto itself. The first person I met who was doing a doctorate in Film Studies (at Bristol U. in the U.K.) was an American theatre Prof at UVic, Frederick Edell. Naturally, he didn't get tenure, had to move along.

I backed into teaching film. I taught workshops on writing stage plays, radio scripts... hmm, if someone wanted to try a film script, go ahead, although I didn't write them myself. Our program had concomitant narrative structure seminars, designed to study important works for how they were put together, and I started showing films in my Structure of Drama course. Pretty soon it became obvious that students were signing up for the movies, so, in order to boost enrollment, movies it was. So I taught the first film course *per se* at UVic.

Part of the politics when government largesse was/is hinged to enrollment figures. Tenured Profs didn't like teaching large courses, lectures especially; some didn't like teaching at all, so beefing up the numbers was passed onto the slaves, the sessionals, many of whom were barely qualified to be teaching anything. Standards? Forget it. So film became a pop culture levee dike for the academic priests to hide behind, pursue their esoteric studies and study grants. Blah blah... blah blah blah. University politics—men as women, women as men... and the ETs who walk the middle.

Y'know, the campus was great in the sixties and some of the seventies. Then it became a tooling station for the Nanny State. Was university a good place for Art to be? Writing, painting, music... performance? I don't think so. Just try sitting on a university committee for a while... Research and Travel, say... or the Committee on Committees. Try it. You either become a Believer and a Parasite, or an Unbeliever and a Parasite.

Some people fake their credentials. Human nature, I guess. Pad the old CV with nebulous publications, awards and the like... some, pure fiction. Many claim degrees they never finished or never had at all. How about the President? A doctorate from Blackstone U., a mail order diploma advertised in the back pages of *Popular Mechanics*. Was the man incompetent? Probably not, but it just goes to show that fiction pervades reality at all levels. This is why story narrative is the greatest art there is because any convincing story will be accepted as reality by others.

Just saying.

Remember when I saw the ad for *Texas Chainsaw Massacre* (1974) on TV, thought, this is genius. When I was a kid, they banned a horror comic which had an old guy with a young doll wife, and the old guy insisted on having a telephone installed in his coffin... and of course when the young wife was getting it on with her young lover, the phone rang, and we got a close up frame of the moldering corpse checking in from the grave. Yes, the Nanny State stepped in and banned it and any other comic that went this far. Well, they were probably right, insofar as this sort of thing shouldn't be sold to children. But there are times when shock theatre can be an effective educational tool. *Texas Chainsaw* was just such a drama... maybe... would scare the bourgeoisie shitless. Anyone who has fired up a chainsaw must have realized its deadly potential for lethal injury... and by extension, as a weapon.

They use them in slaughterhouses, don't they? Oh, I forgot. There are no such places. Meat comes in plastic wrapping, find it in the cooler at your local Supermart.

Went to see a matinee at the Odeon in Victoria—the first showing, actually. There weren't more than five or six people in the theatre. By the time old Leatherface got his saw going on a young guy hanging from a meathook, three people left. The rest of us sat hunched forward in our seats, ready to duck if one of the nubiles got it. Tobe Hooper, director. He actually established some creds with this "slasher" film, got funding for a follow up... uses the old Carnival setting, not as good, but how could it be? The first cut is always the deepest.

Now, of course, in this pornographic universe of ours something like *Texas Chainsaw* and its follow-ups hold no interest for me. It's obsolete, even though it upped the ante in the slasher genre, became a benchmark of sorts. How else can you explain the success and acceptance of that nasty piece of sadomasochism, *Reservoir Dogs*?

Well, I should talk. I wrote one or two nasty absurdist plays with butchers and meat cleavers and people screwing their lights out in abattoirs and other sex and death parables. One, *Black Movie*, was a tape of ugly monologues and duologues, played to an audience trapped in total darkness. In the early seventies I had some plays on at The Factory Theatre Lab in Toronto, remember going outside at the intermission for some air, and a distraught young woman was proclaiming to her friends that these plays were obscene, sick sick sick, and she wanted to go home. I listened to this, thought, it's the director's fault, he scored the negative, bent the scripts to his own need. Maybe so. A director I worked with in my early days in amateur theatre called it "audience fragmentation" and I eagerly grasped onto this idea. Just shock the bastards out of their seats. That's art, isn't it?

Maybe so.

Expanded Cinema

Remember when Paul Sharits came to UVic and showed *Ray Gun Virus* in a science lecture theatre I'd taught a few classes in, and which travelling poets used. Great title, a metaphor for the film projector and the plasmic imagery it projected. Don't know who brought him in, probably the art department. He made himself part of the show, smoking a joint and chugging a bottle of wine, running back and forth like a clown trapped in a sensory deprivation chamber. The sound was produced by two tape loops running independently and going polyrhythmic in random sequences. It was abstract, loud, and totally repulsive, The idea was cool—expanded cinema as a mind-altering event —but the actual experience fell short of its therapeutic desire.

It was like a rock & roll lightshow, but without the great music. Where was the Terry Riley? Where was the Zen Boogie? Astral projection is always the goal, but so seldom obtained, *amigos*.

Gene Youngblood—what a beautiful writer, so deep into the counter-culture, and the synaethesia experiments by artists trying to break the stasis of conventional painting and sculpture by using motion film. These people were following the footsteps of the Russians and Norman McLaren at the National Film Board of Canada. Youngblood was the film critic for the *Los Angeles Herald-Examiner* and the *Los Angeles Free Press*, one of the premier counter-culture papers of the day, late sixties, early seventies.

Expanded Cinema (1970) was Youngblood's most influential book—certainly on me, as I liked his rhetorical expression, his ability to make sense of the avant-garde. Here was a guy who understood Marshall McLuhan, was totally at ease with philosophy and science, technology and art. He was the Joseph Goebbels of the New Age, made you interested in stuff you'd no business liking. Michael Snow—what crap, yet after you read Youngblood's take on Snow's 45 minute zoom from one end of a room to another—*Wavelength*—you felt like you'd missed it completely. "It's the first post-Warhol, post-minimalist movie, one of the few films to engage those higher conceptual orders that occupy modern painting and sculpture," says GY, and you're thinking, yeah, yeah, I'm a dummy... "higher conceptual order", yeah.

But, in this instance, it's my opinion that the real artist is Youngblood, not Snow.

He was a mind-reader, like Freud, could make sense of the insensible. To me, that's art, although this might be my bias for language showing. Suddenly these artists with zero sense of narrative structure, montage or otherwise, were savants on the same level as Edward Teller or J.G. Ballard. Before, you had to have money to mess with film, but these artists weren't shackled by these considerations.

The old Orson Welles adage "the absence of limitations is the enemy of art" comes into play—just draw on the film, scratch it, paint it, put it in the clothes washer, bake it in the oven, go for the random result. August Strindberg had tried some lensless photography, and the Russians (Arseny Avraamov) and Germans were early into "graphical sound" in the 1930s, that is, drawing directly on the film. Anyone could do it... and all you needed was a Gene Youngblood to come along and show the fools how utterly blind they were about you and your experiments.

I'm not saying it was all bad, because it wasn't. But modern art is just furniture unless someone comes along and makes sense of it. It does not stand within its own explanation. There has to be a cipher.

All this was outside the assembly line loop, made the individual artist feel like he or she could embrace the new technology, do something interesting. The thing about film, I felt, was that it was always reverting to the "silent", trying to be pure cinematography. Let the camera do the talking. Even in drama, body language is preferred, talk reduced to ambient noise. Humans... animal, vegetable or mineral, take your pick. The documentary omniscience of film is pure voyeurism. Steve McQueen based his acting career on saying nothing.

There were other film critics I liked, although I didn't read a lot of film criticism. Self-discovery was best for me. Avoid the academic plagiarism, the simple regurgitation of other opinions. But I did like Dwight MacDonald, especially on the Italians. The French guys like Bazin just struck me as ideological jargon... Pauline Kael, some good stuff when you could find it—"action movies are fascist"—but just babbled on too much, the way a lot of those "new journalism" writers did in the sixties. Jonas Mekas... James Agee... Rex Reed... Roger Ebert... others I don't remember. They all had something.

Vietnam

Early in June 1967 my wife's aunt drove us to Bellingham, just south of the US-Canada border. The English Department at Western Washington State was looking for an instructor to teach some lit and creative writing. Somebody interviewed me and then the women dropped me off at the bus station, so I could head back down to Frisco, finish up my grad degree. The place was packed with young guys, draftees, it turned out. There were four of them in a forlorn huddle, about my age, near where I was standing beside my Moroccan bag, the one I'd bought in Tangier the previous year. The tall guy looked at me for a few seconds, then asked me where I was headed.

"Frisco," I said.

Seems they'd just graduated from Western Washington State, and immediately received their draft notices.

"Vietnam," the guy says. "That's where we're headed."

I nodded slowly, said, "You want to go?"

"No way," the guy says. "I just graduated. I don't want anything to do with Johnson's goddamn war."

The others nodded in agreement. I tried to console them, said the war was bound to be over in a few months, no one could resist the god almighty power of the US.

"Guys are coming back in body bags every day," one of the others said. "It's not going good."

My studies had me preoccupied, as I hadn't a lot of money and was trying to wrap up this degree fast, but now and then I picked up a bit of war news through some classmates. One of them was on the G.I. Bill, had served in Germany, was dead against the Vietnam adventure. He'd stand at the window with a glass of wine and a Bogart and rave as the flatbeds rolled past loaded with howitzers and tanks and other weapons going into the Oakland docks for shipment to Nam. He said it was a mess, guys coming back with no legs and badly crippled, guys he knew in the neighbourhood. He had a TV and when the news came on, he'd rave at that too. I didn't know what to think; I'd so much confidence in the US, they'd saved us all in the Second World War, the Red Ball Express, man, this is just a police action, mopping up the mess left by the French. Hey, Elvis did his service, no whining.

But... I just didn't know. Often wondered if I'd been called up, would I have gone? I was curious about it, no lie. Be great for a writer... think of Norman Mailer, James Jones, Hemingway, the others. But then I was also uneasy, as it was a high risk proposition. Canada was full of young Americans fleeing the draft. The right and the wrong of it just didn't seem very clear... other than, I don't wanna die right now, thanks. I was a History major, knew about communism, the relentless imperialism since the Bolshevik Revolution in 1917, messed Germany up, knew that Hitler and WW 2 was part of this fight against international communism, and that Stalin and his successors were bad news. Khrushchev and Castro had damn near got us into a nuclear war, hadn't they?

I just didn't know. None of the young guys at school wanted anything to do with it. So, guess I was glad I wasn't American, was a stranger in a strange land.

The guys in the Bellingham bus station... watched as they lined up and boarded an army bus that was taking them to Fort Lewis, just south of Seattle. Often wondered about them, how they made out, if they made it. Later, when I watched the movie Platoon I thought of them, thought of them getting on the one bus, me getting on the other.

The Vietnam draft had a brutal effect on the American cultural mindset. You see it beautifully in the John Milius SoCal surfing movie *Big Wednesday* (1978). All the young guys were in a quandary: do I report, or do I flee? When I was hanging out on the Costa del Sol and North Africa in 1966, all the American hippies were dodging the fatal telegram. When it came, some went home, some crippled themselves, some fled south into Africa, others north to Sweden. Some even went to the Soviet Union, although they might have been deserters from the theatre of combat.

The Doors' *Light My Fire* was the big hit that summer... was playing on my transistor as I settled into a condemned cabin on the side of a dusty canyon, a quarter mile behind the campus, a joint I had acquired through another creative writer, an English guy with a Berkeley wife, who used it as a shag pad with his mistress, some undergraduate "Betty" who dressed like a clerk from a woman's clothing store. The affair must've collapsed as I never saw them at the cabin... or anyone else at first. One day I realized someone was nicking my food, which I kept in a stone crock to protect it from the mice. There was no front door, you understand, the place was just a property development hold, don't remember who I paid the rent to or if I actually did pay rent.

Two hippies wandered in one afternoon when I was typing an essay at the kitchen table. They had that vacant LSD look, somewhere between the asylum and the voodoo grave. Introduced themselves, shared a joint, and of course I was wondering if they were going to go slasher movie on me. Yeah, they ate my food... just a little... yeah, they were living in the canyon, just sleeping below the wild oaks, digging the butterflies and the snakes, the sun by day, the stars by night, we are all One. They'd "tuned in and dropped out", to use the parlance of the day. No more games, man. Go cosmic, become part of the vegetation.

Eventually they moved along, went downstairs, left via the basement... which also had no door. I continued typing... but after that I never got any sleep at all. The mice were bad, but these stoners were unpredictable. I hid my money, put a kitchen knife below the pillow.

The other big hit in those days was the LSD paean *Sweet Lorraine* by Country Joe & the Fish. Nice guitar. These San Francisco bands were something else. If Kerouac had the jazzers, hell, I had the rockers. It was a good time to be in California.

Vietnam... it seemed forever before the movies appeared. You knew there had to be something. Novels? Seems this wasn't a novel-writing generation. Movies and music, dope and Zen. Rumours abounded. Oliver Stone had been in Nam, he could do it, and sure as hell, he did, one of the best, *Platoon* (1986)... but Coppola's *Apocalypse Now* (1979) preceded it, although its absurdist style and forced ending left it standing dead on its own pretension. *The Deer Hunter* (1978)... now this was something, really ambitious, tuned for maximum identification. Regular guys from Steel Town, USA. Who can forget the tiger cages and the Russian roulette and Christopher Walken's incredible performance? Vietnam zombie. Perhaps *Platoon* has stood the test of time better, although it must be admitted that it has less appeal for women. As a convincing enactment of what it was like, it has to rate. Tom Berenger, the nightmare sergeant, a war criminal by instinct... brilliant. Willem Dafoe, the decent sergeant, Jesus Christ with an M-16... brilliant. There were other films, but perhaps they were undercut by all that television footage, the live action stuff that brought the war into the livingroom and made it impossible to win.

I certainly remember the CBS News broadcast where the correspondent is standing in front of a huge pile of Viet Cong bodies, delivers his report as a large Chinook helicopter hovers, then skylifts the bodies wrapped in a huge net, flies off with its cargo of death. The camera pulls back, and in the distance were a couple of other choppers with their loads, now becoming specks in this convoy to hell. 1968. Vietnam. It was its own movie, reality TV, the genre of the near future.

Early Oliver Stone was incredible as an artistic statement. He made the novel *passé. Midnight Express* (script), *Scarface* (script), *Salvador* (auteur), *Platoon* (auteur), *Wall Street* (auteur)... and a bunch of others like JFK and Nixon and *Natural Born Killers*, later works, more uneven, more unsubtle and polemical, almost unworthy when stacked against his early expression. When he was his own protagonist, he was brilliant; when he was someone's critic, he was parody.

The years went by. I shook hands with Lloyd Bridges on the set of *Joe Forrester* (1975), a cop show he was doing. I remembered him from *Sea Hunt*, where he did a lot of scuba diving. A friend of a friend got me on the set when I was in L.A. having a look around. Saw a lot of movies, taught a lot of movies. They passed through, old and new... *The Manchurian Candidate... The Ipcress Files... The Godfather... Aguirre, the Wrath of God.* The students liked this one, although most didn't have the history to place it. The exotic South American setting, the crazy Spaniards descending through the cloud forest to the Amazon headwaters. Made in 1972 by Werner Herzog, and it made him and Klaus Kinski famous. The story is modelled on the 1560 Pizarro expedition where a detachment of conquistadors enter the jungle to spread Christianity to the natives. Visually spectacular, the film is a hymn to human folly. Would you take your mistress or daughter along on such a trip? In the sixteenth century? They did. To put it in a modern context, these explorers advance towards El Dorado with the crippled uncertainty of plane crash survivors.

Cut To:

Ever wish you could just vamos one place and be in another without the hassle of the journey in between? Just teleport yourself out of a situation, move backwards and forwards through time and space in the blink of an eye, just like the movies? *Cut To:* Nirvana... *Cut To:* the lair of the villain or the boudoir of the hottest sex toy in town or the funky bar where everyone knows your name. *Cut To:* amnesia.

If only life were like that, yet in the movies this is accepted behavior. In action film the cuts can be so fast and fascist that life ceases to exist, and everything is just an impressionist blur. It's all science fiction because the narrative is montage, and narrative is just part of a circuit board. Godard has the famous line, "Film is truth 24 times per second" referring to the predigital era when film shutter speed was usually 24 frames per second. His metaphor is based on the documentary power of film and has nothing to do with the credibility of the story. Yet the heresy has a certain beauty: why use a hammer if you can use a nail gun?

The old classical notion of the unities goes out the window with film, although this subversion didn't start with film. Eisenstein says it started with poetry, but in more recognizable terms, I think we can say it started with the detective (or mystery) novel. The killer's identity is withheld by showing him or her in shadow, or by showing only the hands or the feet, and hearing the scream of the victim or maybe not even that, just hearing the thud as the body hits the floor. Point-of-view is absolutely arbitrary, as capricious as a nightingale, flitting here and there to impossible positions, i.e. those absurd eye-in-the-sky shots that Hitchcock loved... why? The element of surprise? The aesthetic perspective of the cinematography?

Strict POV was a Law in the governance of the later twentieth century novel... unless, of course, it was a murder mystery. But even in that genre where the withholding of information in order to support a plot was considered (and still is) a legitimate trick at the author's disposal, a certain decorum remained. You just didn't flip POV during conversations or wheel in characters by the pallet load to help move the action or tie up the plot the way you see it in the movies.

Cut To: helicopter shot of Bond's Aston Martin driving at speed through the snowy Alpine countryside... well, it's possible that Bond is being pursued by a helicopter, although in this instance—*Spectre* (2015)—he isn't. It's just a groovy landscape-capture by the unknown watcher.

We now allow film to do anything to us, as if we are but dreamers in the darkness of the theatre. Helicopter shots are now so de rigueur we don't even question them when they appear in period dramas when there were no helicopters or CCTV cameras in the streets and malls. Why? Because we accept film as dream, where unidentified omniscience is completely natural. We don't go to the theatre to wake up, we go there to dream. Even a colonoscopy can be a prelude to dream.

Who is this unseen watcher—the omnisicient POV—that we allow in film, yet segregate in writing? The documentary method of film makes it secular in the way that science makes us secular, yet the poetic montage of cutting to improbable camera views suggests a religious sensibility. Within our disbelief we carry the fear of belief.

Yet with the advent of film the idea of being watched moves from the Gods in stage drama to ourselves in film drama. How many times have we seen WW I and WW II intelligence officers examining photographs or watching aerial footage of the enemy's terrain? That was the beginning. And now how many police procedurals or spy films exist almost entirely on CCTV footage, with covens of operatives huddled in bunkers of TV screens following the drama as we watch them watching? In the highly successful TV series *24* (2001-10) "watching the watchers" is taken to a new totalitarian compact of complicity between the audience and the actors. The voyeurism is now a loop, pictures within pictures, a pornographic stimulus of gossip and fear, politics and annihilation.

Cut To: Fall. Early 1970s. I'm on a train somewhere between Toronto and Vancouver, sitting in a roomette looking at a metal 16 mm film canister resting on the opposite seat. It's a horror movie by Tim Bond, the director who has just staged a quartet of my absurdist plays at the Factory Theatre Lab in Toronto. Professional productions, crisp and deadly... although I wasn't happy with the way things turned out. Bond made some edits to a couple of the plays without my consent, and sprung them on the opening night. The edits were simple—in one case, the play ended suddenly with a blackout as two women kissed. As I'd written it, the act was a joke, but as Bond staged it, the act was propaganda.

I was angry, but I kept my mouth shut as I rationalized that no author could ever control how his work would be staged, as the medium demanded creative plasticity. Was I really this nasty? Shock theatre was the thing, but I never thought of it politically—it was all images and sensation to me. I should've known that this is what I might get from Mr. Bond, as I'd read about the riot he had caused when the short 16 mm film he'd shot on Burnaby Mountain (the forest around Simon Fraser University) had been shown earlier that year at a festival in Ottawa.

Yes, he got the infamy that all young dramatists and artists craved. The audience was so disturbed by what they saw that they attacked the projectionist's booth. However, the door was locked as the projectionist had stepped outside for a smoke.

Expanded cinema—this was it, a filmic attack on the cerebral cortex that was considered too dangerous for general viewing. I hadn't seen it yet. Tim had loaned me a copy so I could take it back to the west coast and show it to my students. Did I want to? Maybe I just wanted to heave it out the window, watch it bounce and unspool down the embankment as the train rolled on.

Cut To: a smoky seminar room somewhere on campus as the Bolex projector clicks like a sewing machine. The young man stabs and disembowels a young female in the forest, hangs her guts in the branches. *Et cetera.*

Don't recall how it began, don't recall how it ended. My students had little comment, other than "heavy" or "what is the point?" The term misogyny wasn't in the lexicon of political aesthetics in the early seventies, when artistic expression was still quite innocent. The "killer cannibal" was played by Richard Kelly, a young actor who was living with Bond at that time and had been cast in a couple of my plays.

Tim Bond told me they'd harvested the blood and organs from a butcher or a slaughter house. Pig. This was beyond naughty, yet in terms of what I knew of life (where I witnessed the slaughter of animals) it wasn't completely false. The movie was certainly more taboo than anything Andy Warhol or Michael Snow had attempted—they were merely effette, while Bond anticipated the psychosis of Robert Pickton, the Vancouver serial killer.

Still, what was the point of it? Existential shock? Or was it a homosexual revenge drama, a pathology years in the making? It was a snuff movie for the late night substance abuse crowd, somewhere between Roger Corman and the Marquis de Sade. Well, was I too hip to be cool, or too cool to be hip? Sure, I could write it up, justify it as 'Theatre of Cruelty', quote Artaud:

> "And that is why all the great Myths are dark, so that one cannot imagine, save in an atmosphere of carnage, torture and bloodshed, all the magnificent Fables which recount to the multitudes the first sexual division and the first carnage of essences that appeared in creation.
> "The theatre like the plague is a crisis which is resolved by death or cure."
> [Antonin Artaud: *The Theatre and the Plague*, 1938]

But I didn't write on it and soon lost interest in live theatre, especially as a social milieu. Had no further contact with Tim Bond, although he went on to have a successful career as a TV director specializing in light horror flicks, as if he was existing in some parallel B-movie dimension that catered to junk specialists. Think he did an episode of *Judge Judy*.

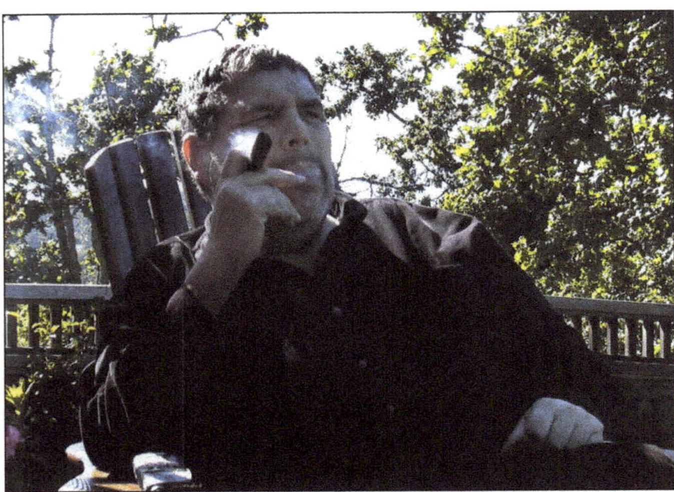

George Cosmatos in Victoria. Photo: Lawrence Russell

George Cosmatos

Sooner or later Hollywood had to call, and of course it did, because a representative was living in town, here in Victoria, George Cosmatos, the Greco-Italian director of the sometimes brilliant *Massacre In Rome* (1973) (*Rappresaglia*) but of course no one thinks of that when one thinks of Cosmatos, he thinks of *Rambo II* (1985), Stallone blazing his way through the Vietnam jungle in search of missing American P.O.W.s. George was a book collector, used to come into the bookshop where my wife worked, so I got to know him, talked the talk, tossed movie ideas around. The Borgias were one idea (with Machiavelli as a character), Benvenuto Cellini another... then I came up with Lord Byron, and he liked that, especially after I wrote a profile, made him sexy, good to hand around to potential money men. George was always flitting back and forth between Victoria and L.A., so we talked a lot on the phone. Phoned from Palo Verde, Arizona, when he was making *Tombstone* (1993), wanted me to come down and hang out.

"I'll put you in a scene," he said. "Put you up in the hotel."

I was tempted, as classes were out, but I knew I wouldn't be getting any lines, doing a scene with Val Kilmer or Kurt Russell. Another time he phoned me from the studio lot, said, "Guess where I am?" He'd taken refuge in Myrna Loy's dressing room, because the soundtrack editing had given him a headache. He was amused about being in this museum of an ancient silent screen star. His voice was hushed, truant. "Smells like musk," he said.

George always spoke with a heavy accent... his father was Greek, his mother Italian.

I asked him how he got Richard Burton for his first film, *Massacre In Rome*.

"Through Burt Lancaster. He was living in Italy at this time, and his daughter was dating Burton. So Lancaster read the script, said he could pass it on to Burton."

It certainly had an A-list cast: Burton, Mastroianni, and Leo McKern, the Aussie actor I'd seen doing a one man play in London, *Boswell For The Defence*. It was a war movie, based on a true story, a German reprisal for an ambush on one of its patrols by Italian partisans. The old 10 to one Nazi revenge thing, total war, even though Italy was supposed to be an ally. They grabbed 335 Romans off the streets, took them to the Ardeatine Caves just outside the city, shot them all. The politics of the time were complicated, so a lot of people wouldn't know the whys and the wherefores, that the Italians had revolted against Mussolini and he was only reinstalled as a puppet ruler in the so-called Salo Republic (the northern half of Italy) as the Germans tried to hold off the Allied advance. A lot of blame, a lot of courage, and of course the Vatican takes it in the nuts. As the Germans prepare to retreat, they loot the treasures of Rome. Perhaps the lack of a female lead made the film less attractive, but hey, if you're going for the truth, then the truth it must be. Although George wasn't so scrupulous when it came to Lord Byron. When I said the story line should have some academic legitimacy, he growled, "Academic, academic... who gives a shit academic."

I asked George about the screenwriter, Robert Katz, who also wrote another Cosmatos film, *Cassandra Crossing* (1976), a thriller about a bio weapons terrorist on a train in the Alps. I assumed Katz and Cosmatos were pretty tight.

He reflected bitterly on what a cut-throat scene Hollywood was, how you couldn't trust anyone, and he certainly didn't, except for one or two old friends.

"The last time I was at the airport in Rome, I saw a paperback of *Massacre*, and there wasn't one mention of my contribution...not even an acknowledgment that I'd directed the film on which the book was based."

I sensed that this was the classic dispute between the writer and the director, wherein the writer feels he gets lost in the auteur shuffle and the director still thinks he wrote the script. Still, there had to be more to it. I didn't really care. I knocked off forty, fifty scenes of Byron in two or three weeks, fully aware nothing was set in concrete. Truthfully, I felt script writing was all pain and no gain unless you had a sure thing contract and there was no such thing here. The hustling and all the bullshit wasn't for me. Film scripts have no literary value, you can't publish them as general fiction reading. You could publish plays, but film scripts, with their weird formatting protocol were like unfriendly schematics. I didn't care if the Byron script ever got filmed... I was more interested in George, listening to him talk about filming *Rambo* in the jungle outside Puerto Vallarta or what some of these actors were like... were they as smart as they appeared to be on screen or were they prima donnas or what.

"Stallone?"

"Disciplined." He chuckled, added, "He's so vain he thinks he can do Puccini."

"Val Kilmer."

"Lovely. Very prepared, takes a lot of time getting ready."

"Kurt Russell."

"Easy to work with. A true professional. I like his wife."

"Goldie."

"Yes, Goldie Hawn."

"You ever meet Nastassja Kinski?"

"Yes, yes, I know her. She lived in Rome for a while, out on the Appian Way. She was living with a producer, was very unhappy."

"I couldn't believe how well she played Tess... I mean, she's German, how could she do it?"

George smiled, said, "Because Mr. Russell she's an actress."

"Her old man is good."

"Klaus? Klaus is a mad man."

GC disappeared for a while, was over in London promoting *Tombstone*. Next time he showed up—Spring of '93, I think—he suggested we have lunch downtown. We were still tossing around other movie ideas, other possibilities.

We were at Milos, a Greek restaurant with a white windmill outside. Maybe it reminded George of when he was a boy, had a bit part in *Zorba the Greek*.

He told me he'd been made an offer to do a remake of *The Informer* with a budget of 6 million. I surprised him by revealing that I knew Liam O'Flaherty's fiction extremely well, and that I thought the remake would have to be updated to the present situation, even changed from Dublin to Belfast.

He agreed that it needed to be set today... said that they wanted to shoot it in Rumania to save money. I said send a second unit to Belfast, get some footage. I told him about some of O'Flaherty's stories, especially *The Sniper*. On hearing my summary, he said, "That would make a good sequence!"

I told him some details about the current IRA, and their opposites, the UVF. I said I thought the plot of *The Informer* was too simple for today's audience, especially after *The Crying Game*, which this project was clearly going to capitalize on. He agreed. I think he saw that I was the person to write this script; when we parted, he said he would be phoning me about it.

Another time I brought up my idea of Christ as a gangster in Rome before he collected the 12 disciples and went on his moral crusade (the thesis being that the 12 disciples came out of a gang in Rome used by a powerful Senator to create political mayhem).

"The missing years," said George.

"Exactly," I said. "One could use Petronius' *Satyricon* as a cultural model...."

We discussed this idea for a while, including Kazanzakis' novel *The Last Temptation of Christ*. I asked George what he thought of Scorcese's film.

"Gritty," he said. "Pretty good... mostly."

I said that I was disappointed in the fact that it was just a *revisionist* view of the Christ we knew, very much within the *realist* attitude of the times. The real challenge was to deal with something new, show how Christ arrived at the posture every Christian believes in.

We drank a bottle of Italian red. The waitress flirted with George, said her friend—another waitress—would love to act in one of his movies, that she was a talent waiting to be discovered. George laughed... a little grumpily.

I said, "I guess you get a lot of that."

George said, "My wife hates it."

When we left, both waitresses hassled him a bit at the till, but he assumed an air of Hollywood royalty, and rolled with it. George didn't drive and he liked to smoke cigars, cursed the new anti-smoking prohibitions and political correctness. As we drove back to his place he railed against Hollywood and American culture, it was all trailer trash, a grotesque philistine world of unrepentant violence and pornography, they had no class, no class at all. Privately I wondered about him working down there but then you have to follow the money, run with the swine, I guess.

"I'd never live there," he said. "I have a condo in Century City, that's it. I like Victoria."

We did lunch a few times here and there, the Faculty Club once because he wanted to meet W.P. Kinsella, get him to sign his first edition of *Shoeless Joe* (*Field of Dreams*). It was a laugh tossing around the names of various actors we might want to use in the Byron project.

"How about Jane March?" I said, thinking she'd be good as Claire Clairmont, Byron's mistress and mother of their daughter Allegra.

He nearly choked, cried, "She can't act!"

"Great body," I said. "Did you see her in *The Lover*?"

"She can't act."

"Good visually, though."

Who would he get to photograph it?

"Vitorrio Storaro... we should shoot around Pisa."

This sounded too good to be true, although GC seemed to be able to get who he wanted when the time came. Didn't hear from him for a while... his wife died, and he went back to Sweden to drop her ashes through an ice hole in a lake near where she was born. He was bitter, blamed her doctor. He wanted me to look after his son's education because he was drifting a bit, needless to say, and George wasn't in town much.

Time passed. The script was now in format and titled *Allegra*. It was a Friday when he called from L.A., said he'd spent the day shooting a scene for the new Bruce Willis movie, the one where he plays a psychiatrist pursued by homicidal chicks. O yes... sounded like my gig as Chair of the Writing Department.

"Just helping out a friend," he said.

"How was Bruce?" I said.

"Very difficult," he said.

"What was the scene?"

"In a cafe where cops go. It is something added to explain what has happened."

"An epilogue."

"Yes. The movie was already cut. It's a piece of shit."

He explained the essentials of the plot. It sounded like an M.P.D. (Multiple Personality Disorder) scene. I mentioned that they were already advertising it on T.V., that it looked o.k.

George was having a snack while he talked.

He said, "You have seen... all there is... to be seen."

The next time we talked, it was about the O.J. Simpson murders, O.J.'s wife and the pizza boy, maybe her lover, their throats slashed on the pathway leading to the house. It was all over the news, and we'd all watched O.J.'s bizarre run down the freeway in his Ford Bronco, followed by several L.A.P.D. cruisers, the whole farrago filmed from a chopper and broadcast in real time.

"It is a tragedy," said George. "He is Othello."

"I don't think he did it," I said.

"No? Why?"

"The style of the murders... it must've been a hit. You know, the Hispanic necklace, throats slashed ear to ear. I think there's a drug connection in there someplace. Maybe O.J. hired someone, but I don't think he did it himself. It took two people. Besides, no one heard anything, and it was only a few feet from the street. Nah... and that business with the bloody glove being found at his place. A plant."

George agreed that it would've required two people to carry out the murders.

"Poor woman," he said. "I knew her. I went to their wedding."

I was surprised, but given George's connections, I shouldn't have been.

"O.J. was in my movie, *Cassandra Crossing*....

It had been a long time since I'd seen that film, the one with the infected terrorist hiding on the train which gets diverted along some old Nazi trunk line, destination some concentration camp in Poland where the passengers can be quarantined.

There was a black man in it, sure. O.J. Simpson. And the incredible irony of it is that he was playing a priest who is in fact an undercover F.B.I. agent. You canny make it up, right?

Last time I saw him we cruised through a couple of antique shops and he bought me a clock out of a Russian submarine, steel, with a red star and a conning tower logo on the face. Windup, still works. I didn't hear from him after that.

Don't know if George made any movies after his wife died... maybe just stand-in jobs. Turns out he wasn't well himself, had a lunger, and died in 2005. Newspaper item claims he said from his hospital bed, "I'll be back."

He went to the London Film School, which might explain his interest in English literature and the great library of rare books and lst editions he put together. He kept them in a cupboard bookcase in his secluded Mount Tolmie cottage in Victoria, where I sat and discussed literature and movies on the back porch overlooking his late wife's garden, and the Gulf Island vistas towards Mount Baker. He had a lot of artifacts there from some of his movies, framed photographs of himself with various stars such as Paul Newman and Stallone, and there was a red English telephone box outside the door. An old time diving suit... movie posters, all sorts of stuff. Great pad. Don't know if his son Panos kept it or not.

Doing It

Over the years, I wrote on all the films I used on my course, just as a matter of habit. So after I took early retirement from the university and started my website *Culture Court*, I had plenty of writing in my notebooks to draw from. Knew film was a magnet and there was precious little about it on the web... well, in 1998 there wasn't much of anything on the web.

Film noir was the craze of the hour, and I had lots of material on the old crime genre. Also coined the term *neo noir* in the late eighties to describe color dramas that followed the film noir plot axiom, as the style wasn't just about theatre sets and shadow and light. Hollywood film had arrived. Students began to understand that a lot of European film by the very film makers they idolized—like Godard *et al*—were heavily indebted to Hollywood, especially film noir.

These European post-modern avant-garde flicks would never have existed without the American cultural model to rebound off.

PART TWO:

Hollywood

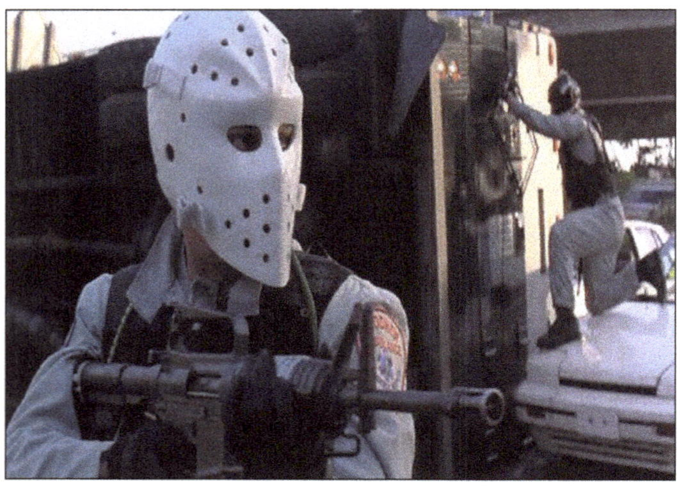

Michael Mann: *Heat*

Heat (1995) writ. and dir. Michael Mann cine. Dante Spinotti music Elliot Goldenthal star. Robert de Niro (Neil McCauley), Al Pacino (Lt. Vincent Hanna), Val Kilmer (Chris Shiherlis), Tom Sizemore (Michael Cheritto), Jon Voight (Nate), Kevin Gage (Waingro), Diane Venora (Justine), Ashley Judd (Charlene), Amy Brenneman (Eady), Natalie Portman, Mykelti Williamson, Wes Studi, *et. al.*

The Final Waltz Of The Cyborgs: Guns, Cars & Planes

A generic armoured Brinks truck is intercepted at dawn somewhere in urban Los Angeles by a gang wearing hockey goalie masks and packing M-16s. The Brinks truck is rammed by a huge industrial tow-truck and knocked into an auto lot, rolling onto its side before being blasted open with strip-wire explosives. It's a rapid action heist in the shadow of a freeway interchange, which sees the ruthless shooting of the Guards and the gang's departure in a stolen ambulance which is later jettisoned and bombed.

The only witness is a hobo called "TV Man" who lives in the concrete palisades of the freeway ramp with a huge television set. Is this some black humor by the writer/director, Michael Mann? Almost certainly, as prior to the heist you see Chris (Val Kilmer) buying the explosives. How will he be paying? "Cash," he says. "Made out to Tax Demolition, Tucson."

As usual with Michael Mann, crime is a game which expresses the attitude of a generation that doesn't see drug dealing as a crime at all, and that most institutions are just criminals who rob from the people. "We're not here to take your money," shouts Neil McCauley (Robert de Niro) as he rotates his M-16 over the cowering customers in the bank. "We're here for the bank's money, not your money—your money is insured by the Federal Government, you're not gonna lose a dime...." The assumption is that beneath it all the money is dirty and that peeling off a few decimal points in the compound rip-off is merely a means of redressing a societal wrong while taking the fast lane to the good life. Here's how it works: after ramming and robbing a Brink's truck, McCauley takes the booty—a package of Bearer Bonds —to Nate the Fence (Jon Voight)...

> Nate: 1.6 mil... 40 cents on the dollar, that's 640 thousand to you... 50 thou front money, get you the rest in three days.
> McCauley: (reads) Malibu Equity Investments...

Nate: Roger van Zant's banks, off-shore drug money... 100% insured. He's a player, so he buys back the Bearer Bonds for 60% of their value, makes 40% on top of the 100%.

So with that taken care of, we're all quite comfortable with what has happened, except for the unfortunate executions of the three Brinks guards, precipitated by the cold-blooded killing of one by the outsider, Waingro (Kevin Gage). Waingro is a thrill-killer, a sociopath who kills as part of his sexual expression. Later, when he murders the sixteen year old black prostitute you suspect he's acting as an apostle of white power as he has a swastika tattooed on his stomach. When McCauley catches up with him in the final stanza, shoots him between the eyes, it's natural justice for the Brinks Guards and the prostitute as much as it's a revenge for his betrayal. Similar to the taciturn Dix Hanley in *The Asphalt Jungle*, McCauley is another loner who isn't afraid to take time out to act against those who break the code of cool or help those soldiers in his unit of desperadoes who are having problems. In some ways, the code of cop and criminal as played by Lt. Vincent Hanna (Al Pacino) and Neil McCauley is exactly the same sort of gentleman's esprit de corps game as represented by the officers in Renoir's famous *The Grand Illusion*. Perhaps Mann is just pushing another sentimental fantasy about those men who are too lazy to get rich by doing real work, although God knows, McCauley and his gang certainly work hard at what they do. Like all clowns and actors, they know how to be someone else if being someone else will get them the attention they need... for, behind every spectacular crime runs the psychology of self-love. *Heat* is a very long film due to the psychology of character and the sociology of landscape. Everyone is in a dysfunctional relationship—or in no relationship at all. Waingro's relationships last maybe 30 seconds past orgasm or first eye-contact. In a way, he's the perfect expression of McCauley's survivalist philosophy—form no attachments you can't walk away from in thirty seconds. While McCauley practices what he preaches—he walks away from his new commitment to Eady—he understands the inability of his demo expert Chris (Val Kilmer) to do this, and in fact intervenes in Chris' behalf with his dissatisfied wife, Charlene (Ashley Judd).

The most peculiar relationship is Lt. Vincent Hanna's. During a mutual admiration meeting between cop and criminal, Hanna tells McCauley he's on the downslope of his third marriage. Some marriage—Justine (Diane Verona) is a Prozac and pot cadet who requires more attention than the good cop can provide. Essentially he's a bigamist, as he's married to his job, the Freudian depth of this condition made graphically obvious by Justine's resemblance to a L.A.P.D. patrolman. Short black hair, black slacks, and black blouse, she's been gendered into a doll, a totem for Hanna's career—"Justine". When he comes home one morning to find another man sitting in his chair, he doesn't pistol whip him, but has his finest speech:

Hanna: I'm very angry, Ralph. You know, you can ball my wife if she wants you to... you can lounge around here on her sofa... in her ex-husband's dead-tech, post-modernistic bullshit house if you want to... but you do not get to watch my fuckin' television set.... He brutally rips the cord from the socket and takes the black portable with him as he exits. At a nearby intersection he boots the set out of his prowl car onto the pavement. Talk about disengagement... although of course he's not done with Justine yet. When her teenage daughter slashes her wrists in the bathtub in Hanna's hotel room, they reach their emotional nadir. But in the movies, good things happen to good guys—the daughter survives and Hanna goes on to take down McCauley.

Typical of the easy money mentality, McCauley's initial plan is to head for the surf and sun in Fiji, but this gets modified to New Zealand. The choice of destination fits with the unspoken sense of McCauley being a revolutionary, someone who knows the American system is corrupt. He's too hip to be a mere thief, too principled to be a murderer. He's an equalizer, that form of the vigilante who acts as a retainer in our dreams. Tailored by Armani, armed by Colt, he's a New Age criminal. Sensitive? You bet. Mercy killings? No problem. Executions? No problem. In fact, if it wasn't for a detour to eradicate that scumbag Nazi killer Waingro, he and his pretty book lover chick would've been home free....

Mann always works within the TV paradigm, that is, a prologue followed by three acts. He dresses the clichés by hiding them in a hip landscape of cool culture—the latest music, clothing and architecture. No wonder so much of contemporary film is poison to the conventional moralist—sex and violence and homicide are montaged into chic gallery hangings of stolen art and stolen souls. Mann is very seductive with his blue landscapes and human isolation. Nice guns, too.

In *Heat*, the sensational action is in counterpoint to moments of stasis—for example, the scene where McCauley leans against the picture window of his beachfront house, gazing at the infinity presented by the ocean horizon. Meanwhile his pistol lies on a table in the foreground, a solution to a problem that perhaps he is yet to see. While the scene is rendered in a deep dream blue, the actual composition is a direct rip-off of Alex Colville's painting *Pacific 1967*. Does that matter? Not at all—Colville himself was influenced by Hopper and other artists—but it serves to remind you that Mann's vision is largely borrowed, even if he masquerades as an auteur. While he follows the Hollywood convention of sex, killings, and the happy ending, there's always enough nihilism within the action to make his drama subversive. *Miami Vice*—his highly successful TV series of the mid-eighties—was laced with nihilism. The objective was always death—the preferred exit of the existential criminal. As executioners, his cops were voyeurs, always around for the next episode. He established a new level of television violence, a dramatic *modus operandi* that rivalled the News, maybe even prefigured it, as the criminals were watching and responding accordingly. "It was like something in *Miami Vice*," became the standard simile for a street shootout.

"Get Clean Shots, Watch Your Backgrounds"

Mann is second to none when it comes to dramatizing a gun battle. When McCauley meets the van Zant contact for the payout for the Brinks job, the rendezvous takes place in the gravel ramp of a deserted Drive-In movie theatre. The point-of-view is shown in the long view, as if seen by the projectionist... although in reality it's McCauley's backup shooter, Chris. The scene is well done, complete with its attempted double-cross, demolition derby and gunfight. It's post-modern, the action a daylight realization of the nighttime fantasy so often shown on the big outdoor screen in the background.

The urban gun battle following the bank robbery is now the seminal scene of that sort. Filmed at the Bonaventure plaza in downtown Los Angeles, the robbery and subsequent shoot-out is 12 minutes of documentary realism performed within the expressionist architecture of pressed concrete columns, marble cladding, terraces, fountains, cone sculptures and mirror glass —the reinvention of one reality by another. What is Nature? Or, more specifically, what is Nature at the close of the twentieth century? An elegant theatre of self-annihilation. We are actors in our own sepulchres. The cops arrive just as the McCauley gang are exiting the bank: Lt. Hanna: O.K. we're gonna have to get 'em in the car. Get clean shots, watch your background. "Watch your background"—indeed. This could be a filmmaker giving instructions to his cameraman. The statement is its own indictment—engagement will happen regardless. The complete recklessness of American law-enforcement is demonstrated by its willingness to turn a city street filled with ordinary citizens into a battlefield as if no other option exists. Justice is not the issue if below your Hugo Boss suit you're wearing *Second Chance* body armor and packing a light machine gun. No doubt about it, the combat is thrilling. The vandalism of property and flesh is outrageous, an ecstatic protest against authority—five patrolmen, two detectives, maybe a couple of civilians killed versus two robbers killed and one wounded. As any student of War knows, you're only as successful as your weapons: McCauley's gang have the good old M-16 assault rifle (Colt Commando) with its thirty round magazine, etc. Meanwhile Lt. Hanna is armed with the very chic Belgian FNC 5.56 mm assault rifle—no doubt this is why he has the confidence to shoot Cheritto (Tom Sizemore) even though he has a young girl clasped to his chest as a hostage. If Hanna had missed, shot the kid through the head... well, who knows how long this movie would've been. But it's the sort of symbolism that isn't allowed, even if it fits within the psychology of the character. As part of the doppelganger with McCauley, Hanna can never injure the innocent. It's part of the systemic lie that allows the culture of violence to increase its free market potential when it's bloody obvious to anyone with eyes that the easy access to sophisticated guns has destabilized society. The fascism of direct action victimizes everyone because it corrupts both sides of the law. In the reductive universe, an action is an imitation of a drama. But this is only a movie, you say... a street gunfight very similar to this one became part of a live television broadcast on February 28, 1997. The two criminals wore full kevlar body armor and when they emerged from the Bank of America on Laurel Canyon in North Hollywood, they immediately engaged members of the L.A.P.D. in what's been described as the biggest gun battle in American police history. The two robbers roamed at will firing their automatics (an AK 47 and an M 16 with 100 round mags and armor piercing bullets). Eight cruisers were shredded, nine cops wounded and others injured along with seven civilians and one dog. Close to two thousand rounds were fired. The police used a nearby furniture store as their command centre, where they were able to watch live television coverage of the firefight on a bank of new monitors. Sound familiar?

"Drama is an imitation of an action," says Aristotle. But in the reductive universe, an action is an imitation of a drama.

The Final Waltz Of The Cyborgs

The ending is really a duel between protagonists, not a set piece of good versus evil where the antagonists fulfill their predictable theatre of propaganda. Oh, there's an appearance of convention because the cop wins the shootout... but when Hanna takes the hand of the dying McCauley, you're left with no doubt as to the unity of purpose. They are merely players in a secular universe, committed to the same objective: death by gunfight. It is, of course, death by orgasm—the preferred exit of the humanist sociopath.

Visually, the finale is very impressive... although it should be noted that it's a reworking of a similar scene in Peter Yates' 1968 Steve McQueen thriller *Bullitt*. Filmed in the flight-path lighting grid as the big jet liners land and take-off, the action exists in stasis. The actors are seen in silhouette against the checkered light boxes and transformers, rendered as *de facto* paintings in this night gallery of contemporary civilization. While neither the hunter nor the hunted are wearing body armor, it is in fact the final waltz of the cyborgs. As humans, Hanna and McCauley are mere simulacra, victims of the architecture that encloses them. They are lost within the machinery—guns, cars and planes. Just as McCauley is finally betrayed by his own shadow thrown by the lights of a passing jet, Hanna looks towards the lights of an on-coming jet—perhaps the one which his alias was supposed to catch.

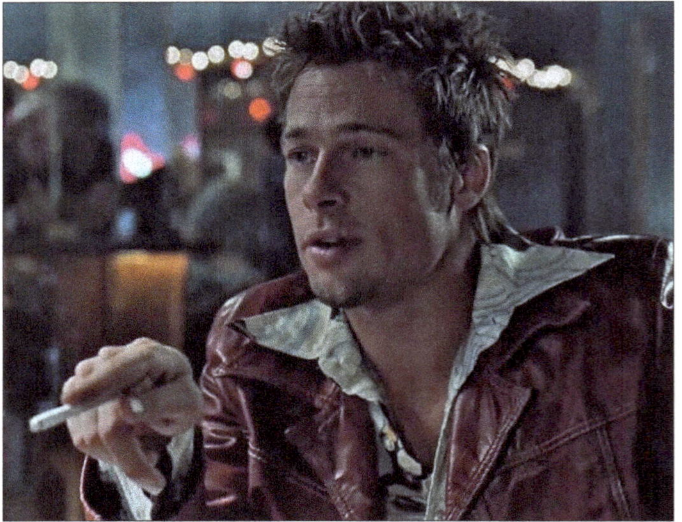

David Fincher: *Fight Club*

Fight Club (1999) dir. David Fincher writ. Jim Uhls (from the novel by Chuck Palahniuk) cine. Jeff Cronenweth edt. Jay Haygood star. Edward Norton (Cornelius/Narrator), Brad Pitt (Tyler Durden), Helen Bonham Carter (Marla Singer), Meat Loaf Aday (Paulson) FOX

The Whiner's Guide To The Universe

Fight Club is one long interior monologue of such self-loathing and masochist self-indulgence that only a late-night caffeine crawler could stick with it to the nihilist overture of its extended, violent ending. Stylistically it's the thinking Gen-X version of *The Matrix*, or another sociological heir of Sid And Nancy—interior, moody, a desperate neo-noir shadow-play, the cynicism of a generation of micro-serfs, gas jockeys and waitresses doomed to be consumer servants in a materialist society they neither care about nor understand, and a moral universe they certainly cannot tolerate. Recently married, perhaps a new parent? Don't watch it. A orphan, a fatherless child, thirty and still single? Light up, lie back and enjoy the ride.

It starts with a kneeling man giving head to a 9 millimeter automatic... well no, it starts with a trippy title/credit montage of the sort of tracking shots that took Douglas Trumbull months to accomplish via his "slit-scanning" technique (i.e. the famous Stargate sequence in *2001*) but is a simple software runup for today's graduates of Adobe Photoshop and the rock vid montage school of editing. Interesting, if you don't mind the raw thudding music of the Dust Brothers. This segues into a kneeling man giving head etc... an image that once again reminds you of the American gun sickness but is so systemic to Hollywood film drama that the script writer probably doesn't think of it as a cliché but rather a convention endorsed by a free-thinking free-acting society legitimized by the Second Amendment. And why not? He certainly has plenty of social criticism to vent through the V.O. ramblings of his victim-hero Cornelius (Edward Norton) and his doppleganger mo-mentor Tyler (Brad Pitt).

Make no mistake about it—Cornelius never spares himself or us from the ugly truth as the ugly truth is to a masochist what a beautiful lie is to a sadist. That Tyler is the sadist in this binary relationship is never in doubt. Like some reincarnated Nazi from a Death Camp, Tyler Durden manufactures soap from the cast-off fat cells of women and sells it back to them at $20 a bar at the cosmetic counters of the high-end department stores. Funny? Ironic? Certainly. It's these moments—and there are many of them—that make *Fight Club* worth enduring.

Essentially Tyler is an anarchist who takes direct action against the corporate and consumer symbolism of the contemporary world. Tyler conceptualizes *Fight Club*, makes it a franchise, initiates Project Mayhem, organizes an army of MIBs who owe more to *The Invaders* than they do to *Mein Kampf*. He's like a terrorist from an art college, armed with attitude, hormones and sexual charisma. He can't draw but he's big on cool games. You might fuck with Tyler but you're never friends with Tyler. In the double-man personality of Cornelius, Tyler is the male persona.

Survivalist or executioner—who is he? To know and discover this is the fate of Cornelius. C. meets T. on a business flight while having a fantasy about a plane crash, discovers that they both share a common cynicism. Cornelius is typical of many generational heroes in the industrial world—he over-achieves in his mind but under-achieves in reality. Thus he—a young man who drifts through a variety of self-help groups as a bogus victim—is an easy mind-rape for the predatory anarchist who sells perfumed soap from a briefcase identical to his.

The idea of the fight club itself is artistically very clever, and its brilliance carries the film through the sludge of its numbing angst and loneliness. Bonding through bare-knuckle fighting is a reinvention of the male identity in a society of manufactured feminists who smoke like men in order to die like men... and what, indeed, is left for a man in a world of Ikea furniture and the motherless/fatherless family? Obsessed with castration to the point of frequenting a testicular-cancer self-help group, Cornelius is typical of the compuvert who is still searching for the father who "moves to a another city every six years and starts a new family". When Tyler asks him who he'd like to fight, he replies, "My father."

The fight scenes in the basement of the grotty local bar are no homosexual delight. Nor are they physical sermons to *machismo*. They exist like a birthing ritual, and it's this ritual that gives birth to the cult in which men experience pain in order to be reborn. For those who favor the cyclical idea of history, the fight club exists in order to replace an absent war, a Vietnam for the soul. Although it's never stated as such, the men who gather there to fight are the orphans of a test-tube culture, a group of unloved castoffs for whom the cure for pain is more pain itself. You can recognize a sexual mysticism here, even if the politics are post-gender.

Or are they? The character of Marla (Bonham-Carter), the chain-smoking vixen who cruises the self-help meetings of the terminally ill as a voyeur looking for a good screw in all the wrong places, is the mother that Cornelius so clearly misses. Her voyeurism is our voyeurism, the addiction of tabloid politics and an appreciation of the grotesque. People love a circus, love a zoo. Far from the cosmetic counters of Macy's and the anal corridors of the Ikea furniture store, these clinics of desperation exist for people without families or spiritual institutions. Marla is after reality-therapy, and she finds it in form of Cornelius/Tyler, another "tourist" like herself. If pain is what makes these people happen, then pain it must be, because it's not long before she's enjoying punch and shout sex with the maestro of pain himself, Tyler. Except for their fucking, Marla and Tyler were never in the exact same room. My parents pulled this exact same stunt for years.

Cornelius endures this like an amnesiac who views his actions by remote viewing, excusing his moral culpability in the 3rd person while declaiming it on the lst. When Tyler launches Project Mayhem and sends out his squad of MIBs to attack objects of corporate art (the vandalizing of the golden ball sculpture is very funny), Cornelius is the first to protest although he is compliant in its agenda. Of course, when you're a double-man you can have a double standard.

And so on. The action continues on through its violent montage of psychedelic events/reality games... and just when you're ready for the second yawn, something is said or something happens to jolt your interest. In this post-God universe of geek-hatred there's always a car crash, a pistol whipping, a bit of thigh or a flash-frame erection to keep it all going.

McVeigh, The Unabomber And Art

There's enough material in this film to have made a masterpiece instead of the aggravating bore it unfortunately becomes. The ending is as hopeless as it is hackneyed. The lisping, low-volume commentary by Edward Norton doesn't help, and neither does the adolescent camp of the director's idea of how this drama should be acted. Perhaps the self-satire is an attempt to make the unpalatable palatable... or perhaps a way of making this angry fantasy appear hip, a form of gallows humor to mess with the altered perceptions of the late-night substance abuse crowd.

Perhaps it's a good thing to have these artistic failings because make no mistake about it, this piece of high romantic nastiness will enjoy a big enough cult of followers as it stands. A shorter, more sincere version might become source code for a new generation of nihilists inspired and fixated by yet another celluloid death mantra. Perhaps we've arrived at that point in our unregulated culture where you need to have a licence to carry a concealed movie like this one.

If McVeigh is a symptom, then this movie is a symptom.

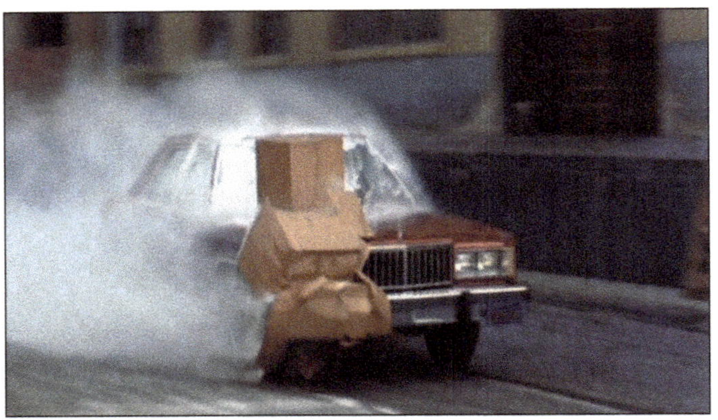

William Friedkin: *To Live and Die in L.A.*

To Live And Die In L.A. (1985) dir. William Friedkin writ. Friedkin and Gerald Petievich (based on the novel by Petievich) cinc. Robby Muller music Wang Chung star. William Peterson (Chance), John Pankow (Bukovitch), William Dafoe (Masters), Darlene Fluefel (Ruth), Debra Feurer, Dean Stockwell, *et. al.*

Expanded Cinema

Although structured like a T.V. pilot, the action in this film is relentless, edited with blink cuts and photographic *mises en scene* in a pure cinematic montage that suspends time and the desire to protest. The narrative is cut like a rock video without the interior histrionics. It's another Gun Drama alright, a pump action thriller of sex, violence and the art of counterfeiting in the degraded atmosphere of chic Los Angeles in the eighties. The model is lifted from *Miami Vice*, the first of the T.V. cop shows to go nihilist, where death is the objective, not the penalty.

The nihilist here is a hipster artist gone bad, Ric Masters (Dafoe), whom we first see in his studio setting fire to a self-portrait in a talismanic anticipation of his fate. His talent for portraiture extends well beyond doing the occasional silkscreen of himself or his lovers into the icons of the Federal Treasury i.e. Ben Franklin and George Washington. He makes money, greenbacks, on his offset press like an art forger makes Vermeers or Picassos. The megalomania is in the subversion, and personal wealth is secondary. The artist's allegiance is to orgasm, so his subject by necessity involves risk.

Masters is another villain who makes the hero look mediocre. In our times the anti-hero criminal has become the object of our fantasies rather than the anal-retentive enforcer like Eliot Ness. In *Miami Vice*, the cops masquerade as criminals, enjoy life on both sides of the divide like high ranking padrones in the Vatican or the Forbidden City. Everyone wants to be "undercover" as it makes his current unsatisfactory circumstances only one half of a double life—you may hang out in the bar a lot, shoot pool and puke, but who knows? You might be a Narc... or a Secret Service Agent. The good guys in this one are a couple of agents who pursue Masters as a personal vendetta and break the law in order to satisfy the need for the only real justice there is, revenge. Thus the agents themselves become criminals, albeit with a higher purpose. It's the gospel of vigilantism again, the idea that personal loyalty is the true spiritual marker when the Law is the horse's ass. It's another one of those Constitutional truths, a paradox like the citizen's right to bear arms while being denied the right to revolution.

The movie opens with a Presidential motorcade moving through the Los Angeles scrapper district, then docking at a hotel which the agents have secured. Reagan's radio voice is heard in the background: "Death and taxes may be inevitable, but not unjust taxes...." As Chance (Peterson) prowls the corridors he discovers there's been an infiltration, radios an alert, heads for the roof. A dead agent lies on the tar and gravel, anonymous and inconsequential in his dark blue jumpsuit. The infiltrator is going over the side on a rope, presumably rappelling for the President's room. He's the *de rigueur* Arab terrorist, a human bomb, dressed for Paradise. As Chance's buddy materializes like the human fly, Chance tries to stall the terrorist:

> Terrorist: I'm ready to die!
> Chance: Nobody's gonna die...
> Terrorist: Death to Israel and the enemies of Islam!

With that he detonates his bomb belt, vaporizes. Agent Hart drags himself onto the roof, groans, "I'm too old for this kind of shit." Indeed he is—he's closing down a 25 year career with the Service, will be retiring that weekend.

Cut To: the credits montage, driven by the new wave chimes of Wang Chung. Various cuts of Los Angeles, the images a collision of industrial strength and weakness. Mostly long shots which flatten perspective and deliver gallery consciousness. A heavy locomotive... a horse drawn cart... thousands of power poles... scrappers... the bloated sun going down or coming up. Flash frames and pans, gradient fills that use the L.A. smog as a natural filter. Agent Hart's last detail on the job is also his death scene. Alone, he scouts out Masters' desert warehouse, and, as he's checking out a dumpster, is ambushed and executed by Masters and his "buddy", the ugly "Jack" who spits rather than talks. When his shotgunned body is found in the trash a short time later by Chance and a squad of agents, the agenda for the movie has been set.

"You Want Bread, Fuck A Baker"

Chance is typical of the extreme sports types who pump themselves on danger rather than drugs. He's always taking "chances". He wears a T-shirt with "52" on it—an ironic inversion of his friend Hart's 25 year stint in the Service—goes base jumping (bungy cord) off bridges on the weekends. He wears jeans and cowboy boots, his bandy legs and tight butt swagger giving the impression that he's either just got off a horse or a woman. Well, he has a woman called Ruth, a blond hardbody check-in lady from a strip club, a minor criminal whom he blackmails for information and sex. "You want bread?" he says to her. "Fuck a baker." In this sense, he's the criminal, and Masters' relationship with his woman, the redhead dancer, looks like love by comparison. Chance gets a new partner, Agent John Bukovitch (Pankow), someone he doesn't want at first, a straight-shooter whose sense of loyalty is so strong (his dad was an agent) it overrides his ethics and common sense... so that eventually he becomes Chance.

Chance and Bukovitch plan to entrap Masters by posing as a couple of money buyers looking for some primo "paper". Chance learns through Ruth that a mule is coming into L.A. on the Amtrak with fifty thousand dollars. As they sit in a bar arguing the ethics of this heist, Bukovitch says, "Steal real money to buy counterfeit money...!" But Chance is a driven man and Bukovitch can only be with him or against him, so they abduct the mule at the station... only to discover later that he's a F.B.I. agent operating as part of a sting.

There are car chases and there are... well, the incredible chase sequences in this film. The gritty authenticity is what makes this more than a gratuitous montage of sensation and impossible stunts. Using the architecture of the L.A. freeway system, Friedkin gives us a choreography of order and disorder, violence and orgasm. It's wild: the "mule" is shot by an F.B.I. sharpshooter with an M-16, the chase continues through the pylons of the elevated freeway, through a truck market, then down the L.A. flood canal, the duo finally escaping against the traffic on the freeway proper.

"You know you're living like a fucking animal in the zoo?"

Meanwhile we also follow Masters' career as he deals ruthlessly with those who try to cheat him. He sends his woman to set up a fence in a trendy townhouse. As the fence and Red get comfortable on the couch, Masters appears out of the rain:

> Masters: First you set me up, then you rip me off... now you're trying to fuck my lady.
> Fence: I swear... she came on to me. I didn't have anything to do with the Cody setup.
> Masters: You know your house is under surveillance? Do you know you're living like a fucking animal in the zoo?

He snap-kicks him in the stomach, they fight, and it ends with Masters shooting him... and recovering his "paper". And the surveillance? Chance and Bukovitch are asleep in their spy-hole across the street. Later he takes out the black hustler, Jeff, in an ugly rumble. He ceremoniously burns the money in his fireplace, naked and occultic in the dancing light as his naked woman lies watching from the bed nearby. It comes as no surprise when Masters eventually dies in the self-inflicted arson of his studio, as the game he plays is really one of predestination.

Chance's sting operation goes bad and he gets whacked by the spitting beast Jack in the locker room at the gym Masters prefers for keeping his body tight and holy. Jack in turn is shot by Bukovitch as Masters escapes in his cool black Testarossa (another "lift" from Miami Vice). To no avail, though, as he's hunted down by B. and killed in his burning studio. The film closes with Bukovitch visiting Ruth, Chance's informant. He helps himself to a beer and with the cynical inflection of his old partner, says, "You're working for me now." We don't really have time to question the stereotypes because of the documentary validity of the style. This is what makes films of this sort subversive, dangerous, because the characters react rather than reflect. It's true that Bukovitch presents an ethical position and his eventual corruption (or conversion) allows us to either sympathize or chastise, but... basically we're here for the sensation and the imprinting. You might ask, what does the Arab terrorist in the hook scene have to do with what follows later? In a complex plot with many interesting secondary characters, this is the only one who exists for effect. The characterizations are quite good for the genre and the cinematography is excellent.

Prime Friedkin: predestination vs. chance.

One of his best.

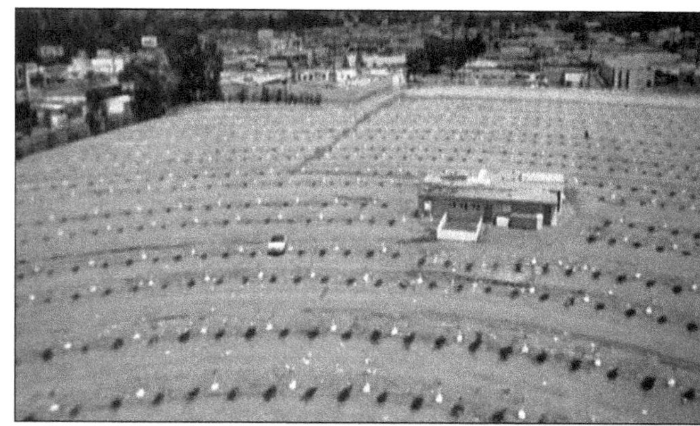

Peter Bogdanovich: *Targets*

Targets (1968) dir. Peter Bogdanovich writ. Bogdanovich (from the story by Bogdanovich & Polly Platt) cine. Lazlo Kovacs edt. Bogdanovich score. generic
star. Boris Karloff (Orlock), Tim O'Kelly (Bobby), Peter Bogdanovich (Sammy), Nancy Hsueh, Arthur Peterson, Mary Jackson, Yanyan Morgan, Sandy Baron
Paramount

Targets operates something like a frame narrative, using Roger Corman's *The Terror* (1963) to create a "movie-within-a-movie". The effect is much more than a conceit, insofar as the subject of art is art itself.

The Terror is a ludicrous dressup fantasy, less regarded today for Karloff's generic appearance than as the vehicle for one of Jack Nicholson's first film roles. Yes, Jack's in it, a mere youth pretending to be a French lieutenant, lost on a lonely Baltic beach as he makes his way home from one of the Napoleonic wars.

And there's Boris hanging out in his castle with his fake raven and coffins, lost in a parody of his former self, that is, the pedigreed psychopath of the Romantic revival.

But it's an excellent counterpoint for the grim, sophisticated story Peter Bogdanovich has to tell in this, his first film.

Thus *Targets* is a story about the B-movie business, which is often the exploitation of fear... and the irrelevance of this culture in mid-sixties America, then undergoing a new kind of fear, a societal subversion from within and without... mass killers like Charles Whitman in Texas... and Sergeant Medina in Vietnam. It was the beginning of something new, the loner with a gun, often with a motive less defined than his urge to kill.

When Orlock (Karloff) decides he's had enough of the movie business, it's not only the ennui of age that forms his decision, but also a measure of self-contempt. The sort of horror he represents is an anachronism, Victorian and fake. It doesn't help when his producer snarls, "If it wasn't for me the only place you'd be playing would be the wax museum."

The closed world of live theatre with its painted sets and crazy aristocrats was never right for the modern dynamic of film with its realistic photography and documentary method. Yet this is what *The Terror* is—a stage melodrama posing as a movie.

The violence of *The Terror* is fraudulent and infantile in the era of Vietnam.

A New Form Of Horror

As Orlock stands beside his limo outside the screening theatre, a young man draws a bead on him from a gunshop across the street. The view is through the cross-hairs of the telescopic sight. Does he recognize the horror movie star? Yes. Will he buy the rifle? Yes. Thus the two protagonists are introduced through a coincidence that turns out to be an instrument of fate. Eventually the stories of Bobby Thompson (Tim O'Kelly) and Byron Orlock will merge in a new form of horror.

When Bobby enters the family home for the first time, he does so as a stranger... or so it seems as his eyes travel slowly around the walls and pictures. His alienation is introduced as spacial, like someone who is moving in two dimensions, the third abandoned when he lost his sense of feeling and humanity. The cold blue walls with their empty spaces reduces perception to a geometric simplicity, where the door becomes an outline, an opening to madness. The evening before the murders, it swings in and out contrary to logic when Bobby enters his bedroom. Directorial touches like this and the use of ambient sound in real-time develop a strong atmosphere of menace and impending doom... perhaps even more than the trunk-load of weapons in Bobby's white Mustang.

Film On Film

Some will say *Targets* is just a film-school exercise made by a young man more interested in dropping names and playing montage games with old movies. Post-modern disease... or a natural milestone in the intellectual development of the Hollywood film? Bogdanovich says critics cite *Targets* as the first American film to have a quote regarding an earlier film. Hmm... what about *Sunset Boulevard* where the Swanson character Norma Desmond watches her early silent screen triumphs? A lot of Bogdanovich's sequences have a familiar feel about them, whether reminiscent of the sniper in the billboard in *From Russia With Love* or James Cagney on top of a gas silo in *White Heat*. Still, there's no disputing the genius of the story-line that allows him to do this.

Bogdanovich, who plays a young writer-director (Sammy), visits Karloff, who plays a horror actor (Orlock). Sammy is drunk and is hoping to coax Orlock into reconsidering his abrupt retirement announcement. Orlock just happens to be watching one of his old classics on TV [*The Criminal Code*, 1931, dir. Howard Hawks]. Semi-pissed, Sammy expresses his admiration:

> Sammy: I saw this at the Museum of Modern Art.
> Orlock: That's right, I am a museum piece.
> Sammy: Howard Hawks directed this.
> Orlock: I know. (hands him a drink) Thanks to him it was my really first important part.
> Sammy: He really knows how to tell a story.
> Orlock: Indeed he does.
> Sammy: (gloomily) All the good movies have been made....

Film instructors and students just love this sort of thing, of course, as it plays directly to their obsession with film culture. It becomes an attractive part of the mythology and employs, some would say, a useful game-model for learning. Conceivably this sort of meta-criticism leads to the over-rating of such films —one need only look at Pauline Kael's love-struck infatuation with the films of Brian De Palma which are jammed with rip-offs and sentimental genuflections to the films of the past. Yes, we groan when a playwright comes up with yet another play about the theatre... yet when it comes to film, such maneuvers are usually greeted as being extremely hip.

Now, instead of saying that drama is the imitation of an action, Aristotle would be forced to say that it's the imitation of an imitation. Is this the signature of the post-modern disease? The condition is now pandemic, the sociology full of intricacies and ironies. The same is true for the psychology of the typical hero, who is now so morally ambiguous even the term "anti-hero" is inappropriate. The stage has been set for lonely sociopaths and gregarious hookers... the fare of prime-time TV in the last stanza of the twentieth century.

What is the psychology of PB's character Bobby Thompson, for example? We recognize that he's imitating something even though the imitation seems rooted in the ageless criminal behaviour of the loser. Although background information is scarce and existential, there are clues. In the DVD director's commentary Bogdanovich tells us that Bobby Thompson was in Vietnam, this possibility set-up by an ambiguous photograph on the wall of the family home. He admits that not many people will notice this, and perhaps the understatement is to avoid comparisons to vet assassins such as the one Frank Sinatra plays in *Suddenly*.

The 1966 campus sniper Charles Whitman is acknowledged as the primary model for Bobby's character, and you don't need PD's admission to spot that. However, it should be noted that Bobby himself doesn't see himself as another Whitman. His model is clearly his own authoritarian father, who comes close to being his first victim... yet, while he is allowed to live, he disappears from the action as if he's been edited out... replaced, appropriately enough, by Orlock. It's Orlock who corners Bobby below the screen at the Drive-In, cuffs him to the ground like an angry father disciplining a truant son.

Dream, Script, Action

Sammy and Orlock get drunk and pass out on the same bed. When Sammy awakes to find himself beside Orlock, the bedside clock says 12:05—which is a transitional device for linking this action to the parallel story of Bobby Thompson, who has just murdered his wife and mother at noon in their modern Valley house—and as he sits up, dazed and hungover, it's as if the murders are but a recalled scene from his script, written especially for Byron Orlock.

This forces us to consider the subsequent action from this point on as Orlock's enactment of Sammy's script... delivered to him by dream transfer. We don't know what the story-line of Sammy's script is, yet the fact that Bogdanovich plays Sammy and Karloff plays Orlock demands that we consider this mystical possibility. Impossible? Imagined events as blueprints for the future are the foundation of existence. Our actions often seem to follow the peculiar ordination of a script, albeit an unknown one. This curious symbiosis is also represented in Bobby Thompson's (script) confessional note, typed in red:

> TO WHOM IT MAY CONCERN:
> It is now 11.40 am. My wife is still asleep but when

she wakes up, I am going to kill her. Then I am going to kill my mother.
I know they will get me, but there will be more killing before I die.

As Bogdanovich freely acknowledges, all of this is lifted from the actions of Charles Whitman, who went on a killing spree in Austin the previous year, 1966. Whitman's parricide has been explained by the fact that he hated his father (his parents had separated some months previously) and that the autopsy revealed he had a brain tumor. Whitman killed his mother first, then his wife. He went to the University of Texas campus, ascended the observation tower, began shooting at 11:48 am.

Essentially Bogdanovich borrowed the actions and some of the psychology... although he chose to leave his character Bobby Thompson existential and elliptical in terms of motive, thereby making him more sinister and symptomatic of the "new" kind of horror. In one way his actions can be seen as a protest against the incomprehensible rat-race of contemporary living, symbolized by the automobile on the freeway and in the Drive-In.

His frustration seems driven in part by the fact that he has no job, is drifting... although there is no sense that this is an issue with his family. We get the impression that he's a child-man, and is regarded as such. His familiarity with guns—an often criticized American standard—also suggests a familiarity with killing. This is easily explained if you assume he was in Vietnam. Whitman suffered from a brain tumor... but the disease that Bobby carries is societal and historical.

White Heat

The fastidious way in which Bobby sets out his weapons on top of the giant gas tank is both anal and infantile, like a boy arranging his toys in a tree fort. He eats a twinkie and drinks a cola before starting to shoot the speeding autos and their occupants on the adjacent freeway. We recall *White Heat* because the symbolism of the madman on the gas tank is the same, although the dramatic style is utterly different. No music, no melodrama here... Bogdanovich's action is as impersonal as a surveillance camera. It's documentary rather than drama, film rather than theatre. This is the cinematic style that develops as the new voyeurism in the later part of the century.

The easy access to guns is still a feature of American life... and gun violence develops at an ugly pace. Bogdanovich says in his commentary that he thought perhaps Targets would have some influence in this regard, notes quietly that "it's still awful easy to get guns". Is he being disingenuous, concerned after-the-fact in a manner all too common with action directors rationalizing the endless Hollywood gun commercial? No. *Targets* is clearly a legitimate intellectual response to the growing phenomena of alienation and spectacular acts of mass violence by individuals using modern weapons. The new horror is upon us... and now, in 2003, we don't need a catalogue of snipers and their targets to recognize this.

The Convergence

It's amazing how Bogdanovich was able to rejuvenate cliches and transcend them. No doubt this is due in part to his work on Corman's *Voyage to the Planet of Prehistoric Women* (1966), which used intercuts from some Russian outer-space footage. If you believe what he says, the script was written on-the-fly, montaging Karloff into the action in five days as a matter of economics.

He acknowledges the ghost writing of the auteur Hollywood director Samuel Fuller, especially for the ending at the Reseda Drive-In. Fuller is off the radar these days, despite classics such as *Fixed Bayonets, Pickup On South Street, Shock Corridor... The Big Red One*... even though he died in France as an American icon, the darling of the *nouvelle vague*. Fuller knew a lot about guns and the behaviour of people around guns. He was also very good at conceptualizing the dramatic moment—the idea of Karloff/Orlock "converging" with the killer sniper at the Drive-In was his, says Bogdanovich. Strangely, Fuller makes no mention of his contribution to *Targets* in his autobiography *A Third Face* (2002)... no doubt a measure of his modesty.

There are many, many fine things about the ending of *Targets*, although "the convergence" is something special. Bobby emerges from the scaffolding behind the screen, spots Karloff/Orlock advancing towards him, dressed in a tuxedo. He shoots at him, misses. He looks up at the screen, sees Karloff, huge and sinister... again in a tuxedo. He shoots at the screen, reconciling the two faces of horror. By now Orlock is upon him.... The symmetry is marvellous, and of course it was all setup earlier in the Beverly Hills Hotel when Bogdanovich and Karloff discuss *The Criminal Code* while getting drunk.

(In *The Criminal Code* (1931), Karloff plays an incarcerated psychopath who kills a prison stoolie called Runch. The hero, who has been wrongfully imprisoned and is in love with the warden's daughter, is Karloff's cellmate but refuses to inform on him, upholding the criminal code of silence... and is thrown into solitary as a consequence. The sequence where Karloff takes care of Runch is used by Bogdanovich as foreshadowing for the ending of *Targets*)

But what can we make of all of this? When Bobby shoots the projectionist as he starts the second reel and *The Terror* continues running, the poetics are easy. When Orlock cuffs Bobby to the ground, the old horror stills the new horror... yet the poetics in this idea are not as easy as they seem. There's a moral here, yes... but illusion and reality are interchangeable, so the extensions are very ambiguous.

This ambiguity is developed beautifully in the closing shot, which is introduced as a lap-dissolve of night into day, the POV from Bobby's shooting hole in the screen. We see the drive-in, the audio posts marking the empty parking stalls like grave stones. A shadow rolls over the gravel as the credits appear.

"Hardly Ever Missed, Did I?"

Targets was Peter Bogdanovich's first film, and Boris Karloff's last. The Gothic romanticism of darkness and shadow is replaced by the breezy 60's California pastels of Pathé color. The simplicity of the cuts (usually on the move) and the canny use of ambient (or source) sound moves the action and delivers a lot of information without a lot being said. Sometimes the acting is a bit shaky, although this can be rationalized as part of the B-movie refit. In all, there are few mistakes, if any.

As Bobby Thompson says as he's been led away by the cops, "Hardly ever missed, did I?"

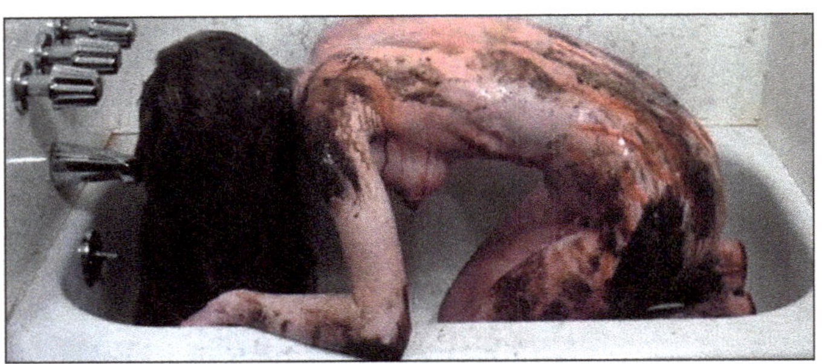

Meir Zarchi: *I Spit On Your Grave*

I Spit On Your Grave (1978) writ & dir. Meir Zarchi cine. Yuri Haviv star. Camille Keaton (Jennifer Hill), Eron Tabor (Johnny), Richard Pace (Matthew), Anthony Nichols (Stanley), Gunter Kleemann (Andy), Alexis Magnotti (wife)

Generic Essay: What I Did On My Summer Holidays

I Spit On Your Grave: the sexual metaphor says it all. A gang of rural louts rape a nice looking young New Yorker who has retired for the summer to a secluded lakeside cottage to write her first novel, but they might as well have ejaculated onto their graves as they pay for their arrogance with their lives. Instead of writing her autobiographical fantasy, she finds herself choreographing a revenge tragedy in which the first person singular becomes the dominatrix in a sado-erotic morality play of such disturbing voyeurism we are forced to dismiss much of the action as infantile and improbable. Zarchi's movie gains as much as it loses from its low-budget primitivism. One camera, no soundtrack music, and a cast of characters who might as well be nameless. The slow real time sequencing evokes both amateurism and voyeurism... as if we are watching something by accident rather than by design. This is good, actually, as we are forced to move past the surface politics of feminist outrage into the sub-text of natural selection and the impersonality of Nature.

What is civilization? Sex by consent, death by orgasm? Hunting in packs, eating in temples? The hunt, the sex, the kill. Everywhere the human spirit appears to be in contradiction with its idea of morality: The Writer points her automatic pistol at the kneeling, naked auto Mechanic on an old logging road:

> Writer: (sneers) Not guilty, of course.
> Mechanic: (indignantly) The thing with you is a thing any man would've done... a man gets the message fast whether he's married or not... a man is just a man. You come into the gas station, you expose your damn sexy legs, walkin' back and forth real slow....

Once again we have the indignation of the sexual criminal that somehow he has been duped, that rape is merely the fulfillment of a universal invitation implicit in the female persona. It's this sort of raw objectivism that makes *I Spit On Your Grave* repugnant to the classic moralist and the contemporary social engineer alike. There's very little dialogue. The action is slow and brutal, like an exploratory game played by bored teenagers. In fact, it's a game that has been played by teenagers. The only variant is the revenge and murder exacted by the Writer (Camille Keaton) which raises the action into the blood consciousness of total war.

Brutalism And The Limits Of Human Consciousness

The rape gang are an association of idiots, of course, and that this is their measurement is represented by the grocery delivery boy Matthew (Richard Pace) who is definitely two bricks short of a load. In terms of ensemble drama, he's the typical buffoon character who tippy-toes around the set like a kid who still thinks it's his birthday party. When his turn in the gang rape comes, he's unable to finish, as if orgasm would commit him to the irrevocable loneliness of adulthood. When the time for revenge comes, he is the first to die: forever the clown, he is lynch-fucked and cast into the lake by the whore he helped create. Orgasm? You bet. Johnny (Eron Tabor), the bored mechanic from the aging gas station (that has the nostalgic appeal of an Edward Hopper painting), is the cunning predator and leader of the pack. His main characteristic is the fact that he never removes his steam engineer's cap even when he stripes down to rape Jennifer... or even later when she castrates him in the bath. His death is a lonely hemorrhage in the locked bathroom of the cottage as Jennifer listens to Puccini, her victim's screams merely part of the opera she is directing. True justice is poetic.

The other two incorrigibles are nondescript, staggered characterizations between the idiocy of Matthew and the predation of Johnny. They are mere outriders, part of the chorus in this evil design, pinions of the visual symbolism. The boat they use to torment Jennifer with is humorously phallic, its bow raised above the water in a crude anticipation of the sex hunt as they circle around yelping. While their deaths are less spectacular, they are no less ironic. Who can forget the image of the wronged woman speeding across the water in an aluminum boat towards the floundering men, an axe raised like a mythological figure from the pantheon of a new civilization? Yes, it's crude. Fantastic? Probably. But certainly not dishonest.

It's the post-rape sequences that test the naturalism and our moral patience. While the rapes are fairly convincing, the revenge is comedy, the director playing to his audience. While it might not have been Zarchi's intention, the Writer's revenge has to be considered part of the novel she is writing. We can accept the fact that she was raped, but her personal therapy can only be accepted as fiction. She has a hand gun, yet never fires it. If she had shot one or two of her assailants, i.e. executed the Mechanic when she had him on his knees on the back road, we would believe it. But that would be too dull, lacking irony and moral possibility. If revenge is the mother of invention, then fiction is the means by which it is fulfilled. The clue that this is so is when Jennifer the Writer reassembles the pieces of her manuscript that her rapists have ripped and scattered. Their sins also include attempted murder. Instead of contacting the authorities when she recovers, she inserts a blank piece of paper in her typewriter and begins typing. Thus the revenge sequences commence. The narrative moves from the masculine imperative to the female imperative. The brutalism of the action commits this film to the Slasher genre, yet it cuts straight to the conscience, focuses the senses. No pretty boy police crusaders mar the action, no special effects dress the reality. It could be considered a crude photo-essay, "What I Did On My Summer Holidays". The genesis? An idle fantasy driven by sexual need. "You come from evil," Matthew says when Jennifer tells him she's from New York. But when he meets with Johnny and the others later, all he can say is, "I saw her tits." Hmm. Men. And the gods who breed them.

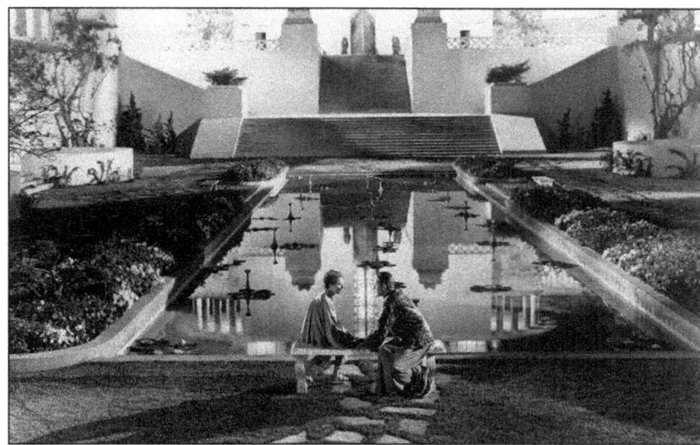

Frank Capra: *Lost Horizon*

Lost Horizon (1937) dir. Frank Capra writ. Robert Riskin (from the novel by James Hilton) cine. Joseph Walker aerial cine. Elmer Dyer special effects E. Roy Davidson & Ganahl Carson edt. Gene Havlick & Gene Milford art. Stephen Goosson music. Dimitri Tiomkin (dir. Max Steiner)
star. Ronald Colman (Robert Conway), Jane Wyatt (Sondra), John Howard (George Conway), Edward Everett Horton (Lovett), Isabel Jewell (Gloria), Thomas Mitchell (Barnard), Margo (Maria), H.B. Warner (Chang), Sam Jaffe (High Lama)
Columbia Pictures

Five people are kidnapped when escaping a local revolution in Baskul, China. Instead of being flown to Shanghai, the DC2 continues east into the mountains beyond Tibet where it runs out of fuel and crashes in the snowy mountain coll of an unknown Himalayan range. The mysterious hijacker dies in the cockpit, the passengers survive... but what could their fate be other than a frozen, anonymous death? Out of the dead light of the endless snow a party of rescuers materialize, led by the enigmatic Chang, who, it appears, has been expecting them. Explanations are left for another time. The five passengers are roped together like slaves and led across the treacherous mountain precipices to a cave, which opens like a dream onto the verdant valley country of Shangri-La.

In fact, as the five are led to the "Lamasery"—a chic modernist villa straight off the drawing board of a Frank Lloyd Wright, situated high in the mountains above the Valley of the Blue Moon—and the reason for their kidnapping is slowly revealed, one might be excused for thinking that these characters were actually killed in the plane crash and that Shangri-La is to be their version of heaven. The idealism of James Hilton's story is yet another in the tradition of closed utopian societies, although the underlying despair of its bourgeois Buddhism is very much a symptom of the 1930s. World economic Depression, the rise of Fascism, technological warfare, ethnic persecution, the rejection of "benign" colonialism and the Christian ethic, were reasons for anxiety among liberals in the western democracies... an anxiety that *Lost Horizon*'s Hollywood director Frank Capra shared.

Lost Horizon opened in March of 1937, the year after Mussolini annexed Ethiopia, Hitler occupied the Rhineland, and the Spanish Civil War started. It was a bad time for those who believed in the egalitarianism of a pluralist society of equal rights regardless of religion or ethnic origin. Capra was among the first of the big Hollywood directors to publicly denounce fascism and its persecution of minorities. For this reason, *Lost Horizon* is an important film, regardless of its clunky narrative and stagey situations (some of which can be blamed on the usual studio politics which led to editing compromises), as it clearly defines the gospel of social moderation that most Americans believed in.

In an early scene at the Lamasery, the hero Robert Conway (Ronald Colman) discusses the purpose of the community at Shangri-La with his host Chang (H.B. Warner):

> Conway: By the way, what religion do you follow here?
> Chang: I would say it was "moderation". It's the virtue of avoiding excesses of every kind... including the excess of virtue itself.
> Conway: Well that's intelligent.
> Chang: We believe that in the Valley it makes for greater happiness among the natives... we all live with moderate strictness... and in return we're satisfied with moderate obedience... as a result people are moderately honest, moderately chaste... and they're somewhat more than moderately happy.

Does this paternalism sound familiar? The benevolent Anglicanism of Charles Dickens, say... or even the naive humanism of Neville Chamberlain. Of course it proved to be ironic that Robert Conway himself was returning to England to assume the job of Foreign Secretary when he was abducted by an agent of the High Lama... and why was he abducted? He was seen as the natural man to become the successor of the High Lama as the "philosopher king" of Shangri-La.

While this sort of secular Buddhism still has its adherents today, there are those who see "moderation" as a social illness. In J.G. Ballard's novel *Super Cannes* one of the characters takes a direct swipe at this philosophy: "The Twentieth Century has ended with its dreams in ruins. The notion of the community as a voluntary association of enlightened citizens has died forever. We realize how suffocatingly humane we've become, dedicated to moderation and the middle way. The suburbanization of the soul has overrun our planet like the plague."

As a man of action, the character of Robert Conway is very much a romanticism of the period. He's like T.E. Lawrence, author of *Seven Pillars of Wisdom*, and hero of the Desert Revolt (against the Turks), as dramatized in David Lean's famous film *Lawrence of Arabia*. Author, scholar, mystic, an uneasy public servant in the colonial extravagance. Another model—the one exploited visually by Capra—is George Leigh-Mallory, the British climber who disappeared near the summit of Everest in 1927. Mallory's disappearance became a mystical event in the imaginations of many: did he achieve the summit of Everest? He was last seen disappearing into the perpetual snow storm wearing a tweed jacket, the quintessential example of a man determined to succeed, regardless of the odds.

And why did Mallory want to climb Everest? "Because it is there." The statement is famous, although we seldom know who said it, and why. Oddly, Mallory's mummified body was found in 1999 on a slope at 27,000 feet, having fallen from a higher elevation... whether during the ascent to or descent from the summit still remains a mystery.

The image of a driven man staggering through the snow in search of Shangri-La is how Capra ends his version of

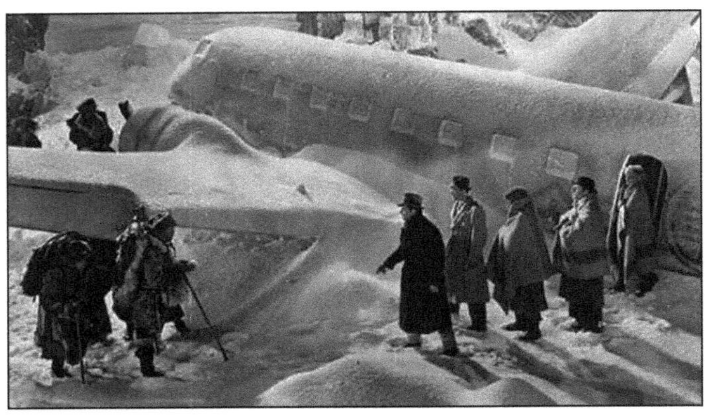

Lost Horizon. Conway's success is that of a man obsessed with recapturing a *deja vu.* Early in their captivity at the Lamasery, Conway tells his disgruntled younger brother George that Shangri-La feels familiar, as if he's been here before. In fact, he has been summoned by a woman, a "young" beauty who has read his books, detected a kindred utopian soul. The implication is that the ideal of a sanctuary within and without this world is a shared ideal because it exists within the collective imagination.

Capra's first cut of *Lost Horizon* used a frame narrative which established the mystical level of Conway's condition. Conway is found a year after his disappearance as an amnesiac who wanders into a Chinese Mission. On his way back to England on the S.S. Manchuria, he relaxes in the ship's lounge with Lord Gainsford, an associate from the Foreign Office detailed to bring him home. Conway hears someone playing Chopin on the piano... he takes over, begins playing in B Minor. When asked, he says it's an unpublished piece he learned from a student of Chopin's.

But how could this be? The student would have to be over 120 years old... the recollection of Shangri-La now comes back to him, and this sequence segues into the Baskul Airport scene which opens the current version.

We return to the frame at the end, where Conway is found by some villagers, and the action resolves as we now know *Lost Horizon.* The recollection is so overpowering, he flees the ship immediately, hell bent on getting back to his abandoned love Sondra in her mountain paradise. He's pursued by Lord Gainsford (like a routine from a Jules Verne novel) who cables details back to London... and when he loses Conway in the mountains, returns to London where he sums up the action over scotch and soda at The Embassy Club. It's unfortunate that the opening sequences of the frame narrative were excised as they contribute a better understanding of the mystical nature of Conway's experience. The DVD reissue of *Lost Horizon* contains a fascinating commentary by Kendall Miller, an expert on the history and making of this film, which includes the missing scenes.

There are a number of curious aspects to this film that Time has brought into focus. For example, the utopia is elitist despite its best intentions. It exists as an example of passive colonialism, complete with a class structure. While the term "native" is just the de facto terminology of the era, it nonetheless reinforces the Eurocentric aspect of the fantasy. Is the story racist? No, although the weary sentimentality of "the white man's burden" is clearly evident. The Lamasery has servants, and they're all Asian. Yet while the High Lama's No. 2 man is called Chang, he neither looks nor sounds Asian (in Hilton's novel, he is Chinese). In fact, he looks and sounds like a head butler imported from the Embassy Club to complete the colonial circle.

While the habitues of the Lamasery are international, they could be a European clique in the Free Port of Shanghai. Maria is Russian, Sondra is English... and the commune's founder Father Perrault is Belgian. The kidnapped group is British and American, as if Art and the ideals of higher civilization are strictly a Caucasian concern. No doubt this was the reality of the period, yet it presents an interesting duality when viewed in context with the period alternative, fascism.

Modernism is really built on the principle of the straight line... and when applied to thinking, can easily become fascism. Direct action appeals to an intellectual elite just as much as an escapist community such as Shangri-La. Just how far is the High Lama's art community of white Europeans and their docile Asian servants removed from the penthouse of the Berlin Chancellory where Hitler and Albert Speer discussed Art and developed The Theory of Ruin Value? The Art Deco isometrics are almost identical when drained of sentiment. As the main players enact their fantasy, the rank and file become ephemeral, mere markers of geometric space.

"You speak English," Conway says almost without surprise to the native grooms who stand obediently with the horses in the pristine morning light of the Lamasery grounds.

When Conway pursues Sondra on horseback from the neo-Egyptian architecture of the Lamasery and finds her swimming naked in an idyllic mountain pool, he could be pursuing Leni Riefenstahl in a Arnold Fanck silent. The fact that she's in a state of suspended youth is part of the illusion and the ideology. His brother George tells him the elixir of Shangri-La is merely a lie to hold him prisoner to a false ideal... but when Maria (George's Shangri-La paramour) reverts to her true age and dies a withered crone as they escape through the mountains, the Truth of the Shangri-La ideal is confirmed. Thus Conway's subsequent amnesia is a metaphor, concealing an ideal that only requires the the right moment to reveal it. For Conway, the *deja vu* is a passage of Chopin in the piano lounge of the S.S. Manchuria.

As a drama, *Lost Horizon* relies on many of the conventions and clichés of the period: a man of action (Conway), a fugitive swindler (Barnard), a terminal cynic (Gloria), a buffoon (Lovett), an impulsive young man (George), a *femme fatale* (Sondra)... all the essential personalities for creating or continuing a castaway society. The main difference between the screenplay and the novel is that the characters are Americanized to suit the target audience. Hilton has four castaways, Capra has five... and the absconding aircraft becomes a DC-2 rather than a small "high-altitude" plane belonging to an Indian Raj. Rooted in the romantic action novel of the late nineteenth century, Hilton's story raids the supernatural elements of Rider-Haggard's *She*, or even H.G. Wells' *The Time Machine.*

Justly famous for its sets—in particular, the Lamasery, and the plane crash—*Lost Horizon* is a great example of 30's Hollywood modernism. The editing, too, uses montage to compress the News headlines and deliver the necessary background information for the story... a style which was later refined by Orson Welles and Robert Wise in *Citizen Kane.*

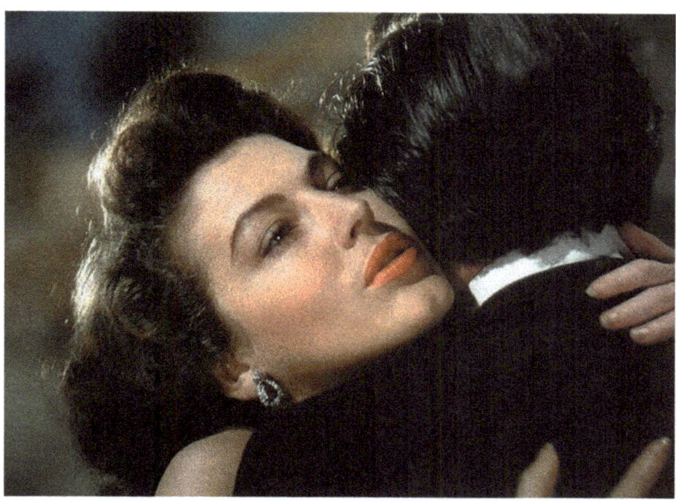

Albert Lewin: *Pandora and the Flying Dutchman*

Pandora & the Flying Dutchman 1951 | dir Albert Lewin | writ Albert Lewin | prod Lewin and Josef Kaufman | cine Jack Cardiff | edt xxx | music Alan Rawsthorne | design John Bryan | Technicolor 1.37: 1 star Ava Gardner (Pandora Reynolds) James Mason (Hendrik van der Zee) Nigel Patrick (Stephen Cameron) Harold Warrender (Geoffrey Fielding) Sheila Sim (Janet, G's niece) Mario Cabre (Juan Montalvo) Marius Goring (Reggie Demarest) Margarita d'Alvarez (Juan's mother) La Pillina (flamenco dancer)

1930. The fishing village of Esperanza on the Mediterranean coast of Spain. An American nightclub singer is hanging out with a group of English friends—an archaeologist and his niece, a drunken poet, and a racing car driver who is about to attempt a new land speed record on the flat sand beach nearby. The singer, a femme fatale who has come here from London with the poet, is a beautiful bitch who suffers from a love hangover or more accurately too much attention from all the wrong lovers. In short, the men just don't measure up.

And just why is she here on the gypsy coast? Is she drifting into an unwise marriage through boredom or is she here for a unknown, fatal rendezvous? Once again, it's the lost generation playing in a lost land. There's something unreal about Esperanza, as if it exists between now and then in a twilight of broken statues and mythological memory. The characters are from the modern, industrialized world, but Esperanza with its gypsy culture and primitive instinct is like a neo-classical garden replete with follies and supernatural possibility. And what stitches the distant past to the existential present? Why, the legend of the Flying Dutchman.

Pandora & The Flying Dutchman (1951) is a peculiar yet fascinating mix of modern art and romantic mysticism. Its pedigree is film noir—i.e. the *femme fatale* and the extensive use of night shadow cinematography—although the story is literary with its European setting and extensive symbolism. Pandora Reynolds (Ava Gardner) is a reset of Hemingway's Lady Brett—pure sensuality in a non-intellectual body (Ava Gardner said that she had no idea what the film was about, even after playing her character to the finish), a refugee from the clubs of New York and London as a goddess of urban noir. Her phantom lover, Hendrik van der Zee (James Mason), is an intellectual of no fixed address, arrives in a crewless yacht dressed in mystery. He paints, he writes, he reads... but where his money comes from is never part of the conversation. He's the anti-thesis of the film noir hard male protagonist, comes directly from the desperate heroes of Romantic literature. He doesn't need a knife or a gun because, like H.G. Wells' Time Traveller, he gets around, regardless.

The Geometrical Hinges Of Death

Evening. Las Dos Tortugas (the Two Turtles), a bodega/cafe on the beach. Pandora is there with her friends, smoking and drinking. A flamenco ensemble performs.

The flamenco interlude might seem to be just a bit of location atmosphere, yet it is more than this. A male dancer takes the floor, then the woman, and then another male, and both males circle the woman. Just as in a stage play where symbolism is used by necessity when verbal exposition won't do, the competition for the woman's attention mirrors exactly the situation at the start of the story. Pandora has two suitors—Reggie Demarest, the alcoholic poet, now on the way out... and Stephen Cameron, the racing car driver, her latest lover. All that is missing from this Lorca-esque routine is the fourth dancer, Death.

After the flamenco performance, she goes to the piano, sings a slow club song, the sort of piano teaser popular for the period. Reggie leans against the upright, pissed and besotted; he thinks this party is a celebration of their anniversary since meeting in London one year ago and when Pandora finishes, he proposes. Her dismissal isn't so much a rejection as it is a deferral. Anything a drunk says can't be serious. However, he is serious; he spikes his drink with some fatal powder, smiles, downs it all, staggers towards the table where their friends sit, has one final poetic declaration:

> Reggie: I know Death has 10,000 special doors for men to make their exits... and they move on such strange geometrical hinges you may open them both ways... and anyway's fine out of your whispering....

He then falls dead in a theatrical flourish. Some gesture, some anniversary. Again, you might think his final words are mere effect, yet their imagery—a direct lift from Webster's play, *The Duchess of Malfi*—fits perfectly with the mystical intent of the story and its surrealist patina. As Geoffrey Fielding recalls, "The moon was at the full, erotic and disturbing." Indeed.

Pandora: in Greek mythology, the first woman. Created by Zeus to punish Man after Prometheus had created the human race (Man). She came with a box or jar in which all sorts of evils and diseases were stored. Bad news woman, and this "Pandora" is no exception. Despite the fact that they should know better, a procession of men compete for her as if she is a mystic trophy in disguise: a poem, a racing car, a bull, or even Jesus Christ.

She is a pure sexual lure, a modernist siren who responds to her lovers' sacrifices with the diffidence of a gentle sociopath. Her cool response to Reggie's death seems baffling, or even appalling, yet the speed of the narrative shift doesn't allow much ethical deliberation. I'm a bitch, therefore I am. Janet—her rival for Stephen Cameron's affections—attempts to call her on it, yet Janet merely comes across as a jealous hysteric.

The Lover As A Futurist Racer

As Reggie suspected, Pandora and Stephen Cameron are already an item, even though Janet thinks Stephen belongs to her. Again, here is another lover as an exotic figure, a man who races with Death... although, possibly, Stephen doesn't see it that way. He's a steady man, not easily perturbed or provoked, even if he thinks he's in love with Pandora. He names his racing car "Pandora"—she's a muse, an inspiration, a mojo.

Stephen Cameron is out of the tradition of British adventurers like Mallory the climber (Everest) Colonel Fawcett the explorer (Amazon)—a "great man" as Pandora tells the bullfighter, Juan Montalvo, when rationalizing her impending marriage.

As the death of Reggie seems to be no big deal, he passes out-of-frame with little discussion, the first of Pandora Reynold's victims, erased as easily as a wet face on a new painting. "Do you think he killed himself because he knew about us?" says Stephen on the boardwalk outside the bodega. "No," says Pandora. She then demands that Stephen takes her for a moonlight drive in his large racer—an absurdity really seeing as the cockpit is for a single occupant, and as the Scottish mechanic cautions, "only has a hand-brake."

Nevertheless the monster is rolled from its shack on the beach and Stephen and Pandora roar away into the gloom. It's fantastic, improbable, yet possible. They leave the beach, follow a winding road to a headland where a megalith stands as a reminder of the pagan sanctity of the location. Down on the bay, the mast light of a moored sloop twinkles. Pandora is intrigued by the mysterious boat, but is distracted by Stephen's need to know what he must do to prove his love. Pandora's reply is preposterous, even vicious—would he be willing to roll his car over the cliff? To sacrifice his ambition is only one step short of sacrificing his life, yet Stephen is willing. He releases the brake, and the car goes over in an elegant moonlit plunge into the sleeping sea below.

Madness? Pandora, like her mythical antecedent, is a natural born destroyer, it seems. The fact that the car—"Pandora" —is later salvaged, and Stephen goes on to set a new land speed record watched by Pandora and her friends hardly normalizes the incident. But the men who love this *femme fatale* are all subject to moments of violence... except the mysterious stranger, Hendrick van der Zee, a.k.a. the Flying Dutchman.

Cars and racing were central to the Futurist obsession with speed. Stephen Cameron is a figure typical of the British racer that emerged in the twenties with Henry Seagrave and Parry Thomas and their record runs on the flat beach at Southport Sands, UK. [both Seagrave & Thomas were killed in separate record attempts in 1930] Sir Malcolm Campbell set a record of 272 mph at Daytona driving the Campbell-Railton Rolls Royce V-12 *Bluebird*—a large modernist machine streamed like a missile, not that dissimilar to the car used in *Pandora & The Flying Dutchman*, which is John Cobb's famous Rapier-Railton.

And the object of all this need for speed? To shrink Time, arrive (paradoxically) at eternal stasis? "And like young lions we ran after Death," says Marinetti, the Italian poet credited with founding Futurism. In the *Futurist Manifesto* (1909), he says, "We affirm that the world's magnificence has been enriched by a new beauty: the beauty of speed. A racing car whose hood is adorned with great pipes, like serpents of explosive breath—a roaring car that seems to ride on grapeshot is more beautiful than the Victory of Samothrace."

This polemical rhetoric could easily describe Stephen Cameron's record-breaking run on the sands of Esperanza, especially when the engine catches fire and his fate is in doubt.

The racing car, salvaged from the sea just like the statues that lie on the beach at the Hotel Isabella or in the garden of the archaeologist Geoffrey Fielding, becomes part of the mythological zeitgeist that extends through time and space... and in dream.

De Chirico And The Flying Dutchman

Drawn inexorably to the enigma of the mysterious yacht (or sloop) anchored in the bay, Pandora drops her clothes, goes buff into the Mediterranean, swims to within hailing distance. The deck is lit, the portholes too, but no one answers. Naked, she ascends the dingy stairs, moves through the shadows to the skylight above the main cabin, sees a man standing before a large canvas, paint-brush in hand. He is deaf to her calls, oblivious to all except the work at hand. She finds the stairs, descends.

This first encounter is the pivotal scene in the film as it not only introduces the principals but also establishes the symbolism that undertows the story's mystical intent. Is the Dutchman surprised by this visit by a beautiful mermaid who insists on his company, transgressing his solitude? No. Or is he surprised that Pandora Reynolds is the literal embodiment of the woman in his painting? No. In the Romantic world there are no coincidences within the architecture of destiny.

His painting—a pure plagiarism (or "appropriation") of the early metaphysical style of Giorgio de Chirico—is drawn by the hand of fate. Giorgio de Chirico (1888-1978) was an influential precursor of surrealism, itself rooted in neo-primitivism and dream. The Dutchman's painting includes the familiar De Chirico classical landscape, an empty plaza with a distant Grecian building... it looks primitive, like a fresco or a print motif for some fabric, and in the foreground the woman is only as real as you allow her to be. It's mythology as expressed in dream, fragments from another dimension.

The De Chirico influence in this drama extends not only through the symbolisms and the color scheme but in the "Nietzche Autumn" lighting that pervades much of the action, i.e. the private matador display that Juan Montalvo gives to impress Pandora, or the love scene between Pandora and Hendrik van der Zee on the beach with the statues. Even the idea for the story is pure De Chirico in its metaphysical recasting of the laws of Time and Space.

Pandora—never shy or particularly well-mannered—decides she doesn't like herself in this painting (surely van der Zee has seen pictures of her in magazines or perhaps seen her in a nightclub in New York), grabs a paint-brush and like an angry, spoiled child, mutilates her portrait with a few ugly swipes.

The Dutchman is unmoved—why? "I was angry once," he says. "But not anymore." He examines the painting, has an idea: "No," he says, "you have improved it." He picks up his brush, removes all the details of the face so that the figure has the faceless mystery of a mannequin. This is more De Chirico. The figure has now become the famous "Manichino", a figure De

Chirico took from the dramatic poem *The Flute Player of Saint Merry* (1914) by his friend Guillaime Appollinaire, the man generally credited with coming up with the term surrealism.

Appollinaire's faceless flute player, both sinister and ravishing, moves through Paris at night, collecting an entourage of hypnotized citizens and beautiful women, who follow him into an abandoned building and disappear. Here, in the Dutchman's painting, Pandora becomes such a figure—beautiful, enigmatic, possibly fatal. Behind her sit relics of the ancient world, dream-like and abandoned.

As a character, Mason plays van der Zee as if he too is part of a painting, and has emerged into this world only by leaving his soul in another. He's usually seen in stasis, intense and otherworldly. When he speaks, he speaks *sotto voce*. He seems indifferent, yet has the manners of a highly disciplined intellectual. A statue or a figure in a painting, he only moves from his pedestal when surprised. James Mason could always play the role of the understated villain to perfection, so his Dutchman has the faint menace of the wounded beast.

When he "translates" the Flying Dutchman's journal for the archaeologist/antiquities collector Geoffrey Fielding—thereby revealing his tragic secret—you know he was a villain, a murderer, and his eternal navigation of space and time is his punishment.

But... a genuine bad man ("I was angry once") or a victim? Hendrick van der Zee's story—a Shakespearean replay of Othello's doubt and despair in the face of blinding moral beauty—isn't a story about murder for venal advantage but rather madness. So van der Zee is a tragic figure, someone to be pitied, a victim not of hubris but rather the capricious hand of Fate. Condemned to wander, a prisoner of a cruel memory, his solitude is the solitude of all men, regardless of situation. He is, essentially, a Romantic hero, a Byronic figure reincarnating through History. His nemesis was a woman, yet his salvation will be a woman.

> "I sing not of this world or other stars/ I sing the possibilities of myself beyond this world and the stars/ I sing the joy of wandering and the pleasure of a wanderer's death" (Appollinaire)

Romanticism And Madness

Madness or the testing of madness is the vocation of the Romantic. Theatrical Reggie or speed-lust Stephen... or the bullfighter Juan Montalvo.

Montalvo is part of the flamenco expression, a professional dancer with Death as his partner. Feted and famous as Spain's greatest matador, he returns to Esperanza to reclaim Pandora. Full of Latin intensity, this confident man is certain he can forestall her planned wedding to Stephen Cameron. He stages a private nocturnal demonstration of his skills in a local bull ring, and then, following this shadow dance, takes Pandora and her friends to meet his mother, a gypsy who reads the cards. In a dimly lit room with a picture of her deceased husband (Juan's father) on the wall, she deals the cards, doesn't like what she sees. As she and Juan argue, Pandora and the others withdraw. Obviously Senora Montalvo disapproves of Pandora, and the future is doom. Juan, enraged, mutilates his father's portrait in a fated reprise of Pandora's action on the Dutchman's yacht. But he knows what's wrong—the Dutchman is what's wrong.

Pandora's romance with the Dutchman is like a blank verse drama by Lord Byron. All is poetry, and perhaps this riddling dialogue is too much for the rank and file to absorb. Yet the beauty of the settings and Jack Cardiff's cinematography carries the action regardless of what is said or what is missed. The party on the beach is more surrealist decor, staged in various De Chirico stylistic tableauxs. The musicians are photographed at odd angles, suggesting various vanishing points, as if their co-mingling with the salvaged statues has pulled them into another dimension where the quake rubble of the ancient world has washed up on some mythological beach.

> Pandora: (as she wraps her scarf around a statue) What do you see out there? The past and the future? Or some fabulous land... I'm interested in the present tonight, the here and now.

The Dutchman looks at the sea, then answers by reciting Matthew Arnold's famous poem *Dover Beach* ("We are are here as on a darkling plain... where ignorant armies clash by night" etc). She's reaching out to him, yet he's a prisoner of too much memory and too much second sight. "I know where destructiveness comes from," says Pandora. "It's a lack of love." What she says is a paradox of course because, if anything, she has had too much love, so... it must have been the wrong kind of love. Reggie, Juan, Stephen... others unnamed, all wrong, all like the broken statues on the beach.

Night. The Dutchman's garden cabana at the Hotel Isabella. Hendrik van der Zee is surprised by Montalvo, who knifes him in the back, leaves him for dead. Montalvo also kills Pandora's terrier dog whom van der Zee has been minding. The action looks supernatural, is supernatural because when Pandora arrives later—aware that Montalvo has murder on his mind—she finds a broken lamp and a fallen hourglass, but no body.

The Dutchman appears, goes poetic: "What strange dream have you had to bring you here at night?" He insists he is unharmed, but admits the dog has been killed. It's a resurrection scene, mystical, yet almost without mysticism. A flying 8 inch dagger in the back should be fatal, but then it might cleanly miss any organ that matters. Anyway, the Dutchman lives, and he lives to see Montalvo die.

Like many of the scenes in P*andora and the Flying Dutchman*, the demise of Juan Montalvo by supernatural intervention is excellent. Although warned by his mother, Montalvo insists on yet another *corrida* to satisfy his local fans and impress upon Pandora that he is a greater man than either The Dutchman or Stephen Cameron. Again the ambiguity between the rational and the irrational is played; Montalvo drinks a good luck potion prepared by his gypsy mother, which doesn't sit well and he seems less than sharp when he meets the bull.

He looks at the empty chair beside Pandora with satisfaction, knowing the Dutchman is dead. But then the Dutchman appears... and Montalvo, stunned, takes his eyes off the bull, and is swiftly gored.

Even the scene at the hospital where the dying bullfighter confesses the murder and describes the supernatural nature of the Dutchman's appearance at the bullfight is excellent; Montalvo accepts his fate, as apparitions and divine judgement are part of his gypsy code, even if the priest thinks he's mad. Pandora, dressed in green, knows he isn't. He kisses her hand. "*Adios*," he murmurs. "*Adios*," she says, leaves, walks towards her fate.

Death As A Romantic Destination

All of Pandora's lovers confront Death as a matter of engagement: Reggie, by poetry; Stephen, by racing; Juan, by bullfighting. And Hendrik van...? Also a poet—just consider his written confession. Or the lines from Matthew Arnold's *Dover Beach* that he quotes when standing on the twilight beach. And he also paints... why not? He has been cruising the seas a long time in search of the woman who will set him free.

Pandora & the Flying Dutchman is an outstanding expression of modern Romanticism, using the powerful twentieth century styles of metaphysical and surrealist art to:

a) suggest that existence is multi-dimensional,

b) suggest that Death is simply a shadow between these dimensions,

c) suggest that true love is fated,

d) suggest that beauty is female,

e) suggest that solitude is male... and that only through the reconciliation of the male and the female is the immortal soul of human existence possible. Old notions, yes, but expressed with a genuine feel for the mystical complexion of life.

Needless to say, the occasional poetic dialogue interferes with the modern need for simple talk and simple solutions. As such, it is not a pornographic film, or is it narcissistic. The darkened settings—that "Nietzche Autumn" pallor—perhaps add to the obscurity of many scenes, yet are essential to the feeling of "enigma".

The story core—the legend of the Flying Dutchman—is all about enigma. While the narrator/archaeologist Geoffrey Fielding initially considers it "a hoax of the period, a literary invention" he—like us—is eventually forced to accept that it might be true. It's a metaphor, and what is a metaphor? A metaphor is one object bonding with another hoping to be real.

While such scenes as the Dutchman's flashback to his renaissance past or even the final scene between him and Pandora on his yacht seem too long and slagged by poetics, it has to be admitted that the narrative structure of the film is superb. Of course it relies on the film noir convention of the frame narrative—a narrator, who begins the story at the end, ends the story at the beginning; of course it steals a trendy fatalism from Hemingway's *The Sun Also Rises*; of course it relies on people who play rather than work, but... scene by scene, the narrative is superb.

The technique of looping—the use of objects, characters and incidents—that somehow repeat further along in the story to ironic and/or revelatory effect is used like the gearing of a magic machine. The Dutchman's hourglass, Pandora's dog, the statues, the portrait of Pandora, the disfigurements, the stabbing—it's all a beautiful blend of metaphor and naturalism.

The writer/director Albert Lewin had a Harvard Master's degree in literature, and it shows. Some will say there's too much intellect and not enough action, that whole scenes and certain sequences are merely posing or just talk.

If so, the wrong man got Pandora.

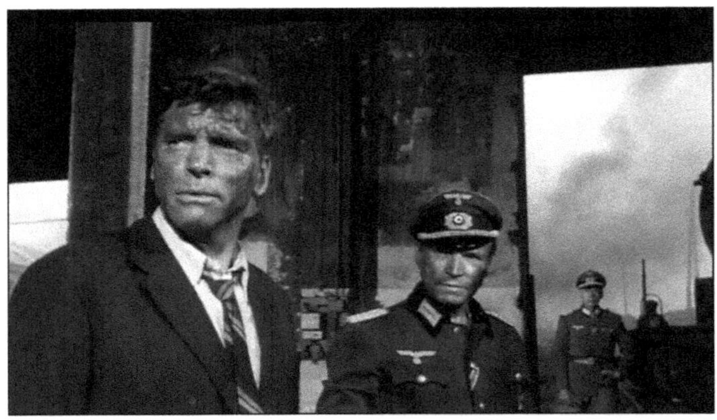

John Frankenheimer: *The Train*

The Train (1964) United Artists dir. John Frankenheimer writ. Franklin Coen and Frank Davis (based on the book *Le front de l'art: defense de collections francaises* 1939-1945 by Rose Valland) cine. Jean Tournier and Walter Wottitz edt. David Bretherton score. Maurice Jarre star. Burt Lancaster (Labiche), Paul Scofield (Colonel von Waldheim), Jeanne Moreau (Christine), Miss Villard (Suzanne Flon), Papa Boule (Michel Simon), Wolfgang Preiss (Herren), Richard Munch (von Lubitz), Donal O'Brien (Swartz), Albert Remy, Charles Millot, Jacques Marin
MGM

With its attention documentary detail, real-time sequencing, minimal mood music, and black and white cinematography, *The Train* is in the tradition of Italian neo-realism... even though it was filmed in France by an American director and features an American star. Films about Nazi villainy tend to be costume dramas with limited characterization, easy propaganda and violent solutions. Exceptions exist: Visconti's *The Damned*, for example, or even Litvak's *The Night of the Generals*.

The Train is violent, but violence is not its vocation. Violence exists as a detail in the industrial landscape, where humans are cultured by their machines and the iron horse they ride. The action is male, the art is female... and once again men fight over her, although this time she is pure symbolism, crated in boxcars heading for the museums of the Third Reich.

The plot is superb. You can have people talk about art and what it means as a physical example of the cultural and spiritual identity of a people, but without a clear example of what it means to be without art, all the talk in the world doesn't do it. The conqueror has always removed booty for his pleasure—Napoleon did it when he invaded Egypt, and no doubt MacArthur did it when he invaded Japan.

The French government protested the looting of the country's art treasures... when one German art expert... dared to call this to the attention of Goering, the fat one replied: 'My dear Bunjes, let me worry about that. I am the highest jurist in the state. It is my orders which are decisive and you will act accordingly.'*

A German army officer called Colonel Von Waldheim (Paul Scofield) decides to ship the best of France's modern art collection back to Berlin before the Allies reach Paris and separate him from his obsession forever. To do this, he needs a train to ship his crated booty... but due to the imminence of the Allied advance, Von Rundstedt—Commander of the German Western Front—has detailed all moving stock for the German pullback. Using the irrefutable argument that "art is money", Von Waldheim manages to secure an old steam engine and sets about press-ganging a French crew to drive the "art train" to Germany. Enter Labiche (Burt Lancaster), the superintendent of the locomotive yard... and French resistance operative. While Labiche might know something about switching freight trains and repairing broken steam engines, he knows and cares nothing about art.

When Miss Vallard (Suzanne Flon) the curator of the gallery approaches him about stopping the theft, he suggests blowing up the train... and the art. When Colonel Von Waldheim approaches him for an engine, he tells him they've all been requisitioned by General Von Rundstedt. Labiche is a pragmatist... and his utilitarian patriotism is the ideal dramatic foil for Von Waldheim's Bauhaus idealism.

While you learn nothing about the personal histories of either man, their characterizations are a brilliant gestalt of body language and visual metaphor. There is really no acting here—both exist as reincarnations of history.

Forget the easy lunacy of comic books and revisionist histories—these are men with a job to do. Sabotage and executions occur with the impersonal objectivity of documentary fact. No one is acting for the camera.

Many more carloads followed... some 137 freight cars loaded with 4,174 cases of art works comprising 21,903 objects, including 10,890 paintings, made the journey from the West to Germany up to July 1944.*

The Colonel stands in the gray industrial landscape, a squad of soldiers stiff in the background, MP 40 sub-machine guns clutched to their chests, the shining empty tracks converging in a distant vanishing point. The isometrics are stunning, like this immaculate patrician in the Nazi officer's uniform.

And the art? Cezanne, Braque, Matisse, Picasso and all the rest? You never really see it. Once crated, it exists as an ideal, and the real art becomes the landscape. *The Train* has to be one of the best photographed films ever. The cool semi-tone renderings of de Sica's *Indiscretion of an American Wife* come to mind but this is way beyond that. Or the expressionist rapture of Welles' last action painting, *A Touch of Evil*... if you think in terms of long tracking shots and uninterrupted sequences. Frankenheimer does it all. And without the easy melodrama of special effects and the pretty face.

Consider the Vaires yard scene. Here you see Labiche in the signal box supervising the line-switching as two trains are organized—the art train and the armorment train. He is also coordinating his movements to a third action—a ten a.m. air attack by the Allies on the German armorment train. At this juncture, he seems willing to sacrifice the entire twentieth century legacy of French art in order to ensure the immediate goal, the defeat and route of the Germans from France. With a Nazi officer at his shoulder, you see him bark out commands to the switching man: "Row 5... Row 8... Row 10...." On Row 10 the shifter jams and the ugly armor-plated engine with its camouflage paint and German cross decals is unable to exit the yard... and thereby becomes an inevitable casualty of the bombing run.

You see all this as if you're watching a squad of carpenter ants organizing their next campaign. The long view is through Labiche's binoculars... later through the bombing window of a B-26. Soldiers move listlessly among the rows of tracks as the flat beds with their tanks and artillery guns await their engine... and Colonel Von Waldheim awaits his art train. The choreography of man and machine here is excellent. It develops like a chess game, ends like what it really is: war.

The art train survives this attack but Von Waldheim suspects Labiche is the real saboteur. He orders Labiche to drive the engine to Germany. Here Labiche and his resistance comrades outwit Von Waldheim completely by routing the art train into a circularity, the deception achieved by changing the names of the stations temporarily as the train roars through. When they eventually pass through "Zweibrucken" it's really Vitry and the Nazis are no closer to home than they were from the outset. They awake at dawn to find themselves boxed between two staged engine wrecks. Usually when Nazis are fools, we are the bigger fools for believing it. But the deception here is so skilfully executed, it becomes symbolism rather than racial politics.

Orson Welles said, "The enemy of art is the absence of limitations." John Frankenheimer would agree, as this deception of circularity was his solution to having only one railway station to work with as his set. Brilliant? Of course.

"Beauty Belongs To The Man Who Appreciates It"

More executions follow. The obsessed Colonel Von Waldheim will not be stopped—he orders in a crane, has the derailed engines removed and the tracks repaired, puts hostages on the front of the art train, and is on his way again. Meanwhile the equally determined Labiche stalks the train, mines the tracks... the finale sees the adversaries facing off beside the stalled train, the art crates littering the cut bank behind the Nazi in a silent irony to the bodies of the hostages behind the patriot. The war, in effect, is over:

> Von Waldheim: Here's your prize, Labiche... some of the greatest paintings in the world... does it excite you, Labiche? A painting means as much to you as a string of pearls on an ape... you won by sheer luck. You are nothing, Labiche... a lump of mere flesh... the paintings are mine... beauty belongs to the man who appreciates it.... (pause) Now, this minute, you couldn't tell me why you did what you did....

While the face-off is a stock situation in film and usually resolves as a fight, the cliché is swept away by the integrity of the acting.

The understated beauty of Scofield's performance is classic. "He's so good," murmurs Frankenheimer on the director's commentary track that comes with the DVD... and of course he's saying what you've been thinking. The same when he observes that Burt Lancaster has the best movement of any actor of his generation... you marvel at the old trapeze artist's casual grace and animal agility. Frankenheimer quite rightly draws attention to Lancaster's swift circus descent from the signal box during the bombing raid at Vaires... and how he jumps onto the passing engine and completes the routine by doing his own fall. No stuntmen here. It's this ability to represent the character entirely that makes possible the long camera shots that make *The Train* a masterpiece of real-time sequencing.

And so according to a report of Bunjes—it is his only appearance in the history of the Third Reich, so far as the documents show—those art objects collected at the Jeu de Paume which are to go into the Fuehrer's possession and those

which the Reich Marshal claims for himself will be loaded into two railroad cars which will be attached to the Reich Marshal's special train... to Berlin.* For students of film, this DVD version of *The Train* is a lesson in the Hollywood method at a time when the Hollywood method still meant something. Watch with Frankenheimer and hear him explain his set-ups, marvel at his actors, recount his experience in France... after, of course, you've ridden the art train.
* William Shirer, *The Rise & Fall of the Third Reich*

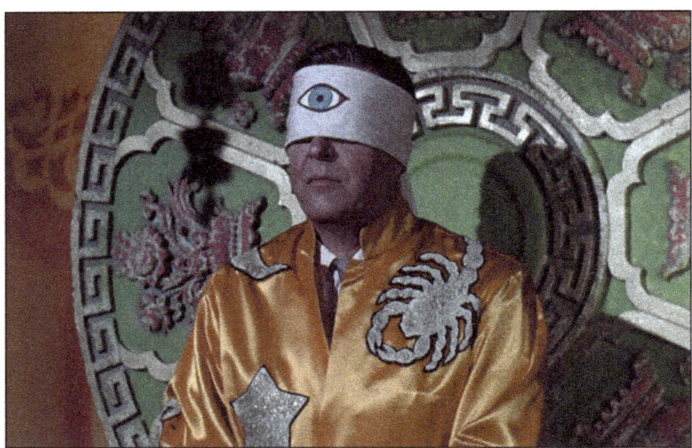

Roger Corman: *X* (*The Man With the X-Ray Eyes*)

'X' (*The Man With The X-Ray Eyes*, 1963) dir. Roger Corman writ. Robert Dillon and Ray Russell (from the story by Ray Russell) cine. Floyd Crosby (effects filmed in Spectorama) music Les Baxter star. Ray Milland (Dr. James Xavier), Diana van der Vlis (Dr. Diane Fairfax), Don Rickles (Crane) et. al.

There's always a raw integrity in a Roger Corman film where parody and melodrama slip into moments of realism, an aesthetic contradiction of crude production values, outlaw characters and surrealist solutions.

The Man With The X-Ray Eyes is just such a film, at times as bad and ludicrous as anything in the thrill genre, at others as brilliant and expressionist as an Antonioni of the same period. It's pop art, the Pathecolor tonality and Spectorama effects anticipating the psychedelic genre, just like the renegade doctor and his quest for a higher level of consciousness.

"Only The Gods See Everything...."

Ray Milland is perfect as Dr. James Xavier, the Los Angeles surgeon and eye-specialist who ends up in a carnival as a mind-reader. In the tradition of a long line of medical scientists (from Bacon to the Hunter brothers) who use themselves as the first human test subject, Milland's rhetorical acting persona has the necessary arrogance to be the single-minded altruist whose obsession drives him into exile and crime.

His role as Xavier is really a reprise of his performance as the glossy alcoholic in *The Lost Weekend*, but with the usual seediness associated with Hollywood's leading men when they fall from grace.

> Diane Fairfax: Dr. Xavier, I've read your report...
>
> Xavier: Yes, but do you understand it? Have you any idea what I'm trying to accomplish here? I'm developing a way to sensitize the human eye so that it sees radiation up to and including the gamma rays....

So Xavier's quest is to break out of the narrow spectral band that forms the current visual reality and expand his consciousness to the atomic limits of light. The first half of the movie shows his conflict with the hospital and contains the tacky drama and crude humor that relegates Corman's work to the youth market and the late-night substance abuse crowd, best represented in *X* by the party scene (Xavier, wired on his eye-compound, sees the interns dancing naked). When he accidentally kills a colleague by knocking him through an upper-story window during a dispute, the real film begins.

"If The Man Was Real, He Wouldn't Be Here"

Cut To: the Carnival on the pier, where Xavier has gone underground and is performing as a clairvoyant under the handle 'Mentalo', his act managed by a predacious hustler called Crane (Rickles). The incarnation is pure born-again American culture, where show business and the religious fringe merge.

Seated on a stage dressed in a yellow satin dressing gown decorated with symbols of the zodiac, his burned eyes concealed behind a blind with a decal of a single all-seeing eye, Xavier/Mentalo runs the gamut of wise guys and the mystically handicapped. Used to con-men and tricksters, even Crane is impressed by Mentalo's unflinching clairvoyance and accurate appraisals. Obsessed with discovering Xavier's secret, he spies on X as he records his Experiment on the Self on a small portable tape recorder. When a woman falls from a carnival ride and X performs an immediate diagnosis, the cunning Crane confronts his act:

> Crane: Mr. Mentalo... you ain't no mind-reader.
> I know what you are....
> X: What am I?
> Crane: A Healer.

Now Xavier reincarnates as a minor Christ-figure, operating a "clinic" from a basement in the old part of the city, performing diagnoses on the sick and the aged, his X-vision bringing in money and renown. With his thick black shades and professional grooming, he looks like a hipster musician from a piano lounge... or a media evangelist whose mystique is both sexual and dangerous.

Diane Fairfax hears of this 'healer', seeks him out. Already in conflict with his greedy manager and distracted from his experiment, Xavier walks out on Crane and drives off with the svelte Diane.

Here we're treated to a Spectorama montage of the cityscape as seen through the altered consciousness of X.

> Diane: What do you see?
> X: The city... as if it were unborn, rising into the sky with fingers of metal... limbs without flesh, girders without stone... signs hanging without supports, wires dipping and swaying without poles...

> the city unborn, flesh dissolved in an acid of light... a City of the Dead.

The montage is an off-focus selection of grids, lights, neon spreads and cellular blots similar to the oil and transparency imagery of a hippy light show. Psychologically, the sequence is similar to an acid trip, perhaps inspired by the mescaline writings of Huxley (*The Doors of Perception*) and/or Sartre (*La Nausee*). "In the Country of the Blind, the One-Eyed Man is King" (H.G. Wells)

Cut To: an aerial shot of a highway in the desert. Like all drug fables, X requires increasing amounts of the X compound to sustain his altered state... and where better to get his hands on the money he needs than Las Vegas? Here the universal fantasy of easy money by beating the odds overwhelms his altruism. Mistaking his obsessive behaviour and fantastic luck as pure criminal deviousness, the casino authorities challenge Xavier when he breaks the Black Jack table.

Cornered, he throws large handfuls of his winnings at the crowd and escapes during the ensuing stampede, highjacks a Lincoln at the door, embarks on a crazy drive into the Mojave pursued by a helicopter, his eyes sheathed in white, the demon blinds that have now become a cliché in occult thrill movies.

He rolls the car but survives to stagger into a revivalist service in a tent on the outskirts of a small railway town. This is a fated rendezvous between the action and the subtext. The scene, with its curious blend of comic strip aesthetics and New Age mysticism, reveals the familiar split between American fundamentalism and science. Here the urgent edge of Milland's performance as the doomed idealist reaches its brilliant zenith:

> Preacher: Are you a sinner? Do you wish to be saved?
> X: Saved? No. I've come to tell you what I see.... There are great darknesses, farther than Time itself... and beyond the darkness, a light that glows, changes... and in the centre of the universe... an eye that sees us all....

Here his eyes seem to blow a fuse and he staggers, raises his hands protectively.

> Preacher: No! You see the sin of the Devil, and the Lord has told us what to do about it... said Mathew in Chapter 5, 'If thine eye offend thee, pluck it out!'

The congregation chants "pluck it out" as the camera pulls back on the scene, X's eyes now black holes as if his consciousness has expanded too far and collapsed, leaving him an isolated shell within a world of superstition and conformity. The police are at the door with Diane, but we're not concerned with crime and retribution, rather sin and contrition.

Anticipating the New Age techno-mysticism of science and eastern philosophy, drugs and inner-space, *The Man With The X-Ray Eyes* is pure American sub-culture, primitivist, historically significant, subversive in the classic Corman manner.

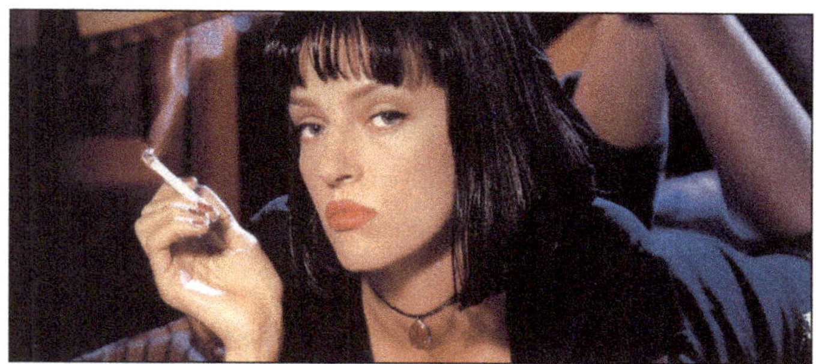

Quentin Tarantino: *Pulp Fiction*

Pulp Fiction (1994) writ. and dir. Quentin Tarantino cine. Andrzej Sekula star. John Travolta (Vincent), Samuel L. Jackson (Jules), Uma Thurman (Mia), Ving Rhames (Marcellus), Tim Roth (Pumpkin), Amanda Plummer (Honey Bunny), Bruce Willis (Butch), Peter Greene (Zed), Harvey Keitel (Wolf), Eric Stoltz (Lance)

Quentin Tarantino: Master Of The Gun Commercial

Nostalgia, n. the need to find comfort in the past when you have no future. This pretty well sums up the retro complexion of this film, and the characters who inhabit it.

Two sociopaths—one white, one black—prowl along in their nostalgic car listening to nostalgic music, their conversation somewhere between the mundane and the irrelevant. You follow them into the lobby of a shabby apartment building, endure their banter about the boss' wife and what a Big Mac is in Europe.

There's a bumbling absurdity to it all, like a buddy cop movie shot by, say, Antonioni. They arrive (eventually) at the apartment of some young men who look more like college students than "business associates" of the beast these two hoods represent. They shoot everybody in the room—sooner or later —after some routine interrogation and humiliation, although they almost get whacked themselves.

Meet Vincent (Travolta) and Jules (Jackson), two more Hollywood clowns with guns. Their ambiguous karma and self-indulgent conversations are quite funny, although they often spend too much time in the script and out of the action. Still, this sort of transitional action is Tarantino's signature style, and is often quite effective in its juxtaposition of the expected against the unexpected. Like workers who spend all morning in the van getting to the job, you just never know when someone is going to die or say something gross.

Tarantino's method is this: never complete a scene if you can cutaway to another and come back later, because that way you can create a plot when there really is no plot at all. Or: how to make a silk purse out of a sow's ear.

It's quite effective. It allows several characters to have their own story rather than be mere vassals in someone else's story, some asshole hero we've seen succeed and fail a million times before. It's an innovation on the commonly used master-slave scene technique of T.V. drama. You're positively amazed when you end up in the restaurant again with Pumpkin (Roth) and Honey Bunny (Plummer) as they conduct their spontaneous robbery. Who would've thought that this droll little prologue would turn out to be the master scene in this episodic collection of vignettes? Like a murder mystery, the action returns to the first person you meet.

The story of Mia Wallace (Thurman), the white drug fiend wife of the big bad black gangster Marcellus is too long. She's a stereotype despite the nineties inversion. Her night out with Vincent—an "assignment" from Marcellus while he's taking care of business—is more black comedy with a mixed message. First Vincent scores some heroin, gets loaded for the date, picks up Mia who's already loaded on coke. They go to Jack Rabbit, a restaurant constructed as a Time Trap, more American pop nostalgia. The Host is an Ed Sullivan dressup, the waitresses various Hollywood sex queens such as Marilyn Monro and Mamie van Doren. The live music? Rockabilly. The booths? Fifties convertibles.

It's amazing how resilient this pop culture of Fender reverb, pastels, glitter and deco soda fountain decor can be. Certainly it fits with Tarantino's *Pulp Fiction* metaphor, although its inclusion is more ephemeral than relevant. They return to Mia's house and she OD's while Vincent is upstairs taking "a piss". He rushes her to his dealer's house and like a bunch of children playing at doctor and nurse, they bring her back with a needle of adrenaline punched straight into the heart. As Mia vaults back into life, the hypo still impaled in her chest, the dealer's wife says, "That was fuckin' trippy."

No doubt. But more trippy than, say, the Twist dance trophy they won at Jack Rabbit's?

"What does it feel like to kill a man?"

The story of Butch (Willis), the boxer who was supposed to throw a fight as a favour to Marcellus ("In the 5th, my ass goes down"), is the most effective despite the absurd scene with the female taxi driver who says she's Colombian but sounds like a Russian mail order bride. It's definitely pulp, alright. As Butch stripes down in the back seat to cool off or reflect upon the value of his flesh, the Colombian chick cabbie asks, "What does it feel like to kill a man?" It seems Butch punched his opponent into oblivion as well as reneging on his deal with Marcellus.

His girlfriend awaits in a bed in a seedy motel. She's another foreign number who sounds similar to the cabbie and is of similar dimensions and intellect. She has forgotten to recover Butch's ancestral watch from his apartment as instructed. Butch gets very, very angry, but spares this dumb little vixen, borrows her battered Honda, heads to his apartment, reenters via the back yard of an adjacent house. He recovers his watch—the one his dead P.O.W. father wore in a Hanoi prison—and slips into the kitchen to make himself some pop tarts when he notices a machine gun with a silencer lying on the counter. It's Vincent's, who's been sent by Marcellus to take care of the treacherous Butch. Too bad Vincent is taking "a shit". Butch strafes him with his own gun as he emerges from the can.

Butch thinks he's home-free now, can collect his bets, head for the South Seas, maybe Mexico. He waits at an intersection as a large black man crosses the street carrying some take-out food. It's Marcellus... who recognizes him, despite the shabby little car. Butch boots the gas, hits Marcellus who bounces onto the hood and over the roof. As he accelerates through the intersection, he gets whacked laterally by a speeding car. As he crawls out of the wreckage, Marcellus—who has survived the hit and run quite nicely—starts shooting. He flees into a nearby pawn shop with Marcellus in pursuit.

Strange how you never know what will greet you on the other side of any door you might open. Butch and Marcellus are taken prisoner by the creepy owner. As he keeps them hostage with his shotgun, he gets on the phone: "Zed... Maynard. Spider just caught a couple of flies." Zed arrives quickly and Butch and Marcellus are taken to the basement, where they meet The Gimp, a masked pervert in a black leather stunt suit who just happens to be living in a large trunk. The Gimp is restrained by a chain which allows him some movement via an overhead rail. As Zed and Maynard bugger Marcellus in the next room, The Gimp moves on Butch who easily beats him unconscious. For some reason he feels sympathy for Marcellus and interrupts the rape, armed with a Japanese Samurai sword he finds in the shop upstairs. Marcellus and Butch make their peace, and Butch exits riding Zed's chopper as Marcellus plans the perverts' torture and death.

More scenes from the comics? Maybe. You can always find an item in a Californian newspaper most weeks that records just such scenes of innovative sex and violence.

"No, this wasn't luck—this was divine intervention."

The narrative drops back to the unfinished business in the apartment of the college kids. This seems strange because you know Vincent is dead (Butch shot him) and you think Time is linear. Apparently not.

Apparently you were left without the moral. Vincent and Jules are surprised by a young man who has been hiding in the next room. He starts shooting but misses with all six bullets. They shoot him, but Jules is now a changed man. As he examines the stray bullet holes in the wall, he decides his good luck isn't luck at all but "divine intervention".

They leave the apartment with the recovered money and a black kid called Marvin, whose fate will be in Marcellus' hands. As they drive along, Vincent's gun accidentally discharges, blows off Marvin's head. Jules decides to drive to the house of a friend called Jimmy (Tarantino), call in the services of a body disposal expert called The Wolf (Keitel). While this sort of bungling is in keeping with Vincent's basic incompetency, the sequence is again overdrawn and even tedious. It seems to be designed to give Tarantino and Harvey Keitel cameo roles. The acting is stiff, the routines beside the point. You've already been sensationalized by several murders and scenes of self-abuse, so the black humour here is marking time, not advancing it.

Like a school principal who makes two vandals clean up their mess, the Wolf makes Vincent and Jules wipe up the blood and brain tissue in the back seat of the car. When the body and the car are finally disposed of at a North Hollywood wrecking yard called Monster Joe's, Wolf says to Vincent, "Because you are a character doesn't mean you have a character." While this piece of advice from the maestro is wasted on a nimrod like Vincent, you also wonder if this is some sort in-joke about

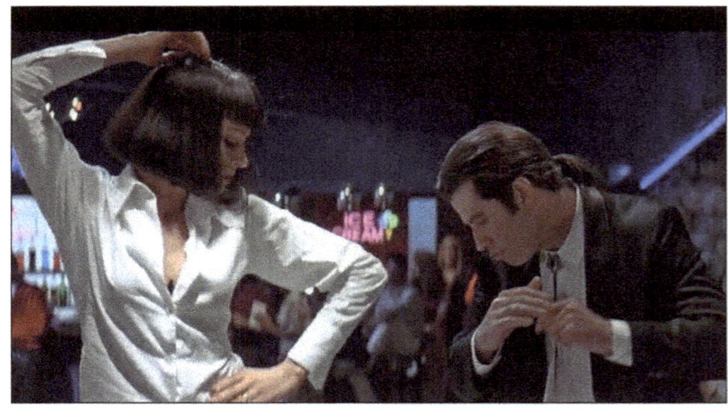

Keitel's cameo. It's a shame to see Keitel as a parody of himself... although by this point just about all the characters seem to be winging it. Improvisation doesn't create character, it merely reveals the actor.

It begins in a cafe, ends in the same cafe. The action is circular and episodic, with a Time shuffle in between. It's taken Hollywood a long time to recognize that the linear Time narrative is a bit of a bore, especially if it ends in a shootout. Tarantino recognizes this, and he uses a shuffle script to deliver a contradictory moral, that is, Jules the Master Enforcer delivers a sermon about the stupidity of crime and violence to the amateur criminals, Honey Bunny and Pumpkin.

As usual, Vincent is taking a shit. As Honey Bunny tries to relieve Jules of his briefcase [loaded with crime money... or plutonium maybe, as this is a "homage" to *Kiss Me Deadly* (1955)] [or ripoff, if you see it as plagarism], he finds himself staring into the muzzle of a heavy automatic. Still believing in divine intervention, Jules tells the two amateurs that they're lucky as "I'm in a transitional period." He actually gives them money before sending them packing. You don't know if they've learned their lesson from "the Shepherd" but you do know that Vincent certainly hasn't.

They casually exit the restaurant, Vincent heading for his death, Jules to "walk the earth like Cain in *Kung Fu*."

If you were to take the guns and shooting out of this script, what would be left? Sex, drugs and rock 'n' roll? Lots of nostalgia and driving around in cars is what. And who does that? The idle young. This appeals to the 9 mm brigade who dabble in Home Invasions and dope dealing. While you know it's only a movie, there's something very uncool about these killers who carry on as if they're simple tradesmen who humiliate and shoot people for a living and have absolutely no conscience about the murders they commit. When Jules chooses to abandon the trade, it isn't because of guilt. He simply recognizes that his hand has run out and if he doesn't quit, he'll be dead.

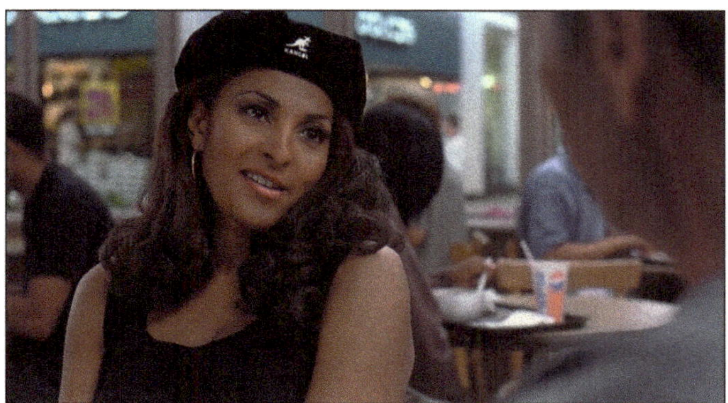

Quentin Tarantino: *Jackie Brown*

Jackie Brown (1997) dir. Quentin Tarantino writ. Tarantino (from the novel *Rum Punch* by Elmore Leonard) cine. Guillermo Navarro star. Pam Grier (Jackie Brown), Samuel L. Jackson (Ordell Robbie), Robert de Niro (Louis), Bridget Fonda (Melanie) (Surfer Girl), Michael Keaton (Dect. Ray Nicolet), Robert Forster (Max Cherry)

It's a truism that any film scripted from a novel is better than those that aren't in terms of depth. Elmore Leonard writes novels of character and setting while Quentin Tarantino writes scripts of attitude and sensation. In theory, this should be a good production combo as a typical Leonard hero is an aging pragmatist fighting it out with a bunch of hoods heavy on attitude, low on intellect.

The hero this time is a woman, Jackie Brown (Grier), a Hispanic black who is fighting the odds as a low-paid stewardess ($16 thou a year) with a record (dope) on a nothing airline doing the surf 'n' turf run between L.A. and Cabo San Lucas, Mexico. Like many minority women trying to escape the birth-curse of victimhood and citizenship without real social security, she's forced into crime as the only means of survival. As is typical of such Leonard characters, she's a sympathetic figure because of her gutsy street-smarts and female vulnerability, a faded beauty on the threshold of middle-age and deepening loneliness. Her sexuality is sustained through the eyes of the alter-hero, Max Cherry, the bail bondsman who becomes her accomplice in crime if not in love everlasting. Max is also middle-aged and single, a straight-shooter whose life on the edge of crime hasn't eroded his spirit with cynicism but given him a secular pragmaticism familiar from American films of yore ie. the soft-talking leader of the waggon train or the team. A loner whose isolation is a matter of integrity, not lovelessness.

In essence, Max and Jackie are typical of many Americans in the nineties, facing the wounding march towards old age unmarried, without meaningful friends or family. The problem is more acute for Jackie.

> Jackie: I ain't going back to jail... how do you feel about getting old, Max?
> Max: I never think about it.
> Jackie: Different for a woman. I always feel like I'm starting over.

Jackie's problem is that she got busted bringing in some crime money from Mexio plus a few grams of coke for Ordell Robbie (Jackson), a black homicidal gun dealer who lives in a beach front condo with a white chick, "Surfer Girl" (Fonda), who now perceives her as a threat to his business. The cops are clearly onto him, as a minor runner is arrested with some guns and they have been stalking Jackie Brown.

Jackson's performance as the "bad ass nigga" Ordell Robbie is superb. First we see him relaxing with a recently paroled associate called Louis (de Niro) watching a video, *Chicks With Guns*, wherein a parade of shapely bimbos demonstrate the fire power of a variety of automatics, from the Tech 9 (the most popular in America) through to the infamous AK-47.

> Ordell: AK-47, absolutely, positively the best there is... when you got to kill every motherfuck in the room, accept no substitutes... that's the Chinese model, I git 'em for 850.

Typical of the black voodoo male, Ordell orders his woman to fix his drinks, answer his phone... and she does so contemptuously, although it's more because it's an inconvenience to her hash smoking than an affront to her pride. She thinks Ordell is full of shit, doesn't know anything about guns, is faking it.

> Melanie: (to Louis) He's not too bright... he moves his lips when he breathes... he's a fuckup.

She doesn't know it yet but in fact she's describing Louis. As an unlikely "white trophy" girlfriend and respondent of Ordell's black jive sexism, she lives in sort of coma, shaped by the hippy past (she drives a VW bus, listens to psychedelic music) and the multicultural present, doomed by her inability to see crime and criminals as more than a sexual fantasy... and to keep her jeering mouth shut. Towards the end, when she's shot in the parking lot by Louis, you recognize the problem as her lack of judgement, not his lack of control.

However, Ordell is soon revealed as a nasty piece of work. In a real time scene typical of many that allow dialogue rather than action to move the story, he visits Max Cherry, posts bond for Beaumont, his recently arrested "employee". There's nothing altruistic in this, as he follows up with a visit to Beaumont, deceives him into climbing into the trunk of an Oldsmobile sedan, drives to a waste lot behind a gas depot, shoots him. He drives to a whore's house, collects Louis, opens the trunk, shows him the body.

> Louis: Who's that?
> Ordell: That's Beaumont, an employee I had to let go... a clear cut case of him or me... and there ain't no motha fuckin' way it was gonna be me. Now, Louis, if you're gonna come in on this deal you better be prepared to go all the way....

By now you're thinking, is this fellow Louis also two bricks short of a load? A man of few words, with basic appetites, primitive like the two bracelet tattoos on his left wrist. Left alone with Surfer Girl, he's soon smoking hash and screwing her—not by his own desire and manipulation but by hers. Sex is just like junk food—he unzips, takes her from behind as if the missionary position would be too personal, too removed from the hit and run reality of life with no fixed address except the penitentiary. He drifts like a mental patient on lithium, his tranquility a false lagoon concealing the soul of a failed criminal. He too is on the broken path of middle-age.

Later, in the Cockatoo Inn, Louis admits he had sex with Surfer Girl.

> Ordell: Ah hope you felt appropriately guilty afterwards. (they laugh) She tryin' to play your ass against mine.
> Louis: Yeah.

The closest to human sympathy and regret Ordell comes is when he shoots Louis after the money exchange scam:

> Ordell: What tha fuck happened to you, man? Your ass used to be beautiful.

Then he finishes him with another bullet.

It seems improbable, but Max Cherry falls in love with Jackie Brown at first sight. Maybe it isn't love. Maybe it's like a *Fata Morgana*, a mirage driven by a middle-age crisis, a desire to be in love but only a trick of distance and the light. He sees her emerge from the shadows, leaving the jail, immediately hits on her, takes her for a drink. She steals his gun and uses it to outwit Ordell who tries to strangle her, solve problem number two. Jackie is too smart, too hip, for the transparent charm that

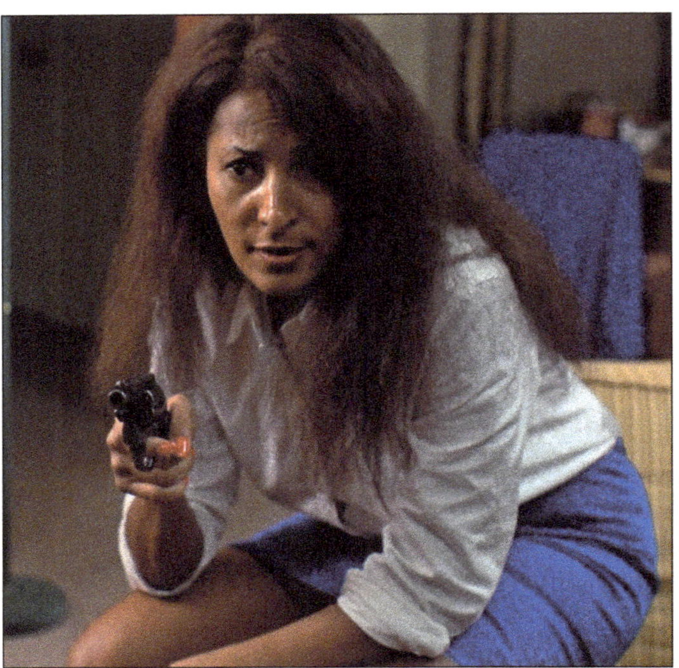

Ordell dispenses like a pimp. Her survivalism is typical Elmore Leonard, who never allows Evil the final hand in his universe. Jackie devises a plan to get free of Ordell, the cops, her lousy job and the slavery of being poor and 44. She will get Ordell's Cabo money for him as part of a sting operation with the cops. With Max Cherry's help, she intends to outwit them all, keep the half mil and—like all movie desperadoes with a dream—go somewhere nice and warm. The complexity of the exchange is handled extremely well and Tarantino demonstrates undeniable talent in the way he structures the narrative at this point.

The action is at a mall in Torrance, involves a switcharama routine with two identical shopping bags. With so many characters and a tradition of real time sequencing the challenge is to make the action comprehensible as well as maintaining tension. Using several cleverly inserted flashbacks within the mall frame, Tarantino manages to reveal the scam and advance the action without compromising story, character or naturalism. In all, it's an excellent example of recovered narrative from several P.O.Vs, using a technique of withheld information and revelation by circumstance.

An old Leonard trick (and one which Tarantino has also used) is to measure characters against their preference in music, invariably nostalgic baggage from their youth. Jackie listens to the Delfonics, while Surfer Girl (Melanie) listens to acid pop. Ordell apparently digs Johnny Cash which, with Max's conversion to the Delfonics, completes the cross-cultural fantasy of both hero and villain.

So much of American film is rooted in the convention of second-time around hustlers trying to get easy money that you expect cliched expositions of violence and casual death as part of the gun-drama fantasy genre. Certainly Tarantino has been guilty of the guns-are-hip obsession. In Leonard's novels, guns are matter of fact, tools used to play the game. There's nothing mystical in Leonard, although Tarantino gets closer to it through sheer ignorance, degenerate stereotyping, the world according to what he saw and read as a kid. But with the solid sociology of Leonard's well-researched novel as a foundation, Tarantino has managed to maximize his true talent as a pop culture dramatist and imagist.

PART THREE:

Film Noir

What is film noir? When I was teaching some of these films in the seventies and eighties, I just saw them as 1940s crime films in black and white, the way Hollywood made them before color stock became viable and—for some—preferable. Then when the French term *serie noire* for hardboiled crime fiction became the same thing for film, I wondered what really defined film noir. Obviously the German expressionist theatre lighting style influenced the cinematography, the chiaroscuro shadow effects and comic book/storyboard montage, but... but what is the black core of it all? Why, the *femme fatale*, and her male patsy who carries out her bidding in their quest for fast, easy money.

The form and style carried into the color crime film by the late fifities, and certainly Hitchcock's *Vertigo* (1958) could be called the first of the neo-noirs, although some might say John M. Stahl's *Leave Her To Heaven* (1945) is the first, even if it lacks the atmospherics and psychology of traditional noir. Today, we even have the *homme fatale*, as seen in Barbet Schroeder's *Our Lady of the Assassins* or Paul Schrader's *American Gigolo*.

But for my money, Roman Polanski's *Bitter Moon* (1992) is the blackest of them all.

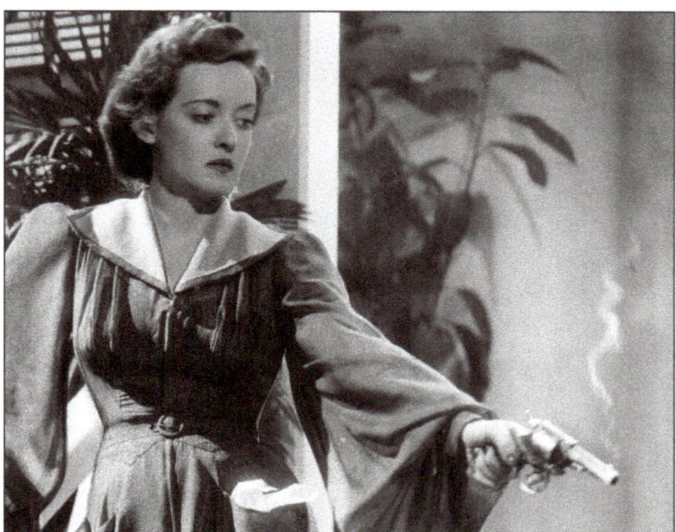

William Wyler: *The Letter*

The Letter (1940) dir. William Wyler cine. Tony Gaudio writ. Edward Koch (from Somerset Maugham's story) music Max Steiner star. Bette Davis (Leslie Crosbie), Herbert Marshall (Robert Crosbie), James Stephenson (Howard Joyce), Gail Sondergaard (Mrs. Hammond), Tetsu Komai (Head Boy), Sen Yung (Ong)

> *"Mandalay by moonlight. The white gateways are flooded with silver and the erections above them are shot with silhouetted glimpses of the sky. The effect is ravishing..."* (Somerset Maugham)

As so much of the action in *The Letter* occurs at night, you suspect that Leslie Crosbie (Davis) is a nympho-somnambulist, betwitched by the moon and the sentient shadows that act as a chorus to her sexual madness while concealing the pornography of her crime. You hear one shot, see someone stagger from the door to the veranda, then fall down the steps before Leslie Crosbie materializes and pumps five more bullets into the fallen victim. You never see the man who was her lover, only Leslie looking downwards as she fires, her face an ambiguous mask, as inscrutable as the moon to whom she eventually raises her eyes.

It's an incredible opening, one in which the lunar atmosphere is a mystic camouflage for a killing whose mystery slowly unravels like the lace work Leslie uses to soothe herself in times of stress. The dead man is Jeff Hammond, another ladies' man in the tight colonial loop of inter-war Mandalay whom no one suspects of having an affair with the solid wife of a rubber plantation manager, Robert Crosbie—another blind love chump. Crosbie immediately sends for his friend and lawyer, Howard Joyce, and despite the fact that Joyce is nobody's fool, he becomes a patsy in Leslie's design to cover up her crime. That he doesn't become a sexual stand-in for her dead lover is probably a matter of fate rather than integrity, as Leslie is as manipulative as she is immoral.

"He tried to make love to me and I shot him."

This isn't entirely an issue of sex and fidelity. Leslie is an accomplished liar. You see her reenact her version of what happened—an uninvited guest, attempted rape, a justifiable homicide, virtue intact. Her husband and the District Officer are duped, for while their code includes men as cads, it precludes women as instruments of evil. Only Joyce is troubled, as his forensic mind anticipates the murder trial that must inevitably follow—why six bullets, when only one was needed?

His uneasiness soon proves justified. When his obsequious clerk Ong tells him about a "friend" who has a letter, Leslie's deception and culpability are revealed. At first she denies having written to Hammond:

> Leslie: We heard about his wife... once, quite by chance, I actually saw her...
> Joyce: What was she like?
> Leslie: Horrible. She was all covered in gold chains... a face like a mask....
> Joyce: So when you knew about her, you stopped having anything to do with Hammond?
> Leslie: (smugly) Yes.

At this point, she means they ostracized Hammond because he had a "secret" Eurasian wife.

> Joyce: I think I should tell you there is in existence a letter in your hand writing...

Leslie admits her lie by creating a bigger one—she invited

Hammond over to ask his advice about a gun for her husband's birthday, she says. A new gun for her husband—Freud would call it the truth. Joyce reads the letter... and the mask is off. Leslie faints, falls to the floor. She has more weapons in her arsenal, however. They reconvene in the First Aid Room:

> Leslie: Are you going to let them hang me?
> Joyce: What do you mean by that, Leslie?
> Leslie: You could get the letter.
> Joyce: Do you believe it's so easy to do away with unwelcome evidence?

They stare at one another like a prelude to sexual intimacy, as if Joyce has now become Hammond. In a film with many great scenes, this is one of the best. While Davis was never a beauty, there's a dangerous vibe in her performance as Leslie Crosbie. As John Huston—who also directed her—says, "There's something elemental about Bette—a demon within her which threatens to break out and eat everybody, beginning with their ears." Howard Joyce escapes with his ears but he loses his integrity. He agrees to get the letter... and in so doing, crosses the line, engages in a criminal act.

Hammond's widow has the letter. The price is ten thousand dollars, exactly the amount that Robert Crosbie has in his savings account. How is this known? You assume that the wily Ong is part of a corruption, a state of affairs systemic to a colonial regime. The price also includes a rider that it must be delivered by Leslie Crosbie herself. While this reversal of Fortune appears to be an unacceptable humiliation, Leslie accepts the conditions eagerly as if it fits perfectly within the design of a larger agenda....

Perhaps this is the best scene in the film. Perhaps it's the best scene in just about any film. It's more than a meeting between two rivals, a rejected mistress and a widowed wife—it's the meeting of East and West, two phases of the moon. Men express themselves through women, and it's through women that culture is born. Maugham would have us believe that the greatest misogynists are women themselves—an embittered view of a failed heterosexual. But the politics in this encounter are as primal as they are territorial, as homosexual as they are sado-masochist. Contrition may be in the ritual.

"Those eyes like a cobra's eyes..."

Ong leads the lawyer and his client to a shop in the Chinese quarter. In a room upstairs they find an old man smoking opium, the apparent "friend" that Ong has been negotiating through. They wait. Glass chimes tinkle... and Mrs. Hammond parts the beaded curtain and enters the room. Her expression is an asexual mask, but like the stone face of a temple idol, it assumes the identity required by the devotee. Now the dominator, she becomes masculine.

The two women stare at one another.

> Ong: She speaks only Malay.
> Joyce: Ask her if she has the letter.

Without taking her eyes off Leslie's, the Eurasian widow tells Ong that Leslie must remove her shawl, the white lace head covering. Leslie obeys. The blood money is passed to Mrs. Hammond but she waves it away. Leslie approaches the low platform, eyes raised as if once again contemplating the face of the moon. Mrs. Hammond draws the letter from her sleeve, allows it to fall at her feet. Leslie kneels slowly, recovers it. "Thank you," she whispers.

While you suspect her intentions, Leslie is now being driven by something much larger than criminal duplicity. While her husband and friends remain anxious about the trial, Leslie sits serenely with her lacework, almost indifferent to the outcome. Her lawyer goes through the moves like a zombie, his values compromised by the fait accompli of the Malayan way. It doesn't matter, as the prosecution gives no rebuttal and Leslie is acquitted.

In the normal scheme of things the drama would end here. Perhaps you would see Howard Joyce succumbing to her in a clandestine moment, his corruption complete. But somnabulists usually follow the same path... and that path leads to Mrs. Hammond and her eyes "like cobra eyes".

There's nothing sentimental in a story by Somerset Maugham. Sado-masochism runs through his work like a river that divides men from women, yet is a common source of Nature from which they must both drink. Despite working under the strict censorship rules of the period, screenwriter Edward Koch manages to sustain the powerful fatalism of Maughan's world-view... and in fact improves upon the ironic potential of the narrative (in Maugham's story, it's Leslie's husband who confronts Hammond's Chinese mistress and recovers the letter). The ending is typically subversive because while it conforms to the rule that adultery must be punished, it posits the notion that women kill just as easily as men.

As her emotionally destroyed husband gets drunk at the bar, Leslie leaves the party and is drawn to mystic solitude of the moonlit garden. The invitation by her new lover has been sent earlier—a dagger on the mat outside her bedroom door. When she returns, the dagger is gone, but the moon draws her into the garden. Mrs. Hammond waits in the shadows by the gate. Whatever spell Leslie Crosbie is under, it controls her sexual being completely. Just as Love must succumb to Death, she is knifed by Mrs. Hammond. Thus the lesbian solution is a phallic solution.

Suicide? As a form of justice, Leslie's death is another example of the mysterious forces that control our sexual identities and shape the religious response. We exist as shadows in the night.

While many people exalt Welles' cinematic opening in *Citizen Kane* (1941), the tracking shot that Wyler uses to establish setting and mood at the start of *The Letter* (1940) deserves attention. The sequence culminates with the shooting of Hammond and that first vision of a woman possessed. It's outstanding, as are the geometrics of light and shadow that characterize this film as something beyond mere melodrama. *The Letter* starts as a masterpiece, ends as a masterpiece—something rare in the translation of literature into film.

* *The Letter*, first made in 1929, star. Jeanne Eagels. In this version Herbert Marshall plays Leslie's doomed lover.

* James Stephenson (the lawyer, Howard Joyce) died a year later. According to Wyler's biographer Jan Herman (*A Talent For Trouble*), Stephenson was recommended to the director William Wyler by Jack Warner.

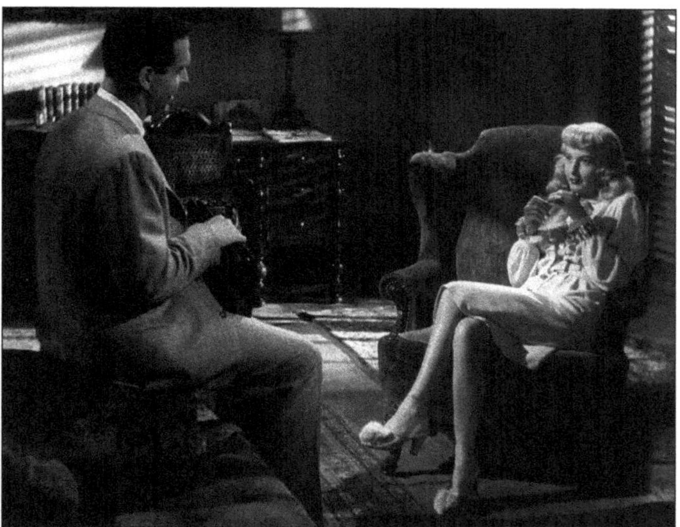

Billy Wilder: *Double Indemnity*

Double Indemnity (1944) dir. Billy Wilder writ. Raymond Chandler & Billy Wilder (from the novel by James Cain) cine. John Seitz music Miklos Rozsa edt. Doane Harrison star. Fred MacMurray (Walter Neff), Barbara Stanwyck (Phyllis Dietrichson), Edward G. Robinson (Barton Keyes), Porter Hall, Fortunio Bonanova, Jean Heather, Bess Flowers, Tom Powers, Byron Barr, Richard Gaines, John Philliber Paramount/Universal

The Cosmology Of Sex

Double Indemnity: is this the definitive film noir? 1. it's in black and white, and 2. it certainly has the pathology: a woman gets a man to commit her crimes on the promise of sex and big money. And that her male dupe is betrayed and takes the fall for the crime is *de rigueur* for the genre. It's an ancient story, older than the Bible and the moralists who wrote it, a mythology from our genes, perhaps.

The frame narrative that contains the story of Los Angeles insurance agent Walter Neff's entrapment and destruction by the fatal sexual magnetism of the ex-nurse Phyllis Dietrichson is classic Wilder, one which he was to repeat with stunning ironic effect in *Sunset Boulevard*... and one which, on the face of it, should be the wrong way to tell a story. If the fate of the protagonist is revealed from the beginning, what's left to keep you watching? A lot. *Double Indemnity* is a trial in the court of public opinion. We know the accused is guilty as he has confessed... but we want to know the details because this man Neff (Fred MacMurray) doesn't look like a criminal even though he's been shot and is reciting his confession into the dictaphone of his boss. The use of the dictaphone is more than a visual prop, as Neff adopts the terse narrative style of an office memo to reveal his role in the murder of the oil industry manager Dietrichson and the attempted fraud of the Pacific All Risk insurance company. It's interesting to note that the script writer—the famous crime novelist Raymond Chandler—used a dictaphone to outline his stories, so the novelty of this new technology was something he was familiar with. So we take sociological/cosmological notice that on the eve of the Second World War, the confession has become a secular ritual between man and his machine.

The cosmology of sex: in a divine universe, sex is the completion of a crime; in a secular universe, sex is the prelude to a crime. *Double Indemnity* exists in a placenta of secular astrology, where fate and chance are subject to the mathematics of an insurance company's actuarial tables rather than to the divine Fortune of a Christian God... or any god for that matter. Fate is a condition of individual intelligence, knowledge of the odds, the mathematics of the perfect crime. In this way the male patsy is invariably an expert, an insider capable of executing his lover's desire with stealth and viral consequence. Walter Neff is just such a man. Walter Neff is the architect of the symbolic matrix, double indemnity, a scripted crime in which the rip-off is a double payoff for double trouble.

As Neff dictates his final memo to his boss—the little man with the big cigar, Barton Keyes (Edward G. Robinson)—the story reverts to the beginning, when Neff stops off at the Dietrichson's Mediterranean revivalist villa in Glendale one day in May, 1938, on a routine car insurance assignment. Dietrichson isn't home but his wife is, wrapped in a towel, fresh from "a sun bath". It's lust at first sight, especially when Neff spots that kinky little ankle bracelet on that kinky little ankle as Phyllis (Barbara Stanwyck) descends the tiled stairway.

> Phyllis: You from the Automobile Club?
> Neff: All Risk....

Indeed. It's not long before Neff is willing to risk all for this luminous blond femme fatale who seems to be the perfect partner for his thrust and parry dialogue:

> Neff: (as they walk to the door) 8.30 tomorrow evening, then...
> Phyllis: That's what I suggested.
> Neff: Will you be here too?
> Phyllis: I guess so. I usually am.
> Neff: Same chair, same perfume, same anklet?
> Phyllis: I wonder if I know what you mean...
> Neff: I wonder if you wonder...

In a society where manners mean discipline, innuendo is the preferred method of sexual engagement. Chandler was a master of this sort of sub-textural dancing, where dialogue is always a hidden agenda about to be revealed. "I wonder if you wonder" is the sort of brilliant mutant palindrome in which the statement is its own mirror—"I wonder if you wonder/ you wonder if I wonder"—a telepathic seal on the perfect crime.

Murder Sometimes Smells Like Honeysuckle

The ambiguous character of MacMurray's Walter Neff... a nice guy, modestly successful, but a loner with a faint smell of cynical opportunism within his persona, a salesman who won't say no to a glass of ice tea... or maybe an extra pair of panties for his closet. While there's no evidence of any previous skullduggery, we sense that his fall from grace isn't from a great moral height. On the walls of his bachelor apartment we might notice the triptych of bare-knuckle prize-fighters... but think nothing of it. He has a nice manner, is respected at work—Keyes wants him to be his assistant manager. Yet, smart as he is, Neff is just another blind love chump: "How could I have known that murder sometimes smells of honeysuckle...."

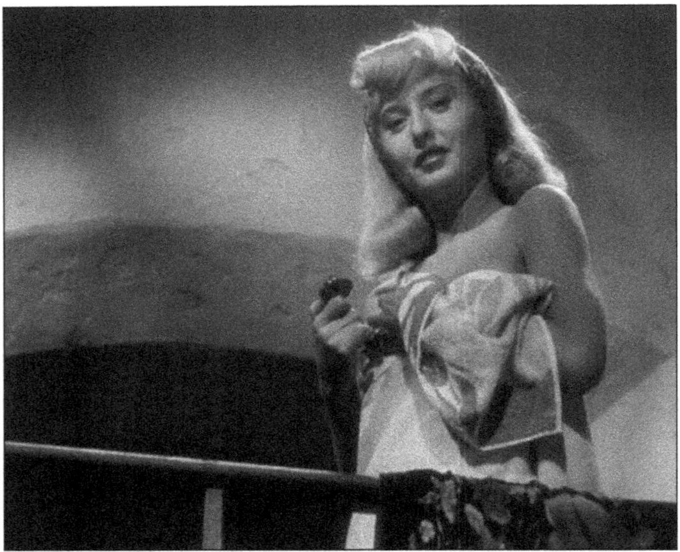

The smell of the Spring honeysuckle on the roads of Glendale remind him of Phyllis' perfume, a scent she says she picked up across the border in Ensenada. Even as he's dying from her bullet, his last action is to try and get to the border, as if this sanctuary might somehow return him to the arms of the woman who betrayed him. Barbara Stanwyck as the *femme fatale* isn't as much a testimony to her beauty as it is to her superb acting and the magical noir cinematography of John Seitz. She's no voluptuary, no garter-belt maw of erotic death, but an atmosphere. Like an animal, Neff recognizes her by smell, not by common sense. Stanwyck's Phyllis has the urgent edge of destiny, the woman who has been waiting for his arrival, and now that he has arrived, becomes his tarot for the future.

In the recently invented culture of thirties Los Angeles, people encounter people without history. It's Neff's misfortune to discover when it's much too late that Phyllis has a history—one that includes the murder of her husband's first wife. Like a black widow spider, Phyllis uses sex as a weapon, and her pleasure is political more than sensual.

Orgasm and death, incubation and replication—this seems to be the bleak mechanistic reduction of it all, the black loveless heart of the matter. Within the modernist sets of the classic film noir sex is primarily an act of self-destruction.

The Murder: The Play Within

A minimized situation as a maximized action is classic Billy Wilder. Consider the scene where Neff visits the acerbic, alcoholic Dietrichson in his house in order to get his signatures on two sets of forms—one for his automobile insurance, the other for the double indemnity life insurance his wife and her new lover have arranged as a prelude to his death. Tired, irritated, distracted by his daughter Lola's unacceptable liaison with a med-school dropout, Dietrichson is easily duped, signs the second form, accepting Neff's assurance that it's merely a required duplicate of the first.

But just as his deception has been initiated, so too the deception of Neff himself. The symbolism is in the chequers game that Phyllis and Lola play nearby. Lola says she's going out to meet her girlfriend, denies any intent of meeting her boyfriend, the penniless Nino Sergetti. Yet when Neff leaves the house, he finds the sexy young Lola waiting for him in his coupe... and once again he finds himself being manipulated by a woman. But who is manipulating who? As it develops, Neff's ambiguous relationship with Lola fits perfectly with Phyllis' second agenda.

The actual murder of Dietrichson is carried out like a play wherein Neff is both his assassin and his understudy. That Neff pretends to be the dead man complete with crutches and leg cast when he boards the train for Palo Alto is both a prophecy and a parody of his fate. Like some latter day Oedipus, his wounded leg is a fatal match for the bracelet that Phyllis wears on her left ankle. So Neff pretends to be Dietrichson and pretends to fall from the Observation Car of the train... and when the police find Dietrichson's body it seems to be a simple case of accidental death, regardless of how rare death by falling from a train happens to be. It's so rare, so improbable, it qualifies as a double indemnity in Pacific All Risk's actuarial scale. So a $50,000 payout becomes $100,000 (which in 1938 would be the equivalent of a million five today or thereabouts). Yet it's the very improbability of this form of death that draws Keyes's suspicions. Edward G. Robinson embraces his role of the little man with a "little man" inside like an old snake guarding a treasure.

While his expression is as sour as the cigars he habitually smokes, he nevertheless has real affection for Neff, and even offers him a job as his assistant. When Neff turns him down, Keyes says, "I thought you were smart, Walter... but you're just a little taller." This reference to size is, of course, a reference to the double-self: big man, little man, moral man, smart man.

Straight Down The Line

The symbolisms make us smile with their forthright ironies. Dietrichson's "double" crutches are incidental compared to the many other instances of "double" imagery, such as Neff's two "crimes" (Dietrichson and his daughter) or his two shots when he completes his role as sexual executioner. The self-serving morality of the situation is often repeated in the phrase "straight down the line", a euphemism that bonds Walter and Phyllis in their murder pact. Whether "rolling a few lines" in the bowling alley to relieve tension or constructing a false accident between the two rails on the train tracks, the line these greedy pair of lovers follows is anything but straight.

And it's through the second woman—Dietrichson's daughter Lola—that Neff learns just how divergent Phyllis really is. It's Lola who reveals that Phyllis murdered her mother, and that Phyllis is now involved with the chippy Nino Sergetti. Jealousy is one thing, but what are we to make of Neff's relationship with Lola? We never see him having sex with Phyllis, yet we assume it, just as Keyes through his intuitive "little man" assumes there is something not right about the Dietrichson claim.

But Neff and Lola? He sees her repeatedly in parallel to Phyllis' "affair" with Sergetti, takes her to dinner, listens to her cry (just as he'd listened to Phyllis cry) on the hill above the Hollywood Bowl... all ostensibly in a friendly way to distract her from those accusations about her cheating lover and her murdering step-mother. In their first scene alone together, Lola says, "I thought you could let me ride with you...." We just know that if *Double Indemnity* were to be remade today, say, ambiguity would be discarded, the sex scenes made explicit.

So is Neff acting sexually or politically? Phyllis thinks it's both. In their final scene she accuses him while admitting her own nefarious duplicity with Sergetti.

Accidentally On Purpose

When Phyllis's double-cross is confirmed for Neff (after listening to a recording of Keyes's analysis of the claim), he realizes one murder is not enough. Keyes has had Sergetti tailed and now Sergetti is viewed as Phyllis's accomplice. Is it jealousy or criminal pragmaticism that sends Neff into the honeysuckle night to settle up with Phyllis in her dimly lit house?

This is one of the great film noir scenes, photographically as well as dramatically. Phyllis, scented and wearing silk pajamas, conceals her pearl-handed pistol below a cushion before dimming the lights. She lights a cigarette, settles back on the couch to await Neff. The shadows of the venetian blinds cast their signature noir bars across the stucco wall. When Neff enters, he is preceded by his shadow, as if this rendezvous is already in the immaterial world.

> Phyllis: We're both rotten.
> Neff: Only you're a little more rotten than me....

Phyllis shoots first but seems unwilling or incapable of finishing the job. Conscience or real love? In their final clinch, Neff fires twice, makes no mistake. *Double Indemnity.* As he leaves the house, he remembers to pick up his hat... that recurring metaphor in this modernist fable of sex and death. No longer will they meet "accidentally on purpose".

Crime And The Impotent Lover

Lola recounts to Neff how she saw Phyllis in the days before her father's death trying on a black hat, rehearsing to be a widow before the mirror. The pre-meditated murder is an act of theatre for the impotent lover. Both Phyllis and Neff are childless loners, individuals who are constantly rehearsing, yet never create anything except death. Both might be rotten, but they are allowed a small measure of redemption. Phyllis's hesitation, her inability to finish Neff off suggests some love, however small. But Neff's second thoughts about his frame-up of Sergetti suggests a much grander love, a real contrition—he might be doomed but there's no reason why Lola shouldn't have a second chance.

Walter Neff carries Phyllis Dietrichson's bullet with him to end like a snake bite. In fact, he wasn't shot in the middle of July when this sordid tale concludes, but rather in May when he first saw and was scented by her. "I loved you, Walter, and I hated him," says Phyllis in the final clinch. "I wasn't going to do anything about it... until I met you. You planed it."

Even today, looking in on Walter Neff as he recites his death monologue into the absurd horn of a primitive recording machine, the whole business looks and feels like an elegant madness. In the noir universe, there's no insurance for an agent who writes his own plan, it seems.

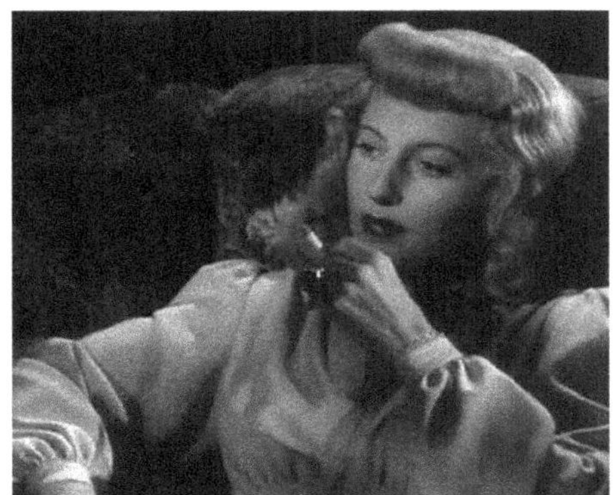

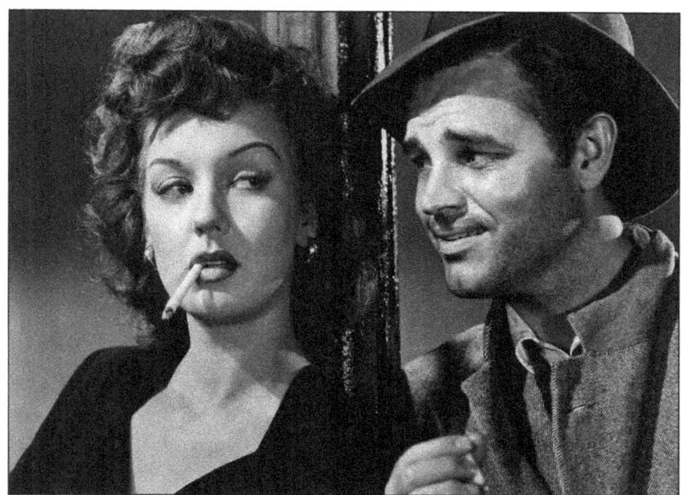

Edgar G. Ulmer: *Detour*

Detour (1945) dir. Edgar G. Ulmer writ. Martin Goldsmith cine. Benjamin H. Kline edt. George McGuire music Erdody star. Tom Neal (Al Roberts), Anne Savage (Vera), Claudia Drake, Edmund MacDonald, Tim Ryan, Esther Howard
P.R.C.

"I Can't Believe You're In Love With Me"

It's amazing what can happen to a person who goes hitch-hiking, especially if he's a jazz pianist from New York trying to hook up with his nightclub singer girlfriend in L.A. Is the hitcher a deviant seeking a victim... or a victim seeking a deviant? You be the judge—if you can handle the crude production values in a film which is often so dark its nitrate must've evaporated before it was printed. For devotees of film noir, this strange film is like a cave painting, a lost artifact of the hunter and the hunted.

With its raw action and raw characters, it becomes a parody of a generational attitude, where women hammer nails for the men who stupidly, eagerly climb onto the cross they construct themselves. Al gets a ride from a bent bookie who has gouges and scars on his wrists—how did he get them? Duelling? "From the most dangerous animal in the world," says the pill-popping bookie. "A woman." That fate should make one man succeed the other and hook up with the sadistic Vera further on up the road seems like a conspiracy... yet, is it?

If you were riding through the desert with a paranoid stranger and he O.D.'d at the wheel just as you're putting up the convertible top for the rain, would you rationalize his death as your fault and dump his body in a gully and drive off in his car? Would you then pick up a woman hitcher and pass yourself off as the dead man in order to impress yourself and the woman? This is exactly what Al Roberts (Tom Neal) does. And of course Vera (Anne Savage) calls his bluff almost immediately, as she's the woman who has ridden and fought with Haskell before Haskell picked up Al. "She must've passed me while I slept," he says in the interior monologue that haunts the narrative like the ghost of a man already dead. Passed me while I slept. Indeed. Everything about this story suggests dream rather than fact.

As a *femme fatale*, Vera is a bleak contrast to the ethereal singer Sue Harvey, the sweetheart Al is pursuing like an ideal he's trying to recover. Hard, cunning, manipulative, this doe-eyed slattern has the volatile nature of a born criminal. Her first move is to blackmail Al into submission. She wants all of Haskell's money, including the car which must be sold to a dealer when they get to L.A. When Al demurs, she snarls, "Just shut-up and remember who's boss here." As they drive into the city, Al observes, "I was further away from Sue than when I started out...."

Just A Piece Of Paper Crawling With Germs

The B-movies of the period often use the frame narrative—the present as an envelope of a flashback or series of flashbacks—and *Detour* is no different. You first see a haggard Al Roberts sitting at the counter in the Nevada Diner—a roadstop in Bakersfield—a paranoid wreck who snarls when another transient tries to strike up a conversation. He exists as a melodramatic caricature, just like a close-up frame from a comic book. His eyes are black rictuses, bad memories erode his face. Through the V.O. his sad story emerges: a piano player at The Break of Dawn club somewhere in New York, in love with a beautiful young singer who leaves for greener pastures in L.A., he decides to bag his gig and hitch his way to the west coast—after all, what was there to stay for? "When this drunk hands me a ten spot for a request I couldn't get excited about," he muses, "it was just a piece of paper crawling with germs. It couldn't buy anything I wanted."

For No Good Reason At All

The full extent of his relationship with Vera is left ambiguous. He's attracted to her or else he wouldn't have picked her up in the first place. He admits that she had a certain fatal attractiveness about her. When she decides to go after old man Haskell Snr.'s fortune by making Al impersonate his dead son, she uses blackmail, and who knows what else? In the 1940s, sex still existed as a hidden ritual, a religious taboo. "Boy," says Vera, "for that kinda dough, I'd let you cut my leg off."

Like Walter Neff in *Double Indemnity*, Al finds himself moving from the impersonation of a dead man to being the dead man. But unlike Walter, Al is no expert and doesn't want to do it, despite Vera's threats. They get drunk, argue, fight. As he relates, "The air got blue... each word from our lips cracked like a whip." It's the amusing street lyricism of Al's narrative that actually sustains *Detour* through the absurd primitivism of its back projections and squalid lighting. When he's driving with Haskell or Vera, the landscape floats like a dream, a hallucinatory effect that isn't always as convincing as it needs to be. Even the frequently used side-wipe transition seems cheap, an anachronism from the silent era. But the cynical V.O. and the tough, street-ass dialogue holds it all together regardless.

Al didn't kill the sleazy Haskell... but he certainly kills the sociopathic Vera, albeit accidentally in an act that is as Freudian as it is ironic. But is it improbable? Who knows. Al's journey has been a series of improbable incidents in search of a probable cause.

Does Al follow through on Vera's plan to fraudulently inherit the Haskell estate? Does he reunite with Sue? Does he ever play the piano again? You expect at least one of these things to happen. But the hyperbole is more important than the plot. In primitivism, coincidence is destiny. It's an odd piece of work, no doubt compromised by a small budget. As a B-movie knockoff, it exists as self-parody in a genre that always plays it straight.

> Al: "Someday a car will stop to pick me up that I never thumbed... yes, Fate or some mysterious force can put the finger on you or me for no good reason at all...."

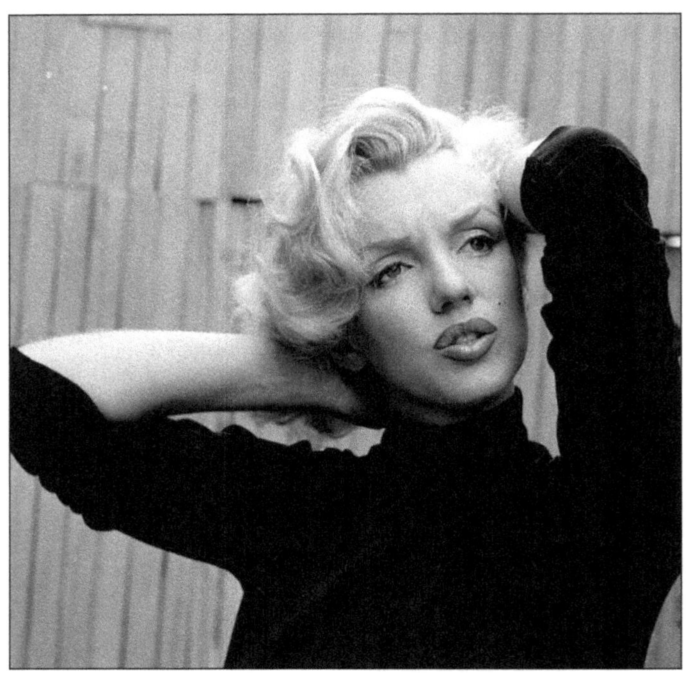

John Huston: *The Asphalt Jungle*

The Asphalt Jungle (1950) dir. John Huston writ. Ben Maddow and John Huston (based on the novel by W.R. Burnett) cine. Harold Rossen star. Sterling Hayden (Dix Handley), Louis Calhern (Alonzo Emmerich), Jean Hagen (Doll), James Whitmore (Gus), Sam Jaffe (Doc), Marilyn Monroe (Angela), Barry Kelley (Lt. Ditich), Anthony Caruso (Louis), John McIntyre (Commissioner), Brad Dexter (Brannon)

The modernism in this drama is in the documentary feel of the settings and the real-time sequences that depend on characterization for emotion rather than music. The style is not unlike the neo-realist drama of de Sica where humans are isolated within an indifferent urban architecture, moving through a semi-tone universe in a gray anticipation of Fate.

In *The Asphalt Jungle*, the streets are empty corridors of stone and concrete, a cage of trolley wires and power poles, where the characters move in a lonely passage between dusk and dawn. Unlike the movie criminals of the nineties, there are people behind them—families, lovers—so their actions have consequences. And unlike most contemporary crime dramas, the story doesn't end with the last bullet, although the last bullet is carried to the end.

Doc Riedensch (Jaffe), a Jewish criminal of German origin, is released from prison and immediately heads to see Cabby (Lawrence), an illegal Bookie, with a plan to steal some diamonds from an upscale jewelry store called Belleteer's. Cabby is the eye of the needle, as it's through him that the essential characters pass who come to make up the gang that performs the heist: Dix (Hayden), the big Irish-American "hooligan" with an obsession for horses and gambling; Gus (Whitmore), the hunchback greasy-spoon operator with a heart of gold; Louis (Caruso), the Italian-American "soup" (nitro) man who can "crack any safe in under four minutes"; and Emmerich (Calhern), the crooked lawyer with an anxiety-invalid for a wife and a "niece" for a mistress.

"Crime Is Only A Left-Handed Form Of Human Endeavor"

The robbery is a simple "hole-in-the-wall" forced entry into the store from the furnace room. The safe is blown with some nitro. The blast disturbs the alarms, which attract the police... and the night watchman who is easily overpowered as the trio of Doc, Dix and Louis coolly make their exit. But as the watchman's gun hits the floor, it discharges and fatally wounds Louis the safecracker in a random stroke of fate. Nonetheless, they slip into the night, return Louis to his wife where he dies later in the company of a priest.

The next consequence has been foreseen by the canny Doc—a double-cross by Mr. Big, Emmerich the lawyer, who is supposed to buy the diamonds before reselling to a fence. Emmerich is waiting for Doc and Dix with his shakedown man, the volatile Brannon who has had one whiskey too many... and is shot dead by Dix, although Dix takes a bullet too. Emmerich confesses that he did the double-cross because he's broke, and invites Dix to shoot him. But Doc suggests he approach the Insurance Company, negotiate a 25% buyback of the jewels. Emmerich is forced to dispose of Brannon's body in the river and use his mistress Angela (Monroe) as a false alibi.

The police visit Emmerich as he plays Casino with his wife, interrogate him about his associate Brannon, whose body has been pulled from the river. When they leave, his wife expresses dismay when Emmerich tells her Brannon may have been connected to the Belleteer robbery.

> Wife: (concerned) Can we go on playing?
> Emmerich: Certainly—why not?
> Wife: Oh Lon... when I think of all those awful people you come in contact with... some of them are downright criminals!
> Emmerich: Oh, there's nothing so different about them. After all, crime is only a left-handed form of human endeavor....

Later, when Emmerich's alibi collapses and the police prepare to arrest him, his child mistress frets about Cuba:

> Angela: What about my trip, Uncle Lonnie?
> Emmerich: Don't worry, baby—you'll have lots of trips.

Emmerich withdraws to another room on the pretext of phoning his wife, shoots himself. Meanwhile Cabby the Bookie is slapped around by the corrupt cop Lt. Ditrich and confesses, betraying the gang for a better deal with the judge. The police descend on Louis as he receives the last rites. Gus and Cabby are already behind bars as Dix and Doc read the papers and realize they have to get out of town. Doc has bonded with Dix, both men recognizing the other's innate integrity.

Doc offers Dix half the loot, but he declines, and gives Doc a thousand bucks to help him get to Cleveland. Dix pulls back the curtain, watches as Doc crosses the street, disappears into the night:

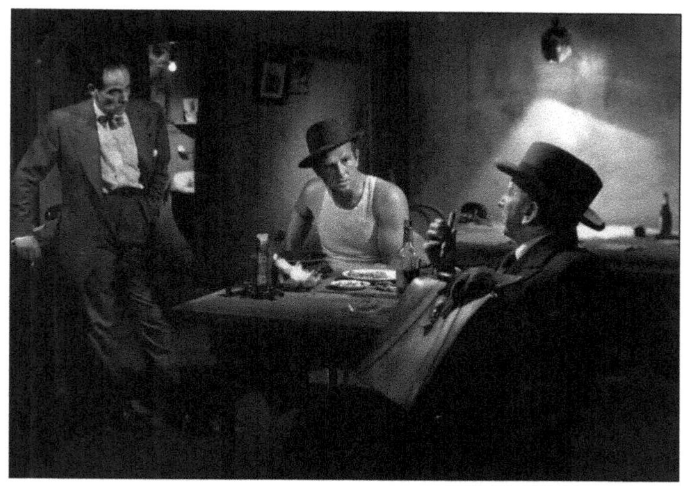

> Dix: That squarehead, he's a funny little guy... I just don't get him at all.
> Doll: Maybe it's because he's a foreigner—they just don't think like us.
> Dix: Anyway, he's got plenty of guts.

Doc is picked up on the outskirts of town when he lingers in a cafe to watch a young girl dance at the jukebox... and Dix dies from his bullet wound in a meadow where he staggers to meet some horses in a hallucinatory quest to complete his unfulfilled dream.

Yes, crime doesn't pay. As the Commissioner tells the Press when they question him about the corruption in Lt. Ditrich's ward: "Suppose we had no police force? The jungle wins."

The approach is out of the tradition of American naturalism as seen in the novels of Norris, Dreiser, Lewis, and others, where character is determined by environment, the architect of fate. The characterizations are driven by the human need for freedom rather than the psychopathic need to kill. Each man has a weakness, but none have a pathology, which marks *The Asphalt Jungle* as quite different from the gangster films of the time, where greed and nihilism presage the future we understand today.

A bit slow for contemporary tastes, it nevertheless has that moody noir feel and raw dialogue that represent the period. Most of the scenes are interiors, so the ambience is controlled by shadow and artificial light, a sunless world where gray is reality.

The opening sequence shows Dix walking through the empty business arcades and alleys of a silent, anonymous American city as a black police cruiser trolls the streets looking for a robbery suspect... "a tall man, Caucasian." The loneliness is pervasive, so crime is an attitude, the only road to freedom when you live in a concrete crypt.

Reinvented as a Western—*The Badlanders*—in 1958, again from a novel by W.R. Burnett. *Cairo* is a 1962 remake set in Egypt while Barry Pollack's 1972 version *Cool Breeze* is a response to the black crime vogue started by *Shaft*.

Influential, as a film by Huston often is.

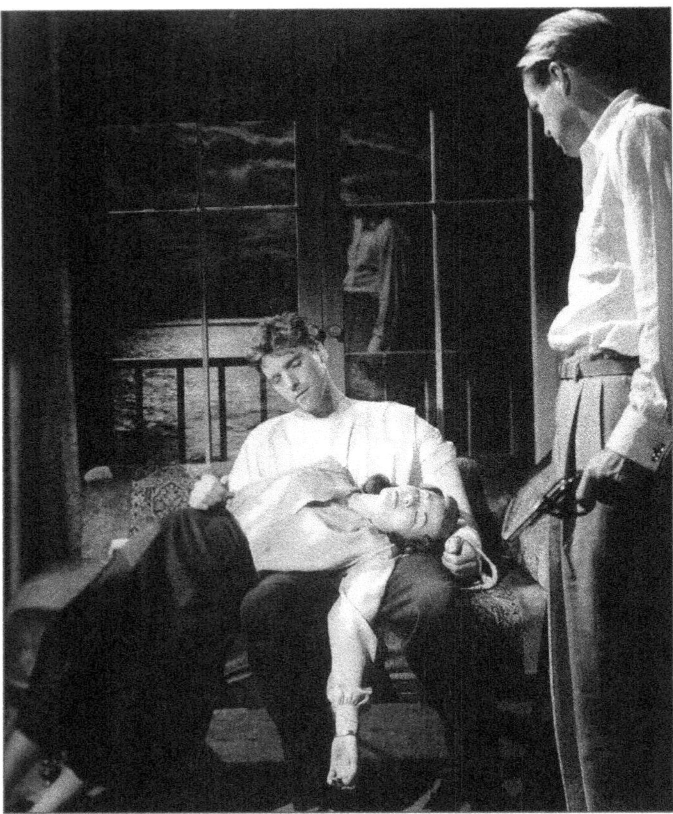

Robert Siodmak: *Criss Cross*

Criss Cross (1949) dir. Robert Siodmak writ. Daniel Fuchs (from the novel by Don Tracy) cine. Franz Planer (special photo by Ted J. Kent) edt. Ted J. Kent music. Miklos Rozsa (with Esy Morales Rhumba Band) star. Burt Lancaster (Steve Thompson), Yvonne de Carlo (Anna), Dan Duryea (Slim Dundee), Stephen McNally (Lieut. Pete Ramirez), Richard Long, Meg Randall, Tom Pedi, Percy Helton, Grif Barnett, Alan Napier
Universal

The Inside Man

This crime drama is typical of the period when motivated characterization is still a consideration, and the execution of the heist becomes a science rather than an act of mere highway brigandage. You might marvel at Yvonne de Carlo's bad-girl beauty or Burt Lancaster's animal vitalism... but what you remember is Siodmak's brilliant choreography of the armored-car robbery. Like a scene from a gas warfare attack, this desperate act is both a reflection of the science of human genocide and a metaphor of urban alienation.

When it happens, the robbery comes as a shock, even though you've been prepared for it, even ride into the action with the armored car as driven by the "inside man", Steve Thompson (Burt Lancaster). You've even been a witness to the gang's plotting of the crime, but the essential details have been withheld. There's no dress-rehearsal, no reconnaissance, no acquisition of weapons, no real warning of the reality and the modernity of the violence when it suddenly happens.

The gang plots just as you see gangs plot heists in the movies that follow—*White Heat, The Asphalt Jungle, The Killing, et. al.* An older man with a basic weakness is brought in to mastermind the logistics—this time it's an old alcoholic who's bribed with a bottle in hand and an account at the local liquor store, a figure you will recognize as the model for Doc, the old sentimentalist in *The Asphalt Jungle*. The robbers aren't just dealing with the capricious hand of Fate, of course, but also their own internal need for treachery, the realization of separate agendas. This is no surprise, as the crime is an alliance between two sexual adversaries, Thompson and Dundee.

The story is told using a frame narrative, where the present sandwiches the past. Thompson returns to his folks' home in L.A. after drifting around the Louisiana-Texas oilfields for three years, trying to shake off the effects of a short, seven month marriage... but of course he hasn't shaken it off, for the first place he heads to is The Roundup, a bar and club where he used to hang out. It's not long before he sees Anna (Yvonne de Carlo) dancing the rhumba... their eyes lock and once again they resume their torrid romance, much to the displeasure of Steve's mother who immediately starts to sabotage it.

His mother might be right, as Anna's character is a bit suspect. An uneducated tough chick who uses her looks to get by, she has another suitor already in the wings, the criminal Slim Dundee (Dan Duryea) who either owns or rents the club. Typical of his ilk, he's surrounded by two or three hoods, two of whom have names—Walt and Vincent. He wears tuxedos, drives a big convertible, is homicidally possessive. So why does Anna suddenly and unexpectedly marry him? Because, as Steve's mother says, "she knows more than Einstein"? Maybe. But it also turns out that Mrs. Thompson uses Pete, the boyhood friend of Steve who is now a cop, to stymie a re-elopement... and, in response, Anna elopes with Dundee.

As sex triangles go, this one is par for the course. While it appears Anna loves Steve, she really loves herself. She begins seeing Steve on the side, unable to break the old habit. As their affair progresses, all the parties become more desperate. When Dundee catches Anna at Steve's house, Steve is forced to invent a story to legitimize the event. "It doesn't look good, Anna," says Dundee as he falsely relaxes with a beer in the living room. Thompson says she's here because he wants to do a "job" with Dundee. Suspicious, bemused, Dundee says, "Why me?" Steve replies, "Because you're the only criminals I know."

The job he has in mind is a six figure heist of an armored car—something regarded as impossible at the time (1948). But as Thompson has been rehired by his old firm, Horton's Armored car service, he will be the inside man.

Criss Cross starts just prior to the robbery. Using an omniscient *Citizen Kane* pan, Siodmak zooms in over the L.A. cityscape to the desperate lovers kissing in the parking lot outside The Roundup. They plan to double-cross Slim Dundee, take all the loot and run away together.

But of course Dundee has a double-cross of his own his mind. When Steve and his co-guard Pops arrive at the industrial plant in San Rafael and unload the sacks of money, a gas bomb explodes, creating a convenient fog in which to stage the heist and the double-cross. Dundee pulls on a gas mask, starts shooting. Pops is killed and Steve, realizing things have gone bad, throws his money sacks back into the armored car. Dundee tries to stop him and both struggle like combat troops in a gas warfare attack. The scene is eerie, a sinister tableaux of impressionism, an inter-zone of life and death.

This action is the centre-piece of the film. While the armored car provides its own novelty, it's the contemporaneous violence which excites your attention. The tools of modern warfare have now become part of the criminal *modus operandi*. Students of film might find an interesting comparison here to the armored car robbery at the beginning of Michael Mann's *Heat*, which no doubt took Siodmak's choreography into consideration. The gas masks become N.H.L. hockey masks and the killings become pandemic.

And Anna? What man wouldn't die for this beautiful piece of work. Still, you might have problems with the ending, despite the solid characterizations and motivations. You might also find Lancaster's V.O. less than satisfactory—disembodied, his voice seems ineffective. It could be the writing, it could be the recording mix, or it could be Lancaster, even though he is effective as the drifting Steve Thompson, the inside man.

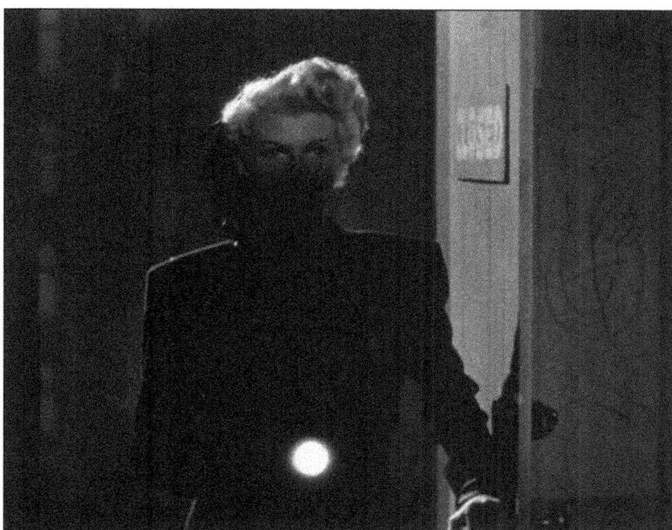

Orson Welles: *The Lady from Shanghai*

The Lady From Shanghai (1947) writ. and dir. Orson Welles (based on the novel by Sherwood King) cine Charles Lawton Jr. edt. Viola Lawrence music Heinz Riemheld star. Orson Welles (Michael O'Hara), Rita Hayworth (Elsa Bannister), Everett Sloane (Arthur Bannister), Glen Anders (George Grisby), Ted de Corsia, Erskine Sanford, Gus Schilling, Evelyn Ellis
Columbia

All film is documentary, is verité. It documents everything the eye can see, so all that remains hidden is dream... and within dream, the subjective truth. While the narrative of Welles' *The Lady From Shanghai* appears obscure at times, its failures are really the material of its success. You read that the original cut was one hour longer, is lost—so this is why it doesn't work. You read that Welles went on a drunken safari on Errol Flyn's yacht, had to scrap most of the location footage as unusable. You read that the studio interfered, brought in its own editor, shot its own inserts. Blah blah—the usual Orson Welles saga of misunderstood genius and creative posturing.

The reason this film has art is because you are forced back into its symbolic subtext in order to understand its logic. The courtroom scene is absurd, obeys its own protocol. The judge plays chess on a huge board that makes San Francisco a mere landscape extension. The defending lawyer is allowed to interrogate himself as a friendly witness. O'Hara escapes by mingling with the jury. Where does he hide? In a theatre in Chinatown where a traditional Chinese play is in progress. The progression of the narrative is a steady devolution from the external world into the internal world. The hero encounters the *femme fatale* at night on the edge of Central Park in New York as she rides in an old world handsome cab. They sail on her husband's yacht to the Caribbean, pass through the Panama Canal, malinger on the Mexican Riviera before arriving in San Francisco and an eventual resolution in the Crazy House in Play Land. While the Acapulco sequences are often lit with bright equatorial light, the settings are stagey, typical of the Welles ensemble method. The characters exist in hyperbole, figures in a nightmare, and O'Hara is the dreamer.

The plot is unconvincing, but succeeds as parody. Two lawyers indemnify their partnership with a life insurance policy covering death by misadventure, but not by suicide. The nuclear bomb paranoiac Grisby schemes to collect on the policy by staging his own murder, then disappearing to the imagined safety of a South Seas island. Elsa (Rita Hayworth), the wife of his partner, is his accomplice, but as per all film noir the lady has an agenda of her own. The double-cross occurs over the *corpus delicti* problem, i.e. O'Hara is paid to write a false confession to the murder of Grisby but will never come to trial if no body is found. But unfortunately bodies are found and as O'Hara (Orson Welles) wryly observes as he is arrested, "The wrong man was shot. The wrong man was arrested...." Etcetera. The love chump goes down. It's all very complicated, more so than *Double Indemnity*... a symptom of madness more than intellectual deviousness. As a device, the crime is decorative rather than functional, a symptom of the characters rather than the story. The action is often fragmented, a landscape of mental disorder. Grisby encounters O'Hara on a small lookout on a precipice above the ocean. He invites O'Hara to "murder him" for $5,000. Overhead angles and wide-angle close-ups render the psychology of paranoia and irrational intent. The grinning parabolic face of Grisby is clearly the face of madness... yet the grim intensity in O'Hara's pin-light eyes also suggests madness. The fatalism of the "black Irish" soul has allowed him to be drawn into an end-game which will decide his fate.

O'Hara has a *rendez-vous* with his lover Elsa Bannister at the Aquarium. They kiss, they walk, the sharks make sinister passes in the illuminated tanks behind. What does it mean? The fragility of existence, the absurdity of reality, the embrace of a nemesis, the lie in love? It means everything and nothing. The historical status quo of reality collapses as the background invades the foreground, the past the present, and the future is proclaimed as symbolism. This scene, in fact, transcends the film by moving you beyond the quotidian into the dream itself.

As a character, Elsa Bannister exists in stasis rather than as action, as an ideal rather as a person. A White Russian born in Shanghai, she's another beauty with a past. She shimmers in white, symmetrical like a magazine model, hallucinatory like a spirit. She never really does anything except pose... and even then, her attitude is passive, her sexuality concealed within the madonna. She's a myth, the naughty lady from the gambling dens of the East, perhaps an entity who is pursuing the brooding O'Hara as a consequence of his accidental homicide in Spain.

Nothing is certain. You are left to make associations, infer connections. In the noir universe, coincidence is Fate.

Dream And Motivation

In 1924 Liam O'Flaherty published *The Black Soul*, a novel about a shell-shocked WW I vet who goes to convalesce on an island off the west coast of Ireland. The hero's name is "O'Connor", and he's a man gripped with the existential torment of the "black soul"—as he prowls the wind-swept cliffs above the crashing ocean, he perceives it to be "all motion without meaning".

Orson Welles was almost certainly familiar with this novel (he did his apprentice theatre in Dublin at the time), so you wonder if in fact he based his O'Hara character on O'Flaherty's autobiographical black soul. O'Flaherty himself was a itinerant cosmopolitan very like Michael O'Hara, a merchant seaman who was familiar with the major seaports of the world.

When Bannister goes to the seaman's hiring hall at the behest of his wife to find the man who saved her from the thugs in the park, O'Hara is seen using a typewriter. As it turns out, he has ambitions of writing a novel, although like many details in this film, this can slip past unnoticed. During the voyage, Bannister says to O'Hara, "Before you start that novel you're going to write, you better learn something... you've been travelling around the world too much to find out anything about it."

Was this aspect of O'Hara's character lost in the post-production editing? The role seems stripped of its motivation—something which perhaps helps the dreamy, associative feel of the narrative. *Non sequiturs* become symbolism. O'Hara offers Elsa a cigarette—she rolls it in a napkin, places it in her purse. In the next sequence O'Hara finds the purse abandoned in the park—and the small pearl-handled gun. Is this a deliberate *quid pro quo*? "I don't know how to shoot," says Elsa when he returns it. "It's easy," says O'Hara. "You just pull the trigger."

So Is The Fix In From The Beginning?

Arthur Bannister is "the world's greatest criminal lawyer". His caustic world-view is that of a cripple well-schooled in emotional and physical blackmail. The drunken exchanges during the Mexican beach picnic reveal that Elsa is his wife by blackmail.

Here the recalcitrant O'Hara delivers his speech about the cannibal sharks, establishing the metaphor which best describes this uneasy band of travelling conspirators. Later, when O'Hara and Elsa meet at the Aquarium, he is well on his way to being eaten by his lover... but still doesn't know it. "Living on a hook takes away your appetite," he says.

As with the injured husband of Phyllis Dietrichson in Wilder's *Double Indemnity*, Arthur Bannister's impotence is made graphic by the two crutches he relies on. But his two most important crutches—his wife and his partner—turn out to be totally unreliable. You can see that Welles supported his narrative with visual symbolism... yet key moments remain verbalized and obscure.

Grisby shoots the blackmailing houseboy/detective/spy Broom... O'Hara shoots into the air as he fakes a murder... Elsa (off camera) shoots her fellow conspirator and paranoid Grisby... in the Magic Mirror Maze, the avenging Bannister shoots Elsa... who also shoots him... and Elsa dies waxing poetic ("Give my love to the dawn"), multiplied and screaming ("I don't wanna die") in the fragmented shards of glass.

This vortex of bungled desires and fatal personae concludes as a tableaux of dream symbolism. Free of his nightmare at last, O'Hara exits the Crazy House.

The superb DVD release of *The Lady From Shanghai* contains a very interesting interview with the film maker Peter Bogdonovitch, a sympathetic aficionado of the Welles *oeuvre*. While drawing attention to the film's innovative scenes and some of the political history behind the making and release of the film, he remarks that when he first saw it, "it blew me away." Exactly. For those people seeking expressionist departures from the rigid formalism of the Hollywood narrative, *The Lady From Shanghai* becomes the watershed film feature of its time.

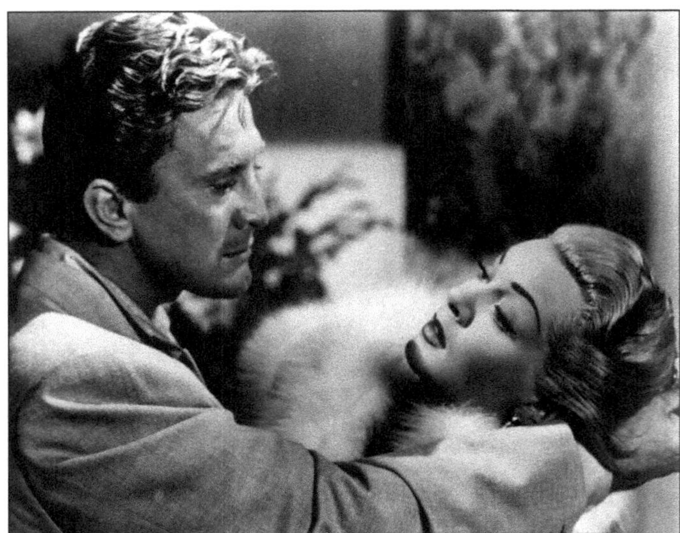

Vincente Minnelli: *The Bad & the Beautiful*

The Bad & The Beautiful (1952) dir. Vincente Minnelli writ. Charles Schnee (from the story by George Bradshaw) cine. Robert Surtees music David Raskin star. Kirk Douglas (Jonathan Shields), Lana Turner (Georgia Lorrison), Barry Sullivan (Fred Ameil), Dick Powell (James Lee Bartlow), Gloria Grahame (Rosemary), Gilbert Roland (Gaucho), Walter Pidgeon (Harry Pebbel), Elaine Stewart (Lila), Paul Stewart (Syd), Ivan Triesault (von Ellstein)
MGM

Despite all the Oscars, *The Bad & the Beautiful* is an uneven, often over-acted piece of work whose dialogue more often fails than succeeds. As a film about the ruthlessness of the Hollywood industry, it's a mere simulacra of Wilder's *Sunset Boulevard*, the film it so obviously stalks like a horse coming late into the race. Yet there are moments that make it worthy of its acclaim and the legends it purportedly exploits.

Consider the scene where the actress Georgia Lorrison (Lana Turner) goes berserk, tries to kill herself in her coupe the night of her first screen triumph. Is this not one of the greatest sequences in the history of dramatic film? Spurned by her lover and mentor, the manipulative producer Jonathan Shields (Kirk Douglas), she writhes in emotional agony as she drives recklessly into the night. Contained within the claustrophobic shell of the car, her body convulses with the nymphomania of death. She shrieks, she screams, she steps on the gas, hurtles at the oncoming traffic, a cacophony of horns and headlights. It's a chilling statement of raw human anguish, a voyeurism you have no business participating in, like the finale of a sex murder.

"I Thought You Were Swell"

Yet this comes on the heels of a scene in which the histrionics are so misplaced you want to laugh. Shields has skipped the opening night party, so Georgia drives to his house with a bottle of champagne. After repeated rings, Shields finally descends from his bedroom, opens the door, admits her into the lobby but no further. She babbles, he evades. A woman appears at the top of the stairs, Lila, a sexy young starlet from the production. "I saw your picture," says Lila as she exits back to the bedroom. "I thought you were swell."

Compromised, Shields lashes out at Georgia in a fury: "You couldn't stay away... you couldn't enjoy what I made possible for you. You've got it all laid out so you can wallow in pity for yourself... the betrayed woman, the wounded doe... with all the drivel that goes with it running through your mind. Well maybe I like Lila. Maybe I like to be cheap once and a while—maybe everybody does...!" After this ugly encounter, Georgia runs from the house, jumps in her car and roars off in another futile attempt at suicide.

The film is structured as a frame narrative which encloses three stories: Shields and his director Fred Ameil (Barry Sullivan), Shields and his star Georgia Lorrison (Lana Turner), and Shields and his writer James Lee Bartlow (Dick Powell). It's unfortunate that the weakest story leads. While certain scenes have undeniable black humor, the screwing over of the director just doesn't have the dramatic punch to keep the viewer involved.

Ameil first encounters Shields at the funeral of old man Shields. When Ameil later asks him why he hired so many professional mourners, Shields shrugs, says, "He lived in a crowd and I couldn't let him be buried alone." This is typical of the man for whom the creative process is a sexual progression of seduction, consumation and post-orgasmic loneliness. As Ameil is later to find out, no friendship with this man includes loyalty or love if it inhibits his ambition.

Georgia's story is much better. Her character has history... and sex which always makes the tension more interesting. Fred is too ordinary, too beside the point to gain our interest or sympathy, whereas Georgia is damaged goods right from the start. The daughter of a screen legend, she lives in a haze of resentment like an Electra who travels with a portable shrine, angry that he's dead and drunkenly seeking his replacement. Shields, who admired her father, sees possibilities in this suicidal bit player, and pretends to love her in order to rehabilitate her and incubate a star. He uses her and, it must be admitted, she allows him to use her. Her character contains the fatalism of tragic genius and the loneliness of the abandoned child.

Non Sans Droit

The third story is no less interesting, and like the other two, also involves the destruction of the self in order to create a career. Bartlow already has a career as a Prof and a novelist, but it's his seduction into the screen writing milieu in order to satisfy the curiosity of his beautiful southern belle, Rosemary (Gloria Grahame), that leads to his fatal wounding. When Rosemary dies in a plane crash with Gaucho—the Latin lover screen star—as a direct result of a machination by Shields, the sardonic Bartlow becomes yet another member of the Shields stable of the used and abused. While the crash is an accident and the extent of her involvement with Gaucho is left hypothetical, it nonetheless appears like murder. Utterly without sentiment, Shields urges Bartlow to keep working because "she's dead and you're alive." With friends like this, who needs love?

The portrait of Jonathan Shields as a very bad man is an uneven exercise of strained one-liners and occasional over-acting. That the script fails the character is obvious—as a writer, Charles Schnee was out of his league in trying to match the stinging cynicism of the Wilder/Brackett *Sunset Boulevard* style.

The problem is that the part is an icon rather than a person, a symbol rather than a character. What Hollywood brute was his template? X, Y, or Irving Thalberg? He's the generic industry villain, the Hollywood producer, he-who-screws-us-all. The role should've been easy for Kirk Douglas but it isn't. Sometimes he's goofy, sometimes he's psychotic, as if he's struggling with the director rather than his fate.

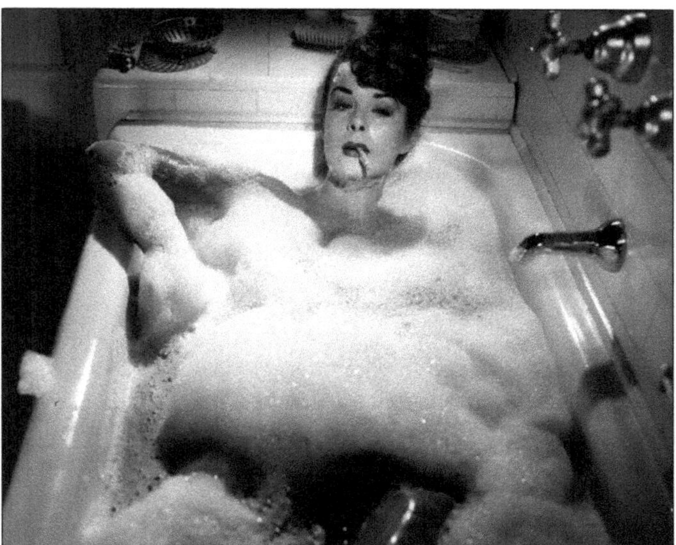

Samuel Fuller: *Pickup On South Street*

Pickup On South Street (1953) writ. & dir. Samuel Fuller (based on the story by Dwight Taylor), cine. Joe MacDonald, edt. Nick DiMaggio, music Leigh Harline star. Richard Widmark (Skip McCoy), Jean Peters (Candy), Thelma Ritter (Mo), Murvyn Vye, Richard Kiley, Willis B. Bouchey, Milburn Stone
20th Century Fox

When Women Were Goddesses

A pickpocket who works the city (New York or Chicago) subway steals a woman's purse but in the process unintentionally ends up with a strip of micro film in transit to a cell of communist agents. He does this in a crowded carriage under the eyes of two cops who are trailing the woman, yet manages to slip away into the streaming throng leaving his mark none the wiser and the cops scrambling to figure out just what's happened.

The execution of this opening scene is excellent. The camera is elevated, as if located in the ceiling, looks down on the passengers who stand tightly bunched, a sea of dreaming heads. You see a statuesque woman in white, could be a shop girl or some doxy on her way to the movies. You see a pickpocket move in beside her, pretend to read his newspaper, proceed to open and loot her white handbag. The action is sexual, as if the couple are enacting a *rendez-vous* in a dream. She's watching him pretend to read while at the same time allowing his hand to explore her intimacy. This ambiguous action is observed by the two cops although their view is obscured. When Skip (Richard Widmark) suddenly exits at the next station, you too are left wondering just what has happened.

Candy (Jean Peters) certainly doesn't know. She's been made love to in a dream but now that she's crossing a crowded street, her reality is her intended dropoff, another *rendez-vous* in which she is a dupe. When she enters the vaulted lobby of a commercial building, checks her handbag, discovers her purse has been stolen, she knows instinctively who the thief is... because, after all, she was a willing participant in the Freudian exchange. She phones Joey, a "boyfriend" for whom she has been working as a courier; this was to have been her last job for him before going her separate way.

Unbeknownst to Candy, Joey is a communist agent. He immediately orders her to do a street search, check out the stoolies, find out who grifted her purse... and recover the film strip containing the top secret chemical formula. Of course the real chemistry in this movie is between Peters and Widmark, and Candy's search is for her natural lover, not a small-time loner thief or a double-agent. Thus the pickpocket Skip McCoy becomes the man with the magic chemistry, and the moral issue one of self-interest versus country.

A lot of the action takes place at night on the waterfront, so it uses the stage expressionism typical of film noir—landscapes cloaked in shadow, humans haloed in light, dialogue-driven action, and a sense of theatre in exchange and gesture. Peters and Widmark in medium closeup is a thing of beauty. When she surprises him in his rathole hideout down on the waterfront—a shack masquerading as a bait and tackle shop—he knocks her out cold... but when he turns on the light, discovers she's the "muffin" he grifted on the subway, he massages her jaw softly as she lies sprawled in his arms. While she regains consciousness, she really enters a dream—they kiss, and she realizes her true agenda is love, not the business at hand.

I'd Rather Have A Live Pickpocket Than A Dead Traitor

Of course, love never runs smooth. Skip still behaves as a sociopath who uses charm rather than surrenders to charm, and his natural cunning quite rightly surmises that Candy is working for someone else and that this film is worth a lot more than a simple negative of some guy's family photos. His main adversary is a cop called Tiger, who has managed to nail him three times already... and a fourth conviction will mean "life". Tiger tries to cut a deal with Skip, tries to appeal to his patriotism, but to little avail—he figures there's a better deal to be made with Candy's "old lady".

When Joey the commie murders Mo (Thelma Ritter), the old stoolie who sells ties from a suitcase as totems for the underworld information she really sells, Skip is moved into his first selfless gesture. In one of many great photographic moments in this film, he recovers Mo's coffin from the death boat before transportation across the river to an undignified burial in Potter's Field. It is the least he can do for this quasi-mother whose last words to him to were, "Stop using yer hands, start using yer head, Skip—the kid loves ya." Indeed the kid does love him... and in fact puts her life on the line for him. Stolen kisses aren't the only loops in this fabulous narrative: Skip's secret stash which he keeps submerged in the Hudson at the end of a rope and pulley just outside his window is later reinvented when Joey hides in the dumbwaiter after shooting Candy... and the opening scene on the train is reenacted in a smooth circularity when Skip picks Joey on his way to a meeting with a communist colleague in the can at the Third Avenue station.

Very much a Cold War psychodrama, *Pickup On South Street* sees small-time hoods as heroes united against the new criminal threat to society, the communist hoodlum. Candy's amusing line "I'd rather have a live pickpocket than a dead traitor" says a great deal about a capitalist society that tolerates petty crime in contrast to its fear of ideology... because, after all, what is commerce but a form of articulate theft? The values here are old-fashioned: the love of a good woman, and the love of a good country.

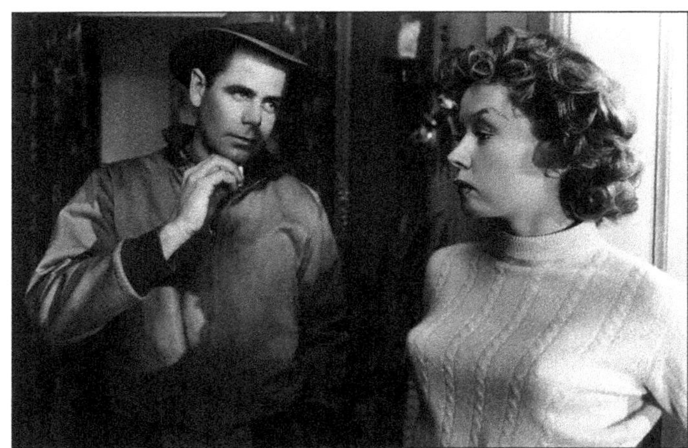

Fritz Lang: *The Big Heat*

The Big Heat (1953) dir. Fritz Lang writ. Sydney Boehm (based on *Saturday Evening Post* serial by William P. McGivern) cine. Charles Lang star. Glenn Ford (Bannion), Lee Marvin (Vince Stone), Gloria Grahame (Debby), Alexander Scourby (Mike Lagana)
Columbia Pictures

Evil Is A Form Of Predestination

This revenge drama is notable for its violence against women—in the course of events, four of them die, always for political reasons, always as a consequence of the men they are involved with. On the face of it, the story is a simple expose of corruption in the Chicago police force, but its raw intensity raises the action to a metaphysical expose of corruption in the human soul.

A detective shoots himself in his study and his wife snags his confessional suicide note, uses it to blackmail Mr. Big, a society hood called Mike Lagana (Scourby), whose racket remains vague but who has not only detectives on his payroll but also the Police Commissioner himself. While this gets our attention, the action is a bit stilted in the opening stanzas, perhaps due to the docu-drama style then in vogue for crime morality tales. The moral force here is Det. Sergeant Bannion (Glen Ford), first driven by principle, later by revenge when Lagana kills his wife with a car bomb. Bannion is established as a family man, a fifties idealism complete with a pretty young wife and daughter, like a dummy family from a World's Fair exhibit or an architectural illustration for kitchen design in *Popular Mechanics*. His simple dream of the good life is a secular dream, a post-war chimera in contrast to the greedy bourgeois dream of his deceased colleague, Detective Sergeant Tom Duncan, and his hardened, manipulative widow, Bertha.

Notice the decor in Duncan's home, compare it to that in Bannion's. Notice too that Duncan had a mistress, one of several according to his widow. Crime doesn't pay? It depends on which side of its shadow you stand. Det. Bannion is motivated by the murder of his wife, an event which raises his mission into a crusade... and as usual in these sort of films there's a clear articulation of good. But when it comes to evil the motivation is left entirely to the imagination.

We never see what makes Vince Stone (Lee Marvin), Lagana's *capo*, into the casual psychopath that he is. We never see the true source of his admiration for his criminal boss or any reason why he treats women as rubbish. His sadism is shown but not articulated, as if evil is a form of predestination. Thus there's a feeling of old-time propaganda in the message, even if we believe the story.

Sisters Under The Mink

The women aren't all paragons of virtue. The corruption is pervasive. In fact, this is best shown in the scene where the mutilated Debby (Gloria Grahame) visits Bertha Duncan to straighten her out about the ugliness of their common situation. Both women are wearing fur overcoats, the feline cachet of success... or is it slavery? The blackmailing widow tries to dismiss her unwelcome visitor, but Debby says "We should use first names—we're sisters under the mink" in a truism that reconciles two victims of a common illness.

While the symptom is greed and materialism, the real illness is lost eroticism. Both women have lost their natural power—one through age, the other through mutilation. Debby then shoots the smug widow, knowing her husband's suicide letter will now become public and ensure the exposure and downfall of Lagana and his rackets.

Symbolism Of The Crippled Woman

It's the crippled secretary at the auto wrecking yard who provides Bannion with the key link to the hood who planted the car bomb that killed his wife. We don't know why she has her affliction, or even if it was caused intentionally or unintentionally by some man as per all the violence against women in this drama. But her injured leg and sympathetic nature casts her as a representative victim of a society of brutes who routinely maim and mutilate their women.

The symbolism runs deeper than a mere testament to misogyny; it reflects the corruption of the human soul that results from a society bent out of shape by sadism and greed.

The Vertical Serpent

In essence, there are only two people to stand up to Lagana's insidious regime: Vince Stone's moll Debby, and Bannion. When Bannion barges in on Lagana at his posh residence during a party for his daughter, Lagana says, "I've seen some dummies in my time but you're in a class by yourself." When Lagana visits his henchman Vince Stone in the latter's downtown penthouse, hears Debby proclaiming them all to be nothing more than Lagana's circus animals, Lagana says dismissively, "You gotta control that woman, Vince—she's too young to be drinking so much." Lagana is an old-time hood, straight out of the Prohibition. His crude authoritarian personality appears to be the product of his recently deceased mother, a matriarch whose painting hangs above his fireplace.

The irony is obvious, yet we can only infer the psychology of this brutal man whose minions terrorize women and who lives alone with his daughter and a crass icon of his mother. Human beings may be divided by gender but in the culture of the jungle, morality is sexless.

Vince Stone has no such history. All we know about him is what we see. We see him extinguish his cigarette on the wrist of a B-girl at his watering hole, The Retreat... thus revealing that he was in on the torture and murder of Lucy Chapman—mistress of the dead cop—whose body was found covered with cigarette burns. We see him throw a pot of scalding coffee in Debby Marsh's face, marking her forever in retribution for her apparent treachery in going to Bannion's hotel room "to play footsie". The tall, lanky Stone exudes a malevolent animal vitality, the confidence that easy money and easy women bring... a sadist without conscience or the fear of supernatural judgement, a vertical serpent in a false Eden. He's a bad piece of work and once again we have to consider the ambiguous nature of sex in relation to death. *The Big Heat* is as much a metaphor about sex as it is about crime and psychosis.

Who can forget his final scene with his lover? They stare at one another, each a mirror of the other's mutilation, two halves merging in a total eclipse of the soul.

You're About As Romantic As A Pair Of Handcuffs

While it's odd that the proto-alcoholic party girl Debby should find Bannion, the artistic symmetry is perfect. When she follows him to his room at The Marlin Hotel, it's like a date with Jesus, as Bannion is stillborn in the memory of his dead wife. "You're about as romantic as a pair of handcuffs," Debby says when she fails to get him into bed.

Nonetheless they bond, as both have been mutilated—she literally, he figuratively. His redemption is through her sacrifice, for she does what has to be done and he can't: kill in order to reveal the truth. When he pins Mrs Duncan against the wall, his hands on her throat, his self-control is admirable... but when Debby visits her later, she has nothing to lose. If Mrs. Duncan exists as a madonna of blackmail, where did she learn it? From Mike Lagana... or in reality, from his teacher, the matriarch?

We don't know, but we can rest easy knowing that a cop who packs his own gun rather than the department's is the best "insurance" a citizen can have.

While Glenn Ford puts in a journeyman performance as the cop who goes vigilante, *The Big Heat* receives its *mal noir* signature from the superb acting of Gloria Grahame and Lee Marvin. Who can forget their sado-erotic heat which ends in their mutual mutilations? As an apostle of the truly bad, Marvin's performance anticipates his casual reprise a year later (1954) as a cowboy bully in Sturges' neglected classic, *Bad Day At Black Rock*.

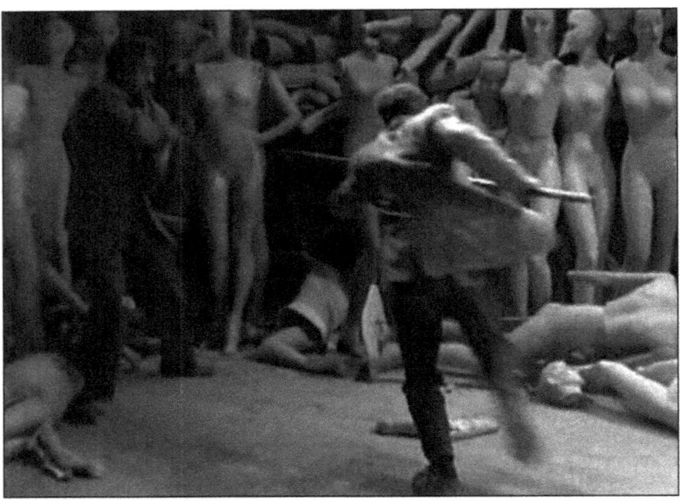

Stanley Kubrick: *Killer's Kis*s

Killer's Kiss (1955) United Artists dir. Stanley Kubrick writ. Howard O. Sackler (uncredited) from the story by Kubrick. cine Stanley Kubrick edt Kubrick music Gerald Fried star Frank Silvera (Rapello), Jamie Smith (Davey), Irene Kane (Gloria)... with Ruth Sobotka, Alex Rubin, David Vaughan et. al.

From The Museum Of Black And White

Do we dream in black and white, or in color? Just as some aesthetes believe silent film is the only cinematic form, even more believe black and white photography is the only true expression of art. The simplicity of a semi-tone universe where space collapses into two dimensions and the material world is rendered in mystifications of light and shadow is not only appealing but is also the way we remember the Industrial Age. Black and white is a marker of history, geometry and technology, dream and depression.

The alienation of 20th Century Man is seen in the solitude of his rectilinear environment, a fascism of vertical and horizontal lines whose machine precision exists in order to help him sleep better.

Consider the young boxer in Kubrick's *Killer's Kiss*: as he lies down on a small bed in a small apartment somewhere in New York, his rest is interrupted by a fracas in another flat in an adjacent wing. He hears a scream, looks through the window, sees a man struggling with a beautiful young woman—another kind of "fight" from the one he just lost a few hours ago in the ring. His loneliness is a frame for dream and reality. Sex is always a triangular relationship—soon he finds himself fighting not only for money but also for love.

His dream is developed as a "negative" print in anticipation of his fate. Is he being pursued or is he pursuing? The onrushing imagery is spectral and fearful, the camera moving like a speeding ambulance down a narrow street between tall buildings that exist only as bone shadows. This simple photographic trick is like an X-ray of the soul.

The rectilinearity isn't confined merely to shadow and light. The characters exist in boxes, like forgotten animals. The Spartan apartments where Gloria and Davey live are boxes. The dancehall where Gloria works as a dance mannikin is a box. Rapello's office is a box, a gloomy den where he watches TV and runs his dancehall. The gym where Davey trains is a box... and the ring where he fights (and loses) is a box. When pursued by Rapello's thugs, he finds himself trapped in a box canyon formed by the drab, abandoned warehouses. In fact, the narrative frame sees Davey "boxed", pacing back and forth in the stone and steel vault of the railroad station as he waits to escape the city with his new love, Gloria.

While the cinematic execution is often self-conscious, this pulp film noir has the contradictory beauty of a fresh cigarette in a fresh mouth. Gloria (Irene Kane) glitters like a silver doll, almost luminous (which makes you realize that the period craze for blonds was probably due to their photogenic allure in the black and white medium) in the shabby world around her. While the influence of the neo-realist films by Vittorio de Sica is strong, occasional inserts such as the ballerina dancing alone give the action a charming expressionism and psychological inscape. These inventions are a means of dealing with unsynced dialogue... and the ballerina sequence a chance for Kubrick to showcase his then current wife, Ruth Sobotka.

While the plot has the lurid simplicity of a Latino comic book melodrama—an impression due in part to the occasional Latin soundtrack rhythms and villain called "Rapello"—Kubrick works the two-dimensionality of the tableaux to artistic advantage. Single camera, single spot lighting, single frame transitions. The m.o. is that of a gallery photographer.

It's easy to forget that Kubrick emerged from the Museum of Black and White, that he shaped his world-view as a Leicaflex stringer for *Life Magazine* before he ever made a movie.

There is one noticeable collapse in continuity: Rapello starts out driving a Cadillac convertible, but ends up driving a Plymouth convertible. He drives away from his dancehall at night, but arrives at his warehouse prison during daylight. Davey follows in a taxi. They must've circled New York, sold the Caddy to pay for the cab and downsize to the Plymouth, or scenes are missing.

More likely, Kubrick ran out of money.

Although the imagery has become cliché now, the scene where Davey and Rapello have their showdown in the mannikin factory is fabulous. These industrial sculptures of the human female form act as an inhuman cyclorama to the primal combat of the Industrial Men. As Davey and Rapello thrash around among the mannikin torsos, this abstraction of misogyny and male despair becomes the perfect statement of civilization. To fight over a woman is as basic as it is biological... but to fight with these dismembered female totems as an audience is as exquisite as it is existential. Expressionist theatre, modernist art, the eroticism is in the symbol rather than the flesh.

So is this why we like black and white photography? Because it symbolizes rather than renders reality? Within its binary cage, it becomes pure imagination, the geometrics of light and shadow, good and evil, the model of a planned universe. Whether through a hole in the clouds or a venetian blind, shadow gives shape to light... and human folly becomes art.

As a film, perhaps *Killer's Kiss* suffers from its derivative situations and consequently a derivative period morality. Between Hitchcock and de Sica, the comic book and the art gallery, Kubrick somehow manages to assert his own personal style. We see all his primary obsessions here, including the beautiful dancing woman and the perplexed, dueling man.

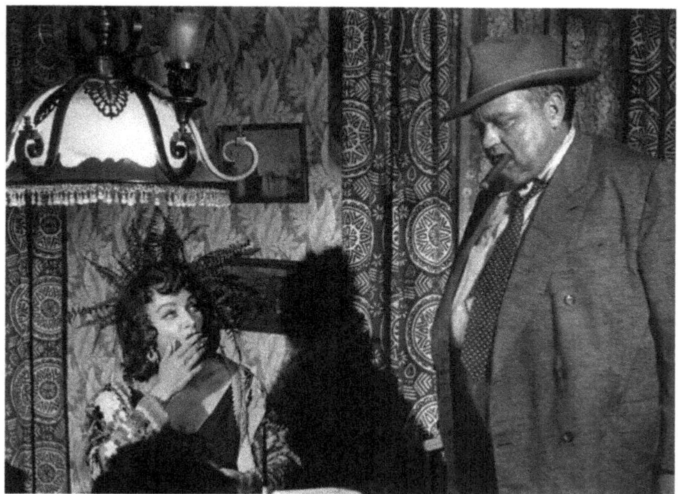

Orson Welles: *Touch of Evil*

Touch Of Evil (1958) writ. and dir. Orson Welles (based on the novel *Badge of Evil* by Whit Masterton) cine. Russell Metty music. Henry Mancini star. Charlten Heston (Vargas), Janet Leigh (Suzie Vargas), Orson Welles (Capt. Hank Quinlan), Akim Tamiroff (Uncle Joe), Marlene Dietrich (Tanya), Mercedes McCambridge (lesbian hood), Denis Weaver (motel clerk), Jospeh Calleia
Universal

Orson Welles plays Captain Hank Quinlan, a detective who fictionalizes his cases in order to make them fit the easy symmetry his corrupted mind requires. All his murder cases have become a replay of his own psychodrama, wherein he plays judge and executioner in the unproven affair of his dead wife and her lover. He strangled his wife... and now he hunts the shadows of the border town Los Robles for the surrogates who must pay the price for his ancient trauma. It's a split jurisdiction—one part in America, one part in Mexico—which act in contradiction, where the lawful and the lawless exist in a sweet co-dependency of oil, drugs, and sex. Quinlan's nemesis is Vargas (Heston), a Mexican cop with a new American wife (Leigh) who just happens to be on his honeymoon in Los Robles, the family home of the Grandy gang whose patriarch is currently under indictment in Mexico City for drug-trafficking.

Night. Los Robles is bustling with border-town excitement, gringos and chicanos in the bars, clubs, and commercial arcades that glow in the shadows of the oil derricks that pump continuously like a chorus of phantoms.

A time-bomb is placed in the trunk of a '57 Chrysler convertible by an anonymous assassin. A couple get in, start driving for the border crossing near the bridge over the river that divides the two countries. At the same time Vargas and his pretty wife are walking along the main drag and arrive at the immigration booth at the same time as the car. The atmosphere is festive, passage a mere formality. Is *Senor* Vargas here to crack another drug-ring? No, just to buy a milk-shake for his American wife. Meanwhile the woman in the convertible protests about a "ticking" in her head... but they're waved through, her consort gunning the car for the bridge.

Vargas and Suzie are walking again, stop to kiss—the bomb explodes, sharding the shiny new auto and its two occupants in a soaring trajectal ball of fire. You later discover the car is identical to the one driven by Vargas, wonder at the meaning of this coincidence that's ignored by everyone, including Vargas himself. The symmetry is even more coincidental when Quinlan arrests a young Mexican shoe clerk for the bombing. The victims are a nightclub dancer and the father of the clerk's American girlfriend, a rich man who was utterly opposed to this love affair.

> Cop: How did you meet Marsha Whittiker?
> Sanchez: I sold her a pair of shoes... and I've been on my knees before her ever since.

Vargas immediately discovers that Quinlan has framed Sanchez by putting two sticks of dynamite in a shoe box. When Vargas finds two sticks are missing from Quinlan's private explosives stash at his ranch, Quinlan is forced into an uneasy alliance with "Uncle Joe", the sleazy brother of the Grady patriarch who has been indicted for drug-trafficking.

Uncle Joe has already drugged and kidnapped Vargas' wife, has her upstairs in his club. But all of this is to no avail, as Vargas has the support of the assistant D.A. and the disillusioned detective, Pete Menzies. It's the disillusioned Menzies who agrees to wear a wire, entrap his former hero Quinlan as they walk together from the brothel through the oil field to the bridge-crossing in a final coda that mirrors the walk of Vargas and his wife at the opening.

It's an ugly ending for an ugly man. This bloated beast of American corruption sinks into a pile of garbage below the bridge as the tape implicating him echoes in the night. He's shot by his lieutenant, Menzies, from the bridge (in a surprise resurrection) and drops backwards into the slimy waters, watched by his old lover Tanya and the Assistant D.A. Meanwhile Vargas is necking with his wife in their convertible, reconciled once more after the nightmare.

> Schwartz: You really liked him, didn't you?
> Tanya: (mistily) The cop did. The one who killed him—he loved him.
> Schwartz: He was a good detective alright.
> Tanya: And a lousy cop.
> Schwartz: Is that all you have to say for him?
> Tanya: He was some kind of man...

Tanya (Dietrich) then exits over the bridge, returning to her brothel as the player-piano mocks the night with its mechanical melody. The ending is an absurd, muddled parody of itself, the actors, and doomed love torch dramas like *Casablanca* or *The Blue Angel*. Within this forced exposition, you learn that Sanchez has confessed to the bombing (so Quinlan was right

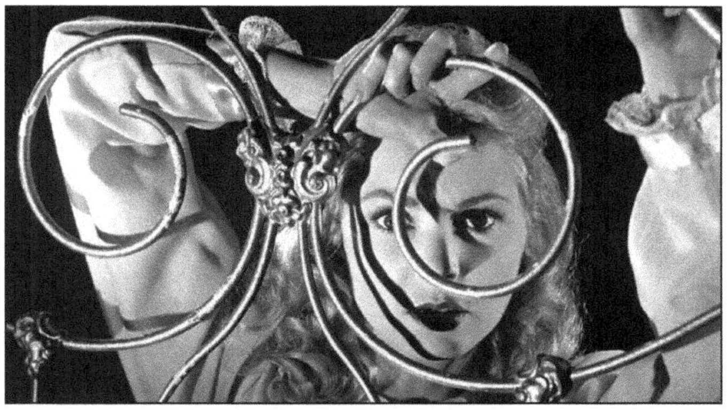

after all) and Susan Vargas wasn't shot up with heroin and Mexicans do have integrity and all's right with the world.

Ugly.

Touch of Evil is perhaps not as good as some of us have thought, have wanted, have believed. It exists in myth, another anti-film despised by the Studio philistines but revered by Orson Welles devotees. The Wellesian signature—the theatre effect—is in full force once again. The actors move and talk as an ensemble, framed in shadow, isolated in spotlight, a Renaissance tragedy complete with assassins, buffoons, go-betweens, madmen and their sexual mothers.

Ugly.

Who's at fault here—Welles? Or maybe the post-production boss Nims who re-edited the first five reels in an attempt to restore linearity to plot and counter-plot? It starts well. Who can dispute the brilliance of the opening three minute tracking shot that remains unbroken until the kiss and the explosion? Who can dispute the atmospherics, the sense of evil in such scenes as Susan Vargas being harassed in her hotel room by a man with a flashlight in another room across the street... or her sado-erotic ordeal in the Mirador Motel with the chicano hot-rod hoods and junky lesbians... or Quinlan's murder of Uncle Joe Grandy, a strangulation by nylon stocking as Suzie V. lies like a drugged nymphomaniac on the bed nearby?

The narrative starts at night, ends at night, a 24 hour cycle in which the waking hours are merely a dream, a hallucination of what is real, what is true.

Yet the film is always struggling with the stylistics of its surrealism, its over-lapping dialogue, improvs and miscast characters. Despite the makeup, Heston struggles in his role as an educated Mexican, lacking the Latino vibe, an emasculated Othello in another American fantasy of racial harmony. And Welles, always re-inventing himself as an aging blimp, isn't as coherent as he should be, is often mumbling to the point of irrelevance. Denis Weaver's celebrated performance as the weirdo motel clerk now seems contrived, a send-up to create character where character doesn't exist, a buffoon masquerading as a demon. As for Marlene Dietrich as the beautiful Madame from the sentimental past, let's admit that her inclusion was a mistake.

It doesn't take much to destroy rhythm and while an alien editor might be at fault, the production values seem compromised, i.e. when Vargas and the Assistant D.A. Schwartz are driving through town, the back-projection suggests they're flying a jet, moving at reckless and improbable speeds. You can cheat on continuity if the rhythm is right, as no audience can ever absorb the full meaning of all the action no matter how linear it might be.

It's a pity, as it's very nice to look at most of the time, the black and white imagery reducing space to the perspectives of woodcut printing, a sort of symbolism of shape and attitude, a theatrical expressionism characteristic of Welles in his best work. The idea of a continuous Master Scene representing 24 hours-in-the-life with cutaways to parallel actions is good. Aristotle would've liked it.

Quinlan's last words before falling into the sewer are, "That's the second bullet I stopped for you." While you can imagine some past anguish between him and Tanya, as likely as not it's probably another in-joke from Welles to his real nemesis, Hollywood.

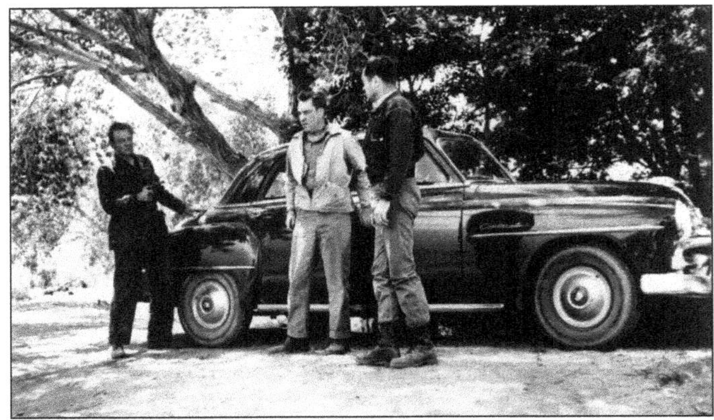

Ida Lupino: *The Hitch-Hiker*

The Hitch-Hiker (1953) dir. Ida Lupino writ. Collier Young & Ida Lupino [adaptation Robert Joseph] [based on material by Geoffrey Howes a.k.a. Daniel Mainwaring] cine. Frank Murusaca edt. Douglas Stewart music. Leith Stevens art. Walter E. Keller
star. Edmond O'Brien (Roy Collins), Frank Lovejoy (Gilbert Bowen), William Talman (Emmet Myers a.k.a. the Hitch-Hiker), Jose Torvay, Sam Hayes, Wendel Niles, Jean del Val, Clark Howard, Nativadad Vacio
RKO Pictures 70 mins 1953

Buscado: The Hitch-Hiker

Ida Lupino wrote and directed this one, an unusual thing for a woman in 1953, even though this was her fourth or fifth film as a director in the masculine world of the B-movie thriller. She was an experienced actress from a theatrical British family, today best remembered for her role in *High Sierra* (1941), where she plays a bad girl love interest of Humphrey Bogart, the doomed bank robber "Mad Dog" Roy Earle who dies in a shoot-out in the rocks way up above the tree-line.

So one is tempted to look for traces of the female sensibility in *The Hitch-Hiker*, which, despite its neo-realist approach, is a modern Western. A harsh impersonal desert replaces a harsh impersonal city, and large period autos replace horses.

Certainly the machismo is low-key, with no absurd shoot-outs and stunts along the way. In keeping with the pseudo-docu style of the times, the film starts with a quick roundup of the coldblooded highway killings by one Emmet Myers (William Talman), who is presented symbolically as "the Hitch-Hiker", his face concealed from the camera, an anonymous figure rendered as Death in a black leather coat. The style is edgy, not dissimilar to the coarse action of Edgar C. Ulmer's 1945 noir classic *Detour*.

The first victims are a young couple in a convertible with a 1952 Illinois license plate. They are shot and robbed at night in a wooded grove, left dead in the car by the Hitch-Hiker who casually leans down, rifles the woman's purse which has fallen on the ground. All you see are his boots as he walks away, like an anonymous dream figure in the ambiguous shadows.

Cut To: a spinning image of a newspaper which winds down like a wheel of fortune locking onto a headline which proclaims "Couple Found Murdered..." and the rampage of the highway killer as he moves across America. An effective, if generic, transitional device typical of the genre. Another murder, another headline: "Nation-Wide Search For Hitch-Hike Slayer!" This time the victim is a man in a sedan... and this time the killer decides to keep the car.

Cut To: dawn, and a similar car merging onto the highway from a back road. But this isn't the Hitch-Hiker, although you think it is... until the camera reveals the occupants to be two men in a 49 Plymouth on their way to a fishing trip in the Chocolate Mountains on the California-Mexico border. The driver is Roy Collins (Edmond O'Brien), a mechanic, and his friend, Gilbert Bowen (Frank Lovejoy), a draughtsman.

On a whim they decide to revise their itinerary and instead take in a little action in Mexicali, then go fishing at San Filipe, Mexico. But Bowen is already asleep in the passenger seat as they pass through the glittering lights of Mexicali as if he's already in dream mode. Daylight... and who do they see standing beside his stolen auto, now out of gas?

Thus Fate Is The Hunter

The lack of a female character limits a wider human dynamic, even though there are women somewhere in the background, as both Collins and Bowen are married. Lupino sticks (mostly) to a single time & space, which can be applauded as artistic, but like most neo-realist films, is actually a condition of economics.

Keep it simple, keep it cheap. One camera, few sets, find nice location settings. In this sense *The Hitch-Hiker* is similar to Spielberg's celebrated first film *Duel*, wherein the characters become the virtual hostages of a truck driver who, by his complete anonymity, becomes a personification of Death.

I'm Gonna Listen To The News

It might be churlish to ask why Myers doesn't kill Collins & Bowen at the outset, just as he did with his previous victims... but he doesn't, prefers to sit in the back with his pistol and have Collins and Bowen chauffeur him south through the desert into Mexico's Baja peninsula, monitor his hunt via news bulletins on the car radio. "This car rides pretty good," he says. "Think when I get where I'm going I'll sell it."

Baja is a fabulous setting, a rugged prehistoric terrain of giant boulders and lava eggs, as if the world of the dinosaurs has been fossilized and abstracted into the landscape. In the brutal sunlight gravel roads and dirt trails evaporate into the cracked mud of the arroyos and dry ravines.

In this way the director Ida Lupino ironically taps the spirit of 18/19th Century Romanticism, which played out its famous dramas & paintings against a gloomy primal landscape of forests, mountains, ruins and supernatural possibility. But here, no castles, just the occasional shabby adobe... no forests, just giant cacti.

Contemporary action drama would have Collins and/or Bowen make an early break for it, no matter how unrealistic, in order to pump the action. Bowen does have a couple of opportunities. First, in the car when they hit a bump, and second, when they stop and open the trunk, when there's an opportunity to grab a rifle.

Myers jerks his pistol, says, "Don't even think about it, you'll never make it." Yet the rifle gives the sadistic Myers an idea. Seems he needs a little diversion and maybe an opportunity for some psycho intimidation.

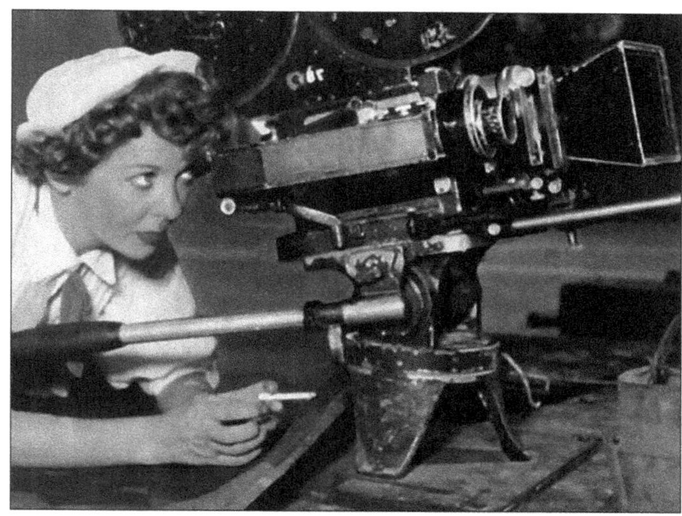

He orders Collins to go and stand beside a rock, hold up an empty can as a target for his friend Bowen. Bowen, although reluctant, proves to be a good shot.

The passivity of the characters in fact is true-to-life, an accurate social profile for the times. The action is psychological—no stunt players necessary. O'Brien—a favorite of Lupino's in her B-movie *auteur* period—is the more resentful of the two hostages, and if he'd been by himself, you know he would've made a quick break or died trying.

His anger crescendos in the scene at the well when he snarls, "If you're gonna kill us, kill us, get it over with." When Myers later decides to reverse identities with Collins by switching clothes, the act is not only a physical match but a psychological one.

Hitch-hiking is one of those continuums wherein the victim and the perpetrator can become reversible entities. The element of chance and the cult of loneliness combine to make it a dangerous pursuit. The predator might be behind the wheel or might be the passenger. Like objects set in motion by an invisible force, the conflict between strangers is both existential and historic, like the nomadic desperados of the Old West or the desert wild-life that never socializes, simply eats or is eaten.

Myers is the classic criminal with an affliction—a paralyzed or "sleepy" eye that never closes, so his face in certain views is like that of a temple effigy, a demon. This is put to good advantage in the scene where he camps for the night beside an abandoned airstrip, watches over his hostages with his bum eye.

The effect is both creepy and chilling, as Collins & Bowen never really know for sure if Myers is asleep when they make their break for it. Visually the scene is very effective as Collins & Bowen are wrapped so tightly in their blankets they look like mummies or spider-food. One eye open, one eye closed... the Spider God never sleeps... and although they roll off into the darkness, their escape is short-lived. He runs them down on the airstrip with the car, and they surrender like rabbits hypnotized by the headlights.

You Guys Are Soft

Myers is a mid twentieth century version of the "Kansas Desperado", presaged by such criminal luminaries as Frank &

Cole Younger (Jesse James gang), Ben Hodges, Billy the Kid (Dodge City), George "Machine Gun" Kelly, *et. al.*

William Talman's subtle though powerful performance as Emmet Myers is best realized in the camp scene when he demands to see Gil Bowen's watch. He's lounging against a tree as Bowen & Collins get a fire going. He examines the watch, says: "I had a watch like this when I was 17... nobody gave it to me... I took it, knocked off a broken-down jewelry store in a jerk town outside of Tulsa. It was a cinch." He draws closer. "You guys are soft. Know what makes you that way? You're up to your necks in I.O.U.s. You're suckers. You're scared to get out on your own... you've always had it good, so you're soft. Well, not me. They never gave me anything, so I don't owe nobody. My folks were tough. When I was born, they took one look at this pus eye, told me to get lost...."

For the most part, though, the action seems a little unimaginative by today's standards. Like many Westerns, the film relies heavily on the magnificent geography of the desert landscape; the occasional cut-aways to some mechanical cop scenes add an unfortunate Keystone tenor to the documentary style, even if the use of Spanish in those exchanges where the Mexican police are involved helps to sustain realism.

Buzzards at the well, a busted oil pan on the Plymouth, patrolling aircraft, a pursuing Mexican Sheriff in a funky torpedo-back [late forties Hudson or Packard]... but no shoot-outs in the rocks. The tension is held completely in the persona of the Hitch-Hiker, who might be a *homme fatale* but for the fact that he hijacked two men rather than two women. He's a bad man with a gun, but a weakling without it, an indictment that seems simplistic by contemporary standards.

The Hitch-Hiker is one of those films that lacks a sub-plot, although this in itself is not an artistic crime. Here, Fate is not a conspiracy... rather, it's a random event. Myers has no plan. He just moves, and when he needs to eat, he kills and robs. When Collins & Bowen become his hostages, he uses them to get food, which is an elementary step up—dare one say a social act—and you can imagine him forming a gang.

At one point Collins asks him if he ever had a job. Myers is circumspect, grips his pistol, looks at the two chumps with contempt. They're married, socialized, whipped... whereas he's a predator and free.

Ida Lupino produced and wrote five or so films for her production company Filmakers [founded with her second husband Collier Young], then went into contract TV drama, directing & writing for such shows as *General Electric Theatre, Alfred Hitchcock Presents, Have Gun Will Travel, The Rifleman, 77 Sunset Strip, The Twilight Zone*... and *Gilligan's Island*. These Family Hour dramas with their clean homicides and general buffoonery are quite distant from her brief but productive career as a female auteur dealing with the ugly in society: rape, bigamy, peer-pressure, crippling illness, homicide and the unhappy lot of some women in the post-war era.

Lap-dissolves, side-wipes, omniscient camera angles, generic dialogue, low-key action, great landscape cine, prototypical villain... well worth watching as a period piece, and certainly as part of Ida Lupino's fascinating career.

Nostalgia might not be enough to make *The Hitch-Hiker* hip, even if Ida is.

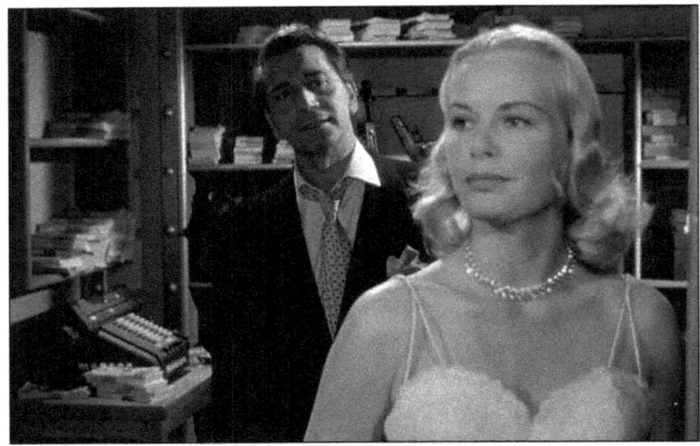

Joseph A. Lewis: *The Big Combo*

The Big Combo (1955) dir. Joseph A. Lewis writ. Philip Yourdan cine John Alton [special effects Jack Rab & Louis Dewitt] prod. Sidney Harmon edt. Robert Eiseer sound Earl Synder music David Raskin star. Richard Conte (Mr. Brown) Cornel Wilde (Lieu. Leonard Diamond) Jean Wallace (Susan Lowell) Brian Donlevy (Joe McClure) featuring Lee van Cleef (Fante) Earl Holliman (Mingo) Robert Middleton (Peterson) Helen Walker (Alicia) Jay Adler (Sam Hill) John Hoyt (Nils Dreyer) Ted de Corsia (Bettini) Helene Stanton (Rita) Allied Artists | b & w 84 mins | 1955

The Shabby Cellar Of American Modernism

The Big Combo. Jazz, sex, crime. Sub-culture, the underworld... and sexual jealousy defines reality in the night-scape of the urban jungle. Pedigreed wasp blonde girl becomes the victim of the Mafia hoodlum Mr. Brown... a script writer's code name designed merely to deflect cries of racism, although "Brown" is as clearly Italian as his Bolemac Corporation is mafioso, part of that bigger combine headquartered in Sicily.

"The largest pool of illegal money in the world," declares Captain Peterson as his Lieutenant, Leonard Diamond (Cornel Wilde), argues the case for going after Brown. And Diamond does go after him, because he's in love with Susan, Brown's victim lover. The symbolism is plain and basic: the values of American society have been seduced and corrupted by the shadowy blood combine, the Mafia.

Just how Mr. Brown (Richard Conte) makes his money isn't clear, except that he runs the Bolmec Corporation from a hotel called "The Bolmec", has a torture chamber in the basement which is filled with whiskey barrels left over from the Prohibition era, and a concealed vault in his upstairs suite which contains stacks of money and a gun rack.

Tommy guns? Revolvers, automatics, sawed-off this and that? Guns aren't illegal and neither is money... but we get the picture. Brown is a gangster, a handsome glistening snake in a suit who sleeps during the day and slithers at night. And he never sheds his skin either, as he's as incorrigible at the end as he is at the beginning.

The beautiful Susan makes him look "legitimate", and as a former prison guard, he tries to keep his friends and enemies close. The film starts with Susan (Jean Wallace) running down a dark alley pursued by two retainers, Fante and Mingo, who corner her in the bleak concession area, back of the arena where Brown is watching a boxing match.

It's the jungle alright, although it's defined by empty monochromatic spaces, shadows, reflected light... a gray world of cigarette smoke and urban fog, the shabby cellar of American modernism.

The Only Thing I Play Now Is Stud Poker

Susan is like a junky without a needle. She craves love, as if her lover is just holding out on her like a crooked dealer in the casino. In one scene, Brown says, "Love? We can talk about love another time." Like a child pretending to run away, she's trying to escape Brown... or her father or her corroding guilt and shame. She wants to be found, even if it means death. The objective of all addiction is death and it soon comes calling for Susan.

Except, of course, she has a saviour, an unknown admirer called Leonard Diamond (Cornel Wilde), a detective at the local precinct. Like some guy in love with a photograph, Diamond's obsession is driven by an unstated cultural idealism, the need to save a pretty blonde from the embrace of this Mediterranean Othello called "Mr. Brown".

Even Diamond's superior, Captain Peterson, knows his crusade is driven by an unhealthy infatuation, and the mafioso business is mere subtext. Brown's criminal activities simply provides Diamond with a legitimate excuse to eliminate a sexual rival.

When asked by the family friend and unlikely nightclub cruiser Audubon why she is isn't at the symphony tonight with her parents, or playing the piano, Susan says, "The only thing I play now is stud poker." While the immediate reference seems to point to the declasse boxing culture of Brown and his enforcers, the irony cuts another way, infers that the sexual victim was not always a victim.

Diamond? He's a bit of a stud himself, has a nice leggy dancer called Rita on tap. Their situation is a bit like Brown & Susan: she's in love with him, desires commitment, but he has an agenda that keeps their relationship simply sensual. Because of her show biz connections, she's also a good source of information about what's going down on the street. He's always after her for updates on Brown. At one point he expresses his anger and bafflement about Susan being in love with a criminal. Rita says, "A woman doesn't care how a man makes a living, only how he makes love."

Obviously she rates Diamond high in this regard, as she later takes a bullet for him.

You Like Crazy Drums?

Brown has a capo called Joe McClure (Brian Donlevy), an older gent who was passed over in favor of Brown by the organization when the previous don, Grazzi, supposedly retired to Sicily. In fact Joe used to run the hotel, feels he was swindled out of it by Brown, harbours a major grudge. He wears a hearing aid, is never spared his boss's brutal contempt. When he displeases Brown, Brown turns up the volume on his hearing aid, has Mingo scream in his ear. Not only jazzers improvise, it seems.

This form of torture is later refined and used in one of the more original scenes in the film when Fante and Mingo snatch Diamond from his apartment and bring him to the cellar of

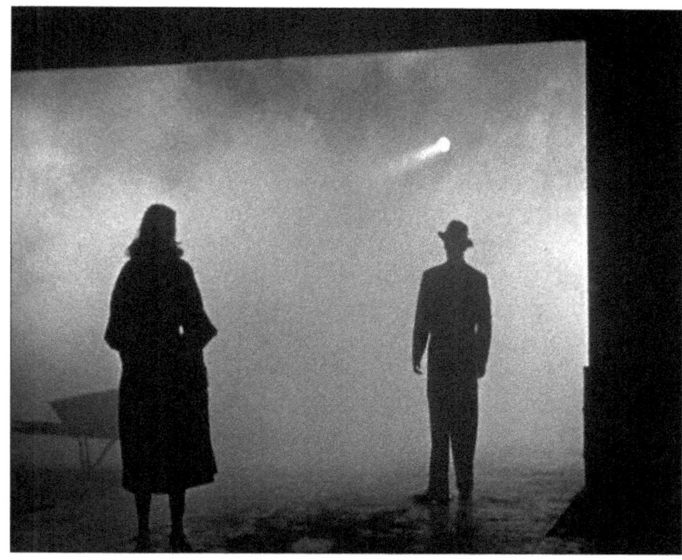

the Bolmec Hotel for some re-education. It's ugly stuff, especially for 1955 when *The Big Combo* was released. McClure decides he's going to break Diamond and proceeds to smash him around, although Fante says "Mr. Brown says he isn't to be touched."

Brown arrives, takes exception, rips the hearing aid from McClure's ear, sticks it in Diamond's. "You like drums, Lieutenant?" says Brown. "Crazy drums?" He takes the radio which is playing some jump jazz drum solo, amps it through the hearing aid, cranks the volume. Tied to his chair, Diamond writhes in agony, a victim of some unknown player's dangerous euphoria. Mingo screams like a crazy vocalist, Brown barks questions. Crazy drums.

It's sublime, if indeed torture can be viewed as sublime, because the symbolism is sublime. Brown and his combo of hoods—old Joe, Fante & Mingo—aren't just criminals, they're hipsters from hell. They liquor Diamond up with some 40 proof hair tonic. Crazy drums. Diamond is dumped in the hallway outside Captain Peterson's apartment. Crazy drums. Jazz is the outlaw music. America runs crazy in the darkness.

For a large part of the action, the plot drag-line is a lift of the Citizen Kane "Rosebud" device; in *The Big Combo*, it's a woman called Alicia. A number of familiar melodrama motifs are used, including insanity, a yacht murder... and an ending in the fog where the blocking—if not the sentiment—is taken from *Casablanca*. Yet despite the unoriginal story, *The Big Combo* is very original as it comes at the close of the film noir era.

Motivation is a post-modern irrelevancy, as assumptions about character and story can be made simply on the basis of history. As a sociopath, Mr. Brown is completely in line with the contemporary criminal villain in film, who acts freely without a conscience. Even when you think Brown is driven by a psychological wound (Alicia), this turns out to be nothing more than an inconvenience on his way to power within the combine.

Even the genre dialogue moves beyond witty cynicism into the existential. When Brown learns that his hunter is in love with Susan, he says, "Diamond in love? That's not possible." Brown assumes that Diamond is exactly like him, just another predator in the night with an organization behind him. Small change, sure, but a realist like him.

Philip Yourdan also wrote *The Conquest of Space* screenplay and a western called *The Man From Laramie* around the same time as he wrote *The Big Combo*, so this might explain the style of science and homicide here. Gadgets... Diamond dictates his memos into a reel-to-reel tape recorder, Brown misuses Joe McClure's hearing aid. There's an element of submerged parody throughout the action, from Brown's monologues about power, strength and weakness, to (some think) an implied homosexual rapport between Fante and Mingo. And the *Citizen Kane* motif: "Alicia, Alicia... don't know if it's a horse, a boat, or a girl," cries an exasperated Captain Peterson as he and Diamond discuss the latest lead.

And how serious is Diamond's declaration of love to Susan in an empty nightclub as an unknown pianist hammers out a mad overture in the shadows? It's a pulp fiction zaniness where nothing is normal except the abnormal. Even Diamond's stalwart associate Sam has the scarred face of a circus freak, as if he stepped straight from the drawing board of a comic book illustrator.

Photographically *The Big Combo* is theatre, where the landscape is pure illusion, shaped by light and shadow. Much is always made of this chiaroscuro aspect of film noir, although the "art" is always an issue of economy, and the fact that this is how it was done in live theatre production. John Alton's cine is justly celebrated, however, for its deco angles and porous backgrounds which retain definition while merging with the foreground. It's like lino cut art or wood block engraving, where the symbolism of shape advances image articulation.

I'd Rather Be Insane And Alive Than Sane And Dead

Richard Conte is superb as the malevolent Mr. Brown who always has to be number one. "First is first, second is nobody," he lectures a boxer who sits bloody and demoralized after losing a fight. Conte's character has some great lines, which mostly celebrate his strength in contrast to the weaklings around him.

This was his best role after playing a stubborn truck driver in Jules Dassin's 1949 crime drama *Thieves Highway*, and certainly better than his largely cosmetic part as Don Emilio Barzini in *The Godfather*. Although he was small in stature, Conte, like Alan Ladd or James Cagney, had an outstanding physical presence. As a movie hoodlum, *The Big Combo* puts him in the gallery of gangster greats (Cagney, *White Heat*; Ray Danton, *The Rise & Fall of Legs Diamond*; Lee J. Cobb, *On the Waterfront*; Lee Marvin, *The Big Heat*; Al Pacino, *Scarface*; Lawrence Tierney, *The Hoodlum*, etc etc).

For Cornel Wilde, his urgent character is quite different from the passive novelist in love with a manipulative beauty that he played in *Leave Her to Heaven* (1945). Diamond is a familiar and dangerous mix: a missionary posing as a cop.

He's trying to save Susan Lowell with the urgency of an evangelist. With the advantage of hindsight, you can see that while he lives in a secular world, his narrow idealism is imprinted by a previous generation... and you wonder if he wasn't in love, how concerned with evil would he be. Still, it's a dangerous world.

As Brown's wife says: "I'd rather be insane and alive than sane and dead."

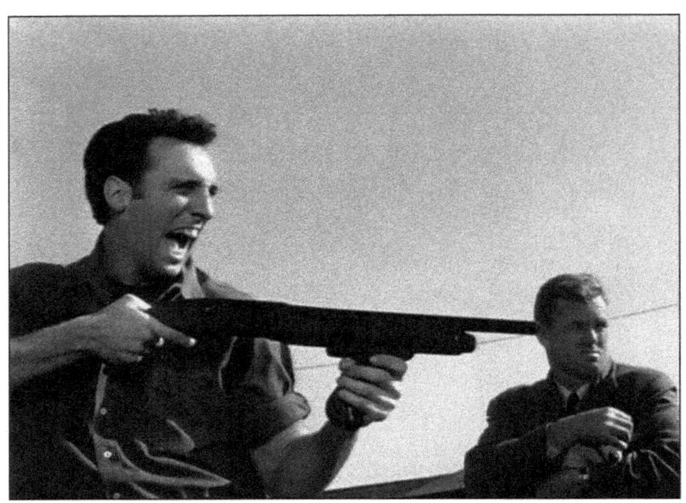

Stanley Kubrick: *The Killing*

The Killing (1956) writ. and dir. Stanley Kubrick (from the novel *Clean Break* by Lionel White) cine. Lucien Ballard (horse race footage by Singer) edt. Betty Steinberg music Gerald Fried star. Sterling Hayden (Johnny Clay), Vince Edwards (Val), Marie Windsor (Sherri Peatty), Elisha Cook (George Peatty), Jay C. Flippen, Ted DeCorsica, Joe Sawyer, Timothy Carey, James Edwards, Kola Kwarian
United Artists/ MGM

Movie *Deja Vu*: The Hollywood Remake

The narrator in this one sounds like a spokesman for God—the deep theatrical tones of the righteous describing death by human greed and stupidity. It's the voice of propaganda, the institutional warning to the children of the State that crime does not pay. Omniscient, it lacks the sardonic worldliness of the robocop reports in *Dragnet*, yet is as essential to the non-linear narrative as a surgeon's log is to reconstructive surgery.

The uniqueness of *The Killing* isn't so much in its setting at a racetrack as it is in its method of telling—a reconstruction of the events leading to the robbery—lifted faithfully by Kubrick from Lionel White's novel *Clean Break*... and subsequently appropriated by Quentin Tarantino in *Reservoir Dogs*. *The Killing* is a cipher from the Hollywood past—technique by *Citizen Kane*, plot by *The Asphalt Jungle*.

Exposed like this, you might think this movie is a mere remake, part of the chain of plagiarisms that Hollywood uses like a spiritual tradition... but no, it's more than that. Coming at the end of the black and white era, the monochromatic claustrophobia of shadow and light is opened up by the anamorphic view, the widening of the world and what you see.

It starts at the track where you see Stopwatch dueling it out with Lucky Arrow and Purple Shadow as they take the final curve into the home stretch. The credits roll... then you see the first of the conspirators, Marvin Unger—an older man with no interest in horse racing or gambling—place a bet, then make his way to the track bar. As he did with the betting clerk, Unger passes on an address and a time to the barman—thus establishing that the heist will be an inside job.

Like *The Asphalt Jungle* you meet the various gang members in a sequence of tight scenes that reveal character, circumstance, and motivation. Patrolman Randy Kenan, a corrupt cop with a gambling debt, tells his Bookie, "I'll take care of myself, mister—that's my specialty" but no sooner is he out of uniform and ready to collect, and he's dead. Mike O'Reilly, the track barman, has an invalid wife, but the flowers he buys for her remain in his locker, a corsage for his grave. George Peatty (Elisha Cook), the betting clerk, has a dissatisfied vixen for a wife (Marie Windsor) who reveals the robbery plan to her lover (Vince Edwards) in a double-cross that costs them all. And the leader, Johnny Clay (Sterling Hayden) with his devoted girl-friend who has remained loyal during his five years in prison, her sacrifice so pure it makes you believe he's Robin Hood, not a cheap hustler too lazy to get a job and pay taxes.

Like *The Asphalt Jungle* there are two "specialists", men paid up front for their "special" talents. There is Maurice, the Russian chess-player and wrestler, who starts a fight in the the track bar in order to draw away the track police.

This is some fight. It has the raw brutality of the Bogart barfight in *The Treasure of the Sierra Madre*, not a stylized choreography from Bolshoi. Maurice is bald and shirtless, a roaring plinth of meat, discarding his assailants like pieces of useless furniture. It takes all the track cops to subdue him, and by then Johnny Clay is inside the money room with his 12 gauge watching the bookies fill his duffle bag with the two million.

Nicky is the other "specialist". You first see him pump three silhouette targets full of lead, then stand fondling his puppy as Johnny commissions him to shoot a horse. Of all the hoods, he's clearly the most homicidal, like some twisted hipster jumped on amphetamines. When the time comes, he's a good shot—he takes out Red Lightning in the 7th at exactly the moment when Johnny makes his entrance into the money room wearing his rubber clown mask. But Nicky is the first to die—he never makes it out of the parking lot.

Nonetheless, the robbery goes as planned... until the gang assembles at the room on Olive St. to wait for Johnny and the loot. This is where Sherri Peatty's treachery is their undoing. Her lover and an accomplice arrive, hold the gang at gunpoint, expecting Johnny Clay to arrive at any moment. When Val reveals that Sherri tipped him off, her husband emerges from an adjacent room, starts shooting. The action is sudden and lethal, a brief gunbattle that leaves them all dead. This scene is reblocked and adapted to his own needs by Tarantino in his postmodern gun-drama *Reservoir Dogs*.

And George? Badly wounded, he survives the shoot-out long enough to stagger home and shoot his cheating redolent wife before collapsing beside the bed, dead at her feet.

The Master Scene: Past, Present, And The Predictive Future

The use of flashbacks to interrupt the linear, forward-moving narrative was a source of concern for many people—including Sterling Hayden's agent—and United Artists were slow in releasing *The Killing*. But it's this very technique that marks the film as different from its predecessors. While the technique is common today—especially in television drama, where the Master Scene often involves cutaways to a parallel present or the past—it was perceived as confusing, and anti-dramatic.

But it's a completely logical narrative form, just like the reconstruction of a crime by various witnesses at a trial. It's really just a variation of the frame narrative, popular in nineteenth century literature and used quite successfully in Siodmak's 1949 crime drama *Criss Cross*. Kubrick uses it to establish the principals and their common purpose, then repeats the technique during the execution of the robbery. Far from betraying the moments of dramatic significance, it in fact sets you up for unexpected drama and irony.

While you anticipate the shooting of the horse, you don't anticipate the shooter's swift death. While you anticipate the intervention of Val, you don't expect the sudden deaths of the gang. Thus the narrative continues to be omniscient, the replays part of the bigger game, like the tracking shots that ignore the walls that separate the characters, the action, and the notion of linear Time.

As a film, *The Killing* is a technical masterpiece that set a new standard for editing while using familiar characters in an exotic setting. Is robbing a racetrack a crime? In a society where crime is often a political definition, it somehow seems like justice.

You want Johnny and Faye to beat the odds, escape on that plane to Boston with that over-stuffed suitcase bought in a hurry from a pawnshop. The closing sequence would make a good ad for Samsonite luggage—don't go cheap when you can afford to go rich. They made a killing, alright....

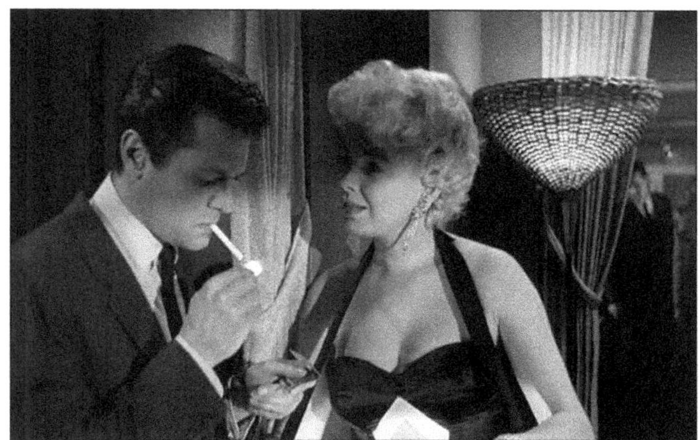

Alexander MacKendrick: *Sweet Smell of Success*

Sweet Smell of Success (1957) dir. Alexander MacKendrick writ. Clifford Odets and Ernest Lehman (from Lehman's novel) cine. James Wong Howe music Elmer Bernstein (and the Chico Hamilton Quartet) star. Burt Lancaster (J.J. Hunsecker), Tony Curtis (Sidney Falco), Susan Harrison (Susie), Martin Milner (Steve), Sam Levene, Barbara Nichols, Jeff Donnell, Joe Frisco, Emile Meyer, Edith Atwater
United Artists

Winter. Night. Manhattan, somewhere on the Broadway axis. Pretty-boy press agent Sidney Falco (Curtis) is on the hustle. Picks up an advance copy of *The Globe*, scans J.J. Hunsecker's column, doesn't find what he wants, tosses the paper into a pavement trash bin, adjourns to his nearby apartment/office where he proceeds to vent his frustration on his homely, love-struck secretary.

> Sec: I wish I could help you somehow.
> Falco: (snarls) You could help with two minutes of silence.

Sec: Sidney, if you feel nervous....
Falco: (turns, hissing) What? You'll open your meaty, sympathetic arms?

Like a character from an Italian revenge tragedy, Falco is a go-between desperately trying to manufacture success by the manipulation of his clients, friends and lovers. He's a parasite, a good intention gone bad.

When he tracks down Hunsecker (Lancaster) holding court in the 21 Club, he bears bad news from The Elysian Room, the club owned by his Uncle Frank. But first he has to gain an audience, so he phones Hunsecker's table from the lobby. But Hunsecker is displeased with Falco's failure to carry out his assignment, namely, break up the romance between his young sister Susie and an up-and-comer jazz guitarist. "You're dead, son," Hunsecker barks into his table phone. "Get yourself buried."

But like all court jesters and starving animals, Falco is willing to play the masochist if gets him what he wants. He slithers up to Hunsecker's table, and the columnist proceeds to humiliate him in front of his companions—a senator, a blond "singer" and her "pimp", a vacuous male who might or might not be an agent.

There's no nicer way to say this—Hunsecker is a prick surrounded by flies. To see Falco cavorting at his shoulder is a lesson in ancient court politics. Later, as Hunsecker and Falco stroll the street, Hunsecker says, "I love this dirty town, Sidney... conjugate me a verb. For example, I promise...."

Well, Falco promises to six Susie's impending betrothal to the guitarist who looks like an ivy leaguer on the slum. He will slander Steve Dallas (Milner) by planting fictitious slurs in a rival column. "Cat's in the bag, bag's in the river," he purrs as he exits into the night.

There are a number of first-rate scenes as Falco goes through the machinations that will allow him to destroy this romance, become J.J.'s understudy, write his column while the tyrant is on holiday. Lies, blackmail, and pandering are the weapons of choice. In order to get Otis, Hunsecker's rival, to include the slander about Steve in his column, Falco sets him up with a vulnerable cigarette girl from his uncle's club. The politics of this sexual exchange make you cringe, and stand in dramatic contrast to the true love of Susie and Steve.

As study of what is bad in human behaviour, *Sweet Smell of Success* is marvellous in its detailing... but, it must be noted, it's less successful in showing us the alternative. Susie is "good" because she's young, apparently innocent, the clear victim of her possessive older brother J.J., who is a control freak of the first order. Her beau Steve is quite unconvincing as a habitue of the club scene. He looks like he was parachuted into the Chico Hamilton Quartet directly from the frat house. Their characters are drawn by omission rather than by inclusion, their love supported by the cliches of history.

There's a feeling of edgy insomnia about much of this film, as if sleep is to be feared. It's an inverted world of late-night venues, where winter cuts the souls of the principals like an X-ray. Manhattan looks like an industrial dump, a grayscale saturation of angst, loneliness and corruption. The police are corrupt, mere pawns in the extended game of blackmail and nepotism purveyed by J.J. Hunsecker, the man in the penthouse over Broadway. Falco is corrupt, driven by his infantile desire to not only be near his idol J.J. but to actually be J.J. And of course Hunsecker is utterly corrupt, his morality merely another form of bad egotism.

"My right hand hasn't seen my left hand in thirty years," says Hunsecker metaphorically, as if his halo is so bright that darkness no longer exists.

Like many masterpieces, *Sweet Smell of Success* was considered a failure at the time (1957) because it lost money at the box office. Yet over the years many have recognized the brilliance of Curtis's performance as the handsome sycophant Sidney Falco, a man who calls himself a press agent. As for Lancaster, what can one say? Another defining performance from his Golden Period (which includes *From Here To Eternity, Apache, Trapeze, Gunfight At The O.K. Corral, Elmer Gantry, et.al.*).

"Hunsecker"—pronounced as sucker the very name itself is a classic of the sexual and/or racial insult. As the king of the show-biz columnists, the character has the lonely elegance of today's talk-show host, courted by clowns, politicians, and cops. As a demigod, the persona is a lethal cocktail of the understated epigram and the skull-faced stare. Like all tyrants, he believes he rules by divine right. "I wasn't really playing a columnist but a heel," Lancaster says. "No, I just played a heel who happened to be a columnist." (as quoted in Gary Fishgall's 1995 Burt Lancaster biography *Against Type.)*

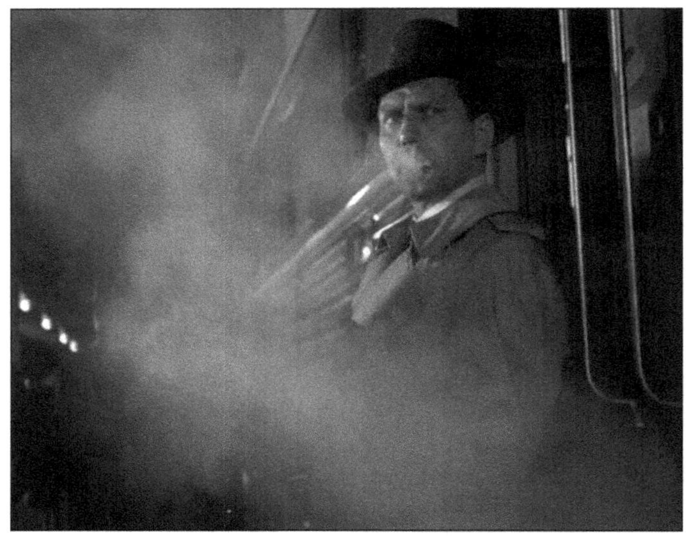

Richard Fleischer: *The Narrow Margin*

The Narrow Margin (1952) dir. Richard Fleischer writ. Earl Felton [story by Martin Goldsmith & Jack Leonard] cine. George E. Diskant art. Albert S. D'Agostino & Jack Okey edt. Robert Swink sound. Francis Sarver & Clem Portman
star. Charles McGraw (Det. Brown) Marie Windsor (Mrs. Neall/ Sarah Meggs) Jacqueline White (Mrs. Sinclair/ Mrs. Neal) Gordon Gebert (Tommy), Queenie Leonard, David Clarke (Joseph Kemp), Peter Virgo (Denzel), Don Beddoe (Det. Forbes), Paul Maxy (Jennings), Peter Brocco (Vincent Yost), Harry Harvey
RKO Pictures 70 mins 1952

Just A Job, And No Joy In It

As the credits roll: the intercontinental pulls into Chicago at night, and two detectives, Brown (Charles McGraw) and Forbes

(Don Beddoe) disembark. Forbes is older, plump, wears a dark overcoat, smokes a cigar. Brown... masculine tough, fedora, trenchcoat, chain smokes cigarettes. No sooner are their suitcases on the platform than Brown shows the conductor a return ticket, instructs him to have the cases re-boarded as he and his partner will return within the hour to take the train back to L.A.

Why the quick visit? The widow of the Chicago gangster Frank Neall has a list of names that she has agreed to turn over to the Grand Jury looking into organized crime in Los Angeles. Brown & Forbes have been sent by the D.A. in order to ensure a safe passage for Mrs. Neall back to L.A. When they get to the apartment where she's being held in protective custody, she's chain-smoking and listening to dance music on a small windup phonograph. She certainly looks the part: an aggressive full-figured gangster's moll, "a 60 cent special", a cheap date who was probably a rent-a-dance girl before marrying dirty money. As they exit the apartment they are ambushed on the stairs by a hood wearing a *de rigueur* Prohibition overcoat with a fur-collar. The hit is bungled, although Forbes is killed and the assassin escapes over a back-yard fence into an alley where a getaway car is waiting.

While this action might seem generic for the genre, the expressionist cinematography is the best of its kind. You want noir shadows? Check out how the stair-rail bars ripple shadows over the ascending cops, the chiaroscuro poetry between light and darkness. The set is angular & tight, like a comic strip frame... and establishes the medium shot/close-up photography that dominates the train sequences and makes all the characters large and intimate.

It's a bad start for Det. Brown. He's lost his partner, and his consort is a yappy self-centred bitch who's always in his face. This "Mrs. Neall" is a party doll who hyper-spaces between paranoia and flirtation as easy as igniting a match. She fills a stereotype and all your expectations. Brown would have an easier time concealing a horse on the train... yet through a series of amusing antics he manages well enough until they are almost in L.A. He also manages to romance a certain blonde called "Mrs. Sinclair" who is travelling with her young son and a nanny. For a man whose partner was just shot by the mob, and who have him marked as the bodyguard of the witness, he does o.k.

Deception, Reflection, And The Art Of Revelation

This film is all about style: the way it looks, the cine, the editing, the sets, the costumes, the attitude. The use of optical reflection is taken to a dramatic and aesthetic extreme, becomes the signature of the action, more so than the plot. "Reflection" ties directly into the theme as well as being an accurate visual dynamic of train travel. Nothing is what it seems, especially with certain key characters, who reverse identities with Aristotelian precision [i.e. Marie Windsor & Jacqueline White].

Like a double or triple exposure, the imagery in the windows contains layers, dimensions, motivations, premonitions. You know how it is on the night train as you relax with a scotch & soda in the club car, spying casually on the other patrons via the reflections in the window... reflections which inter-weave with the shadowy rushing landscape outside... the subtle blend of the past & present tenses, of memory and the evolving status quo. It's through the use of reflection, in fact, that the resolution of the story is achieved when Det. Brown does some fancy shooting.

Yet there's nothing intellectual about *The Narrow Margin*, despite the geometric precision of the cinematography and the editing. The montage conceals the simplicity of the characters and their business. Mrs. "Sinclair" is a bourgeois fix, a charming victim who dismisses her complicity in crime by saying, "Who knows what kind of woman marries a gangster?" Suspension of disbelief is required at least twice here: one, that no one in the syndicate knows what Frankie Neall's wife looks like, and two, that the widow needs to courier a list of names to L.A. when the U.S. mail would do just nicely. True, she needs to testify before the Grand Jury... but the "list" could've been delivered separately. The Marie Windsor character's deception of her colleague Det. Brown is a thing of beauty, yet seems improbable, unless the real mission is to test his loyalty.

Her volatile character is played to perfection by Marie Windsor, the former Vargas model and beauty queen, who played many noir tramps and vamps such as this one or her corrosive whipper role in the great Kubrick racetrack heist film *The Killing*.

The DVD of *The Narrow Margin* contains the now obligatory commentary version—in this instance by the accomplished Hollywood director William Friedkin who more or less declares himself to be an understudy of Richard Fleischer in terms of technique, especially on how "to move the action." Friedkin draws parallels to his famous New York-Marseilles drug movie *The French Connection* (1971)... and you can also see a similar narrative drive in his *To Live & Die In L.A.* (1985).

Narrative semiotics aside, Friedkin's commentary is outstanding, both as an insider's view and for its positioning of *The Narrow Margin* within the history of film noir. Who, for example, can dispute his observation that there's a missing scene/sequence at the end? To deal with Marie Windsor's character? It is so. Aesthetics & propaganda demand it.

Despite the hard-boiled characters and the grim action, most of it is strictly theatre. The closed space of the train is theatre. The burlesque entrances and exits are theatre. Ducking into washrooms, wrong compartments, alcoves... all this is theatre. The character tableaux is theatre. The gangster's moll, the fat man railway cop, Denzel the Prohibition assassin, Brown in a trenchcoat... in the reductive universe, it's almost paint by numbers.

Yet withal the realism is impressive. As Friedkin observes, Brown's fight with Kemp in the washroom compartment is seminal, was copied in the James Bond movie *From Russia With Love*. It was also copied by Ken Annakin in *Across the Bridge* (1957) when Rod Steiger needs to kill and assume the identity of another man. Claustrophobic and real, shot with a handheld camera. It's also one of the longest scenes in the film, almost four minutes if you include the fight and its aftermath interrogation. All the while the sense of being in a speeding train is sustained by the strobing light & pulsing shadow lines typical of the experience... and of course the rolling vertigenous sound of the train.

You could call *The Narrow Margin* pseudo "neo-realism" because it affects a documentary naturalism by using no music, and by simulating ambient sound. The sound of train—within and without—with its machine rhythm and doppler transitions is worthy of *musique concrete*. The train sets, too, are so realistic, so authentic in detail, that you assume all sequences are filmed on location.

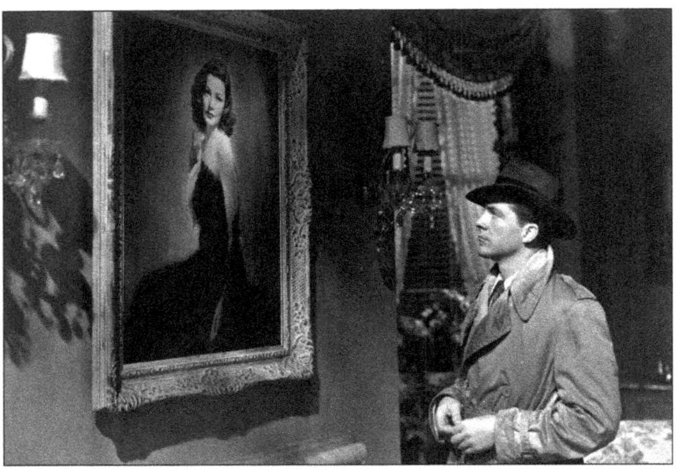

Otto Preminger: *Whirlpool*

Whirlpool (1949) dir. Otto Preminger writ. Ben Hecht & Andrew Solt (based on the novel *Methinks the Lady* by Guy Endore) cine. Arthur Miller (effects by Fred Sersen) audio Winston Leverett/Harry M. Leonard (Western Electric) art Leland Fuller & Lyle Wheeler edt. Lois Loeffler music David Raksin
star Gene Tierney (Ann Sutton) Richard Conte (Dr. William Sutton) Jose Ferrer (David Korvo) Charles Bickford (Lieutenant Colton) Barbara O'Neil (Terri Randolph) Constance Collier (Tina Cosgrove) Edward Franz (Martin Avery) Fortunio Bona (Baron Parveau) *et. al.*

A statuesque beauty exits a Wilshire Blvd department store and gets into a new 1950 Ford convertible which the car-hop has just delivered to the sidewalk loading zone. Before she can start the engine she's confronted by the store detective who accuses her of theft. He grabs her purse and sure enough, finds a new costume pin. A kleptomaniac in an Oleg Cassini suit? Seems so... although surely there must be some mistake. The incident is observed by a man with a vague Mediterranean pallor who might be there by chance... or by design.

The thief turns out to be Mrs. Ann Sutton (Gene Tierney), the wife of a well known local psychiatrist, Dr. William Sutton. This information is revealed when David Korvo (Jose Ferrer) intervenes, saves her from the manager and the store detective. Korvo knows who she is, although she doesn't know him. The manager knows who Korvo is, although he doesn't know Ann Sutton, apparently, one of his store's valued customers. It's all possible, of course, although most people would recognize immediately that Korvo has an agenda.

What? At first Ann Sutton thinks it's blackmail, then seduction. "I'm not looking for a lover," she says over martinis, but Korvo isn't easily dissuaded. He tears up her "gratitude" cheque [5,000 dollars], then gives her the Wilshire Store's shop-lifting file which he has somehow managed to get. See? his interest is purely professional. She tears up the file, smiles. How can she repay him?

Although married, Ann agrees to meet him at a party being hosted by one of his friends. Here, in an adjacent room, he proceeds to analyze her discontent, her neuroses, then, as a quick-fix therapy, hypnotizes her. Presumptuous in the extreme, this man has no boundaries, uses insult like a sex-whip. He commands her to give him her hand. She extends it slowly, as if from another dimension, then withdraws it. *Non plussed*, he tells her to fall asleep, and she does... so he wins one, loses one. It seems that no hypnotized subject can be persuaded to do something that isn't in her basic nature. Or at least this is the thesis that the writers advance.

It's this ambiguity of game, intent, crime and sickness that drives the action as a modern melodrama, stylistically similar to a stage play with closed, static sets, lengthy conversations, a beautiful female whose virtue is on the line, and a fascinating man whose villainy knows no bounds.

In fact, *Whirlpool* owes its cachet to the superb performance of Jose Ferrer (fresh from an acclaimed Broadway stage stint as Iago) as the villain David Korvo, for, without the novelty and vitality of this vicious character, the film would be a failure. As many have observed, Richard Conte is a bit too street coarse to be comfortable in his role as the sensitive psychiatrist William (Bill) Sutton, and you keep expecting him to revert to his famous hard man persona, go nuts, choke this insolent slime Korvo for messing with his wife.

But more fatally, perhaps, the narrative structure is handicapped by director Preminger's live theatre sequencing, especially as seen in the absurd ending where all the principals show up and have their say. Perhaps the writers can be blamed for this, although it must be noted that Preminger was also the producer, and received his training in the theatre in Vienna... and was under heavy pressure to reprise *Laura* (1946), his previous hit with Gene Tierney. The DVD reissue has a scene-by-scene commentary by the canny film historian and critic Richard Schickel who discusses the problematic aspects of the final scene (at Theresa Randolph's house), but admits a fondness for the unreality as befitting the film period. He might be right. You could argue that the stage expressionism fits the chic psychological landscape of a bourgeois zombie and her crazy hypnotist.

David Korvo. *Homme fatale* or clown? Like most movie characters, he arrives without a history, so motivation remains circumspect. In this instance, he exists as a gothic noun. "Corvo" is Latin for "raven", an image that sits perfectly with the sinister gloss of the pandiculating mentalist, healer & hustler. This is the key to his character, which is clearly based on the peculiar English writer Frederick William Rolfe (1860 - 1913), who often wrote under the nom de plume Baron Corvo. Rolfe/Corvo was famous for his venomous tongue, and the settling of old scores in his roman a clefs. As a means of reinventing the stock upper-class brute who uses and abuses all who get in his way, the character of David Korvo is a stroke of modern genius. Alienated, embittered, this fluent individual exists as a shadow player on the fringe of the new and wonderful world of institutional psycho-analysis. Here he stalks the wealthy society of post-war Los Angeles as an intellectual werewolf, not unlike the occultist Aleister Crowley, another brilliant apostate dedicated to seduction and criminal begging.

A tantalizing yet inclusive hint of his background occurs at socialite Tina Cosgrove's party, where he does a quick analysis of "the Baron" (Fortunio Bona), then later, when exiting the house, addresses him in fluent Italian. This is a direct lift from the actual Baron Corvo (via the novelist Guy Endore) who spent some time under the patronage of the Duchess Sforza-Cesarini in Italy, knew Italian, wrote on Italian subjects, including the Borgias and the sexual possibilities of Venice. Yet there's a missing sub-plot action here, as the Baron's blonde fiancé is supposedly one of Korvo's "proteges". As Korvo tells Ann, she supplied him with the personal information necessary for his impressive diagnosis of the Baron at the party. This suggests the ancient grifter scam employed by a charismatic couple who conceal their relationship in order to seduce & scam others. Yet this part of the "plot" was either undeveloped or edited out. The blonde protege and her mark the Baron just disappear, yet remain as a dangling modifier for the uneasy and mostly invisible back-story.

"Your Eyes Are Full Of Fear & Tension"

As head-game bullies go, Korvo is typical, plays on insecurity, exploits neuroses, seeks power and sensual gratification... which contrasts dramatically with Dr. Bill Sutton, who simply wants to free people of their psychological trauma. Sutton is scientific, institutional, committed to the common good... whereas Korvo is an outlaw, a predator, by his own ironic definition "a mere humble astrologer". His targets are usually women, although men aren't immune from his vicious, manipulative invasions... which is dramatically evident in the scene where, after Ann is arrested for murder, Dr. Sutton confronts Korvo in his hospital bed. Here Korvo uses innuendo with the corrosive cunning of Iago poisoning Othello's mind about the loyalty of Desdemona. Sutton is rattled, but refuses to abandon his belief in his wife. It's a good scene, made all the more memorable by the fact that Korvo has just had a gall-bladder operation, is in great pain.

Korvo's control over Ann has it limits, although the true extent of it is left to your imagination. A re-examination of the opening events suggests that just possibly Ann Sutton was already hypnotised when she stole the $300 Mermaid pin. When she is apprehended and led back into the store, Korvo is nearby, watching... trolling or maybe already con-trolling. She faints in the elevator (which is about the only justification for the metaphoric title *Whirlpool*) and when she recovers, finds herself in the manager's office on a couch.

The female clerk says, "I could clearly see her reflection in the glass—" but is interrupted by the arrival of David Korvo, who intervenes smoothly on Ann's behalf. The manager reacts respectfully as if he believes Korvo to be a man of some professional and moral significance. Mrs Sutton has an account here, has she not? Indeed. Etc. In a later scene, Korvo auto-hypnotizes himself using a mirror, so if he could do this, he could have hypnotized Ann by using the glass of the display as a mirror, ordered her to steal the pin.

Was such a sequence written and/or filmed, then edited out? Possibly, as there are a number of missing transitions elsewhere that suggest either forced or creative editing, i.e. Ann's hypnosis when she "steals" the recordings of her husband's analysis sessions with Theresa Randolph, then, in alpha rhythm, zombie drives to the Randolph mansion, finds her murdered.

"Wire-Tapping The Sub-Conscious"

Whatever you might feel about the ending, the scene that prefaces it is very good, has a crazy pulp fiction allure. Korvo, alerted by a nurse—probably intentionally, although this is another ambiguity in a very ambiguous story—that the police are on the verge of finding the missing Theresa Randolph recordings, is forced to leave his hospital bed and go to the Randolph house where he knows his automaton Ann has left them by his command. He's had major surgery within the last 24 hours, so his ability to walk would be neigh impossible. Like a freak incident chronicled by Charles Fort or Ripley's Believe It Or Not, Korvo performs self-hypnosis using a vanity mirror, wills himself to leave his bed, dress, then drive to the Randolph house where he takes an ill-advised time out to actually play and listen to the recordings of his mistress denouncing him to her therapist Bill Sutton. Because of this "relationship" we are left with the impression of a man driven by a homoerotic jealousy of his former mistress.

"She may be telling the truth or laying the foundation for an insanity appeal," says the police shrink after Ann confesses her thievery. Childless, she exists as a trophy wife, and typically blames her husband for her malaise. Yet the automaton woman is a classic male fantasy, and in this context is subversive. A criminal somnabulist or bi-polar victim can always find moral refuge in institutional psychology. Innocence becomes a question of redefining the crime. Motivation supplants act, sickness supplants motivation.

A secular Jew from Vienna, a couple of Hollywood Blacklist writers... the real backstory to *Whirlpool*? Hecht was initially credited under an alias while Guy Endore who wrote the source novel *Methinks the Lady*—himself an experienced screenwriter—wasn't part of the team. A committed Stalinist until the Kruschev renunciation, Endore is best known for his pulp classic *The Werewolf of Paris* (1933) [the film version was made by Hammer in 1961 renamed *The Curse of the Werewolf*, starring Oliver Reed], and you can see a lycanthropic element in his character of David Korvo. While Korvo doesn't feed on children and virgins, he has the viral appetite of a mind parasite.

Methinks the Lady—a play on the Hamlet line—was also published as *Nightmare*, a more direct and generic title than the film version's metaphoric *Whirlpool*. Consider *Nightmare*'s subheader: "She led a double life—wife to one man, wanton to many" and you can see that, conversely, Preminger's film navigates the Hollywood Motion Picture Production Code with the stony virtue of a nineteenth century melodrama. The secret hypnosis therapy of Ann Sutton uses sex as innuendo, as if the lavicious scenes have been excised, and you are convinced of her victimization and innocence only by the lack of visual evidence. Blackmail is replaced by a frame-up, as Korvo is reduced to murder in order to solve his problem.

Interestingly, William Irish's (a.k.a. Cornell Woolrich) story *Nightmare* was filmed in 1947 as *Fear In The Night* starring DeForest Kelly as a bank teller who is manipulated into committing a murder while hypnotized... and least anyone thinks Preminger's *Whirlpool* owes nothing to this moody B-noir mystery, let him/her compare the scene where the villain Bellknap hypnotizes his patsy DeForest Kelly using a pocket watch as a mirror to the scene where Korvo auto-hypnotizes himself using a small mirror. Cinematically, both shots are identical.

This plagiarism is the sort of theft that gets a student expelled from the academy but in Hollywood usually rates an Oscar nomination.

Whirlpool is now being marketed as "film noir" and while it does have a couple of scenes that use shadow & light expressionism—Ann's night drive, and Korvo's night exit from the hospital—it isn't film noir. Preminger flood-lit his scenes, used live theatre blocking, followed the verbal style of the drawing room drama. These various stage conventions include "theatrical

Time", static scene blocking, verbal exposition, and secrets known to the audience but with-held from the characters. Thus the virtue & reputation of the heroine are in jeopardy, exacerbated by a "misunderstanding", i.e. her relationship with David Korvo (itself a secret from her husband), and the secret of her kleptomania.

Director Preminger's apparent distrust of cinematic montage probably explains some of the absurd time & space transitions, although the dysfunctionality of the narrative can be rationalized as a hallucinatory point-of-view, the so-called "subjective Time" of the hypnotic state.

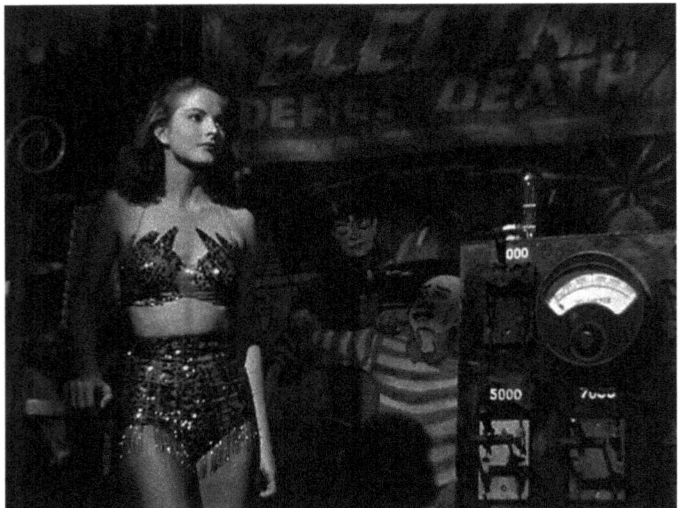

Edmund Goulding: *Nightmare Alley*

Nightmare Alley (1947) 111 m. dir. Edmund Goulding writ. Jules Furthman [from the novel by William Lindsay Gresham] cine. Lee Garmes [special effects Fred Sersen] edt. Barbara McLean art. Lyle Wheeler & J. Russell Spencer music. Cyril Mockridge cost. Bonnie Cashin prod. George Jessel
star. Tyrone Power (Stan Carlisle/the Great Stanton) Joan Blondell (Zeena) Colleen Gray (Molly) Helen Walker (Lillith Ritter) Taylor Holmes Mike Mazurki Ian Keith et. al.
20th Century Fox 1947

Depending on who you believe, Edmund Goulding either died from a heart attack or by suicide in 1959 following a depraved life of bisexual adventurism. The conflicted nature of his personality is certainly evident in the gloomy patina of *Nightmare Alley*, especially in the night-shadow sequences of the carnival action that occupy the first half of the film.

Despite the obvious live theatre stylings—ensemble acting and static setting—the film could be classed as neo-realism because of its real-time scenes, minimal music, and documentary detail. Yet despite this naturalism, we see the psychology of inner space, occult mysticism and Freudian hucksterism beautifully revealed within the atmospheric poetry of the semi-tone cinematography.

This 1947 film influenced the style of David Lynch's *The Elephant Man* (1980) and the content of Roger Corman's *The Man With the X-Ray Eyes* (1963), and, despite its uneven narrative, has to be considered one of the best examples of black and white photography as visual metaphor in modern film drama.

The carnival is in town... although we see no town, only the dilapidated theatres of the travelling freak show. It's a closed, deceptive world of curtains and shadows, where concealment and revelation are as ritualized as the culture of a New Orleans voodoo cemetery. One by one the principals are introduced as the camera patrols: The Geek, for now seen only as a brutal caveman on a marquee poster, blood dripping from his fangs; Zeena the Seer [Joan Blondell], lounging on her stage, watching the gathering crowd with the sleepy slattern eyes of a fallen Tarot priestess; Bruno the strongeman in a leopard-skin wrap... his young assistant Molly, pretty and wholesome enough to be a Sunday School teacher on the lam... and Stan Carlisle [Tyrone Power], a young buck moving through the throng as if he's just another voyeur here for a good time, not a working member of the carnival. Thus the point-of-view is established as that of Stan, the neophyte carny, his fresh young arms unblemished by tattoos, his bright eyes on the thrilling edge of corruption.

The Geek? Of course Stan is fascinated by the Geek, the number 1 attraction. He approaches the handler, hustles him for information. Why would anyone play the part? He gets a dirty look. The subject is taboo, as if our ugly ancestry as just another blood-lust animal is the real question, the contaminated sub-text of human pornography. The handler exhorts the crowd to line up for the ghastly show, then tosses a couple of live chickens into the throng with the clincher, "And now, folks, it's feeding time!"

Another Exotic Animal In The Night

Stan moves on, flirts with Molly, the young presenter for Bruno/Hercules, the strong-man act. It's Molly who tells him about "The Code", the jealously guarded secret system of words and correlative numbers that Zeena (the Seer) and her partner Pete use to "read" the minds of the naive. And it's Pete, the derelict prompter who lies beneath the stage or in his crib in a perpetual drunken daze, who reveals the common wounds within the common mind that can be exploited by a crafty mentalist on the hustle.

Pete hustles no more, of course. Kept by Zeena, but broken by her in the past when she took up with a younger, sexier Magician in a failed attempt at post-carnival stardom, he now earns his keep through guilt and acting as a prompter concealed below her lectern. He has been replaced by Stan, who now wears the stripped jacket, white gloves, spins the cane, works the crowd. Stan is also Zeena's latest lover, another sexual apprentice in the ancient art of fortune telling. She's just past her prime, but nonetheless we can see that she's still a good piece, still got something. She's one of those bad ladies who's not really bad at all, just another exotic animal in the night.

Zeena has no illusions, although illusion is her act. "I'm about as reliable as a 2 dollar coronet," she says as they drive through the darkness to the next anonymous town, Pete lying in the back of the truck like a crippled dog, Stan driving. Stan wants to learn the secret of the blindfold code, start a new act outside the carnival, work the society chumps, hit the big-time. Zeena is uncertain, is considering selling the code in order to finance treatment for Pete. Still, life goes on... and she's smitten with Stan. Ever the eager learner, he persuades her to reintroduce mind-reading to the act and thus learns the blindfold code. But one day during a tryst in a hotel room, Zeena looks into the future with the help of the Tarot and sees Death as the draw for Pete. Distraught, she tells Stan that she can't abandon Pete or the carnival, head for the bright lights.

The Art Of Trance

It's an interesting triangle with more-than-interesting implications, as the quasi-outlaw culture of the carnival draws into focus the ancient spiritual protocol of man and woman, wherein the woman is the oracle (or cipher) who reads both the past and the future, and the man is her wand, always craving divination. This is something which reaches back into paganism, yet has been politicized out of the civilized personality. Yet our fascination remains, however, with the imagery of the crystal ball, especially when combined with the erotic. It's the jaded Pete, who, in a moment of lucidity, delivers a hypno monologue while staring into the "crystal" of his whiskey bottle, in a funny yet fascinating demonstration of the art of trance as a weapon of manipulation. Again, Stan absorbs the lesson... and unknowingly, his fate. He also starts an affair with Molly which is quickly discovered by Bruno, who forces the couple to marry by choking Stan into submission. So strange is the code of the carnival, everyone concerned accepts this shotgun judgement as fair and right—even Stan, who actually sees this "expulsion" as a chance to become the star mentalist of his dreams, adopting Zeena's role as the blindfolded seer and using his new wife Molly as his telegrapher.

The death of Pete is an accident designed by destiny... while it might seem contrived, it's certainly plausible. As in all carefully plotted narratives, the event is both ironic and causal. Stan buys a bottle of moonshine from another carny, hides it in Zeena's prop trunk when Pete approaches... but, swayed by the broken man's desperation and willingness to divulge techniques and secrets, he opens the trunk and gives Pete the bottle. Later Pete is found dead from drinking the kerosene Zeena uses for burning the trick notes in their routine—the bottle, identical to the moonshine bottle, was also in Zeena's trunk. Zeena's trunk... symbolism? Possibly... although we don't need it to appreciate her fatal charm.

Zeena, Zeena... perhaps we see Zeena as a victim of the allure she once held. In her grief she cries out that she'd made up her mind the previous evening to sell the secret of the blindfold code, use the money to get treatment for Pete least he ends up completely insane like the Geek... who seems to be the final tragic incarnation of all carny hustlers who mess with the occult.

Who is to blame here? The priestess who messes with her messengers, or the messenger who messes with the priestess? If the carnival was Eden, we could blame the serpent. The crystal ball, the whiskey bottle, the wounded child within... yes, we learn that Stan grew up in an orphanage, graduated from reform school. In this script, all the characters have a background to accommodate their motives. It's the psychology of American naturalism whereby a man's fate is shaped by his social environment. He's usually allowed one chance for redemption, otherwise he's sent to hell. This "born-again" psychology, so fundamental to the American experience, is always waiting in the wings in such stories as this.

The second half of the film concerns Stan's rise to fame as "The Great Stanton", a slick player who reads the minds of the rich and vulnerable in the Spode Room, a nightclub in

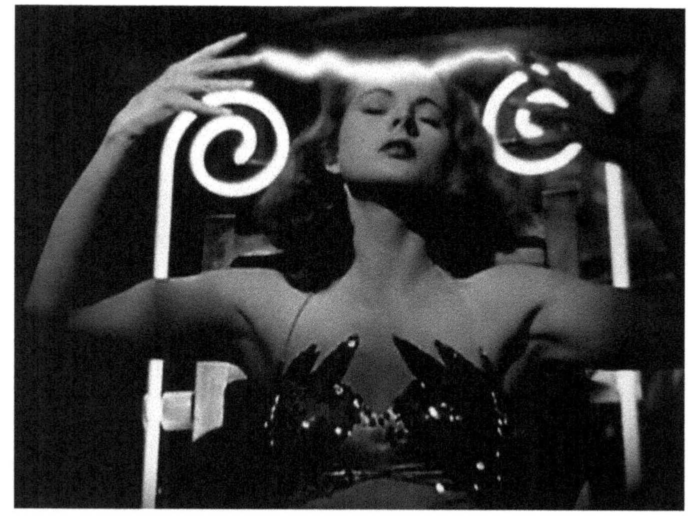

Chicago's tony Hotel Sherman. Now he wears a natty black evening suit complete with tails and matching black blindfold. Wife Molly takes the questions, telegraphs the code via set phrases and voice inflections. He's absorbed Pete's actorial monologue style and Zeena's sexual karma, blending their tricks into his persona of the Scottish boy with the gift of the second sight. Why has he been chosen? He doesn't know. He's an agent of a higher being, and everyone wants a piece.

It's in the ocean liner setting of the Spode Room that he encounters the next characters to shape his fate: wealthy widow Mrs. Peabody, industrialist Ezra Grindle... and the beautiful psychologist Lillith Ritter. The attraction between Stan and Lillith is immediate, presents an interesting conurbation of the old and the new, that is, the outlaw tradition of mentalism and its modern child, institutional Freudian psychology. Lillith tries to trick the Great Stanton with the following question: "Do you think my mother will recover from her present illness?" By now Stan is so on top of his game, he immediately intuits a trick. In a ritual unmasking, he removes his blindfold, stares at the woman who will be his nemesis. Their eyes lock, a test of wills, a sexual meld. Finally Stan says he can't answer the question as her mother is dead. Is he right? Of course. Impressive? Of course. Second sight? Who knows.

Within The Edits

Later, when Lillith invites him to a meeting in her office, he shrugs it all off as a pragmatic guess. Their affair is conducted within the edits—we never see them kiss or leave a bedroom together... or even share drinks and smokes in a lake-side lounge. It's a pity, as we sense there's something crazy about their relationship, just like that between Phyllis and Walter in *Double Indemnity* (1944), two hustlers on the road to hell. Stan discovers that Lillith records her patients' couch sessions with a concealed machine (acetate record cutter, state-of-the-art for the early forties), brutally insists that she's no different than he. Yet it's not long before Stan ends up on her couch, confessing his involvement in the death of Pete. Says Lillith, "You're completely normal... selfish and ruthless to get what you want... and when you have it, kind and gentle."

Now Stan trusts Lillith completely, just as he once did with Zeena. Mrs. Peabody wants to give him money, a radio station... Grindle outbids her, gives Stan thousands, which he passes on to

Lillith for safe keeping. Lillith is quite the mover—in one clandestine rendezvous on the lakeshore, she arrives in a speedboat. Sex is subverted to the excitement of a scam, and the millionaire Ezra Grindle is their mark. We've already seen how Stan can find the insecurity in a person when he manipulates the old Marshall who comes to shut down the carnival. Like Iago, he is a natural master of 3rd party paranoia.

While there are many good things about this film, it does have some weaknesses. The narrative is a bit hurried at times, especially at the end when Stan returns to the carnival as a broken drunken wretch. This is not unusual when a script is based on a novel, which by nature is verbalized and covers a lot of history/time. The symmetry, achieved at the expense of real Time, might appear convenient with its literary loops, even when these loops are effective. We might laugh at the stagey morality and at so many characters with hearts of gold as all this seems out of step with contemporary living, even if we sympathize with its Biblical certainty. Yet withal the ensemble flow suits the "nightmare" quality of the action, most of it internalized to night settings, so that we can easily accommodate the superstitions of the characters and the unrealistic closing sequences.

The film was a box office failure, despite being a Zanuck response to the austere docu style of the neo-realist films coming out of Italy at the time. Rock Hudson surmised that the public didn't believe it as "A man as handsome as Ty would never be reduced to eating a live chicken." [as quoted in Hector Arce's *The Secret Life of Tyrone Power*] True enough as far as the hollow theatrics of the ending go... yet somehow Power is extremely effective as the ambitious orphan loner willing to exploit the criminal edges of the occult. He has the look—dark and handsome, like a gypsy without a toothpick. Apprenticed with Zeena, he becomes another of Satan's handsome sensualists. "Why am I like this?" he asks Lillith, alluding to his shifty penchant for using and abusing.

But as womanizers go, he is hardly the worst, as his women are merely part of his Oedipal hunger and a professional necessity. The one we know least about, really, is Lillith who is arguably the real criminal. Compared to Zeena and Molly—neither of whom commit any crime—she is a genuine charlatan, unable to satisfy her clients, yet willing to defraud them of their wealth and mental health.

However, her liaison with the Great Stanton is ambiguous enough that we might see her as a woman trying to impress a lover who just might have the fabled gift of the second sight despite his own cynicism and dedication to the art of the hustle. Still, it takes one to catch one and while Lillith doesn't quite live up to the the Biblical implications of her name [Adam's wife before Eve was created and/or a female demon who attacks children in deserted places], we can imagine her later in life hosting a radio or TV Talk Show.

PART FOUR:

Neo-Noir

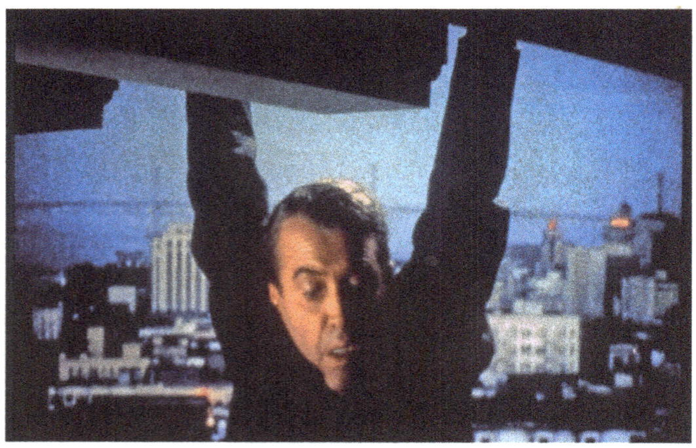

Alfred Hitchcock: *Vertigo*

Vertigo (1958) dir. Alfred Hitchcock writ. Samuel Taylor (and Alex Coppel) (based on the novel *D'entre les Morts* by Boileau and Narcejac) cine. Robert Burks edt. George Tomasini art. Bumstead and Pereira costumes Edith Head music Bernard Herrman
star. James Stewart (Scotty), Kim Novak (Madeline/Judy), Barbara Bel Geddes (Midge), Tom Helmore (Gavin Ellster), Henry Jones, Ellen Corby, Lee Patrick, Raymond Bailey, Konstantin Shayne
Universal

Misogyny And The Make-Over

John "Scotty" Ferguson is a middle-aged San Francisco detective gripped with a psychosexual obsession that manifests itself as a fear of heights or vertigo. His phobia appears to be a dream phobia, as the opening sequence shows him hanging from a gutter several stories above the street. Another cop has just fallen to his death trying to save him... and the criminal they were pursuing gets away. While we are expected to take these events literally, they are the stuff of common human nightmares and the recurrent imagery of Mr. Alfred Hitchcock, a director well-known for stranding his dreamers on the edge of a cataclysm.

Following this event, Scotty takes early retirement to convalesce, but is soon contacted by an old alma mater, one Gavin Ellster, a local shipbuilder who fears his beautiful young wife is about to commit suicide because she too is possessed by a dream. Madeline believes she is the reincarnation of her great grandmother, Carlotta Valdes, a beauty who committed suicide after she is separated from her child and abandoned by her rich lover. So now Madeline's days are given to "wandering" in a trance, visiting the graveyard where Carlotta is buried or viewing her portrait in the San Francisco Art Gallery. Scotty is detailed to follow Madeline, make sure she comes to no harm.

His quest seems legitimate enough at first but such is the curious psychology of this story, he ends up as her stalker, a lover in search of an obsession.

In pages 242-44 of his 1978 Hitch biography, *The Life And Times Of Alfred Hitchcock*, John Russell Taylor opens up the uneasy core of this emotional film as well as anyone. "*Vertigo*... is alarmingly close to allegorical autobiography," says Prof. Taylor, and although we reply what fiction isn't? we nod in agreement when he goes on to say that "Hitch seems (to be) the great exponent of male sadism." Taylor sees in *Vertigo* an allegory to Hitchcock's obsession with blondes (his leading ladies) and their "make-over". When Scotty forces Judy to become a blond and dress as Madeline, his actions are like that of a director manipulating an actress into a theatrical ideal. That this game sequencing has a sexual pathology goes without saying. Hence Taylor sees a strong streak of misogyny in the films of Alfred Hitchcock.

We see more, however. We see *Vertigo* as the transition from the old technology of film noir into the technology of neo noir. This technology extends beyond Technicolor and Vistavision into the psychology of post-modernism. What Taylor describes is really the self-referencing typical of the culture of contemporary art—if Fellini had made *Vertigo*, James Stewart would've been playing a movie director, not a detective.

In noir, an expert is required to complete a crime. He has to be in love, and he has to be a dupe. In a sense, the woman who uses him is an idealization of his art. We could be describing Walter Neff in *Double Indemnity*, Ned Racine in *Body Heat*... or Scotty Ferguson in *Vertigo*. While Neff and Racine are willing criminals, Scotty isn't, unless we view Madeline's final fall from the Mission tower as a homicide. Scotty suffers from a mental illness, so it's easy enough to profile him as a sex killer, no matter how kindly Jimmy Stewart's persona appears to be.

The question of his guilt is submerged in the apparent accidental nature of her demise. Demented, he drags her up the stairs into the Belfry, rages at her as he recreates the crime... and of course a full reenactment requires Madeline to fall from the portal, just like the cop in his nightmare or the real Mrs. Madeline Ellster in his deception. We can leave the symbolism of the Nun for another time. Hitchcock, the old bourgeois, has just legitimized a murder.

The brilliance of the ending is of course in the finality of it... when there's nothing final about it at all. Madeline lies smashed on the terra-cotta tiles while Scotty, frozen in his dream orgasm, is left transfixed in the tower. Where does he go from here? Does he finally awake... or does he simply return to San Francisco, find another woman, do it all again. From what we've seen, his dream appears to be a serial dream.

Sex is an off-stage act in the movies prior to the sixties. What are we to make of Scotty's actions following his rescue of Madeline from drowning in San Francisco Bay? Instead of taking her home, he takes her back to his place, undresses her, puts her in his bed. She is pretending to be in a trance, pretending to drown... and we must wonder, is he pretending to be a gentleman? Between the melancholy and the sentiment, the dream and the reality, they become lovers.

We don't see it, but we know it.

The deception calls for it, and the dream determines it. There are four kisses: two when Madeline exists as Gavin Ellster's make-over, two when she exists as Scotty's make-over. "He made you over, Judy—just like I made you over... but he made you over better...!" Scotty raves as they embrace in the tower. Their final kiss is the prelude to her death.

One or two unlikely aspects of this supernatural conspiracy are easy to overlook or rationalize. That the smooth patrician Gavin Ellster is able to keep his real wife in the dark while publicly choreographing his mistress as her understudy is one. Another is the somewhat incredible performance of Judy, a coarse shop girl from Hicksville, Kansas, as a pedigreed society woman with lovely diction, manners, and a desire to act.

While nothing is impossible, her relapse from Madeline—the reincarnated *fatale* Carlotta Valdes—back to Judy the chick who lives out of a suitcase and works at Magnum's is, uh, incredible. That she could be bought off with a piece of Carlotta's jewelry and dumped, devolving gracefully from her persona of ghost fatale is even more incredible. Having attained that character, she would've stayed in it and found another lover.

We note, of course, that she did find another lover... or rather, he found her. Only in our dreams can we create a totem and bring back the dead. This is exactly what Scotty does. He revisits the places of his former surveillance detail—Ernie's restaurant, the graveyard, the Art Gallery, the flower shop... and it's on the street outside the florist's that he has his moment of *deja vu*, spots Judy.

He stalks her back to The Empire Hotel where he immediately impresses himself upon her. In the normal course of events only a boor or a sociopath would be as insistent. We accept his actions as those of a grieving man (who has never shown any conscience about being in love with another man's wife) although he is clearly on the lunatic fringe. Our tolerance, our sympathy, comes from the fact that we recognize this game within ourselves. Alfred Hitchcock isn't the only person to do a make-over on a ghost masquerading as a ideal.

Sex, Civilization And The Cargo Cult

The make-over of the persona is at the core of civilization. We hunt, we kill. We dress, we undress. Actions become art, and art becomes a cargo cult. Scotty Ferguson turns Judy into a cargo cult object—and it works. Madeline returns, willed into existence by a man who has been waiting for her all his life. He was briefly engaged to Midge while in college... but he was unable to commit. Midge paints a picture of herself as a parody of Carlotta Valdes but the gesture fails miserably.

In fact, Scotty is so far gone he sees it as a desecration. "That's not funny, Midge," he says tragically. "Not funny at all." Following Madeline's fake suicide, he ends up a traumatized zombie in a clinic listening to but not hearing Mozart. He doesn't hear Midge either when she fusses around trying to cheer him up. No totem, no power. We last see her walking away in sad defeat down an empty corridor.

Scotty's madness is an elegant and beautiful thing, because it manifests as an elegant and beautiful thing, namely, Madeline. She visits the grave of her incarnate as the morning mist renders her ethereal. When she emerges from Scotty's bedroom for the first time, she shimmers... but the greatest shimmer of all is when she emerges from her bathroom after Scotty's make-over. The effect is supernatural and Freudian.

Thus the crime in Vertigo isn't the murder of the real Mrs. Madeline Ellster but rather that of her masquerade.

A Prologue followed by 3 Acts—so goes the melancholy romanticism of Bernard Herrman's hypnotic score, perhaps the single most unifying element in this mystical film. Music is the best means of engaging the supernatural, and this score is a descendant of a number of such astral dramas. Wagner's *Tristan And Isolde* is the most obvious, or even his *Pandora And The Flying Dutchman*. Those opening minor chords immediately draw us into the acrophobia of Scotty Ferguson, although the flattened couplets and spiralling colorations develop a metaphor for something far more sinister than a mere fear of heights.

Music is the means by which we make contact with the spirit world. Wind in the forest, waves on the beach, beating hearts in a lovers' embrace, these tones exist in Eternity. If the music is right, we don't give a damn if what happens next makes any sense. Through Herrman's fabulous score, we enter the dream of two somnambulists in search of one another. The ritual is elaborate, involves deception, but this deception is merely a game used to excite the perception of one for the other. Love is, as they say, a masquerade.

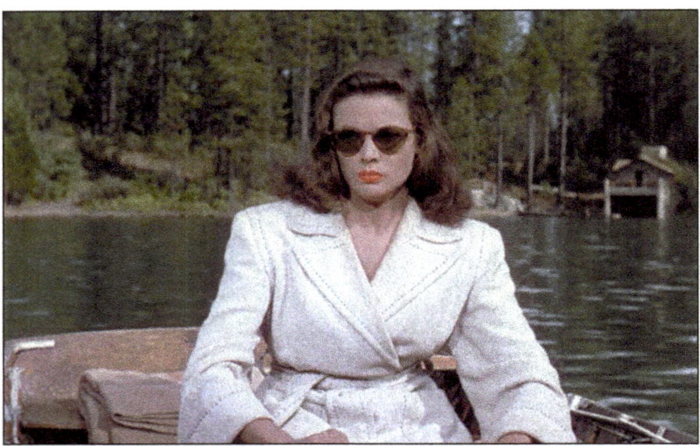

John M. Stahl: *Leave Her To Heaven*

Leave Her To Heaven (1945) 110 m. dir. dir. John M. Stahl writ. Jo Swerling [from novel by Ben Ames Williams] cine. Leon Shanroy [effects by Fred Sersen] [Technicolor by Natalie Kalmus & Richard Mueller] art. Lyle Wheeler & Maurice Ransford edt. James B. Clark music. Alfred Newman sound. E. Clayton Ward & Roger H. prod. William A. Bacher
star. Cornel Wilde (Richard Harland) Gene Tierney (Ellen) Jeanne Crain (Ruth) Vincent Price (Robie) Daryl Hickman (Danny) May Philips Ray Collins Gene Lockhart Chill Wills
Twentieth Century Fox 1945 | Technicolor 110 mins

Two men stand on a landing beside the placid water watching a launch approach: here comes Richard Harland [Cornel Wilde], novelist, just sprung from two years in jail for withholding information concerning the death of his wife. Although they are supposed to be in rural Maine, everyone is wearing a fresh suit, like store window dummies on display in a big city. Even Harland, who, after an exchange of subdued pleasantries, skilfully slips into a canoe without scuffing his shoes or losing his hat, starts paddling for his writer's retreat, a funky log house known as "Back of the Moon" where Ruth [Jeanne Crain], the sister of his dead wife, awaits on the dock, dressed as if she's just stepped out of an ad for sensible clothing in the *Ladies Home Journal*.

Even Nature itself seems groomed and artificial, like an illuminated model in a museum, an idealized form of quarantined beauty that exists only for contemplation. Even though much of this film was shot on location, the use of deep focus Technicolor renders the landscape as Elysian as a Maxfield Parrish painting. The actors, the sets, the lighting, are all locked into a strict art design, so that the color code of green and blue declensions suggests magazine ad art, people modelled to defeat death by virtue of being clean and sensible... just like a 1940's *National Geographic* layout. Too weird? For some, yes... but for others this is part of the directorial style that harnesses the stiff emotions of the characters and the technology of Technicolor to create a fascinating study of human psychosis.

Richard and Ruth embrace, reunited after the nightmare... and the rest of the film is a flashback, told in sequential Time.

Act 1

Cut To: the lounge car of a train moving through the desert landscape of New Mexico. The beautiful Ellen Berent [Gene Tierney] is reading a novel called *Time Without End*. Sitting opposite (by chance) is the author, Richard Harland. This fated meeting—which has probably happened to every author at least once—is just the stuff of fiction. Quite possibly his novel starts with this exact romantic encounter, although we never find out. Yet there seems to be some sort of spiritualist vibe within coincidence, because Ellen stares at Harland as if she's rediscovered someone she already knows.

Love at first sight, some will say... but when we learn that she's *en route* to Rancho Jacinto to scatter her father's ashes, another level of obsession is introduced. And while some will say Tierney and Wilde are barely competent as actors and sleep-walk their way through their parts, the restrained quality of their emotions fits the bourgeois culture of mid-century consumer America. The values are from the previous century, befitting an itinerant Jamesian society of female comfort and modulated beauty.

Who is Ellen? A sex-bomb in a rayon suit, a daddy's girl who is already engaged to a young District Attorney called Robie (Vincent Price), a man who is more concerned about the damage to his political persona than to his mental health by her desertion. As a *femme fatale*, her objective isn't money and dangerous sex, but rather possession, complete and utter. Her father was a scientist, a man with a lab in the attic. His ashes are now in a silver chalice. Ellen rides through the incredible New Mexican sierra, chalice aloft like an Olympic torch, releasing the ashes into his favorite view spot, while her new lover stalks her in the distance, a Freudian protege painted into the landscape.

The craziness of it all is reminiscent of Capra's *Lost Horizon*, where the characters ride and frolic in the splendid wilderness of Shangri-La divorced from pain and death. Despite the well-stacked gun-rack that shows up in several scenes at Rancho Jacinto, this is an American paradise... and in fact the only dangerous animal around is Gene Tierney. She buries her father, dumps her fiance, marries her lover—all in a matter of days. While her mother seems concerned, she likes her new son-in-law, says nothing, even though we realize she knows something he should know.

The exact history and politics of the family remain obscure, so we know nothing of Ellen's mother, who apparently preceded the current Mrs. Berent. Ruth [Jeanne Crain], her adopted sister (a cousin), is another model of restraint and concealed emotion, who puts duty first and personal gratification second. She's a stock character in such dime novel romances, the good sister who plays second fiddle to the older, more glamorous sibling. Here she sits at the piano, although she could be knitting.

Electra

Married, the happy couple leave Jacinto and visit another paradise, Warm Springs, Georgia, where Harland's younger brother Danny is receiving therapy for polio. Truly a dependant, Danny represents the first blight on the happy couple's marriage, although his condition is romantic, without disfigurement and contagion, so that we don't immediately understand why Ellen doesn't want him around. Her character as a selfish bitch is now established, even though she does an about face, and Danny accompanies the couple to the Maine paradise on Deer Lake, *Back of the Moon*. Her selfish, possessive nature is reinforced when she discovers Harland has invited her mother and sister to visit. The script or perhaps the editing has left out important information here, as Ellen's neurotic behaviour is clearly at odds with her breeding and the facts as presented. For example, if Mrs. B. is actually her step-mother, then we might allow some justification for her erratic spoiled-brat actions. Stahl's direction is to cast her as evil and manipulative, rather than as an insecure child-woman with an Electra complex who should be cut a bit of slack. No doubt her "daughter of Satan" persona comes from the Biblical rhetoric of the southern writer Ben Ames Williams, who wrote the novel, but as the script goes, little room is left for us to sympathize with her situation.

The famous scene from this film shows the drowning of Danny as the beautiful Ellen sits in the rowboat nearby, does nothing. According to Daryl Hickman, who played the part of Danny, the studio boss Darryl F. Zanuck was so impressed that when he viewed the rushes, he proclaimed this scene to be the greatest in all film to that date. For 1945, it certainly pushed a moral button. Homicide by negligence, or malign opportunity? As Danny struggles in the cold waters of the lake, cries for help, Ellen sits motionless in the boat like a *Vogue Magazine* sphinx, eyeless behind her sunglasses, a prisoner of the trance that binds her in its Oedipal shroud. Is the crippled Danny a proxy for Ruth, the sister she suspects is in love with her husband? Or is she simply too vain to get her clothes wet, her make-up mussed.

"I'll Never Let You Go—Never"

Act 4 sees the "action" move to the Berent family home at Bar Harbor on the coast of Maine. It's in this *Ladies Home Journal* setting that Harland finishes his Mexican novel, *The Deep Well*. When Ellen discovers that he's dedicated it to the gentle gardener Ruth with the inscription "to the gal with the hoe", she decides that they are having a secret affair, plan a rendezvous in Mexico. She engineers a fall down the stairs, has a miscarriage, then poisons herself, making her suicide appear to be murder by the hand of her sister, knowing that her discarded fiance Robie will indict Ruth for murder.

Evil? That's what everyone calls this piece of twisted Hollywood algebra. The young Vincent Price, who plays Robie, prosecutes the case in a final courtroom Act with that *faux* gothic malevolence that was to become his signature style. The fact that as a prosecutor he's in a conflict-of-interest, and that an absurd confession of love while on the stand by Ruth make the denouement both contrived and propagandistic drifts past in the sweet studio light. When Harland declares his deceased wife to be "a monster", it's out of character because he seems incapable of anger, and for a writer, incredibly naive. Miscasting? Possibly. Perhaps we don't care because the photographic splendor of the courtroom distracts us with its artificial complexion and symbolic tones. Once again the color green... green walls, green dresses, green trains. It's a powerful visual motif, one which integrates the action even when the action appears to be illogical or missing scenes.

Leave Her To Heaven can be called a costume drama, because the artistic direction makes it so. Like a group of peasants called in to be extras, the cast is always in its Sunday best, in contradiction with everyday reality. Whether he's at his typewriter in the blazing poolside heat of New Mexico or on the veranda of his cabin in Maine, Richard Harland is dressed formally. Outside the movies, Gene Tierney was a model, so of course she looks great in the endless series of avant fashion gear, and again we don't care if she always looks as if she's on a runway. The visual idealization of the Technicolor cinematography overpowers us with its erotic symmetry, that consumer pornography that Hollywood so often aspires to... as if the producer is selling sections of the screen to various products. The beautiful settings demand statues, not people... hence the action appears neo-classical, with a certain mythological imagery re-played within a modern American context.

Great as a mural, weak as a drama. A woman resents a man's time alone, which, because he is a writer, is dream. He writes his, she acts hers.

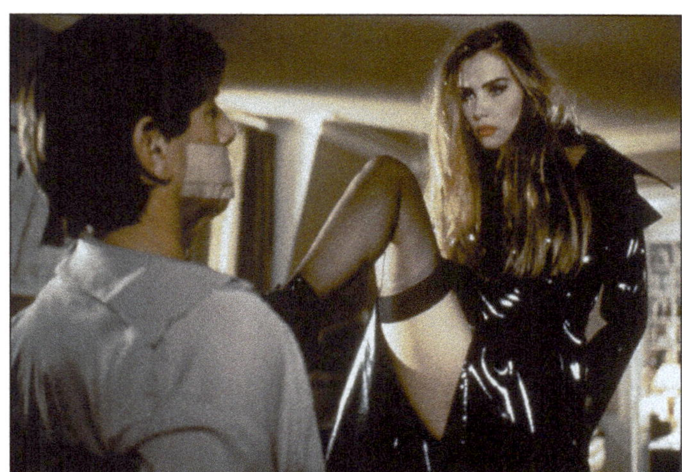

Roman Polanski: *Bitter Moon*

Bitter Moon (1992) dir. Roman Polanski writ. Polanski, Brach, Brownjohn (based on the novel *Lunes de Fiel* by Pascal Bruckner) cine. Tonino Delli Colli edt. Herve de Luze music Vangelis star. Peter Coyote (Oscar), Emmanuelle Seigner (Mimi), Hugh Grant (Nigel), Kristin Scott Thomas (Fiona), Stockard Channing (Beverly), Luca Vellani, Boris Bergman, Victor Banerjee
Fine Line Pictures

Polanski's first feature *Knife In The Water* (1962) was about sex games on a boat, so you could say he's returned to his roots with *Bitter Moon* and the elegant nihilism that pervades its closed system reality. Imagine a small ocean liner somewhere on the Mediterranean, en route to Istanbul. Imagine a crippled American writer and his stunning French vixen wife encountering a staid English couple, involving them in their sexual nightmare... the end-game of Scott and Zelda Fitzgerald? Sure. Or how about Hemingway's Jake Barnes and Lady Brett? It seems that the impotency of the Lost Generation is still extent at the close of the 20th Century.

"You're exactly the listener I've been waiting for," says the crippled American writer to the Englishman. Remember how the Ancient Mariner apprehends the Wedding Guest en route to the wedding, forces him to listen to his tale of despair and self-loathing? How he killed the pure white albatross and endured a voyage through the spectral oceans of Hell? Bitter Moon employs a similar narrative method wherein one man is taken hostage by another man's tale of misery.

Oscar (Coyote) is the author of three unpublished novels, but the story he tells is his greatest novel to date... and his last. The voyeurism is exquisite. His brutal cynicism is the gallows humor of yet another artist doomed to be a comedian in his own failed desire for endless attention. Love? What is love—a pig mask, black vinyl and a whip? Love is an unexpected encounter on the No. 96 Montparnesse bus when Oscar first sights Mimi (Seigner) and slips her his ticket, rescuing her from the contempt of the ticket inspector. Thus Oscar allows himself to be expelled from the bus, and smitten, watches as his new love disappears towards the boulevard of broken dreams. This is his first and last selfless gesture, alas, for what follows is a painful exercise in the corruption and degradation of the human spirit.

Of course Polanski is an established master of such gamesmanship... *Repulsion* was made long before the mutilation and murder of his wife Sharon Tate by the Manson Family or his flight from the USA to avoid prosecution for the corruption and rape of an underage Valley girl. While it would be nice to view a Polanski film without recalling these tragic events, you cannot help but examine his psychodramas in the nuclear light of these sensational traumas. Yes, it must be tiresome for Polanski to have these events cast up as proof of a sick mind, yet when you read his forthright 1984 autobiography, you realize he's quite prepared to die in the crossfire.

This out of the way, it must be recognized that Roman Polanski is a reasonably honest man, and that as an artist he is fearless. The sadomasochism of the Oscar-Mimi relationship isn't unique to the decadent bohemian *zeit geist* of the Left Bank... for really, who hasn't seen just such a black comedy acted out in the midlife holocaust, even in the hick cities you call home. There's something very contemporary about *Bitter Moon*, both in its secular despair and frightening nihilism. Oscar's contempt finds its perfect foil in the English twit persona of Nigel (Grant), the young husband bound for India on a holiday designed to give his seven year marriage some new karma. He stutters, he twitters, an anachronism in a preposterous universe.

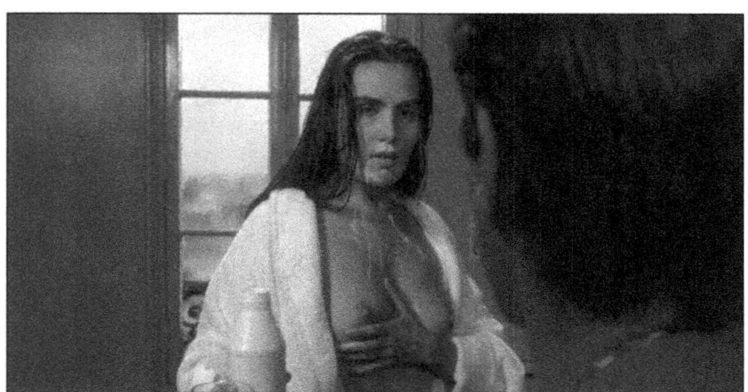

As an American playing the expatriate writer role, Oscar is a combination of New World honesty and Old World cynicism, this duality made clear by the fact that he's paralyzed from the waist down. Nigel on the other hand is still an innocent, protected by the discipline of English middle-class manners, a man who is too polite to tell a cripple to go to hell, too polite to be in any other role than that of the masochist. He endures Oscar's sadism with the stoic English fatalism of the wounded hero in Waugh's seminal novel of cruel love, *A Handful Of Dust*, wherein a man who is held hostage in an Amazonian hut is forced to read Charles Dickens for the rest of his life to appease his captor, that denizen of evil, the village chief.

Of course Nigel is also a victim of his own sexual desire, stricken by the sight of Mimi in a red dress dancing solo in the ship's lounge to Peggy Lee's classic love cry, *Fever*. As a *femme fatale* Mimi seems committed to the destruction of the entire male sex as if sent from Eden as a virus. There's nothing subtle about her act, both on-stage and off. Trained as a dancer, she exists only as foreplay, like a nymphomaniac from *The Circus of Hell*. The choreography of submission and bondage is her business. And while Nigel quickly recognizes that she and Oscar are playing a game, he is powerless to disengage. Oscar, once her lover, is now her pimp. The two men sit drinking in Oscar's cabin. Meanwhile Nigel's wife remains in their cabin seasick while Mimi flirts in the bar or does dance exercises in her separate cabin. Nigel is galvanized by Oscar's story, becomes a voyeur to love and pornography, the twin sisters of civilization. Thus Polanski uses the trusty old frame narrative, the favorite story device of film noir...although the blackness in *Bitter Moon* isn't in the cinematic mystification of shadow and light but rather in the utter blackness of its world-view.

You know that Polanski has learned his lessons from the history of film. He revisited film noir with his period crime drama *Chinatown* (1974). While old noir left its sex to the imagination, neo-noir makes it a pornographic priority. This is essentially a historic movement from a religious culture into a secular culture. In film noir, crime is the surrogate of sex, whereas in neo-noir voyeurism has replaced the crime. Impotency remains, and death as a destination.

Thus Oscar's story is a dialectic of sex and corruption. He corrupts Mimi, he corrupts Nigel... and finally he corrupts Fiona. Essentially, Mimi is degraded from innocent love to sexual slavery by a man who is too selfish to set aside his fantasy of himself. Spiritual sex, grudge sex, healing sex, bondage sex—it's all the paradigm of impotency. With no particular destination in mind, how could Oscar end up any other way than bored out of his mind? The romantic boulevards of Paris become avenues to further promiscuity. Yet his blatant infidelities and cruel innuendoes pale in comparison to his heartlessness when he tricks Mimi onto a jet bound for Martinique and then sneaks off the plane before takeoff, like a man abandoning a pet at the city dump.

Yes, Oscar is another American jerk. Yes, you smile with

satisfaction when he unexpectedly gets whacked by a taxi when leaving a club intent on a private orgy with two girls. And yes, you smile with delight when Mimi reappears fresh from two years on Martinique and dumps him from his hospital bed onto the floor to writhe in the first overture of a new-found agony.

In his famous treatise on Tragedy, Aristotle elaborates on the essential narrative device of dramatic reversal. The reversal of Fortune in *Bitter Moon* is a reversal of power of superb ironic consequence. If Mimi was too stupid to be Oscar's muse, she's certainly smart enough to be his torturer. Back in his chic apartment, locked by paralysis in his wheelchair, he can only watch and sip his Bordeaux as Mimi dances with the feline negro Carl, then engages in intercourse. He can only watch and suffer when she medicates him with a dirty needle... and he can only suffer when she abandons him in the bath to talk dirty with some unknown lover on the phone. In fact, this scene is the crucible of what they've become: as Mimi babbles on the phone, Oscar rolls out of his bath, drags himself naked across the floor like a wounded animal seeking a warm place to die.

Yet this bleak farce has further dimensions of degradation. They get married... and they take a cruise. "You think I enjoy being a rubbish dump for your unsavory reminiscences?" says Nigel at one point... but obviously he enjoys it better than he cares to admit as he's already trying to establish a rendezvous with Mimi. It also doesn't take long for the suffering Fiona to figure out that the attraction is Mimi, not pity for the crippled Oscar. Her first response is to flirt with a handsome Italian who looks like an Armani model... but a simple tit for tat isn't what Polanski has in mind. While you expect ruin for Nigel and Fiona, you don't expect it for Oscar, as he's been destroyed already.

So what are you to make of the lesbian solution—is it the ultimate revenge of woman on the sexist pig? Or is it merely the science of birth control and the natural consequence of the impotent heterosexual... as the East Indian traveller advises the English couple, "Children are a better form of marital therapy than any trip to India." This old fashioned wisdom is as close to a redeeming moral as Polanski comes in this black farce on the high seas.

Have You Ever Seen Such An Allegory of Grace & Beauty?

It's an ugly ending... befitting, some would say, the final decade of an ugly century. "You were just too greedy, baby, that was all," says Oscar before putting the 9 mm automatic in his mouth. You wince at his desperate exit, yet realize it was scripted by his muse, the bitter moon in red who gave him the gun as a birthday present.

The soundtrack by Vangelis is excellent, is pure onomatopoeia with the ocean, the moon, the bitter spirit that pervades this story of poisoned love. But the film's power comes from its narrator. Peter Coyote moves through his role as if he is no mere fiction but rather an eloquent subject of *cinema verité*. His resemblance to that well-known poetic undertaker Leonard Cohen (or even Pascal Bruckner, author of the novel) perhaps helps some of us suspend our disbelief... yet the fact remains that Coyote is utterly convincing as Oscar, an American writer as horny as Henry Miller but without the humanism of his famous precursor. You wonder if there is any irony intended in the name "Oscar". Paris: you get your kicks on Route 96.

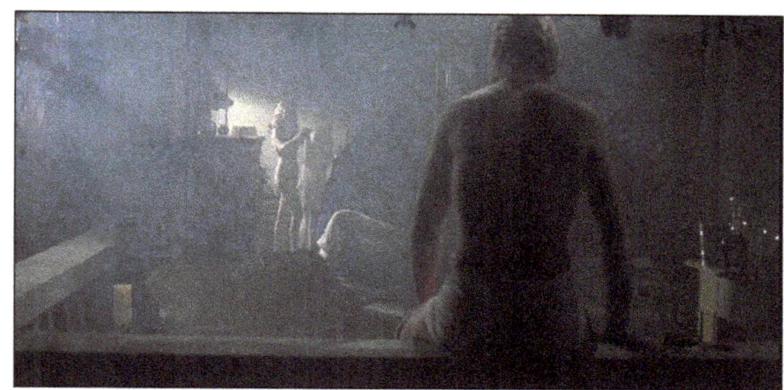

Lawrence Kasdan: *Body Heat*

Body Heat (1981) writ. & dir. Lawrence Kasdan cine. Richard H. Kline edt. Carol Littleton music John Barry star. William Hurt (Ned Racine), Kathleen Turner (Matty Walker), Richard Crenna (Edmund Walker), Ted Danson (Ass. D.A. Lowenstein), Mickey Rourke (Teddy), Kim Zimmer (Mary Ann), J.A. Preston (Oscar)
Warner Bros.

Sex And Identity

Are you who you really say you are? Are you living under an assumed identity? Such identity masking is usually the cover-up for a crime, but in *Body Heat* it's the prelude to a crime. Yet the question of identity goes well beyond such maudlin pursuits as greed and fast money. The architecture of fantasy is sex. And the *femme fatale* is the architect.

Ned Racine (Hurt) is a thirty something lawyer working the seedy side of the street in Miranda Beach, Florida. You first see him standing on a small balcony looking at a column of fire in the distance as a casual lover dresses and banters in the room behind. He's naked from the waist up, his slender body sweating from the tropical heat. He assumes the fire is arson, a real-estate swindle. "History is burning up out here," he says, and you sense that he is the cynical post-modern replacement... even if his Creole name and the fact that he grew up here suggests otherwise.

Racine is presented not so much as careless as casual. As a single male, his slow talking sensuality and hip cynicism mark him as a man whose first priority is sex, his second, business. While he's a womanizer, you don't get the feeling that he's an abuser or a crook. He's just an opportunist, a drifter in search of something he has yet to define. "Next time you come into my courtroom, I hope you've got a better defense... or a better class of client," says the Judge in his reprimand. So perhaps when Racine encounters Matty (Turner) that evening at the concert down on the beach, he's following the Judge's advice, moving up from his waitresses and female cops into a higher class of lover.

And who would think that this encounter was anything other than chance? As usual, it's lust at first sight. An elegant woman in summer white leaves her seat near the stage, walks slowly towards where he stands on the boardwalk overlooking the beach. She pauses for air, leans on the railing. He moves in swiftly like the hustler he is. Their exchange is bold, the innuendo sexual. "I'm a married woman," she says. "You didn't say happily married woman," he says. He quickly intuits that she's from the upscale Pinehaven neighbourhood and just as quickly seems to be in control of the situation. He buys her a Cherry float... she spills it on her dress. He takes the cup from her, heads for the can to dump it. "Don't you want to lick it?" she says. When he returns, she's gone.

Matty is a woman on the nub of discontent. The grass widow of a shady businessman who only comes home on the weekend, her elegant body unmarred by children or bad diet, her restlessness is the classic signature of the neglected woman. Or so it seems to Ned as he hunts her down in Pinehaven and begins a raunchy affair under the chimes that move softly in the sea air, seem to represent the mystery of this exciting woman. They screw here, they screw there, they screw like humans, they screw like animals... and so how long can it be before they're scheming to get rid of her husband?

"He's small... and mean... and weak," says Matty. Later, as they lie on the beach under the stars, she says, "I'm afraid... because when I think about it, I wish he'd die." And Ned, greedy and pussy-whipped, says, "It's what we both want."

Noir, Sex And The Totemic Woman

Matty's manipulation of events is standard for the film noir genre, of which *Body Heat* is the redefining drama of the post black and white era. At first you think of *Double Indemnity* as its ideological model, but in many ways *Body Heat* is closer to Hitchcock's transitional noir masterpiece *Vertigo*, as Matty Walker's deception uses masquerade as a form of totemic sexual hypnosis. Like Hitchcock's detective, Kasdan's Ned Racine is pursuing a woman who is masquerading as an ideal when in fact she is anything but. The similarity is also atmospheric, as John Barry's beautiful score is clearly in the dream sonata tradition of Bernard Herrmann's *Vertigo* theme. There are differences, of course, the main one being that Hitchcock's *fatale* (Kim Novak) is the agent of another man while Matty is strictly the author of her own agenda. In this regard, she is like Phyllis Dietrichson in *Double Indemnity*.

It's Matty who insinuates the problem, then suggests the solution even though Ned thinks the solution is his. While the death-fight with Edmund Walker in the hall of his opulent home is a fitting parody of Ned's first sex with Matty, the disposal of his body by arson bomb in the abandoned beachfront club The Breakers is sublime. The method is crude, yet the desired insinuation is that Walker died as part of an on-going real-estate scam engineered by the shadowy criminal investors with whom he's associated.

Yet even Teddy (Rourke) the bomb maker and client warns Ned against this audacious act. "Don't do it," says Teddy.

Cut To: a slow pan along Matty's legs, ass, naked reclining body. "Don't do it...." Sure. "Next time I see you," says Ned to Matty, "he'll be dead."

As per all film noir, the woman's patsy must be an expert. What's interesting about *Body Heat* is that Ned Racine is chosen not only because he's an expert but also a fuckup. The criminal rewriting of Edmund Walker's will requires an expert, of course, but also one who might make the mistake essential for Matty's plan to be fully realized. For the perfect crime, perfection must interact with its silhouette, imperfection. So it is that Ned thinks he's a partner in the grand deception when in reality he's merely a part.

Yet... why doesn't he recognize this before it's too late?

When an accidental encounter with Matty and her husband at a local restaurant turns into wine, dinner and conversation, you recognize that Ned is perhaps a junior version of Edmund. "I was a lawyer," says Edmund. "Don't practice anymore." Edmund goes on to mock the man Matty was with before they got married. "You wouldn't believe the dork she was with," he says. "Tries to make it with one score... but can't do what's necessary." Ned nods slowly, says, "Yeah, I know that kinda guy... I hate that kind." Then he smiles, adds, "I'm a lot like that." Both men laugh but neither, in fact, recognizes the true extent of their tragic symbiosis.

The police know that Edmund Walker was murdered and Racine knows they know, as he's a buddy of Lowenstein, the Assistant D.A. (Danson), and Oscar (Preston), the investigating cop. He's warned to stay away from Matty but, convinced that he has what it takes "to do what's necessary", he boldly continues his affair with the new widow—after all, she is his client. But when he discovers that she tampered with the will that he forged in such a way that the mistake makes her the sole heir of her husband's estate, he's so whipped he fails to see the fall before it happens. "I love you," she says... and she bought him a fedora, didn't she? Here the director Kasdan makes a sly allusion to the blind love chump Walter Neff in *Double Indemnity*, another "expert" with a fedora.

During the affair, certain incidents threaten to spoil their idyllic repose. Ned and Matty are caught in a sexual act by Heather, Matty's young niece... but when the critical moment comes, the niece fails to identify the man with the erection. More significant is the disappearance of Edmund Walker's glasses, which later factor as blackmail and the setup for Racine's elimination. Vaguely symbolic, Walker's glasses become both the talisman of death and male myopia.

As the story plot is synonymous with Matty's plot and this plot is both complex and sophisticated, understanding just what happens and how it affects Racine's disintegration isn't always easy. For example, you know that while Racine screwed up a previous will (the Gurson case) you wonder if in fact he screwed up the Edmund Walker forgery or if the devious Matty tampered with it to play on Racine's history of incompetence. Her admission, when it comes, can slip past you in the heat. Either way, of course, Edmund Walker's will becomes invalid and in the State of Florida "in testate" means the widow gets everything.

Part of the will deposition is the "missing witness" factor, which also figures significantly in the action and the crunching ironies of the ending. The witness is Matty's friend Mary Anne Simpson, now absent, supposedly on holiday in Europe. Somewhere in here Mary Ann is supposedly murdered by Matty and her body stashed in the boathouse in anticipation of her lover Racine's death by boobytrap bomb—the same type as Racine used to dispose of Edmund Walker. While the symmetry is neat, you wonder why Matty would use Racine's friend and client Teddy to supply the information for such an act... after all, Teddy picks up the phone and calls Racine... so Racine expects the boathouse to be booby-trapped.

Matty has shown herself to be smarter than that. But in the arcane movement of the final sequences, you might overlook such plot conveniences, marvel instead at the sweet irony.

Clairvoyance, Symmetry And The *Femme Fatale*

Incarcerated for two murders, Racine has a moment of clairvoyance, knows instinctively that Matty is still alive. His friend

Oscar, the black cop, visits him in prison. "Her teeth, man," Oscar says by way of incontrovertible evidence that Matty died in the boathouse explosion. But Racine has it figured out: Matty is a masquerade. She has switched identities with her high school friend and is really Mary Ann Simpson. So naturally Matty (Walker) Tyler's teeth are found. "Matty sees a way to get rid of us both at once... two killers, dead."

The symmetry is indeed a thing of beauty—just like the fatal allure of the *femme fatale* herself. This symmetry forms the visual logic of the climactic scene, in fact. As Matty a.k.a. Mary Ann stops on the grassy fairway near the boathouse you see Racine in the distance and beyond him Oscar the cop, the three characters arranged like markers on a moral map. Matty is wearing the same close-fitting white dress she had on the first night she and Racine met. She stops, isolated like a white flame in the darkness. "Whatever happens," she calls. "You must believe that I love you."

Relentless? A person who could do whatever was necessary? Better believe it.

The performances in *Body Heat* are superb, from the principals to the secondaries. Ted Danson as the friend and Assistant D.A. who lives vicariously off Racine's sexual exploits and whose nature is so whimsical that he dances across parking lots and piers as one might doodle is a classic example of movie minimalism and the art of characterization. But Hurt and Turner as the reckless lovers are a thing apart, beautiful and crude, sexed and unhinged, just like their generation.

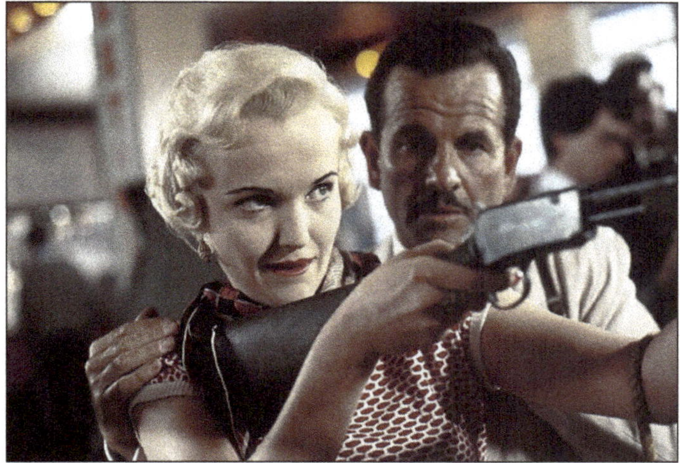

Mike Newell: *Dance With a Stranger*

Dance With A Stranger (1985) dir. Mike Newell writ. Shelagh Delaney cine. Peter Hannan music Richard Hartley star. Miranda Richardson (Ruth Ellis), Rupert Everett (David Blakely), Ian Holm (Desmond Cussen), Joanne Whalley, Tom Chadbon, Stratford Johns, Mathew Carroll

What is passion? A perfect fit between a sadist and a masochist? Human beings appear to be lost somewhere between the solar codes of their animal origins and the religious rituals of their toilet training. Love is a tragedy, a disease whose symptoms are sex and violence. It begins in lust, ends in death. So go the politics of *Dance With A Stranger.*

If anyone ever deserved to die from a lover's bullet, it would have to be David Blakely, the swinish young prat who drives racing cars for a living and drinks as a profession. He's a typical upper class wastrel whose self-hatred is symptomatic of aristocratic loneliness and is measured by speed and sexual violence. If Ruth Ellis hadn't come into his life, no doubt Blakely would've brutalized a few prostitutes and died in a car wreck, as his destiny is another form of suicide.

The Ruth Ellis story is essentially a sex-triangle. The film opens with Blakely and a few drunken friends at an after-hours club somewhere in London. He's been led here by Desmond Cussen, a working-class man who is also a member of the British Automobile Racing Association, and an admirer of Ruth.

While it isn't stated, you get the impression that Cussen is a wealthy automobile dealer. He's the opposite of Blakely—shrewd, calm, plain, a self-made man. He begins as a go-between, ends as another victim of the class war this doomed romance obliquely represents.

> Blakely: You've brought us to a den of vice, Desmond. These places are glorified brothels. (to Ruth behind the bar) And who are you?
> Ruth: The glorified brothel keeper.

It's lust at first sight, and soon the urgent Blakely is on top of Ruth in her convenient suite above the club. Like the self-flagellants they are, their screwing is another attitudinal exercise in sarcasm, a sado-masochistic dialogue of attack and thrust:

> Blakely: I love you.
> Ruth: Everybody does. Why should you be different?
> Blakely: Has Desmond ever slept in this bed with you?
> Ruth: No... come to think of it, he must be the only man.

So the stage is set for an affair between animals, as their humanity and common sense is shed like dead skin as they slither into their fate. Soon it's a battlefield of grudge fucks, healing fucks, actions without a purpose, love without a future. Ruth accompanies Blakely to Silverstone, watches him race, watches him kiss his pedigreed fiance.

Later she forces Desmond to take her to the Racing Association's annual ball where she watches Blakely drink and socialize with his clique, dance with his fiance. Is she stalking him... or is he stalking her?

He has a key to her apartment, breaks in when he feels like it, always drunk and abusive, always acting by divine right. Her "key" to his "apartment" is Desmond, the patsy go-between in this tragic parody of the courtly love convention.

Blakely has no apartment. He sleeps in his garage with his racing car, *The Emperor*, another doomed project, an ideal that echoes the failure of the British auto industry and his absurd romance. He takes *The Emperor* to Silverstone but it throws a rod, fails to complete the race. He has another chance, though—the elite Bristol Racing team invite him to drive one of their cars in the Le Mans 24 hour race.

Ruth sits in an empty cinema with her son watching the *Pathe News* montage of the race as an anonymous male sits watching her watch like a predator who can smell the heat.

What does Ruth see? She's a myopic who needs to wear glasses but knows she looks better without them. So her world is narrowed to the spectral band of smell and touch... and the sound of racing engines. She isn't artless—she sings in her club, even if her song isn't much more than a tone poem, a talking blues for effect rather than design.

Blakely arrives with his fiance, throws a tantrum, gets into a fight, gets Ruth fired. Later she trashes the club in a final act of despair and anguish, closing her theatre of desire.

They reconcile. Blakely drives her into the country in his Jag, shows her his ancestral home. She refuses to go in, recognizing that she will never be a Cinderella in this story. Blakely promises to take her son on an outing but fails to show... Ruth has Desmond drive her to the country village pub where she confronts Blakely in a humiliating scene of recrimination and denunciation. Blakely scuffles with Desmond outside. It appears to be over.

But Ruth is pregnant. Blakely is the father but he prefers to suspect Desmond, the loyal, ever-suffering understudy. In the most dramatic scene in the film, Blakely encounters Ruth in the London smog, has sex with her in an alley. They're like plague victims, the shrouding smog their passion, a disease for sentinels.

Ruth moves in with Desmond, who has a nice flat and pays for her son to attend boarding school. He also has his service revolver in a drawer. You see the revolver as Andy—Ruth's son—explores Desmond's study, opens the drawer, a Freudian pawn in a game he will never understand... so the detail is casual, the possibility vague. Blakely continues to visit Ruth, even in Desmond's flat.

> Desmond: Are you sleeping with him?
> Ruth: Yes.
> Desmond: You're disgusting!

Nonetheless, the enslaved Desmond drives her to the street where Blakely parties with his friends. She sees him leave with a young woman. Ruth goes berserk, the police arrive, but Desmond spirits her away.

But this isn't the end. One evening she waits for her lover outside a pub and shoots him as he emerges. She puts five bullets into him with Desmond's revolver... and thus, in 1955, becomes the last woman to be hung for murder in the U.K.

This time she's wearing her glasses.

Well-written, directed and edited, with a marvellous music score by Richard Hartley. The beautiful scaling runs of the saxophone are introduced as thrilling transitions, accurate emotional triggers for the deadly ecstasy of these doomed lovers. In terms of dramatic form and emotional engagement, it's a much better film than its 1958 American antecedent, *I Want To Live!*, Robert Wise's docu-drama about Barbara Graham who was also sentenced to death in 1955 for murder.

Both movies end with letters from the executed women. Barbara Graham's reveals nothing whereas Ruth Ellis's reveals everything: "I have forgiven David, I only wish I could've found it in my heart to have forgiven him when he was alive...."

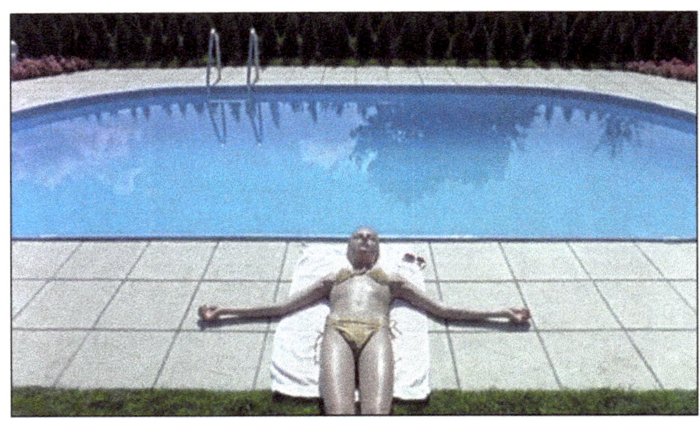

Ulrich Seidl: *Dog Days*

Dog Days (*Hundstage*) 2002. dir. Ulrich Seidl writ. Seidl and Veronika Franz cine Wolfgang Thaler edt. Andrea Wagner & Christof Schertenleib star. Maria Hofstatter, Alfred Mrva, Gerti Lehner, Franziska Weiss, Rene Wamko, Claudia Martini, Victor Rathbone, Christian Bakonyi, Christine Jirku, Victor Hennemann, Georg Friedrich
Seville - Allegro

Angry Men And Crazy Women

Lower Austria in August, when the heat is suffocating in the suburbs and the constellation Orion (the hunter and his dog) is directly overhead like some sort of malevolent deity. In the gardens and patios people lie facing the sky like sacrificial offerings. Things are tense. In the washroom of a club a young man called Mario threatens another young man for ogling his girlfriend, one of the dancers they pay to watch as they drink and smoke.

Later Mario goes after another young male, and they scuffle outside on the steps. The fight is broken up by the bouncer, a lanky tattooed character called Lucky, who later figures in an adjacent scenario as a peculiar moral arbitrator. Mario leaves with the dancer, a slim eroto-adolescent called Claudia, engages in some dangerous driving in his rodded metallic blue coupe, then parks below an underpass as the long-distance night haulers roar past in their trucks. Sex? Sure, but Mario doesn't want it. Claudia is a whore, a pussy-peddler who can't trusted. He heaves her off his lap, slaps and punches her, throws her out of his car. She stands a short distance away, isolated in the false moonlight of the freeway, sobbing... the first and youngest of several female victims in this ugly yet brilliant movie by the documentarian Ulrich Seidl and his writer Veronika Franz.

There are six parallel stories that occasionally overlap, share a common symbolism... best recognized, perhaps, in the strange rituals of Mr. Walter, a lonely widower who wanders his garden like a lost Adam, with only his aging dog for company and protection. When his dog dies, the event not only presages the end of the heat wave but also works as an illustration of the dysfunctionality in the alliance between the sexes. By and large, all the women are victims in this confused and brutal world of men. Or, if not of men, then of Nature.

The most didactic example is "crazy" Anna, who is offered up as a sacrificial totem by Hrudy, the home security salesman, to appease his clients. Who vandalized their property, their cars? Who knows... but this crazy child-woman who spends her days hitch-hiking back and forth between malls on the same stretch of highway, spouting TV commercials and singing banal pop songs, will do. Following her rape, the thunderstorm starts, the heavy rain breaking the drought as if the gods have been bought off. The primitivism is instinctive, a condition within the contemporary *homo sapien* that can only be described in ritual and symbol. Angry men and crazy women stagger along the industrial highway like zombies driven by private traumas dispensed by fate and fortune. Free will? Doesn't seem like it. The behavior of the beasts is the behavior of the Gods.

Like Dummies On Exhibit

For a hundred years or more, alienation has been a major theme in western art. Human beings divorced from the natural flow of Nature by the industrial landscapes they incubate within.

Dog Days has a number of shocking incidents and situations that tests its audience, and the orgy in the mall is one of them. It's one thing to go to a party where booze and dope break inhibitions, lead to a mass sexual grope, yet quite another to go to a mall where an orgy is always underway in what appears to be commercial gym.

Seidl drops us into this in a sudden cut to: like turning a corner in the museum, looking into an arboretum exhibit to see dozens of naked men and women of various ages and erotic sophistication screwing and fellating in a staged Eden of tacky wallpaper and elevator music. Who is responsible for this absurd ritual? Here Seidl is arcane and crafty... we might notice "Euro-pimp's" smiling face reflected in the peep-window but probably not. This bloated hustler with his gold chains and rings shows up later as the drunken pig lover of the schoolteacher, so the causality is curious and intriguing. But... the psychology of the editing is such that we merely react rather than connect.

The style of *Dog Days* is one of fragmentation, even though the narrative is connected and determinist. Even when the action lingers within set *tableaux*, we are focused on the grotesque. The ugly beauty of these cameos is reminiscent of the erotic *mise en scenes* of Helmut Newton, the German fashion photographer... or even the set quotidians of Edward Hopper, where people sit facing the sky like dummies on exhibit. The ordinary, the mundane, is hereby dramatized in an extraordinary sequence of loneliness, desperation and faint hope. Sadomasochism? Yes. Every human compact here is described in such terms. Funny? Yes... some of the time. Fact is, Seidl simply doesn't give us much room to turn away when these private hells are best left private.

The Pornographic Exposition Of Human Despair

The voyeurism is therefore exquisite and relentless. The schoolteacher returns to her apartment, ogled by a short man as they ascend silently together in the elevator. As she sits on the toilet, she listens as her mother whines on the answering machine about being neglected... and we watch as she then examines her declining body in the mirror, goes about trimming her pubic hair. The vanity seems ridiculous, all the more so when we realize all of this is in anticipation of an evening with her lover. This isn't the sex of advertising and eternal life... yet the hunger and the madness is just the same as that of Mario and Claudia, the tormented teen beauties who screw in a car parked on the highway. When Euro-pimp and his friend Lucky arrive, they find the teacher kneeling on a chair, her ass raised like an animal in heat. The men are drunk, proceed to humiliate the woman. We cringe at the exhibitionism and the cruelty. They drink more and more, play an idiot word game, the inexplicable culture of bullies and victims on the edge of nihilism. At one point the teacher is sitting below a Gustav Klimt picture, *The Idyll*. Irony? We probably don't even notice.

Bad behavior and exhibitionism does have a certain lure, yet some of this will be too much for even the more sophisticated voyeurs among us. Sometimes intelligence is the author of pain, not unconsciousness. Yet unconsciousness is what they seek. Anything to escape the heat and the gnawing sexual angst. Or the ugly rhythm of other people's problems.

An old man leaves his lawn-mower running in order to mask the sound of his neighbors' domestic dispute... a cleaning lady sits on the toilet behind a locked door to have an unauthorized smoke... a man hammers a tennis ball off the walls of an empty swimming pool as his wife cavorts with her lover nearby... or a man sits all night in his car watching for the vandals who never come.

Everyone is waiting to be released, like people trapped at an airport, hostages of an unknown terrorist. Sound like Beckett's *Waiting For Godot*? The *ennui* is the same, and here and there the situations certainly have the Godot feel, especially the power-reversal between Lucky and his boss, Euro-pimp. Of course the styles are vastly dissimilar, as Godot is theatrical expressionism whereas *Dog Days* uses the documentary posture of *cinema verité*.

Dog Days: quite possibly the best feature film of the last two or three years. It won at Venice, if that means anything. Yes, it's the pornographic exposition of human despair... but it's not devoid of humor or even compassion. The cinematics are brilliant, and the acting likewise, even though these characters remain submerged and starless in the documentary *raison d'etre*.

They say the wheel is the greatest invention... but it isn't. The mirror is... if indeed it was an invention. A pool of water, a piece of silvered glass... and now the instant replay monitor.

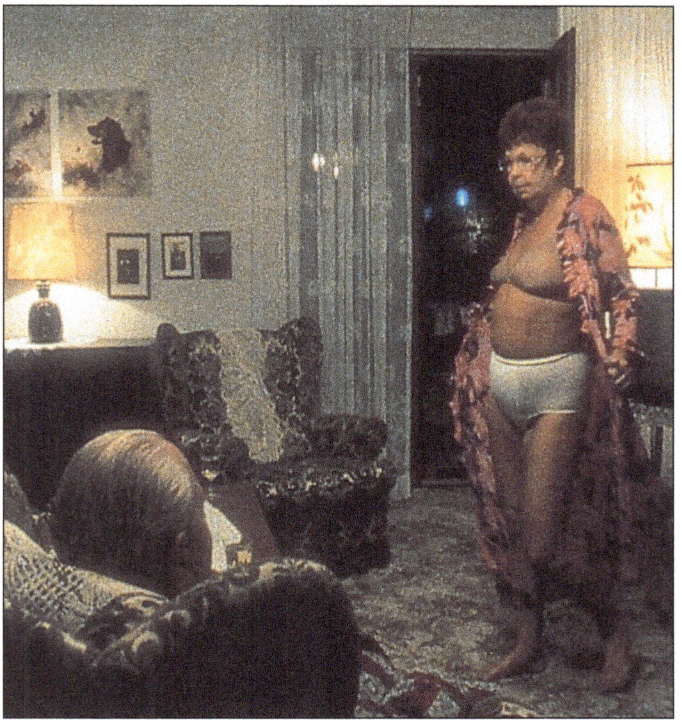

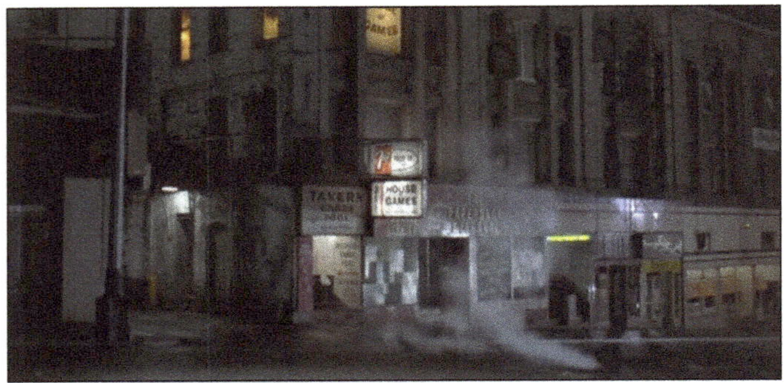

David Mamet: *House of Games*

House of Games (1987) writ. & dir. David Mamet (from the story by Jonathan Katz and David Mamet) cine. Juan Ruiz Anchia edt. Trudy Ship music Alaric Jans star. Lindsay Crouse (Dr. Margaret Ford), Joe Mantegna (Mike), Steve Goldstein (Billy Hahn), Mike Nussbaun (Joey), Ricky Jay (George/Vegas Man), Lila Skala (Dr. Maria Littauer), J.T. Walsh (business man/cop)
Orion

House of Games is a deception-within-a-deception, just like *Double Indemnity* and other classics of film noir. Most of the action takes place at night, in dimly lit taverns, back rooms, streets and alleys, the standard venues of film noir crime. While Mamet is less concerned with creating a stylistic votive to the film masters of the past, his dramatic method is nonetheless a basic inversion of the noir film. The dupe is a woman rather than a man, while sex remains the real currency in the transaction, even though money remains the *modus operandi.*

If the noir thirties and forties saw a man as the professional who gets used, the eighties has a woman. Dr. Margaret Ford (Lindsay Crouse) is typical of the American cultural inversion... and typically she's a psychologist, the favorite refuge of the female occult personality. If her entanglement with the slick conman Mike is a searing attack on the notion of female emancipation, then Mamet seems to confirm the feminist dialectic by allowing the doctor a measure of revenge, even if it comes from a bullet rather than a psychiatric end-game.

When a young male patient called Billy Hahn (Steve Goldstein) visits Margaret Ford in a panic, telling her that he's incurred a gambling debt of $25,000 to a man named Mike and will be killed if he doesn't pay it, the psychiatrist is placed in a put-up or shut-up situation:

> Billy: (bitterly) You do nothing... you and your book... it's a con-game... you know dick.

He pulls out a gun and threatens suicide.

> MF: (firmly) You give me the gun and I will help you—I swear to help you.

And why not? Dr. Margaret Ford (MF) is the model of the eighties educated female: a smart, professionally empowered member of the secular priesthood of psychiatry who has recently published the hip tome, Driven: obsession & compulsion in everyday life. Nice little book, nice little practice, nice little life.

But... if you were her, would you respond to the challenge? Would you be equipped to handle the jungle?

When Billy leaves her office, MF checks her notes, sees the address of The House of Games, the gambling club where her desperate young patient hangs out. That evening she heads out into the wet, shadowed noir streets, finds the seedy pool hall/tavern that hosts the gambling den... and thereby enters The House of Games and comes face to face with the seminal challenge of her life. His name is Mike (Joe Mantegna). He materializes from the smoky back room like a demi-man, shrouded in shadow.

> Mike: Wha tha fuck is it?
> MF: You threatened to kill a friend of mine... he's a sick kid.

Thus the pedigreed mistress of the head game enters into a wild adventure with the street-coarse master of the con game... and who is to say what is the difference and what is the reality? Once again the mystical pulse of sexual attraction arranges the dominant and the sub-dominant, the deceiver and the deceived, the sadist and the masochist within the peculiar chromaticism of the sexes. And once again the action exists as a play-within-a-play, a game-within-a-game.

"You Want To See How A True Bad Man Plies His Trade?"

The street savvy Mike quickly draws the insular MF into his world by revealing some of the secrets of the con game. First he enlists her aid in reading the body language of a poker player from Vegas—she enters the back room, poses as his girlfriend, enters into the con. According to her new friend Mike, if the Vegas player fidgets with his gold ring, then that's a "Tell", a sure sign that he's bluffing. Sure enough, the Vegas man twiddles his ring while Mike is in the can, and on his return MF urges Mike to call the bet. The bet is now $6,000 and MF, the affluent voyeur, quickly agrees to guarantee Mike's hand.

> Mike: (spreads his cards) Triple aces, beat 'em, my friend.
> Vegas: (spreads his) Club flush... (rakes in the chips) Thank you very much. Next case....

Next case. MF has been had and when the volatile Vegas gambler pulls out a gun and demands her check for six grand, the ugly reality of the situation almost has her conned... until she recognizes the gun is fake, merely a plastic water pistol. You might think this is odd, as the gun MF confiscated from her patient Billy Hahn is real, and as Hahn is part of the con, why is this gun fake? The symbolism is its own justification, as the plot will be a dialectical movement of the real and the unreal. "The necessity of dark places to transact a dark business...."

MF accepts this attempted deception good-naturedly, is soon sharing coffee and secrets with the boys. It's also not long before she's in bed with the chameleon Mike, the man with a deck of personae to suit whatever scam the occasion calls for. Good subject for a book? She thinks so. The user and the used is a game in which identity is a matter of perception.

The action throughout is driven by Mamet's characteristic dialogue, that fusion of brutal idiomatic conversation and the mannered exchange. Not everyone likes it. It often seems stilted, even dysfunctional, like a failed attempt at the theatre of manners. Yet it's this contradictory formalism that makes a Mamet drama a deeper exchange in human communication, like a combination of speech and thought. The language of the inner being is formal, a dream code of nuclear thinking... whereas the language of the outer being is metaphor, all raw emotion rather than academic reason.

In *House of Games*, language is more than just talk. As Mike instructs MF in the methodology of the Confidence Man, you realize he is the Archetypal Man, a predator who exploits the psychology of body language. A tip of the nose betrays which hand a coin is concealed in, a blush a sexual desire... some you know, some you think you know. There's an infantilism in the method, a forgotten or suppressed way that you only use by occasional instinct. A female patient says, "He says, I can make any woman a whore in 15 minutes." She is a victim of some man, some trauma, some double-think. Her condition is a condition she will share with her therapist.

Night. Rain. Charlie's Tavern. MF writes in her notebook: "The necessity of dark places to transact a dark business...." And Mike materializes at her table masquerading as a waiter. He says, "You want to see how a true bad man plys his trade?"

Inversion, Projection, Compression, Elaboration

The ending of this superb film drama begs comparison with the benchmark *Double Indemnity*. When Walter Neff shoots his double-dealing lover Phyllis Dietrichson in the final clinch, his action expresses the cynicism of a generation who have committed and lost. Love in a free market economy is a Freudian hedge fund, a strategy of loser takes all. The *femme fatale* is the manipulator and her men are her marks. In *House of Games*, Mike is the *homme fatale*, a ruthless inversion of a tradition, yet a very familiar figure in the culture of love and crime.

But patsies will revolt if given a chance. Just as Walter Neff is allowed to set up his own final double-cross, so too Dr. Margaret Ford. Of course MF's is a con and she works it with the driven precision of a top graduate in the school of revenge. Mamet's sociology here is more ambitious and overtly political than Wilder's, a paradigm of the eighties if ever there was one. MF enters Charlie's Tavern by the back door, listens in as Mike and his gang of con artists joke and mock her gullibility as they pass around a copy of her book *Driven*. One of the boys asks Mike how he knew MF would go for the 80 thousand con. "Go for it? says Mike. "The broad's an addict."

MF the addict is waiting for Mike the grifter at the airport that night with a bag she says has a quarter of million in it, her entire savings... and the silver automatic she confiscated from Billy Hahn. This gun is not only a part of the first con, but also her first theft (as Mike the Master once said to her: "I read a book once. It said this: if you get fired from your job, take something from life, something, a memento, a pencil... assert yourself."). When she cons Mike into a "restricted area" of the terminal and shoots him, it's not only an act of hatred but also one of political opportunity.

Mike dies an incorrigible. He even taunts her, the depth of his male contempt a misogynist war-cry: "Please sir... give me another." As he lies twisted and dying in the corner, his pain is his sneer. And she gives him another bullet—inversion, projection, compression, elaboration. Gender inversion is one thing, phallic projection another. In the American free market, a woman with a hand gun is the first sign of a post-gender economy. Utterly unsentimental, the ruthless feminist gestalt is the flavor of the era. Whereas Phyllis in *Double Indemnity* dies in love or feigning love (Walter doesn't believe her), Mike dies a pure criminal, a loveless entrepreneur who steals trust as a profession. But he's a classic Mamet male—a reptilian operator who only sheds his tail in order to conceal his position.

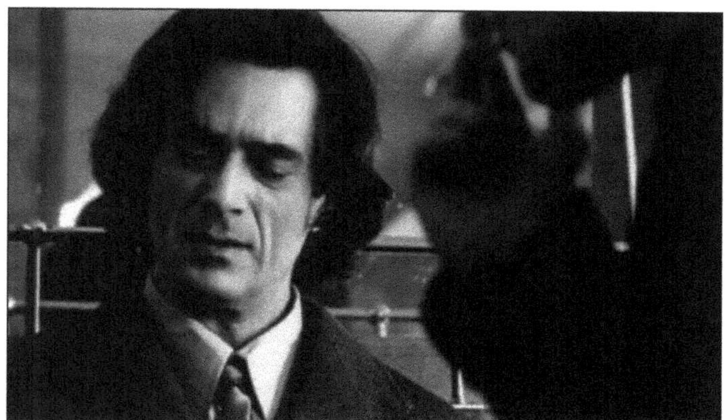

Gerard Mordillat: *My Life & Times With Antonin Artaud*

My Life & Times With Antonin Artaud (*En Compagnie D'Antonin Artaud*) (1993) dir. Gerard Mordillat writ. Mordillat and Jerome Prieur cine. Francois Catonne edt. Sophie Rouffio music Jean-Claude Petit star Sami Frey (Artaud), Marc Barbe (Prevost), Julie Jezequel, Valerie Jeannet, Clotilde de Bayber, Charlotte Volandrey, Alain Broissard *et. al.* Fox Lorber

"...A Patient Breaking Into A Nuthouse"

Theatre of Cruelty—what is it? "Everything that acts is a cruelty" says Artaud in his essay on the subject. "It is upon this idea of extreme action, pushed beyond all limits, that theatre must be rebuilt." If you look at his subjects—the Marquis de Sade, Bluebeard, the Fall of Jerusalem, the Conquest of Mexico—you get some idea of the crypto-fascist cosmologies that run behind the revolutionary expression of this French poet, actor, medium and madman who advocated the artist as a Creator rather than as a writer or director. Visionary... or just another ass with an act? Gerard Mordillat's black comedy on the subject gives you some idea. The narrative frame for the action is an unrecognized poet's journal which records his meeting and later enslavement to the great man. If masochists exist in order for sadists to express themselves, then Jacques Prevel (Marc Barbe) must be a masochist. In a sense this poet who says he writes "for people who will be alive when I'm dead" is Artaud's understudy, and ironically a sadist by default to his suffering wife and superbly suffering mistress.

Prevel has sent some of his poems to Artaud in the asylum at Rodez (outside Paris) and receives a polite letter back. It's a measure of Prevel's desperation or delusion that he thinks that if he could publish this letter, this in turn will help him get recognized as the sensitive genius he knows he is. Crazy? That's French literature in the post-war climes, folks. And this Left-Bank mentality is far from dead, as you can find it on nearly any campus in North America today. For this reason, *My Life & Times* is likely to be seen as hip rather than tragic, a model rather than a moral.

There's no question that despite the immediate squalor of madness, there's also something attractive about it, especially for the poet as savant. It's like reverse language therapy, an occultic means of breaking through the spectral walls that enclose our reality. As this involves an assault on the senses, drugs are nearly always involved. It was true for Nerval and Alfred Jarry, both obvious precursors of Artaud. They say Jarry was found dead on a bed of straw, a cylinder of ether nearby. For Artaud—the man who looks like a fresh cadaver in a stale bistro—his death might've been accelerated by any one of the different drugs Prevel delivers to him. Once, during one of their many transits of the Charrenton bridge, Artaud says to Prevel, "All the opium in Paris must be at Artaud's disposal... so he can finish his work." Thus spake the Master. And such is Prevel's sycophantic desperation, he continues to supply Artaud (Sami Frey) with laudanum—that ancient staple of the visionary poet i.e. Francis Thompson, *City of Dreadful Night*—or nearly anything else that will give the man a buzz. Artaud wants ham—Prevel gets it for him. Artaud needs woman—Prevel's wife might do. Artaud needs his visions recorded—Prevel will write them down. Artaud needs an audience for his theatre—Prevel will be that audience.

"Make It Vibrate Til The Fibre Of Life Squeals"

In a delineating scene, Prevel approaches through the asylum garden, hears the pained voice of the actress that Artaud is rehearsing in his room. "There once was a King of Thule," she recites... over and over. "No!" shouts Artaud. "Louder... louder...!" She stands stiffly like a truant schoolgirl, accepting her humiliation from the Master like the slave she is. "There once was a King of Thule," she shrieks, "whose faithful courtesan gave him a talisman!" "No!" shouts Artaud. "The sound must squirt out! Make it vibrate 'til the fibre of life squeals!" Tears stream down her face, her body trembles... and the madman circles. Avant-garde? Yes. Theatre of Cruelty? You bet.

Artaud's relationship with Colette the actress is left ambiguous, like much of the metaphoric language that the poet excels at. He tells Prevel that Colette was brutally raped and that he will slit the man's throat "if (he) can find him." You wonder if Artaud is the assailant, as he frequently refers to himself in the 3rd person... the mind-body dualism of a spiritual coward? Yet his immersion within his own act of self-destruction is so complete, a certain integrity prevails. For example, he's not too far gone to suggest to Prevel that he's treating his wife badly and that Jany his mistress "is an evil influence". Prevel's situation is so absurd that it can only exist by omission of detail. His wife and children live in apartment while he lives down the street in a hotel with his mistress. There never seems to be any money... and why would there be? Prevel never works. When she's not stoned, Jany is out "trying to sell (Prevel's) poems". Somehow Prevel seems to be able to keep this menage trois going between writing in cafes and running dope to the madman. All the while only one thing matters: recognition that he, Prevel, is a significant poet. While Artaud is evasive, a publisher is not—he says Prevel's poetry reveals a certain "laziness". Funny? We think so.

Prevel is ostracized by the literary disciples who await the sporadic visits of their Christ in one of the many smoky cafes they hang around in like hyenas. They resent his relationship with Artaud, the fact that he supplies the maestro with drugs. Prevel is killing Artaud, they feel. Meanwhile Prevel continues to walk the walk with Artaud, listen to his stream-of-consciousness (or is it vomit) with the dead-pan rapture of a nicotine zombie.

"Everytime a man and a woman have sex, I feel it," intones Artaud. "They deprive me of something." He advises Prevel to give up sex. "Avoid it. One day it will no longer be desired or necessary, or exist anymore."

> Prevel: Drugs do that to you?
> Artaud: I take drugs to rid myself of sexual obsessions! (Prevel demurs) Only a hermaphrodite knows what love should be, the rest just saps energy.

One night they return to the asylum but Artaud has lost his keys. When Prevel is giving him a "leg up" onto the wall, two gendarmes come by, demand to know what's going on. "A patient breaking into the nuthouse!" one exclaims. They help Artaud climb the wall in an act that symbolizes the absurd *modus operandi* of the modern poet in search of understanding.

The film is in black and white, no doubt to help lock it into history and the bleak cultural confusion of forties France. It works, as Paris looks like an industrial nightmare, a perpetual shunting yard of locomotives and Metro transit. Cafes, streets, buildings, even nature, are drained of color, reduced to shades of gray and black as if filtered by the smoke from the endless cigarettes everyone is smoking. The principals are excellent in their roles. Sami Frey is so within the character of Antonin Artaud you think this is a documentary. Mordillat's film isn't that funny if you have no sympathy for transcendental language, and indeed many will find its self-indulgent characters tiresome. But for the curious with no previous knowledge of Artaud, it might draw attention to his brilliant collection of "essays" collected as *Theatre And Its Double*. Here you will find such interesting gems as "No More Masterpieces" and "Towards a Theatre of Cruelty".

Artaud died in 1948, a month after his war-guilt radio play *To Have Done With The Judgement of God* was broadcast to an indifferent public, his manisfestos misunderstood, his exorcism withheld.

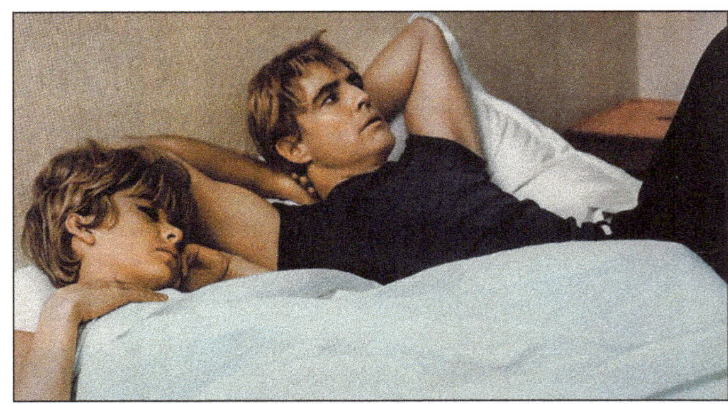

Hubert Cornfield: *The Night of the Following Day*

The Night Of The Following Day 1967 dir Hubert Cornfield writ Hubert Cornfield with Robert Phippeny (based on the novel by Lionel White) cine Willi Kurant music Stanley Myers edt Gordon Pilkington art Jean Boulet | sound Ken Scrivener
star Marlon Brando, Richard Boone, Rita Moreno (Vi), Pamela Franklin

(Dupont's daughter), Jess Hahn (Wally), Gerard Buhr (gendarme), Hughes Wanner (Dupont), Jacques Marin (Cafe owner), Al Letteri (pilot)

Crime fiction is a recreational fantasy for the meek or a game plan for the outlaw. So what exactly is Hubert Cornfield's *The Night of the Following Day*: The story of a crime, or the story of a fantasy? A teenage girl (Pamela Franklin) daydreams on a transatlantic flight, eyes closed, headphones on. Her image is double-exposed against the typical in-flight view of clouds and the earth far below. She is drawn from her reverie by a pretty stewardess, who asks her to fasten her seat-belt—the plane is descending towards Paris. An anonymous young boy across the aisle plays a flute. Like her, he appears to be travelling alone, yet never recurs in the story, remains significantly insignificant.

The plane lands, the girl disembarks, is met by a handsome chauffeur (Brando), in a black uniform who tips his hat and smiles. His lips move, but, assuming her point-of-view, we hear nothing, as she's still dreaming. The chauffeur takes her bags, chaperones her to a waiting Rolls limo. The suitcases are put in the trunk, he opens the back door, she gets in, sits quietly as the limo leaves the airport. Throughout, the sound is ambient—traffic, aircraft, the coming rain. The limo pulls in behind a wasted blue Peugeot sedan on the exit road; both cars stop on the shoulder, a man (Boone) gets out of the Peugeot and climbs roughly into the back seat, crowding the girl. The girl looks in alarm at the chauffeur, who merely looks away, activates the glass partition as he pulls the Rolls onto the freeway. End of the romance?

The convoy ends up in a discreet spot in the winter woods where the girl and her luggage are transferred to the Peugeot. To her surprise, she sees the stewardess (Moreno) in the front passenger seat, no longer friendly, her face cold and tense. Clearly this is a gang, this is a sophisticated kidnapping. The driver of the Peugeot (Hahn) now swaps cars with the chauffeur who proceeds to drive the hostage, the enforcer and the stewardess to a lonely coastal location somewhere on the Atlantic (in actuality, Le Touquet in Brittany). Lit by the dull light of the overcast, they pass through the pines and dune grass onto a vast beach, drive a short distance, park on the sand. On the wide, distant ocean the black clouds of a thunder storm; on the wind-swept dunes, a lonely white villa. Night approaches, menace has arrived.

Even though the story-line of *The Night Of The Following Day* is an action cliché, the execution is elegant within its simplicity. The real-time sequences, the moody coastal light, the Left Bank jazz score, and the A-production acting make this film much better than the cheap action drama many believe it to be (including Marlon Brando). Although the production is American, it was shot in Brittany and (ironically) has the reverse-engineered complexion of a French neo-noir such as Jean-Pierre Melville's *Un Flic*.

The title has a poetic mystery to it, like a dramatist's scene tag, and it actually fits the time frame of the story. The title has, of course, a mixed astrological/religious significance in terms of the "12th Night" of the winter festival (the Winter Solstice to New Year's Day followed by the Feast of the Epiphany) although this allusion does not in itself make this film good or clever. Clearly the director Hubert Cornfield and his script collaborator Robert Phippeny exploited some aspects of the seasonal holiday—most notably the idea of role-reversal—and also took cues from Shakespeare's play *Twelfth Night*. Rita Moreno's character (the stewardess, sister of Wally) "Vi" is a casual reinvention of "Viola", a *Twelfth Night* character, and there are several significant reversals along the way. Still, as a technique, "reversal" is as basic and ancient as *Oedipus Rex* within the history of drama, so there is nothing especially clever here, although this shadow intellectualism in no way intrudes upon the telling of the story. We don't need to recognize any of it, but if we do, the imagery deepens.

As in many crime dramas, the gang implodes, due to the usual duplicity, weakness and greed. Moreno's character Vi is a coke-head, insecure in her relationship with Brando (unnamed, although at one point he is called "Bud"), which echoes their off-stage romance which they carried on for many years. As the enforcer, Boone's character is a sadist and natural-born killer, can share with no one, except Death. Wally—Vi's brother—is a sentimentalist, is in for the last caper, the perennial easy pension plan of the doomed. He's bonded to Brando through his sister and the fact that B. feels indebted to him. "If it wasn't for you, I'd be doin' time in Sing Sing," says Brando. The caper appears to be Wally's idea, as he was the one who recruited Boone. Details of life before all this remain scarce, however. As in most movies, characterization is by visual impression, not biography.

Brando creates an impression, no question. *The Night Of The Following Day* is the last film wherein he appears as a slim, viable hipster before surrendering to the tragic obesity that would eventually make him a freak. His character is really himself, a mid-fifties beat replete with emotive jive talk and de rigueur sexual cool. No scene shows this better than the dispute with Boone over their hostage. Brando understands immediately that Boone is a sexual sadist, intends to rape the girl somewhere along the line. They argue:

> Brando: What's going on, man?
> Boone: She tried to leave.
> Brando: (raised) I was upstairs. I saw what you did.
> Boone: (snarls at the sobbing girl) Shaddup!
> Brando: Listen, man, if you wanna get freaky you don't do it with her—
> (Boone laughs harshly)

Or there's the fight with Moreno. When she sees him leaving the girl's room, she makes a paranoid assumption (fueled by coke), loses it, attacks Brando. Brando does no explaining (although we know he's innocent), merely challenges her by smashing a bottle and handing it to her, urging her to disfigure him if she really thinks he doesn't love her. Because of the real-life tension between Brando and Moreno, the scripted fight becomes a real fight. According to Peter Manso in his bio of Brando, Brando was flying in various women to help him pass the time off the set and still messing around with Rita. "Even though she lost the script, she stayed in character." (as quoted in *Brando, the Biography*, Peter Manso, p. 645)

This ability to improvise within context in order to give an edge to character and scene was something that both Brando and Moreno were familiar with; Brando had studied the Stanislavski "Method" under Stella Adler, Moreno under Jeff Corey. In those days everyone wanted to see Brando lose it, go psycho, do his Stanley routine, knock a woman around. The angry man was a period figure, a universal post-war male trauma. Anger was the root sexual power of the modally hip, the release that precedes the release. In his now almost forgotten 1957 essay *The White Negro*, Norman Mailer says: "The unstated essence of Hip, its psychopathic brilliance, quivers with the knowledge that new kinds of victories increase one's power for new kinds of perception.... In short, whether the life is criminal or not, the decision is to encourage the psychopath in oneself."

So to understand the Brando style, we have understand what it meant to be hip. Dress him in black, with jack boots and a chauffeur's uniform, he's undercover; dress him in black, tight T-shirt and slacks, and he's hip, the existential bohemian with a machine gun and a chick to protect. The chick of course is the hostage, Dupont's daughter. His character is a moralist—just as Brando was, albeit in the instinctual sense, not institutional. Certainly, he's a criminal, but a nice one; here he's Left Bank gone bad. We never see the gang discussing strategy—events just happen. Boone flies from Le Touquet to Paris, enacts the elaborate "clean money" scheme, instructing by phone, then shadowing Dupont (father of the kidnapped girl) as he exchanges the marked bills for clean ones at two different banks, then flies to Le Touquet with the money. Events happen—familiar scenarios need no prompting. Brando unwraps a brick of plastique, wires it, then has Vi drive him to the airport beacon which he ascends like a man on a personal mission of revenge, not some local plan. But this, of course, is this point: everyone has a personal agenda. When Brando blows the tower, it's an expression, not a tactic. When Boone tortures and rapes (off-camera) the girl in defiance of political logic, it's an expression, not a tactic. When Vi and her brother die in flames... it's merely an expression of their respective desires, where Fate is an accomplice, not a Hunter. Thus the action is existential throughout.

The soundtrack relies mostly on the ambient presence of Nature, the ubiquitous ocean, the rain, traffic, distant reverberations. Scene transitions use sympathetic music welds—moody jazz figures reminiscent of mid-sixties Miles Davis tones. Minimalism is the art-style throughout, whether it be the vast empty shoreline with its staggered dunes and lonely villa, or the gang's shabby Peugeot station wagon with its corroded blue Picasso paint job. The characters are minimal, their relationships private. Even the friendly local gendarme/fisherman whose appearances seem coincidental remains a mystery, his role reduced to ambiguity and visual tension.

Pure film? Or simply a weak script rescued by style and edit... certainly an argument can be made either way, although the atmospheric power and the latent mysticism makes *The Night Of The Following Day* a very interesting film. A box-office failure and disparaged by its star, it has none of the zany intellectual chit chat that made Godard's films such a hit, and was doomed to be greeted as a shallow exercise in fake exoticism.

Yet despite the setting, the filmic style is more Antonioni than French. The ambient sound, the real-time indolence within the action, the sense of a waking dream reminds us of certain passages in *L'Avventura*, that most anti-dramatic of films.

Yet *Night* is a dramatic film. Brando's performance is much better than he believed or cared to believe. His idea of a good film was one where the dialogue achieved a social ideal, raised the weak, destroyed the strong... like *Queimada* (a.k.a *Burn!*), his personal favorite (and 12th box-office failure) which he made in 1969, two years after *Night*. His idea was a stage idea, not a pure cinema idea.

Pure cinema removes the actor, exalts the landscape.

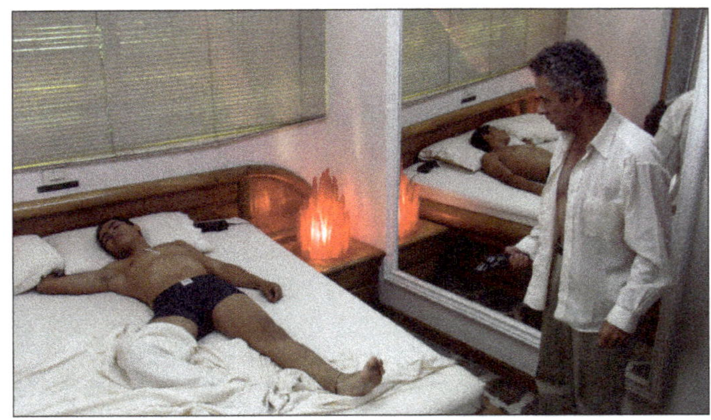

Barbet Schroeder: *Our Lady of the Assassins*

Our Lady of the Assassins (La Virgen de los Sicarios) 1999 dir. Barbet Schroeder writ. Fernando Vallejo [from his novel] cine. Rodrigo Lalinde edt. Elsa Vasquez music Jorge Arriagada cost. Monica Manlanda star. German Jaramillo (Fernando), Anderson Ballesteros (Alexis), Juan David Restrepo (Wilmar a.k.a. The Blue Lagoon), Manuel Basquetes, Cesar Salazar, Jean Goudier, Dominique Hennequin
Studio Canal/Losange/Vertigo/Tucan production 100 mins
Alliance/Atlantis DVD

To Love A Murderer...

Medellin: the place where Pablo Escobar started out as a reseller of stolen tombstones before forming the cocaine cartel that put Colombia, S.A., on the map. A violent place, *amigos*. Maybe you read about it in Gabriel Marquez or saw it on T.V. You don't need to know that Barbet Schroeder lived near there for a short time as a kid to understand why he'd want to make a movie about it or why he'd be drawn to the writing of Fernando Vallejo.

Remember Barfly? Where Charles Bukowski is the central character in his own desperate, drunken devolution? *Our Lady of the Assassins* is also about a writer on the skids—Vallejo himself, no less. Yes, he too is from Medellin, although these days he lives and writes in Mexico.

The title, of course, is keyed to the infamous masturbation classic by Genet, *Our Lady of the Flowers* (1943). Reactionary, subversive for the times, this novel by the inmate of cell 426 exalts the murders and sexual proclivity of his fellow inmates as a spiritual triumph. No longer banned or even expurgated in most countries, *Flowers* set the standard for creative blasphemy and pornography.

Now that pornography actually leads the creative arts, many criminal literates have found fame. Want to be a famous writer? Get incarcerated. In a sense, this is what the protagonist "Fernando" does in *Our Lady of the Assassins*—he incarcerates himself in the criminal city of Medellin. By his own admission, he has returned there "to die". Fact is, you never know what his status is as a writer. He doesn't do any writing, says what he has written is "rubbish".

If the films of Godard are post-modern fantasy, then this film is post-modern reality. Call it nihilism, homoerotic fatalism... call it misanthropic, misogynist, mystically challenged... call it bullshit, call it genius. For you, no middle position is possible. If offending the audience is art, then this is art.

To use the gay sex culture as a paradigm for exploring the

culture of the teenage assassins is, well, brilliant. Their fleeting lives have about as much value as the binary combatants in a video game or a film fantasy such as *The 10th Victim*... yet a peculiar feminine dignity becomes them when they seek love....

The Most Fabulous Boy In Medellin

Fernando (German Jaramillo) goes to a gay party somewhere in the city. Because he's been away in Europe for 30 years, the host gives him a young boy as a present. They adjourn to the "Butterfly Room" and undress. Fernando checks out his present: nice teenage hardbody, amulet necklace, shoulder tattoo... scarred ribcage... hmm, how come?

The boy says it's from a shotgun blast. A 9 millimeter automatic slips from his shorts, bounces on the floor. What's this? His "heater". Seems some dudes are in love with him... "in a hateful way."

Fernando orders him to lie down on the bed. They have sex. Afterwards Fernando hands him some money, goes back to the party to get him a drink. As F. mixes a rum and coke, he overhears some men talking. Seems the boy is the only survivor of an Escobar gang that got wiped out... has three or four murders to his credit.

Does this deter Fernando, the middle-aged sophisticate?

A Walking Tour Of Our Fine Churches, *Senor*

The narrative is more or less an existential travelogue, wherein the two "lovers" walk around Medellin visiting the various churches and hilltop towns. By this method Fernando instructs Alexis (Anderson Ballesteros) in the early history ["it was just a pig farm"] and Alexis instructs him in the current [the Metrallo drug gangs & youth scene]. Their first date is a pilgrimage to the church at Sabaneto, near Fernando's old family farm, now gone. However, the old cafe is still there and the jukebox still plays "Serendito". As he listens to the music, he's overcome with sentiment, weeps.

This stroll down memory lane takes an ugly turn when they witness a shoot-out on the steps of the church. One gang is massacred by another firing automatics from motorcycles. Alexis knows the participants, of course, casually shrugs the incident off.

This establishes the pattern of violence: everytime they visit a church, death follows.

What Do We Do Now?

Like a priest who finds love in an orphange, Fernando is both a mentor and a moral compass for the uneducated Alexis. Yet it is Alexis who actually corrupts Fernando into embracing violence, as a point comes in the increasing vigilante action whereby he is stimulated, despite his civilized, pragmatic nature.

They return to F.'s apartment. Alexis notes with amazement that "it's empty" ...and of course this is symbolism for F.'s current spiritual state. Nonetheless, it has a great view of the city. At night fireworks explode over the hilltowns. What's this? "They got another shipment of cocaine into the U.S.," Alexis says.

They leave, come back, stand in the empty room. "What do we do now?" says Alexis, as if he's in a Samuel Beckett play..

Buy him a stereo, of course. The only thing he wants other than Calvin Kleins and a mini-Uzi.

Turn That Faggot Off... It's More Noise

Fernando has a noise phobia, which is really a cultural phobia. When Alexis' speed-metal music becomes too much, F. grabs the stereo, tosses it over the balcony. Alexis thinks this is cool... what the hell, his indulgent lover will replace it anyway. When a skinhead in an adjacent apartment angers F. with his evening drum practice, Alexis shoots the offender dead in the street. Like the stereo, problem solved. Shocked, F. asks why? Alexis shrugs, says, "He was a dickhead."

Oddly, perversely, F. carries within him the same corroding contempt. He kneels in chapels, curses the saints. He mocks the statue of Simon Bolivar, the liberator of South America. He sees the President of Colombia on a cafe T.V. promising better sewers, barks, "Turn that faggot off... it's more noise."

He rides in taxis, fights with the drivers because they won't turn down the samba music. The aggravating noise of disrespect and free-market anarchy is everywhere in Medellin, except at night when the city sleeps or within the dim candle lit sanctuaries of its many churches. "If there is a God, he's a scumbag," hisses F.

We Were Born To Die

The fatalism of the young is succinctly expressed by The Pest, a young street orphan who is friendly with Alexis. He tells them he's knocked-up his girlfriend. Why? The kid will avenge him when he's dead. Does he expect to die soon? Yes, because, "we were born to die."

Another member of this street clique is called Death Boy. Tall, skinny, with long tattooed arms, he wanders the malls and streets. He wears a hooded sweat-shirt and shades like some sort of heavy-metal ghoul... and is always around to warn Alexis of an impending hit.

The hits are always the same: a speeding motorcyclist with a shooter on the pillion. Alexis faces them head-on, just like a cop on a T.V. show, legs apart, feet firmly planted, both hands on his Berreta... blows them away, yeah. One attempt is just across the street from the Fine Arts Building, where F. took piano lessons as a kid. As Alexis restores his gun to his crotch and slips away, a pregnant woman starts screaming at the sight of the mutilated assassins dead and bleeding on the sidewalk. By now inured to this daily violence, F. mocks her, says, "This isn't Switzerland, this is Medellin, Colombia!"

Mockery Of Pregnant Women

F. and Alexis regroup later in the apartment. Alexis parodies the distress of the pregnant woman. He stuffs his stomach, dances, whines hysterically. He's encouraged by F., who rants about the stupidity of these women, asserts that "having kids is a sin." So much for the Pope and the Catholic position. As they laugh and cavort, his logic about poverty and indiscriminate pregnancy might be correct—especially in this context—although it does sound like familiar gay propaganda.

Still, it must be noted that F. isn't devoid of some sympathy for women... it's just that he prefers them as boys. When Alexis is eventually killed, he makes a melancholy journey to the hilltop town where Alexis' mother lives with her kids above The Kingdom of Heaven grocery store, gives her some money in memory of her fallen son. She's pregnant, been deserted by her husband. Again, poverty is seen as the purveyor of reality.

The Dumping Of Cadavers Is Prohibited

The natural beauty of Medellin's location in the mountains is always ironic, especially as the violence plays out. Again, they're in a taxi. Again, F. tells the driver to lower the music. The driver flips, stops, curses them as faggots, orders them out... then attacks F. with a machete. Again, Alexis is handy with the gun... and they wander off like two tourists admiring the view, the taxi abandoned, doors open, music playing, the swarthy driver sprawled on the road in his death repose.

Where are the cops? You never see them anywhere, anytime.

A sign warns that *se prohibe arrojar cadavero* but of course bodies lie festering on the rocks as the vultures circle. Ludicrously, the view from this spot is especially beautiful, as if Death has the best real-estate in town. Below, the city buzzes like any modern metropolis... new highrises, freeway, rapid rail system.

Once again, the unreality is in the contrast of the living with the casually dead.

Next, they're on the train, heading into town. Two mestizo workers curse them as cocksuckers, perhaps aggravated by F.'s sarcastic remarks. As they attack, Alexis shoots them. No respect? In Medallo, happiness is a warm gun, amigo.

Europe, Elitism & Civilization

Even though he's an iconoclast, F. makes a number of attempts to dissuade Alexis from violence. "Can't you distinguish between thought and action?" says F. "What separates the two is called civilization." Alexis just smiles... but agrees to leave this evil city, get a new life, despite the generation gap between him and F. The problem is to some extent racial, as poverty is mainly an Indian and mestizo problem. F. might be from Medellin, but he's white, out the colonial class. His idea of civilization is European and elitist. The implication that morality is art is there, but as such, not really explored. They buy a new stereo, and F. plays Maria Callas singing an aria. "Sounds like she's being strangled," says Alexis. Exactly—what is the perfection of beauty to F. is just "noise" to Alexis. Like his young contemporaries, his culture is the videogame and T.V.

Symbolism Of The Wounded Dog

There are many great scenes in this film, and the one with the wounded dog might well be the most telling. Alexis has successfully avoided assassination. It's night, they're walking along the road as the traffic roars past, when F. spots a dog lying in the big concrete culvert. The dog is whimpering, unable to escape the sewer... F. determines that it's been hit by a car, is beyond rescue. He tells Alexis to shoot it, but ironically the boy who can shoot people without regret or guilt, is unable to do a mercy killing. F. takes the gun, shoots the dog. They climb out of the sewer, continue walking.

This scene is symmetrical with the death of Alexis, and the imagery contains the entire lesson and moral of this movie. As they used their last bullets on the dog [and lost the gun in the culvert], Alexis has no defence against the next hit. All he can do is sacrifice himself to save F. by standing in front of him and taking the bullets in the chest.

F. rushes Alexis to hospital in a taxi... but the only charity he gets for this is, "How dare you drop a corpse at our hospital?" people who aren't on T.V. don't exist

Despondent, F. drifts through nightmares and solitary walks. In the Patio del Tango, the old singer/owner Don Hannibal sees him sitting alone, comes over, says, "You're the writer... where's your son?"

Your son. F. says he left for the U.S., departs into the night.

F. is determined to track down The Blue Lagoon, the boy who killed Alexis. Eventually he finds him in the doorway of a video store... although at this time he's unaware this boy is The Blue Lagoon. Now he's known simply as "Wilmar".

> Wilmar: Haven't I seen you on T.V.?
> Fernando: People who aren't on T.V. don't exist.

They go for lunch. "We should indulge in every vice to make sure we're alive," says F. , repeating the well-known de Sade maxim. And so a new affair begins... with the same absurd culture of death.

F. is pissed by a whistling man on the street—Wilmar takes out his .38, shoots him. No more whistling. They do the church routine. Later, The Pest asks why F. is hanging out with the guy who killed Alexis? By now F. is "in love" with this boy, has agreed to buy his mother a Whirlpool fridge. F. takes him to a motel as part of his plan to kill him. When Wilmar is asleep, F. points the .38 at his head....

Self-Portrait

"The exceptional value of the work lies in its ambiguity. It appears at first to have only one subject, Fatality: the characters are puppets of destiny." So says Sartre in his essay about Genet's *Our Lady of the Flowers*. He could just as easily be talking about the Schroeder/Vallejo film, which isn't to say that it's a plagiarism of the Genet novel. Indeed, you might think Genet is crap, just more stream of vomit from the secular Left. There's nothing hallucinatory or narcissistic about *Our Lady of the Assassins*. The realism denies fiction, even if fiction is used.

Schroeder's style is always documentary, as film documentary contains the objective truth. Recently interviewed about his documentary on Idi Amin, he says, "For me, the making of non-fiction films is the same as making fiction films... all of the New Wave, which I was surrounded by, was influenced by documentary film-making."

This implies voyeurism, and there is certainly that feeling in this film. For this reason, the outstanding acting of German Jaramillo, Anderson Ballesteros and Juan David Restrepo passes unnoticed, because you don't believe it is acting.

And Vallejo, the writer? Is this truly a self-portrait?

> "To love a murderer. To love to commit a crime in cahoots with the young half-breed pictured on the cover of the torn book. I want to sing murder, for I love murderers. To sing it plainly. Without pretending, for example, that I want to be redeemed through it, though I do yearn for redemption...."
> (Genet, *Our Lady of the Flowers*)

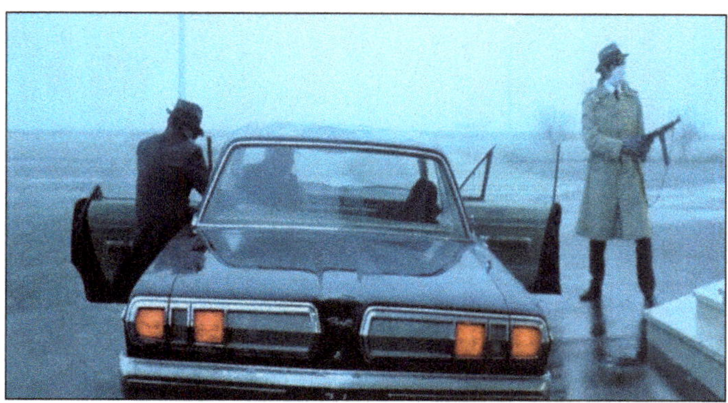

Jean-Pierre Melville: *Un Flic*

Un Flic (1972) (a.k.a *Dirty Money*) writ & dir Jean-Pierre Melville cine Walter Wottiz edt. Patricia Neny music Michel Colombier star. Alain Delon (Inspector Eduoard Coleman), Richard Crenna (Simon), Catherine Deneuve (Cathy), Ricardo Cicciolla, Michael Conrad (Costa), Paul Crauchet (Paul), Simone Valere, Andre Pousse, Jean Desailly Studio Canal

Death Is A Blonde

You're in France. It's winter, and you want to rob a bank. You're thinking a lonely coastal branch, a place where the seas are heavy and the fog closes in, eliminating the near distance, witnesses, memory. The gulls cry, the rain and wind increase. An Atlantic gale is on the way. The condos are shuttered, the owners invisible, perhaps back in Paris watching a movie about French gangsters who dress like Americans from a previous generation. Well, it could be you and your three associates, all wearing fedoras and black overcoats... although you wear a trenchcoat, just like Bogart in *Casablanca*. In this kind of weather you might pass for businessmen, except for the fact that you arrive in a black American sedan, a '62 Plymouth....

From a sociological perspective, there are two questions: is Melville's *Un Flic* about criminals and cops who take their professional cues from American noir movies and behave accordingly, or is this film simply an example of art for art's sake?

Even though *Un Flic* was Melville's last film, he wears his influences like a young painter exhibiting for the first time. Besides film noir, there is the unmistakable minimalism of Italian neo-realism: ambient sound, real-time sequencing, documentary validity. The atmospherics of the opening action are brilliant—the pastel blue tint of the cinematography, the intercutting of the crashing waves with the silent architecture, the fog, the bank, the robbery. It's a dialectic of opposing sensibilities—the noir acting, the neo-realist action—which produces a drama that's very beautiful to look at. No psychopathic behaviour here, just the familiar French fatalism, the existential rapprochement of the living with the soon-to-be-dead.

The title suggests that Coleman the cop (Delon) is the protagonist, although his role is a doppelganger with the character of the club owner and robber extraordinaire Simon (Crenna), as they both share a mistress (Deneuve). This appears to be a designed strategy by Simon in order to stay one step ahead of the law, although in the end it does him no good. There's a certain ambiguity about this triangle that leaves you wondering just exactly who is manipulating whom.

Delon's character is tough, often sadistic. He might be a cop, yet he isn't above a little blackmail. One of his informants is a blond transvestite, a dancer from Simon's club. For some reason she's clearly in love with him, yet he treats her as street meat. He drives a 63 Dodge Dart, she a Jaguar with the English right-hand drive (symbol of her reversed sexuality). Their meetings are clandestine, suggesting something, although you just don't know what. He backhands her across the face, blaming her for the "Suitcase Matthew" fiasco: "From now on, dress like a man."

He has a thing for blondes—the first crime you see him investigating involves a murdered blonde in a hotel room. She's naked, her eyes wide, her expression more sad than fearful. Coleman stares as if he recognizes something... but what? You never see her again, so she becomes symbolism, part of a chain of sexual criminals. "We're doomed victims," says a homosexual art collector, a paroled pedophile on the verge of relapsing. Again, Coleman says nothing, just stares at infinity. While his sympathies are always political on the outside, you sometimes wonder what's going on inside. He has a working relationship with "criminals", yet as he drives the night streets of Paris in Car 8, his destination is always Loneliness.

The Boulevard Of Broken Dreams

Simon is a man for whom crime is an art—typically, a French sentiment. How else can you explain his actions? He has a club, a beautiful mistress, a cash flow, youthfulness... and most importantly, a vibe of cool. His masculinity is predicated on action, whether or not some of these actions make any sense. The robbery of the heroin courier on the Paris-Lisbon train makes little sense. Essentially a set-up by Coleman and his squad, the intricacy of this robbery is pure existentialism at the expense of consequence.

You might laugh when you watch it, but watch it you will. Simon is lowered from a helicopter onto the roof of the train, manages to get into the washroom, where he removes his jump suit, revealing his elegant dressing gown and cravat. No music here, just the rhythmic rattling of the train as it speeds through the night. He makes his way along the swaying corridor, stops for a cigarette. An older gentleman passes, says, "Difficult to sleep..." and Simon murmurs, "How right you are."

Simon produces a large horse-shoe magnet from under his dressing gown, uses it to move the inside chain and break into the carriage of the slumbering heroin courier, a corrupt customs agent by the name of Suitcase Matthew. This ritual—and everything during the robbery—takes place in real time which gives an undeniable documentary realism to these absurd events. Suitcase—himself a powdered blond of suspect gender—is stunned by a blow to the head, then taped and drugged. Simon removes the heroin from the two suitcases with their false bottoms, puts it into his, returns to the washroom, puts on his jump suit, goes outside where... lo! The helicopter is still up there, still stalking the train. The heroin is winched up, then Simon.

The helicopter lands in a field at dawn, the gang disembarks, speeds off for Paris in a black Mercedees. Crazy? Of course. The magnet trick is schoolboy stuff, adolescent, out of the comics. The helicopter heist? You know it can be done, except here the director is using models. Again, schoolboy stuff. You understand the expense and difficultly for a French director in 1971 trying to stage this, yet you wonder if the whole mise en scene is deliberate, an artistic choice. It's like watching a magician saw a woman in two—you know it's fake, but the woman is so beautiful, so real, you watch and marvel.

A French Kiss, A French Death

Like everything French, death has a protocol in this movie. A wounded gang member ("Louis Albouis") surfaces from his coma only to be dispatched by an injection from Cathy (Deneuve) in order to ensure his silence about the bank robbery. Coleman breaks in on another gang member—previously an assistant bank manager—just as he's putting a pistol to his head, withdraws, allows the fallen bourgeois the dignity of suicide. When Simon is intercepted on the street, moves as if he's got a gun, Coleman obliges by shooting him. When another detective observes that Coleman was a bit quick on the draw, Coleman says (elliptically), "I wasn't sure if he would commit suicide."

These stagey rituals are rooted in ancient codes, where choice is a matter of honor. When Coleman visits Cathy for a lover's rendezvous, the ambiguity of their situation is acted out. "You're under arrest," he says as he descends the steps into her hotel room. They stare for a moment before she reaches under his jacket, snaps his pistol from its holster, points it at him... then tosses it onto the bed as they embrace, kissing desperately.

When he shoots Simon, Cathy watches from the escape car. Does Coleman arrest her too? Not at all. Their complicity is masked by the symbolism: death is a blond.

Theatre Of The Self

Theatre is always a parody of the self. Thus parody appears as fiction, even if the parody is part of an event. In film, fiction exists but is always hidden in the documentary effect, which you take for the truth. Melville seems to understand this aspect of human behaviour—conscious and unconscious action—when he exploits the consciousness of film noir and neo realism. Here, everyone is an actor. Coleman's street informant is a man pretending to be a woman. When Costa is ambushed in the Chez Luce restaurant, the diners are all police masquerading as citizens. As for Simon... he's always pretending to be something to suit the occasion.

You're in France. It's now June, six months since you robbed the Banque Nationale De Paris in St. Jean-De-Monts. You're in the Hotel Splendid with a suitcase of heroin, thinking about escape. Gone is your gang, gone is your nightclub. You pick up the phone, call your svelte blond mistress. How could you know her phone is tapped, your conversation recorded on a Swiss ReVox reel-to-reel for the pleasure of the police, especially your nemesis, Inspector Eduoard Coleman. You tell her to pick you up at the door. She arrives on time in an Austin 1100, scattering the pigeons. You exit the lobby on cue... but Coleman is waiting on the sidewalk, pistol in hand. What was it the wise man Francoise-Eugene Vidocq said? The only sentiments a man is never incapable of inspiring with the police are ambiguity and derision... or something like that. The woman you both share is across the street. You suspect she has already made her choice, although nothing is certain. Judas might be a man, might be a woman.

One thing is certain, though: she's a blonde. What the hell. Existence precedes the essence. You make as if you have a gun below your trenchcoat... Coleman fires and you die as only the cool can, a handsome desperado in a beautifully photographed movie.

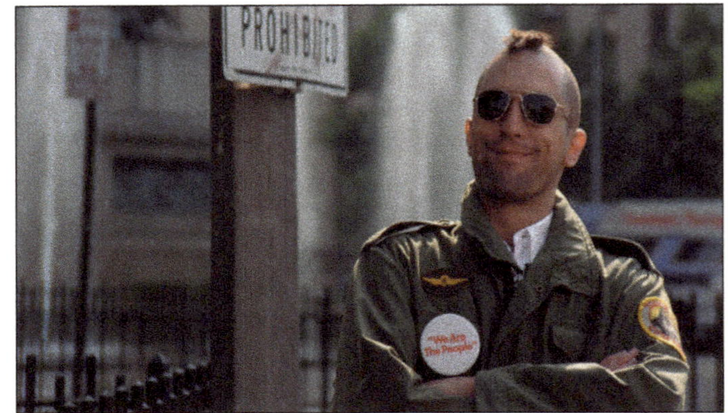

Martin Scorsese: *Taxi Driver*

Taxi Driver (1978) dir. Martin Scorsese writ. Paul Schrader cine. Michael Chapman music. Bernard Herrmann star. Robert DeNiro (Travis), Cybill Shepherd (Betsy), Jody Foster (Iris), Harvey Keitel (Mathew/ Sport), Albert Brooks (Tom), Peter Boyle (Wizard)

Christ wears a cowboy shirt, jeans, boots and a combat jacket. He packs a 44 Magnum in a special holster concealed below his armpit and a Colt 25 automatic up his sleeve. He has a 38 snub-nose tucked into his pants above his ass and a 12 inch hunting knife taped to his right boot. Not especially literate, he manages to keep a diary between watching TV and visiting a 24 hour porno theatre down on the strip. This is what he does when he's not working—and he works a lot, driving a generic yellow taxi through the habitual rain and neon night.

Working within the established tradition of American vigilante movies, Scorsese and Schrader give us Travis Bickle, insomniac vet, a direct action loner who decides to rid the streets of the scum he sees on his nightly tours of New York in his cab. Although it's never stated categorically, the trauma of Vietnam runs through the psychology of this movie like the rain that continually blurs the details of the city nightscape in a confusion of love and pornography, patriotism and loneliness.

We know this: he was discharged from the Marines in May, 1973... and his diary begins May 10 (although what year?). While he shaves his head into a Mohawk cut in the manner of a Vietnam Special Operations commando, the only reference to Vietnam comes in Senator Palatine's speech at a rally ("...we the people suffered in Vietnam....").

Why is Bickle's background left so enigmatic? Without Vietnam, his motivation is existential rather than political. While he professes to support Palatine's populist run for the Presidential nomination, his participation is circumstantial rather than intellectual. He thinks he's in love with Betsy, the campaign worker who "appeared like an Angel out of this filthy mess" but when he takes her to a pornographic movie in his idea of a date, she mistakenly thinks that their agendas are different. She walks out on him, and he's forced to find another madonna to complete his fantasy: the pubescent whore, Iris.

"Oh look at the size of that... oh looking good, it's getting harder... and harder, oh!" (porno soundtrack). The link between sex and violence is categorical. Yet—like Bickle's background—there's an ambiguity in his method of operation just as there is in the Scorsese/Schrader paradigm. Bickle's isolation is anal-retentive, a white man's fantasy of reality. If you believe his card to his folks on their anniversary, his mission is constructed in delusion. He tells them he's working for the government in "the utmost secrecy" and that he has "a girlfriend whose name is Betsy". Yet he toys with the Secret Service Agent at the rally in the ambiguous way that sociopaths express themselves—sincerely manipulative. Are these lies merely a camouflage for his course of action? Or is he another one of the insane working hard to legitimatize himself....

> "All the animals come out at night. Whores, skunk pussys, buggers, fairies, queens, dope pushers... sick, veno." (Bickle)

There's no question that many people would agree with Travis Bickle's assessment of the state of the city and the spiritual confusion that comes with the de-regulation of sexual identity. Is it crime, or is it freedom? On the one hand he's a crude moralist, a retrofit whom we suspect is also a racist, while on the other hand he's a man of principle, an American individualist not unlike the populist politician he appears to be stalking. Like the veterans who returned from Nam expecting to find recognition and a disciplined and prosperous society, he finds himself marginalized and dangerously obsolete.

The gunfighter is a familiar figure in American culture—a rugged individualist whose principles often fall between the conflicting shadows of homicide and sacrifice. Bickle listens to the client in the back of his taxi rave about the power of a 44 Magnum, what it will do to his cheating wife's face, pussy—as they sit and watch her silhouette in the "nigger's" apartment. While there are a number of classic scenes, the one where he buys his guns probably tells us all we need to know about a society built on the right of the individual to bear arms. Andy the salesman puts two suitcases on the bed, opens them.

> Andy: (the Magnum) Stop a car at a hundred yards, put a bullet right through the engine block. (demos the gun) There you go—a premium high resale weapon. (spins the chamber) Lookit that, lookit that... that's a beauty.

He hands Travis the Magnum.

> Andy: I could sell those guns to some jungle bunny in Harlem for 500 bucks... but I just deal high quality goods to the right people.

Travis snaps off a "shot".

> Andy: How about that? This might be a little too big for practical purposes... I recommend a 38 snub-nose... look at this... that's a beautiful little gun... snub-nose but otherwise it's the same as a Service revolver. That'll stop anything that moves... the Magnum, they use that in Africa for killing elephants.

Travis sights the 38 on a car in the parking lot.

> Andy: Some of these guns are like toys, but that 38, you can go out and hammer nails with it all day, come home and it'll still cut dead centre on target everytime. Got a nice action to it, and a heck of a wallop. (holds up an automatic) You interested in an automatic? That's a Colt 25 automatic, a nice little gun....
> Travis: How much for everything?

What's the message here? That we have a society where men use guns as women use birth control pills? When Bickle suits up with his weapons, he turns himself into a cyborg, a killing machine where the gun is integrated into the motor-system of the human body. He manufactures a spring loader, a prosthetic limb that replaces his right arm, propels the Colt automatic into his hand like a hidden ace in the hole. The Magnum hangs across his heart like a sex organ waiting to be discovered. He's all stealth technology, a Magician of Death.

While there's certainly nothing romantic in the bloody shoot-out where the pimps are killed, there's certainly something of the existential hipster in the cool persona of Travis Bickle, avenging angel, Christ in a taxi. Indeed, he survives the carnage, becomes a folk hero on the street, in the media, and is so cool he can drive away from the angel of his dreams, Betsy, who is now aroused by the apparent political correctness of his actions. At the time (1978), this was funny, an irony as unlikely to happen as it was prophetic. Since then, Chapman (John Lennon), the Subway Vigilante, McVeigh, the Trenchcoat kamikazes, and a cast of other armed desperadoes have been writing history and establishing the mythology of contemporary culture. The true sexual karma of the altruist predator is enshrined in a new secular code of the unconscious, which seeks to reconcile perpetrator and victim as reversible entities.

Question: is *Taxi Driver* as lethal as the gun it exalts?

In the long tracking sequence reminiscent of an Orson Welles stylistic, the camera retreats from Iris's sex room over the bodies and guns. The John, the Master Pimp, the Street Pimp, the bloody walls a violent testimony of their day of judgement. This fresco of degenerates fixed in death allows us the moral superiority our legal system denies us.

"Listen you fuckers, you screwheads... here's a man who wouldn't take it anymore, who stood up against the scum, the filth, the deadheads." It's the paradoxical nature of Travis Bickle's character that allows a wider range of society to identify with his utterly illegal and reprehensible actions. It's easy to forget that he exalts women as madonnas at the same time as he cultivates his loneliness in a porno theatre. It's easy to forget that he's a bit thick, yet he's extremely cunning when dealing with authority. He's sensitive, occasionally charming, doesn't smoke, seldom drinks, never has sex. A fundamentalist without a scripture? Certainly. But he's also a sociopath with a diary... and a taxi, and a gun. Imagine this film without Bernard Herrmann's score. The music tracks Bickle's manic mood swings in sudden downward glissandos and floating sax allegros that recall the atmospherics of prime Hitchcock thrillers. Despite the excellent acting and direction, the movie would be a non-sequitur without it. It fits as subtext, counter-points Bickle's voice-over diary, and the occasional lazy real-time dialogue improvs. A hippy pimp from a commune. A child prostitute who measures time with a burning cigarette. A deranged man who screams "I'll kill you, I'll kill you" as he lunges anonymously down a crowded sidewalk.

A cabbie trying to sell a tile from Errol Flynn's bath tub. Lots of contradictions, alright—just like this movie and its message.

PART FIVE:

The Italians

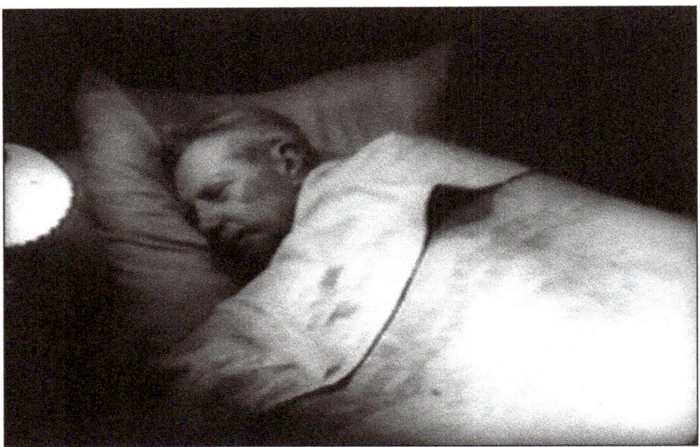

Vittoria de Sica: *Umberto D.*

Umberto D. (1952) dir. Vittorio de Sica writ. Zavattini and Sica cine. G.R. Aldo star. Carlo Battisti (Umberto) Maria Pia Castilio (the maid) Lina Gennari (the landlady)

This is a very sad film, falsely criticized for its sentimentality by the political status quo of the time in Italy. The story is about a retired civil servant Umberto D. Ferrari and his dog Flick who are evicted from their Roman pension by a self-absorbed landlady because he has fallen behind with his rent. Forced into the streets, the elderly pensioner feigns illness in order to live rent-free in hospital, tries street begging but lacks the resolve, contemplates—even tries—suicide, but his beloved dog distracts him from the explosive passage of the express train.

This powerful narrative in the classic social realist style has a universal application regardless of period or cultural setting. The loneliness of the aged and their marginalization in society is still a problem in affluent industrial states, regardless of social welfare and political paternalism. Perhaps it's a mechanism of Nature, although Sica and Zavattini certainly seem to place the blame for Umberto's plight on the Italian government.

The opening shot of a tolling bell and the marching pensioners to a spontaneous demonstration is certainly a political act, as is their quick route and dispersion by the army. There's a sad comedy in this opening scene which in turn establishes the melancholy pattern for the rest of the film. Many scenes are coolly ironic, while others are outright farcical.

When he tries to use the Catholic hospital as a free boarding house, he ingratiates himself with the supervising nun by asking for a rosary (on the advice of the experienced hustler in the next bed) and is allowed to stay despite the doctors' recognition that he's faking it. When he tries begging, he puts his cap in Flick's mouth, then conceals himself behind a pillar and watches as the dog sits obediently on the sidewalk waiting for the largesse of the passing citizens.

But like the clowns at the circus, nothing Umberto does turns out right. He returns to his room, finds the landlady has rented it by the hour to illicit lovers; he returns to his room, finds the landlady has gutted it for a major renovation. He abandons his dog, later saves it from the gas chamber; he abandons his dog, but the dog quickly finds him in the street.

The routine of abandonment and reconciliation is a continual motif within the film. His only friend, the pretty maid Maria, is abandoned by her lover(s) (is it the man from Naples or is it the man from Florence?). Like Umberto, she is also a victim of the times and society's attitudes.

Pregnant, facing an uncertain future, her condition is symbolic of the State's indifference to the well-being of the weak. Umberto's parting words to her are, "Give up the man from Florence." One gets the feeling that there is a veiled ellipsis in this reference.

There are a number of notable scenes, including the Animal Pound when Umberto recovers Flick and saves the hapless mongrel from certain death, or there is the stunning attempted suicide at the climax. In a final attempt at solving his dilemma, Umberto tries to give away Flick (pronounced "fly-k") to a little girl who is playing in the park but her young, vital parents intervene, say no.

Umberto tries to walk away, crosses a bridge... but Flick follows, finds him by the tracks, jumps into his arms. The train whistle howls, the express blows past as man and dog are bisected in shadow and light, as if framed in transition between this world and the next.

It's a brilliantly conceived and executed piece of film, one of the greatest sequences ever, anywhere.

The dog escapes and Umberto totters back over the footbridge into the park where he finds Flick hiding behind a tree, suspicious of his master's intentions. But Umberto lures the dog out with a familiar routine and the film ends with the man and his dog gamboling into the distance as if happily reconciled to each other and their very uncertain fate.

It's largely a silent film in real time with action and few words. The soundtrack is mostly ambient—street traffic, ambiguous industry, and beautifully—in Umberto's lodgings—the operatic *soiree* the landlady conducts in her chambers. It's a monochromatic world of shadow and half-light, often evening and dawn locales rendered in the black and white film stock typical of the neo-realist period.

Despite the strict naturalism of the action, there are some interesting images with metaphoric or ironic possibilities: the cat on the skylight above the maid's bed, Umberto's gold watch, the "dog hotel", the express train, etc. The juxtapositions of humans and buildings is continually ironic in terms of past, present and future.

Even the dialogue has occasional sub-text: "Take him (Umberto) to see yesterday's dogs," says the Pound official to a worker.

What is there to criticize about this film?

Nothing.

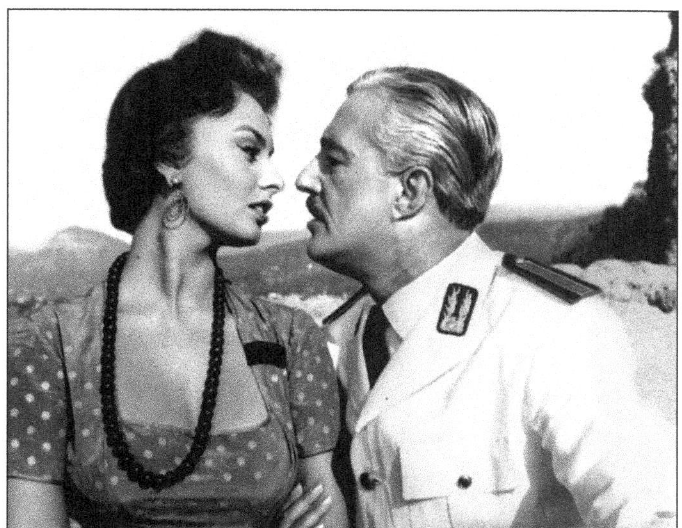

Vittorio de Sica: *Two Women*

Two Women (La Ciociara, 1960) dir. Vittorio de Sica writ. Zavattini and Sica (based on the novel by Alberto Moravia) cine. Gabor Pogany star. Sophia Loren (Cestra), Eleanora Brown (Rossetta), Jean-Paul Belmondo (Michele), Raf Vallone (Giovanni)

The uneven dynamic of the narrative is due, perhaps, to the neo-realist aesthetic of linear time. Given that the action occurs over several months in 1944 during the Allied advance into Italy, and the desire to protect the integrity of Moravia's story, the action is episodic rather than integrated, flattened rather than dramatic. However, the film is saved by the outstanding performance of Sophia Loren as the widowed shop-keeper who leaves Rome and returns to her native village in order to spare her daughter from the bombing of Rome... and, of course, a number of scenes shot in the de Sica/Zavattini trademark style.

The story begins with an Allied attack on Rome, and the fear and chaos that the bombing brings. Eager to protect her young daughter Rosetta from the violence and horror, Cestra (Loren) decides to pass the care of her shop and property to an adjacent fuel merchant (and friend of her deceased husband).

The deal is sealed, typically, with a sex act in Giovanni's sunken coal cellar. The isometrics of the light and shadow are typical de Sica as is the ambient sound (children playing, traffic). Giovanni casually shuts the side door (closing off the light) and then the overhead dump door from the street (again closing off the light) before he climbs onto the widow of his best friend in a friendly Italian manner.

> Cestra: Giovanni... think about your wife.
> Giovanni: I wish a bomb would fall on her so I could marry you....

He sees her off on the train but the train doesn't get far because the tracks have been bombed. The widow and her daughter decide to walk the rest of the way to San Eufemia, the village of her kin. In a portent of things to come, the women are strafed by a passing fighter plane. They survive but witness the death of an elderly cyclist from whom they've just taken directions.

They find their mountain village (the daughter is fondled by a couple of low-level fascists en route) and altho' the near-relatives have left, they manage to secure a place to sleep for a month. Here they meet the young socialist Michele (Belmondo), the idealist who initially wanted to be a priest. His disgust and loathing for the confused and demoralized condition that Italy finds itself in comes out in a number of lines, most acutely in, "The uncivilized people are in the cities... they are the evil ones... the peasants could build a new society...." Etc. When Loren says that escape is possible, that they are safe here in San Eufemia, he replies, "There is no escape. You can't even escape from yourself."

Of course the village turns out to be no refuge at all. Italian fascists, British spies, German soldiers all pass through as the chaos of the war develops. The news of Mussolini's imprisonment comes from two angry fascists who threaten Cestra, Rossetta, and Michele on a mountain path. Michele is attracted to Cestra, and again, during a bombing attack, she finds herself in the arms of a man. Although the symbolism of the spilled flour suggests sexual completion, the editing of the scene leaves the full extent of the love-making ambiguous. Shortly thereafter a hungry and dehydrated group of German soldiers stumble into the village and abduct Michele as their guide. He's herded into the mountain mist, never to be seen again. Cestra decides to return to Rome. The day is hot, the road dusty, jeeps and tanks occasionally pass. The women look for shade in a bombed-out church which is where they experience the full indignity and degradation that often happens in war: they are raped by some Moroccan (Allied) soldiers. The final shot (overhead) shows a bomb crater in the middle of the chapel, a black spot that is a metaphor for the horror and the failure that has overtaken the mother and child... and perhaps the failure of Italy's institutions.

The rape places a wedge between Cestra and Rosetta. In the beginning, they were mother and daughter; now they are two women. There is a reconciliation, but only after Rosetta briefly runs off with an Italian truck driver and "singer".

"You can't even escape from yourself," says Cestra in despair, repeating Michele's line. The closing shot is a pull-back through a hole-in-the-wall, isolating the mother and daughter as they embrace, their misfortune no doubt typical of many.

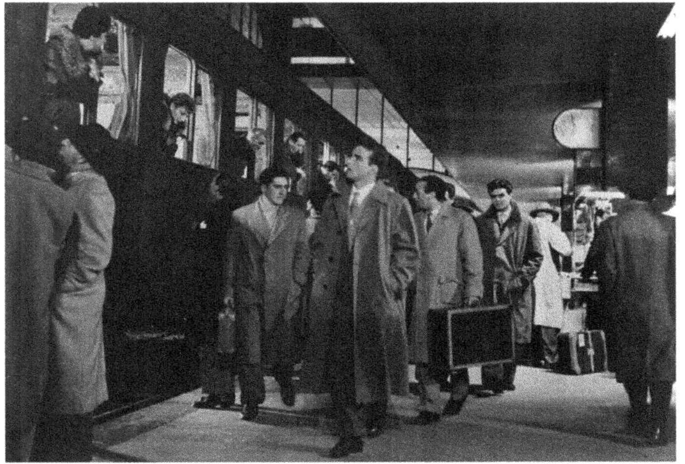

Vittorio de Sica: *Indiscretion of an American Wife*

Indiscretion of an American Wife (Stazione Termini, 1953) dir. Vittorio de Sica, adapted from the story *Terminal Station* by Cesare Zavattini, dialogue by Truman Capote. star. Jennifer Jones (Maria), Montgomery Clift (Giovanni)

The American version was (apparently) severely edited and the title changed without de Sica's permission. Perhaps Selznick, who put up some of the money, thought it would be confused with Coward's *Brief Encounter*, another love-on-the-run story set in a railway station. There's no denying that *Indiscretion* has more of a bite and gives the film a lurid appeal that it doesn't warrant. Now, maybe if a remake were to be set in an airport with some hot sex and American feminism under examination, well then the title could be made to live up to its sub-text.

As it stands, the "indiscretion" is entirely oblique as per 1950's mores. When Maria (Jones) and her lover Giovanni (Clift) are discovered by the railway police in the first-class compartment of a side-lined carriage, they aren't naked, and they aren't going at it, although the implication is that they were.

The plot is simple and the action is close to real time. Maria, a housewife from Philadelphia with relatives in Rome, decides to return to the States suddenly, hoping to put an end to her brief affair with an Italian academic, Giovanni Doria.

Set entirely within the modernist rectilinearity of the Rome railway station, the movement of the crowd is constantly framed by reversing diagonals within the familiar play of light and shadow as favored by the neo-realist cinematographers. It's against this continuously changing chorus of humanity that Maria and Giovanni act out their sexual pantomime.

> Giovanni: What am I? Some Guide Book you don't want anymore?

This statement is the key to the understanding of the power reversal in the male-female relationships of the era. America is the dominant power and its women use foreign men like men use women in Italy... evidently. Furious at being walked-out on, it's Giovanni who slaps Maria, not she who slaps him.

In many ways, it's the spectacle, the incidental characters who are merely passing by that carry this drama. Four priests ordering "four cups of tea", a well-dressed woman and her toy dog, singing football fans, soldiers, business men, railway workers... the movement of the public through the marble concourses of the station.

There are two remarkable photographic scenes: one, when Maria and her nephew Paul are taking refuge behind a pillar following the "slap", and two, when Maria and Giovanni are being led to the Station Commissioner's office and their shadows elongate as they ascend the staircase to answer to their "crime".

The social criticism, of course, is based on the hypocrisy of the situation. Italian males like to be seen as lovers but conversely want to be as pure as priests. This paradox of gigolo and moral ceremony is evidenced by the smirking men and the gossip that follows the lovers as they are "arrested" and taken in. The short, humiliating interrogation by the Commissioner is reminiscent of truants facing a school Principal. While he has the wisdom and humanity to let them go, his gesture is really an expulsion, not an acquittal.

Maria and Giovanni are allowed to leave, walk together to the train. He sees her to her compartment, and they exchange more fevered expressions of love eternal. As the train starts to move, Giovanni falls from the door to the platform. A man helps him up, asks "Are you hurt?"

As with all good writing and direction, we are left with only the characters to criticize, not the reality of their actions.

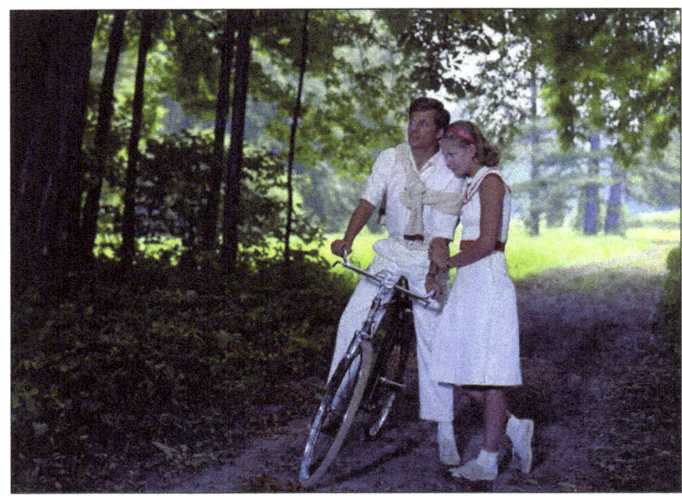

Vittorio De Sica: *The Garden of the Finzi-Continis*

The Garden of the Finzi-Continis (1971) dir. Vittorio De Sica, writ. Ugo Pirro & Vittorio Bonicelli (from the novel by Giorgio Bassini), cine. Ennio Guarnieri, edt. Adriana Novelli, music Manuel De Sica
star. Lino Capolicchio (Giorgio), Dominique Sanda (Micol), Helmut Berger (Alberto), Fabio Testi (Malnate), Romolo Valli, Camillo Cesarei, *et. al.*

Summer, 1938. Ferraro, a town mid-way between Venice and Bologna, perhaps best-known as a former duchy of the Borgias. A group of young Italians have just been invited to a tennis tournament in the splendiferous walled garden estate of the Finzi-Continis, a family of reclusive Jewish patricians.

As the group waits for the gate to be opened, the question of why they have suddenly been honored with this invitation comes up. "We can thank our Fascists for the privilege," says one. In fact, Micol Finzi-Continis and her brother Alberto have just been expelled by the local Tennis Club. But these competing agendas seem like minor social politics as the group cycles leisurely along the meandering avenue below the ancient trees. They're young, beautiful, dressed in tennis white, laughing and chattering as they ride their black Italian bicycles... except for one, whose bicycle is red. This is Malnate, a university friend of Alberto Finzi-Continis, now living in town as an industrial manager. You soon learn that he considers himself a communist.

The centre-piece of the action is really the imagined romance between Micol and Giorgio, a childhood friend who lives just down the street, a young Jewish man with poetic aspirations also in the process of completing his degree. Giorgio's family is also wealthy but not on intimate terms with the Finzi-Continis. As his father bitterly sees it, "They basically welcome the anti-Semitic laws... with their broad smiles, low bows... and the garden finally opened to everyone... converted into a ghetto under their noble patronage." A merchant, he's also a member of the Fascist Party, and stubbornly believes that Mussolini is no Adolf Hitler. Initially, you think he's deluded, although it gradually becomes obvious his actions are defensive, and he has clear insight into his son's abortive romance and the deteriorating situation that it ironically mirrors.

Giorgio seems tight with Micol. Everyone expects them to get engaged, although their contact has been sporadic as she has been studying in Venice. She sits on the handlebars of his bike, they tour the garden, get reacquainted. She points to a tree, says, "That plane tree... could've been planted by Lucrezia Borgia. Imagine! It's nearly 500 years old...." This reference to the Borgias is both a clue to the symbolism of the setting and Micol's complex and contradictory personality. She's beautiful, she's clever... and she's cruel. Her thesis, she says, is on the American poet Emily Dickinson, but somehow you know she has more in common with Lucrezia Borgia.

It starts to rain, the tournament suspended as everyone runs off. Micol and Giorgio take shelter in an old building now used to store a car and an old horse carriage, the one she rode in to the synagog with her mother and grandmother in the days of her childhood flirtation with the naive Giorgio. She invites him to sit in the carriage with her. "I feel like I'm a woman," she says, looking him in the eyes. Her pet, a great Dane called Jor, suddenly appears, sticks his face in the open window as if he has been sent by her parents... or their manservant... or her brother... or... who knows? The dog—who always seems to be where she will be—becomes symbolism, elusive, part of Micol's mystery.

Impassioned and encouraged, Giorgio puts his hand on Micol's bare thigh... but she rebuffs him, slips out of the carriage, disappears in the rain and the lush blur of Nature in the Finzi-Continis garden. Poor Giorgio! While he can read the signs of the impending diaspora, he simply can't read Micol. In a childhood flashback scene, she invites him to climb into her garden using the "nails" she has inserted into the wall. Still, her rejection seems merely part of the game, and at her invitation, Giorgio calls on her again, only to discover that she has returned to Venice to finish her thesis.

This setback is one of two: Giorgio is told he can no longer use the university library as a consequence of Mussolini's enactment of the anti-Semitic laws. He turns to the Finzi-Continis, is allowed to use their extensive private library. As Micol's father says, "We have everything they have... a bit more selective perhaps." On the desk is a photograph of Micol. Strangely, Giorgio has yet to realize that she's carrying on an affair with Malnate.

Meanwhile her brother Alberto remains secluded in the estate, bedridden and slowly dying of consumption. His condition is a direct barometer of the condition of the Jewish community in Ferrara.

The futility of Giorgio's love for Micol is like the collective futility of his community in its love for Italy... or their religious icons. Within the simplicity of the action, there is a vast complexity of social and psychological politics at play here. The villain is depersonalized, a chimera of crooked hope as represented in propaganda newsreels and disembodied public address broadcasts. You expect a traitor in their midst, a Mussolini in embryo, but de Sica chooses an oblique approach, appealing to the collective guilt of his fellow Italians. The beauty of the "garden" is the beauty of Italy, and the slow movement of evil is like the coming of winter, when the Finzi-Continis estate is invaded by snow, then police, and the family is finally rounded up for deportation.

The elegance of it all is stunning, like a total eclipse of the sun... and nothing is left but the inhuman symmetry. The camera seems to float in the dazzling diffusions of light, harmonizing with the melancholy score and the intrigues of the doomed. Like an art exhibit, a generation is cancelled to suit a political agenda. Even Malnate, the outspoken Marxist friend of Alberto and Giorgio is killed on the Russian front—as an Aryan, he was not barred from the armed forces like his Jewish friends. Oddly, everyone looks Aryan, the exclusivity of their pale bourgeois complexions oddly in harmony with the fascist racial ideal.

De Sica's films have always dealt with human isolation, and the agony of withdrawal. In *Umberto D.* a retired veteran and civil servant is forced into poverty and homelessness within Il Duce's fascist society. In *Two Women* a mother and daughter are forced to flee Rome and wander the countryside as refugees. False paternalism and the victimization of the innocent are his recurrent themes. Like Pirandello, his situations appear simple, yet contain a complexity of symbolisms that are both supernatural and political, sexual and cultural, tragic and comic.

There's always hope within a De Sica situation, an appreciation of the cyclical nature of human affairs. Giorgio may have lost in love, but it's just possible that he escapes to live another day. As his father says to him (about his rejection by Micol), "In life... to understand the world, you must die at least once. So it's better to die young when there's still time to recover and live again...." You know he's speaking from experience when he retires to his room alone... and you know, too, that he's anticipating the future.

The Garden of the Finzi-Continis was awarded the Oscar for the Best Foreign Film in 1971. De Sica would only make one more film, *The Voyage*, released in 1973.

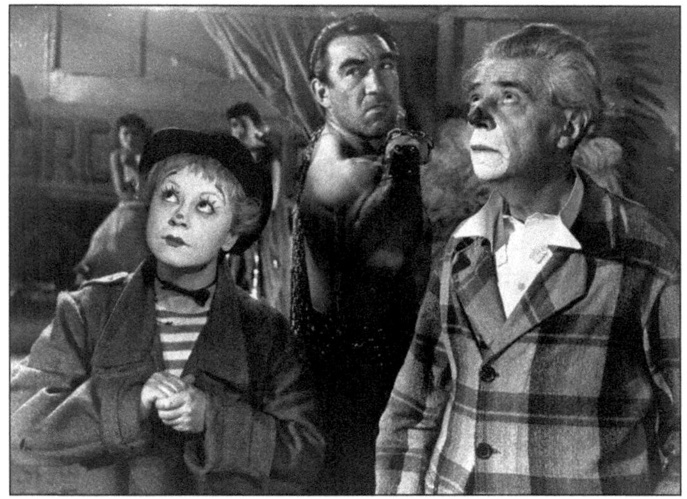

Frederico Fellini: *La Strada*

La Strada (*The Road*), 1954 dir. Frederico Fellini writ. Fellini, Tullio Penelli, Ennio Flaiano cine. Otello Martelli music Nino Rota star. Giulietta Masina (Gelsomina), Anthony Quinn (Zampano), Richard Baseheart (The Fool), Aldo Silvani, Marcello Revere, Liva Venturini

Fellini says this film isn't neo-realism but if it isn't, what is it? It certainly has that look—a linear-time narrative in gritty black and white whose itinerant characters exist in a world of squalor and fatal consequence. It starts with Gelsomina (Masina) being sold by her mother to the "strolling player" Zampano (Quinn) for 10,000 lire as a replacement for her sister Rosa who has died under unexplained circumstances, then follows her shabby career "on the road" as the strongman's assistant, slave, and bogus wife in a series of realistic scenes that mark the beast and exalt the innocent. Zampano's profession of gypsy-artist and circus performer really belongs to another time, another century, as do his values. He performs his trick of expanding his lungs and chest to break a girdle of chain in waste lots, yards and grubby circus rings in a simple Promethean fable of Man breaking free but his personal world depends upon the abuse and slavery of others.

> Mother: Take care of her...
> Zampano: Sure—I even teach dogs.

> "...for me (La Strada) became real when I drew the circle on paper that was Gelsomina's head" (Fellini)

Gelsomina is as simple-minded as a pet, although she has the innocence of a child with the human need for love and recognition. Although she is willing to go away with Z., confident that she can succeed as a performer, she is soon broken by his womanizing and containment of her artistic ambition. She can sing but her favorite melody is an annoyance to Z. She runs away from him, follows three musicians into a town where an Easter parade is underway. That evening she witnesses a tightrope walker performing his act above an enthralled mob in the square. Z. later recovers her from some tormenting drunks and she wakes up the next morning in a circus encampment. This is where she meets The Fool (Baseheart) who is playing her melody on a violin in the tent and recognizes him as the tightrope walker.

This melody, which is the basis of the sound score, represents the bond that exists instinctively between Gelsomina and The Fool who has had a previous run-in with "Gummy" (Zampano's character in the duck-hunter sketch) and proceeds to taunt him. He seduces Gelsomina, and although he gives her his necklace, he sends her back to Z. who has been briefly jailed for trying to knife The Fool. When The Fool is later killed by Z. in an assault intended to humiliate rather than eliminate, his death fulfills his own earlier prediction. Z. dumps the body in a gully, then rolls The Fool's car after him in an attempt to disguise the murder as Gelsomina watches and wails inconsolably.

Cut To: winter in a frozen, dreary town. Z. performs his chain-act to a small crowd but distracted, Gelsomina is unable to provide the drum roll. They travel a narrow road through the snowy mountains. Z. pulls his truck into the lee of a ruin, sets up camp. But Gelsomina remains desperate and broken, falls asleep beside a wall. Z. decides to abandon her and in a sentimental gesture, leaves the trumpet beside her before rolling his truck down the road and slipping away....

Cut To: Z. performing his chain-act in a circus on the beach. Afterwards he strolls the promenade, buys an ice-cream, then hears a woman humming Gelsomina's melody as she hangs out her washing. Z. approaches her, learns that the woman picked it up from a "crazy woman" who came to town and one morning didn't wake up.... Disturbed, Z. visits a bar, gets drunk, fights in the street between a fork in the train tracks, then ends up on the beach where he collapses in misery and remorse on the edge of the surf. He raises his eyes heavenwards as if following the transit of Gelsomina's soul or the Hound of Hell.

The action is tedious at times, with observable lip-sync problems caused by using American actors in an Italian script and Fellini's preference for dialogue dubbing. The uneducated characters are perhaps devices of a conveniently determinist universe, easy to manipulate, even easier to judge. Yet there's a historical authenticity in the milieu and a metaphor in the story of players in the world rather than in the theatre. Masina plays Chaplin into her character rather obviously, but it's undeniably effective in supporting Fellini's stated intention of creating an innocent betrayed.

You can certainly see the roots of Fellini's later move into cinematic expressionism—not in the structure, but in his choice of characters and subject. A strongman escapes his chains, a Fool walks a tightrope... and their version of society is a circus.

Because absurdist theatre is so often a play within a play—without revealing one or the other—the action is always a mimicry of something hidden or something anticipated. Thus Zampano and Gelsomina are like animals, performing simple tricks with ceremonial intent and human possibility, but disconnected from society. Like the abandoned tramp/clowns in *Waiting For Godot*, they can leave the circus, but the circus doesn't leave them.

La Strada starts on the beach, and ends on the beach in a circular motion between being and nothingness. Zampano's contrition might satisfy the Pope, but the true extent of his guilt extends beyond his blunder with The Fool into the enigma of Rosa... and the death of Gelsomina.

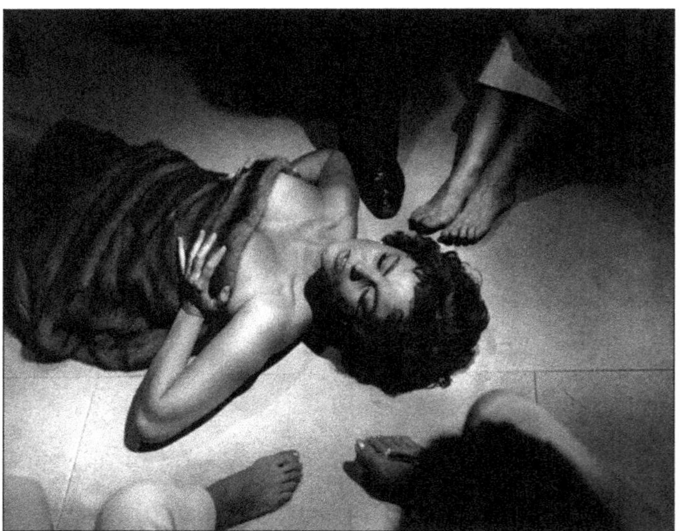

Frederico Fellini: *La Dolce Vita*

La Dolce Vita, 1960 dir. Frederico Fellini writ. Fellini, Flaiano, Pinelli cine. Otello Martelli music Nino Rota Star Marcello Mastrianni (Marcello), Anouk Aimee (Maddalena), Walter Santesso (Paparazzo), Yvonne Furneaux (Emma), Anita Ekberg (Sylvia), Lex Barker (Robert), Alain Cuny (Steiner), Annibale Ninchi (Marcello's father), Nadia Gray (Stripper), Valerie Ciangotti (Paola, the innocent)

There aren't many opening sequences that match this one: a helicopter flies over a broken Roman viaduct, a statue of Christ suspended below its fuselage like an effigy from a cargo cult. A second helicopter shadows it, bearing a journalist and his photographer. Their journey is not only a mission for the Vatican but also a progression through Time. They fly over ancient ruins, then over construction sites and the new cluster housing units on the edge of the city before closing on St.

Peter's Square. The journalists linger briefly above a rooftop patio where some pretty women are sunbathing, engage in a brief flirtation with shouts and sign language as the chopper hovers. The women want to know where they are taking the statue. Where else—to the Pope. It's this atmosphere of religious cynicism and cultivated decadence that drives *La Dolce Vita*. The heresy isn't a political articulation but rather one of indifference. At the core of the movie is the suicide of Steiner, musician and intellectual, which marks the collapse of contemporary culture like an abyss between the secular left and the religious right. And it's along this abyss that Marcello, gossip columnist of the rich and famous, charts his rite of passage in a determined attempt to remain a child disguised as a man.

Marcello lives for sensation, evades commitment. He's always on the move in his chic little English sports car between trendy Roman sidewalk bistros and nightclubs, seldom at his apartment which remains undecorated and unfurnished in an obvious expression of his spiritual indifference. When he writes, he writes in empty cafes. When he loves, he loves in the flooded basement suite of a prostitute or in the darkness of a ruined villa. His women are transitional, secular icons of the affluent world he covers, fantasies of the moment, patterns in the night.

> "I like lots of things, but there are three things I like most: love, love... and love." (Sylvia the movie star at her press conference)

His live-in girlfriend Emma overdoses on sleeping pills but is saved when he races her to hospital, has her stomach pumped. But he might as well not have bothered, as he continues to neglect her in his continuous drift through the socials and press assignments that become parties, ambiguous destinations in a false reality. He pursues the visiting American/Scandinavian filmstar Sylvia (Ekberg) into a bell tower, into a fountain, but their brief affair comes to nothing. He visits the scene of a Madonna vision, endures the reenactment for the media and a rain storm, but no miracle is forthcoming. He talks with Steiner about the meaning of life but Steiner kills his two children, shoots himself in the head. His pursuit of sensation is degenerative, climaxes at a drunken party in the seaside villa of a movie producer—another agent of fantasy. The revellers are a collection of thespian drifters, queens, artists, international party animals drawn together on the thin excuse of celebrating Nadia's "annulment". The metaphor of separation continues. Marcello—wearing a white suit like some sort of secular priest—is the ringmaster of the dissipation, urging the guests into exhibitionism. Nadia performs a striptease, but even this isn't enough. Marcello offers to perform public sex but the best he can do is ride a woman like donkey. He throws bottles, smashes furniture, rags pillows, throws chunks of chicken over the naked shoulders and breasts of a woman.

"Maybe One Day We'll All Be Homosexual..."

The scene is pathetic, like the infantile defiance of adolescents smearing excrement over tombstones. The producer returns home, expels this rabble from his villa, some migrating through the woods to the beach where some fishermen have caught a "sea monster". Marcello and the others watch as it's hauled onto the beach, a membranous blob with a single eye that seems to be alive, maybe scrutinizing them. Are they looking at themselves in the prehistoric past? The image is Darwinian, secular, a dramatic denial of the false miracle of the Madonna. "Maybe one day we'll all be homosexual," babbles one of the Queens in an unrelated observation. But, in fact, it is related, as Fellini is the master of oblique innuendo.

Someone is calling Marcello. Further down the beach a girl is waving. He walks towards her but is stopped by a small river that separates them. It's Paola, the young "innocent" from the cafe where Marcello sometimes goes to write. They try to communicate but the surf is too loud, a primal noise that divides them as effectively as a child leaving the womb. Marcello smiles, waves, turns away... leaving it all behind.

The "it"—the indefinite article—has the plastic possibilities of several meanings. As symbolism, this sequence is brilliant, resolving the two primary themes of religious disbelief and secular solipsism. Marcello is the Modern Man, unable to believe, unable to commit, a lost child in the body of a monster. "We live in a state of suspended animation... like a work of art."

Steiner's suicide is pivotal. Is Man the only animal for whom suicide is an option? Is it a detachment from God? Or is it merely another part of the mechanism that binds us within the cosmic plan. Steiner appears to have it all: a beautiful wife and two beautiful children, an upscale condo and the favor of the Church. His "party" includes an intellectual elite of international and local artists and thinkers. He has "committed", yet he is another version of Marcello. "I'm too serious to be an amateur, and not serious enough to be a professional." He urges Marcello to get serious about his writing, move beyond these "semi-fascist scandal sheets". The guests listen to a tape montage of Nature: birds, wind, water, rain, thunder. They also tape their conversations, creating instant "art". "Art," says Steiner, "has left nothing to chance." This avant-garde milieu appears to be the summit of mid-century culture... yet Steiner is a troubled man.

He suffers from nuclear anxiety, the fragility of life in the Cold War. He is cosmopolitan, yet Italianate, a contradiction of principles. He dotes on his children, blesses them as they sleep like a parody of the Pope. That he later kills them so that they will be with him in his transcendental sleep is an act of religious arrogance as much as it is a gesture of secular despair. He consigns his wife to Hell in order that he may be free. Later the investigating Detectives listen to his taped conversation, Dialogue Between Feminine Wisdom and Masculine Uncertainty as Steiner sits nearby, leaning forward as if in rapture, the bullet hole clearly evident in the side of his temple.

Each side of the abyss has separate but inevitable routes to loneliness, despair and death. Marcello investigates the scene of the miracle sighting of the Virgin but when the stampeding crowd has finished, only the corpse of a trampled man remains in the mud. In the ruined villa adjoining the castle, a possessed woman at a seance moans, "I want to love... life, everything there is..." but minutes later his mistress Maddalena cheats on him after proposing marriage through a wall like a spirit. When he confronts his prehistoric self on the beach, can he be anything other than an apostate? Religion is the denial, art is the testament.

Night. Marcello and Emma sit in his sports car, arguing:

> Emma: You'll end up alone, like an animal—
> you'll see!

Marcello: I hate your selfishness... it's not love, it's animalism!

She bites his hand as he drags her from the car, then drives off. He returns at dawn, finds her still pacing, a bunch of flowers in her hand. They reconcile... for the moment. Marcello's not a bad man, even if he lacks character. His flaw is rooted in the mid-century sickness, that is, the redefinition of the supernatural by science. He's a victim of paranoia, a species on the verge of self-extinction. He thinks he has free-will, yet moves like an automaton. Soon the world will be full of people like him, child-men driven by cynicism, always on the move or waiting for something to happen. The film opens with a statue of Christ, closes with an ingenue version of the Virgin. The heresy is sublime, coded in the imagery—but who is to say it isn't the truth? Fellini is never monolithic, propaganda. Yet like Shakespeare, there's a sense that the genius of Fellini is not the genius of a single mind. While the Fellini "style" is clearly evident, you wonder how much of its intellectual fabric comes from his main writing collaborator, the novelist Ennio Flaiano.

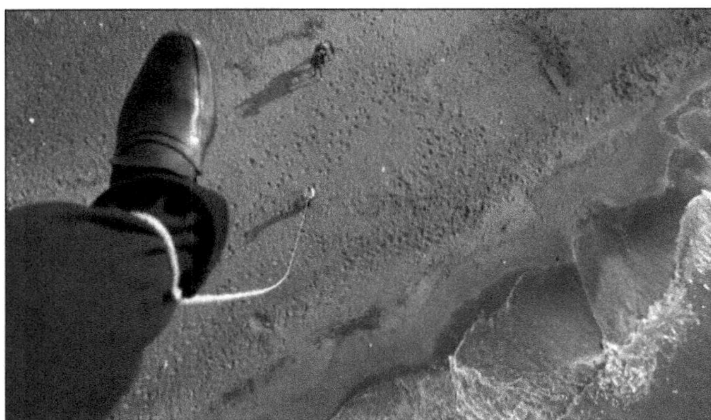

Frederico Fellini: *Otto e Mezzo*

8½ (*Otto e Mezzo*) 1963 dir. Frederico Fellini writ. Fellini, Flaiano, Pennelli, Rondi cine. Gianni di Vernanzo music Nino Rota star. Marcello Mastroianni (Guido/Director), Anouk Aimee (Luisa/wife), Sandra Milo (Carla/mistress), Edia Gale (La Saraghina), Guido Alberti (Producer), Claudia Cardinale (Claudia) *et. al.*

In 1963 autobiographical expressionism wasn't new in literature or the plastic arts but in feature films it was unheard of, thought impossible because: 1. film is a collaborative art, 2. film costs so much money. But due to the international success of *La Dolce Vita* Fellini was able to gain the necessary *carte blanche* to make a film on the highly personal theme of an artist who makes films and is confronted by writer's block. Fellini was able to extend his symbolisms into a narrative that alternates between the exterior and interior worlds of the protagonist Guido (Mastroianni) without warning, presenting an integrated reality of past and present—even the future, perhaps—but within the usual beginning, middle and end narrative structure.

"It was self-centered of me, I suppose, not only that my own ideas seemed more attractive to me, as our own ideas seem attractive to all of us, but I believed I could carry them out with greater feeling, I could stay with them and give them a unity because they were born of me, and I could achieve the greatest understanding and intimacy with my characters." Drama requires crisis and *8½* starts with one: Guido suffers a claustrophobia attack when he finds himself trapped in his car in a tunnel during rush hour. As he claws at the windows, watched by the impassive passengers in the other stalled vehicles, he astralizes and floats clear of his car and the tunnel until he is over the beach, anchored by a rope as if he is a kite. Then, in the classic anxiety dream-fall, he crashes towards the beach....

Cut To: a doctor's office where Guido is being tested.

Doctor: Well, what are you working on now? Another film without hope? Now you recognize that Fellini is slyly creating an autobiographical commentary on his previous work as well as presenting the universal artist confronting a guilty past within a confusing present. Soon Guido is consulting with his writing collaborator, his producer, his cast, his mistress and various incidental characters at a health spa which also shares time and space with the film studio... and incidents from his past as well as his dreams and fantasies.

The doctor recommends 300 milligrams of mineral water every day before breakfast and every second day a mud bath. The Spa is sited at a spring which is to be the opening sequence in his film. Meanwhile the elderly and the infirmed line up for this elixir in a continual confluence of theatrical possibilities with his cast and family. Guido's older friend Mario is there with his young mistress, his folly a more advanced case than his own, a biological anomaly between the sexes, institutionalized in Italy but here presented as part of the multiple personae of the artist rather than a chauvinist double-standard. Guido meets his own mistress at the railway station, although her materialization is as much an erotic dream as it is a literal event. At the Spa, his "collaborator" harangues him about the script:

Collaborator: This film is merely a series of senseless episodes... oh, their ambiguous realism is perhaps quite amusing... but what is the writer's real intention? To make us think? To frighten us?

Again, this elliptical commentary fits perfectly with Fellini's own experience and the actual film you are watching. This sort of personalism, where the play within becomes the real structure, and the play without a dismantling of the old determinist model, is both existential and revolutionary. It abandons the fixed certainties of a religious universe in favour of the uncertain topographies of a psychological one where dreams and trauma shape the soul of the individual. Guido is often in narrow spaces, hotel corridors, tunnels, between buildings... even a cemetery where the ancient walls enclose a pasture that seems more like a forgotten roadway between past and present. Here he meets his mother at his dead father's tomb... his father, in the bizarre logic of dream, is inspecting his own tomb. As they part, his father shakes his hand, sinks into the ground and disappears in a surreal event as natural as the propitious arrival of the Producer and Mario. Ergo: Guido might be dreaming in the arms of Carla or postulating a scene in the film he assembled this cast to make.

And so it goes. There are a number of amusing scenes which make no political distinction between dream and actuality, memory and the status quo. The Catholic Church is satirized, criticized, even chastised. Guido submits his script for approval, but the Cardinal says "I don't believe film is the proper medium for some subjects". In the long sequence in the steam baths,

Guido's friends and associates exhort him prostrate himself before the Cardinal and he does... but the Cardinal simply says "There is no salvation outside the Church". The window closes on the Cardinal's private steam room, effectively shutting Guido out. "I was a little shocked when I saw on a church door a poster that had my name on it that had a black border... the poster said, 'Let us pray for the salvation of the soul of Frederico Fellini, public sinner.'" The Church and trauma: the Seraghina episode is Fellini's payback. The boy Guido and his friends visit a coarse voluptuary known as The Seraghina and give her a few coins to dance for them. Seraghina comes out of her cave—an abandoned concrete gun box on the beach—and performs on the sand. She is swarthy and obese, yet retains the vestiges of her sexuality and the desire for attention, even if it is only a boy's. She vamps, she shakes her boobs, she shimmies... and a couple of priests from the school show up in pursuit of the truants. They are hauled back to school and Guido is selected for special punishment by the tribunal of Holy Brothers—to the chants of "For Shame!" he is forced to wear a conical dunce's hat in the company of his classmates. It's a great sequence, photographed in that familiar Fellini imagery, humans as performers, life as a circus.

Is the film too long? Yes. Guido's condition cannot be resolved, unless by suicide or by accident... and this fatalism isn't in Fellini's world-view. By the time Guido is faced by a revolt of the women in his "harem" and he quells it with a whip—like an animal trainer—the action has already reached a *cul de sac* of analysis and counter-analysis, symbolism and contradiction. Despite the secular heresies along the way, Fellini is merely a neo-Catholic who reinvents the nightmare of his histrionic paternalism (as Director, lover, family man and hypochondriac) into a *c'est la vie* fatalism that allows him to avoid compromise and get past the ethical considerations that go with the job.

"Having always loved the circus, I saw the resemblance between movies and the circus. As a boy, my greatest dream would have been to be the director of a circus. I love the fantasy and the sense of improvisation in both."

The ending is at the launch-pad for the huge rocket that Guido has built, the only tangible evidence that he actually has something "real" that a producer can relate to. The closing sequences are a montage of crowd scenes (the cast of his movie, his family, hangers-on, *et. al.*) around and on the scaffolding that supports this phallic fantasy. Guido holds a press conference, but ignores the questions of the journalists in favour of some head-talk with his wife. Eventually he gets the show on the road, "directs" everyone onto the low perimeter of a circus ring that just happens to be on the sand... and they flow around him like a zoetrope in the dance of life. He links hands with his wife in an apparent reconciliation and they too join the flow....

It's a cluttered conclusion that resolves nothing, a smoke and mirrors montage of psycho-babble dialogue and photo cut-ins which might accurately reflect a day-in-the-life of a movie director but does very little to make sense of the psycho-drama to this point. But—where else could it go? Guido orders the dismantling of the space ship set and the scaffolding begins to fall—just like the determinist structure that is the cladding of all conventional film. Highly original, the first of the mass-market "art" films to succeed. Like many of the great Italian and European Catholic muralists, Fellini's personal symbolism fits perfectly within the orthodoxy some claim he opposes. (The Fellini quotes are from *I, Fellini* by Charlotte Chandler.)

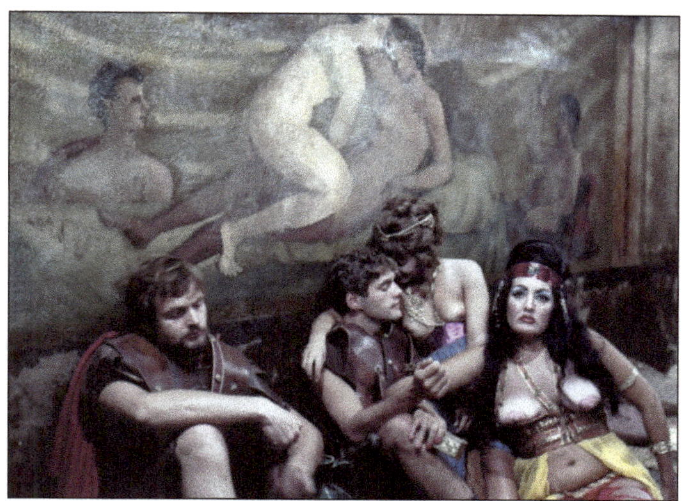

Frederico Fellini: *Fellini Satyricon*

Fellini Satyricon (1969) dir. Frederico Fellini writ. Fellini and Bernardino Zapponi (based on the writings of Petronious) cine. Giuseppe Rotunno sets Danilo Donati and Luigi Caccianoce music Nino Rota, Ilhan Mimaroght, Tod Dockstader, Andrew Rudin star. Martin Potter (Encolpio), Hiram Keller (Ascylite), Max Born (Gitone), Salvo Randone (Eumolpo the Poet), Il Moro (Trimalcione), Magali Noel (Fortunata), Capucine (Trifena), Alain Cuny (Lica), Fanfulla (Vernacchio), Luigi Montefiori (Minotaur), Joseph Wheeler (suicide: Petronius), Lucia Bose (suicide: P's wife), *et. al.*

Figures In A Fresco

The "theatre effect" is often the sign of primitivism in film drama—except when it's Orson Welles or Frederico Fellini. *Satyricon*'s sets are spectacular, neo-modernist constructions that combine both the pictographic art of the past with the angular sensibility of the present. Characters declaim their lines to phantoms beyond the screen or to decadent aristocrats in the burlesques that are frequently featured within the playhouses, feasts, tombs, temples and the other venues that carry the action of this mythical adventure.

The film begins with the "hero" Encolpio (Martin Potter) monologuing in front of a fresco, bemoaning his fate:

> Encolpio: The earth has not dragged me into the abyss... nor has the tempestuous sea engulfed me... I have fled from justice, from the arena... I have even stained my hands with blood... to end up here, banished and abandoned.... Who was it that condemned me to this solitude? He who knows every vice... who himself admits he deserves banishment: Ascylitus!

Who is he speaking to? The obsolete convention of live theatre is resurrected by Fellini in order to break the alienation between the viewer and the subject, thus moving away from the aesthetic of cinematic voyeurism into audience complicity.

It's a clever directive, one which establishes not only the dramatic method but also the visual style. An atmosphere of history is integral to the audience's acceptance of the story. Proceeding as if the world is an art gallery is often the kiss of death in drama, but under Fellini's direction it's a brilliant fugue of modern expressionism and interpretative mythology.

> "In *Satyricon*, I was influenced by the look of frescoes. At the end, these people, whose lives were so real to them, are now only crumbling frescoes." (Fellini)

Encolpio: student, pretty boy bisexual adventurer, and creature of fortune whose present misery is due to the theft of his boy lover Gitone by his friend and fellow student, Ascylitus. We are also introduced to Ascylitus (Hiram Keller) by way of a monologue and quickly learn that he's no sentimentalist:

> Ascylitus: (hoarsely) Encolpio is looking for me, he wants revenge. (gloats) Friendship lasts as long as it is convenient.

They fight, and Encolpio holds Ascylitus's head over a steaming culvert.

> Encolpio: Where is Gitone?
> Ascylitus: (gasping) I sold him to Vernacchio the actor...

Their dispute over the boy-toy Gitone (Max Born) is another one of those peculiar passions that make love an illness, sex a disease. Gitone is a treacherous little ponce whose affections are political rather than spiritual, so we are forced to consider him as a symbol of Encolpio's cruel Fortune. While Encolpio's fascination with Gitone is pathetic, the masochism is part of the complexity of his friendship with A.

> "Because of the picture's open, non-judgemental portrayal of homosexuality, some journalists seized upon the tempting notion that I myself must be a homosexual or at least bisexual...." (Fellini)

In one of the many great scenes, Encolpio confronts Vernacchio (Fanfulla), the actor who bought the boy and is training him for female roles ("Helen of Troy, the faithful Penelope, Cornelia..."). Typical of the Roman arts in the time of Nero, Vernacchio's playhouse stages not only obscene farces but also the "theatre of the real thing"—a blasphemer has his hand chopped off as part of the evening's entertainment. The audience laughs at Encolpio's attempt to regain Gitone, begin bidding for him. But a Senator intervenes, and Encolpio is allowed to lead Gitone away.

They wander the city, which is a warren of the grotesque, a bizarre brothel, a merchant mall of the unconscious. A huge head is being dragged through an alley, a nightmare from a beheading, or an icon of the local Caesar (the megalomaniacal Trimalchio, as it later develops). They retire to Encolpio's room, make love, but in the morning are found by Ascylitus. Instead of fighting, they decide to go their separate ways, split their possessions, but when asked who he wants to be with, the faithless Gitone chooses Ascylitus. Encolpio barely has time to dwell upon this treachery when an earthquake hits, and the city collapses, blocks splitting from the huge dream walls, burying citizens, animals and the collective memory.

Cut to: an art gallery that looks perhaps a little too chic for the ancient world, but nonetheless sustains the film's neo-primitivist/moderno style. Here Encolpio meets up with the poet Eumolpus (Salvo Randone), an older gentleman, also down on his luck. As the camera patrols the hangings:

> Eumolpus: The masters in this gallery... are indicative of the apathy of our times. Nobody paints like this anymore.
> Encolpio: What caused this decadence?
> Eumolpus: Lust of money...

How did you get here? While the continuity is outstanding in terms of tone, the narrative progression is difficult to comprehend unless one is familiar with Petronius, recognizes the stories, the characters and the Fellini fictions. This isn't a major problem, as the action exists as a Fellini expressionism as much as it is a history, is a literature. Petronius' *Satyricon* is also a collection of fragments, memories of the original work, an incomplete oeuvre, like the plays of Sophocles or the writings of Cicero. In this sense Fellini's narrative imagery is internal, fragments of music from the id.

The next major scene is the feast at Trimalchio's, another Caesar who considers himself a poet, wit, *bon vivant*—a subject of envy, contempt and rage from Eumolpus. The scene is raw, the characters coarse, the action bizarre to the point of revulsion. Eumolpus and Encolpio watch, participate, but are really observers in this casual orgy of sexual theatre, gluttony, and megalomania.

The aging Trimalchio (Il Moro), who, like Truman Capote, can do anything at his party, humiliates his slaves and his guests as dwarves stagger in with smoldering cauldrons of flesh—ambiguous torsos from ambiguous creatures in an ambiguous universe. A pig is brought forth, gutted, releasing an avalanche of hens, snails, pigeons—verily, all the small animals and fowl of the known world. The guests drink, dance, insult one another under a huge icon of the host. Trimalchio's belches, farts, snores are decoded as maxims of wisdom and divinations by a vulpine secretary. At one point Trimalchio denounces the drunken Eumolpus for having stolen his verses, orders that he be thrown into the ovens. Eumolpus is dragged up the steps to these open pits of hell, but allowed to retreat, intimidated and debased. Trimalchio is a tyrant of the flesh, the soul—a tumorous ego.

His feast is a farce, as is the next scene, his rehearsal for death—a play-within-the-play which is an existential homage to the occult. The party adjourns to the plutocrat's tomb, a Roman theatre-set of heavy megalithic blocks, a stone garden of the soul. Here Trimalchio rehearses his funeral and internment, has his guests weep and deliver their sycophantic perorations as he lies smugly in the vault.

Telescoping the narrative within itself even further, Fellini now inserts the story of *The Matron of Ephesus*. A beautiful widow makes love to a young soldier who has been guarding a crucified thief on a nearby ridge. When the body of the thief is stolen, the widow aids her lover by replacing the thief with the body of her husband... which allows Trimalchio to proclaim his grandest witticism, "Better to hang a dead husband than a living lover." Thus Fellini uses the theatre-effect to cobble together an episodic narrative that has the spacial architecture of consciousness, an anecdotal progression of memory, cause, and effect. Art can't exist without history. It exists as a perception of the Past, which in turn becomes an anticipation of the Future.

"It was like speculating about life on Mars, but with the help of a Martian, so *Satyricon* satisfied in me some of my desire to make a science-fiction film." (Fellini) Now the dynamic changes, moving away from the closed, interior city sets of perpetual night into the open, exterior landscape of the ocean and the unknown. The transition here is thrilling, like arriving on another planet—albeit as a prisoner.

A huge barge sits on the ocean, its black hulk a fantastic metaphor of evil, a contradiction in the face of Nature. The V.O. by Encolpio tells us "we had been taken prisoner by the terrible Lichas of Tarantum." By "we" he means himself, his friend Ascylitus and toy-boy Gitone. How? It doesn't really matter. As Encolpio moves, so goes his nightmare, so goes his fate. These sequences are among the most brilliantly executed in all film drama to date. The photographic compositions isolate Nature and exalt the machine. The screen is sectionized into the geometrics of ocean horizon and the raised oars of the slave galley—dramatic simplicities that give imaginative and emotional depth to the historical reality. No matter how fantastic the characters and their actions, there's a raw authenticity continuously seeping from the expressionism. This, says Fellini, is how it was.

The bowels of this war barge are a hellhole of chained slaves working the huge chorus of oars as acrobats perform on the walkway between the bulkheads, musicans play lyres in droning harmony with the pitch and yawl... and Gitone sings in the tradition of the Arabic boy soprano. The master Lichas (Alain Cuny) amuses himself and his cast of cutthroats and slaves by wrestling selected victims in a sexual overture to death. His insane, reptilian eyes turn to Encolpio:

> Lichas: (rasps) Come to me, O tender fawn...

The androgynous Encolpio is no match for the sadistic Lichas. But instead of snapping his neck, Lichas' death embrace becomes one of love. "What eyes, what clear blue eyes," he intones as he pins Encolpio to the deck and kisses him. And this is no mere one-night stand—Lichas and Encolpio are married in a hastily convened ceremony on the top deck and celebrate their love with the slaughter of a young calf. Lichas wears a veil in a peculiar gesture of submission and dominance, as if he is both male and female, his homosexuality a primal twining, an omnivore from the deep. Time passes... the ship is seen passing through sleet and snow. A sea-monster is captured, raised to the deck, butchered. Then, as they draw close to the island where the young Caesar has his home, armed vessels surround them. As they watch, the young Caesar is hunted along the shoreline onto the sculptured white rocks where, cornered, he draws his sword and kills himself. His body is then impaled on a pike to the cries of "The Tyrant is dead!" The invaders confront Lichas on his ship, sneer, "We've drowned your emperor like a pig!" A sword is drawn and—in one of those cinematic moments you forever recall in your dreams—Lichas is decapitated, his head flying into the ocean where it sinks beneath the waves, his broken eyes rolled upwards in a frozen moment of ecstasy.

You last see Gitone being hustled away ("We'll keep him") as you expect Encolpio and Ascylitus to either die or remain in chains. But no... here Fellini changes the mood dynamic again.

You see an enclave bounded by a rock face, a sand garden adjoining the villa of Petronius, which is where he slits his wrists after freeing his slaves and sending away his children. You don't know it's Petronius, although Fellini has said elsewhere that's who it is. Does this matter? You know suicide was a Roman option, an occultic solution to a political fait accompli. Again, the episodic narrative emulates dream, articulates history.

In this broken paradise of softly falling water, chirping birds and frescos, they find a beautiful Ethiopian slave girl hiding in her kennel, share her for the night. Encolpio awakens at dawn to sound of departing horsemen, and the roar of flames. The bodies of Petronius and his wife are being immolated on their funeral pyre.

Cut To: Another desolate landscape where the wind stirs the dust around some tethered horses near a covered wagon. This is the encampment of the Nymphomaniac, who lies bound in the wagon, writhing in a perpetual state of indiscriminate arousal. Her position is more cruciform than missionary, her desire more occultic than mad. A crone tells them her husband is taking her to the "Hermaphrodite" at the oracle for a "cure"... but in the meantime he would be pleased if the young men would help soothe his wife's hermetic fever. Forever the incorrigible opportunist, Ascylite is only too happy to oblige, and he mounts the Nymphomaniac in an act that simulates ecstasy, but seals his fate.

They journey with the husband to the Oracle. The plan is to steal the Hermaphrodite, a sickly grotesque who lies in a crib beside the healing pool in the cave. The Hermaphrodite is a transgendered being who mirrors our origins, realizes our fears, fixes myth with biological fact. All come to this "demigod" seeking a cure for what ails them. War amputees, seniles, the insane... and the wandering voyeurs of history. Encolpio stabs and kills the old man who is the Hermaphrodite's guardian, and the trio flee with this sacred creature lodged on a hand cart. But like some fragile experiment from the stud farm, the Hermaphrodite dies, and the nympho's husband, enraged, attacks Encolpio and Ascylitus. What now? Fellini's complex, episodic narrative continues to scroll.

Somehow Encolpio finds himself rolling down a slope into a crude arena, the lair of the Minotar. And, true to form, his "friend" Ascylitus is somehow the grinning intimate of the Caesar and his entourage who will watch this piece of mythological theatre. The Minotar is a seven foot giant wearing a bull-ram headpiece, and awaits his trophy in his labyrinth. Once again Encolpio finds himself on-stage against his will.

He escapes death by appealing to the Minotar's humanity:

> Encolpio: Dear Minotar, I will love you if you set me free...

The Minotar removes his headpiece, smiles, laughs, addresses the crowd:

> Minotar: (to the pro-Consul) This isn't cowardice... it's the commonsense of an educated youth!

They embrace and instead of being killed, Encolpio is given Ariadne, a trophy harlot who lies willing and able on a stone bed nearby. But Encolpio finds himself incapable of performing and is tossed contemptuously into the surrounding trench by the disgruntled Ariadne. And as he crawls out, who should appear on a travelling litter, reborn as a wealthy noble with an entourage of women? His old mentor Eumolpus, The

Poet... in a crazy reversal of Fortune that makes him the heir of Trimalchio! They retire to Eumolpus' harem, a fantasy quadrangle of the senses. Encolpio has his bum smacked by a bevy of voluptuaries in a futile attempt to restore his potency as Ascylitus stands arrogantly on a giant swing, riding it back and forth in a vulgar foreplay as infantile as it is theatrical. This respite—like an interlude from *One Thousand and One Nights*—is brief, and presently Encolpio journeys beyond the Great Swamps in search of the Witch who will restore his lost sexuality.

Oenothea is a plump negress, another vagina on a slab. Her magic is to morph into fire in a basic metaphor of potency. Once again Encolpio is invited to perform—and this time he seems to have better luck. As Ascylitus lingers outside by the river bank, he is attacked and killed by a man who might be the Nymphomaniac's husband or merely a bandit who preys on the clients of the Witch. Ascylitus calls out to Encolpio as he's fatally stabbed, then mysteriously enters the Witch's cave, urges Encolpio to leave. Delighted with his restored powers, Encolpio follows the ghost, finds Ascylitus dead in the saw grass. The incident is contradictory, occultic, and left unexplained. The scene closes with the shocked Encolpio framed against a solitary stone megalith. The final episode sees Encolpio encounter a ship heading for Africa. The Master lies dead on the shore, surrounded by crates, friends and retainers. The Master's will is read, the lucky inheritors told that they will have to eat his body if they want to share in in his wealth. Meanwhile the crew invites Encolpio to join them, and as they run happily over the dunes towards the ship, the Master's body is eaten. Although there's no Christian intent, the situation appeals to the cynical who will recall The Last Supper. The film ends with Encolpio's V.O. telling of his odyssey, the islands, the cities... then, in a lap-dissolve, he and his friends transmorgrify, become figures in a fresco on a broken wall in a set of ruins.

"'What a pity,' some archaeologist laments, upon viewing something called *Fellini's Satyricon*. 'It seems to be missing its beginning, middle and end. It is so strange... what kind of man could this Fellini have been? Perhaps he was mad.'"

Fellini's narrative has an interesting image/symbol sub-text, one which integrates the action in a series of loops. There is the head, at first a mysterious icon in the street, later a mural at the Feast of Trimalchio, finally the severed head of Lichas sinking below the waves. Lichas is first seen wearing an animal head piece, a totemic mask similar to that worn by the Minotar. There's the white horse, sleeping on its feet in a sunken court prior to the earthquake, a thing of beauty and innocence in a city of polymorphic decadence. Horses recur in elegant pursuit of the horizon or in captive poses, more beautiful than the human, closer to the Gods, never grotesque, never decadent. Women on their backs: the Nymphomaniac, Ariadne, the Witch. Always on altars, sexual transponders of Fortune and reincarnation. And the frescoes....

Paganism: Religious Order And The Secularization Of Form

The pagan form is episodic, mythical, anthropomorphic, open. The religious form is determinist, codified, atomic, closed. *Fellini Satyricon* is the perfect post-modern testament, a de-construction of the determinist model in which the hero is the author of his fate in favor of the episodic model where Fate is a subject of Fortune etc. By interpreting the past, it predicts the future: the end of religious order, the secularization of Form. When a priest posted a black edged bulletin of the door of his church denouncing Fellini as a sinner, he was responding instinctively to the heresy of art and the fatal movement of history. But Fellini is only the messenger, not the messiah. (Fellini quotes from *I, Fellini* by Charlotte Chandler.)

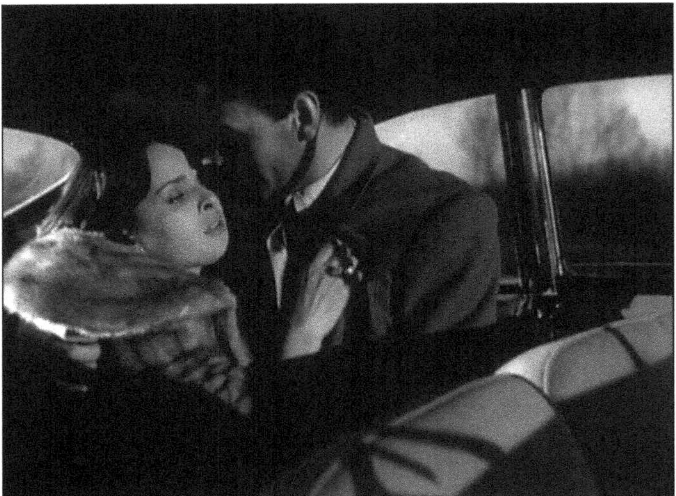

Michelangelo Antonioni: *Story of a Love Affair*

Story of a Love Affair (*Cronaca di un Amore*) 1950 dir Michelangelo Antonioni writ Antonioni, Citto Maselli, Daniele D"Anza. Silvio Giovenetti, Piero Tellini cine Enzo Serafin edt Eraldo Da Roma, Raffaello Vianello, Antonioni score Giovanni Fusco (sax Marcel Male, piano Arnando Renzi) production design Piero Filippone costume design Ferdinando Sarmi prod Franco Villani
Cast: Lucia Bose (Paola) Massimo Girotti (Guido) Ferdinando Sarmi (Enrico Fontana) Marika Rovsky (Joy) Gino Rossi (Carloni), Anita Ferrara, Bobi d'Alma, Carlo Gazzapini, Nordo Remediotti, Renatto Burrini, Vittoria Mondello (Matilde), Franco Fabrizi (fashion presenter)

As The Crimes Are Not Directly Witnessed By The Camera, They Are Circumstantial, Symbolic And Fated

Although Antonioni's first feature film T*he Story of a Love Affair* (*Cronaca di un Amore* 1950) looks as if it comes from the prevailing Italian neo-realism of the period, it actually owes more to American film noir. The black & white documentary landscapes of neo-realism are there, of course, and the atmosphere is driven by the bleak industrial edges that sit in the floating fog of the Milanese winter. There are plenty of shadows, though—literally and figuratively—and the core action is driven by a beautiful femme fatale who is as wilful and impulsive as her beauty allows. And there is the gumshoe element, the use of a private investigator who provides us with those details of the past that help us understand the present.

Typically for such narratives, the present is a montage of parallel Time scenes in which events seem predestined, especially when viewed in the light of the past. Antonioni always understood the poetic freedom of film montage, and used it subversively even in these days of post-war realism. Despite the classicism implicit in the Italian settings—some of the action is in Ferrara, that walled city of Renaissance dream palaces and wide ethereal streets—Antonioni is already a modernist on the edge of expressionism. Milan is modern among Italian cities, and Antonioni loved its new straight-line architecture, even the fouled irrigation canals with their distant vanishing points.

Atmosphere is everything, that pure barometer of instinct and psychology. Consider the score by Giovanni Fusco, a minimalist atonal dithyramb for piano and sax, which haunts the scenes like the cries of a deranged burlesque performer. Even as the credits roll, and we watch Paola Fontana pull away and enter the traffic flow in her silver coupe followed by the private investigator Carloni in a black saloon, we hear the grim staggering of the saxophone, beautiful yet tormented, rational, yet irrational. The idea of crazy love in the urban world is established immediately, despite the documentary scenes and the casual conversations of the bit players that follow.

The sex-triangle plot seems simple enough, although the circumstances make it psychological rather than venal, so that by the end everything is more complex, more ambiguous. Money does matter in this story, yet money is not the primary motivation. The two principals—Paola (Lucia Bose) and her lover Guido (Massimo Girotti)—are fated rather than devious. Guido is a victim, although it would be superficial to say he is Paola's victim. Even though Carloni wonders at one point if Guido is guilty of murder, he just drifts, bumped along by the current. The bigger scheme of life is at work here, lovers as elegant automatons, prisoners of an invisible order. This isn't an Italian Catholic thing either, as religion plays no part in this drama, despite the fleeting view of the Domm de Milan (Milan Cathedral) in the first few frames.

Initially Paola is a reinvention of herself, fast moving and existential, disguised and hiding in the moment; as the film progresses and the past catches up, she is exposed, although this unmasking is psychological rather than criminal even though what happens is criminal.

The 1948 Bellentani Affair

According to the Assistant Director Francesco (Citto) Maselli, *The Story of a Love Affair* took its inspiration from the 1948 Bellentani murder case, which thrilled Italy at the time, including Antonioni. The similarities between fact and fiction are fewer than we might expect—the high society Milanese setting is the same and Pia Bellentani's lover was a silk merchant but that's about it.

Paola is a different type altogether, a voltaic social climber from the middle class with no apparent artistic inclinations except for looking good and staying warm. Pia Bellentani was a mother, a poet and a pianist, and there was nothing ambiguous about her crime. Pia was confined in an asylum for ten years and we can imagine a similar fate for Paola.

The daughter of a "professor", Paola was raised and educated in Ferrara, the once famous principality of the Borgias, and it's there that Carloni the investigator discovers her "secret". For some reason her husband—the wealthy Milanese fabric manufacturer Enrico Fontana—has decided to check her past (on a "whim" according to the detective agency) as they were married after a very swift courtship.

He found some photos—Paola alone, Paola with girlfriends, Paola with a boy, or part of a boy, mostly out-of-frame, yet just enough to make him jealous. Many families were shattered by the war, and reinvention of who or what a person used to be was probably common. Fontana himself had done well despite (or because of) the war, become part of the *nouveau riche*, making his wealth in the fabric industry... and while he might've just picked her up in a bar or at a party, we fill in the dots, suppose that Paola was a model, or perhaps wanted to be a model—even then Milan was a nascent fashion hub—came into contact with Fontana in March 1943, married him within 2 months. She was 20, recently a school girl, so masquerading as her "uncle" the first place Carloni checks is her old school.

There Carloni learns about her friendship with two girls, and the sudden death of one, Giovanna, two days before she was to be married to a student called Guido. Carloni visits the other girl, Matilde, now living in stressed circumstances with a cynical professor ["Like Petronius, I rise late"]. This time Carloni poses as a "colleague" of Paola's father, now deceased, hoping to pass along some letters of "a spiritual nature". Matilde isn't home but no matter, her husband knows all about Paola and how she stole Giovanna's boyfriend Guido. Love at first sight, apparently. Then the accident... following which Paola disappeared, surfaced in Milan, married to wealth. When Matilde arrives home, she's immediately suspicious of Carloni, and he quickly makes his exit. Matilde then sits down, writes a cautionary letter to Guido, now a car salesman somewhere in Milan.

The Illusion Of Flesh & Blood

As with all the scenes involving Carloni the private investigator, there is a subtle humor here. The dialogue is sharp, moves the action, reveals information and character. The professor wears a dressing gown, hangs around the apartment as an eloquent unemployed layabout, and Matilde wears a black masculine suit, like a nun forced to do business outside the convent. "(Matilde) came to see me once," says Paola later. "She was boring, badly dressed. Then she vanished." Matilde's distrustful manner and her pale, haunted look raise questions, suspicions about her part in what happened between the three girls in 1943, although she never reappears in another scene. Perhaps she too was in love with Guido.

The story is now set. Carloni continues his investigations, and the Master Scene now assumes the primary action, that is Paola, now seven years married to Enrico Fontana, a man who often wears his overcoat as a cape and smokes heavily as per the fashion of the day. Moustache, slight build, walks quickly with short steps, as if the appearance of speed equates with efficiency. In this sense, he and Paola are a match, as she moves impatiently through her scenes, elegantly dressed in the latest fashions, smoking and chattering like a model from a glossy fashion magazine. Paola is a pure *femme fatale*, with her dark eyes and pale complexion, tall and slender like a ghost woman whose reality depends entirely on the vagaries of light & shadow and the exotic clothes that sustain the illusion of flesh & blood.

A trophy wife for Fontana? Without doubt, for his is the world of high fashion, business deals and parties, where image and social exclusivity mean everything. "Luciani made me a business proposal," he says. "Let's hear it," says Paola. "It involves you," he says. "He said I'll buy your wife for 300 million lira." Paola is sitting at her dresser, doing her face. "Only 300?"

she says. "You know what an Eastern Prince would have said...." "What?" "You can have my wife for free... then I'll kill you." Fontana is sitting nearby in an armchair. "Maybe he would," he says. "But a Milanese industrialist, for free...? Hmm, he'd say, Give me the money, you can have her... then I'll kill you." Fontana then adds the raison d'etre: "He earns the money, avenges the insult, gets rid of the wife."

It's of interest that Fontana was played by an Italian aristocrat, Count Ferdinando Sarmi, a designer of high fashion clothing, and it's his dramatic haute couture that Paola and others wear in the film. This use of clothing as art fits well with Antonioni's predilection for using landscape as art, or art itself as landscape in his films. Despite the prevailing neo-realist credo of harsh documentary settings, Antonioni is able to psychologize both the landscape and his characters by using art. This method becomes the *de rigueur* Antonioni style by the time of *La Notte*, where it becomes more difficult to distinguish the internal from the external landscape. For some, this dissembling of conventional story narrative in favor of a personal expressionism is troubling... but here, in his first feature, there is no such difficult abstraction.

Paola is always dressed as if she has just left a fashion runway and is often seen dragging her tresses through the rough streets and gutters. There's an absurdity to it, although the upper classes—especially the *nouveau riche*—have always indulged in the absurd. We first see her emerging from an opera house (probably the famous La Scala) just after midnight, a glittering Cinderella in a shimmering white coat and white fur, stepping onto the pavement of the arched portico.

It's here that she sees Guido watching her from across the street, the first sighting in seven years. She hurries off to catch up with her husband and their friends. Guido phones later that evening, says it's important that they meet. She agrees and the next day picks him up at a kid's rugby practice and they drive to a nearby lake (probably Lake Como). Many scenes are pivotal in terms of the plot, and some, like this one, are remarkable for their judicious choice of locale. Set on a descending terrace beside the gray water, the steps extend straight to an off-screen infinity like the risers of a vast theatre. The location is real, yet the modernism is theatrical. It's anti-romantic, yet there's something fantastically romantic about this setting, this troubled *rendez-vous*.

Guido shows her Matilde's letter warning him about Carloni's investigations. Paola is concerned, and her anxiety seems incriminating even though it's unclear whether Giovanna's fall down the elevator shaft was accidental or something else. The complicity of Guido & Paola in the tragic event is clear, yet the nature of this complicity isn't. Were they accessories to a murder or a suicide or a clumsy accident? At the time of her death, Giovanna was to have married Guido within two days. Yet Guido was now in love with Paola. Motive, desire, and opportunity are all there, yet in what was to become a signature motif in the Antonioni style, all this becomes part of a deliberate mysticism.

Now, on the terrace by the lake, their old intimacy returns as they sit side by side, share the histories of their past seven years. She notes that he smokes the same old cheap Nazionale cigarettes. They ponder what to do about Carloni. It isn't long before their affair is resumed, fated, as it were, by Fontana's ill-advised probe into his wife's past. Guido goes to Ferrara, finds out Carloni has visited Giovanna's old apartment building, examined the elevator. His anxiety is compounded by the fact that's he broke, that he hasn't been able to do anything significant with his life following the war. Paola offers him money, but he declines out of pride. She has an idea, suggests that he sell her husband an expensive car as he'd promised to buy her something special for her 27th birthday.

This seems like a practical idea, if dangerous. Fontana can't know that she knows Guido or even who Guido is. Guido has an associate, Valerio, who can acquire a new model Maserati, and they can work through him. The subterfuge requires a chance meeting, and they arrange to do this at a charity clothes auction to be held in a club called Esperia. Valerio's mistress is a blonde model called Joy who will be working at the auction, and who already knows "Mrs. Fontana" from client modelling jobs at a Milan clothing store.

But just like the machinations of the lovers in *Double Indemnity*—the Noir classic that probably had some influence on Antonioni—things do not go exactly or easily to plan. Paola is jealous when she sees Guido dancing with Joy, is convinced there's something between them, and indeed we wonder if she's right. Paola outbids all for the dress Joy is modelling and when the leggy model peels it off (in a very sexy choreography) and presents it to her, Paola throws it back, snaps, "Keep it." Meanwhile she ignores Valerio, despite the agreed need for an occasion to introduce him to Fontana. In an angry encounter near the washrooms, Guido snarls, "What's wrong with you, stupid?" Paola tries to slap him but he grabs her wrist. "I don't get you," she says angrily. "A deal so you can go with a tramp?" It's all a jealous misunderstanding, of course, but unlike the Countess Pia Bellentani, Paola doesn't take her husband's gun and shoot her lover.

Cut To: ...a bleak winter road in the country with two giant liquor bottles on either side, billboard facsimiles on a long straightaway. A Maserati A 6 slopeback races past as the camera draws away to reveal the familiar Fontana sedan parked on the shoulder, Paola and Guido kissing passionately in the back seat. Fast cars, fast women—life on the edge. When the Maserati returns, it goes into a dangerous skid as a feral dog unexpectedly runs across the road. The screech interrupts the lovers, who disengage reluctantly. Guido gets out, straightens his overcoat as the Maserati pulls up and Fontana and Valerio get out. Shaken yet cool, Fontana says, "You can be dead before you know it in a car like this... unsuitable for a lady." We laugh, of course, but perhaps uneasily. The analogue between the car and the woman is easily recognizable, yet it might not be the only symbolism in this incident. (Just after the release of the film, Count Ferdinando Sarmi who played Enrico Fontana moved to New York where he became the head designer for Elizabeth Arden, abandoned acting even though he appears to have been a natural. Of possible interest is that his character's surname "Fontana" is the same as that of the Fontana sisters, a trio of Italian designers who became popular with movie stars & the aristocracy.)

So the car deal goes south... and Guido remains the victim as he is always responding to rather than initiating events. Although Antonioni—speaking about this film at the time—says "I abolished 'the victim', 'the hero', 'the good man' and 'the bad man'" the fact is the creation isn't always what you intend. In the same interview he also says "(The) environment always stayed in the background. And it's this, I think, which distinguishes *Cronaca di un Amore* (*Story of a Love Affair*) from other Italian neo-realist films in which the environment is in close-up and the characters are nothing more than an excuse to show that environment." While his balance between subject and setting is superb in this film, he did allow himself to diminish story and character in some later films in his pursuit of post-modern abstraction. Here, in Cronaca, while there are no lingering landscape transitions, there are landscapes whose judicious geometrics do prefigure the mindscapes of his later work.

Paola does get her birthday present nonetheless, a snappy little Alfa Romeo 6 C coupe, the sort of *barchetta* model that was popular with Italian coachmakers at the time. When the keys are delivered, she immediately skips outside, dismisses the chauffeur, drops behind the wheel, drives off. From down the street, Carloni the P.I. pulls out in his black saloon, follows.

This appears to be the commencement of the opening sequence in the film (which is used to introduce the title credits), when we see this tailing from an overhead view. Paola knows she is being followed, and when she parks downtown, she ably loses her stalker by slipping into a department store. She then doubles back, crosses the street, enters a building for a showing of some new dresses. Once again she encounters Joy, the blonde she thinks is her rival for Guido's affections. Paola is already rattled by Carloni's snooping, and now, seeing the shapely Joy modelling the new dresses, she is even more rattled.

She paces, she smokes, she looks through the window at her car in the street below and the baffled Carloni on the corner. She slips away, meets Guido in a hotel room, where they discuss Giovanna's death. Paola is distressed, seems to suggest her friend's death was an accident which they allowed to happen, an opportunity seized by passive duplicity. Paola's guilt is both sexual and religious, the hunger and the sickness. "Giovanna separated us in life and in death," says Paola. The irony here is heavy, as Fontana's investigation has driven them together again, as if Fate is the Hunter.

Symbolism Of The Elevator

This sense of determinism, of their fate being the consequence of linked events, is reinforced by the symbolism of the elevator. In order to avoid Fontana, Guido and Paola are forced to retreat up a grand set of stairs that spiral around the hotel elevator. Emotional and fearful, the lovers argue in chorus to the ascent & descent of the elevator cage, as if they are part of a guilty dream concerning the death of Giovanna. Does desire kill? Is desire a spirit form? Is one person's desire/spirit stolen from another's? Etc. Ancient personifications, ancient questions scroll. This psychology, this sense of the unconscious controlling their lives is also apparent in the role of Joy, who later tracks down Guido, tells him that she's finished with Valerio, and that she merely used Guido in an unsuccessful attempt to make Valerio jealous... so we can see that she has been acting as an unconscious agent of destiny. Her part is pretty effective for a write-in, a character created to satisfy the desire of the film's major financial backer to help a young woman (Marika Rovsky) who was "special to him".

As in all serious film noir sex triangle scenarios, the time must come when the femme fatale will suggest to her lover that they must kill her husband in order to be free. This moment comes after Paola and Guido make love in his rented room. Guido suggests that they run away together. "I feel like a new man with you," he says. Paola is more realistic. "With me you'd come to a standstill." (he's been complaining that he's achieved nothing since leaving the army after the war)

Then Paola says, "You ever think deep down what it would be like if he died?" It isn't long before they're out in the country, scouting a bridge as the best place to shoot Fontana on his way home from work. The bridge crosses an irrigation canal, is approached by a long straight section of road running parallel to the canal, so all drivers must slow down to cross. Again, we are reminded of Antonioni's fascination with straight lines, the sense of infinity implicit in the existential now.

The ending of this film is a classic of the sort of ambiguity that Antonioni was/is to explore time and time again in his later films. He is like a magician who is dissatisfied with his disappearing act and continuously tries to improve upon the trick architecture of his cabinet. Compare, for example, the ending of *Cronaca* with that of *The Passenger* or *Blowup*. Mentalism, metaphysics, and mysticism.

Having Ascertained The Intimacy Between Garroni And The Subject

One night Guido Garroni waits for Fontana at the bridge, whom he knows will return home by this route to join his wife. But as it happens, Carloni has delivered his report, and Fontana has read it. Disturbed, Fontana stuffs it in his briefcase, leaves his office. In an eerie sequence we see the Gateman roll back the factory gate on its rails, and Fontana's car passing through, bumping over the puddles as it vanishes into the darkness. His assassin awaits... but is it Guido Garroni? Some might consider what happens next to be an unbelievable coincidence, a crude exercise in authorial intrusion. Yet the action is inevitable, especially when linked to the ambiguous death of Giovanna.

There is no question that Guido has set out to shoot Fontana. He has cycled to the bridge and is waiting with his automatic in his right pocket. Dogs bark, typical sounds in the deep ambient reverb of the rural countryside at night. In the distance, a car is accelerating, the engine tuned to a racing snarl. Guido is briefly illuminated by the headlights of a passing car heading the other direction... then he hears two bangs, which could be shots or backfires... startled, he takes out a cigarette, then hears two more. He looks down the road, sees two headlights, gets on his bike, rides that way.

A car is overturned and burning in the irrigation canal, and a man's body lies on the embankment. Another man—perhaps the driver of the car that just passed Guido—is reading the victim's license or identity paper: "Enrico Fontana... etc." Another man appears, and they lift Fontana's body onto the shoulder as Guido arrives. "Look at that," says one. We don't know it at the time, but he's referring to a hole in Fontana's throat.

What is this? A self-inflicted wound? An assassin's bullet hole? A wound from the crash? We never find out, and the hole becomes a mysterious stigmata in a mysterious finale.

Technically this is the climax of the film, not the ending. There is an epilogue, where Paola, fearful and desperate, dressed in a long cocktail dress and swathed in fur, meets Guido on a dingy back street, tells him the police are looking for her. Guido tells her she's mistaken, that her husband is dead, but not by his hand. They get into her taxi, and he delivers her to the doorway of her mansion before continuing to the railway station alone. Abandoned on the steps, Paola writhes in despair like an inmate waiting admission to the asylum, beautiful and mad—a widow by both accident and design. As Guido's taxi disappears down the street, perhaps we notice a figure emerge from a parked car. Who is it? Was this scripted or is it just an event at the location? The credits roll, and the action closes on black.

In The Architecture Of All Things Real & Unreal

The film is non-judgemental, is as objective as the narrative allows, although we all know that an edited event must proclaim some sort of bias. Religion plays no part in this film, as it would, say, in a Fellini drama. The action is entirely modern, although guilt drives the principals. The psychology of Paola suggests a child dressed up, although she has no obvious Freudian modus operandi. The fact that Lucia Bose was just 19 when she played the part supports this impression. As for Guido, he appears absolutely normal, and Italy was probably full of similar young war vets struggling to get by in the late forties. Neither devious nor greedy, he just drifts like someone whose potential was stymied by the war, and when he sees Paola again, it's like winding the clock back to the days before the death of Giovanna. Unfortunately Paola is fatal for him, although not so fatal that he can't disappear into the night. This isn't *Double Indemnity*, where everybody must die.

The sociology of time and place is very interesting in this film, delivered as it is by the neo-realist locations and the modernist action. It is the world as Antonioni found it in Milan, Italy, in 1949. A little shabby, still hungover from the war, still in the emotional winter, yet with a fantasy class living in their upper floor world of fantasy fashion and endless parties. The underclass is there, represented by Valerio the car dealer and his mistress Joy, the Professor and Matilde, Guido and even Paola, as she is a fugitive hiding in the nouveau riche. The middle class is trying to reestablish itself, edge closer to that luxury that Enrico Fontana represents—nights at La Scala, drinks at the "Little Bar", cigarettes and cinzano, Maseratis and Alfas.

In the architecture of all things real and unreal, there is nothing like the aristocracy, a living symbolism of the way it can be for all Italians. While neo-realism's signature is the face of the underclass, drama has historically dealt with the affairs of kings and queens, the aristocracy and those we elevate as heroes. In the 1920s, European expressionist drama was full of ideology and modernism, and frequently dealt with the industrial classes high and low. Industry is a fantasy of the future, identifiable as it is with an easier way of living, playboys and playgirls and their toys, their romances, their tragedies. These are the people who can afford art, and live as if they're living in an art gallery, a sensibility Antonioni established very clearly in many of his later films, including *La Notte, Blowup* and even *Zabrieski Point.*

This gallery consciousness isn't exclusive to Italian post-war directors, as it is a lingering legacy of live theatre set design, and even Hollywood exploited landscapes in this manner with its film noir cities and geological westerns. All film has sociology, yes, but Antonioni also has style, and the balance of his style, his personalism, against or within the rigors of documentary neo-realism is impressive.

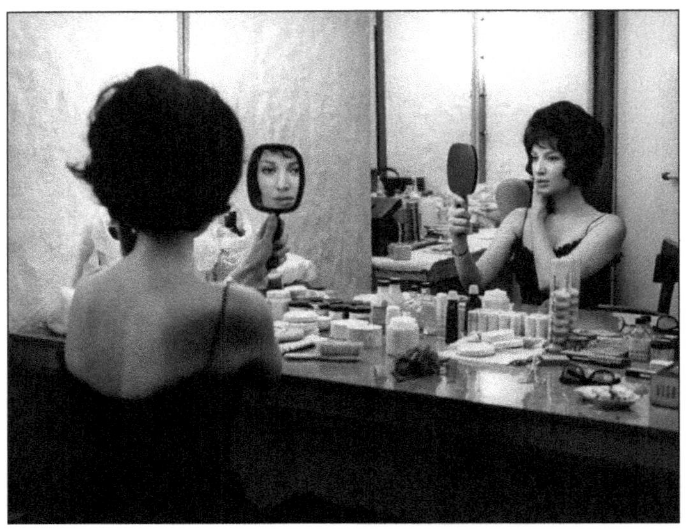

Michelangelo Antonioni: *La Notte*

La Notte (1961) dir. Michelangelo Antonioni writ. Antonioni, Ennio Flaiano, Tonino Guerra cine. Gianni de Venanzo edt. Eraldo da Roma music. Giorgio Gaslini art/design. Piero Zuffi production. Paolo Frasca produced. Emanuele Cassuto
star. Marcello Mastroianni (Giovanni), Jeanne Moreau (Lidia), Monica Vitti (Valentina), Bernhardt Wicki (Tomasso), Vincenzo Corbello (Gherardini), Maria Ra Luzi (crazy patient), Rosy Mazzacurati (Resy), Giorgio Negri (Roberto), Ugo Fortunato (Cesarino)
Nepi Film/Sofitedip/Silver Film 115 mins b & w

Chance, Form & Dimension

It's a world of reflections... of dimensions, where the past and present coexist in the architecture, inhabited by ghosts and dreamers. Windows become murals, and murals become windows. The place? Milan in the summer of 1960, in the boom of its post-war reconstruction.

The camera gently descends the black glass facade of a new tower as if you're in an external elevator, can see the panorama of the city, the reconstruction zones between established buildings, the railway tracks entering the modernist Stazione Centrale like a demarcation between the old and the new. Reflections, imagery... chance, form & dimension. As space becomes hallucinatory, banality becomes art.

Cut To: a hospital patient awakening in agony. This is Tomasso (Bernhardt Wicki), a writer who is dying of cancer. A Doctor and a nurse arrive, inject him with morphine. He moans, says, "What am I going to do?" He rolls to his right, stares through the window at the building across the street, as if some sort of transcendental escape is possible. The doctor picks up a novel from the bedside table, examines the jacket....

Cut To: the street outside the hospital. A small Alfa Romeo approaches, carefully navigating a construction zone, avoiding a demolition bucket, then turns into a small parking area. Giovanni (Marcello Mastroianni) and his wife Lidia (Jeanne Moreau) get out, enter the hospital, take the elevator to Room 103. As the doors open, you see a woman spying from her room just across from the elevator. She slips out and calls to Giovanni, asks him for a light.

There's a craziness in her dark eyes, a tuberculin sexual hunger. Giovanni obliges. She says, "My phone is out of order,

I wonder if you...." A nurse appears, and she scurries back into her room. Giovanni and Lidia continue to Room 103.

The visit with Tomasso is a strange interlude, conducted in "real time"—as indeed all of the action to this point and thereafter appears to be—with all the tension you would expect in an encounter with the dying. The sound is ambient... modulated conversation, a passing helicopter, the pop of a champagne cork as they drink in honor of their doomed colleague. Tomasso's mother arrives, sits quietly in the corner as her son and his friends reminisce. Tomasso has a copy of Giovanni's latest book, *La Stagione*—he says he's read 50 pages, feels it's some of Giovanni's best writing. Speaking of himself, he says, "The advantage of premature death: you escape success."

Tomasso is full of gallows humor, nervous desperation, impeccable manners. Giovanni meanwhile is like a sleepwalker... he murmurs, he defers... almost as if he is viewing a double-figure in the bed, a dream version of himself. In fact, Tomasso's self-doubt is a direct mirror of the malaise that you come to recognize in Giovanni as the film progresses. Says Tomasso: "I regret that my presence has spoiled so many delightful evenings... I wonder if I've ever done anything useful... I lacked the courage to probe deeply... probably I never had enough intelligence anyway."

The self-doubt of a doomed animal is to be expected, yet the impotence within the despair is typical of the European intellectual in the mid-twentieth century. Alienation and the paranoid Self. The characters are awake in the existential moment, yet wander through the action as sleepwalkers... which in fact is the title Giovanni finds later at the party: *The Sleepwalkers* (1933) by Hermann Broch.

Antonioni used two scriptwriters to help him develop the scenario for *La Notte*—Ennio Flaiano and Tonino Guerra—and you wonder if they based this scene on the death of Curzio Malaparte who died in a Rome hospital in 1957 from lung cancer. Certainly Malaparte would've enjoyed the surrealism in the following scene when Giovanni, on leaving Tomasso's room, is lured into the nymphomaniac's room and molested.

Again, because of his passivity and the absurd contrast to his visit with Tomasso, the action is dream-like, despite the documentary style of the direction. She becomes a reincarnation of Tomasso, a Freudian personification. Because the cine is black and white, and the characters and settings filmed on location, the naturalism associated with Italian neo-realism subverts the whole idea of fiction... just as the superb cinematography with its art school geometrics and metaphysical symbolisms subverts the whole idea of documentary.

Giovanni rejoins Lidia, who, overcome with sentiment, left Tomasso's room earlier. There is a sense that she and Tomasso shared a special relationship, although its exact nature remains circumspect. Giovanni immediately confesses the incident with the crazy woman. Lidia dismisses it, says, "You were taken by surprise. Let's forget about it."

But Giovanni still feels the need to justify what happened. Lidia, sotto, says, "Good story material. I'd call it *The Living & The Dead*." This dead-pan witticism draws into focus the sub-text behind the incident. The madwoman with her nympho desire is an existential trigger, a proof of life. Yet despite the primal drama, resurrection eludes him.

They drive to the offices of his publisher [the famous Bompiani company] where the book launch for his latest novel is underway. As Giovanni chats and signs copies, Lidia lingers on the periphery, leans against a pillar, watches. All attention is on Giovanni, even though he drifts through the ceremony like an afterthought, connected yet disconnected.

Lidia slips away unnoticed, starts walking through the streets. Men appear... in offices, on the street... various classes of workers, sexual possibilities, or accidental witnesses to her aimless stroll. There's a similarity here to the sequence in Antonioni's previous film *L'Avventura* (where Claudia leaves her hotel in a small southern town, goes for a walk). In fact there are so many similarities in this and other sequences that many critics dismiss *La Notte* as a reprise of the controversial *L'Avventura*.

The similarities are in the psychology of the characters and in Antonioni's painterly style. And while both films are travelogues of the soul, *L'Avventura* is rural whereas *La Notte* is urban.

Distant Tracks Arrive In The Present

Lidia's amble takes her to a suburb where she and her husband started out. She witnesses a fight between two punks on a waste lot. She watches some young men firing model rockets in a field. As dusk approaches, she has a drink in a small bar, then phones Giovanni, who has long ago returned to their chic apartment and is now prowling the darkened rooms. He drives to their old district, and they engage in some mutual sentimentality about the area.

Lidia is either watching him or waiting for something to happen. Consciously or unconsciously she has drawn her husband here to rekindle their early affection and intimacy. You see them beside a old wall and a stretch of overgrown railway tracks, another setting which suggests much more than mere documentary. Antonioni is a symbolist, his imagery metaphysical. [his protagonists are always suffering from disengagement, represented by disappearing women, and intimidation by the supernatural] Here, the past is almost obscured, the track abandoned... and yet you might recollect the opening of the film where the distant tracks arrive in the present.

They return home. Lidia takes a bath, puts on a new dress. The banality of it, the pure quotidian—the stuff that would remain off-stage for most dramatists—continues. Montage is not an option for Antonioni. His real-time action is an extension of live theatre, just as his sophisticated cinematography is an extension of theatre set-design... itself an extension of mural/fresco painting.

They stop at a night club, watch some erotic choreography by a couple of African dancers. This scene is reminiscent of one in Fellini's *La Dolce Vita* (1960), filmed the previous year with Marcello Mastroianni in the lead. But not only do Fellini and Antonioni share a leading man, they also share a script writer: Ennio Flaiano. It's Flaiano's sophisticated dialogue with its dry edginess and Pirandelloesque sub-text that make their films of this period appear to be the work of a single auteur.

As usual, the night-club scene is masturbatory, suggests decadence through ennui. Faintly narcotic, definitely cynical, it's the reinvention of a song-and-dance interlude in live theatre. The choreography is ancient, although the spin is modern. Again, Giovanni fails to be aroused. It's now late in the evening and they proceed to the party which is somewhere on the outskirts of Milan in a huge contemporary villa owned by a millionaire industrialist. Perhaps you sense that Lidia is steering her husband into situations that might draw them closer together... but of course every time they enter a crowd, they move further apart.

Antonioni and crowds: Dwight MacDonald, who wrote better than anyone on the films of this period when they first appeared, says, "He is the Veronese of films, a master of calculated composition. His groupings are, like Veronese's, both austere and luxurious, classical in design but baroque in surface and texture. He is able to show a complicated scene without any cluttered effect." (Antonioni: *A Position Paper*)

Nowhere do you see this talent for dramatizing large groupings better than in the villa sequences, although the Stock Exchange sequences in his next film *L'Eclisse* (1962) are also very good. Dramatically, the choreography in both instances is for the same purpose, that is, the point-of-view of an outsider looking in.

In *L'Eclisse*, the Monica Vitti character hangs around the fringes of the stock exchange floor watching her mother trade. In *La Notte*, Jeanne Moreau drifts through the edges of the party watching her husband socialize and flirt. In both dramas, there is a failure to engage and a longing for love. The naturalism is as impressive as the alienation is modern. No one in contemporary film has ever matched Antonioni in showing loneliness in the social context of a large gathering.

Do You Still Hang Around With Intellectuals?

When they enter Gherardini's villa, no one seems to be around. "Are they all dead?" says Giovanni as he and Lidia pass through the empty rooms. Appropriately, he sees a copy of *The Sleep Walkers*, wonders who here would read it. While this is a setup for his later encounter with Valentina (Monica Vitti), the daughter of the Gherardinis, it's also a metaphor for the milieu he inhabits. This is reinforced when they step outside, and Lidia meets an old friend from her schooldays who says, "Do you still hang around with intellectuals?"

Giovanni meanwhile encounters a blonde woman—Signorina Resy—who says, "I'm your greatest admirer in Italy... I'd like a novel about a woman who loves a man... but the man doesn't love her. But he does admire her intelligence and her character. They live together... but how could such a story end?" Giovanni says politely, "It could end many ways." You wonder if he recognizes the analogy here to his own relationship. You certainly do, as by now you are also wondering how this story can end.

Will another mad woman step out of the shadows and seduce him... and would anyone care. Still, the voyeurism sustains us, replete as it is with post-modern irony and ambiguous visual realities.

Reflection

Once again Antonioni explores the use of reflection as a means of visual sub-text by using the extensive glass surfaces that make up the walls of Gherardini's designer villa. Despite the rationalist architecture of glass, steel and concrete, the irrational functions as a supernatural counterpoint. When Giovanni watches Valentina amusing herself with a game of solo bocci (shuffleboard) on the patterned tile floor you see him as a reflection in the plate glass. And what you see, really, is a spacializing of the past and the present, as there is a Renaissance landscape mural on the wall.

This natural multiple exposure has about it the stuff of spirits, the sense of passing from one world to another... of romanticism and idealization. Symbols abound. In the garden the patrician Gherardini admires his roses, and a cat is transfixed by the disembodied head of a statue on the grass. It's indeed fitting that Lidia slips away, phones the hospital, finds out that Tomasso has died.

It's now raining heavily. Disheartened, Lidia allows herself to be spirited away by Roberto, a lead-footed Cassanova in a coupe. They drive through the night, an impressionistic blur in the downpour. They stop for the lights at a level-crossing, get out of the car, dally. A passenger train glides past. Roberto attempts to kiss her but Lidia disengages, abandons the Hemingway rain, gets back in the car. Roberto returns her to the party.

She knows Giovanni is making love to Valentina. She knows this because she gave him to her. She knows Valentina is reading *The Sleepwalkers*, is vulnerable. But despite all the head-talk and a couple of half-hearted kisses, nothing comes of it. Instinctively, Valentina knows he's a dead soul.

Although she won her "game" (of bocci) with Giovanni, she says sadly, "At least I'm clever enough not to break up a marriage." She adds, "Now you can spend the rest of the evening with your wife." Giovanni protests, then concludes, "It's so dark. How can I find her?" Thus Giovanni is left with his own reflection in the rain-streaked glass.

A Melancholy Shuffle Of Weariness

Excluding death, it becomes obvious that the action can only be resolved by metaphor... and when it comes, it better be good. First, Giovanni refuses Gherardini's offer of an executive position in his company. While he doesn't need it, this becomes another example of the artist's inability to commit. There's a verbal confrontation between Lidia and Valentina, but quickly they decide they actually like one another.

As the dawn breaks, Lidia tells Giovanni that Tomasso is dead. As they walk away from the villa, the jazz combo is still playing in the garden, a slow and melancholy shuffle of weariness as if the cruise ship has left without them. Signorina Resy, rejected by all the men, consoles herself with a woman on a bench. So it goes. The surrealism is in the muted light and the banality of the lateral events.

Giovanni and Lidia walk onto the private golf course, keep going until they reach a sandtrap. Lidia takes a typed page from her purse, reads what is a *de facto* love rhapsody, then weeps. Moved, Giovanni says, "Who wrote that?" and Lidia replies, "You did." Finally, after a long day's journey into night and beyond, Giovanni is aroused. He embraces his wife, pushes her to the ground, she protesting. He climbs on top of her, and they roll in the sand. Up music and *exeunt* on the long view.

Mastroianni's restrained performance as Giovanni has been criticized in the past, even though passivity and creative frustration is what defines his character. This passivity is often a sign of the child-man, a role Mastroianni plays to perfection. Here he looks like a boy in a man's suit, and he relates to his wife

Lidia with the affectionate indifference of a boy to his mother. As an intellectual, his role is anti-dramatic, lacks physicality.

This isn't just a question of a bourgeois type in Antonioni's films, as the mechanic played by the American actor Steve Cochrane in *Il Grido* (1957) exhibits a similar sort of passivity. Women become detached from the Antonioni "hero"—just like mothers relinquishing their sons. The sociology begs analysis, such as the modern secular male detaching from the maternalism of Catholicism... or the childless bourgeois artist in a hopeless search for fulfillment. Still, while Giovanni's condition is a fact, its true nature remains as provocative as the symbolism of Tomasso's death.

An obvious comparison is to be found in Mastroianni's previous role, that of a playboy gossip journalist in Fellini's *La Dolce Vita*. Here again he plays a child-man, but a man of action, even if that action is trifling. As "Marcello", Mastroianni again finds himself as a man who is unable to commit, a man of talent unrealized. As Giovanni, he finds his talent realized, and yet it brings him nothing. Both characters are left on the edge of a spiritual abyss, studies in the infantile self.

While the success or failure of *La Notte* should rest only on a viewing of the film itself (regardless of production politics), it will come as no surprise to fellow voyeurs that Mastroianni thought it was a failure. "I didn't like the script of *La Notte*. I never believed in the crises of my character," he says.

Despite his disenchantment with Antonioni [who was having an affair with Monica Vitti], he says he agreed to do the film "Because at the beginning I had the impression that the writer character was someone at the very edge of the conventional. He reminded me of my writer friend Ennio Flaiano. But that wasn't Antonioni's idea at all."

As a consequence, Mastroianni got into a heavy dispute with the other screenwriter Tonino Guerra. These quotes come from Donald Dewey's book *Marcello Mastroianni: His Life & Art*, and while it all sounds like typical gossip from a movie shoot, the detail about Ennio Flaiano should not be overlooked.

Ennio Flaiano (1920-72) was a novelist, playwright, screenwriter, theatre critic... editor of *Il Mondo*... author of the superb novel *Short Cut* (1948) about Italy's Ethiopian war, filmed in 1991 by Guiliano Montaldo as *Time To Kill* starring Nicolas Cage. Without question, Flaiano is the significant intellectual force behind Antonioni's *La Notte*... and, as it happens, many of Fellini's best: *La Strada, La Dolce Vita, Otto e Mezzo* [*8½*].

Alberto Moravia, Flaiano's famous contemporary, says about him: "Flaiano was a little man, originally from the Abruzzo, dark and stubby, with a core of pessimism, of negativeness. He was witty, and he knew he was, with keen intelligence.... As a writer, he oscillated between surrealism and a British black humor." [as quoted in *Life of Moravia*].

It must be said that Monica Vitti's role as Valentina is intriguing, if a bit indulgent. She seems far too clever for an eighteen year old, too full of world weary wisdom even if she is the sophisticated daughter of a millionaire.

As for Jeanne Moreau, her screen presence is perfect for the mystery within her character. But of course she too didn't like her character or *La Notte*.

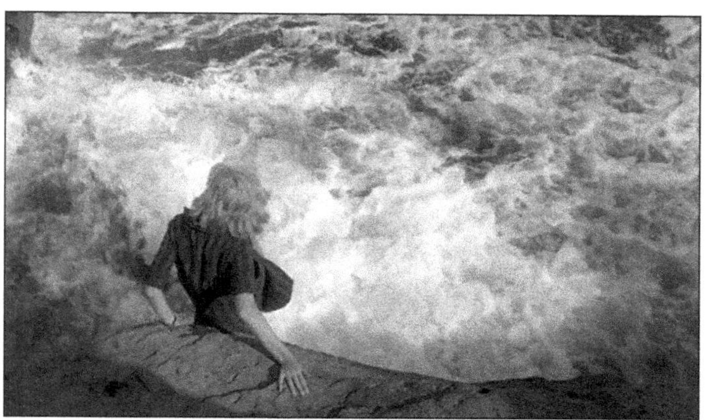

Michelangelo Antonioni: *L'Avventura*

L'Avventura (1960) dir. Michelangelo Antonioni writ. Antonioni, Elio Bartolini, Tonino Guerra (story by Antonioni) cine. Aldo Scavardia music Giovanni Fusco star. Monica Vitti (Claudia), Gabriele Ferzetti (Sandro), Lea Massari (Anna), Dominique Blanchar *et. al.*

This film was marginalized at the 1960 Cannes Film Festival by Fellini's brilliant *La Dolce Vita* (which won the big prize) and it's easy to see why: at 145 minutes playing, the indolent real time sequences are a real test of the viewer's patience, despite the marvellous imagery and the incidental decadence of the characters along the way. Ironically the theme and symbolist imagery mark it as extremely similar to *La Dolce Vita*—the difference is in the editing method.

Real Time Or Montage Time

L'Avventura is like the literary novel where the plot is simple and the imagery complex. The landscape continually threatens to overwhelm the characters who are afraid to commit in a reality of rapid social change as measured by the new architecture as versus the old. In the opening scene we see Anna emerge through a Roman arch from her father's villa onto a road lined with new cluster housing. The road bisects the screen, marking the old from the new, and in a brilliant touch vanishes into the distant mirage of a Renaissance dome.

It's interesting to compare this sequence to the closing one where the screen is once again divided in two, with the couple (Sandro and Claudia) framed like a gallery painting in an uneasy reconciliation between a wall and a landscape, near and far, present and past. Space collapses back into two dimensions, Time into stasis. Their relationship is represented perfectly by this artistic mise en scene.

Antonioni's narrative symmetry is as perfect as the palindrome that characterizes the heroine's name. And Anna is the heroine, despite the fact that she disappears 25 minutes into the action and the next two hours are preoccupied with her disappearance. As her lover and her friend go on a search through southern Italy, their exploration is one of the Self, where they try to recover innocence as they rediscover the past. This is best realized in the character of Claudia who takes up where Anna leaves off, wears Anna's dress, becomes Sandro's lover, and finally—perhaps—becomes Anna.

Sandro is a child-man with the typical compulsive sexuality of the artist, a man of suspect allegiance and charming disposition. Perhaps 40 years old, his unrealized self is hinted at in a scene in the gallery below his apartment. As he makes love to Anna, Claudia passes the time by wandering through the gallery, overhears an American couple in one room proclaim "he really knows how to paint" while in the next an Italian says "he's got a long way to go".

Again the screen is bisected by the wall between the rooms in a visual palindrome that is mirrored by Claudia's stroll through the building.

The Multiplication Of Self: Time, Dimension And Stasis

Sandro's character is represented by three versions of himself: at the beginning, the successful artist/architect who is despised by Anna's father, a diplomat of the Old Order; later as the 17 year old Geoffredo, the young artist who seduces Guilia, sensualizing her with the raw, urgent sexuality of his nudes ("Women like to show themselves"); and finally as the angry 23 year old tourist artist who sketches historic sites in Palermo. As Sandro waits for the Cathedral to open, he knocks the drawing ink over a church sketch of the absent artist in a gesture that is as accidental as it is inevitable, an eradication of the past by the clumsy hand of the present.

Doors opening, doors closing. People in groups as people alone and isolated. People arriving, people leaving. People seen in the mid-ground between viewer and horizon. Landscape rather than story, photography rather than action... perhaps this is reason for such frustration with *L'Avventura*.

The film is both neo-realism and expressionism, exploiting documentary Time with spacial Symbolism. It's this static action, with its compositional style taken from the academic tradition of painting, and the intrinsic omniscience of photography and ambient sound, that defines the Antonioni method.

Anna and her friends visit a bleak island in the Eolian chain, swim beneath the intimidating cliffs until Anna claims a shark is in the vicinity. They land, explore the rocky abstractions, hunt for some ancient ruins. Meanwhile Anna is gripped with sexual contradiction, argues with Sandro, and while this seems like the typical neurotic game-play of love, the sub-text suggests a deeper rationale in Anna's polar yearnings of love and repulsion.

Sandro offers to marry her but she says she wants to be alone... Sandro lies back on the rocks, closes his eyes as Anna turns, looks at him... or at eternity in the breaking waves and horizontal ocean. This is the last we see of her as the sequence lap-dissolves into various views of the women of the party reclining on rocks to the doppler hiss and roar of the troughing waves... and the mysterious sound of a boat engine which makes Anna's disappearance more extra-sensory than real.

Did she fall or jump? Did she escape the island freely or was she abducted?

Commitment: Sex And Identity

A long search ensues, Anna's friend Claudia being the most committed. Sandro joins her, although his concern seems to be one of form rather than spirit. They search the lava beds of the small island but the only thing they find is an "Australian" hermit and piece of ancient pottery which is dropped and broken as soon as it is found. Claudia goes to the mainland, takes a train, goes south as rumors of sightings are reported in the newspaper. Sandro follows and quickly transfers his fascination to Claudia.

> Sandro: I have no desire to sacrifice myself... why? It's idiotic to sacrifice oneself... why? For Whom?
> Claudia: For me things are just the same as they were three days ago... you and Anna. Three days! Is it possible it takes so little to change, to forget?
> Sandro: It takes even less.

Sandro is a creature of transition, a man who is unable to commit because he is a man. Antonioni's idea of commitment is female, as represented by Claudia, even if his films are full of disappearing women. The existential reflex is confounded by an implicit criticism of the status quo, the developing impotency of the modern male.

As their affair develops and they penetrate the sub-tropical south, they arrive at destinations which continually draw them into confrontations with themselves and history. Anna might be in Noto, so they drive there, but find a modern church as deserted as the small town itself. Claudia presses against the shutters, calls, "Is there anyone in there?" but all she gets is an echo of herself. As they drive away, they leave the frame, the camera in fixed contemplation of the bland modern facade of the empty church.

In another town, they expect to find Anna in the only hotel. Sandro enters alone, ascends the stairs, disappears as Claudia waits in the street in a ritual that she expects will mirror the opening of the film: Sandro will find Anna, they will make love, Claudia (again) will wait. In an incident that is more to do with Claudia's psychology of sacrifice than the crude sexism of the Mediterranean male, she is surrounded by dozens of insolent leering men as she strolls back and forth. Sandro returns, descending the stairs from yet another rendezvous with nothingness.

They rejoin Corrado and their other affluent friends from the yacht in a luxury hotel. Exhausted, Claudia elects to stay in their room and rest rather than join the reception in the lobby. Sandro encounters a young brunette of similar erotic dimensions as Anna and quickly engages her in sex.

Claudia finds him missing at dawn and as if she has never left her dream, searches the corridors of the hotel, eventually discovering Sandro with the brunette on a couch in a deserted lounge. Distressed, she runs from the hotel, ends up in a plaza where Sandro finds her. The film ends with their ambiguous reconciliation as Sandro sits weeping on a bench and Claudia places her hand on his head.

Art, Time, And Stasis

While stasis is obviously part of Antonioni's artistic *raison d'etre*, the reduction of human activity to its trivial interludes can seem pointless unless unless you follow the sub-text. Many scenes depend upon beauty and symbolism to justify their inclusion. Sandro and Claudia make love in the grass as a train passes and we witness the trail of fresh steam rather than the lovers' climax. Or Sandro witnesses a paparazzi scrum as they interview a young female "writer" whose brash sexual persona is a living example of Geoffredo's assertion that "women like to display themselves".

And Anna? She's never found, her disappearance another mystery like the ruins on the island, or the selves we shed like lovers.

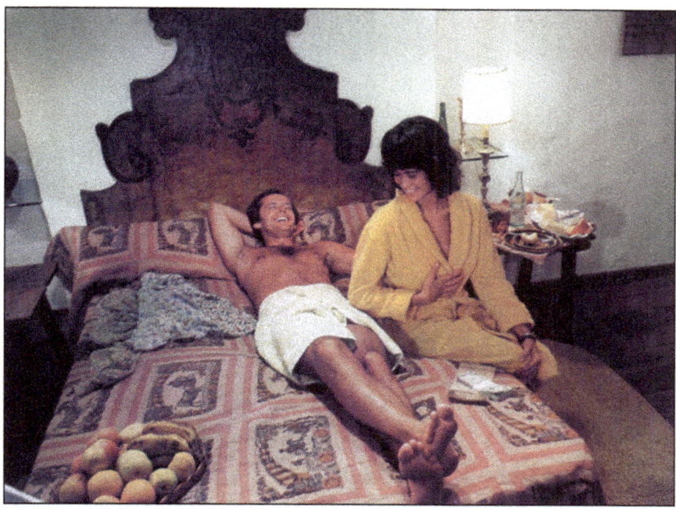

Michelangelo Antonioni: *The Passenger*

The Passenger (1975) (aka *Professione: reporter*) dir. Michelangelo Antonioni writ. Mark Peploe, Peter Wollen, M. Antonioni cine. Luciano Tovoli edt. Franco Arcalli & Antonioni art. Piero Poletto music. Ivan Vandor costumes. Louise Stjernsward
star. Jack Nicholson (Locke/Robertson) Maria Schneider (Girl) Jenny Runacre (Rachel Locke) Charles Mulvehill (Robertson/dead man) Ian Hendry (Martin Knight) James Campbell (witch doctor) Ambroise Bia (Achebe) Manfred Spies (German) Jean-Baptiste Tiemele (thug) Angel del Pozo (police inspector)
MGM 1975 anamorphic widescreen 126 mins | color

About Coincidence & Fate

The anticipation which Antonioni's film *The Passenger* generated prior to its release in 1975 owed something to the counter-culture's fascination with the desert, its mystery and natural minimalism... and of course Antonioni's reputation as a dramatic artist on the same level as Samuel Beckett and Harold Pinter, unconventional stage writers who seem to have had at least a passing influence on the great Italian muralist. Autistic dialogue, indolent action, mental and spacial alienation... in small doses, dysfunctional humans acting out their psychodramas within beautiful landscapes and designer plazas was an appealing art style.

There was something of science fiction in it, an alternate-world gestalt, like a zombie colony on another planet. The opening scene of *L'eclisse* (1962) is so slow & non-verbal, it's as if the actors are waiting for the director to arrive while the camera runs. Yet the style—good for the one-act play format—was fatiguing in a two hour drama. Even the prof and the students got weary in the darkness, longed for a gun fight and a sexual rendezvous. Is this why *The Passenger* received a lukewarm reception on its release? Too slow, too arcane and self-conscious in its attempt to be hip?

Fall 05, you read that the star, Jack Nicholson, owns the master print and is organizing its release as a remastered DVD. Your first thought was, hmm, is Nicholson, the guy who started out as an ivy league ingenue in the bent flicks of Roger Corman now seeking some academic recognition because, let's face it, Hollywood still doesn't have the same cachet as Old Europe? So you buy a copy, let it lie on the floor beside the plasma wide screen for a couple of days before settling down with a glass of shiraz, skeptical yet hopeful. Thirty years ago maybe you smoked a joint before entering the theatre as you believed insight = THC squared. Thus the lingering prejudice that *The Passenger* was/is a derivative mistake, the first clear marker of Antonioni's decline and fall as a significant filmmaker.

Wrong... or mostly wrong. True, much of it looks like a Godard road movie (*Pierrot le Fou* in particular) but now perhaps you can see it properly. You were looking at a 16 mm print back then. If Antonioni went dark, it wasn't due to the creative failure of *The Passenger*. Not only does the film look good (despite those wobbly, human pans) with its multi-cultural settings and characters, the story is an excellent example of the non-linear narrative. Plot? There's a plot alright, even if you are forced into the ellipsis that surrounds each incident in order to understand it. And how difficult is this? At times, watching an Antonioni film can be like watching a surveillance video, and *The Passenger* is no different. It takes the same patience and attention that an afternoon in the art museum requires.

A journalist called David Locke (Jack Nicholson) is in North Africa, trying to make a documentary on some rebels in the southern Sahara (probably the Polisari). A failed attempt at contact leads to him abandoning his Land Rover in the sand and walking back in the scorching heat to his one star hotel in a village oasis with no name and few inhabitants. He needs a shower but the hotel has no soap, so he decides to ask a fellow guest, a man called Robertson. He finds Robertson lying on his bed, dead. As he goes through Robertson's belongings, some aspects of his identity are revealed... but not all. It's as if he's a stencil for an identity—one which Nicholson decides to assume when he sees how easy it would be to swap their passport photographs.

Yes, there's a facial resemblance between the two. But at this point, you don't really know what Nicholson is doing here or what his relationship is to Robertson... who later turns out to be a gunrunner with a bad heart. Later on a flashback reveals that Nicholson is a a journalist making a documentary, although it's much later in the story that you learn what Robertson is/was up to way down here where the Blue Men roam. Thus Nicholson's new identity is both a process of discovery and abandonment.

The Doppelganger

Why would he do this? Why, in a remote hotel in North Africa, would he exchange identities with a stranger? A bad, frustrating day in the desert to be sure, but what would induce a moderately successful journalist (that even Robertson has read) to do such a thing? The with-holding of information is usually subject to the point-of-view. Thus, as the cast come one by one or two by two into the action, the mystery is (paradoxically) both deepened and illuminated... and thus a thriller format is used to disguise an ambitious paradigm about coincidence and fate.

Cut To: Locke's London townhouse where his wife is watching TV and a group of fellow journalists discussing her husband's death in Africa. There's no great distress in her expression. Later, you learn that she has a lover... and there, at least, is one motive for Locke/Nicholson's actions. More information is revealed when she goes to the studio, watches rushes from the documentary, etc. The viewer is now catching up, although he/she has come into the story late. This is the classic *in medias res* narrative form, i.e. starting in the middle of

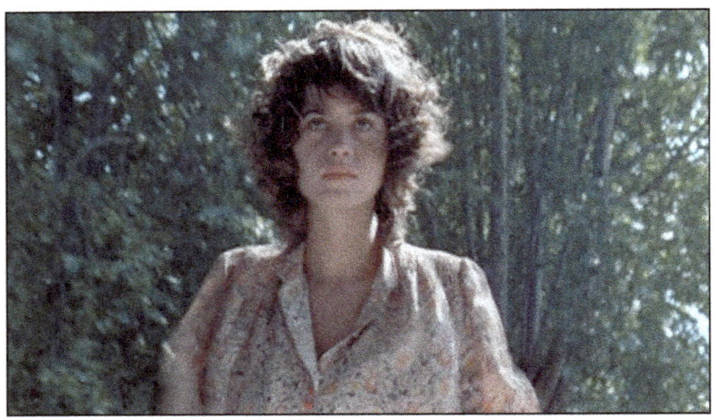

the story. Thus Locke becomes a "passenger" in Robertson's identity. He returns to London, burgles his own house, gets some float money and then, using Robertson's date book, follows Robertson's itinerary, flies to Munich, meets with two brokers for the rebels, receives payment in an old church, agrees to meet them in Barcelona on September 5 for further business. He rents a car, drives to Barcelona, wanders into a post-nouveau building designed by Antonio Gaudi, encounters a young woman (who is never named) who says she's a student of architecture.

She looks pretty good, seems to have an intuitive grasp of just what "Robertson" is all about... or at least enough to go along for the ride. Maria Schneider. You recall her previous movie, naturally: *Last Tango In Paris*. Shocking stuff at the time and perhaps it clouds your perception of her acting. Possibly you anticipate a pornographic incident, although it never happens. In truth, she acts well, and her character is convincing. She has a natural persona, an aspect of non-acting, that softens the often heavy dialogue with its pointed sub-text and malingering pauses. In this sense the literary medium of language innuendo is partially concealed by the documentary medium of real-time film. Nicholson's character has something to hide, whereas Schneider's is ambiguous. You're never sure if she's innocent or part of the hunt. Even by the end, her role in determining Nicholson's fate remains ambiguous. She might be an agent of Destiny... or she might be a casualty of coincidence.

One thing for sure: she's nice to look at. It's easy to follow along with her and Nicholson as she first aides in his escape from Barcelona, then becomes his accomplice in his run down the Costas del Brava and del Sol... following the itinerary set forth in Robertson's date book. A dangerous stranger? What does she care. So maybe Nicholson/Robertson's a gunrunner, maybe he isn't. Romance requires fiction, a flight from the past... although, typically the past is in pursuit of the present. Not only are government agents (of the Saharan republic where the revolt is taking place) closing in, but also his wife and Martin Knight, his documentary film associate, the latter determined to make a tribute documentary about him in lieu of their stalled African project.

Nicholson's wife discovers the passport switch whenever she recovers his gear from the African consul in London. Her suspicions deepen as she views the footage returned with the camera, listens to a conversation on the Uher. Most of this "play-within-the play" is elliptic, has more to do with symbolism than story exposition, and, as a narrative device, will remind some of the darkroom photo blowup sequences in Antonioni's London film, *Blow Up* (1967). Consider Nicholson/Locke's interview with the "witch-doctor": "Mr. Locke, there are perfectly satisfactory answers to all your questions... but I don't think you can understand how little you can learn from all of them... your questions are much more revealing about yourself than my answers can be about me." A head-game artist in dreadlocks? At this juncture, you, the viewer, is the one asking the questions, the one desiring clarification.

Thirty years later, certain aesthetic choices made by Antonioni and his collaborators seem less problematic. At the time, Jack Nicholson seemed wrong for the role of a UK TV journalist. He seemed to be a stand-in or an understudy, a need to appeal to the American market by using an American actor. And casting Maria Schneider as the love interest seemed nothing more than a crass production ploy to mate *Last Tango In Paris* with *Easy Rider*... and behind that, a tap of a standard Godard pairing such as Belmondo and Anna Karina. Big on fantasy, low on detail, these characters were as slight and existential as stolen shadows.

Today, of course, you can see it all in the post-modern context, cut it a bit of slack, compare it to Hitchcock, and marvel at the Antonioni touch. As always, there are a number of scenes in *The Passenger* that could only have been drawn by Antonioni. Nicholson's first sighting of Maria Schneider on a bench on an elevated plaza in London... Nicholson/Locke's discovery of Robertson's body & recognition of the doppelganger... the failed rendezvous at the white geometric village known as the Plaza de la Iglesia... and the brilliant ending at the Hotel de las Glorias.

How You Begin, How You End

The ending of *The Passenger* is a masterpiece of real-time cinematic articulation in the same way as, say, the famous opening three minute tracking shot of Orson Welles' expressionistic *Touch of Evil* (1958). As any serious narrative hustler knows, only two things really matter when telling a story: how you begin, how you end. Antonioni has always favored symbolism and mime, two things film can use very well... rooted, as it is, in the silents. To be sure, an Antonioni ending doesn't always work as well as it should [i.e. the mysterious ritualism of the tennis game in *Blow Up*], but usually it does. The endings of *Il Grido*, *L'Avventura* and *La Notte* are like paintings, full of stasis, symbolism and mystery.

The ending of *The Passenger* has all the mystery and potential of a metaphysical painting by Giorgio de Chirico, and is so provocative it could function by itself or as the opening of the film. The point-of-view is everything, a line-of-sight from the foot of Nicholson's bed through the barred window that overlooks a dusty gravel plaza and the wall of a bull ring that looks like an ancient Roman amphitheatre. The sound is ambient and desultory... the only music a faint distant trumpet, as if an unseen bull fight is underway... or the memory of a bull fight. As in a zoetrope, various figures appear, stage right, stage left... disappear, reappear... an old man and his dog... Maria Schneider, pacing... the bad guys crawling past in a small Fiat... the cops arriving... and Rachel Locke.

And so on. It's a convergence, as in a thriller... but unlike a thriller, the action is anti-dramatic. It could be a dream-fever, the past and the present coming together as the mundane. It's an inversion of a dramatic tradition, a reversal like the visual and verbal palindromes Antonioni uses so effectively in *L'Avventura*. Here, identities reverse, roles reverse. Locke's wife is a widow in a fiction, yet also a widow in a fact. The action is as remote and impersonal as slowly passing clouds. And all the while you're unaware that the camera is moving gently towards the window and through bars into the yard. Magic? Some will recall a similar astral move at the beginning of *Citizen Kane*, but if you want to know how it was done, listen to Jack Nicholson's commentary track. As for the compositional style, de Chirico's famous 1913 painting *The Red Tower* is worth comparing or any of his early street/plaza paintings.

The cop says to Mrs. Locke, "Do you recognize him?" No. He asks Maria Schneider (who still remains unnamed), who says, "Yes, I knew him."

As usual, the DVD contains commentary tracks, although none by Antonioni. Mark Peploe, the main scenarist, reveals a lot of interesting stuff about how the script was written, what Antonioni added or changed, and even talks about an aborted project which preceded *The Passenger*, a film to be shot in Sardinia and Brazil starring Jack Nicholson as a journalist, and using a narrative of two parallel stories intercut. Called *Technically Sweet*, it seems from Peploe's brief description to have been a dry run for *The Passenger*. A comparison of the scripts will make an interesting study for some film student.

Look Through Any Window

Jack Nicholson's commentary (separate) is also excellent, reveals that he knew exactly what this film is about and quite understandably rates *The Passenger* as his greatest experience as a film actor. "In an Antonioni film you see things rather than hear them," he says as he explains the difference in method between the maestro and directors of the usual music-driven melodramas of the commercial cinema.

He's right, of course, as the audio is virtually all ambient noise from beginning to end [consider: the clever use of the running shower as Locke discovers Robertson's body & eventually drags it into his room to switch identities]. And while Jack has had some terrific roles over the years, the cool documentary persona that Antonioni introduced him to perhaps deserves reconsideration. He is good as Locke/Robertson—and not just because he was able to prop up Maria with a hidden hand....

You want the details? Listen to his commentary.

The Passenger should be a sad story, but the objective distance—the spacial alienation—of the Antonioni method flattens our emotions. Somewhere in the narrative he includes documentary footage of a real execution in some African nation. The writer Mark Peploe admits he has moral issues with this... but the fact is that it looks no more or less real than any other scene in *The Passenger*. Some will even rate the parable of the Blind Man that Nicholson/Robertson relates to Maria Schneider in the orchard as more emotionally provocative because, after all, language excites the imagination while film excuses it.

Look through any window, and what do you see? "A little boy and an old woman. They're having an argument about which way to go." This exchange between Nicholson and Schneider is an analogue for their own situation, of course, but it also encapsules the Antonioni method.

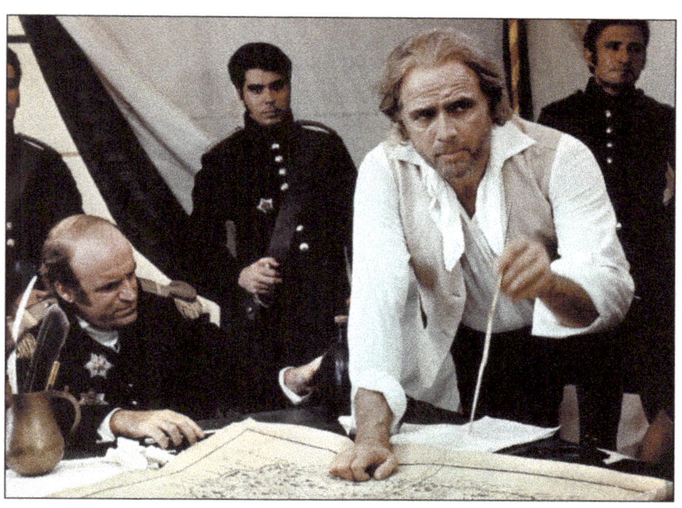

Gillo Pontecorvo: *Queimada*

Queimada (a.k.a *Burn!*) 1968 dir Gillo Pontecorvo writ Francos Salinas & Giorgio Arlorio (story & screenplay) prod Alberto Grimaldi cine Marcello Gatti & Giuseppe Ruzzolini edt Mario Morla music Ennio Morricone
star Marlon Brando (Sir William Walker) Evaristo Marquez (Jose Dolores) Renato Salvatore (Teddy Sanchez) Norman Hill (Shelton) Thomas Lyons (Gen. Alonso Prada)

Credits appear over a montage that sums up the violence of the sugar rebellions in the Antilles Islands of the Caribbean in the 18th Century. Burning plantations, bodies, soldiers, fleeing slaves, the population in tragic turmoil, etc.

The motifs of fire and blood—repeated throughout the film—are immediately established. A sailing ship approaches the Portuguese island of Queimada [meaning: fire or burnt rum] bearing Sir William Walker (Marlon Brando), a handsome agent provocateur retained by the British Admiralty. When he steps onto the quay a muscular black man approaches him in the crowd, says, "Your bags, senor?" Thus Walker meets Jose Dolores (Evarista Marquez), the man who will become his friend, then enemy and nemesis.

The meeting is brief, however. From his hotel room, Walker witnesses the death by garrote of the black rebel Santiago; when his widow and children come to collect his body with a hand cart, Walker follows them on horseback.

Their home village is in the hills, and the way is steep. Walker dismounts, helps them pull the cart, tries to engage the widow in conversation. He wants to meet a friend of Santiago's, "a man like Santiago." This eventually leads him back to Jose Dolores, who is kneeling in prayer in a church. Walker accuses him of stealing his bags, then sequesters him for some white man discipline.

Walker isn't a sadist or even a *de facto* racist, he simply has an agenda. He challenges Jose by smashing him around, by provoking the instinctive rebel within him. It's an interesting scene, as it establishes the power differential between the master and the slave, the white and the black.

It's a rapid education—perhaps too rapid to be believable—and might be an example of why many consider Pontecorvo's didactic style *agit* propaganda. Soon they are exchanging drinks—Walker's habitual flask of whiskey and Jose's saucer of rum—and Walker is grooming Jose to lead the next insurrection.

Walker is crafty, though. At first he makes the mission personal, not political. They will rob the local Banco Esprito Santo, split the gold, escape on a ship Walker says he has waiting, and then they can go their separate ways. "Even to Africa?" says Jose. "Even to Africa," says Walker.

They rob the bank, and Jose and his gang return to their village in the hills. Walker meanwhile is working the other side of the subterfuge. He meets with the principal plantation owners, suggests they overthrow the puppet Portuguese regime, and tells them where he believes the stolen gold is. In essence he's setting up an alliance between the disgruntled local ruling class—many of whom are *mestizo*—and the slave class, the blacks who work the sugar plantations and suffer the brutal indignities of colonialism.

This is all to the advantage of the British Admiralty within the complex history of European competition in the Caribbean and central America, and the contagion of the French and American revolutions. The narrative here isn't easy to follow, and even the alert viewer might lose the plot. Voice dubbing, quasi documentary time shifting, multiple characters (with little characterization), and expositional dialogue heavy with politics obscures the action within the spectacle and the tragedy.

Walker arrives at the village with horses and rifles, just ahead of the Portuguese slave soldiers sent to track down the robbers. At this point he convinces Jose Dolores to stand and fight for the freedom of his people rather than escape with the gold, assume the dubious life of a pirate. The magic of his fantastic persuasion doesn't end here: even though the soldiers appear to be only minutes away, Walker has enough time to a) persuade the villagers to stay and fight, and b) demonstrate to the men how to load and prime a musket.

Cut to: a bunch of dead soldiers scattered on the scorched ground. Whether hours or days elapsed between the lesson and the event matters not—this is history by dialectical montage.

Walker then meets with the planter Teddy Sanchez (Renato Salvatore), tells him, "England wants what you want—Free Trade." Their goals coincide with progress and civilization, etcetera. Thus Walker manipulates everyone like a god playing both sides against the middle and no one disputes the wisdom of his agenda.

Teddy agrees to a putsch with the support of Jose that will make him, Teddy, President; afterwards he meets Jose Dolores—now General—to discuss a new constitution. Jose sits on a throne in a bare room, wearing a shabby uniform in a sad parody of the colonial culture he has rebelled against. In the streets, the people celebrate to the beat of the voodoo drum.

Of course paradise doesn't arrive, although Walker leaves Queimada for 10 years to take care of business elsewhere, still no aficionado of rum, a cynic who deals in the art of real politic while retaining a soft spot for Jose Dolores.

This 10 year hiatus lacks dramatic power as the decline of the new republic isn't adequately shown [it's summed up in a sidebar during a meeting between Walker and the planters]. So the decade goes missing with both sides of the story. Rather simply two agents of the sugar growers track down Walker in a seedy London tavern where he's in the middle of a brawl.

They offer him money, and he agrees to return to Queimada and hunt Jose Dolores who has rebelled against the new government and is carrying on a guerrilla campaign from the sierras.

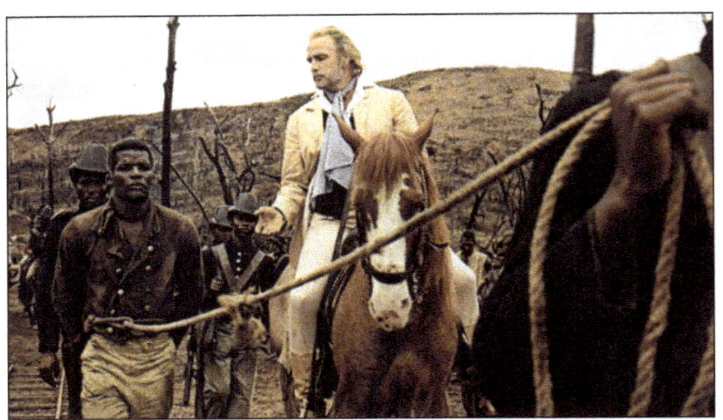

It's a big story to be sure, and a romantic one, although not romantic in the feminine sense. There are no significant female characters, only fighting men and dead bodies, horses and dogs. While Pontecorvo's objective was to blend the romantic adventure and the film of ideas, Walker exists as a poet without a lover. He has the words, he has the horse, he has the politics, but he has no woman. Jose Dolores has the look, the words, and the machete, but no woman. Of all the principals, he exists as an idea rather than as a character. If the goal here was to create Lord Byron meets *Black Orpheus*, then the romance definitely goes missing.

In some sequences, Ennio Morricone's score with its harmonium and mad revivalist-tent choruses suggests parody rather than realism, seems at odds with this somber story.

However, the fact that 20 minutes was cut from the director's original 132 minute Italian version doesn't help, and perhaps one day this version of *Queimada* will be available in North America. You can see the brilliance in the authenticity of period and setting, and it would be helpful to see the entirety of what Pontecorvo created.

There's a lot of panorama in this film, as Pontecorvo is the master of the long shot. Much of the action is at a distance, seen through a telescope, seen from a hillside looking down or looking up. Or the wide view, the omniscient view... a running slave pursued by dogs, emerging from the stand of mature cane... or Walker standing with his back to the burning field and the low bloated sun. It's a documentary view, a newsreel view, an ideological view... at times an authentic view.

In the second half, Pontecorvo finds the rhythm of his story in the tension between dialogue and landscape, irony and history. Walker and the redcoats hunt the rebels in the sierra. The drums keep beating, the fires burning, and Jesus rides a white horse. The sayings of Jose Dolores are repeated by the black population as maxims for a future revolution.

While the highly superstitious Pontecorvo might've been a lapsed Marxist, he wasn't adverse to the deification of his victims, and Jose Dolores goes to the gallows secure in the knowledge that through his legend he will rise again. If you compare his character to that of the amazing Toussaint-Louverture, the black freeman who fought a guerrilla war against the French (and the British & Spanish) in the 1790s that led to the establishment of a black republic in Haiti, you will recognize clear similarities; in fact the entire story of *Queimada* owes much to the story of Haiti.

The character of Sir William Walker is quite similar to that of his namesake, William Walker the American mercenary who staged a coup in Nicaragua and had himself made President for a brief period. This followed similar stunts in the Mexican state of Sonora and Lower California. He was executed by firing squad in Honduras in 1860, an incorrigible apostle of Manifest Destiny. Again, the idea of a man of action, he who can manipulate people, shape history, become a legend. The difference, of course, is that Brando's character wants no power for himself.

He doesn't know why he does what he does, and he just wants to do it well. An artist? The alter-ego of Pontecorvo himself? While Pontecorvo isn't credited with the screenplay, you suspect a great deal of the story came from him, especially when you compare it to his most famous film, *The Battle of Algiers* (1966).

Your Bags, *Senor*?

Why would *Queimada* be Marlon Brando's favorite film? Especially when he hated Pontecorvo's obsessive direction of (up to) 49 takes per scene, and in fact deserted the shoot in Cartagena, Colombia, before the film was finished? Problems with bandits, heat and horrible conditions, a stoned-out crew... miscommunication.... (Pontecorvo spoke no English & packed a pistol) made the experience less than ideal for him. But "you have to separate people from their talent," said Brando in his acerbic recollection of Pontecorvo in Lawrence Grobel's *Conversations with Brando* (1991).

According to Peter Manso in his Brando biography, this wasn't a good period in the actor's life. He was in a middle-age skid, drinking heavily, doing acid, and binge-eating while holed-up in his Mulholland Drive house, and when the Pontecorvo film came along he welcomed the project as a chance to re-legitimize his career.

Action films like *Morituri* (1966) and *The Night Of The Following Day* (1967) were hack jobs done for money—*Queimada* was something else, a serious script that fitted well with his social activism on behalf of the American Indian and the black civil rights movement.

While he played his fake Nazi agent provocateur in *Morituri* to perfection, his portrayal of Sir William Walker seems less effective, although it allowed him to be both a thug and an intellectual, exploit the strengths of his acting style. He has the look, no question—the stocky English bulldog, arrogant, cynical and dangerous, yet behind it all, a humanist. No clowning, just serious work.

"Now listen to me you black ape," says Walker, "I didn't start this. I arrived here and you were already butchering one another." Jose, who has refused to speak to Walker, just spits in his face. At this point he gives up trying to save Jose, goes to the site of the gallows where he finds a worker trying to make a noose.

Walker takes the rope, deftly applies the hangman's knot, says, "You see, Paco, this is how they do it."

Indeed.

Walker mounts his horse; he doesn't wait around for Jose's execution, as he must hurry to his own.

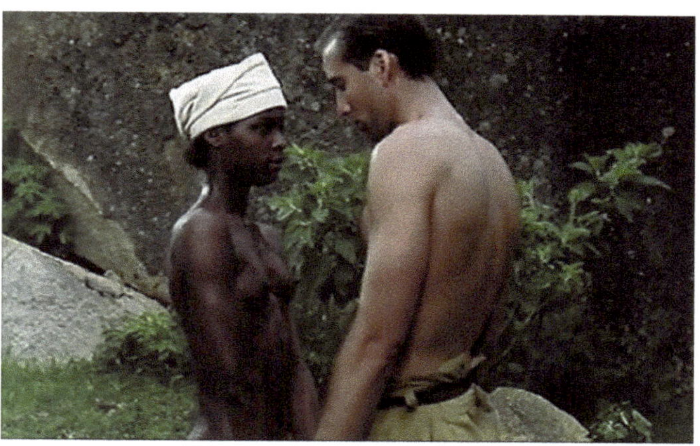

Guiliano Montaldo: *Time To Kill*

Time To Kill (1991) dir. Guiliano Montaldo writ. Scarpelli, Virzi, Montaldo (adapted from the novel *Short Cut* (1948) by Ennio Flaiano) cine. Blasco Giurato music Ennio Morricone star. Nicolas Cage (Lieu. Enrico Sylvestre), Ricky Tognazi, Patrice Flora Praxo, Gianlucca Favilla, Georges Claisse, Robert Liensol, Giancarlo Giannini

Lieu. Enrico Sylvestre (Cage) resting on his cot, recovering from a bad tooth ache. A large moth buzzes the lamp.

> Enrico: Jesus Christ... what a nightmare!
> Narrator: ...the landscape out here is indifferent, it's got nothing to do with us, doesn't even know we exist. This dream of Africa—what was it? A huge space to fill with our dreams of grandeur... and what did we fill? Nothing. If anything, it's Africa that's filled almost 100 pages of my diary.

Set against the background of the Italian-Abyssian war of the mid thirties, this largely ignored film is one of the clear masterpieces to emerge in the nineties. Perhaps the setting and politics are too dated, or the frame narrative with its shifting POVs and symbo-allegorical story-line is too complex for wide appeal. Nevertheless, it's the literary complexity within an authentic setting that give depth and meaning to this story far beyond the usual cryptic fare of the action/grunt genre of film making.

Cage plays a young officer with a toothache as inconvenient and real as the Italian involvement in Africa. Disregarding his roommate's warning (a junior officer who is the authorial "I" behind the diary that frames the narrative) (Flaiano, who wrote the novel, is well-known for his writing collaborations with Fellini ie. *La Strada*), he leaves camp at dawn to find a dentist at another army base. His truck crashes, so he decides to walk the rest of the way. He passes through a construction site where a mysterious young Italian directs him into a beautiful valley, the "short cut" from which Flaiano's novel is named.

The short-cut takes him through a false Eden, a tropical landscape of scattered boulders, giant cacti, saw grass and ubiquitous vines. First thing on the path is a decomposing horse, second a lizard which startles Enrico into drawing his pistol. His directions tell him to look for a lake, but he finds a secluded pool fed by a waterfall instead... and the beautiful Christian native girl, Mariam.

Enrico calls to her, asks directions. He throws her a bar of soap. The sexual tension is as immediate as is its fulfillment.

Rape and submission, love and contrition. The act is ambiguous, yet undeniable. This is a riveting scene, devoid of pornography or shame, an interracial bonding where the metaphor goes beyond politics and religion into the ill-understood mechanisms of Nature and existence.

When they finish making love, he gives her a Bible and his watch (which has stopped—as if he has left Time, entered myth). When he hoists his backpack and tries to leave, she runs after him, implores him to stay. As dusk descends, they retreat to a cave where the clean fractures of the stacked rocks form a prehistoric vault of dim petroglyphs and geologic codes. They lie down on the sand but the eerie cries of a marauding hyena awaken the uneasy Enrico. He draws his pistol, tries to shoot it but only succeeds in mortally wounding Mariam in the stomach with a ricochetting bullet. She dies and he hides her body in a cleft in the rocks. As he leaves, he sees some pilgrims in white approach the waterfall. He doesn't know it at the time, but they are Christians, and their leader is Johannes, Mariam's father....

This Eden-sequence forms the second "frame" and his "confession" to "Flaiano", his roommate.

Did he dream it, or was it real? Later, on a hunt for the rebels who overran and killed the workers at the bridge construction site (including the mysterious young man who told Enrico about the short cut), it becomes clear that it was no dream. Bodies of the pilgrims are scattered in the grass, casualties of the cultural "bridge" that linked them to the rebels and the Italians. There's an uncanny feeling of reliving a nightmare, a *deja vu* of events experienced but somehow forgotten.

As luck would have it, Enrico's toothache is replaced by a hand wound, a stigmata from the truck crash... or his careless shooting in the cave.

He receives his furlough back to Italy, celebrates with the black marketeer Major, "Little Ceasar", who takes him and "Flaiano" to visit three women in white who turn out to be lepers. Ceasar, enjoying his joke, says: "Stick no dick in a white turban—another maxim." But Enrico is filled with apprehension—Mariam was dressed in white, was she also a leper? Is his hand wound a sign of contamination?

This vision of the Italo-Ethiopian world is like the New Testament, the Ethopian Christians overwhelming these new Romans with their native purity. The irony is typical of the movement of cultures and history.

Enrico goes to the coast but before boarding his ship, he visits an army doctor in his tent clinic on the beach.

> Enrico: I have in mind a novel about a man who comes to Africa, gets infected by a mysterious disease. Africa has been described as the land that heals but instead all he finds is death... (the doctor laughs, appreciating the irony) I was thinking you could give me some suggestions for this character's disease... something like leprosy.
> Doctor: Why not?
> Enrico: In my opinion, the character might get it from sleeping in the bed of a native man. Could something like that happen?
> Doctor: Why doesn't he simply go to bed with a native woman? But you realize it takes 10 to 20 years for leprosy to show up in the human body. Of course there are recorded cases where it has showed up rapidly, sometimes in a matter of days....

Now Enrico is truly unnerved. As he hands him a small book on *Hanson's Disease* the doctor says, "The best novels are always a bit subversive." When the doctor lifts the phone to call another clinic, Enrico draws his pistol, shoots the phone, fearing betrayal (lepers are quarantined). He flees, tries unsuccessfully to board the ship without his discharge papers stamped, and then, as fate will have it, runs into the Major who is dropping off a load of stolen army supplies. They get drunk, visit a brothel, start back for camp... Ennio decides to steal the Major's profits.

In the last great scene, the two men have it out on a dirt road as a column of rebels pass into the valley below. Their parting—in which the robber is robbed—essentially dramatizes the two views of Italians about their war.

"You're insane," roars the Major. "You're anti-fascist... you're gonna die here!" But it's the Major who dies, unable to defend himself against the rebels because Enrico has removed the bullets from his gun.

Delirious, Enrico stumbles into Mariam's village, finds Johannes alone among the dead. The old man tends him in Mariam's hut but Enrico can only recover after he confesses. Johannes' first instinct is to kill the Italian, but his Christian discipline triumphs. In a touching scene of reconciliation, father and "son" return to the cave, build a wooden altar and consecrate her grave.

The film concludes with the Italian withdrawal, the color drained to newsreel black and white. The diarist (the Flaiano alter-ego) encounters Enrico for the last time on board a troop ship. His hand has healed, Africa is behind him, his wife awaits his return.

> Narrator: For years I could smell that hair lotion he used... it was sweet and cloying, like flowers in a cemetery... we all thought the killing time was over, we were all going to change our swords into tractors, get back to raising our families, but it didn't turn out that way.

Obtuse, certainly; bordering on the sentimental, certainly. But the depth of characterization within the symbolist narrative, excellent acting and atmospheric soundtrack make Montaldo's film a masterpiece despite the awkward framing of past and present Time.

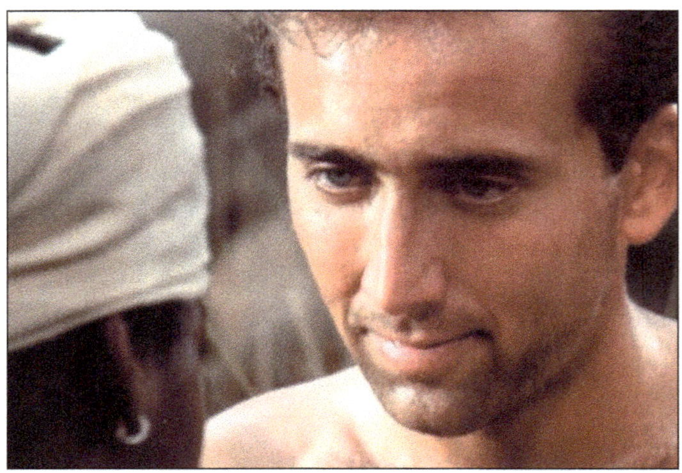

PART SIX:

Miscellaneous Film & TV Drama

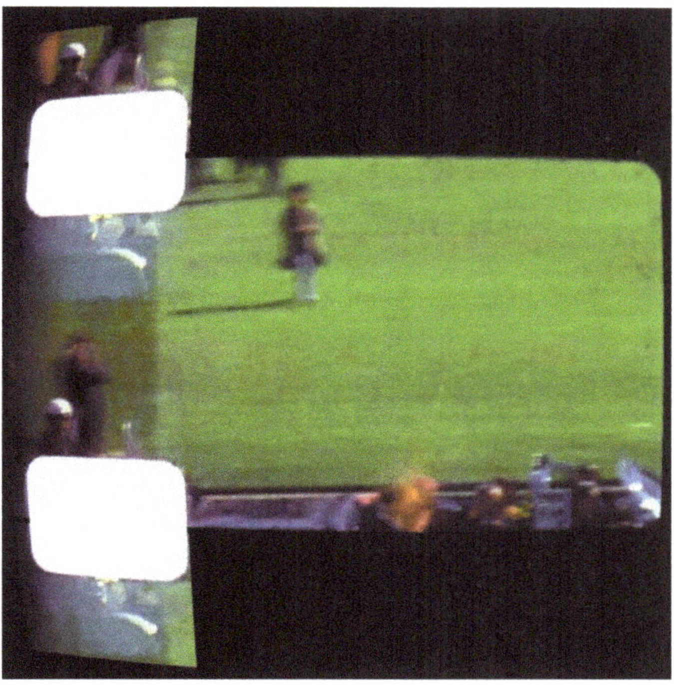

The Zapruder Film

The photographic image has become the sacred relic of our times. The Zapruder film is more important than Kennedy's grave or even his bones. It begins as history and ends as theatre, an interactive movie for the global voyeur.

Frame 230—Kennedy is shot, slumps to his left as if seeking solace in his wife's bosom. Frame 313—the right side of his head is blown off in a blood burst. Jackie scrambles onto the wide trunk of the Lincoln convertible, extends her hand to Secret Service Agent Clint Hill who has jumped onto the bumper. Governor Connally sags down in his seat.

Zapruder is panning left to right, following the motorcade's transit through Dealey Plaza. It's 12.30 pm, the shadows of the onlookers extending north like astrological spokes. The man with a black umbrella absurd in the high noon sun... the Woman in Red... the Woman in Black... a man leaps forward into a crouch as if in a ballet... and the Lincoln disappears into the tunnel of the underpass, moving into symbolism forever.

We search the crowd trying to distinguish players from audience, guilt from innocence, fate from chance. One shooter, two shooters or many shooters? Kennedy is dead, shot by the Secret Service, the FBI, Texas nationalists, the KGB, Fidel Castro, the Mob, Lyndon Johnson—everybody has a motive. Better still, they all have metaphor

"I saw his head come off... but I kept on shooting" (Zapruder)

Just as it's an opportunity for Oswald to shoot the President, it's also one for Zapruder. Which player is operating in metaphor? As Oswald's role is circumstantial—seen, but not recognized as the shooter—he also becomes a metaphor in the interactive movie. Like Zapruder, he is also a voyeur, a sentinel on the 6th floor of the Book Depository. He sees what Zapruder sees: two men in a black Lincoln getting shot. His role as a metaphor is completed when he's arrested in a movie theatre just over an hour later, and his role as a player is completed when he's shot dead by Jack Ruby two days later at the Dallas jail, the killing broadcast nationally on NBC.

Film is a dialectic of documentary and fiction. The Zapruder film is the seminal gun drama on which the world has imposed its fantasies, developed its fictions. The time: November 22, 1963. The place: Dealey Plaza, Dallas, Texas. The action becomes fated rather than circumstantial. Zapruder moves like a director instructed by his unconscious, sets up his camera on a concrete pedestal, the best position for filming the execution. How far does his design extend? Is Oswald in the sixth floor window with his Mannlicher-Carcano 6.5 mm rifle by direction? Is he a player... or is he a stuntman standing in for another player, the real adversary in the scenario?

Behind Every Brutus Stands A Cicero

Zapruder provides the documentary, we the fiction. Perhaps it started with Garrison and his bootlegs, although he was always playing to a gallery of believers, fellow citizens eager to exchange guilt for conspiracy. Reality is always the struggle of opposing fictions. Oliver Stone gave us his extravagant fantasy, just as the Warren Commission gave us theirs 35 years ago. Books, movies, seminars, conferences, and now web sites help drive the fiction like a serial drama rotating its characters while maintaining its setting.

The Man with the Black Umbrella stands between Zapruder and Kennedy like a professional mourner hired in anticipation of the event. Partially hidden by the Stemmons Freeway sign, his symbolism is enhanced by the conjunction he creates. As the Lincoln emerges from behind the sign and Kennedy grimaces in pain, it becomes obvious: Zapruder, MBU, Kennedy = Death.

The Woman in Red—who is she? To some, she has a name: Jean Hill, Dallas schoolteacher and "the last dissenting witness". As the conspiracy momentum develops, her story alters, embraces the symmetries suggested. She hears multiple shots. She hears Jackie talking to a non-existent dog. She doesn't see SS agent Clint Hill jump onto the trunk of the Lincoln but she sees Jack Ruby on the grassy knoll. She isn't there for Kennedy but for a police outrider in the Presidential motorcade, a guy she fancies. What does this all mean? Triangulation? It engages the imagination, a sexual undertow like Zapruder's "assistant" holding him from behind as he films the tragedy.

Dealey Plaza resembles a theatre. Consider the Texas Book Depository rear centre stage. Pergolas with their pseudo-classical columns extend right and left as Elm Street cuts the stage diagonally. You can be in the pergolas or on the railway overpass or on the grassy knoll or even in the Book Depository.

You might have a camera, you might have a gun.

Some say the Zapruder film is a fake, part of the conspiracy. More specifically, the original 8 mm print has been tampered with, frames removed, frames inserted in a deliberate prevarication of the truth. In the "claw shadow" and "claw flare", in the image ghosting and the obvious frame splices the conspiracists see tampering, take comfort in these technical avenues to further fiction. It's not good enough to accept that *Life Magazine* technicans damaged the original print while making stills for publication. Evil exists in the off-frame shadow between the sprockets, concealing players waiting to be unmasked.

The Groden Movie: Anonymous, Muchmore, Nix & Zapruder

Perhaps the real Kennedy assassination movie is the Robert Groden montage. Here the symmetry becomes mystical, the intention religious. In 1968 Groden clandestinely copies the Zapruder original when it's sent by *Life* to the lab where he works in New Jersey. Like the photographer in Antonioni's *Blowup*, Groden believes the truth can be discovered by improving upon the original. He softens Zapruder's camera jitter and makes the assassination the climax of a longer narrative by incorporating footage by other shooters who filmed the motorcade prior to its swing into Dealey Plaza. Thus Zapruder becomes one of four cameramen—Anonymous (commercial footage), Murray Muchmore, Orvil Nix, and Abraham Zapruder.

By extending the narrative without substantially leaving real time sequencing, Groden enhances the atmosphere of the setting and controls the anticipation of the killing. His montage was shown on the Geraldo Rivera show, *Good Night America*, March 6, 1975. "It's the most horrifying thing I've seen in the movies," says the reigning high priest of media hip, Geraldo, as they rerun the Zapruder sequence in slow motion. Frame 313 becomes the indictment—anyone with eyes can see that Kennedy is thrown backwards by the impact of the bullet that tears the right side of his head off, *ergo*, the shooter is to the South, probably on the railway overpass, or in a sympathetic vector to the railway. And as everyone knows, Oswald is sited in the rear, to the North....

The obfuscation is in the spacial perception. Whatever else it might be, Zapruder's film is two-dimensional. The plane of viewing is flattened, the isometrics deceptive. As it doesn't include the Book Depository, Oswald is off-stage, his angle of fire fantastic, improbable when considering the fatal head shot. It doesn't matter if the rank and file know nothing about ballistics or gun-shot (nervous system) trauma or whip-lash—Groden's movie becomes another optical version of the truth for the citizens of Flatland.

The off-stage action in the Zapruder movie is just as troubling and extra-sensory. How many shots are fired? We don't hear any, of course, as this is a silent film. The Lady in Red says four or five. Oliver Stone says six. A man in the underpass is wounded by a piece of shrapnel. A bullet in the Lincoln, a bullet hole in the infield, a bullet hole on the sidewalk.... Three cartridge shells are found with Oswald's abandoned rifle but it seems impossible that he had time to get off three shots. If indeed (as William Manchester reports) a bullet can be chambered and fired in a rifle like Oswald's in 2.3 seconds, and Zapruder is filming at 16 frames per second (the minimum for persistence of vision), then Oswald has lots of time. If the first shot precedes 230—when Kennedy's Lincoln is masked by the Stemmons Freeway sign—then it really doesn't matter what speed Zapruder's camera is running at or if Oswald was ever in the Marines or if there are two or three Oswalds.

Evidence is still being found, the script revised: guns, shell casings, another 8 mm movie. Like totems at a shrine, every offering becomes an artifact. Expect a rise in death-bed confessions.

To pose such questions engages you in the fiction. You enter the ambiguities, assign character and motive, invent geometries, trajectories, solutions. Re-enact the drama on location: load a black Lincoln convertible with dummies, send it down Elm Street at 11.2 mph with a shooter in the Oswald window. Take 2: send it down Elm Street at 11.2 mph with a shooter on the railway tracks. Take 3: repeat sequence with shooters everywhere. Film everything at 96 frames/sec or faster if possible. You want to know the truth? It's in the re-run, in the *deja vu*.

The LMH Digital Zapruder

After thirty-five years of all those spectral bootlegs, will the hallucinating stop now that we have the latest techno revisionist Zapruder in the form of the LMH digital copy? Stabilized, balanced, rendered, this version gives us everything, including the imagery captured outside the projection frame. There are five digital versions in the MPI release of the LMH remaster, including the original 8 mm 4:3 frame view, outside frame view (sprocket track imagery), slow motion versions, and a grand finale centre frame version.

Frame 313? It seems incredible that Jackie isn't hit. Again, the spacial depth is difficult to imagine, the image as flat as a pop art painting by Roy Lichenstein. There's a flash—not unlike a lens flare when catching the sun head-on—which shrinks back to Kennedy's head and the red halo. This implosion certainly helps insinuate that the bullet has come from the South. And as the head snaps backwards, can there be any doubt?

Absolutely. There has to be a parallax problem. It might be frontal... or it might be side shear and recoil, the final heave of a scrambled nervous system. Despite the digitization, despite the resurrection, the moment remains existential.

The production is distributed by MPI under the title *Image of an Assassination: a New Look at the Zapruder Film*. Some frames appear to be missing or reversed, as if the reassembly is designed to mess with our minds, infuse our fictions. We see more, understand less. In this way it appeals to our sense of tragedy, agitates our desires. Impressive? Of course. Interactive?

As always.

The compilation details the history of the Zapruder film through a series of interviews and VO narration. The WFAA-TV (Dallas) interview with Zapruder the day of the assassination is especially interesting:

> Zapruder: I got out there about a half hour earlier to get a good spot to shoot some pictures... and I found a spot, one of these concrete blocks they have down there at that park near the underpass... and I got on top and there was another girl there from my office, she was right behind me... (inter-

> viewer adjusts Z's mic) And I was shootin' as the President was comin' down from Huston Street and makin' his turn... he was about half-way down there when I heard a shot (makes a down angle motion with his left hand) and he slumped to the side... like this (mimics left slump). I heard another shot or two — I couldn't say if it was one or two — then I saw his head open up... (hand to head) all blood and everything... and I kept on shootin'....

Zapruder is like a benevolent Erich von Stroheim: bald, double-chin, glasses, black bow tie, enigmatic pin in his lapel. The interviewer is smoking, his jowelled face and raccoon eyes evoking a Nixon parody. Isolated in time from its cultural ethos, the scene seems false, succumbing to the improvisation of the moment. What else could it be? Incompetence and duplicity are always in tandem, like guilt and innocence in a running child.

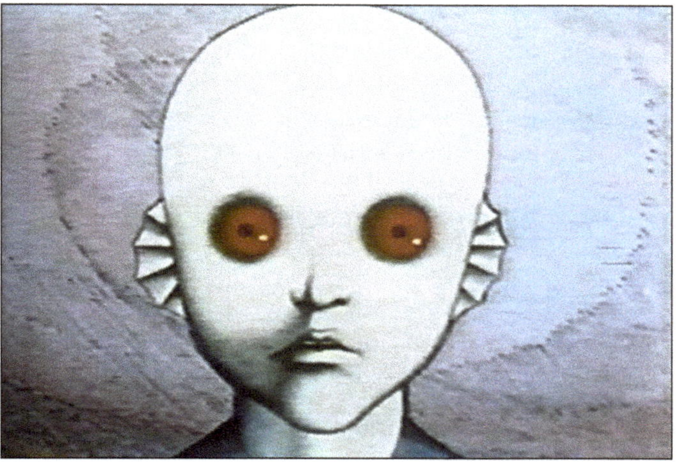

Rene Laloux: *Fantastic Planet*

Fantastic Planet (1973) dir. Rene Laloux writ. Roland Topor and Laloux (based on the novel *The Savage Planet* by Stefan Wul) cine. Lobomir Rejthan and Boris Baromykin graphic design Roland Topor graphics: Joseph Kabrt (characters), Joseph Vania (backgrounds) music Alain Goragner

"Our planet Yon possesses a single satellite, Fantastic Planet. We utilize this uninhabited planet for meditation. Yon is divided into several ouvas. Two of the ouvas, Strohm and Yaht are natural and symmetrical...." This peculiar work is frequently dismissed by North American viewers as primitive, lacking the technical sophistication of fluid movement animation and integrated foreground / background isometrics. Yet this allegory of human regression and rebirth which uses the speculative fiction convention of symbolism by scale (the human Oms are the pets of the giant transcendentalist Drogs) demonstrates a psychological sophistication and art tradition that moves beyond the infantile animations of Disney and the American method.

The Oms have self-destructed on their planet Terra and are now in a Stone-Age state on the planet Yon. The domesticated Oms live in the Park, the wild (outlaw) Oms live beyond the walls in the forest. The status quo is quickly established in the opening sequence, where a giant blue finger flicks an Om woman and her baby down the slope like a bug. The woman is killed and her baby is later discovered by two strolling Drogs, Tiva and her father, a member of the Drog ruling cabal. Like the Pharaoh's daughter finding and adopting the infant Moses, Tiva takes the baby home and inadvertently educates it during her subliminal Info lessons.

It's a world of continual irony, based upon a reversal of fortune as elementary as that in *Planet of the Apes*, but in this instance showing human development in polar opposites: where we have come from (the wild Oms) and where we expect to evolve (the mystical Drogs). The human experience is expressed in both master and slave, thus the expected historical progression of revolt, war and political settlement occurs.

While there are many amazing scenes and graphic whimsies along the way, the climax on the *Fantastic Planet* itself is the most interesting. Escaping "Omization" (gas extermination), two Om rocketships make it to the satellite that orbits Yon and find giant headless torsos standing like the forgotten effigies of a lost civilization on a Daliesque plain.

This is the "Fantastic Planet", a conjunction for Drogs everywhere in their galaxy, a place for mating and reproduction. Drog youth navigate to this rutting field of the demi-gods in glass spheres that float like spore bubbles and attach themselves to the shoulders of a statue of the appropriate gender. The statues then begin to dance in pairs, a ritual that allows these astral beings the necessary physicality for reproduction and the continuation of their species. In danger of being crushed, the two Om ships open fire with their ray guns and wipe out the mating couples... causing a parallel chaos back on Yon, where the Drog elders are in telepathic contact. Faced with disaster, they immediately open negotiations with the Oms and peace follows, based upon a New Order: an artificial satellite (state) called Terra (in honour of their ancestral planet) is launched and henceforth both cultures are free to progress in harmony but with independent spiritual sky-cults.

> "...contrary to what one may think, the needs of graphics do not necessarily correspond to the needs of movement... consequently the American school ties drawing to animation... the European school to graphic imagery... Americans a taste for curved lines, quick movement and comedy, as well as an emphasis on character. In Europe, the emphasis on graphics favored the straight line, slow movement, fantasy and a lesser emphasis on the psychology of individual characters." (Rene Laloux)

This reinvention of the Egyptian/Israelite mythology (combined with the more recent experience of the European Jew with the Nazis) uses the color blue as a symbolism for the astral consciousness for the Drogs and their sky-cult allegiance to the *Fantastic Planet*. While the micro world of the Oms is scaled to the organic topography of root tunnels and plant forests, it is also as bizarre as the interior of the human body, with roving creatures that resemble organs, and where red is the color of fear.

The graphics are obviously drawn from the tradition of gallery painting, compositions structured in terms of stasis, two-dimensional space, and the symbolist artifice of the surrealists. The sub-text is driven by history and politics, the text by dream and expressionism.

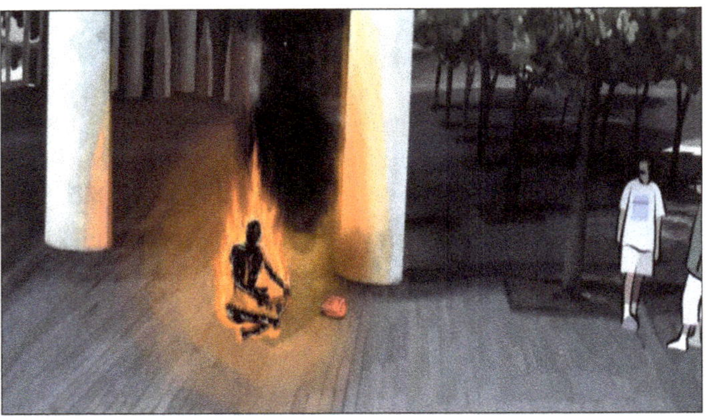

Richard Linklater: *Waking Life*

Waking Life (2001) "written" and dir. Richard Linklater cine. R. Linklater & Tommy Pallotta art dir. Bob Sabiston edt. Sandra Adair music Tosca Tango Orchestra (score by Glover Gill)
animators: too many to mention
star. various profs, comedians, actors & sundry from the Austin, Texas, community
20th Century Fox 100 mins

You're living in Austin, Texas. You want to make a movie... but not the usual Lone Star vigilante action feature. Howz about an animated essay, sorta French New Wave... like Jean-Luc Godard run through Adobe Photoshop or some other digi software. Solarize, posterize, fantabulize. Remember the way Godard interviews Belmondo or an extra, has him respond to a bunch of questions that you never hear? Splice these monologues into the action... cryptic, elliptic, *tres mondo mystic*.

You could do this, and you could have some other guys do their own routines, splice them in too. Music? Just do what Godard does in *First Name Carmen*, get a string ensemble, include them in the action too. Hand-held camera, spontaneous action/reaction... the dialectic of fiction and documentary. Narrative? Easy. What the hell is narrative but a procession of events. This could be cool, guys....

Richard Linklater's *Waking Life* is "cool", exploits the plasticity of digital photography and impressionist landscape painting in a very powerful and provocative way. The animation is a type of rotoscoping where the characters are photographed and the backgrounds replaced with drawings. The blending of digital and analogue, techno and human, is great. While a team of animators is used, the documentary effect of straight photography is humanized (or psychologized) by good old-fashioned art.

And this isn't just some retro expanded cinema exercise in synaesthesia for the night trippers. The entire architecture of the style supports the subject: is life a dream? Or, as Linklater puts the question, "Are we sleep-walking through our waking state or wake-walking through our dreams?"

Mind-Body Dualism

A generic young American man—could be 1970 vintage, could be 2000—called Wiley Wiggins seems to be "sleep-walking" his way through life. While most people dream of peculiar sexual assignations, ambushes and various forms of treachery, Wiley seems to be trapped in an academic hellscape where various profs and other experts declaim on sundry subjects including existentialism, language and communication, evolution, free will and choice, trans-this and trans-that... a lot of awfully clever qua qua qua stuff that might remind you of the table of contents of *The Encyclopaedia of Ignorance* (Pergamon Press, 1977) or pot parties with Profs X , Y and Z.

His astral journey starts as a child when he observes a comet in the sky, has to grab the door handle of the family sedan to keep himself from floating away.

The beauty is in the ambiguity. He takes the good old Freudian train to some city and finds no one is there to meet him. He's eyed up by a foxy chick but keeps moving. He steps out of the station, looks for a taxi. A boat-car pulls up, and a dodgey looking fellow offers him a ride. As Wiley doesn't seem to know where he's going, he's dropped off somewhere at random... and so his adventure goes.

Whatever you think of these anonymous profs, writers, comedians and other dream figures, there's a fascinating level of obsession within their monologues. New, exciting ideas... or just plain old *deja vu*, you do notice that the sane and the clearly insane sound very similar. Linklater: "The aesthetic of ideas, information... is coming at us, 100 miles an hour... for example, the Internet."

This dream noise makes for interesting random possibilities. Wiley encounters a social malcontent (J.C. Shakespeare) wearing a black T-shirt, and they walk the walk like old friends, arrive at a gas station where the man fills up a gas can. He never stops monologuing, so when he asks Wiley for some matches, you might not even notice. They arrive at the entrance to some public building where he douses himself with gas, immolates himself in some vague protest just like a Buddhist monk in Saigon, 1966. Yes—"extraordinary ideas require extraordinary solutions."

You're All Gonna Die

One of the best sequences features Charles Gunning as an anonymous prisoner in red ranting in his solitary cell about the revenge he's going to exact on persons unknown when he gets out. The hatred is sublime. The scene is a lift from Hubert Selby Jr.'s *The Room*. "You're all gonna die," growls the man in red, his voice heavy with vengeance. Who is he? What's his problem? He's merely another random incident, a piece of channel surf, more noise.

A similar scene has Stephen Prince [you might remember him as the gun bootlegger in Scorcese's *Taxi Driver*] telling a barman about what happened in the desert outside of Vegas. This routine is like something out of Charles Bukowski, ends with both men shooting each other. This slice of American death counterpoints with another bar conversation, featuring Prof. Louis Mackey, expert on the SF writer Philip K. Dick, talking about Time, dream and reality. If you happen to pass through Austin, stay clear of Lala's bar.

Two women authors discuss aging... a man drives through the urban streets in an old Plymouth, declaiming his philosophy through a hailer like some political propagandist on the hustle... meanwhile Wiley wanders through rooms, offices, public places trying to wake up or at least make sense of life. For the most part, his dreams are fairly innocent. The synchronicity of ideas does not include the atomic bomb.

So does he wake up? Where does this meta-dream lead? Well, where can it go if circularity is the subject....

The *Decoupage* Of Comic Books

Waking Life is certainly one of the most interesting films of this sort since Rene Laloux's 1973 *Fantastic Planet*. For people who failed in school or for whom school failed, it's not likely to be of much interest. You might think it's too long at times, repetitive in its discourse, even though there's no question about the uniqueness of each character. Linklater addresses these criticisms in his director's Audio-Commentary (included as "Bonus Features") when he says that ideas can be revisited whether or not you use them today. The nostalgia for debate, say.

Waking Life is what a large part of film culture will become—a synthesis of photo realism and hand-crafted detailing. Oddly, it's an old-fashioned concept, just like painted sets for live actors in the theatre. Now, the sound stage becomes the computer.

You're in Austin, Texas... and for some reason you're real thirsty and you're in LaLa's. Jesus... who's that guy in black wearing the poncho, standing, other end of the bar? Stevie Ray Vaughan? "You're right, man," he says. "Human vibrato beats a software oscillator anytime, any place." And over there... isn't that the beauty you met in a dream three, four years ago? Yes. She recognizes you. She's with Godard, the movie director. "The *decoupage* of comic books is the preferred method for montage," he says. "As for Louis Malle, you know and I know he's...."

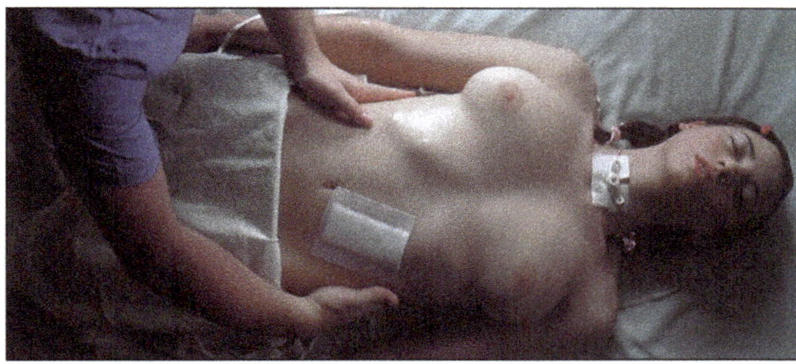

Pedro Almodovar: *Talk To Her*

Talk To Her (*Hable Con Ella*) (2002) writ. & dir. Pedro Almodovar cine. Javier Aguirresarobe edt. Jose Salcedo art. Antxon Gomez music Alberto Iglesias
star. Dario Grandinetti (Marco), Javier Camara (Benigno), Rosario Flores (Lydia), Leonor Watling (Alicia), Geraldine Chaplin (Katerina) *et. al.*
Sony Pictures

They're Bound To Become Friends

You're a journalist who writes for a publication in Madrid and who travels overseas to exotic locations writing travel brochures... and who cries easily in the theatre or when listening to music. Your excuse is that you're trying to get over a woman who was freaked out by a snake in Africa when you were having a romantic sleepover by an oasis. Sound promising? There's more: you replace her with an androgynous female bullfighter called Lydia who gets gored and ends up in a coma. Tabloid? Perhaps... but certainly not cheap, as there's lots of sub-text and mytho-symbolism in your unhappy situation. Your name? Marco.

Or maybe not. Maybe it's Benigno, another lonely guy who lives in an apartment just across the street from a dance studio... and who falls in love with one of the dancers, a girl by the name of Alicia whose old man is a psychiatrist. This is interesting as your behavior is a bit suspect, definitely obsessive. You break into her apartment, steal one of her hair clips... she discovers your unauthorized entry as she steps out of the shower but you assure her you're harmless. You make an appointment with her father for some counselling, although this is merely a ruse to get closer to Alicia. Alas, one rainy day she gets hit by a car and ends up in a coma... end of story? No. Fate is the hunter. You just happen to be a male nurse who works in a hospital that handles just such cases. The father, who believes you're a homosexual, hires you to look after her. A case-history gem? Perhaps... but certainly not cheap, as there's lots of sub-text and mytho-symbolism in your (unhappy) situation.

Two women in a coma, two men in attendance—they're bound to become friends.

The Shifts In Fragmented Time

As the past is always trying to catch up to the present, more than half the film elapses before the action claims the future. Think of it as a breaking newscast story. In the casts, followups uncover information from the past. It's a montage narrative typical of the media noise of our era, although the artistic presentation makes it appear to be something else. It's an absolutely natural form of narrative; after all, when we remember the past, we don't necessarily recall events in linear Time.

The story starts at dance performance (Cafe Muller) which opens the film with the male principals Benigno and Marco sitting in the audience. The metaphor of blind women and custodial men is introduced. The idea of dancing through a world of obstacles is repeated throughout the action [Alicia's fated jaywalking most obviously], and the film concludes on a cyclical motif, once again at the dance theatre... although this time in the future at a different performance.

The second stage [or "theatre"] is at the clinic where the two comatose women are attended by their devoted lovers. This is broken by flashbacks which show how the men (Marco and Benigno) meet their women (Lydia and Alicia) and the evolution of these relationships until the accidents that leave the women in comas. In essence, these flashbacks are a sharing of information between the two men as they become friends, united by a common dilemma.

Although the structure appears complex, it has a beautiful montage rhythm and is perhaps the only way to deal with the internal world of these characters without stopping the action for impossible exposition. The sense of personal loneliness on the existential scale is enhanced by the melancholy score of Alberto Iglesias, and helps guide us through the shifts in fragmented Time.

Some scenes, though, add little to the action except mood. An example would be the party/concert at the country villa, where the Brazilian tropicalismo singer Caetano Veloso sings a sensitive song as Marco, deep into his romance with the bullfighter, is once again moved to tears. It's a beautiful cameo in a beautiful setting [Almodovar's country retreat, apparently], although nothing happens here to advance the story. We already know Marco is a sensitive soul... and that Lydia hangs with the international Latino artistic elite. Directors often include their friends as extras in their movies... and no harm is done here, as the atmosphere is charming.

Media Noise And The Meaning Of Art

We now have an entire generation of film makers whose idea of reality is a movie theatre. It's a behavioral reduction in both psychology and culture. They can't tell a story without the movies somehow being involved... and Almodovar is no different. But it certainly can be argued that movies are an integral part of today's reality and their celebration doesn't always signal a post-modern conceit.

The character of Benigno is certainly reminiscent of Adrian LeDuc, the cloistered cinephile in Donovan's *Apartment Zero* (1988) who lives with his sickly mother and spends far too much time at the movies. Both Benigno and Adrian have a distinct homoerotic posture in terms of infantilism and fantasy. In both situations a political symbolism coexists with a Oedipus complex. And both use a "double-figure" or doppelganger motif. For cultural purposes (Spain vs. Argentina), the comparison is intriguing.

Almodovar does a clever exposition of Benigno's mental state with *The Shrinking Lover*, the silent movie cut-in that serves as an analogue for B.'s rape of Alicia and which is also a lesson in symbolism. Cocteau... Dali... even Jack Arnold (*The Incredible Shrinking Man*) and countless cartoons that use the shrinking motif come to mind. Benigno recounts the action of this silent film to the comatose Alicia like a patient confessing the sordid details of a mad dream to his shrink. It's far more effective than a documentary view of her rape, yet the surrealism is sexual voyeurism nonetheless. Almodovar is like a bad schoolboy whose crude graffiti of stolen images and neurotic symbolisms allow us to laugh in the darkness while retaining our sense of moral superiority.

Apostasy And The Make-Over

Lydia's character is really a bisexual foil... can be viewed as a fantasy figure for straights and gays alike. The pure tabloid unreality of her character is established from the outset when Marco first sees her on a TV talk show trying to fend off a crude personal invasion by the host, which ends up with both women grappling like juvenile deliquents. A female bullfighter —why not? That holiest of Spanish institutions is certainly open to sexual revisionism by the artist in search of revulsion. That Lydia should receive the bull who gores her on her knees is a sado-masochism worthy of a drag queen giving head to a homicidal potentate.

Sacrilege? Naturally. It's all prepared in the idle conversation before the fight as Lydia is dressed by her valet. Her sister is tending a small candle and photo shrine [of Lydia], asks if anyone read about the nuns being raped by their priests in Africa. Marco says that before AIDS, the priests raped the local women instead. A man says not all priests are like that. No, says someone, some of them are pedophiles. The sister is shocked. Another man shrugs, says, everyone enjoys fucking. Cynical, secular... yet absolutely true to the casual conversation of those who make money from the superstitions of others.

The parallelism of Alicia's father and Lydia's old lover El Nino (also a bullfighter, played by the actress' father) introduces a level of kink to this Freudian nightmare. The sexual chessboard that Almodovar likes to play on is typical of a graduate of a post-fascist state free to shock and scandalize... and luckily enough, all this passes as surrealism in other places like North America where the political context is likely to be overlooked.

He Won't Be The Last Warlock In The Green Room

This is a very funny film, often close to mockery—people, situations, institutions. By default, it's Theatre of the Absurd, although in practice it's Life... a bit like tabloid TV perhaps but Life nonetheless. The situations constantly challenge convention and reality itself. The symbolism is always leading the observer into the more ambiguous aspects of gender, identity and societal function... at times it's a bit like following water down the drain into the hidden geography of the gutter. Role-playing... infantilism... apostasy and the make-over. Too weird to be practical? Almodovar isn't the first and he won't be the last warlock in the green room. Hitchcock has been diagnosed as a sadist for his "make-overs" of his leading actresses as if this is some sort of special crime, even when we know the make-over of the persona is central to the creation of art.

And art, of course, is civilization.

Almodovar's make-over of his actress into a bullfighter is less interesting as a political act than as mythic transformation. To say that art as he sees it is homosexual would be a simplification, although the sub-text often suggests it. Women made comatose by snake-phobias and abandoned men driven crazy by loneliness can only have a homosexual conclusion, unless some sort of mystical union beyond physical sex is possible. The unlikely friendship of Marco and Benigno is a case in point, and while they are never lovers, they become a doppelganger by the time B. is imprisoned. They are the reconciliation of opposites, which is what art is all about. Think of the conditions and implications of Lydia's pregnancy—these are irrational and mythic. Think about this, and we see a Trinity shaping up. A bit unholy, yes, but who knows... in another life, Pedro Almodovar might be a Catholic theologian.

Nothing Is Simple

Conceptually the script for *Talk To Her* is very good and deserving of the Oscar it received. The acting is great, and the direction is definitely audacious. More successful than its predecessor, *All About My Mother*? Yes... the level of heresy has been raised, the sadness refined, the pain exorcised.

"Nothing is simple" says Katerina (Geraldine Chaplin), the dance instructor. The last line of the film could be an oblique comment on the complex psychological paradigm that sits behind the story. Too complex for language alone, yet made accessible by music. The finest passage in Alberto Iglesias' score comes at the conclusion. *Hable con ella* features some beautiful flamenco blanco guitar by Vicente Amigo... as the London Session Orchestra tangos softly. Some call-and-response between the violin and the guitar... and the animal lament of *El Pele*. The atmosphere is melancholy and lonely... hallucinatory, like the passing of a ghost.

Talk to her, Pedro.

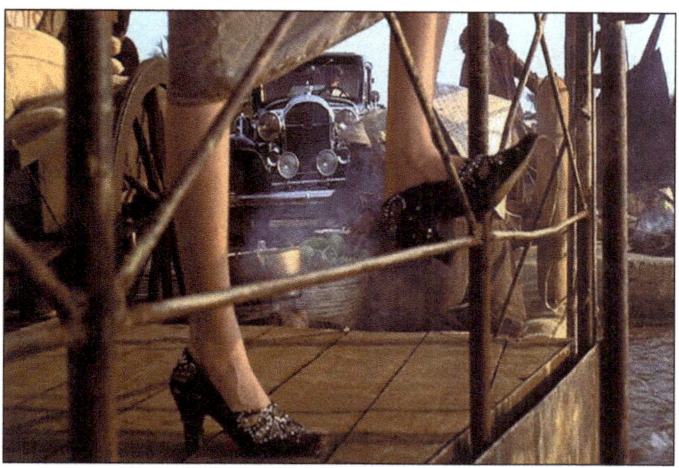

Jean-Jacques Annaud: *The Lover*

The Lover (1992) dir. Jean-Jacques Annaud writ. Gerard Brach [based on the novel by Marguerite Duras] cine. Robert Fraisse edt. Noelle Boisson music Gabriel Yared art/design Thang At Hoang costumes Yvonne Sassinot De Nesle
star. Jane March (French girl), Tony Leung (Chinaman), Frederique Meininger (mother), Arnaud Giovainetti (older brother), Melvil Poupaud (younger brother), Lisa Faulkner (Helene), Xem Mang (Chinaman's father)
Jean Moreau (narrator)
RENN/BURRILL/A 2 co-production
MGM Avant-Garde Cinema 115 mins

Vietnam *Mon Amour*

Ladies... you know you had another life, one in which romance and desperation were your fate. You're 15, almost 16, a loner in a lonely land. You're on a small ferry, just about to cross the turbid waters of the Mekong... yes, you're in Vietnam, French Vietnam, back before the colonial dream all went to hell. You're leaning on the rail, one foot hooked on the scupper, a girl dreaming of being a woman. As the peasants swarm aboard with their bicycles, carts and livestock, a large black Citroen C 6 limo eases itself slowly onto the deck. Already you're being observed by its hidden occupant.

And what does he see? A French girl in a cotton dress, a school girl with a loose girdle and rhinestone cabaret shoes... her pigtails partially concealed by her favorite hat, a man's Fedora. Forget the pouting mouth and slim adolescent figure. Think of dream, think of Freud.

As the ferry starts moving out, the chauffeur steps down, opens the rear door... a man emerges, an oriental man in a white suit. He leans on the railing nearby. He glances your way, takes a gold cigarette case from his jacket, flips it open, offers you one... naturally, you don't smoke... and just as naturally, you know this routine is merely a prelude....

And so it starts... although, actually, we've been chauffeured into this action by the writer, an older woman who is sitting somewhere in Paris writing this story. Based on the "autobiographical" novel by Marguerite Duras, *The Lover* lingers somewhere between the sentimentality of doomed love and the flesh-eating horniness of sexophilia. Behind this, though, is a political gestalt of the French and Chinese colonialists in Vietnam. Prejudice is cultural, destiny ancestral. Recall that Duras wrote the script for Resnais' famous deconstructivist paen of western guilt, *Hiroshima Mon Amour* (1959), where again we see her familiar story of forbidden love in an interracial context. A grim montage of nuclear anxiety, Hiroshima is more like a photo-essay than a drama. But... not so *The Lover*. Director Annaud and scenarist Brach never allow the background politics to overwhelm the sensuality... or the landscape the characters. Yet *The Lover* is a beautifully photographed film, where the surrounding squalor simply heightens the exotic elegance of the lovers. Fact is, we can never rest easy in anyone's arms after seeing the superb skin of Tony Leung and Anne March. Is it pornography? If pornography is sex that we watch, then yes. Is it art? If art is the sexual perception of an object, then yes. Can pornography be art? If you've ever made love in a dream....

The black car is speeding along the dykes and dusty roads towards Saigon. You're in the back with this stranger. He's twice your age... and Chinese. This is dangerous stuff. But what the hell... you're young, starting to crank. You have breasts, legs and hands... and you want to use them. You have no father, your brother is a sadist, your mother a doting old schoolteacher in a swamp up country. You exchange banalities. He confesses he has no job, no prospects... his father is an opium addict who hasn't left his bed in ten years since the death of his wife. Do you care? No. You dream of writing novels in which you revenge yourself on your brother, your brutal, psychopathic brother. You watch the landscape flow past... villages, rice paddies, needle forests, horizons. His hand moves timidly to meet yours... first a finger touch, then a hand... finally, like a full sexual embrace, his fingers interlock with yours.

Gerard Brach got his big break as a screen writer working with Polanski... and *The Lover* is the sort of film we would expect Polanski to make. *The Lover* seems an odd project for Annaud [*Quest For Fire, Name Of The Rose, et. al.*], especially when viewed in tandem with his follow-up, *The Bear* (1994). As Brach wrote the screenplay for this too, we might wonder if there are any similarities. Ludicrous? *The Bear* is about an orphan grisly pup trying to survive in the British Columbia wilderness when hunting was a career and environmentalism non-existent. Stripped of setting, though, both stories are the same: survival of a young free spirit in a dangerous world.

Looking Towards The Mountains... And The Sky Of Siam

While there is no mention of the crash of '29 and the subsequent world-wide economic depression, both characters are affected by bigger events in the bigger world. Perhaps the pivotal scene is where the lovers discuss their hopeless situation at a ruined plantation on the edge of a mud desert... perhaps the former property of her parents. "My mother was killed by the land registry agents and robbed by government officials," she says, looking towards the mountains and the sky of Siam. The dawn wind moves the palms. Yes, he went to his father, told him the situation. His father said, "I would rather see you dead than know you were with a white girl." His father, the opium addict. His father, a financial patrician from the 1 million Chinese minority in Vietnam.

The Vietnamese are merely background in this movie... rickshaw runners, market vendors, paddy workers, servants... landscape. The lovers represent the two competing colonial cultures. The Chinese, of course, ruled Vietnam for a 1,000 years

("Indo-China")... and financed and supplied the communist Vietminh in their fight with the French. The French divided Vietnam into two (North & South) in 1954... to little avail as history as shown. Now they only go there to make movies.

The Chinaman, though, has his problems. His family was displaced by the Japanese in Manchuria. While his father profited by selling his lands and jewels to them, it seems this led to his mother's death. We're not directly informed of the circumstances, must infer them from conversational fragments. We know, of course, that Japan occupied Manchuria in 1931 following years of meddling and fighting with Russia over domination in the region.

Trapped by the Buddhist code of ancestor worship, he can do nothing but follow the dictates of his father. While this seems absurd in today's mobile, secular society, things were much different then. As a character, he presents a curious paradox of cultural passivity and animal vitality. His manners are, yes, impeccable. His generosity outstanding. His integrity... well, the seduction of a young school girl might be distasteful, yet the historical and cultural context is quite different from, say, the lavicious paedophilia of H.H. in *Lolita*. As it turns out, it's quite possible that he is the one who was seduced.

Your boarding school is like an orphanage, where little French Madelines and their half-caste sisters cluster in mosquito tents within long, humid dormitories. Your friend Helene walks naked, a model without an artist, joins you in your tent, tells you about Alice, a classmate who has been slipping over the wall in the evenings, prostituting herself with the passing men. You smile, say, "It's always appealed to me... going with someone you don't know." You pass through the gate, leave the school, briefcase in hand. You're walking below palms in the dusky light... and there he is, the big black car, parked. What is there to say? He takes you to "the Bachelor Room", a street-level apartment in a rough Chinese district. Slatted windows, green deco armchair, table... and the bed. The ruckus of the street is close, immediate. He says he can't do this, you're too small... but you, working with the intuition of an ancient talent, help him get past his charming apprehension.

Sexual Attraction And The Perception Of Art

This film is about sex, make no mistake. It's about sex and the politics of sex... and politics are in some measure about the manufacturing of lies. Lies only exist when we are afraid of some raw, defining truth. The ease with which the French girl lies to her family is typical of sexual hunger and the need to conceal its ritual. Brother Pierre knows better, of course. When he sees the diamond ring, he knows. Why would this Chinaman give his sister the diamond belonging to his dead mother? Sex. He grabs her discarded panties from her bed, sniffs them, says, "Smells of Chinese..." The humour here slides past in the black absurdity. They fight, as hate is a condition of poverty. His mother can never give him enough money, and now his sister is the provider.

We see only brief moments of this unhappy family as they struggle to exist on the income of a rural schoolteacher. The mother favors the brutish elder son in an unreasonable and pathetic fashion. Why this is so, she doesn't know. When the family is invited to dinner at a restaurant in Saigon, the crux of the matter is clearly defined. The affair must not be mentioned. Call it pride, call it racism, call it dumb... but for some, identity can only be maintained by taboo. The impoverished French get drunk, behave badly. The brutish brother challenges the Chinaman to fight... but he merely defers, like a monk with no regard for the material world. Yet the material world is where they are.

Afterwards, the lovers retire to the Bachelor Room. It's now time for some grudge sex. He's angry, because good manners and Confucious can only take you so far. He backhands her, rips her panties off, goes straight to work. As we watch, we have to admit this young girl is quite good at the art of whorish detachment.

> She: How much would this cost you in a brothel...
> what we just did, I mean.
> He: How much do you want?
> She: My mother needs 500 piasters....

To pay the boarding school, apparently. When is a mistress a whore, or simply a lover? The power in the relationship is constantly shifting. Her mother, in a moment of truth, asks her, "Do you only go with him for the money?" and she replies, "Yes." Her mother nods, although her expression reveals that she knows otherwise.

The monsoon rains hammer down... and in the blue Bachelor's Room he tells her that he is to be married. He's now smoking opium, just like his father... imprisoned and desexualized by convention, astral travel is his only means of escape. What's the bride like... is she pretty? "She's rich," he says. "Covered with gold and jade and diamonds...." He could be describing a temple idol. The French girl takes this all in stride, has only one request, that he meets her one final time one week after the marriage. Does he show up? Or does the rigid racial lock of ancient culture still hold him hostage.... Well, this can be said: a lover always has a way of reappearing.

If You Believe Marguerite Duras

Throughout, the cinematography/visual design is superb. The symbolisms are always oblique, subtle details in the action. For example, the woman in white [the Administrator's wife, another *pussy fatale*] in the back of another limo, always travelling in the opposite direction, boarding the ferry when the French girl is disembarking... or vice versa. Or when the French girl puts her lips against the glass of the limo window, forms a kiss to which he responds... two people reaching out from different solitudes, different cultures. Or the failed plantation, with the broken dams....

The moods, too, are very sympathetic to the emotional core of the story. The rains internalize the action, mythologize the sex. The dusky light, the sense of memory, things remembered, fantabulized. As characters, the lovers act almost in contradiction to their gender: he, fashionably dressed, the trembling lover; she, casually dressed, the ambiguous lover. She seems older, almost cynical. He was in love... but was she? The ocean liner moves out of frame, leaving a contrail of black smoke above the waves, which gradually fades... time, memory, reality.

Yes, you're a writer, living in Paris. You smoke cigarettes now, your lizard eyes masqued by heavy glasses. You'll win a big prize for this confession, the Prix de Goncourt. You'll do it the old way, pen on paper:

"One day, I was already old, in the entrance of a public place, a man came up to me. He introduced himself and said: "I've known you for years. Everyone says you were beautiful when you were young, but I want to tell you I think you're more beautiful now than then. Rather your face as a young woman, I prefer your face as it is now. Ravaged."

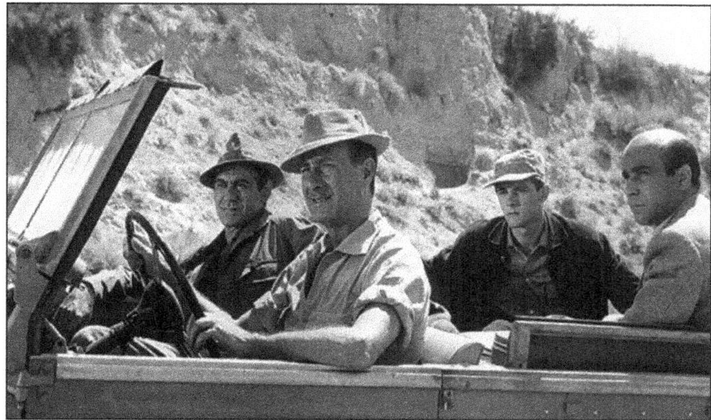

Carlos Saura: *La Caza*

La Caza (*The Hunt*), 1965 dir. Carlos Saura writ. Saura and Angelino Fons cine. Luis Cuadrado music Luis DePablo star. Ismael Merlo, Jose Maria Prado, Emilio G. Caba, Violeta Garcia, Fernando Sandez Polock

Four men assemble for a rabbit hunt on the desert property of Jose, a business man and host of the hunt. The arroyo where the hunt takes place just happens to be a battlefield of the Spanish Civil War in which three of the men took part. As the temperature rises and the three veterans begin to disintegrate from the heat, continuous drinking and pill popping, their separate agendas converge in a bloody finale that turns the hunters into the hunted and reveals the psychoses of a generation... and, perhaps, Nature itself.

La Caza—an ugly piece of work with the visceral authenticity of a snuff movie. While the Hollywood film culture is driven by the Gun Drama, this is the only film I've ever seen that truly deserves to be in the genre. The four men are defined by their guns: Jose and Paco, vets, businessmen, uneasy friends, use double-barreled shotguns, their chambers sheathed in silver plating, the ornate scrolls like the new-found pedigree of their wealth.

Luis, vet, the business partner of Jose and science fiction aficionado, has a sniper rifle, its telescopic site clearly designed for targeting humans, not rabbits... aliens, not Spaniards. And young Enrique is armed with his father's pistol, a German Luger from the Civil War.... Like all exercises in human realism, the humour is in the bizarre, the madness in the detail.

And these men are mad. When they arrive in the arid river valley and begin setting up camp, Luis tells Enrique: "Many died here—it's a good place for killing." In a metaphor for this valley of death, much of the rabbit population has been destroyed by myxomatosis, a disease introduced by humans to control the "rabbit invasion". The first rabbit turned up by Cuca the dog is dead, its eyes hanging from the sockets of its bloated face, the definitive signature of myxomatosis. As they sit in their sun tent preparing their weapons, they discuss the nature of the hunt:

> Luis: A real hunter isn't interested in cowardly, inoffensive rabbits.
> Paco: (shrugs) Neither weak nor crippled have a part in life—it's the law of Nature.
> Enrique: You're not serious.
> Jose: He's right as far as hunting goes... rabbits are defenseless. The more defenses the quarry puts up, the better the hunt.
> Luis: That's why someone said the best hunt is the manhunt.
> Paco: (jittery) What's that? (Luis shrugs) The hunt is like life—the strong take out the weak.
> Jose: Sometimes the opposite happens....

It turns out that Jose's motive for the hunt has been to hit up Paco for a loan. Jose's life is in crisis—he's left his wife, taken up with a young beauty called Mirabel, now has a financial problem. In an analogue to his own situation (and Spain's) the crippled gamekeeper Juan asks Jose for five thousand pesetas to help deal with his mother's illness... and of course Jose refuses, just as Paco later refuses him. Jose's refusal is conditional, however, unlike Paco's.

The first hunt is like a military patrol. The men fan out, and as they follow the dog through the sage, the dialogue becomes interior, arguments with the Self, or in the case of the young Enrique, a *deja vu:* Seems to me I've been here before... the scent of the thyme... was I ever in such a place? The subsequent montage of rabbit kills engages the poetry of violence in a sequence that anticipates (and probably influenced) Peckinpah's famous ambush montage at the beginning of *The Wild Bunch.* Drums roll in military meter as the men fire at will and the rabbits roll down embankments, convulse, die in what is clearly the real thing. The contradiction of ugliness and beauty is perfectly actualized in the action and the contemplation.

This could be used as a basis for a theory of art—but is it art or merely documentary?

It's cinema at its best, where the voyeurism places the beholder into an ethical crisis. From here on the film becomes relentless. It might not suit everyone to see life in terms of the famous Hobbesian credo of "nasty, brutish and short" but this world-view is dramatized by Saura in convincing detail. The second hunt wherein we see a ferret terrorize the rabbits in their tunnel warren is pure cinematic genius. The tunnels are shown in cross-section and we see the ferret—which has a chiming bell tied to its neck—trap and kill a rabbit before flushing the others out to be massacred in the cross-fire. It's like looking in on a laboratory experiment—ugly, but an undeniable characteristic of the human experience, just like the daily slaughter of cattle in abattoirs everywhere.

Is it blood fever or an reenactment of the past? The men recall the old days and the camaraderie of an old associate, Arturo (the youngster Enrique is really his replacement in the hunting party), who takes on the atmosphere of a ghost. In a pivotal scene Jose tells Paco he has "a secret in these hills" and takes him up to a cave which has a padlocked door. Inside, Paco is shocked to see a skeleton sitting against the wall, and quickly withdraws.

Jose: I found it years ago.
Paco: Then why not bury it as God ordains?

A good question. The identity of the skeleton is as ambiguous as is Jose's intention. Later, as the men eat lunch at the camp:

> Luis: It's like a funeral. He must've shown you the dead man.
> Enrique: Who? Arturo?
> Luis: Jose's big secret: a war casualty he keeps hidden in a cave.
> Enrique: Which war?
> Luis: Any war—which do you prefer?

Luis's madness seems more advanced than that of the others, as he uses Science Fiction like a Christian fundamentalist uses the scriptures in his perception of the impending Apocalypse.

> Luis: You haven't much time left. A day will come when the rabbits will invade, form a new civilization. And as they're smaller than us, there will be room for all. The class struggle will disappear, and so will envy. First, though, there will be a war with the rats....

As they settle in to sleep through the afternoon siesta, the men become more edgy, events more primal. Paco and Jose doze in the tent as a melodrama between a man and a woman plays softly on the radio, their fevered dialogue like an expose of the hunters' desperate dreams. Meanwhile Luis circles the dummy of a woman (brought from the village for target practice), muttering his maxim for living: A thing is moral if you feel good after it... and immoral if you feel bad after it. He spikes a beetle, pins in the chest of the dummy, takes aim, obliterates it after several shots. He seems to be acting out a hatred for his cheating wife or all women, whom he likens to vampires and ferrets. The shooting startles the sleeping hunters in the tent. Enraged at this and other indiscretions, Jose punches Luis, hammers his "partner" to the ground—as if Luis alone is responsible for his nightmare. Thus the circle of humiliation widens. Meanwhile Enrique is paning the horizon with binoculars, sees the caves, then sees the young niece of the gamekeeper bathing outside their adobe. His discontent is sexual and elementary. He starts a fire with a pinup magazine. Luis joins him, throws the dummy onto the fire... which—like the emotions of the hunters—gets out of hand, spreads through the sage... and is only put out with difficulty.

Paco—who was the cause of Arturo's death (whether it was murder or suicide)—has also crossed the line. As he watches the gamekeeper struggle with the ferret cages, he says to himself, "The cripple looks like a ferret." When he shoots the ferret at the end of the hunt, it's obvious to both the gamekeeper and Jose that it's a deliberate execution. As Paco examines his face in a vanity mirror, Jose takes aim on him but is distracted by the private hunt of Enrique and Luis, a bizarre ritual in which the youth stalks through the sage with his Luger pistol accompanied by Luis in the Land Rover. When they flush out a rabbit and start shooting, the others join in by reflex... and Jose uses the opportunity to blow Paco away.

The gunfight between Luis and Jose is short and brutal, completely realistic. Enrique, stunned at this turn of events, runs away, escaping the arroyo and the battlefield. The film ends with a freeze frame of his flight as he gains the top of the hill.

If there's a victim, it's Jose, as he's the only one of the three veterans with any humanity. He can't help Juan the gamekeeper with cash, but says he'll help with medicine and hospital bills. He recognizes Luis's lunacy, tries to manage him and can't, and even after he strikes him, he begs Luis's forgiveness. Luis is clear cut in his homicidal nature, his code a simple rationalization of death by numbers. Paco is cunning and no less homicidal, a natural fascist who views life as a triumph of the strong over the weak. Jose is really a sentimentalist, a man who keeps a skeleton in a closet (cave) because he needs to remember the past in order to blackmail the present. But if the guilt is meant for himself or Paco remains circumspect. In the end, he's a victim of his own machinations, a Don of Guilt, Bankruptcy and Death.

When this film appeared in 1965—ten years before Franco's death—Spain was still a society under armed guard. The Guardia Civil stood on street corners in every town of significance with sub-machine guns, a sort of welfare army for the fascist regime still living the fantasy of the Conquistador. *La Caza* is only obliquely anti-fascist. The red and the black schism of Spain—like some sort of special Latino schizophrenia—runs its political and spiritual arrow right through the souls of these characters, although hunting and killing can be found in any country, any culture. Excellent acting, beautiful editing rhythm, sophisticated story, subtle cinematography....

It's hard to find anything wrong with this film, save that it might not be what you want to see. There's no fantasy in the use of guns here, just as there is no fantasy in the outcome of the story. The only fantasy exists within the characters—and this, after all, is what delineates the human within the animal.

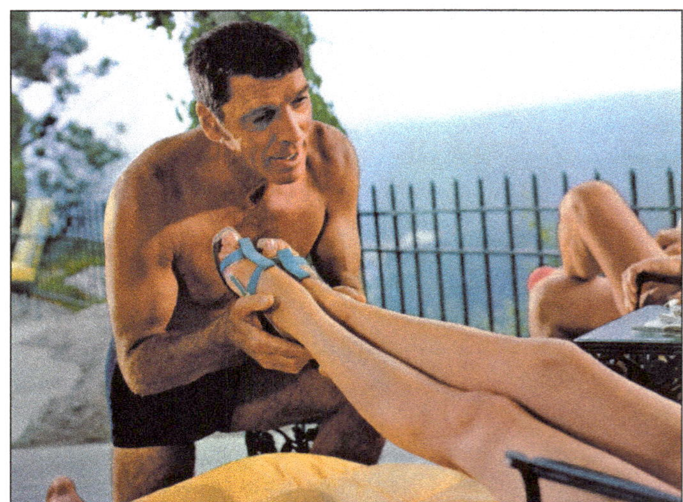

Frank Perry: *The Swimmer*

The Swimmer (1968) dir. Frank Perry writ. Eleanor Perry (based on the short story by John Cheever) cine David L. Quaid edt. Sidney Katz, Carl Lerner, Pat Somerset music Marvin Hamlisch art Peter Dohaus star. Burt Lancaster (Ned Merrill), Janet Langard (Julie Anne Hooper), Barbara Loden (ex-mistress), Tom Bickley, Bill Fiore, House Jameson, Kim Hunter, Janice Rule, Bernie Hamilton, John Garfield Jr., Charles Drake, Dolph Sweet, Marge Champion, Nancy Cushman, Diana Muldaur, Joan Rivers, Diana Van Der Vlis

Cheever Surrealism: An American *Midsummer Night's Dream*

A man emerges from a dry forest of scrub oaks and haunted wildlife in a slow long distance lope, naked except for his tight swimming trunks, enters a garden dominated by a large feminine swimming pool. His entrance is mysterious and primal, like a dream figure leaving one memory and entering another. He dives into the blue, swims a couple of lengths, rises sensuously onto the apron of the pool where he is handed a fresh cocktail by a beaming woman leaning forward from her recliner:

> Helen: (purring) Neddy... where've you been keeping yourself?
> Merrill: (marvelling at the sky) Oh here and there, here and there... what a day... have you ever seen such a glorious day?

Thus starts the odyssey of Ned Merrill (Lancaster) through the rural Elysian yards of upstate New York and the perpetually stoned society of party animals who own them. An amnesiac with no memory of his fall from grace (quite possibly suffering from a bad case of chronostasis), he stands sipping his drink, glimpses other yards, other pools in the cascading landscape of forest and dale. He has an epiphany:

> Merrill: If I take a dogleg to the south west, I can swim home....
> How? Why?
> Merrill: Pool by pool they form a river... all the way to our house... I'll call it the Lucinda River, after my wife.

A noble, romantic gesture from the lips of man dressed in self-deception. At first he appears to be an incorrigible optimist, the very epitome of the American child-man driven by bourgeois altruism and free market determination. But as we follow his progress pool-by-pool towards his stated destination, his God-like persona gradually decays, and the essential schizoid nature of his reality is revealed. He swims the pool of his former mistress, has an ugly encounter. He swims the pool of his former baby-sitter, takes her with him for part of the journey. A storm threatens, he injures himself cavorting in a horse paddock. He disrobes completely for a swim in the pool of two nudist patricians, limps off into the dimming light.

If You Make-Believe Hard Enough, Then It's True For You

In a key scene, he encounters a solitary boy playing a flute at a lemonade stand below a tree. The boy's parents are away somewhere. Merrill has no money but cajoles the boy into giving him a drink. He asks the boy if he can use his pool... but when they arrive at the pool, they find it empty. The boy says he can't swim very well. Undaunted, Merrill gives the boy a lesson, and they simulate different strokes across the floor of the dry pool. "If you make-believe hard enough, then it's true for you," Merrill tells him, and the boy is suddenly delighted by his apparent success in swimming an entire length.

But as Merrill departs, he hears a sinister reverberation... he turns, sees the boy bouncing on the spring-board above the deep end.... Yes, in this low tech but high concept film, symbolism is everything.

The screenplay is by Eleanor Perry, at that time the director's wife. It should be noted that it's no mere photocopy edit of the John Cheever story and is arguably better. Cheever's talent was for writing realistically about his social milieu in a very unrealistic way. He was an American surrealist. Events happen, nothing is rational. A product of disfunction in his writing method? His stories are really condensed novels because they use summation and long time-frames. In fact, they read like social essays, their style slightly archaic in the manner of the scented rhetoric of Henry James. *The Swimmer* is typical in this regard, its Biblical tone and elliptical humor quite anti-dramatic.

Eleanor Perry solves this by dilating the action into a series of symmetrical scenes at a series of symmetrical swimming pools. She also accelerates the symbolism by introducing new characters and reinventing others, and all this works despite a modest debt to the expressionism of the Italian filmmaker Antonioni. What is a Hollywood film without sexuality? Julie Anne (Janet Langard) the nubile baby-sitter is a clever departure from the original story, yet the invention is pure Cheever. This character allows us to see Merrill through eyes of an innocent on the edge of corruption, for elsewhere the characters are already corrupted. Everybody drinks, pretending success, but in fact they are anticipating failure. Although Merrill's failure is an unstated business debacle, the bigger failure is something that's both abstract and physical, spiritual and natural, that deals with the coming into and the going from life itself. As Merrill advances, he thinks he's evolving, but in reality he's devolving.

In the Cheever story, Merrill starts out with his wife but leaves her at the first pool; in the Perry film, she exists only as an ideal, a device to drive the action towards its paranormal ending.

Post-War Sexist Ass-Slapping Triumphalism

So while *The Swimmer* uses a paradigm rather than a plot, the narrative is nevertheless very visual and metaphoric. For some, the heavy reliance on sub-text will be a delight; for others, a bore. Rooted in the episodic tradition of Bunyan's *A Pilgrim's Progress*, the action seeks to be instructive and moralistic. At times, it's like watching a National Geographic documentary about the rites and customs of some forgotten tribe in the Amazon jungle. It's pure anthropology.

Is life a dream? Is there such a thing as a collective unconscious? The director Frank Perry uses some interesting montages and double exposures in the bridges that link the scenes. Merrill stares at the sky, sees a river of pools... or, Merrill stares... and from his eye a dark horse emerges. These art-house saccades are elementary in this age of computerized special effects, but they are effective and accurate indicators of Merrill's psychological condition.

And how about Burt Lancaster... did he ever make a bad film? Probably... but *The Swimmer* isn't it. His attitude (post-war sexist ass-slapping triumphalism) and his physique (the trapeze artist in middle-age) are excellent for the role. Yes, he's the star (he's in every scene) but his role isn't sympathetic. Typically he conflicted with the director (who thought Lancaster wasn't right for the role) during filming and even came to believe what everyone else at the time said about the film, i.e., it was a disaster.

Echo Harbour

Some Thoughts On Errol Flynn And Other Sailors

Years ago, late sixties, early seventies, we used to visit an island near Campbell River, the famous salmon fishing area off the west coast of British Columbia. The island was one of many in the archipelago and was becoming a hippy refuge for all sorts of itinerants and fugitives up and down the west coast, many escaping the Vietnam Draft or just escaping the general madness. This was rain forest country, big trees and deep inlets, and miles of raw, unexplored country, and the eastern horizon was one long jagged line of snowy peaks where the Coast Range stretched all the way to Alaska.

We knew a young guy there who had an old fishing boat and an old cabin, was doing some guide work when he wasn't growing weed and investigating the cosmos... and the cosmos was beautiful there on the island with its unpolluted air and forest meadows. Eddy. Jack of All Trades, was good at carpentry, knew a bit about electronics, could mess with cars and trucks... all sorts of stuff. Black hair, bad acne scars on his face, but out-of-focus he looked alright, photographed well regardless. Looked Russian, the way an Apache Indian can, but as he got older, more Indian. Bit of an Oedipus inversion too, clashed big time with his old man, and we saw the similarities right away, even if Eddy just didn't have the discipline and fealty Edward Senior required. But this is neither here nor there—Eddy had this boat he'd fixed up and we took a couple of cruises around the island on it.

On one of these cruises Eddy took my wife and I to this abandoned property at the head of a small inlet with its own pebble beach and wooden dock. The low walls of this inlet were smooth granite, like they'd been quarried and the quarry had sunk, forming a a small channel which made an excellent harbour, and had a fantastic echo, so we immediately called it Echo Harbour, although what it was really called or who had owned the property, we didn't know. Eddy figured Americans, a hunting and fishing retreat.

The only way you could get to it was by boat, so not many people knew about it, and the house—well, it was just a big cedar summer cabin—was left to subside and collapse onto the beach in the uncharted silence. Shake roof, some corrugated zinc... broken windows, two storeys, facing south east, although this was on the north end of the island. There was still some furniture—kitchen table, chairs, some drawers... crockery, utensils... upstairs I found some magazines from the late forties and early fifties lying on the floor with some large black and white photographs... nine by twelve large. One drew my attention—not the salmon trophy pictures but the one with the man and the woman on top of Mount Whitney, smiling from the triumph of their ascent. How did I know it was Mount Whitney? Not because I recognized it or knew it was just north of Death Valley or that I'd ever climbed it myself. It said so on the back, written neatly in pen and ink: Lynn and Pat on Mt. Whitney, elevation 14,505 feet, June 21, 1950. Good looking couple, if they were a couple, and they were standing close enough to suggest that they were. My first thought was 'movies' as they looked really familiar, like I knew them. He was the safari sort, wearing khakis and sunglasses, had a Hemingway beard, off-duty camouflage maybe. And her, 'Pat', could be any of those sirens from back then, the crime doll and nightclub singer, the pinup in the G.I. bunkhouse. Wearing shades too, and blonde, with her hair pulled back and the belt on her hiking tunic tight on her waist. Whoever took the photo must've stood on a rock as they were looking up at him—not much, just enough to make the angle and get the rugged mountain vistas behind. Twin reflex Rolli or a Leica M3, I figured, as the blowup quality was so good. Professional, not amateur. Could be Susan Hayward using an alias, I thought. Read somewhere she'd visited Campbell River back in the days when John Wayne brought his yacht up to do some fishing. The WW II minesweeper he had fitted out with a bar and sweet accommodations. *Wild Goose*, he called it. I could see it coming in here, no problem. Or perhaps whoever owned the property came in by float plane. There were some 40 gallon drums lying near the dock, just rusting away where they lay. Could be aviation fuel, could be diesel.

As I studied the picture, I wondered if the guy was Errol Flynn. I went to the window, looked at the inlet, tried to imagine his yacht anchored out there, *Zaca*, the 120 foot schooner. She'd pull too much water to come to the dock but she could anchor out there just like the *Flying Dutchman*. But did Flynn ever sail this way? Who knows... the *Zaca* was big enough to sail anywhere, and Flynn died on a beach or in a hotel in Vancouver 1959, didn't he? In the arms of a fifteen year old, quarter of his age and that was o.k. because he was Flynn and could break any rule he liked.

The others were on the beach, trying to skip some crockery they'd looted from the kitchen, saucers and plates. Eddy was pretty good, had them bouncing over the water, and was giving instruction to his latest, who was giggling lots. She was fifteen too, half his age, still in junior high and he was getting away with it because on this island in these times you could get away with quite a bit. Maybe not as much as Flynn, but quite a bit.

Her name was Lucy, I think... but I might have that wrong. Does it matter? Forty, nearly fifty years ago and the echo is quite faint, although in other ways clearer than ever. It was Spring, there was a freshness in the air, and the alders were pushing hard in the swampy depressions along the logging roads and the dogwoods were blooming wherever we came across them. There were one or two behind the house and several crab apple trees and they were flowering too. Nice, quite mystic.

Lucy was hippy basic, a few beads and buckskin, and jeans that kept slipping over her ass when she bent over to throw her saucer at the water. My wife couldn't talk to her, because what was there to talk about? The girl was already proficient in rolling joints and writing poetry—so Eddy said. Joints I could believe, poetry... well, Eddy was no poetry expert, but had a keen sense of smell. Hippy oil did it to him every time. When he left his first wife, it was for a chick who was into aroma therapy and reckless sarcasm. When he left her, it was for my wife's cousin, and when he left her... well, I can't remember. Maybe it was this Lucy, although she wasn't the sort you leave anyone for. Think he was just passing the time with her as she was hanging around the dock when he was working on the boat, and they shared a joint and you know the rest.

My wife was paddling in the surf, holding the hem of her cotton Cleopatra dress up. Bare midriff, long hair. You'd never know we had two kids. She liked swimming and I could see she was thinking about it, was up to her knees and looking over the water, which was quite still, almost like a lake. I wondered if 'Pat' had stood there like that, statuesque and shapely, like a goddess looking for Neptune. I watched through a broken pane. Insects were buzzing around, recently hatched from their long slumber. My wife waded a little deeper, swinging her hips. Then she yodelled... and listened for the echo to come back. It was marvellous, like someone unseen was returning the call, concealed in the forest or—as I fantasized—on a phantom yacht at the mouth of the harbour. What was she calling? It sounded like "love", long on the first syllable. But it was just a nonsense yodel, an experimental cry into the past. I understood this when the others joined in, launching their own yearning signals, delighting in the long, slow delay... once, twice... (faintly) thrice.

Weird place. It was like the occupants had just boarded their boat or climbed on their float plane, left in a hurry... why? Why would they leave personal stuff like these photographs? Just forgotten in the haste? Or perhaps they meant to come back but something intervened... they crashed or sank or maybe back in L.A. they got divorced, went bankrupt, committed suicide or something. There was a lot more text on the back of that Mount Whitney photo, written in neat pen and ink:

> 4.2 mile climb to Cottonwood Pass. (11,160 ft), then camped at Rock Creek. Next day we made the nine miles to Guitar Lake, the last water before Whitney. Peaceful and beautiful. We hiked on during the night, no clouds, no moon, so you could see the Milky Way across the sky. Our world was defined by flashlight. Anything off trail was in a dark abyss. Trail Crest (13,500ft) was the dangerous part. Babs developed altitude sickness. Made it to 13,900ft and had to turn back. She felt disoriented and the cold air hurt her lungs. But as you can see, we made it!

Who was Babs? The woman of the guy who took the photo? Maybe they were doing a location trek for a movie project.

Getting out of Echo Harbour was a lot tougher than coming in, as the engine gave out and we drifted through a gap in the rocks, completely at the mercy of the tide, which was running pretty fast and this was a notorious danger spot, turns out. It was a tense couple of minutes but we made it, and Eddy managed to get the engine going again with his girlfriend holding the wheel. Later, when we talked about it, my wife said her dad was probably a fisherman, so handling a fishing boat wasn't new.

The other night I was lying alone in bed, couldn't sleep because of the moon which was near full phase and coming through the skylight like someone was shining a lamp in my face. Could hear some sea lions flopping around and yapping the way they do in the moonlight when they form a circle in the water for some reason I've never been able to figure out. Mating? A salmon trap? Mimicing the face of the moon? The reverberating splashes made me think of Echo Harbour, back forty years to those times I hadn't thought of in some time, even though I kept that photo of the couple on Mount Whitney long enough, intrigued by its mystery. Somewhere along the line I'd come to the conclusion the couple had to be Errol Flynn and his second wife Patrice Wymore, based on the fact that they starred together in a 1950 movie called *Rocky Mountain*, in which the mountain was supposed to be an Indian "ghost mountain" on the edge of the California desert. Mount Whitney, right? And the woman's name was Pat and his was—best as I could make out—Lynn. This was good enough for me, made my fantasy complete.

Flynn wanted to be a writer and I was a writer, wasn't I? And I'd done a bit of acting and could've gone on with it if I'd wanted. Delusional or not, this was the way I was thinking. Flynn said somewhere sometime, "By instinct I'm an adventurer; by choice I'd like to be a writer; by pure, unadulterated luck, I'm an actor." That's it, isn't it? Chance. Life is just chance, and chance gives, and chance takes.

Chance certainly kept on giving for old Eddy. We fell out of touch years ago, had an argument about something, maybe my wife's cousin. Last time I saw him he'd decided to become a painter, and confidently asserted that he'd be famous "within six months". Abstract stuff. Fat chance, I thought. The only way he'd be famous in six months would be if he took a gun and shot someone famous. Come to think of it, he was like Flynn, as the women just kept passing through, even though you could never call him handsome or admire the way he walked along the dock. His boat was no sleek beauty like the *Zaca* and he didn't throw money around like Hollywood. In fact, he was really good at holding onto what he had, despite the marriages and the endless follies of this project and that. He was crafty, the sort of fellow who could use his hands for feet, and his feet for hands.

Eddy's still going, last I heard, had a gig as a carpenter doing sets for a movie they shot recently in the Campbell River area, a piece of nonsense with Antonio Banderas, called *The 13th Warrior.* Supposed to be Scandinavia during the Viking period, which would make it the 8th or 9th century. Well, Eddy would fit right in. Could hammer a nail real straight, keep the echoes coming.

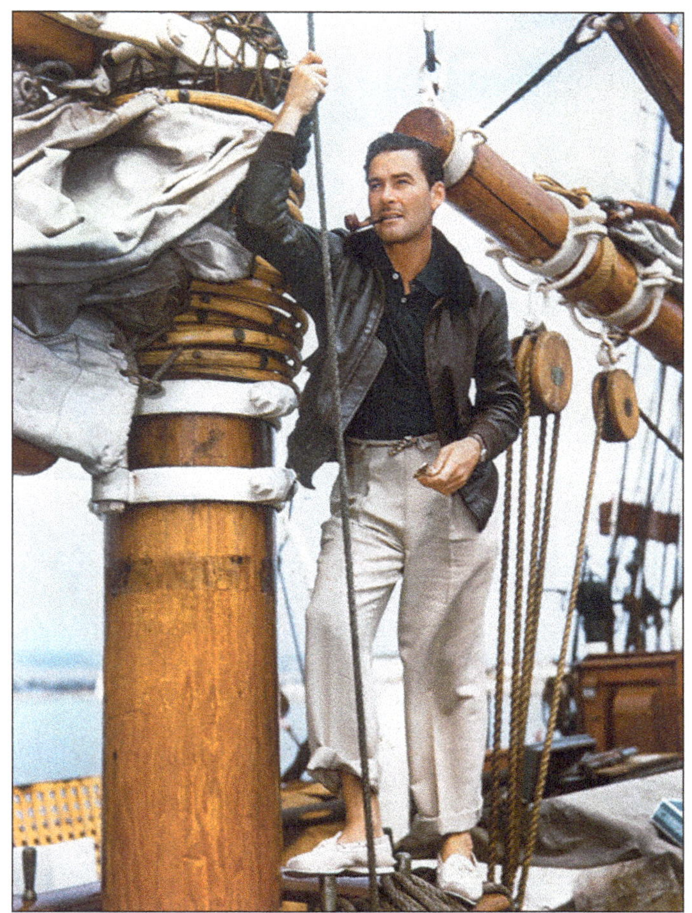

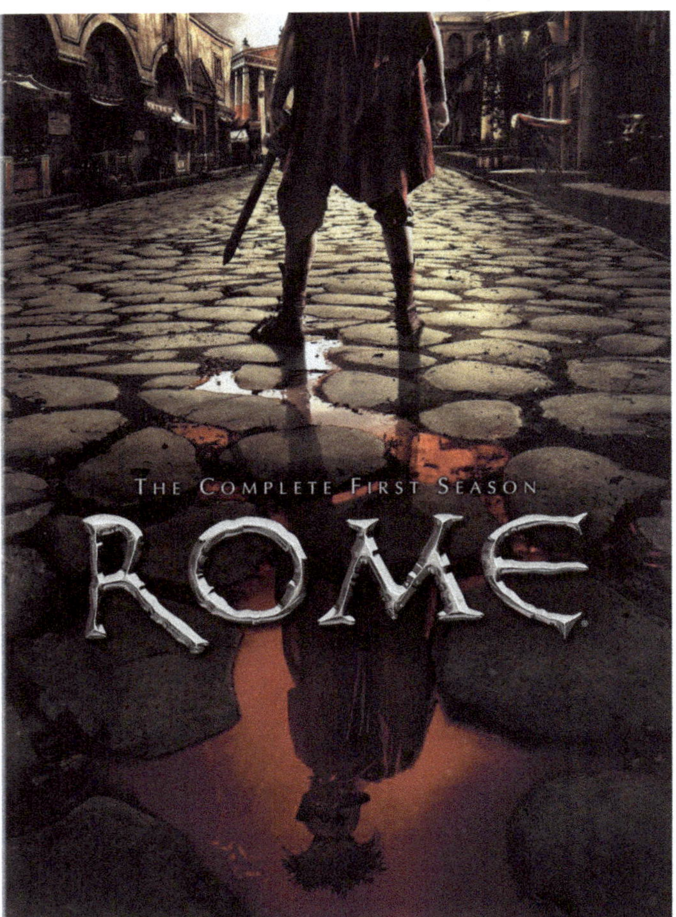

Rome
The HBO-BBC series
Season 1 2006 DVD box set

Written by: Bruno Heller, John Milius, William J. MacDonald, David Frankel, Adrian Hodges, Alexandra Cunningham
Directed by: Michael Apted, Allen Coulter, Julian Farino, Jeremy Podeswa, Alan Poul, Mikael Salomon, Steve Shil, Alan Taylor, Tim van Patten
Cast: Ciaran Hinds (Caesar), James Purefoy (Antony), Max Pirkis (Octavian), Kevin McKidd (Vorenus), Ray Stevenson (Pullo), Polly Walker (Atia), Lindsay Duncan (Servilia), Kerry Condon (Octavia), Indira Varma (Niobe), Kenneth Cranham (Pompey), David Bamber (Cicero), Tobias Menzies (Brutus), Lee Boardman (Timon) *et. al.*

Fiction Struggling To Be Truth

At times *Rome* looks like a soap opera, an absurdist view of life today with history as a stylistic rather than an archaeological fact. Roman vulgarity is indistinguishable from contemporary vulgarity in manners, speech and action. Life in the count-down of the "Before Christ" era (52–43 BC) is occultic and tabloid, and as bloody as the six o'clock News. Sex is the greatest obsession, even when you think politics are, or even the concomitants such as war and economic advantage. Voyeurism is a way of life, "express yourself" the only real credo. Like today, just about anything goes, although in this production paedophilia is left in the shadows, a casualty of contemporary ambiguity and the marketing concerns of Prime Time TV. But as for the rest... hey, it's full frontal.

Sound interesting? It is interesting, even if students of history will carp at the Anglican revisionism. When you measure this BBC-HBO series against the great Fellini *Satyricon*, say, the cultural appropriation/deviation is obvious. The secondary characters—the full fiction characters—could be out of *Coronation Street* or *Cracker*. Is this an aesthetic failing? Not necessarily. A creative writing cliché is that you should write only what you know or what your audience knows. The real bitching will be about the primary characters, those Roman icons who exist in historical fact, such as Gaius Julius Caesar, Marc Anthony, Cleopatra, Pompey Maximus, Brutus, Cicero *et. al.*, those stalwarts of your early school history classes. Some of you even studied them in Latin... if not, for sure you read the Ladybird profile of Julius Caesar. You know these people like you know your relatives and your catechism.

The 12 episodes of Season 1 of *Rome* are primarily the story of Julius Caesar, although they in no way come close to telling the complete story of this amazing man. Forget that he stole 3000 pounds of gold from the Capitol, concealed this major crime by substituting gilded bronze in its place. Forget that he bribed his way into the office of Chief Pontiff and later Consul. Forget that he plundered the votive offerings of the temples of the defeated, although he was a priest of the Temple of Jupiter. Forget his homosexual escapades, bi-sexual delinquencies. Forget that he plotted continuously against the Republic. The script writers did and maybe they should, as it might all be hearsay. After all, history is a fiction struggling to be truth.

Yet... the story as presented could've benefitted by at least one motivating incident to explain his egregious ambition. For example, the famous dream wherein he rapes his own mother, then, after consulting the soothsayers, adopts their interpretation that he would conquer the earth [our universal Mother]. This would help, as his actions would then seem less the ambiguous moves of a nice guy who really loves people. After all, in this Anglican version, Caesar is not really a tyrant but a misunderstood democrat. He's a populist, just like Clinton, although he could easily be written as Nixon.

The Sentimental Ghosts Of Charles Dickens & Sid Vicious

Episode 1. 52 BC. Caesar has just defeated Vencingetorix, the King of Gauls, has him prisoner, makes him kiss the Standard, a gold eagle which shortly thereafter is stolen. While he has been sending wagon loads of booty back to Rome, the jealous senators consider this Gaullic war and Caesar's action to be "illegal" and order him to disband his legions. Of course he doesn't and soon crosses the Rubicon river (or stream, as shown here) and marches on Rome. His opponents, led by Pompey, flee the city, hoping to out-manoeuver Caesar at a later date when his money and popularity evaporate.

So much for the facts. The rest of the action is fiction, much of it effective and clever. Such as: following the story of the "13th Legion" and two of its soldiers, the steady Centurion Lucius Vorenus (Kevin McKidd) and his loyal party-hearty Legionaire Titus Pullo (Ray Stevenson). As Caesar's fortune rises, so do theirs. These are the high-identification figures for today's international TV audience. Vorenus is almost Christian in his values, and Pullo is like a wayward brother who really has a heart of gold. They recover the Eagle, and they rescue young Octavian from Pompey's hired thugs, the "blue Spaniards".

When they return to Rome, we follow their fortunes as they try to adjust to peace time outside the Legion... and they do have problems. Yet somehow both remain at the centre of the action (by the scriptwriters' artifice). Just like a decom vet returning to *Coronation Street*, Vorenus has problems with his pretty wife Niobe (Indira Varma), and Pullo manages to get himself messed up by a pretty slave girl... at the same time slitting a few throats along the way. Ah, it's life among the plebs longing to be bourgeois. Forget the history lesson here. This is tabloid fiction and good laughs are had by all. The sentimental ghosts of Charles Dickens & Sid Vicious sit behind the writing.

Caesar is played by the Belfast actor Ciaran Hinds, and in this interpretation he plays him well. Hinds looks the part, talks the part, walks within the benevolent persona of the dictator with just a hint of menace. The sensibility is very modern, projecting a civilized and pragmatic leader. The brutality that exalts his power is stage managed, so that he plays good cop to the generic Roman bad cop in pursuit of imperial grandeur. This Caesar delegates crucifixions rather than orders them, so he's always seen as the merciful warrior. While the Hinds Caesar isn't adverse to using force, he prefers the politics of bribery, delegation and reconciliation. He's too big to hold petty grudges or avenge big-time treachery (mostly), as if these things are part of an agreed political game for which everyone has rehearsed.

You can see why he goes easy on Pompey (related by marriage) and Brutus (his nephew), although you might wonder about Cicero, the real intellectual behind the opposition. Omitted from the script is the fact that they corresponded, and that the Hellenist Cicero admired Caesar's oratory, considered him the greatest public speaker of their times... yes, even though he conspired in Caesar's eventual murder. Historians tell us it was a personal grudge, actually, as at one point Caesar had Cicero demoted to the plebeian classes. Thus Ciaran Hinds becomes Caesar as the tragic hero rather than Caesar the homicidal megalomaniac who would be King.

Sex As Politics: Every Woman's Husband And Every Man's Wife

Love? Caesar loves... to a point. His wife is described as "a species of statue" by his male secretary, so he's given a semblance of moral license here. While Suetonius in his touchstone work *The Twelve Caesars* suggests that Caesar was a womanizer, here he is played as no licentious sexist pig. Servilia (Lindsay Duncan) is his mistress, and the mother of Brutus, the man forever associated with the assassination of Caesar. While she has a husband, her position is also precarious, seasonally subject to the violent politics of the time. Shortly after their reconciliation (when Caesar arrives in town), pornographic graffiti depicting the couple appear on walls in the vicinity of the Forum, and Caesar, stung by this ridicule, ditches her.

Caesar was "every woman's husband and every man's wife," Cato the Elder said, but here he's just a man who digs power more than love.

Hell hath no fury like a woman's scorn is the theme followed. Servilia goes voodoo in the temple, puts a curse on her absconding lover... and Atia, who she discovers was behind the graffiti. This misfortune provides the most personal of all the motives that drive Brutus away from his uncle and into the plot. Atia—Caesar's social operative in the city—tries to compensate (and protect her own position) by passing on her daughter Octavia as a "companion" who becomes in fact a lesbian substitute. Typically, the line between expediency and humiliation is a shifting marker. The affection between Servilia and Octavia is shown as genuine, despite the politics of the situation. In fact, a time comes when Atia engages one of her lovers (a horse dealer) to dispatch a gang of thugs to ambush Servilia in the street as she's being transported in a curtained litter. The litter is overturned, the slaves put to the sword, and Servilia left to crawl in the filth and blood in an ugly, public humiliation.

So much for the gentle spirit and the feminine mystique. And while intrigue is their forte, the Roman women here are shown to be good with a knife too.

Recoil Or Yawn

Marc Antony. Maybe you recall Marlon Brando's engaging version of this playboy swine who, in history, was actually related to Julius Caesar. All accounts have him as a dissipated individual, and this is the position assumed by the script writers. In 50 BC he became a tribune of the plebs and went to Rome to represent the interests of Caesar... and this is shown in the opening episodes with effective dramatic clarity. On his way to town he stops off to shag a shepherd girl beneath a tree as his detachment waits nearby, watching with varying states of amusement and impatience.

Voyeurism? Spectator sex is the most obvious modernism of this BBC-HBO production which treats us to many such incidents of chic porn during the 12 episodes, and Marc Antony is the star in a number of them. It certainly helps to keep you alert for the history lesson. James Purefoy is the actor, and he must've had fun. As Antony, he has the same submerged malevolence as Richard Burton, that five o'clock shadow of the soul. He has the engaging nastiness of a born predator—you never know if someone is going to have his throat slit or get it up the ass.

In Rome, he sets himself up in Pompey's villa (abandoned in his hurried exit from the city), passes the time in extortion and violent sex. One scene has two naked women sword fighting as Antony lolls on the bed, urges them on, eager to lick their bloody wounds. You might see this vampirism as gratuitous sadism, or you might see it as a nifty sociological truth about the effects of hand-to-hand combat on the mind of a Roman war veteran. However, whether you recoil or yawn, there's no doubt about the effectiveness of this character who, as the number two, plays bad cop to Caesar's good cop.

A Large Penis Is Always Welcome

Atia. This is a very contemporary character—the single mother who is an excellent example of the maxim that politics is the manipulation of the strong by the weak. She too is a relative of Julius Caesar, although this doesn't mean that she's secure in her position as a leading aristo hostess in the city of the seven hills. Atia pimps not only herself and various trophies but also her daughter Octavia (Kerry Condon), whom she forces to divorce her husband (who she loves) in order to marry Pompey (as a gift from Caesar). Sadly, Pompey merely has public sex with Octavia and then marries someone else. Of course these in-house liaisons and forced marriages were normal protocols within the tight aristocratic class of Rome, used as political hedges and clan breeding formats. Atia's charming ruthlessness is a thing to behold, and without doubt Polly Walker's character is one of the most interesting in the drama, unshackled by fact, freed by fiction.

Brutus. A pivotal character in the story, yet the interpretation here perhaps leaves him under developed and/or under utilized. Torn between familial loyalty and the special interests of his friends, he has the potential of a Hamlet, but here drifts between the two camps like a horse without a rider. Tobias Menzies wears the saddle.

Octavian. This is the most successful character in the drama... because, while we know a lot about him later in life as the Emperor Augustus (Season II or III?), his childhood leaves plenty of scope for creative fiction. As the great nephew of Caesar, his education in the ways of the Roman *zeit geist* is a complete amalgam of his mother and his uncle.

Although still a boy when we see him in Episode 1, his ruthlessness is demonstrated early on when he kills one of his kidnappers with a club. His intellectual grasp of the politics of the Senate, the Roman street and his own family is clever and audacious, and a perfect fit for the man who would one day become the great Augustus, the Emperor of the Roman world. He's good with the books, not bad in a brothel, and perfectly capable of engineering the murder of a Roman citizen in order to protect Lucius Vorenus from finding out about his wife's indiscretion.

Murder as altruism—the reality of this action can slip past you in the speed of the montage, especially when you like the murderers. Incest? We get that as well here, passed off as an act of familial love. As for Caesar's famous affliction—epilepsy — Octavian is able to keep it as a secret, despite his youth. Great character, great new young actor, Max Pirkis.

When You Ride With Destiny

One of the best dramatizations occurs when Vorenus and Pullo are shipwrecked en route to fight Pompey's army (in Greece) and end up on a sandbar island with little hope of rescue. Vorenus notices the floating corpses of fellow legionnaires in the surf and uses them as floats for a raft, thus escaping the island. This leads to a major use of "coincidence" in the scripting, when they just happen to encounter Pompey on a beach where he's encamped for the night, *en route* for Egypt in disguise. While not impossible—there are no coincidences when you ride with Destiny —it certainly makes plot points easier to map. Vorenus & Pullo seem to buffoon their way into history as if Cervantes runs the story board. Still, the action is good, is kept visceral. But with such lengthy dramatic absences from Rome, no wonder Vorenus's wife lives as if in a parallel universe....

Cleopatra. Yes, she shows up, a short-haired pussywhipper who looks like a graduate of the heroin chic school of modelling. For some reason, she's omitted from the cast at the HBO *Rome* website as if she's too hot for even them. In style, she's the most revisionist of all the characters in sensibility. You might meet her in a L.A. boutique or a Paris trance club.

This interpretation of the Egyptian queen who almost destroyed imperial Rome by bedding both Caesar and Marc Antony is certainly a pornographic one, and one that will divide Old School from New School in terms of acceptability.

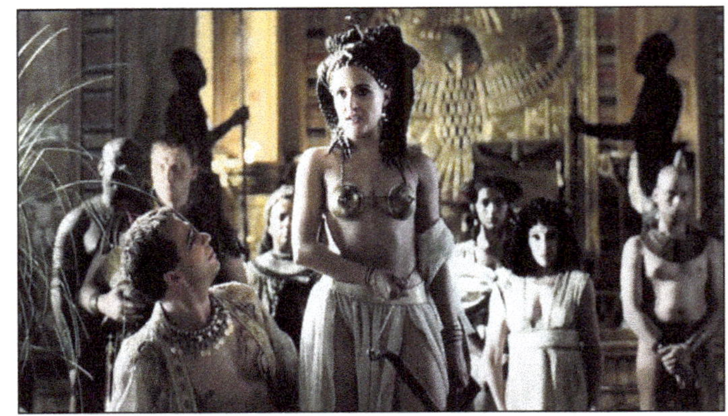

Mind you, if Old School has hung in there long enough to see her Triple X romp with the Legionaire Titus Pullo—Episode 8—then maybe Old School is past textural fundamentalism. This aside, the Egyptian scenes are well-written and staged, with great costumes, sets and sight-lines.

Cicero. If you ever have the occasion to read it, you'll see a clear obsession with Caesar running through some of Cicero's correspondence which teeters between admiration and fear, and while this fear is usually read as Cicero's fear of tyranny, there's something more to it. In this dramatization, this character is the most unrealized, especially in view of how much we know about him. Here he's portrayed as an ineffectual hanger-on, with none of the incredible forensic talent and verbal brilliance he displayed in fact.

Missed opportunity here, people.

Italian Light

The producers/directors made the best of the tonal lighting of the ancient world. The oblique back light, the sense of the pre-electric... the natural light of Italy, the pastels of the eastern Mediterranean etc. While Fellini's view of the Roman world is a landscape view, emphasizing the mid-field and the panorama, this view is closer, photographed for the small screen, a sequence of back-lit interiors, alleys, plazas. Even when landscapes are used, they are often framed in tight by walls, trees, aqueducts, or seen through windows and arches, using vertical rather than linear perspective. There's a beautiful look to it all, no question. The Italian light has that old Hellenic idealism about it, that softening of the harsh edges of reality. Marco Pontecorvo is the cinematographer, obviously another in the line of Italian greats.

The directors. Well, there are a number of them, just as there are several writers. Michael Apted unfortunately directed *Gorillas in the Mist*... but he also directed *Gorky Park*. And now, luckily, he has *Rome* in his CV. Bruno Heller wrote (or co-wrote) eight of the episodes, so he has to take most of the credit for the attitude in the British dialogue. He's also listed as one of the series "creators", so if the series stank, he'd be the first to fall on his sword.

John Milius (one of the *triumvir* producer/creators) wrote/directed such classics as *Red Dawn* & *Big Wednesday*... and *Apocalypse Now*. So some good old American violence is put to good use here (they should consider bringing in Michael Mann for an episode down the line). William J. MacDonald — not to be confused with Peter McDonald, who directed *Rambo III*, in case you think the style fits—directed Episode 8, which features the raunchy Egyptian sequences. So these are experienced Hollywood professionals mixing it up with UK stage pros and Italian techs.

The writing is pretty good. You wonder why no Latin is used, the odd phrase here and there for flavour, remind us that this is Italy, after all, not Chelsea. But most people could probably care less. Shaped by 4 centuries of King James I rhetoric and the blank verse of Shakespeare, British dramatists do have a cachet when it comes to historical subjects, and the UK writer Bruno Heller appears to have carried the most of the writing.

If you compare *Rome* to another HBO series, the western soap opera *Deadwood*, you can see that they march in lock-step in terms of visual and verbal sex and violence. *Rome* with its sober Royal Shakespearean pedigree is far better than *Deadwood* with its Yankee wise-ass cool, yet both are revisionist. If all history is "revisionist" because we can only see it in terms of the present tense, so be it.

The world view is left-of-centre, a social democrat's guide to the Roman world. The bad guys are clearly those 300 or so aristocrats who make up the Senate, in particular those patricians who backed Pompey and later murdered Caesar. Cato is written up to look like a fool, like some nasty English clergyman who gets elected by forging votes from the death register. Cicero, one of the most brilliant men of the period, is rendered as little more than a spear carrier.

To be sure, an attempt is made with the character of Brutus to move beyond an ideological stereotype, and Pompey is only as venal as he has to be... indeed, we feel sympathy for him as he and his wife and children attempt to escape to Egypt. But he's rendered as weak, lacking true sexual karma. Caesar has the pop-culture mojo. Like Clinton or Kennedy, he can be forgiven while Nixon remains a criminal, LBJ a pariah.

Religion & The Rebel

Julius Caesar claimed descendancy from Ascanius, and therefore from Venus, ergo, he was a legitimate patrician and a chief priest. A *pontifex maximus* was a lifetime appointment, carried great political significance. You do see him in the temple, communing with Jupiter, and other characters making offerings to their personal gods. You also see "the reading of the signs" at various junctures, and while some Romans are devout believers, there are instances of artifice and cynicism.

When Caesar visits the auguries (a committee of priestly clairvoyants in shabby togas), they say the "sign" will be the appearance of the birds of peace... and indeed the day he is proclaimed emperor, a flock of doves is released from a hidden cloister in the temple. Divine intervention is stage-managed if the politics are auspicious.

It's interesting to see how this aspect of Roman living is dramatized, the idea of personal gods within a pantheon. Everyone has a shrine in the house, or has access to one in the street. You wonder if Christianity (when it arrived in Rome) was a fad that suited democracy, a plebeian checkmate against the old gods of the patricians. While there's no hint of this in Season I, it might come by Season 3. The struggle between the plebs and the patricians was 300 hundred years old and still going when Caesar emerged.

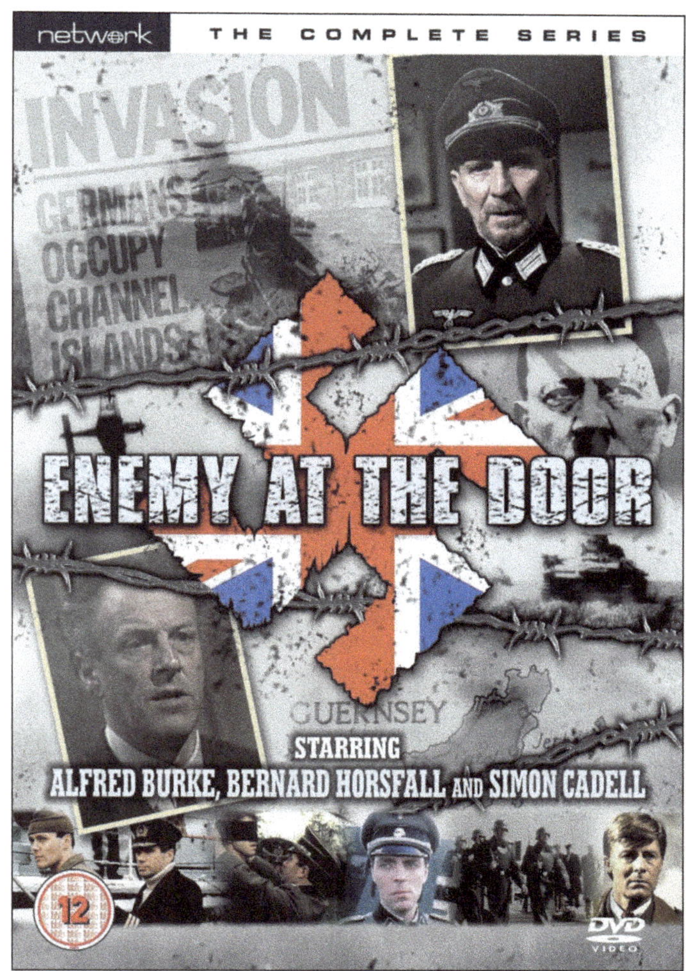

Enemy At The Door: A View From The Inside

Michael Chapman | James Doran | Kenneth Clark | NJ Crisp writers | star Bernard Horsfall | Alfred Burke | John Malcolm | Simon Cadell | Helen Shingler | Antonia Pemberton *et. al.*

The New Order

> "This Island has been declared an Open Island by His Majesty's Government of the United Kingdom. There are no armed forces of any description. The bearer has been instructed to hand this communication to you. He does not understand the German language." [letter from the Bailiff to the first Germans to land on Guernsey by Junkers transport aircraft, June 30, 1940]

A sunny day sometime in 1944. A powerful Mercedes Cabriolet—top down—is surging along a country road on Guernsey driven by a German soldier in uniform. In the back are two civilians, a handsome blond Swedish journalist in a immaculately tailored silver-gray suit; beside him, a beautiful brunette who could be a German UFA film star but who is in fact a monitor from the Nazi Propaganda Ministry in Berlin, a hand-picked escort by Dr. Joseph Goebbels himself. As the car slows for a corner, the woman—Fraulein Trudi Engle—becomes excited when she spots a roadside sign outside a cottage garden, exclaims, "Oh look... 'Afternoon Tea'... we're in a little part of England!"

As we all know, England was never invaded by Hitler, although his troops did seize the Channel Islands on June 30, 1940. It's this military occupation that provides the setting for the little known (North America) but superb UK (Granada/ London Weekend) TV drama series *Enemy At The Door* (1978-80). While the Channel Isles were the only part of the British Empire to fall under Nazi rule, the drama does give some idea of what the situation might have been like in England had the Germans successfully invaded. In this way *Enemy At The Door* stands as "alternate history" view, a metafiction in the tradition of Philip K. Dick's *Man In The High Castle* (1963) or the more recent Nazification novel *Fatherland* (1992) by Robert Harris.

While this "objectivity" humanizes the Germans—and consequently glamorizes them—the result is an interesting (and often vexing) Anglicanization of the Hun. Do they not all speak immaculate English? That the Wehrmacht officers sound like graduates of the Royal Shakespearean Theatre Company now and then contradicts the stereotypical Nazi who emotes like a wanked out robot and thinks like a parallelogram. The political correctness of National Socialist slogans are so dear to those of us who learned all about them through our comics, movies and mutilated historians, that we think, these aren't Nazis... and indeed, most of them aren't. *Enemy At The Door* draws a clear distinction between the soldiers and officers of Wehrmacht and those who belong to the attached SS unit.

The Channel Islands: an archipelago of islands off the Northwest coast of France (Cotentin Peninsula) that have been British Dependencies since the Norman Conquest in 1066, although full Anglicanization was slow as many French found refuge there following the Revolution of 1789. Even the famous French author Victor Hugo was exiled on Guernsey in 1855, lived there for 15 years. The area is therefore quite bilingual and many of the established family names are Norman French. It was used early in WW II as a staging base to bomb Italy but was abandoned by Churchill in June 1940 with the fall of France, left as a demilitarized zone. About a third of population—mostly from Jersey and Guernsey, the largest islands—was evacuated to the UK, among them thousands of school children. It was just as well they left as any islanders who were British born were shipped to KZ camps in France and Germany by the new occupation regime.

Essentially the idea was to make the islands part of the Atlantic Wall defence. Islanders with knowledge of what the Germans did to Belgium in 1914 would have every reason to be alarmed. Seemingly abandoned by Westminster to fend for themselves, what, really, should they do? Resist or collaborate? And if they collaborated today, would it be Nazification tomorrow? This is certainly what happened in France under the 'New Order'. "Passive compliance" is what Westminster advised. While it stuck in the craw of many Islanders, this is the course their liaison Committee decided to follow.

Yet while the series is fiction, many of the incidents and characters are based on fact. Were there commando raids? Yes. Did local women fraternize with the Germans? Yes. Were there concentration camps? Yes. Was there resistance? Yes. Were there executions & deportations? Yes. Was there a curfew under military law? Yes. Property confiscation? Books banned, free speech curtailed? Naturally.

And then, the more difficult questions: were the Islanders cynically abandoned by Churchill? The more recent—and some would say revisionist—series *Island At War* (2004) which tells the same story as *Enemy,* but reloaded to the Islanders' point-of-view, says yes. Were the German occupiers a pack of insensitive homicidal brutes? *Island At War* follows the more conventional line (with some cause) but while the production values of the earlier series *Enemy At The Door* are low tech, the beauty of its political and moral illumination is that it alternates the POV between the Islanders and the Germans.

Dr. Philip Martel (Bernard Horsfall) is invited by the Bailiff to join a negotiating Committee in anticipation of the occupation, leading his daughter Clare (Emily Richard) to accuse him of collusion. After the Germans arrive Dr. Martel and the Committee face the invaders under Major Richter (Alfred Burke), who refuses to recognize the island as a demilitarized zone and puts it under martial rule. Thus, Martel and Richter are immediately at loggerheads... yet while raised voices and shouting are a frequent part of their encounters over the next three or four years, these two principals develop a pragmatic working relationship which for the most part seems to work. Just like the black market the Germans are forever trying to shut down, both parties function within a necessary *quid pro quo*—you scratch my back, I'll scratch yours... or, you slap me, I'll slap you... somehow.

The approach here is to set one "family" ensemble off against the other: the Islanders, represented by Dr. Martel, his wife, son and daughter (and fiance) versus the German administration command under Major (later Colonel) Richter. Richter —who was a Cambridge professor for nine years, knows the British well—is a cultured Wehrmacht Officer, is sensitive to the situation, and is determined to set up a functional administration that will see the Islands' eventual integration into the Third Reich. It's not that he would rather be somewhere else but war is war and, as he says later, "human evolution is an obstacle race". A moralist, but in the crunch, a realist.

Things don't start well. The Martel's prospective son-in-law, an affluent local land owner called Peter Porteous (Richard Heffer), tries to escape the island for England at night in an open boat; his accomplice, a local fisherman, is shot and killed by a shore patrol, and while Porteous survives the machine gun fire and swims ashore, he is forced into hiding. In the second episode, the local librarian Miss Brown gets two years from a military court for refusing to apologize for injuring an SS officer during a dispute over "decadent" books proscribed by Berlin, and is shipped to a KZ camp in France. And in the third episode a young Viennese soldier is sentenced to death, tied to a tree in a garden, then shot for raping a young local girl, the daughter of a lawyer, John Weston (Ray Smith), a WW I vet who despises "the Bosch". The story is interesting as there is some ambiguity about the rape, the daughter's psychology, her uneasy relationship with her father (single parent), and his bitterness over the appropriation of his Rolls Royce by SS Haupsturmführer Reinicke (Simon Cadell). Beautiful girl, beautiful car, bad Germans. Yet Kommandant Richter doesn't hesitate in approving the death sentence, ambiguity be damned, and we're left wondering if the young soldier was a sacrifice for the New Order, a signal to the Islanders that German justice plays no favorites.

The fourth story is not only peculiar but pivotal. *Steel Hand From The Sea* (writ Kenneth Clark) explicates the tragedy and the cost of war for both sides in a brutal yet mystical way. Martel's son Clive returns secretly to the island to spy on

German fortifications but is betrayed by his old business partner at the motor cycle shop, Teddy Lupus, a Judas in league with a German soldier involved in the black market. Instead of being shot, Clive is sent to a P.O.W. camp in Germany out of sympathy for Dr. Martel by Major Richter and his deputy. But this is really just a back-story to that of Clare Martel and Leutnant Willie Kessler (Martin Jacobs), a disfigured Luftwaffe Stuka pilot fresh from combat in Poland.

Spring day... Clare arrives at the local chapel to place some flowers at the wall plaque/shrine commemorating her fiance's father, Captain Ralph Porteous of the 56 Squadron, Royal Flying Corp, lost in action, 1918. When she realizes she's being watched by a German sitting in a nearby pew, she angrily challenges his right to be there. He turns to face her, reveals his disfigurement, a crash burn that has left his right eye closed and his cheek hideously scarred. He says, "I am Catholic too... don't I have the right to be here?" Alert viewers might notice that, despite the Luftwaffe uniform and burns that mask his face, Kessler bears a close resemblance to her fiance, Peter Porteous, and could be a prefiguration of what might happen to him should he succeed in escaping from the island to join the RAF, say. Although she's shaken by the encounter, her anti-German resolve hardens, especially when she learns that her brother Clive is hiding on the island.

We know Kessler is contemptuous of the Nazi dream and the process of war from his cynical recapitulation of the Polish campaign at the officers' nightly schnapps gatherings. It was fun at first, but later it was not. It's obvious to all that Kessler is passing into treason or suicide. Richter and his deputies recommend he visit a certain promontory, scout it as a possible emplacement... or perhaps it's a suggestion that it would be a good place to throw himself into the sea. There's an ambiguity to the order, as if it's code for an officer's right to "fall on his sword" if need be. It so happens Clive Martel is hiding on the beach and when Clare shows up they spot Kessler standing on the cliff smiling down at them. As Clare believes Kessler overheard a conversation about Clive, she assumes his appearance is connected, panics, urges her brother to "Kill him! Kill him!" Clive hesitates; Clare picks up stone and hurls it at Kessler as he turns away, causing him to stumble and fall onto the rocks below. The tide rushes in, and Kessler's body is drawn into the surf, then floats in a trough, bloody and inert. The incident is quick and hallucinatory, as if part of a private nightmare Clare has carried since the incident in the Chapel.

So starts the beginning of Clare's disintegration. Anyone familiar with *Hamlet* will detect undertones of Ophelia in her character, and certainly anticipate her fate. She carries the guilt of Kessler's murder through the next few episodes by becoming more withdrawn and depressed. However, she and her boyfriend Peter, frustrated by the pace of the war and not being able to escape the island, get involved in domestic espionage, mapping gun emplacements and photographing military equipment. When Peter successfully photographs a new class of German torpedo boat in the harbour, they conspire to get the photos and diagrams to the French resistance. In order to do this, Clare—forever smug and blindly impetuous—asks her father to pass an envelope to a certain Francois Duval, a resistance courier who works on the ferry, and is a relative of the young Martel housekeeper. Dr. Martel has been given papers to travel to Paris to pick up some essential medical supplies for the island hospital and is unaware of Clare's agenda. During a routine boarding search, the espionage materials are discovered. Martel is arrested, along with Clare and Peter Porteous. When Martel begs to take the rap alone, that Clare and Peter are naive, Richter barks, "War is for professionals, not enthusiasts!"

But it's clear to Major Richter that Dr. Martel has been used, was a dupe, and in order to avoid a tribunal under the new Kommandant Major General Mueller (where all would've been found guilty and shot) due to arrive on the island at any moment, Richter sentences the Doctor to six months and Peter to twelve in the infamous Paris prison Cherche-Midi; as for Clare, he dismisses the charges, knowing that she is the cause of her father's misfortune, and perhaps connected to the death of Leutnant Kessler. When the SS Hauptsturmführer Klaus Reinicke expresses surprise at the leniency, Richter replies sagely, "I suppose you could call it the Judgement of Solomon."

Indeed. It's not long before Clare wades into the sea, tries to drown herself in a final Ophelian act. However she washes up on the beach and in a fitting irony is resuscitated by a German soldier, then taken to a German hospital. When she recovers, she enters the true prison of the spiritually damaged, a nearby nunnery. Not really a sympathetic character, the symbolism of her role spares us from gloating too much. Quick to judge and chastise her father, her fate was forged by her immaturity, sexual neurosis, impatience and inability to see the bigger picture. As Major Richter said, "War is for professionals, not enthusiasts."

When her father returns from prison, she refuses to see him.

In all, a clever and impressive story, and not just because it conjures Shakespeare and Freud, but because of the mysterious transformational nature of 'being' in the time of war. Some people adapt, some revolt, some die in the crossfire.

Women certainly don't do well in this series... except perhaps when Louise Gardner is a last minute replacement for her ailing husband Arthur in the Islands' chess championship final and defeats General Mueller, denying the German "New Order" its Master Race victory. Clare Martel defies her father, goes mad; Marie Weston (Sheridan Fitzgerald) defies her father, ends up raped and humiliated; Ms. Brown the librarian gets two years in a French KZ camp for 'injuring' an SS officer and refusing to apologize; her successor is also threatened with internment; Chantal Loutrec (Meg Davis) the jilted lover of Hauptsturmführer Reinicke, is reduced to working in an Island brothel, gets murdered by a German soldier; Betty Ridge (Norma Streader), works as a cleaner for the Germans, gets pregnant by one and ostracized for being a 'jerrybag'; Lily, the black Nigerian housekeeper is run down and killed by three SS thugs in their Kubelwagen... etcetera, etcetera. In the end, even Richter's wife back in Berlin is imprisoned by the Gestapo for slagging Hitler.

But do the men do any better? Does anyone? Maybe Foster-Symthe, Martel's replacement Committee liaison, who, after his black marketeering is exposed, his property confiscated and his housekeeper/lover murdered by the Germans, burns his house to the ground before escaping by boat to England. Interesting character... one of those colonial rascals who take life as it comes, crafty and pragmatic behind a facade of officious bluster. As he torches his house with black market petrol, he cackles, "I'm departing in a blaze of glory!"

The brilliant James Doran episode *The Prussian Officer* recalls a personality type from the past, a Junker class aristocrat who once formed the officer elite of the German Army, and which provided the Nazis with a cultural root to model their arrogance on... even though the Nazis were socialists. Hauptmann von Bulow arrives on Guernsey with the 396 platoon for a bit of training before being deployed to the new Russian front. He's such a larger than life character, his manner so dramatic, we think he has to be satire, that we're watching an episode of *Fawlty Towers*. Introduction? He snaps to attention like a shotgun. Need a drink? He snaps fingers like a pistol shot, barks "Schnapps!" and the waiter reverses direction like a salmon being yanked from a river.

He's not pleased to learn that Reinicke has the same rank as himself, albeit in the shabby new SS, a unit without tradition or class. He knows Reinicke from Paris and is surprised to run into Reinicke's old girlfriend Chantal on the street. He investigates, discovers that Chantal is working as a prostitute for the benefit of the German military. It seems Chantal has fallen on hard times. Her father—a wealthy Parisian doctor—was arrested by the SS on the charge of running a communist cell, quite possibly on information provided by Reinicke, for whom love always ranks second to career advantage. Von Bulow is inspired by this misfortune, recognizes a means of humiliating that upstart Reinicke. He orders his batman (Ordonnanz) Klinski—a chump peasant from his family estate—to go to the brothel that evening and have sex with Chantal. Chantal laughs at Klinski, refuses his custom; Klinski gets drunk, gets angry, gets even—he murders her with a bayonet in an alley as she walks to her lodging. It takes a while but Richter's in-house policeman, Oberleutnant Kluge (John Malcolm) traces the murderer back to Peter Porteus' house, where von Bulow and Klinski are billeted. Reinicke is humiliated when Klinski is arrested and the whole sordid story comes out. He goes to the officers' evening schnapps gathering, seeks out von Bulow, slaps him lightly with his gloves, his lop-sided face exaggerated by his seething anger. A duel? Von Bulow is only too happy to accept the challenge, although Major Richter intervenes, forcefully advises them to forget it.

Cut To: a sloping field ringed by bare winter bushes where the two adversaries check their Luger pistols as their seconds stand nearby; Reinicke goes left, von Bulow right, and they face one another about 40 feet apart. Slowly they raise their pistols... Reinicke aims, fires first, misses. We think, well that's it for him... and do we care about the malicious little SS bastard? Well, we don't care much about the elitist von Bulow either. He aims, his arm as straight and steady as an extended sword... then, after a little time torture, jerks his pistol to one side, fires into the air, dismisses his adversary with classic Prussian contempt: "I am an officer and a gentleman... you're only a bad shot. Come, gentlemen, I'm off to a real war where the real soldiers are."

You'd think this would be the end of Reinicke, that he'd be a laughing stock, want to leave Guernsey, but no, the sun shines on fools and lizards alike... and loyal Nazi SS officers even more, for shortly thereafter Himmler has him promoted to Major—the same rank as Richter! No wonder he later exhorts Oberleutnant Kluge to join the Nazi party ("It's a question of loyalty")... Kluge, the ex-Hamburg cop, feels it isn't for him. "It's a question of loyalty...." Richter asks if the adverse is also true. Reinicke has no answer.

We know D.H. Lawrence wrote a homoerotic story called T*he Prussian Officer* and wonder perhaps if the writer James Doran took anything from it. Was the von Bulow-Reinicke animosity the residue of a lover's quarrel? A Freudian scan of the subject is inconclusive... although aspects of the Lawrence story do have echoes here. A Captain and his Ordannanz compete for the same woman, although the Captain prefers the sensuality of his Orderly. This leads to a sadistic abuse of the Orderly, who then seeks revenge during some maneuvers.... It's almost the back-story for what happened in Paris, say, before Guernsey. But, as we know, both men die in the Lawrence story—

It's impressive the way the writers/producers/directors have adapted factual incidents from the occupation with literary patterns of the past to form the narrative. While the dramatizations may seem old tech at times, out of step with the rapid montage methods of today, the fact is the real-time action is refreshing, provides real characterizations and human psychology rather than flash image fantasy hypnosis. Essentially the narrative is basic Master Scene/Slave scene TV drama, with Major Richter's office being the main Master Scene locale (he and his subordinates are always trying to solve a problem, either political or criminal), so all action returns there. Sometimes Dr. Martel's kitchen is the Master Scene locale, although generally he's in reactive mode, trying to get drugs or pardons or whatever favors he can from the German administration.

The episode stories usually start with a hook scene—skulking commandos, a body on the beach, the arrival of a General or repatriated Islander, a murder, a burglary... the usual dramatic fare that arouses the voyeur... but always within the atmospheric context of the series and its setting. Occupation and martial law have the effect of reducing an entire society to an integrated fantosis of concentration and holiday camp. There are watch towers (Marine Pelistand towers) but of course they face the sea. A case could be made that Patrick McGoohan's surrealist series *The Prisoner* (1967) owes something to the German occupation of the Channel Isles.

Who is the protagonist? Well, there are two: Richter and Martel. Martel, we assume by his name, is Norman English, is so English he never thinks of himself as French in much the same way as Lady Diana Spencer's family consider themselves real English (i.e. pre Windsor/Saxe-Coburg and Gotha) even though they're Catholic. But there's no trace of racial bias about Martel; he's a doctor, bound by the Hippocratic oath, and as such is an ideal cipher for the humanist point-of-view. Occasionally more nanny neurotic than George Bernard Shaw (understandable, given the situation) he is nevertheless an excellent advocate for not only the Committee/Islanders but the fabled British characteristic of fair play. The fact that he becomes a victim of his daughter's patriotic machinations only temporarily dampens his spirit, and the measure of his character is found in the respect that his German adversaries afford him, so much so that when he returns from the Cherche-Midi, Richter and his subordinates scheme to have him reinstated as the Committee point-man.

And this isn't because they view him as a collaborator—after all, his son is in a German POW camp, his daughter in a nunnery (and her fiance still in the Cherche-Midi prison). He seems to be one of them, that their ethics can accommodate his ethics, and they can get things done. The respect of your enemy is in some ways more valuable than the respect of your friend. The fact that they persuade him to take a bath in their facilities, shake off the stink of the prison, is like a baptism into the "New

Order' of the Third Reich. Martel agrees to take the bath reluctantly, swayed by the argument it would spare his wife more unpleasantness. But he won't give up his battered suitcase, and he won't agree to being driven home by a German military chauffeur. In a sense he's been "snookered" by Richter, yet the real politik of the situation favors both parties. Major Richter gets to play good cop, Dr. Martel gets to play martyr. Because of his immaculate English, it's difficult to see how Richter's character differs from, say, your well-educated British colonial administrator like F.D. Lugard or Chinese Gordon.

He knows might is on his side, and while there's no evidence to show that he's a believer in the Nazi "New Order"—the contrary, if anything—he's not shackled by simple jingoism and easy 10 Commandments morality. He has the mind of a German philosopher. He could be Hegelian ("human evolution is an obstacle race') although we can see Immanuel Kant in his actions, where morality is a product of reason rather than dogma. *Noumenal, nein; phenomenal, ja*... i.e. reason without experience equals illusion. We know he was a member of General Ludwig Beck's staff before his Guernsey posting, and that Beck led the Hitler assassination conspiracy, for which he was shot on July 20, 1944. We also know that Richter wants to be reposted to North Africa, join General Erwin Rommel's staff. General Mueller denies his request, however, just as he denies Richter's request for leave to go to Berlin to help his wife Anna when she gets arrested by the Gestapo.

Anna is a regarded literary translator, well-known for her work on August Strindberg, the Swedish playwright. Richter was an academic in Cambridge, so he's an intellectual, although in all regards he appears to be the quintessential Wehrmacht officer; he accepts Mueller's reasoning about the futility of any mission to Berlin on his wife's behalf with a relaxed fatalism.

> Muller (scoffs): "What could you do? When a bomb explodes near the Fuhrer's bunker and she says pity it didn't hit the bunker, what are you going to do? What power do you have with the SS?"
> Richter: "I am an officer in the Wehrmacht... that must count for something."

Later, when his deputy, Major Freidel, asks him what he's going to do, Richter shrugs, says, "Anna is going to have to look after Anna". The fortunes of war are reversing; he knows it, senses it, the maelstorm that will carry them all towards an unknown destiny. His wife? The Russian Front? Daylight bombing raids on the Fatherland? Dying Todt slave workers on Aldernsey? Seems the Atlantic Wall will be another Maginot Line—a lot of ugly work for very little use.

Alfred Burke's move from playing the soft-boiled private detective Frank Marker (*Public Eye*) (produced by *Enemy* writer/producer Michael Chapman) to playing the Commandant of a German occupied island is very like Parick McGoohan's move from being a British secret agent in *Danger Man* to playing an imprisoned agent in *The Prisoner*. The dramatic art styles are quite different: *Enemy* is realism, *Prisoner* is surrealism. But both are variations of the same theme; the visceral occupation has become a psychological occupation; WW II has become the Cold War.

The last episode has the body a German soldier lying in a muddy, rain-swept field, as a farmer digs a grave. The soldier was a thief, was caught and killed by the farmer. The burial is interrupted by a German search party... but no matter, the symbolism of the collective German fate has been signposted. Even when Peter Porteus is killed trying to escape the island, Richter deputizes the task of telling his mother to Martel. We don't know Richter's fate, or any of the others, yet we know it's all over for the New Order.

While *Enemy* does give us some idea of what life might've been like under German military rule if they'd successfully invaded mainland Britain, the differences in geographic size and population would've made enforcement far more difficult, even under a "10 for 1" reprisal law. The natural criminal expression of any large city coupled with organized patriotic resistance would've made any such occupation very difficult to sustain without a fast sexual and ideological integration... although we don't know what would've happened if some Nazi "human farming" actions were part of the subjugation. Like the tide, what comes in must go out.

Many of the actors in *Enemy At The Door* have died since 1980... Alfred Burke (Major Richter) recently at 92... Simon Cadell (SS Hauptsturmführer Reinicke) at 46... John Malcolm (Oberleutnant Kluge)... Cassandra Harris (Trudi Engle) *et. al.* Others continue, even in related dramas, i.e. Richard Heffer (Peter Porteus) in *Night Of The Fox* and John Nettles (Sergeant Lewis) who actually played a feral young investigator in the cult 70's UK series *Bergerac*. While *Bergerac* was never shown in North America, Nettles is recognizable here as Inspector Barnaby in *Midsommer Murders*, still shown on the various PBS stations. Likewise people might recognize William Simons who plays Kapitanleutnant Erlich, a German patrol boat captain in Episode 5, *The Laws & Usuages of War*; Simons played Alf Ventress, the indolent chain-smoking constable in the popular series *Heartbeat*.

As mentioned, the natural comparison for this drama is to *Island At War* (2004) which tilts towards a sexual rather than political dynamic. While Stephen Mallatratt's script is built on the bones of *Enemy At The Door*, the story starts pre-invasion and shifts focus to a newly widowed shop keeper Mrs. Mahy and her three daughters, all of whom become involved with the Germans in dramatic counterpoints to one another. Business love, true love, blackmail love, and no love.

The "adopted" daughter Kay/Zelda, a Jew, becomes the obsession of the self-described "decent, honorable Aryan gentleman" Leutnant Walker, a monomaniacial bigot who comes on like a death camp Nazi even though he wears no SS lightning bolts on his collar. This predatory relationship sharply contrasts with Angelique Mahy's love affair with the fatalistic Luftwaffe bomber pilot Bernhardt or the mother's "one might eat a rat if starved" shag with her blackmarket partner, the German harbourmaster Wimmel.

Again, the Commandant (the "Baron") is another German who struggles with the mechanized impersonality of military law and the ideological imperative of the New Order; in the end, like Jesus, he finds some sort of humanity to salve his aesthetic loneliness. *Island At War*: nice to look at, with good and bad and the shades between clearly dramatized. "Coincidence" is abused now and then, and occasionally the "improbable" displays its smiling face... but all in all, quite a powerful drama.

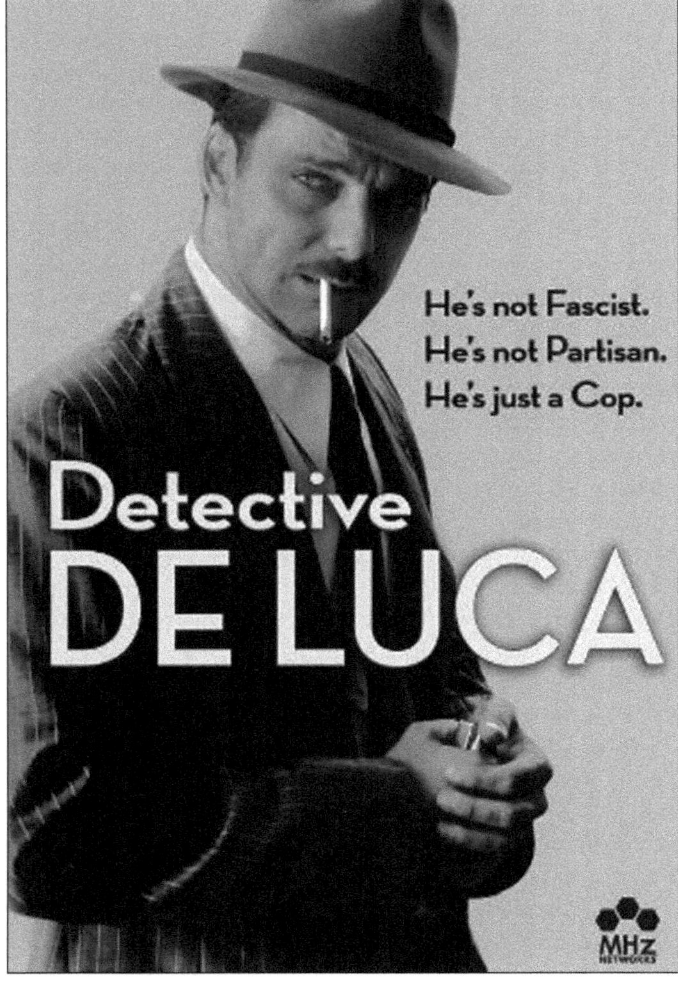

Detective De Luca: The View From The Other Side

Antonio Frazzi director | Carlo Lucarelli writer | Alessandro Preziosi star

Let's Hope It's Not A Political Homicide

Italy. August 1938, the resort town of Riccione (Rimini), on the Adriatic coast where Benito Mussolini has his fun villa. The body of a young woman in a black floral print dress is found lying on the beach near some fishing net racks by a group of children out for some early exercise with their teacher. The local detachment of the *Carabinieri* (military police) is alerted, immediately dispatch a squad of detectives in two black cars to the scene. Among them is *Commissario* Achille De Luca (Alessandro Preziosi), a lithe handsome man in a gray double-breasted suit and fedora, said to be the youngest detective in Italy, a man of integrity and no obvious political persuasion.

We learn, along the way, that his father was a policeman, killed in the line of duty, and that the young De Luca studied law briefly before deciding to join the police himself following his mother's death.

Two members of Mussolini's bodyguard are already at the scene, drawn by the commotion after a patrolling policeman's two dogs and the convent children discover the body. One wears a white suit and a black shirt, the civilian uniform of a fascist thug. While they remain neutral, their presence accelerates the political atmosphere and the need to find a quick solution to the crime. The girl has been shot through the heart with a 7.65 millimeter bullet. A boy finds the shell casing, gives it to De Luca, who meanwhile recognizes the victim as a local hooker called Miranda Rubino a.k.a. "Lucious Butt".

We never see Mussolini in this episode, yet his presence haunts the action of the entire De Luca series as an off-stage character, a phantom deity by whom all actions are judged. In Episode 1, *An Unauthorized Investigation*, his villa sits above the beach like the temple of an invisible god awaiting whatever sacrifices the sea will offer. The detectives play cynical games with the fascist protocol, seek solutions with fast salutes, easy justice with expedient politics. The paranoid speed of the prevailing political correctness is a bullet in the dark or a demotion to the provinces. Who killed Miranda? Why, obviously her pimp, a man called Tabanelli. They speed to his room, but he has fled. They speed to the bus station and there he is, back seat of a coach just about to pull out for the big city of Bologna. White suit, white fedora, black goatee, black pistol. The gunfight among the buses ends when he cornered face-to-face by De Luca. Tabanelli fires his Glisenti 1910 point-black at the detective but he's out of bullets and is quickly subdued.

Lucky De Luca? Young, handsome Italians with a strong sense of moral justice are lucky is the message. Back at the precinct the Chief Commissario congratulates the squad, reads a message from Mussolini who's pleased by the swift conclusion to the Miranda murder case. The Chief raises his glass, leads the detectives in a choral salute to *il Duce*. Heels click, arms extend, and like a wolf pack they howl "'Duce!" Even De Luca—who, of course, knows the case is anything but solved, even though his compagni try to beat a confession out of Tabanelli in the rubber room—salutes. Later, when he realizes the bullet casing from the bus station shooting doesn't match the casing found by the little boy on the beach near Miranda's body he doggedly pursues the investigation in defiance of the Chief. No, it's not solved. The boss doesn't want to hear it, as political expediency trumps any idea of justice for the pimp of a dead hooker, never mind the girl herself who turns out to be the mistress of a young Count close to the fascist circle of power.

Game over, case solved? Not a chance. This drama, and the three others that follow in the series, is an excellent way to see Italian society on the heady run-up to WW II, then, later, during the collapse and its aftermath. You see it from the street to the aristocracy, see it within the secular halls of power. It's 'the view from the other side', free of the post-war bias that haunts the typical outsider view of what went on in Italy under Mussolini. What is/was fascism but a style of thinking, another way of doing business: reactionary, technocratic, futurist, aggressively nationalist and full of moral relativism, an ideology rather than a culture, yet seeking to become a culture nonetheless... a tradition. And what is tradition? The illusion that protects us from the jaws of reality, the rituals and repetitions that bind us like mummies in the living tomb. So while some of the characters in *Detective De Luca* are committed fascists, most just play the game, try to get by in the world they find themselves in. A good example is the landlady in Episode 2 who keeps her radio on Berlin for fear of being reported as anti-fascist, but dials in Milan orchestra music after De Luca tells her to relax. The absurdity of life in a collapsing order, although the collapse must run its disorderly course through intrigues, bombings and the European sickness, that is, what are we to be: a nation, driven by national interests (fascism), or a vassal, part of the Bolshevist collective (communism)?

The shoot-out is one measure of De Luca's charm, because he is obviously one lucky man (no bullets), but it's in his first encounter with beauty that we recognize his full measure as a 'lucky man'. He receives a phone call from an anonymous female about a burglary at the Villa Maria, a beautiful white house set in a beautiful garden, the home of the young elitist Count Utimperger, a member of Mussolini's social circle and up for a ministerial position. The Count's name conjures associations from the pre-unification days (1861) when the northern states of Italy were Austrian dependencies, and the strong influence of Germanic culture on Italy, so it comes as no surprise when we meet the black shirt Camerata Silvestri (Richard Sammel), a Consul in charge of the local fascist militia who is a friend of Paolo Utimperger and his femme fatale wife Laura (Kasia Smutniak). Chicanery is *de rigueur*, even if the fascist mindset is techno modernism. Intrigue, duplicity and murder aren't left behind in the revenge tragedies of the Renaissance. The Law is a set of shutters, unfolding light and shadow within which these political players dodge and plot.

Yet it's all sunlight and splendid decor in the Villa as Laura Utimperger descends the stairs with the leggy couture/allure of a Milanese model, even though her answers to De Luca's questions are evasive, as if she is hiding in a shadow. For a rags-to-riches story, she plays the Countess well, alternately hiding behind the haughty verbal noise of class protocol and modulated anger, well aware that her only real power is her beauty. Detective De Luca—who knows from the maid that a valuable brooch is missing—plays it cool, suppressing his desire with the discipline of a committed professional. But we know that both parties to this conversation carry a secret weapon that only the other can disarm, regardless of politics and the law. A favorite cliché in both life and film noir—where the manipulation of desire is often a form of suicide—we eagerly anticipate the inevitable. Who is the sacrifice, who is the checkmate, who is the victim?

Miranda is from Romania, Laura from Croatia—the low and the high, the story for two female migrants fated to cross in their hungry desire for a piece of the fascist action. It's a good plot, the story entirely as possible then as it is now. The narrative pattern is stock detective fiction—bodies, clues, fights, with a bit of romance and class warfare en route... yet the setting is unique, the culture classical. It's like visiting a museum gallery and exploring the mystery of western civilization.

Silvestri, the Consul in charge of Mussolini's security squad, is a pivotal figure, not only because of what he represents but also because you think he's trying to cover up the murder. Why? To protect his friend Paolo Utimperger (who in turn is a protege of the ill-fated Count Ciano, the Italian Foreign Minister and son-in-law of Mussolini) who's in-line for a ministerial appointment? What does Silvestri want? He wants the crime scene pistol. So while he's the boss of Mussolini's protection squad, just whether or not his investigation is authorized or unauthorized remains conjectural. When De Luca fails to find it, Silvestri, dressed in a white summer suit and accompanied by the *il Duce* squad, threatens to shoot him. He seems particularly upset by the fact that De Luca—a mere *Carabineiri* who rides a bicycle when a driver is unavailable—has bedded the Countess Laura, so his motivation becomes personal as well as political... although, of course, we don't know which takes priority. It does, however, throw suspicion on Laura.

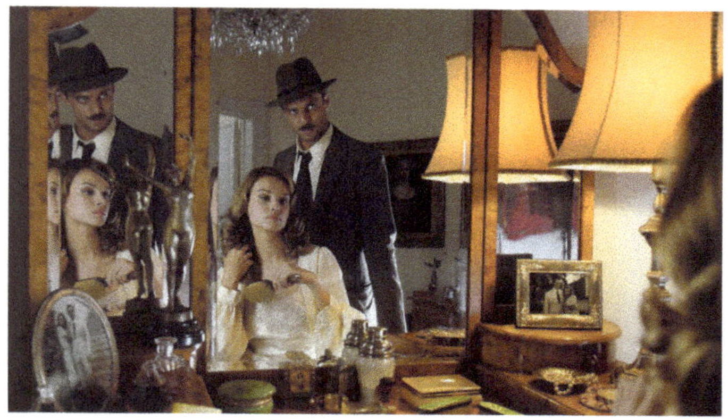

It's Said That If Necessary, You'd Arrest *Il Duce*

As a culture, De Luca's Italy just exchanges one salute for another (fascist hand for a communist fist)... yet there's a nice aesthetic distance in this drama, where communist and fascist are given equal measures of approbation and/or understanding. Perhaps the Left is given a bit more sympathy, although the centre path is definitely De Luca's way. As with much of Italy in those times, the *Carabineiri* were politically all over the map. They helped Mussolini gain power (1923/5), and they removed him in 1943, only to be subverted by the fabled Waffen SS rescue whereby Hitler made *il Duce* a German puppet in what Italian territory remained unconquered by the advancing Allies. Mussolini was under *Carabineiri* guard at the Campo Imperatore Hotel on the Gran Sasso alpine region in Northern Italy. Certain *Carabineiri* fought with the Yugoslav partisans (mostly communist) against the Nazis. So they were no mere monolithic fascist police organization... just as De Luca is no mere romantic revisionist fiction of the post-war Italian mind, although he certainly is romantic. He's a secular Catholic, guided by law and tradition, yet modern enough to stand apart from the institutional *zeitgeist* when justice demands it. He's not Jesus Christ, yet he has the key Christian virtues: humility, compassion, charity... and the steadfast use of authority for justice.

He's in no way corrupt—unless love be corruption—yet corruption surrounds him. In one way he's a slow-moving action hero cliché, yet in another a sophisticated navigator of *realpolitik*. He learns as he goes, like a tightrope walker who follows the dead. In Episode 1 he clashes with the fascist orthodoxy. Episode 2, the Nazi occupiers. Episode 3, the communist partisans. Episode 4, the new post-war order (will it be Moscow or Washington... Communist or Christian Democrat). The movement is dialectical: Rimini, Bologna, the northern Apennines, Bologna... the death of one Order, the birth of another. Behind the ancient arcades and marbled villas of these neoclassical players, chaos simmers.

He's not a blunt instrument, is pragmatic, takes beauty at face value, and remains pragmatic even if beauty is revealed to be flawed. Laura is revealed to be a hustler, in bed with evil, yet there are extenuating circumstances. Most of the characters in the De Luca series are hustlers, high and low, *de facto* pimps and whores to some necessitated degree. Definition is merely a matter of power or proximity to power.

In Episode 2, *Carte Blanche*, the women throw themselves at the German-Italian Riccardo Rehinard, either excited by the couture of his "New Man" persona or his social position with the Germans. Just what he is remains vague. He could be a satire. The symbolism of the situation sums up the Italian paradox: sell-out greed or adaptive survivalism? For the beautiful Slavic fortune teller Valeria, it seems to be a matter of survival, whereas for Laura (of Rimini) it could be either, with greed rationalized as survival. In the third episode, *Cloudy Summer*, Francesca, the daughter of a widowed innkeeper, has her head shaven by the CLN because of her romance with a blond, blue-eyed German soldier, yet she is also the girlfriend of the hot-headed communist partisan leader Carnera. Francesca is another strong-willed woman who "does what she likes" in order to survive. It's definitely a trend with novelist Lucarelli's romantic characters, especially the females: strong, stubborn survivalists who will vamp any man if he can improve their situation. Francesca is perhaps an exception, unless she really beds De Luca in order to protect Carnera. She has no ideology, no materialism, is just one degree beyond the peasant.

Can one infer that fascist totalitarianism advanced women from domestic entrenchment through its adaptive modernism? Or is this mere revisionist thinking, a fiction of the present imposed on the past? Or—as seems clear in this drama—is it the chaos behind the New Order that gives the opportunity to women? Of course it's beautiful women who have the power, and that power is ancient. The young women that De Luca encounters in the line of duty do what they like... Laura, Valeria, Francesca... even the peripherals like Sonia and Lea, and the ladies who play at the Grand Hotel. There is, of course, a degree of crime fiction fantasy whereby the women are *femme fatales* waiting around for outlaw men packing guns, and while he's a government cop, Achille De Luca is something of an outlaw within a system that bends to the whims and imperatives of the politically powerful.

The Man Who Saved *Il Duce*'s Life

In *Carte Blanche*, De Luca arrives for his new posting in Bologna in the back of a National Guard truck, and is dropped off in the street as a (fascist) funeral cortege passes. As he walks through the arcade, suitcase in hand, a bomb goes off, tossing him to the ground and wounding some of the GNR militia, who engage in a brief gunfight with some unseen partisans on the roof. When the shooting stops, De Luca recovers his suitcase, continues to the Pensione Dal Raduce. But hardly has he checked in when an officer from the precinct arrives with orders that De Luca come at once as there's been a murder that requires immediate attention. The victim turns out to be a fellow by the name of Riccardo Rehinard, a known dealer and womanizer in the local high society circles.

By now Commissario De Luca is famous because he was recently in the newspapers as "the man who saved il Duce's life" —he thwarted a street assassination attempt simply because he was passing by—which turns out to be an embarrassment for him, and later, a curse (the partisans put him on their death list). Even the Italian SS have a use for him, and it's with their blessing that he proceeds with his investigation, even though the high placed Count Zaccari will be compromised.

Italian SS? De Luca, now a fascist hero because he saved

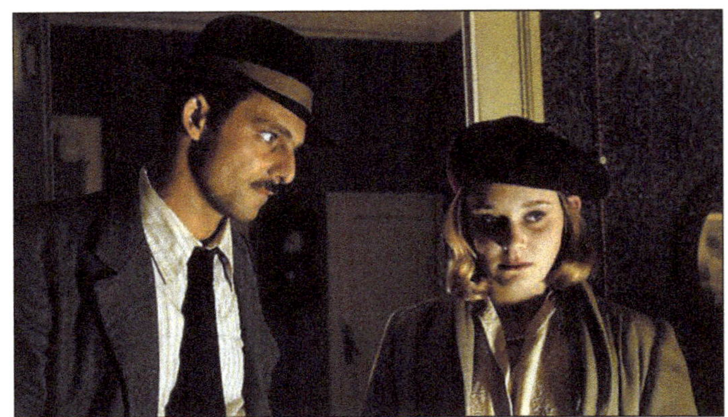

Mussolini's life, is given "carte blanche" by Vitali, a slim figure in a natty Italian SS uniform standing near the heavy curtains in the Chief's office, an older gent replete with the grim politeness of a vampire bat who may or may not visit De Luca some night and draw blood if he doesn't nail Count Zaccari. You do wonder why the SS has turned on Zaccari, a well-placed diplomat in the Mussolini regime. De Luca does but nonetheless gets on with the case.

Riccardo Rehinard is a dope dealer gigolo whom all the women love like some magic mirror that flatters. Rehinard is part of a local high-roller clique that holds seances on Friday evenings at Count Zaccari's villa. With his Germanic surname, his character assumes a symbolic function like a corrupt movie star from Berlin always available for Italian fascist romance. Vaguely Theosophical, the neo-paganism of Reichsfuhrer-SS Heinrich Himmler and other Nazis was seen as the hip way of rationalizing fascist exclusivity, so seances hosted by the local aristocracy in Bologna would fit with the European tradition of secret societies that exercise the real power.

Rehinard is a silhouette character, a D'Annunzio without the poetry, a corpse whose true history and appeal remains with the women who loved him. What little we do see allows us to believe he deserved what he got: a stab in the heart, a stab in the balls. The fact that he deals in contraband British morphine is almost beside the point, as the real crime is the fact that his fascist accomplices dream of escape to Switzerland. As a plot, this is very similar to that in the excellent ZDF (Germany) TV miniseries *Dresden* (2004) where a hospital administrator is hoarding British airdrop morphine and selling it to the SS in order to have money to escape to Switzerland. Copied? Or a common story from the Axis defeat?

In their first encounter, Count Zaccari (Jose Maria Blanco) barks at De Luca, "I am a personal friend of Mussolini!" It's a claim that others will make as they try to intimidate the servants of justice. Is/was Rehinard really connected? For once De Luca has *carte blanche* to pursue the case with official blessing (unlike the Miranda/Rimini case). Carlo Lucarelli, who wrote the novels on which this series is based, must surely have been thinking of the time when the Duce sent a telegram to Cesare Mori, Prefect of Palermo, Sicily, stating that Mori had "carte blanche" to take on the Mafia.

There's a sense that Count Zaccari is more than an ultra conservative. The fact that his addled daughter the Contessina Sonia is a morphine addict is one clue, his obsequious clerical secretary Don Vincenzi Peroni another. Perhaps the fascist elite distrust him as an old school elitist because, after all, the root of fascism was/is socialism. Zaccari's class arrogance has a criminal dimension that reaches beyond the occult and a cellar of vintage wine. The fact that De Luca uses a squad of GNR (National Guard) to haul the Count in for questioning might be reason enough for an oligarch to have a nosey cop killed, but obviously there's more to it. The plot thickens.

De Luca also has occasion to tangle with the local detachment of the German SS police, the Gestapo. They have detained and tortured Oreste Galimberti, a criminal associate of Rehinard's and when De Luca arrives to question him, he finds Oreste already dead. You are left to assume that this rough justice was the goal, not any confession or useful information per se. This sequence also reveals the uneasy relationship between the Italians and their German overlords in the puppet state (the Italian Social Republic a.k.a. the *Salo Republic*, 1943-45), only weeks away from total collapse. Allied bombing, partisan attacks, Nazi cruelty and easy murder makes daily life in the Republic existential. Law and order become theatre, survival reality. One of De Luca's sergeants is murdered, tied to a railing above a fast running sluice that photosizes the chaos, and De Luca himself is hunted through the night shadows of the arcades of the Via Nosadella. Once again gunfire, and De Luca saves himself from Count Zaccari's assassins by seeking refuge in the apartment of Valeria (Raffaella Rea), the beautiful Balkan clairvoyant.

Valeria is also pivotal, as she recurs in Episode 4, resumes her romance with the charming Detective De Luca. As with all the *femme fatales* in this series, there's a madonna-whore aspect to the relationship. The male cop is the figure of virtue, not the woman. Referring to the times, Rehinard's landlady says, "There are no decent girls anymore." When beauty is the only currency you have, sometimes you must spend it to survive. Valeria lays it out with forthright modern simplicity when she admits she slept with Rehinard: "So what? I slept with you, didn't I? I'm a grown woman and I can do what I like." Once again it's the *realpolitik* of the moment, of the time... and De Luca is shown to be pragmatic, especially when it comes to women. He allows Laura Utimperger to walk, and he allows Assuntina to walk... and as for Valeria, well, love trumps all. Their relationship is stormy, to say the least. One visit is preceded by a gun battle, another interrupted by a bombing raid. Both sequences act as psychological analogues to their fated romance.

The interrogation that turns into a love scene during the nighttime bombing raid really sums it up. The mutual fear of uncertainty undermines the professional distance, closes the human gap between being and nothingness. Mortality is focused and real in the time of war when everyone becomes a patsy. While bombs are democratic and impersonal, bullets are always personal in Bologna, April 18-21, 1945.

Cloudy Summer

Captain Rassetto (Rolando Ravello) is a sort ghost figure who runs behind the series as a parallel but alternate moral view to De Luca. Rassetto is a committed fascist and fellow detective at the precinct in Rimini. He's always friendly with De Luca, helps him out with inside information, even though De Luca teases him about his politics. Yet there's a mutual respect which in turn forces us to be less judgmental about the Italian situation. Public servants can never be fully neutral and in totalitarian regimes this is almost impossible. The fact that the De Luca series ends with the *Carabineiri*/OVRA policeman Rassetto about to go on trial for the unlawful killing of a communist partisan underscores the Italian divide and the fascist fiasco. We know the circumstances, we see the shooting, but we don't know the outcome of the trial. The fact that he was a member of OVRA (secret police) during the war won't auger well and quite possibly he could implicate De Luca in some form of plea bargain.

Because he's "on the list" as a fascist *Carabineiri* policeman that the partisan CLN want to apprehend and execute (probably because he 'saved Mussolini's life'), De Luca goes into hiding with Captain Rassetto and some other colleagues. Episode 3, *Cloudy Summer* starts with Rassetto and De Luca leaving their farmhouse hideout in the Moden Appennines to escape the advancing British Eighth Army. They run into a partisan roadblock and a shoot-out occurs. Rassetto has a sub-machine gun (Beretta Model 38A), kills the partisan who orders them out of the car, but as they attempt to escape, their driver is shot. They bail from the car, Rassetto going one way, De Luca and another Carabineer going another.

De Luca eludes his pursuers but quarrels with his companion on a river bank. While they have false I.D., De Luca thinks it's foolish to carry weapons, as displaced citizens don't carry guns. He tosses his pistol aside, much to the contempt of the other cop, who seems more committed to the ways of the past. He pockets De Luca's discarded pistol, while threatening to shoot him.

The best policeman in Italy? The man doesn't believe it. De Luca shrugs, walks away, crosses the river by wading the shallows and using stepping stones.

This crossing is symbolic in the sense that he leaves the world of the political Right and enters the Left.

Will he be investigating the shooting death of a communist partisan at a roadblock? No such irony. It's not who killed who that matters in this drama—after all this sort of jigsaw fetish is just an excuse to present other ideas—but rather the characters, the landscape, the times, the past slipping forward into the present.

Instead, he encounters a partisan policeman, Brigadier Guido Leonardi (Stefano Pesce), while waiting with some refugees for the British army to clear the road ahead. Leonardi examines De Luca's ID—he's passing himself off as a government engineer called Morandi *—and while he thinks he recognizes De Luca from somewhere (that news photo, "Italy's Best Policeman"), offers him a cigarette and ride to a local inn. On the way they check in briefly with Leonardi's second, who's guarding a rural house, scene of a recent murder. The cat-and-mouse game proceeds, with Leonardi installing 'Engineer Morandi' at the inn and having dinner with him. They are served by Francesca (Ana Caterina Morariu), the landlady's shapely daughter. She looks pretty chic despite having had her hair sheared by the partisans for having a German lover. She's unrepentant and incorrigible, yet even Leonardi is forced to admit she has "a nice ass". While Leonardi is a serious communist, he is also a man.

* In Episode 1 there was a painting at the Utimperger villa by the Bologna artist Giorgio Morandi (1890-1964), so we recognize that De Luca chose his alias in memory of Laura.

He's also pragmatic, recognizes he has neither the training nor the logic to solve the murder on hand. He more or less holds 'Engineeri Morandi' hostage while co-opting the fugitive detective's aid in solving the murder. He recognizes De Luca is a Carabineer, yet has empathy, as if he recognizes another idealist—not an ideologue, but an idealist nevertheless—whose goal is not that different from his own: the common good and a better Italy. So he offers De Luca a *quid pro quo*: help me out and I'll return your I.D. and deliver you to wherever you need to go.

While this is northern Italy, the local politics are Sicilian: a corrupt mayor, homicidal partisans, a village society with ingrown traditions and a dissembling present. The Germans have just left, the British have just arrived. The mysterious disappearance of the English Lieutenant Witherspoon is as symbolic of the situation as is the death of a goat in the minefield near the village.

Francesca too as the trophy woman of Carnera (Massimo Venturiello), a reclamation from the Germans of the village integrity, and in the wider context, the Italian. When she seduces the handsome fugitive Carabineer, this places him in an interesting (if familiar) situation when it comes to arresting Carnera for the murder of the Count. When faced with the growing evidence, Leonardi expresses apprehension, admitting that he's afraid of going up against an Italian hero. De Luca isn't. The irony is sweet: a Carabineer of the old regime versus a Communist Partisan of the new.

Who really speaks for Italy?

> people didn't care about the future... they lived in
> the present... so I had to stop being a fortune teller

Episode 4. April 14, 1948. Via Delle Ocha is the brothel district in Bologna and this is where De Luca finds his assignment after his 'rehabilitation' in the provinces. A young brothel worker has hung himself, apparently... but as De Luca points out to Pugliese the space between the chair and the toes of the deceased are a couple of hands (8 inches), so it must be murder.

The victim is the brothel's handy man/muscle who the girls call Ermes. Once again—as if the war never happened—Deputy Chief D'Ambrogio (Carlo Cartier) wants the case wrapped up immediately as a suicide despite De Luca's suspicions of murder because Ermes was a communist and his death might have something to do with the elections underway in which the Communists are neck-to-neck with the Christian Democrats (Moscow vs. Washington as the street hailer proclaims) and D'Ambrogio is a Christian Democrat. In fact, he has already written up the death as a suicide, so he tears up De Luca's report.

It's simple, really: if the Christian Democrats win, the current Chief will move along and D'Ambrogio will ascend. The fix is in.

Not only is De Luca reunited with Sergeant Pugliese (now a full detective with the Homicide Squad) but also Valeria, the fortune teller, from "Carte Blanche" who is now a cynical "madame" or prize hooker at Number 22 (but "23 on the papers"). Again, their scenes are fraught with sexual tension wherein the interrogations are just a form of foreplay. Why is she now a prostitute? "People didn't care about the future," she replies. "They lived in the present, so I had to stop being a fortune teller."

Of course she is hiding vital information. Of course the murder is political and of course Valeria's position is political. This becomes obvious when the body of another communist called Usvaldo Piras is found lying in the street. D'Ambrogio prefers to see it as a robbery, De Luca as 'suspicious'.

But when De Luca and Pugliese investigate Osvaldo's apartment they interrupt an intruder. A gunfight ensues. De Luca pursues the man across the flat roof. The man uses a rough fire escape but wouldn't you know it, one of the metal rungs gives way and he falls to his death. Before the squad arrives, they find a number of sentimental photos of Ermes with various girls (girls from Via Delle Oche as it turns out). A stud? No. Seems the girls used him as a substitute fiance to fool their families back home.

Shortly thereafter Valeria is moved to the best brothel on the Via Delle Orso, a reward apparently for her silence. Nevertheless, her affair with the relentless detective continues with the erotic elegance of an undergarment modelling show. Love might be sweet but it isn't easy. Both are carrying a cross that only the other can remove.

Suspicion eventually falls on Antonio Abatino, a fascist masquerading as a Christian Democrat. Did he have a hit man take out three communists? Is he connected to Deputy Chief D'Ambrogio? It's a fascinating scenario that develops, perhaps a bit obscure for outsiders today to follow, yet utterly credible. Blackmail is the order of the day and even De Luca isn't immune. When an angry mob attacks Abatino's back street H.Q. office and De Luca finds him burning sex photos of the dead communist politician Orlandelli, Abatino sneers, "If the gods have fallen, the angels will too... your turn will come next, De Luca."

God Can See You, Not Stalin!

De Luca is also reunited with Guido Leonardi, the CLN brigadier policeman from *Cloudy Summer*. Leonardi now holds an administrative position with the Bologna Police and being a communist, is fully cognizant of the local political situation, both in the force and out. He sees a cover-up under way, and welcomes De Luca's appearance.

But with the victory of the Christian Democrats and the elevation of D'Ambrogio to Chief of Police, Leonardi is immediately transferred to Rome, the graveyard of all communists. As for De Luca, it's the night shift.

Production

The production values here are of a very high order. Antonio Frazzi's direction is superb, the cinematography and editing likewise. Carlo Lucarelli—whose novels were the basis of the De Luca series—was involved in the scripting of all four episodes, although he was aided by a dozen other writers. The costumes, the music, the sound all have the bona fide period feel. The acting—extremely good.

The women—watch out. While we've seen dozens of cops and their faithful buddy sergeants, the rapport between Alessandro Preziosi (De Luca) and Corrado Fortuna (Pugliese) is a thing of beauty, more like an artist and his student. Police procedural ugliness is softened by the period fresco, so there's not only an engaging honesty in their story, but also a real humanity, both in terms of characterization and history.

Get yourself a bottle of Primitivo and check it out. Salut!

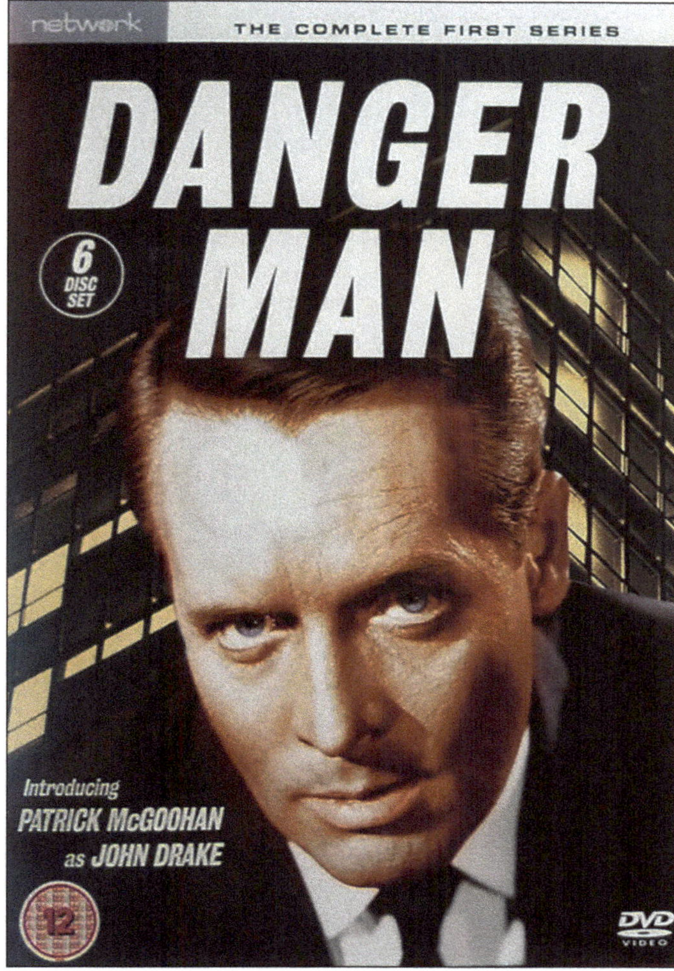

Danger Man/Secret Agent: TV Noir

Patrick McGoohan | Ralph Smart | Brendan J. Stafford | Don Chaffey | Donald Jonson

Danger Man (later, in the USA, *Secret Agent*)... two steps from Enid Blyton, one step from Dick Barton, Special Agent? Certainly the pedigree of the first 39 half-hour episodes has the raw semitone simplicity of a comic book thriller, embedded in the inter-war UK pulp fiction culture of writers such as Sapper McNeile, John Buchan, Leslie Charteris, Eric Ambler, Helen McInnes, Edgar Wallace... later, Ian Fleming and Graham Greene, so that you might be thinking it's pop-culture rubbish.

The character of John Drake owes a lot to Sapper's Bulldog Drummond—a pared-down modernist version, hi-tech, moral, subtle... a Cold War version but a Drummond version nonetheless. In *The English Lady Takes Lodgers* (Series 3, 1965) agent John Drake (Patrick McGoohan) is posing as a penniless novelist in Portugal, when Commander Collinson (Howard Marion-Crawford)—a criminal who is selling secret weapons technology—asks him what sort of fiction he writes. Drake is modestly evasive. "I prefer Bulldog Drummond myself," says Collinson, in an amusing sub-textural dig at the character of his adversary.

The early episodes (1960-2) often have a back lot B movie look about them, with certain actors and props rotating through the stories like a travelling theatre troupe. The same 1956 Desoto... the same 1960 Thunderbird... the same German MP 40 sub-machine gun... the same pistol, the same helicopter, the same sandpit and the same old gray sky.

"The Eternal Quest For Melodrama And Romance"

If the hunter once rode a horse, in the 20th Century he drives a fast, nimble car. Drummond drives a M.G. sports, and John Drake drives a stable of models, starting with an Aston Martin in the series pilot, *View From A Villa*... later you see him in an Austin Healy, a Mercedes 190 SL (in his NATO guise), a MGA. and a Mini Cooper (in his *World Travel* London days)... and in *The Prisoner*, a Lotus 7.

Despite the rough drama of the early episodes, their budget exoticism is enhanced by a number of familiar actors early in their careers. Honor Blackman (James Bond, *The Avengers*) as Joan Bernard in *Colonel Rodriguez* (1960); Jackie Collins (Hollywood novelist, sister of Joan) as Lucia in *The Contessa* (1961); Robert Shaw (James Bond, *A Man For All Seasons*) as Tony Costello in *Bury The Dead* (1961); Howard Marion-Crawford (*Fu Manchu, Lawrence of Arabia*) as Archer in *Yesterday's Enemies*... Lois Maxwell (James Bond), Charles Gray (James Bond), Donald Pleasance (James Bond, *The Night of the Generals*), Peter Arne (*The Pink Panther*), Bill Nagy (*Coronation Street*, James Bond), Bernard Lee (James Bond, *The Third Man*), Yvonne Furneaux (*La Dolce Vita, Repulsion*)... and on and on. Fifty years later, there's a pleasant sense of *deja vu* when watching *Danger Man*.

Danger Man follows the conventions of live stage drama closely, favoring interior locations and dialogue-driven action. For example, while the later offshoot series *The Prisoner* adopted Theatre of the Absurd, *Danger Man*'s absurdism/expressionism is muted by social realism, where the characters are often driven by class anxiety as much as Cold War ideology. The spy gadgets and *femme fatales* often distract you from the sociology, the post-colonial rapprochement and the new liberalism. Treason has become a crime of class revolt, legitimate for some, easy cash for others. While the class argument is never as full-blooded as in *Look Back In Anger*, it is often present in the clash between characters and countries. If George Orwell had been a secret agent, he would've been John Drake.

One superb example is *No Marks For Servility* where Drake goes undercover as an English butler in a Roman villa rented by the sociopathic Balkan villain Grigori Benares (Howard Marion-Crawford). Benares is essentially a high-level swindler and misogynist, and unfortunately his manipulative charm has allowed him to bag a pretty young English wife. While his international graft is serious enough for M 9 to send in Drake to thwart his latest scam, all this becomes secondary to the clash between Benares and Drake, between master and servant, and the fate of Helen (Suzan Farmer).

"Let's See What I'm Paying $1500 A Month For"

Benares obtains a short-term lease on a Roman villa from Sir Charles Fielding, a collector of antiquities who happens to be a friend of M (Peter Madden), Drake's boss. M decides to insert Drake into the Benares household as a butler to spy on Benares and if possible thwart his criminal activities. Drake has an immediate empathic relationship with the pretty but insecure Helen Benares, which does not go unnoticed by her domineering husband, who is always in a high state of alert... quite possibly because, like Drake, he too is an imposter. As M says, "Benares, nationality unknown... he carries many passports... a vulgarian who likes to display his wealth."

When Benares arrives at the villa and finds only Drake the butler there to greet him, he says to his naive wife, "I would've liked all the servants here to greet you." When she demurs, he says, "It's a civilized custom, honey." He turns to Drake, says, "Perhaps you haven't come across it, Drake."

Drake: Oh yes I have, sir—in the cinema.

Benares: (stiffens) What exactly do you mean by that—

Drake: Forgive me, sir. I didn't wish to be facetious.

Benares: I'm glad to hear that, Drake. I'm the one who makes the cracks around here and you're the one who laughs.

Joe Orton? Not quite, although the menace and farce unfold in a similar manner. Benares left Athens in a hurry—interrupting his honeymoon—because he'd driven a compromised local politician to suicide. Predators have no conscience.

His character is brilliantly portrayed by Howard Marion-Crawford, an effortless UK actor well-known in the 30s, 40s and 50s for his radio drama work (he played Watson in Sherlock Holmes), and to a lesser extent as Dr. Petrie in the Fu Manchu films. Of passing interest is that one of his ancestors, the American sculptor Thomas Gibson Crawford, moved to Rome in 1830 where he lived and worked for a number of years in The Villa Negroni, which might have given Ralph Smart, the DD series creator and writer for *No Marks For Servility*, the idea for his Renaissance noir setting. Marion-Crawford was also a friend of Winston Churchill, and indeed they have similar intonations. There's a sense, too, that Benares might've understudied an American gangster. As a cunning bully, his characterization of Benares is a perfect foil for McGoohan's John Drake, and a true test of the agent's pragmatic self-discipline. When Drake hears Benares slapping his young wife around, he's only stopped from intervening (and blowing his cover) by the sound of the doorbell.

When the British financier Armstrong (Mervyn Johns) arrives with his pretty daughter Judy (Francesca Annis), the class-barrier once again dissolves as Judy, attracted to Drake, decides he's too hip to be a butler. It's as if she senses the masquerade, or recognizes the redundancy of the entire social convention. So now Drake has two women to protect, and protect them he does. After 40 or 50 or so episodes of *Danger Man*, you might be immune to the humour of his spy gadgets and techno subterfuges, yet is there anything as funny as Drake the stately butler descending into the wine cellar where he pours himself a tall glass of Primitivo red, lights a cigar, settles down in an armchair to watch and listen to Benares pitch his scam to Armstrong after dinner on the patio... or the two young women discussing whatever, all this over a retro CCTV unit of 4 monitors installed in a wine barrel? For the times, it was science fiction, yet credible and possible. Drake's unflappable manner becomes the epitome of cool. He is still in the thrall of the secret agent life-style, has not reached the Orwellian black hole that surveillance and counter-surveillance becomes in *The Prisoner*.

The Film Noir aspects of this episode become really apparent when Drake spots Benares using a semaphore lamp to signal to someone in an abandoned property several blocks away. Using a local street map and some basic triangulation, Drake determines the locale. The action is all moonlight and shadows. Drake scales the wall, drops into the ruined garden, gains entrance to the house, wearing his butler's black bowler hat and packing an umbrella (surely a model for Patrick McN in *The Avengers*). An owl cries. Like a well-dressed truant looking for someplace to kip, he cases the joint, moving stealthily through the noir geometrics. An unattended pot of soup simmers... an empty gun holster hangs from a peg... the stairs ascend into darkness... a dimly lit corridor, a sinister door... the house hangs in the void like a monument to cubism.

The chiaroscuro cine is superb. A lot of TV drama was shot in Super 16, but for *Danger Man/Secret Agent* it was all 35 mm (4:3 ratio) under the excellent direction of Brendan J. Stafford. In the 60s, watching this on a 21 inch vacuum tube television simply didn't reveal the true beauty of the cinematography, the monochromatic artistry that lies within every frame. Looking at Danger Man today on a 40+ LCD or plasma screen is like exchanging a postcard for the real thing.

Why is Drake here? When Armstrong rejected Benares' bribe of an easy stake in a Circassian coast real-estate development as a quid pro quo for an easy foreign aid loan, Benares reacted to this righteous snub by kidnapping Judy, Armstrong's nubile daughter, holding her captive, bound and gagged to a chair in this moldering den of shadows. The rescue is no problem for Drake—he has done it before, will do it again. The two thugs are easily tricked, despite the fact they are armed. As usual, the fight choreography has the athletic simplicity of a circus routine, reinforces the anglican view that guns are seldom required for law enforcement. Patrick McGoohan had a Jesuit's insistence that guns rarely needed to be used, as if he feared television violence would imprint the next generation. In fact, *No Marks For Servility* is one of the few episodes in which he actually fires a shot, yet when he does, it's just a warning.

Strong characters, great dialogue, outstanding sets and art design, interesting story... *No Marks For Servility* was written by Ralph Smart—the series creator and executive producer—and directed by the accomplished Don Chaffey (who, in a later life, directed—to his everlasting credit—Raquel Welch in *One Million Years B.C.*).

Danger Man Modern Gothic

Don Chaffey directed a few of the better *DM* episodes, including *The Not-So-Jolly Roger*, about a den of spies sending coded messages from a pirate radio station in the North Sea. As a set, the old off-shore WW II forts that house the station allow some excellent photographic imagery. Anchored on stilts and connected by suspended gangways, the minimalism of the architecture—geometrics in modern gothic against a blended horizon of sea and sky—is reinforced by the black and white cine. Much of the action takes place during a storm, and the cast of villains operate as an ensemble, complete with a fake drunken buffoon (Corrigan), a hulking goon (Mullins), a predatory wife, and a sexy DJ called Suzy. Drake pretends to be a DJ, replacing a dead jockey called Andy, who was shot because he'd tumbled the Blue Danube code. Better music would've helped, although the style fits the Swinging Sixties period and most likely the ITC *Danger Man* budget. You can easily imagine the power this episode would have if the sound track was refurbished with some A-list UK rock from the likes of The Kinks, The Yardbirds, The Stones, Cream, etc.

Episode 1 of *The Prisoner* was directed by Don Chaffey, so his imprint on the style of this cult series is significant. Chaffey went on to direct four *Mission Impossible* episodes (a series that clearly owes a debt to *DM*), some *Avengers*, some *Charlie's Angels*, some B movies.

In the *Danger Man* series, there's often a Somerset Maugham feel to many of the settings and characters, although the context is post-colonial. It's a Cold War world, a shrinking world—Drake is often jetting to Bagdad or Beruit or Prague... Greece, Italy, Portugal, Spain... Hong Kong, Tokyo... the Caribbean, Central America, Africa. He's like Graham Greene, slightly to the Left, a loyal loner, pedigree vague. You suspect his lineage is British SAS even though he now wears a jacket and tie. His diction is staccato, clipped and iambic as if trained in officer military speak. In the acting world, you might think of Burt Lancaster.

Modern English is a military-industrial diction as much as it is an aspirational upper-class nuance. Rhetoric disappears in favor of brevity, stacked syllables barked out in a drill yard or sketched out in a short-hand memo. Patrick McGoohan's John Drake is a master of brevity, the punchy iambic (where subjects disappear in favor of the predicated object). In close he might be a gentleman in a gentleman's suit, but in silhouette he's pure military. His adversaries are usually more obvious (as fascist enforcers are) even when masquerading as legitimate business men like Grigori Benares. Benares has rhetoric, but his arrogance is fuelled by sadism, so he longs to dominate, even when it would be in his best interest to be more subtle. While justice is served in the end when he's led away by the Roman police, you do (perhaps) long for a deeper humiliation with a truly ironic twist. But in *Danger Man*—as in the post-modern world—udgement is often left to the legal lottery of the faceless State.

Not all the damsels in distress are women—it can be a trapped diplomat in a foreign embassy, a journalist falsely imprisoned for spying, abducted scientists or even a compromised British accountant working for a middle-eastern druglord as in the early 30 minute episode, *A Position of Trust*. While inserted ostensibly to subvert the flow of raw opium, Drake is soon working on the rehabilitation of Captain Aldrich (Donald Pleasance) who works in "the Ministry of Health", which has become a conduit for the illegal trade. The locale could be Pakistan, and Mr. Big is in fact the Minister. Pleasance's portrayal of a colonial Englishman laid low by snobbery and cultural isolation is excellent. "More British than the British—Anglo-Indian," says Sandi Lewis, a statuesque US operative. Manipulated by his employer and then by Drake, he nevertheless redeems himself by "doing the right thing", turns over a list of names associated with the drug trade. Lois Maxwell plays Sandi Lewis as a cool 440Hz flirt in much the same way she does later as Miss Moneypenny in James Bond. Pleasance as Captain Aldrich is excellent, and the depth of his character is remarkable for the few scenes he's in. Thanks to Drake, he's not thrown to the wolves, and his self-esteem is restored, and he can continue to wear his old Southminster school tie with pride.

As has been well-documented, gays were often compromised for intelligence purposes during the Cold War. In *Don't Nail Him Yet* Drake masquerades as a lonely school teacher to trap an Admiralty clerk called Rawson (John Fraser) who has been selling submarine technology secrets via micro-dot film reduction. Here Drake mirrors his victim's enthusiasms—soccer, records, music—in yet another virtuoso double-role performance. Although left ambiguous, homosexuality is suggested through the loneliness of the characters, art, books, poetry... and the fake Canadian book dealer, Dian (Sheila Allen), whose masculine charm includes a secret radio transmitter and a pilot's license. When Drake confronts her and Rawson in an upstairs room at Eglington Rare Books, Rawson laughs bitterly at the idea that they might be lovers. When Dian angrily asks if he is a policeman, Drake replies, "I could never be a policeman... too many rules and regulations... I'm like you... I work outside the law."

Dian attempts to escape back to the east bloc (with Glasgow as a fake flight plan destination) in a De Havilland DH 104 Dove, abducting an unwilling Rawson and Drake at gun point. As usual, Danger Man thwarts the plan. Using the plane's fire extinguisher as a weapon, he escapes as the takeoff begins, then uses the spies' abandoned Zephyr 4 to block the runway. Dian, at the controls, screams as the plane collides with the car, explodes, and we're left with the latent satisfaction that butch Marxist traitors burn in hell, no matter how sensitive to micro dot poetry they might be. Written by Philip Broadley, directed by Michael Truman.

Blueprint For *The Prisoner*

> "Once people enter Colony Three, they cease to exist" (*Colony Three*, writ. Donald Jonson, dir. Don Chaffey)

Fuller—glasses, hat, raincoat—exits a London terrace house, boards a double-decker bus, which is followed by secret agent John Drake (Patrick McGoohan) in his Mini. Fuller eventually gets off the bus, enters a building with a door plaque reading Citizen's Advice Bureau. In a room, he starts packing a black duffle bag; perhaps we notice his reading for the journey, a book called *The Theory of the Neutron Ray* by Boris Turgenev, a modest clue that perhaps he's heading for the Soviet bloc [Boris Turgenev was a Marvel comics Soviet super-villain who wore the Crimson Dynamo exoskeleton body armour for his fights with Iron Man]. Drake enters, surprises Fuller, says, "My Principals want to have a word with you before you leave, Mr. Fuller."

Cut To: Drake and his boss M watching a sweating, dishevelled Fuller, over a TV monitor in M's office. Fuller is denying that's he done anything wrong, reiterates his itinerary. M shuts off the monitor, tells Drake that over 400 UK citizens have disappeared "over there" since the war... why? "We're switching the records on Robert Fuller—you're going out there to take his place."

So Drake becomes Fuller—raincoat, glasses, doctored passport and resume. Drake takes a Comet 4C airliner from London to an unnamed location (perhaps Prague) behind the Iron Curtain. Drake/Fuller is met and hustled into a black van, which takes him to the loading dock of a bland railway station. Armed unfriendly soldiers check his credentials, and he is escorted quickly to the train. Drake—inhabiting the Fuller persona—blusters about his treatment, says, "This isn't what I was led to expect in London." The official replies, "Mr. Fuller, you are here to work for us and you must accept that there is a good reason for what we do."

Indeed. While it's no Nazi death train, Drake quickly discovers that the carriage windows have been blacked out and sealed, and that his fellow passengers have no idea where they are going. The totalitarian denial of freedom has been established. He shares a compartment with a chippy Australian communist called Randall, and a young female librarian called Janet Wells. As the train gets underway, Drake does a crossword and Randall does most of the talking. "They want me to work with a combat school... well, I was with the Special Brigade in Spain... I'm an electrician, well, really an engineer." Etc. You quickly get the idea that he didn't get the respect he felt he deserved in London. He speaks some Russian, is optimistic about the future. Drake nods towards the sleeping girl. "Her?" says Randall. "I think she made a mistake."

It turns out that Janet is looking for a boyfriend called Alan Bayliss, who used to work in the same library. When his letters stopped coming, she decided to follow. "I'm rather fond of Alan," she tells Drake [who, as per all *Danger Man* episodes, is always sympathetic to a damsel in distress, even if he never takes advantage].

The train arrives at a bleak wasteland, an east bloc prairie in pre-winter. As they disembark, a London double-decker bus approaches [similar to the one Fuller takes in the opening scene]. To everyone's surprise, the route sign says, "Hamden, New Town, 12." They board Number 12, and Randall tries to engage the driver, find out where they are going. He uses Russian, but the driver ignores him. Quickly they arrive in Hamden, New Town, and as they get off, Randall says, "We seem to be right back where we started."

The true absurdity of the situation is later reinforced by a brief appearance of a London bobby, none other than Constable George Dixon from another popular UK TV drama series of the mid sixties, *Dixon of Dock Green*. While it's just a moment, and to some extent an in-joke, this clever detail nonetheless helps reinforce the madness of the social paradigm that is *Colony Three*.

Their handler appears, says, "Welcome to Hamden. My name's Richardson. I do hope you had a comfortable journey." Richardson (Peter Arne) has the smooth manner of a born PR hack, yet with a hint of menace, a man with a hidden switch that can render him as an instant psychopath. When asked about the impossibility of this being an English village, he goes straight to the metaphysical nub of the situation: "Geography is a matter of physical illusion... lines on a map, words on a signpost." He clinches with: "Mr. Donovan says all countries are countries of the mind." This might be some hip Zen-think or self-serving Marxist propaganda, yet the facts are soon clear: Hamden New Town is a culture-simulator, a staged society for programming Soviet agents in "Englishness".

Incredible? This brilliant 1964 *Danger Man* script by Donald Jonson owes its genesis to the Cold War notion that Potemkin Spy Villages existed in the Soviet Union for training agents to infiltrate British and American institutions. Whether urban myth or Cold War fact, these life-style immersion locations took their name from Prince Grigory Alexander Potemkin (1739-1791), the favorite minister of Catherine the Great. He created a number of new towns and villages in the southern steppe regions and the Crimea, not all of which were entirely real. Painted facades were used to simulate real villages, perhaps to intimidate the ungovernable Cossacks or impress Catherine on her tour.

For those who know the cult McGoohan series that followed *Danger Man/Secret Agent* in the fall of 1967, the similarities between *Colony Three* and *The Prisoner* will be obvious. Patrick McGoohan has said that his idea for *The Prisoner* came primarily from its Port Mereirion (Wales) setting, as four or five *Danger Man* episodes were filmed there, starting with the pilot, *View From the Villa*. *Villa* is set in Rome, yet the Port Mereirion locales look legitimate enough, especially as most of the action is interior. The plasticity of the architecture—which McGoohan described as looking like a holiday resort—was a convenient passport to the surrealism that *The Prisoner's raison d'etre* required. *Colony Three* wasn't a Port Mereirion location, yet its closed-system world is the prototype for the Kafkaesque no-exit asylum that is *The Prisoner*. *Colony Three* is real, *The Prisoner* is surreal, yet both function as a metaphor for all that is incomprehensible about life in much the same way as Samuel Beckett's famous stage play *Waiting For Godot* does.

The Season Is Winter

It should be noted that Don Chaffey, who directed *Colony Three*, also directed the first episode of *The Prisoner*. Don Chaffey also directed *Such Men Are Dangerous* (writ. Ralph Smart, *DM* series Producer), which also has some narrative similarities to *The Prisoner*, and especially to *Colony Three*. Here Drake masquerades as a con in Wormwood Scrubs, and when released, infiltrates a political assassination squad run by a rogue general from a gated estate somewhere outside London. Again, Drake gets there by train; again, the season is winter as if the Cold War is stuck permanently in one psychological season. Again, as in *Colony Three*, one of the inductees tries to escape after becoming paranoid about what is being asked of him i.e. be part of an illegal hit-squad to kill undesirable foreign heads-of-state. Drake is sent by "the General" to kill the defector—Taylor, his roommate at the estate—but through his usual secret agent *modus* is able to save Taylor and spoil the nefarious plans of Major Latour (Lee Montague) and the General (Jack Gwilliam). The General's pretty wife gads about the estate in a jeep, and always seems to intersect with Drake whenever he's dodging through the rhodos sending messages to M or spying on The Order. As usual, Drake's crafty charm keeps him one step ahead. As is often the case in *Danger Man*, the action is coolly satiric (the country estate, the duck hunting, the class system).

The acting in *Colony Three* is excellent, especially that of Peter Arne as Richardson (the prototype for "Number 2"). As his character is by training an act, the ambiguity of his actions are a perfect foil for those of Drake masquerading as "Fuller". The scene where he invites an overly curious Drake to sit in an interrogation chair, then tortures him with electric shocks (by way of a demonstration) is very good. He extracts a confession, yet the agile Drake is able to hold character, throw the confession into doubt. When he eventually tries to kill Drake to prevent his return to Section 1, but dies in the attempt, you have no sympathy... and of course it will come as no surprise that in real life Peter Arne—who played villains in many TV dramas and feature films, including *The Pink Panther*—was bludgeoned to death in his London flat in 1983 just like Joe Orton. His personal story is not a pretty one, yet he was a very good actor.

The character of Randall, the electrician, played by Owen Glyn is a morality tale onto itself. He doesn't like Fuller a.k.a. Drake, and eventually betrays him, although this can be excused as he thought he had no choice. He mistakenly thinks Fuller/Drake is a sycophant, cozying up to Donovan, the director of the village, and his *capo* Richardson, and an unfeeling swine when it concerns Janet Wells and her fiance, Bayliss, the man who died trying to escape Colony Three. However, the village is a big disappointment for him. His ideological arrogance is such that he thinks he can do what Bayliss couldn't, that is, successfully escape. When he finds a couple of English aristocrats who recently defected from the UK still living and acting as aristocrats, his pure socialist principles are absolutely compromised, and he has to escape. Janet knows and approves of his plan. "He speaks the language—he stands a better chance," she tells Drake. Drake goes after Randall, catches up to him in a sandpit. They argue, they fight... and of course Danger Man wins any such fights. A helicopter patrol spots them, and both men are returned to the village. Randall denounces Fuller/Drake, Drake denounces Randall. "He's mad," says Fuller/Drake. Donovan, the Director, nods, says, "Certain English socialists are...." One is reminded of the paranoid hopeless of *The Prisoner*, the interrogations, the surveillance, the futile attempts at escape... Number 6 (McGoohan) being hunted and defeated by a meteorological balloon on a flat beach, measured by infinity as in a dream.

Virtually all of the *Danger Man/Secret Agent* dramas have no epilogue scene at the end, no summing up, no blanks filled. The action invariably ends on the climax, with Drake escaping towards home. *Wrong Number* by Ralph Smart would be a good example of mission accomplished, no explanation needed. A car, a boat, a plane... swimming with a beautiful woman, as in the atmospheric *The English Lady Takes Boarders*. Not so *Colony Three*. Successfully repatriated back to "Section 1", then to London, Drake confers with his boss M, asks if anything can be done for Janet Wells. "We've never even heard of her," says M. Indeed. "Once people enter Colony Three, they cease to exist."

Readers of British fiction from the 1960's will no doubt notice the similarities of *Colony Three* to some of the short stories by JG Ballard, as if Ballard and script writer Donald Jonson were drinking from the same well. Ballard's 1962 story *The Watch Towers* has an English village (or suburb) monitored by unseen watchers from concentration camp towers, yet the locals carry on oblivious to this fact as if it's just another day on *Coronation Street.* Surrealist stories such as *Colony Three* or *The Watch Towers* wherein spatiality is collapsed in favor of a global psychological landscape are an accurate bioptic of Cold War paranoia; you might live in England or America, but in your mind the Iron Curtain is just next door. "All countries are countries of the mind"—

Jonson wrote several excellent *Danger Man* episodes, including *The Outcast*, which looks like a counter-espionage version of Tennessee Williams' *The Night of the Iguana*... and *Judgement Day*, which anticipated today's more sober view of Israel's automatic right to justice. Here Drake goes to Jordan to save a German biochemist who did some experimental virus work for the Nazis using Jewish detainees as lab subjects. Drake intends to fly Garriga (Paul Deghy) to safety in Oman, but the small plane is hijacked by a beautiful Israeli-American called Jessica (Alexandra Stewart) who is posing as an archaeologist. When the plane crash-lands at an abandoned airstrip in the Sinai, Jessica is joined by three armed members of an Israeli Holocaust justice group. Before they can execute Garriga (who is pretending to be an innocent Spanish scientist), Drake demands that he be given a fair trial, and in a rough, quick court facsimile staged in some desert ruins, acts as Garriga's defence counsel. In a fit of self-righteous arrogance, Garriga admits his crimes (all for the higher good) but not before Drake exposes the fascist hypocrisy of execution without a fair trial. Nice visuals, good characters, and definitely going against the tide of western public opinion in 1966. And once again, directed by Don Chaffey.

The Outcast uses the exoticism of Gibralter and the Costa del Sol as its setting. Although it deals with espionage, it's essentially a study of character. A nice looking Wren officer involved in intelligence work is murdered and Drake flies in to investigate. The suspect is a navy cipher clerk called Leo Perrins (Bernard Bresslaw) who flees to the Costa del Sol, possibly Marbella or Torremolinos, finds a temporary sanctuary in the kitchen of a bar run by an Englishwoman and her teenage daughter. Drake poses as a tourist, observes the sordid love triangle involving the alcoholic Nora, the Lolitaesque Helen, and the Spanish waiter Xavier, a Latin opportunist of the most obvious sort. Meanwhile Drake befriends Leo, saves him from a Russian assassin, gains his confidence and a confession. Leo was part of a triangle himself, it seems. He was in love with the Wren, knew she was passing classified secrets to her lover, the guy in the Triumph sports car. She laughed at him, he lost it, he shot her. How Drake manipulates Leo into this confession is both credible and in the end, touching, because even though Drake deceives his new "friend" out of professional necessity, you know that he regrets the fact.

Again, as with many of the *Danger Man/Secret Agent* episodes, there's a stage feel to the action, which, rather than being a distraction, allows characterization to develop in real-time without cheating by montage.

The Prisoner: "No Exit"

Despite Patrick McGoohan's denials, it's obvious that No. 6 in *The Prisoner* is John Drake... otherwise why repeat the same sort of *Danger Man* credits montage at the beginning of the first episode? The *Danger Man* series creator, producer and lead writer, Ralph Smart, had the copyright on the character "John Drake", so some sort of pretence had to be maintained in order for the producers of *The Prisoner* to proceed. The diction, the look, the attitude... these nuances show that McGoohan was still "in character" as he launched the new series. *Danger Man*'s cool has snapped, and now he is condemned in perpetuity to a daily psycho-drama enacted in an Orwellian resort village.

In Jean-Paul Sartre's famous 1944 play *No Exit* a man is locked in a room with two women. They are all dead, and perhaps this room is an ante-chamber to hell. Occasionally they are visited by a valet, who is the son of the Head valet, therefore No. 2 in the scheme of things. McGoohan, who emerged from the Sheffield Repertory Theatre, would've been familiar with *No Exit*, just as he would've been familiar with Beckett's *Waiting For Godot* or even Harold Pinter's derivative *The Caretaker*, all symbolist dramas that set the intellectual standard for the dramatic arts.

And of course there was the seminal *Danger Man* episode *Colony Three* propelling the idea, whether McGoohan cared to admit it or not.

As McGoohan said in various interviews, his original concept for the series was for just seven episodes, but that Lew Grade the CEO of I.T.C. said that he couldn't market such a mini-series in the USA without more, so it ended up as seventeen. This was unfortunate, as the idea was diluted beyond its dramatic horizon, with many of the later episodes being mere game playing, repetitive without real tension... although, to be fair, a lot of absurdist theatre reduced human action to infantile game playing. Despite this, the series has a zany stylistic charm not unlike the 1965 Elio Petrie film *The 10th Victim* (*La Decima Vittima*). But the series was losing its narrative thread, falling further into parody and montage. Regarding the infamous Western (episode 14) *Living In Harmony* (which caused the series script editor George Markstein to quit), you wonder what—if any—influence it had on Michael Critcheon's 1973 seminal killer-robot western *Westworld*. As has been stated elsewhere and often, the influence of McGoohan's *The Prisoner* on TV and film drama was immense despite the fact that at the time its real audience was still in the future.

The 2009 US remake of *The Prisoner* is narrative by montage rather than episodic scene shifting in linear time. Eisenstein might dig it, not Aristotle. Claveizel's No. 6 spends a lot of his time reacting to his situation whereas McGoohan's 6 is nearly always setting the agenda. The metaphysics of the 2009 remake have been tailored to fit the post-911 American trauma, and has a parallel world version 1 *Planet of the Apes* feel. It has romance—No. 6 gets to roll around with the English actresses Haley Atwell and Ruth Wilson—and an uglier sense of violence, as if the American condition has been inserted into the original 1967 Village of quaint British cars and bicycles. The beach becomes a desert, and sink holes appear like magic in the empty lots. While the symbolism seems focused and effective, at times the narrative becomes a grim psychedelic soap opera, presenting a challenge to even the most hardened aficionados of the irrational.

Why not, you say. Surely this was the purpose of McGoohan's 1967 original. Legend has it that the actor Leo McKern—one of McGoohan's No. 2s—had to be hospitalized after the stressful workout of his role, even though the action was a theatrical sendup.

In the 09 version, Ian McKellen's No. 2 is cool, with the malignant benevolence of a grammar school principal who shares a smoke with the prefects as a devious act of good politics. In some ways the 09 remake is an improvement, but in others it's just American TV. The theme music—at first mated beautifully with the landscape cine—becomes an annoying distraction (you'll notice that the refrain sounds like Mark Knopfler's score for *Local Hero*).

The End

It's hardly to his credit, but Peter Yates—famous as the director of Steve McQueen's *Bullitt*—directed *Shinda Shima*, the ridiculous last episode of *Danger Man/Secret Agent*. You can suppose he was only following orders.The last two episodes, written by Norman Hudris, were filmed in color and teamed into a feature for showing in theatres. The first of the two, *Koroshi*, had some potential. Set in Tokyo, with Drake investigating a murder cult (an ex-pat clique of mad Englishmen into "the poetry of death"), this episode is now remembered for its Kabuki version of *Hamlet* and the art props of Albert Witherick.

The style of these Japanese episodes had clearly been infected by the pop fantasy burlesque of James Bond, so it's no surprise that Patrick McGoohan wanted to go in another direction. Judging by *The Prisoner*, he wanted to bring the intellectual poetry of live theatre into television drama, rather than play to the kids in the "scratchies" (front row matinee cinema).

So, obviously the real Series 4 of *Danger Man/Secret Agent* is/was *The Prisoner*.

No question, Patrick McGoohan had the mojo for the *DM* character of John Drake, Secret Agent, and his artistic determination drove the series beyond its medium cool espionage imagery. The Cold War kept people alert. The cultural anxiety bred deep insecurity and systemic madness. The notion that someone could maintain his composure and control desperate situations was appealing in the age of nuclear dreams and easy obliteration.

Cultural brainwashing was just another television channel, and people, desperate for some tasteful sexual pacification, could easily identify with the ambiguous fantasy of *Danger Man*. Ironically, Patrick McGoohan ended up a prisoner of sorts in Hollywood, never able to completely escape his character of John Drake.

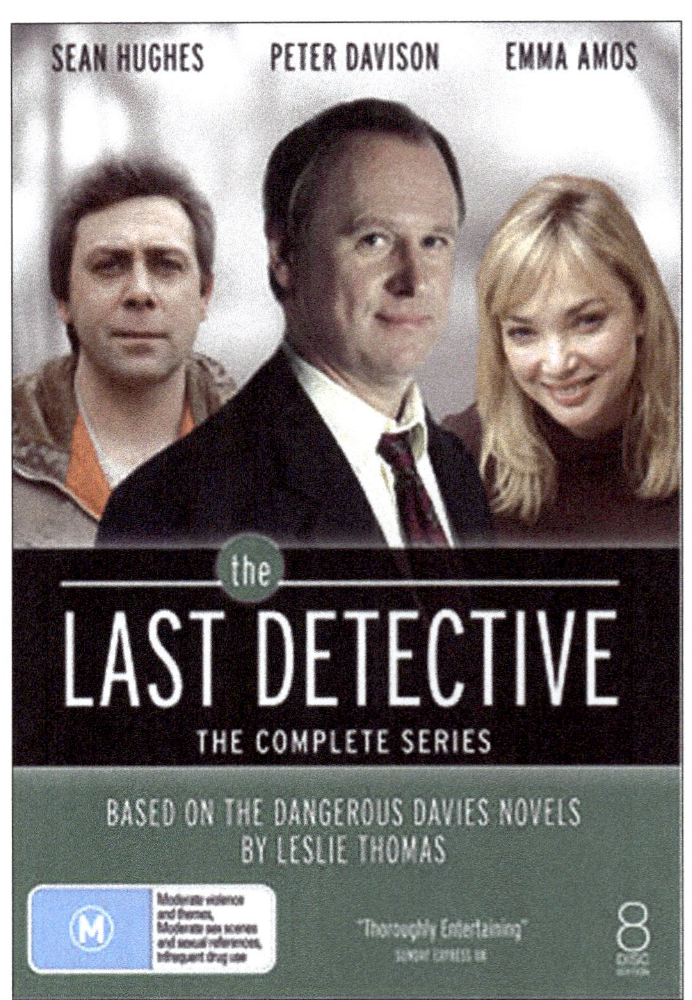

The Last Detective

Last Detective. DC "Dangerous" Davies (Peter Davison) Mod (Sean Hughes) Julie Davies (Emma Amos) DI Ray Aspinall (Rob Spendlove) DS Pimlott (Charles de'Ath) DC Barrett (Bill Geraghty) PC Zsa Zsa Kapoor (Vinetta Rishi) WPC Cheryl (Michelle Austin)
writers: Richard Harris, Michael Atkins, Russell Lewis, Tim Vaughan
directors: Pip Broughton, Moira Armstrong, Matthew Evans, Rick Hurran, Ferdinand Fairfax, Douglas MacKinnon, Gavin Millar dir. of

photog: James Aspinall, Kevin Rudge edt. David Head, Paul Garrick, Paul Richards *et al* music: Rupert Gregson-Williams prod. by Julie Clark, Julie Keir, Robbie Sandison

As of 2006 17 episodes shot in wide screen stereo. Frst broadcast on ITV. Series based on the novels of Leslie Thomas. Granada International

Imposed Upon The Past

Low tide on the river. *The Last Detective* staggers over the fresh mud in an industrial bivouac to interview an associate of the victim as a welder works in the shadow of a listing boat... it could be a painting by L.S. Lowry but it isn't. Or: A flooded quarry on the Welsh border. *The Last Detective* stands on the smooth rocks watching a police diver search the green water... this could be a painting by David Hockney but it isn't.

Or: A comedian stands like a carnival doll in the footlights playing to his harem in a seedy Willesden social club, drinks a glass of wine laced with rat poison, drops dead on the stage... it could be a painting by Francis Bacon but it isn't. These understated but fascinating visuals belong to Dangerous Davies, *The Last Detective* (the latest incarnation), an ITV series created in 2002/3 to fill the family hours just after sundown on a winter evening.

Family viewing? You have to wonder, because while the gratuitous violence is mostly off-camera, and there is occasional buffoonery, make no mistake, this is adult drama. *The Last Detective* was first filmed in 1981 as a single drama, and this updated series retells the same story in the pilot episode. Although it's all in color, the documentary finesse of the locations gives the action a neo-realist feel, so that it looks like a sociological expose worthy of Vittorio de Sica.

True, the stories unfold in the usual way as a series of interviews with witnesses and suspects, but there's something going down here beyond mere novelty. A sense of Time is in the faces of the characters, as if Dangerous Davies (Peter Davison) is interviewing the complete cast of British society, where everyone is either a suspect or a witness or a squealer.

Everyone has a tragic flaw, a secret, and has probably murdered someone somewhere sometime. It's a society where the Present is imposed upon the Past like another coat of paint, an existential concealment staged in the endless camouflage of shabby buildings and second hand light. It seems England is a memory obscured by the present. An abandoned horse stands on the pavement as if the suburb has just materialized, supplanted its pasture... a pram rises from the dirty waters of the canal... a porno vid is found in a drawer... and the victims: bodies in the garden, the trash heap, the canal, the railway tracks... a secret chamber below the greenhouse... burning studios and exploding cars, women who are mad, bad, and dangerous to know. And the lead character is afflicted by the romantic memory of his marriage and its failure in the present, as if he's trying to recover the way it was once in sleepy old middle class Albion.

The Last Englishman

Despite his handle as "The Last Detective" (a cynical witticism by his boss: "You're the Last Detective, Dangerous... the last one I'd ever think of.") Dangerous Davies is actually The Last Englishman. He prefers a pint rather than a Bud, an ironic rebuttal rather than a reactive fist. His composure is dangerously obsolete, as are his values and his methods. "You're decent man in an indecent time," says his pal Mod in the pilot episode. Here, the murder he solves is a police crime—a sex crime—and he finds himself shunned for his good work, and the real crime seems to be that he broke the collegial code, not the mystery of a teenage girl murdered by a cop.

He can't understand his wife's sexual restlessness or the attitude of today's women in general, even though women like him, give him tea and sandwiches... and the stripper with the boa who lives on a barge probably gave him more. He's always working from the bottom up, from the outside in. He's merely "Detective Constable", a bumbler who's never made the grade, and yet at the end of the day it's the good old yeoman fortitude of Dangerous Davies that solves the crime.

The primary English virtues of perseverance and fair play are written in his source code. Sympathy, steadiness, suppression of self—these codes predate the "Me Generation" yet this is his generation. No malingering rebellion gone bad with middle-age, no self-pity... he's just a humble servant of the people in a raincoat and a station wagon that sometimes won't start, the Columbo of London N.W. 10.

A Drifter With An Address

While In North America the "buddy cop" script paradigm started with the Robert Culp/Bill Cosby series *I Spy* (1965-68), it could be argued that it reaches back into the Conan Doyle Sherlock Holmes stories. It's certainly used a lot in recent UK TV crime drama, such as *Inspector Morse*—another English type facing obsolescence—which is set further up the Thames Valley from the west London suburb of Willesden that D.C. Davies inhabits.

Of course Davies' "mate" isn't a cop—he's a drifter with an address, a flat which he sometimes shares with Davies when DD's wife or landlady won't have him around. He's on the dole, occasionally takes ludicrous temp jobs which are more like acting gigs. Mod is typical of his generation, unable to graduate to reality, full of paperback ideas, educated and lazy, a gentle soul too nice to be called a loser, although he loses frequently.

What is "Mod" short for? "Modesty," says Dangerous to an old lady who asks. It certainly isn't because he's a snappy dresser, a holdout from the "Mods" of sixties England, although anything is possible, as we know nothing about his past. He likes books, often has one on hand, such as a collection of Oscar Wilde. "I don't care who he shagged," says Mod. "He wrote a bloody good essay." And when he and Dangerous are mistaken for a homosexual couple on the canal towpath by a petty criminal, Mod snaps back, "How dare you—I was once engaged to Miss Galway Bay."

Thus his Irish pedigree is revealed, and Willesden does have its community of Irish transplants, a movement that started seriously during WW II. So he's an Irish dreamer, should be a writer himself, escape the curse of the leprechaun. Sometimes DD discusses a case with him—in the pub, the car, the park, on the towpath, somewhere between the bricks & the trees, walking the big dog—and more often than not Mod has some insight that proves useful. It might be spotting a revealing imprint on an old photograph (as in *Lofty*) or setting up an association in DD's mind by an off-hand remark.

The crimes are almost irrelevant in this series because the

action is carried by the strength of the principal characters and the documentary Willesden setting. Nothing unusual in this, as it follows the tradition of the English murder mystery, which is more like a game of *Snakes and Ladders* than a grim decoding of homicide. The crimes are invariably indiscretions, never cold-blooded slayings such as the exotic killings in *CSI: Miami* (Las Vegas, New York), for example. The mercy killing of the Balkan war vet Frank Moore in *Towpaths of Glory* (episode 10) is as brutal as it gets; the point of nihilism hasn't been reached.

However, the breaching of the cultural fabric that allows British common sense to always triumph might be on hand, as DD's colleagues seem to have surrendered to a xenophobic cynicism as a matter of machismo or caste survivalism. An alert comes into the station about a load of Chinese illegals being smuggled into Willesden but when they stake out the dropoff, the operation is a bust. There are no illegals this time.

Occasionally the crimes act merely as a background to Dangerous' personal life, his problems with Julie. The pilot episode pretty well lays it all out. Dangerous is in the can washing his hands, a fellow detective at the urinal.

> Barrett: Did I see you walking your dog yesterday, Dangerous?
> DD: You probably did.
> Barrett: I thought she had custody of the dog.
> DD: She can't handle him.
> Barrett: Oh? What I heard was she can handle just about anything... no offence, Dangerous.
> DD: How can anyone take offence at you, Barrett?

Of course this cameo nails the situation exactly. DD collects his dog like a father getting visiting rights to his kid just as an airline pilot arrives at the house to spend the evening with Julie. As they pass on the path DD's restraint is old school middle class England, the sort of Anglican fortitude that drove a generation of missionaries into Africa without complaint. No punch outs here, no head butt, no knee to the groin or dog attack, just some ironic remark... as if he recognizes this latest rival to be just another victim like himself.

A decent man in an indecent world indeed.

The Dreamy Madness Of The Living

As body dramas go, *The Last Detective* goes light on the dead, heavy on the living. Corpses are seldom figurative art studies and when they are, there are no lingering photographic autopsies (well, one maybe... the has-been rocker Teddy O'Connor in *Three Steps To Hendon*). The dreamy madness of the living is the real subject.

In *Dangerous by Moonlight* an old terminal ballroom dancer refuses to believe her husband is missing, but rather on a philandering vacation, and dies happily unaware that she killed him during a drunken squabble. In *Lofty* a successful female executive starts an impulsive affair with a young married employee who accidentally causes the drowning death of an old vagrant war vet and in turn is killed in an auto accident while talking on his cell phone to his lover.

A cop lives the last 20 years of his working life devoted to a crippled wife even though he killed a teenage girl in a fit of sexual madness... the various lovers of a murdered comedian delude themselves as to his fidelity and talent... a female gardener and man-hater lives in art and dangerous obsession... a kindly old violin master kills in order to possess a classic instrument, etcetera.

The various episodes are a study of loneliness and involuntary disengagement. The context is multi-cultural, a society where even the natives seem like foreigners. Black cops & street criminals, European au pairs & Balkan refugees, gypsies, Hong Kong exiles & Indian exotics, uptown cockneys & Yorkshire bikers, they all look like passengers who wandered out of Heathrow and got lost in Willesden. It's the ebb tide of the colonial experience, a patriation of collaborators and victims, and a multi-cultural reinvention within the European Union. It's no longer the BBC, it's the BBC World.

DD's boss is Detective Inspector Ray Aspinall (Rob Spendlove), a beautiful study of the functioning alcoholic. He carries a flask in his pocket, keeps a 26er in his filing cabinet, and is often the only guy at the bar in the police club. Tall and nicotine thin, he carries his darkness well, even when hung over and fixing himself a bromo & milk. He might have fits of sarcasm, he might be occasionally insulting, but he is always fair.

His subordinates respect him regardless and none more so than Dangerous. It's a beautiful thing to watch how the bond between the two men develops within the episodes, goes from no confidence to brotherly love. By episode 11, *Three Steps To Hendon* (story of the murdered rock star), the reversal is almost complete; Aspinall says he's been asked to head up a new regional squad outside London, suggests that DD comes with him as his "bagman".

A promotion? Dangerous checks around, finds out something is wrong. He sees Aspinall in his office says, "Guv... don't do it, it's a setup... they can't get the man they want, so they're putting in a temp... if you take the job, they'll get rid of you." The revelation hits the Inspector like a bullet; he stares silently at DD, then pulls a whiskey bottle from a drawer in his desk, pours a shot. So much for going tee total. DD throws up his hands, exits. Stress, politics, the shaft. Last exit from Willesden is a vertical rise to the bottom.

By the next episode, *Willesden Confidential* (12), the circle closes. A boozed up Aspinall loses a confidential police file in a pub, and Dangerous offers to take the fall "because I'm never gonna get promoted now, am I?" So there it is, Dangerous Davies, the quintessential foot-soldier who makes the sacrifice, "falls on the grenade" to protect his boss. Respect? A tongue lashing from a female superintendent doesn't help, but he gets respect where it matters, from his friends and colleagues.

Iago & Iago

Detectives Pimlott and Barrett are always standing around like conspirators in a Renaissance revenge tragedy... Iago & Iago. Wise guys in suits drinking Buds. Pimlott (Charles de'Ath) is a sort of cockney dandy, always spiffed out in a new suit & tie, maybe the latest overcoat. His car is new, good for extra mileage claims. Because he's a Detective Sergeant, he outranks DD, and is always quick to "take the piss" out of him with a nasty little game or taunt.

Like so many in police forces everywhere, Pimlott could easily be mistaken for a hoodlum, although he's nowhere near as macho as he puts out. His day of reckoning comes early in the series when he gets stabbed by the crazy female stalker in *Tricia* (episode 3); the irony here is that she is trying to get Davies. When DD visits him in hospital, Pimlott says, "What are you here for? You don't even like me." DD looks away, smiles, says, "No, I don't." DD doesn't hold grudges, is loyal to his unit, and things between him and Pimlott aren't quite so rude thereafter.

Yet this near-death experience doesn't completely divest Pimlott of his sexist bully persona when interviewing women, and there is one memorable scene where he gets slapped by the widow of the victim when he moves in a bit too close and personal. "What are you?" she snarls. "A tit man? Arse, leg, what?"

D.C. Darren Barrett: he has very few lines, communicates mostly in the body language of smirks and quizzical glances. He could be a poster on the wall, a piece of cultural sub-text... which isn't a criticism, as this is how the producers want him played. Barrett at his desk, Dangerous at his. He's like a bored teacher watching his delinquent student writing an essay in detention, both victims of a mutual contempt. He's an effective prop, although as an acting gig, it's money fer nuthin', yer chicks fer free.

Between The Dots

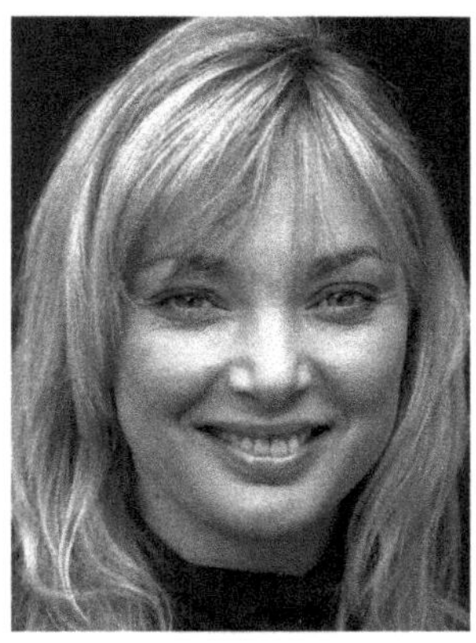

Julie (Emma Amos). "I can still remember the first time I saw her," says Dangerous (mistily). She's a very common type these days, in many western countries, part of the first generation of women to be liberated by the birth control pill. There's no analysis of her confusion here: she just is. Between the dots we recognize that the big St. Bernard dog is a substitute in a childless marriage now beached in middle age. A bit plump, lynx eyes & rich mouth like a Madame. She still has her erotic potential, although her best days are behind her. Clearly she's the one who called it quits — she has the house, the dog, the vague agenda.

And her husband's crime, if any? Being a bumbling loser who can't get promoted? Lousy in the sack or just a push-over, he who never slaps back? While she can date other men, whenever she suspects another lady is interested in Dangerous, she gets jealous. A pilot, an oil rig diver, a pandiculating executive... these substitutes, these stand-ins, are invariably gentle souls like Dangerous, Englishmen drifting through middle age like clergymen without a church.

Only the dog collar remains—invisible, perhaps, but it's there, a shackle to some, a life-belt to others. Their world has become a dumpster culture (they call them skips), a modulating era of the continuous discard. No wonder murder is viewed as just another form of divorce.

Of course you want Julie & Dangerous to reconcile, and as the series progresses Dangerous eventually makes his way back into her bed. There are many hiccups along the way—the cell phone interruptions, the blundered remarks, the fake rendezvous... well, they even meet in a local pub, play it as a pickup between two strangers, but within minutes they argue, split.

"Ah the games people play," sighs Mod somewhere, sometime when discussing one of DD's cases. In this sense, the biggest mystery in the series is the slow flying death of DD's marriage.

> Dangerous: (choked) So we've had three years of foreplay leading precisely nowhere.
> Julie: I just want life to sweep me off my feet.

Does it? Perhaps. Watch *Willesden Confidential.*

The series is laced with nostalgia. All the characters carry their past like a b & w photograph, and for most it was taken in the seventies. The target audience for this show is definitely those in middle age or investigating retirement. The best episodes? They're all good, although "Lofty" with its brilliant cameo of an old vagrant played by the veteran actor Norman Wisdom stands out.

His character has a clever back story that reaches into a Nazi prison camp and an apparent hit list, although his fate turns out to be far less glorious & disconnected from the strange German beauty whose secret drives the action. And Dangerous has a romance of sorts with another lost soul like himself, a slim social worker who disappears back to Trinidad to find her son and husband before we find out if indeed love has come again. Great plot, great characters, and the Willesden locations refine the vibe. Written by Richard Harris, directed by Matthew Evans.

Tricia (3) is also good, although some will say the featured character is just a British reprise of Glen Close as Alex Forrest in *Fatal Attraction* (1987); of course anyone who has worked downtown or in a university in the last 30 years will know that Tricia (Eleanor David) is an all too common type, the anti-male harridan calling herself a victim, longing for love, a romantic stalker on the edge of psychosis. Bad attitude, dumb ideology? Here the character is realistically shown transferring her obsession to the sympathetic Dangerous. Political correction 101. Written by Richard Harris, directed by Pip Broughton.

In *The Last Detective*, contemporaneity is sustained by its clear-view study of female and male confusion. You want strange? Try getting a read on the mysterious widow (Susan Vidler) in *Christine* (5), who rattles the cages of all the boys in the precinct. Nostalgia is working hard on the hearts and minds in *Three Steps To Hendon* (11), which deals with the suspicious death of Teddy O'Connor, the lead singer of the defunct pop band The Overnight Sensations.

His demise?

The usual vomit choke after a night of dissipation in a Willesden pub. This story touches on a couple of pattern-areas of male irresponsibility, i.e. the callous sexual exploitation of young girls and boys. A groupie commits suicide and her friend seeks revenge... and a young drummer is sexually violated by a creepy manager known as Mr. Wonder... "the entry fee" to the world of glamour. There's a lot of cynicism in this drama, so it will be of no consolation to the target audience.

So while *The Last Detective* is mostly a Comedy of Manners, it does have some of the same grim socio-psychological reality that made *Cracker* the greatest detective series of the nineties.

What next? A dead-ringer for Lady Diana Spencer shows up in Willesden? Death is always a murder mystery, even if the facts suggest otherwise.

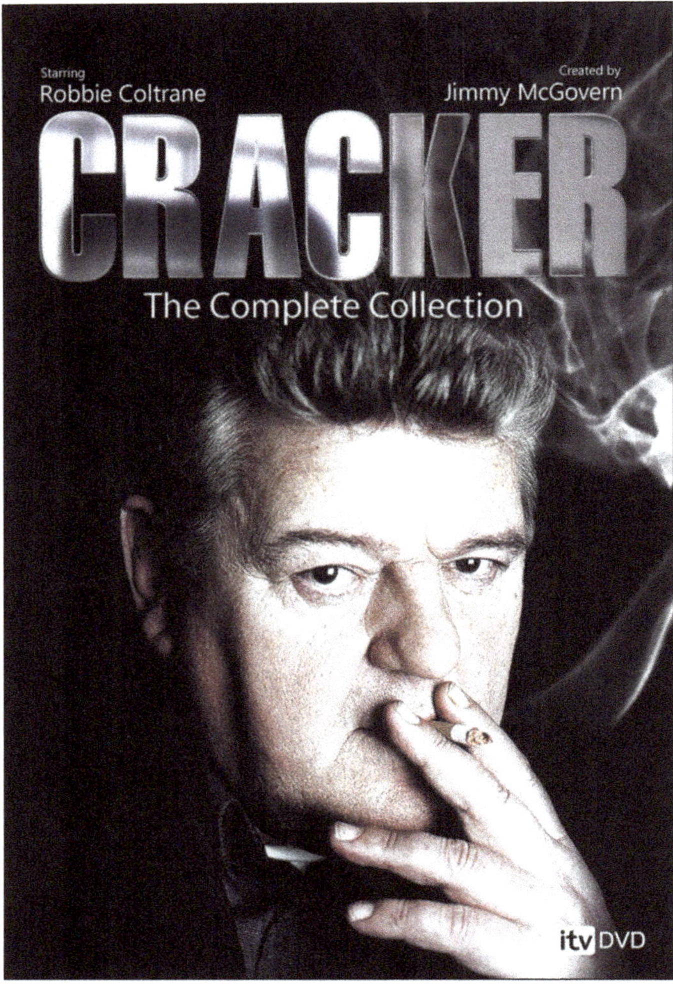

Cracker

Cracker (Granada Television in assoc with A&E Network) 1993--96 star. Robbie Coltrane (Dr. Eddie "Fitz" Fitzgerald), with Barbara Flynn (Judith Fitzgerald), Geraldine Somerville (D.S. Jane Penhaligan), Lorcan Cranitch (D.S. Jimmy Beck), Christopher Eccleston (D.C.I. David Bilborough), *et. al.*
The Mad Woman in the Attic writ. Jimmy McGovern dir. Michael Winterbottom
To Say I Love You writ. Jimmy McGovern dir. Andy Wilson
One Day A Lemming Will Fly writ. Jimmy McGovern dir. Simon Cellan Jones
To Be A Somebody writ. Jimmy McGovern dir. Tim Fywell
The Big Crunch writ. Jimmy McGovern & Ted Whitehead dir. Julian Jarrold
Men Should Weep writ. Jimmy McGovern dir. Jean Stewart
Brotherly Love writ. Jimmy McGovern dir. Roy Battersby

20th Century Schizoid Man

"Cracker" is a dangerous beast, no matter what side of the law you view him from. While he despises the Church and organized religion, he conducts his criminal investigations with the vicious intuition of a renegade priest from the Inquisition. Indeed, as one priest says to him, "I take it you're a lapsed Catholic...." Why? "Because you're so serious in your mockery."

If the forensic psychologist is the new secular confessor of our era, then "Cracker" is the epitome of the self-love and loathing our civilization is constructed to conceal. "I smoke too much, I drink too much, I gamble too much... I am too much," he admits to another priest he is investigating in relation to a sex killing. With his street savvy and bloated body, he denies being a victim of his self-abuse while berating his suspects and colleagues with an endless list of psychological illnesses: penis envy, Oedipus complex, religious psychosis, libido dysfunction, neuroses gratification, guilt transference, etc etc. While giving a university lecture, he tosses copies of Spinoza, Descartes, Hobbes, Locke, Freud, Jung, Adler and others at the students in an iconoclastic display of theatrical cool, although we never see him jettison his first primary reference, the Bible he claims to have walked away from thirty years ago. As he knows, "it's all in the head."

"Cracker" is Dr. Eddie "Fitz" Fitzgerald (Robbie Coltrane), another in a long line of Scottish thug geniuses from Deacon Brodie to Alexander Trocchi. He's middle-aged, badly overweight, an oral compulsive who supports his chain-smoking and drinking with frequent trips to the dog track, the slot-machine arcade and the casino. He embraces one-arm bandits more frequently than the suffering wife and children he claims to love. His role loyalties are split between playing the legitimate husband and professional counsellor versus the illegitimate masquerade of the gambler and working class hustler. For this fat coal-miner's son from the hard streets of outer Glasgow is also in the grips of the hidden deviant persona of the male menopause. If, as Colin Wilson continually asserts, the sex-killer is the true hero of the twentieth century, then Fitz is the perfect bourgeois embodiment of 20th Century Schizoid Man.

Fitz is a reinvention of a cliché, whether it's the eccentric detective of the Anglo-French tradition, or the outlaw P.I. of the Hollywood hard-boiled genre. He's an outsider, a savant with a flexible code and dossier of criminal fantasies. He's pleasantly familiar with the fix of instant gratification and the role this infantile reflex plays in the modus operandi of the contemporary criminal. Still, it takes more than a Ph.D in the art of needling and gifted innuendo to become a stringer for the Manchester police force. So how does he gain access to the homicide unit and move from being adjunct player to being the primary means of solving the crime? When one of his pretty female students gets murdered is how....

The Mad Woman In The Attic

It's summer in the city, 1993, and Fitz (Robbie Coltrane) is on a losing streak. He's losing at the track, he's losing in the arcade, and he's kiting cheques to pay cabbies. His wife Judith (Barbara Flynn) is approaching ground-zero in their marriage and his son is a listless voyeur to the disintegration. As he performs for his class of university students ("I rehearsed the death of my father for years"), an absentee has her throat slashed and her body mutilated by an unknown assailant in a train carriage approaching Manchester.

When the police fail to arrest a suspect, the parents enlist Fitz's aid, requesting that he be part of the autopsy and subsequent investigation. The cop in charge of the investigation —Detective Chief Inspector Bilborough—reluctantly engages his services. Some children then find an unconscious man lying in the bushes by the tracks in the general vicinity of the murder. The man has no identification and when he regains consciousness, he's suffering from amnesia.... Is it real, or is it feigned?

With this clever move, the premier script writer for the *Cracker* series Jimmy McGovern creates the number one suspect—and a clean, symbolic interface for Fitz to fabulize into existence the real killer.

One is reminded of the Borges story, *The Circular Ruins*, wherein the dreamer in the mysterious ruins dreams into existence a man only to realize that his creation is merely a part in an infinite series of dreams. The amnesiac is a contradiction: he has the coarse hands of a manual worker and the vocabulary of an intellectual. For Fitz, the man is a blank page, a scenario waiting to be written. It's not long before you realize that he is Fitz's alter-ego, a sort of spiritual garbage dump of his own tormented past and evolving present. "Prove to me I did this and I'll confess," says the man.

Fitz tries—his signature monologues are brilliant extemporizations in the art of creative psychopathology. The male predator finds the young woman alone in the carriage. She moves slightly, shows a bit of thigh, touches the crucifix around her neck... but: "She's dismissed you the way every woman has... you'll show the bitch." Fitz's monologue climaxes with the incantation "Kill the bitch/ kill the bitch/ kill the bitch" in a rhythmic fugue with the repetitive clatter of the train wheels hitting the expansion joints. The moment is cathartic—yet the suspect does not confess, does not recover his memory from the bog of silence or the mask of cunning. "It's you that needs the psychologist," says the man.

Who could this invisible man be? He doesn't know who the Prime Minister of England is or who wrote *Catch 22*. He missed the Falklands War, he missed the World Cup. He's like a UFO abductee reinserted into this world without his memories but retaining the curse of Christian guilt. When it turns out that he's an Irishman by the name of Kelly (Adrian Dunbar) and that he's a hard-time monk who just recently left the monastery in a sudden fit of curiosity, his purity stands in dramatic contrast to the atheist cynicism of the lapsed Catholic, Fitz.

The police publish the amnesiac's photo in the media under the code name "Sweeny", appealing for the public's help.

Other victims are linked to the killer. In a typical McGovern move, an anonymous caller claiming to be a "priest" tells the police he knows who "Sweeny" is and that the body of an earlier victim is lying at the bottom of the canal... and sure enough, when police divers check, they find a young woman near Clayton Wharf, dead two months.

"Better To Kill Than To Penetrate"

D.C.I. Bilborough—never a fan of the arrogant buffoon Dr. Fitzgerald—dismisses him from the case and he's forced to appeal to Detective Sergeant Penhaligan (Geraldine Somerville), a young redhead whose slim figure and cultivated silence makes her an odd match for the obese motor-mouthing Fitz and unlikely successor to his alienated wife. Penhaligan is often the third person in the room during the "interviews", a silent witness who becomes the ghost of the dead girls as Fitz goes about his psychic reconstructions.

A farm woman claims she recognizes Kelly as her husband... but her claim turns out to be false, this being another example of the well-known fascination of women for violent criminals, masochists finding their natural sadists to complete their identities. Frustrated by this blind lead, Fitz takes a swig of scotch, fantasizes about a soap opera with a cast of murderers, "fifteen million viewers, all women, no problem". It's this sort of raw commentary devoid of social engineering propaganda that makes *Cracker* a drama of character rather than facile spectacle and vicarious gratification.

Yes, Fitz solves the crime—but loses his wife. *The Mad Woman in the Attic* (a metaphor that Fitz tosses at Kelly when challenging his amnesia and his "crime": "You lock it away like the mad woman in the attic") is the first episode in the series and perhaps the best because it so powerfully introduces the protagonist and his milieu, so skilfully establishes the boundaries of the psychodrama. And—what is more Freudian than sex and death on a speeding train?

Excellent direction by Michael Winterbottom, great cine by Ivan Strasburg, and (as they say) "seamless" editing by Trevor White.

To Say I Love You

The second episode reveals script writer McGovern's obsessions and influences more clearly, while extending Cracker's study of the dark side of human nature and the contemporary expression of social and spiritual alienation. *To Say I Love You* is an accelerated version of Sid and Nancy wherein a couple of young losers express their disillusionment by murdering their enemies instead of murdering themselves with heroin. Tina (Susan Lynch) the murdering vixen has a poster of the spree-kill classic *Badlands* on the wall of her flat. While the Fugate-Starkweather m.o. has been an inspiration for a number of wannabes, you wonder if Fitz's appreciation of American movies is really Jimmy McGovern's.

Yet who can deny the generational imprinting of popular culture in today's secular society? You first see Sean (Andrew Tiernan) at a karioke pub fervently singing the sappy ballad *To Say I Love You*—but when he is joined by Tina afterwards, you realize that he is the victim of some inner trauma that renders him dumb—at best a stuttering freak—unless inspired to sing.

In film noir the female manipulates her male patsy into committing her murders on the promise of sex and big money. This is how it goes in *Double Indemnity* and in *Body Heat*—just to name a couple. The squalid, government-welfare-driven world of Tina and Sean is no different, although the relationship is bonded in love, no matter how twisted. Tina's resentment is towards her bourgeois parents and their enshrinement of her blind, beautiful sister. That Sean is a surrogate for her sister is as obvious as their respective afflictions—but one she can manipulate in her quest to humiliate her parents for their big mistake in loving Sammy more than her.

They steal a car, they steal a bus, they murder a loan-shark. The murder of the loan-shark is a raw sex/death sandwich, where Tina lures the man into a back alley for sex and Sean materializes from the shadows to smash his head in with a brick. Sean then takes the man's place for a frenzied act of intercourse against the wall (a "knee-trembler") as the body of their victim bears silent witness. All in all, this scene is a thing of beauty when viewed in terms of psychopathological behaviour—one which forensic Fitz immediately and clairvoyantly describes during his subsequent interview with Tina.

Yet despite his battering interviews, Fitz elicits no confession and the police are forced to let her go. It's now that

Evil becomes the true mother of invention: on the promise of a friendly romantic evening, Tina lures D.C. Cormack to her grotty flat which has been converted into a murder chamber by cladding the walls and floor with black plastic. Together Tina and Sean dump the naive cop's body down an embankment... but instead of dropping into the canal, it's found the next morning on the tow-path wrapped tightly in a white shroud....

This is the episode in which the separation between Fitz and his wife Judith is clearly established. Fitz arrives at a restaurant with Jane Penhaligan to find Judith dining with her new lover, another psychotherapist. Judith views Fitz's appearance as a crude attempt to make her jealous while he swears it's a coincidence. After a bitter exchange between husband and wife which Penhaligan is forced to endure like a mistress in a Strindberg play, she gets up and dumps a jug of iced water over the big control freak's head. Fitz takes it well, considering his ubiquitous cigarette is extinguished.

You wonder what the attraction is between Penhaligan and Fitzgerald, considering that he plays on her insecurities with a certain unprofessional candor. But he does have that confidence that goes with genius. Oedipus and Lord Byron might have Achilles tendon problems, but Fitz has his large Ubu body, a romantic affliction as dramatic as any. If Fatty Arbuckle could dazzle the ladies, why not Eddie "Fitz" Fitzgerald?

Again, Fitz solves the crime, he's there at the big moment. Sean has made his Hollywood move, taken the beautiful blind sister hostage and is intending to burn her alive. Fitz arrives, goes alone into the house, makes his pitch....

It's a good episode, even if you pause when Tina tries to set up Fitz for the kill by asking him back to her place to read her thesis. What would a 20 year old drop-out know about post-graduate theses on any subject? It's a funny scene, though... and the rapid editing helps secure our belief when disbelief turns to laughter.

The Big Crunch

The camera is tracking through the bushes of a light forest like an animal closing in on its kill. You hear the small cries of a woman in apparent distress. A well-dressed man, his trousers down around his ankles, is having sex with a young girl whom he has perched on the crooked bough of a convenient tree. The POV is that of a middle-aged woman who has a concealed camera in her handbag. You see her eyes glisten with the ambiguous intensity of indignation and lust as she begins photographing the rapturous event....

Is this a good hook scene or what?

"All Flesh Is Grass"

The villain in this piece comes complete with his own school and his own church—the ultimate establishment disguise. Well, almost. His church is a little less than orthodox, even if its members look like the usual assembly of suspects. A large man, going a little round at the shoulders, his black hair and piercing eyes mark him in the mould of Rasputin, although he is really another English fraud in the tradition of the occultist Aleister Crowley. Meet Kenneth Trant (Jim Carter), by day a successful school principal, by night (and on the weekends) the leader of a cult which is like a parody of Christian Science or Scientology. God has been replaced by the Big Bang (hence the title, *The Big Crunch*) and the usual mumbo of occult symbols and candle mysticism.

Each *Cracker* episode is a *de facto* attack on organized religion. Whenever Fitz faces off with a priest, he becomes the secular successor confronting his past. Trant is the perfect whipping post for this assault, because his fundamentalism is really just a psychosexual pathology in disguise— something we suspect is the archetype of all religion. His recruits are nearly all damaged goods, peer paranoids and daddy girls. Joann(a) (Samantha Morton) is his favorite of the moment, but when he is confronted by a friend of his wife's with the photographs of his infidelity, he evokes the Devil. Joann is unwilling to fade into the back pews—she's pregnant, believes "Kenneth" will divorce his wife, marry her. The inner cabal decide to dispatch this silly little schoolgirl in a ritual murder....

Things go wrong, of course. When Dean Saunders (Darren Tighe), the young mental defective who is assigned the task of feeding Joann into the industrial shredder at the packing plant where he works (at the discretion of a church elder), has second thoughts (because, well, he fancies her) and opens the box before it hits the blades, Joann escapes and the Trant empire unravels. It's an interesting scene: Joann—traumatized, her naked body decorated with the cult's cryptolog—staggers off into the night like a zombie, wandering through the traffic until she finds a bank of TVs in a mall. "All flesh is grass," mutters Dean.

This episode allows Fitz one of his finest monologues in a Western-type showdown between him and Trant during a service. "Your religion is a sham," snarls Fitz as the photos of Trant impaled in Joann are circulated to the stunned congregation. "A theatre for your dreams of power... a hopeless shag in a godless universe!"

Clearly, Trant is no match for a boogie blues shouter like Fitz, and "The Fellowship of Souls" is another New Age cult whose leader is doomed by his dick.

This one was written by Jimmy McGovern and Ted Whitehead.

Detective Sergeant Jimmy Beck

There are always two storylines in *Cracker*: the crime of the moment, and Fitz's struggle with his personal and family life. Sometime during the third episode—*One Day A Lemming Will Fly* —a third storyline starts, and is partly responsible for its diversionary, elliptic ending.

A mob of enraged parents is hungering to kill a suspected homosexual school teacher who is under suspicion for the murder of a student he admits to corrupting, so he's given into the custody of Dr. Fitzgerald. Fitz, the teacher and D.S. Beck hole up in a hotel room, which becomes a Pinteresque Theatre of Innuendo as Fitz and Beck attack one another. Ego and homophobia become the crime and the punishment.

"This is posh," says Jimmy (Lorcan Cranitch) looking around the room, waving the TV remote. "Shall I tell you why I can't stand lesbians?" Fitz rolls his eyes, the Teacher suspect remains stoic. "Queers are o.k—s'long as I don't turn me back on you, that's o.k. Two queers doin' it, that's two women goin' spare... but two women doin' it, that's two men goin' short."

When Fitz suggests that a moustache is a homosexual affectation, Jimmy shaves his off the next day. But he also takes credit for the Teacher's confession (which turns out to be false) and even when Fitz tells their boss the confession is false, the man is charged with murder anyway... the implication being that because they think the Teacher is queer, he deserves to be charged regardless. Ergo, guilt is a question of agenda.

So sexual neurosis is alive and well within the police force.

Genital Man Will Sacrifice Rectal Man

It's no surprise that the homicide investigation cadre resent the insertion of Fitz into their unit and have general contempt for his psycho-mystical approach. The most vocal in his contempt is Jimmy Beck, a Belfast migrant who has assumed the cop persona so incompletely it never occurs to him that rape is a crime and violence prohibited. To him, Mike Tyson was railed-roaded, another patsy for the system. During interrogations, he zealously plays "bad cop"—something you ascribe to simple role-playing—and appears to be an unquestioned loyalist to the code. When D.C.I. Bilborough is murdered by the skinhead Albie Kinsella in *To Be A Somebody*, Jimmy becomes guilt-ridden and dedicates his down-time to looking out for Bilborough's widow and daughter. His distress affects his judgement.

It's Jimmy Beck's inability to recognize Albie (Robert Caryle) as the killer that greases the skids for his own decline and fall. As the marginalized white male who finds himself socially and culturally redundant in the new secular morality, Albie's hatred and cunning is too much for the conventional cop-thought of Jimmy. Albie has a system, a mathematical paradigm based on the 96 victims of the infamous Hillsborough soccer riot in 1989, and his mystical identification with the persona of his old man, the recently deceased war vet, Albert Kinsella. Father and son—the name is the same, but the generation is different. "We're not queers, we're not not black," Albie later tells Fitz. "We're gettin' treated like animals... and some of us are gonna start actin' like animals when the cages go up."

The Pakistani shop-keeper, the psychology Prof with his social engineering cliches... Jimmy Beck should've been the third victim, not his boss and pal, D.C.I. Bilborough.

When Beck eventually catches up to Albie in an alley and beats him unconscious, he suffers the New Age indignity—he's sent for "sensitivity" training by Bilborough's replacement, D.C.I. Wise (Ricky Tomlinson). If he didn't know it before, he knows it now: he's in the same "cage" as Albie.

To Be A Somebody is a brilliant social commentary, one which ends on a disturbing apocalyptic prophecy: "You're lookin' at me," says the shaven-headed Albie, "and you're lookin' at the future."

In *Men Should Weep* the wife of a taxi-dispatcher is raped, a humiliation directed at her husband. You know who the rapist is: a young black called Floyd Malcolm (Graham Aggrey), a part-time cabbie with a huge grudge against white society, women, and life itself. Like many of the criminals Fitz and Jimmy Beck hunt, Floyd's mental wound has a concealed, physical symbolism—his body is scarred from childhood when he immersed himself in a bath of bleach in order to become like his white mother. This macabre baptism becomes part of his m.o. After he rapes the dispatcher's wife, he immerses her in the bleach blue night of a public swimming pool, which—symbolism aside—is an expedient means of destroying evidence.

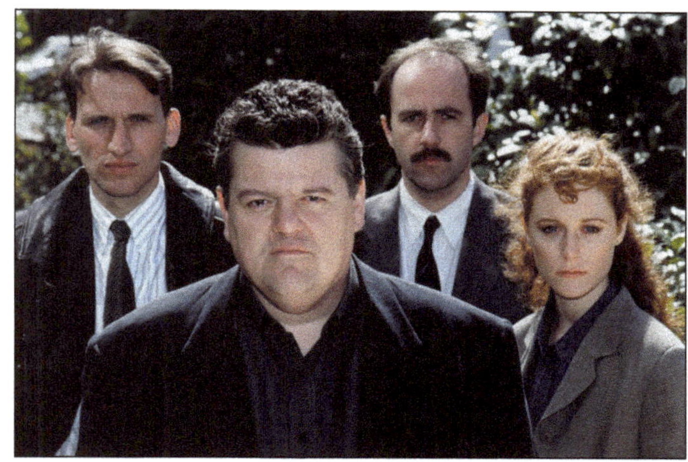

Jimmy immediately accuses the caretaker of the pool, an old loser with a criminal record of petty crime. Even when Fitz pushes the caretaker into the pool and Jimmy is forced to jump in and save him, Jimmy still believes the caretaker is the guilty man. When the dispatcher pays the caretaker a visit and almost beats him to death in the elevator, Jimmy is sent to arrest the demented husband. Jimmy says to him, "If it was up to me, I'd give you a medal."

Floyd is also an early suspect, and is interviewed by Fitz. What you know and Fitz doesn't is that Floyd has phoned Fitz on his open-line radio show, claiming to be the rapist. Masking his voice in a Jamaican accent, Floyd asks what should he do—should he kill his next victim?

Fitz and his police colleague (and "mistress") Jane Penhaligan join the other members of the squad in a local pub. The subject of the rape crimes quickly passes into a discussion of the sex war and rape as a natural condition of existence. Jimmy says, "Subconsciously (women) want it." Later "Panhandle" tells Fitz that Jimmy asked her, "Do you fantasize about rape?"

The irrational zones of human motivation with their contradictory semaphores of sex and death are Fitz's forté. Yet, when D.S. Penhaligan becomes the next rape victim, neither she nor you suspect the work of a second rapist... although the canny Fitz is quick to deduce it. While the exposure and arrest of Floyd Malcolm continues to drive the action, this becomes secondary to Jane Penhaligan's trauma. When she accuses Jimmy with her rape (on the basis of smell), no one is willing to take her seriously, and even Fitz is inclined to be skeptical.

"Just As Every Cop Is A Criminal/ And Every Sinner Is A Saint"

It's this disintegration of the unit integrity that forces us to consider the absolutely brutal way that sex makes civilization a mere mask for animal instinct and animal action. As Jimmy's depression deepens, you wonder if it's the office politics he can't stand or the misery of Bilborough's death.

Because of the D.S. Jimmy Beck storyline, you have to view *Men Should Weep* in tandem with the next story, *Brotherly Love*. Here prostitutes end up murdered by an avenging Irish housewife—a plot that has similarities to the *The Lady Killer* by the Japanese novelist Masako Togawa (perhaps taken indirectly via *Presumed Innocent*, itself indebted to Togawa). In order to spare her husband from a charge of murder, the good Catholic wife kills another prostitute, then inserts her husband's sperm with a

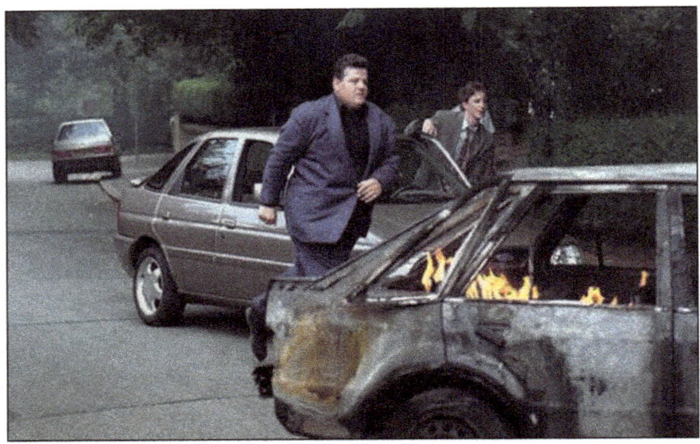

chisel into the prostitute's vagina while he is being held by the police....

This "impossibility" means nothing to D.S. Jimmy Beck, who insists that the husband did it. By now Beck is a mess. He is shocked to find that his dead friend and colleague's wife, Catriona Bilborough, has shacked up with another man. He suffers panic attacks, hyperventilates. Fitz head-butts him in the face, frustrated that he won't confess to raping Jane Penhaligan... when he eventually does confess, he makes Fitz swear an oath of secrecy. "Women need rage," Jimmy tells Fitz. "It's their weapon."

McGovern wrote this script—again the scenes and dialogue are swift and brutal, the action following the maxim, drama is the juxtaposition of the expected against the unexpected. Jimmy snaps, abducts the husband—a pathetic creature addicted to sex with prostitutes who will dress up as little girls (a "Shirley Temple")—and heads for the roof of Manchester's Ramada Inn. You could say this is a classic Hollywood move, as countless crime features see their criminals head for the roof... but in this context, in this locale, the cliché is unexpected. Before he jumps with his hostage, he shouts to Penhaligan: "I raped you."

On the bleak, uncompromising image of both men falling down the face of the hotel to their deaths on the street thirteen floors below, this episode ends.

When we fall in our dreams and awake hyperventilating, are we rehearsing our deaths or escaping the infantile self? The vigilantism is upstaged by its own theatricality, and spectacle becomes the only meaning in an existential universe. When Beck takes "Shirley Temple" with him on their plunge into Hell, they become the complete Freudian package.

Beck's act of murder-suicide is clear proof of the lunatic within us, the illegitimate masquerading as the legitimate. A female Catholic killer is completed by a male Catholic killer—could McGovern's displeasure with religion be any clearer? This act of contrition is also an act of megalomania. Perhaps the writer can ironically disguise his world view in his protagonist. Jimmy Beck isn't the complete story, and neither is Jane Penhaligan. You have to watch big Fitz.

Resistance, Rebellion, And Death

If murder, rape and mutilation can't stop Dr. Eddie "Fitz" Fitzgerald, then what can? The death of his bingo gambling mother maybe. Just as the birth of Bilborough's son opens the door for his death, we expect the birth of Fitz's child to open yet another door in this temple of life and death. Sure enough, his brother appears with the news that their mother is dead, struck down that morning by a heart attack. Fitz is mortified. He has been negligent of late, preoccupied with his own middle-age binge. His brother doesn't help minimize the guilt—together they bury their mother, bickering and fighting all the way as they resurrect the imperfect past and nearly bury the perfect future. They get drunk at the wake, and later reconcile when they get into a fight with some sober people on a tram.

This occurs in *Brotherly Love* as a cutaway to the Madonna-whore action of "Shirley Temple" and the disintegration of D.S. Jimmy Beck. Poor old Fitz—he takes down the newspaper clippings of his successes his mother has pined on the wall, a simple shrine for an absent son. When he speaks at the service, his recollections are personal, the history that shaped the man in the spirit of his mother. Ah, we all want to weep with him.... This death also marks the true moment of resurrection in his marriage. Judith encounters Jane Penhaligan, who congratulates her on the birth of her child. Judith asks Penhaligan if she is finished with Fitz:

> Penhaligan: I was only ever interested in his body.
> Judith: (stung) There's a certain poetic justice to it... your rape, I mean.

So—just when you were getting sentimental about it all—you realize there are no madonnas in *Cracker*.

Non-Adaptive Cultural Imperialism

A great deal of *Cracker*'s success as a series has to be ascribed to its editing method. Instead of using the typical television compression format of the dominant "master" scene with cutaways to a sub-dominant "slave" scene, both actions are flattened into an alternating montage that moves the action with remarkable speed. It creates a shared psychology between cop and criminal, an essential feature of the overall *Cracker* persona.

Instead of the long, real-time sequencing with its live theatre feel typical of British television drama, you get a large screen action feature drive expressed in the the smaller 4:3 screen format. As this is "public television", it's also freed from the lock-step Act structure with commercials interrupting the narrative. The large screen drama with its origins in "silent cinema" always defers to photography, landscape and action; television drama with its origins in "live theatre" always defers to dialogue, close-up and stasis. The *Cracker* series is a hybrid, an inevitable narrative evolution at this point in history.

With *Cracker*'s moldering documentary landscape and brilliant crypto-fascist characterizations, the question has to be asked: Has the television serial drama replaced the large screen film feature as the serious dramatic venue of our times? As Hollywood continues to pander to adolescents with its retinal strobing and fantasy imprinting, the lack of substance in its stories is obvious from the empty spaces between the propaganda and the thrill-kills. With its endless conscious and unconscious remakes, the corporate Hollywood tunnel-vision has compromised cinema narrative as you know it. It has become non-adaptive, a grandiose cultural imperialism. If violence exists without psychology, then the universe exists without Man.

Today culture is popular culture—movies, rock music, television, sex and death—the only subject of discussion and emulation among the rank and file. Spontaneous, reactive, fantasy and event merge in tabloid politics. Between the weather and the sports roundup, crime is the heart and soul of the daily news.

Coda

What is crime? The imposition of a personal fantasy in opposition to the group fantasy? The infantile reflex of quick gratification asserts itself in the Schizoid Man, a creature driven by invisible particles dedicated to his survival and sexual pleasure regardless of the status quo.

The tired commandments of the Church fade into mere mysticism when measured against the new secular intensity of the scientific humanist who absolves us from Guilt by making new existential victims in the pew. Fitz says: "You lock it away like the mad woman in the attic."

If one animal kills another in a fixed—yet natural—cycle of predator and prey, then what is human sexual hunger but a homicide anticipated by Nature? As Fitz says to a suspect about sex: "Better to be the first... and the last."

To hell with the Pope, feminism and the right to clean air —Fitz is a classic protestant rebel in a classic catholic body. Robbie Coltrane is so completely within his character, it's difficult to believe that he's fiction, another theatrical conceit. In a post-series interview, Coltrane says, "The original description of Fitz was a small wiry man who looked as if he'd spent a lot of time in the army. So, naturally they found me." (Fitz is apparently characterized after Prof. Ian Stephen, an expert in the psychological profiling of criminals) This was a good move by the producers, as a large man automatically becomes symbolism, especially when measured within the shallow depth-of-field of television photography.

Fitz alone in a tram... in a taxi, moving through the urban nightmare, considering the options, the odds, the shifting shadows of Fate. A line of divers moves slowly through the fouled waters of a canal... his wife sits with a therapist pretending to be a lover... his race dog fails on the home stretch... a masked man drags his victim into a darkened swimming pool... a man crouches in a cage as a woman circles with a whip... he shoulders his mother's casket towards the grave... two men fall from the roof of a high-rise. The death clock of the millennium?

We Share His Melancholy, Crave His Defiance

It's not a happy world. Society is coming apart at the seams. Cop and criminal share Original Sin... or is it Original Freud? Kelly (*The Mad Woman In The Attic*) left the monastery because he had doubts about his vocation, wanted to see the world. "Now that I've seen it, you can keep it."

What is Guilt?

Penhaligan: "I've got evidence beneath my fingernails."

A good thing to remember... little men of the world. The Big Man remains undeterred.

* Series concludes with these non-McGovern scripts:
Best Boys writ. Paul Abbot dir. Charles McDougal
True Romance writ. Paul Abbot dir. Tim Fywell
White Ghost (movie special, 96) writ. Paul Abbot dir. Richard Standeven

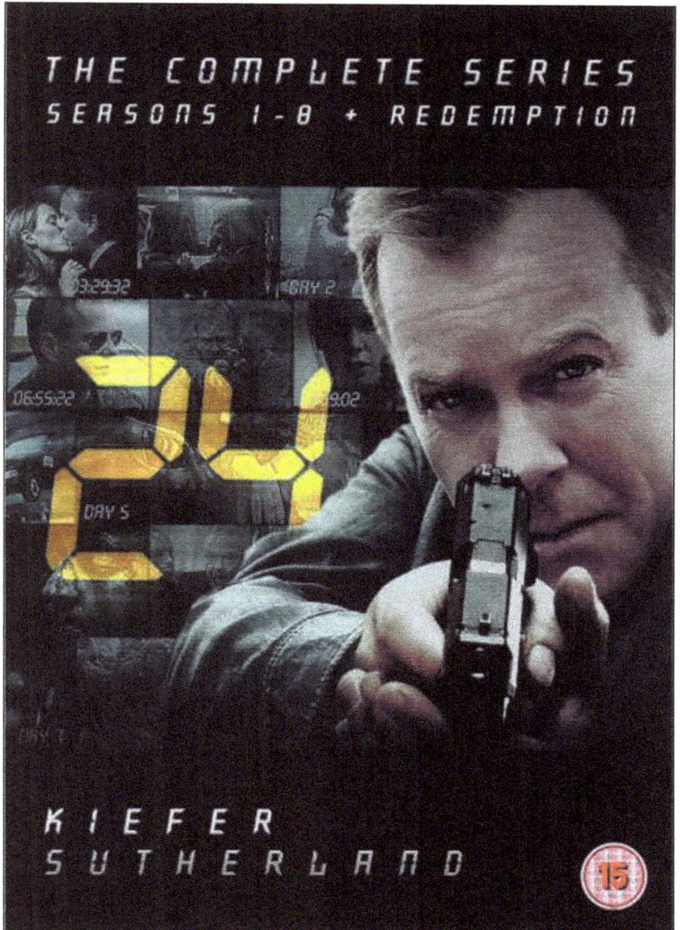

24: Parallel Stories Must Converge

24: created & produced by Joel Surnow & Robert Cochrane written by Surnow, Cochrane, Loceff, Gordon, Aubuchon, Grant, Cosin, Williams, Ehrman, Katz, Hurley, Johannessen, Newman, Hertzog, Cohen, Chernuchin, Kronish, Demetrius directed by Hopkins, Kolbe, Spicer, Guggenheim, Cassar, Keller, Shapiro, Cassar, Whitmore, Charters, Toynton, Turner, Hooks
star: Kiefer Sutherland, Elisha Cuthbert, Dennis Haysbert, Sarah Clarke, Leslie Hope, Penny Johnson Jerald, Carlos Bernard, Xander Berkeley, Kate Warner, Dennis Hopper, Lou Diamond Philips, Reiko Aylesworth, et. al.
www.fox.com/24

It's no coincidence that Jack Bauer's initials are the same as those of James Bond. Historically speaking, Bond was a projected fantasy of the near future, whereas Bauer is the blunt realization of the sordid present. The Bond dramas were dreams, products of the sleeping mind; the Bauer dramas are insomnia, the paranoid clippings of surveillance cameras. If Bond was Demerol for the Cold War and nuclear anxiety, then Bauer is an amphetamine fix for the Age of Terrorism.

Bond was a form of social control, a way of disguising reality as absurdism, a purge for the mind, a forgetting. Bauer is absolutely the reverse, a cardiac resuscitation, a preparation for the apocalypse. The psychic structure of *24* is concomitant to 911, a game model that interacts with the hyper voltaic transfer of information by TV, cell phone, computer and the occult senses twenty-four hours a day. Circadian rhythm is no longer a bio vibration of the planets and Nature, but rather a binary pulse as people are hard-wired into the electro-psycho megalopolis of the 21st century. Synaptic overload? Hallucinations? Better believe it. Welcome to the world of pro-active nihilism and moral relativism.

24: Season 1
Parallel Stories Must Converge

Midnight, Pacific Standard Time. Word comes from an operative in south Asia that an assassination attempt on Sen. David Palmer, the first black candidate for the Presidency of the United States and odds on favorite to win the California primary, will happen within the next 24 hours. CTU (Counter Terrorism Unit) in Los Angeles is alerted, and the section chief, Agent Jack Bauer [Kiefer Sutherland] is called in to deal with the crisis. Perfect casting here: he's not pretty, he's not ugly, he's on the edgy side of generic... as if the sculptor left him slightly unfinished. He drives a domestic guzzler SUV and packs a couple of automatics... and cell phone which is connected to both heaven and hell. He's masculine, with a feminine declension: no son, just a wife and teenage daughter.

Very quickly you learn that Bauer's unit is compromised, that someone on the inside is working with the terrorists. Who can he trust? He shoots his immediate superior George Mason [Xander Berkeley] with a dart gun, because Mason denies him information, and when Mason revives, blackmails him, gets the information. Is this the guy to get the job done? Better believe it. Yet other actions are moving to thwart his determined modus operandi. Split screen, triple screen, quad screen, matte-box boogie, the P.I.P's insert the parallel actions in real time. A jumbo jet is blown out of the sky over the Mojave as it approaches LAX, the female terrorist using the bomb blast to bail the carnage, rendezvous with a rogue operative who has a media lab in a shack somewhere in the desert. Two metal punks kidnap his daughter Kimberly, and his wife Terri is snatched by a terrorist masquerading as a concerned parent.

Meanwhile Senator Palmer [Dennis Haysbert], the intended assassination victim, gets no sleep either because a female journalist is threatening to expose his son as a murderer. As he tries to figure out what to do, his retainers and wife plot and scheme with such smug deviousness the approaching assassin(s) might be the lesser of his problems. Bauer in parallel motion just shoots and hacks his way through the issues and problems as they happen. His lieutenants plot and scheme too, spy on one another through computer screens, surveillance monitors... channels between furniture, windows, fellow workers, bodies. The watchers are watching the watchers.

The paranoid gestalt of the CTU work deck is like the gloomy stone vault of a Renaissance court... yuppy workers troll corridors of light and shadow between flickering desk monitors and large suspended LCDs, hunting evil in the collective electronic mind, their own actions and motives often indistinguishable from those of the enemy. Sometimes the action is a montage of eyes, faces, silhouettes... you read expressions, ignore dialogue. Techno-gothic, crypto-fascist. Go-betweens shuttle back and forth between work-stations, offices, hotel rooms, malls, parking lots, wrecking yards, bunkers... yet, virtual or real, this is no courtly love convention. Like an executive secretary in love with her boss, Nina, Bauer's No.1, works the subterfuge of good and evil with psychic efficiency. Tony, No. 2, watches every move with the jealous obsession of a teenage hood in love with teacher. Yet the true chain of command always remains in doubt—orders are routinely disobeyed or reinterpreted, agents killed, bosses reassigned.

The same is true in Senator Palmer's court. His wife Sherry [Penny Johnson Jerald] is as snake-bitten as Lady MacBeth, ruthless as Delila, indispensable as Cortez's mistress Marina... or Ms. Hilary Clinton. Intrigue replaces sex, power replaces orgasm. She gets tossed like the Comtesse du Barry, but returns for the Revolution. The truth within her character makes you squirm, forces you right of centre, then hard left of the abyss.

Bauer? Well, he has two balls, because as often as not, he's shooting with two automatics, German SIG-Sauers [occasionally S & W's, Glocks, assorted] tuned to his body and mind like cardiac implants. He's a familiar American ideal, an unblinking patriot who functions as an official outlaw, now incarnated as a cyber-punk for the new millennium. Perceived by his rivals as an unstable vigilante, and by those who love him as an indispensable fixer, he cuts through the bullshit and political disease like a radiation pellet. Licensed to kill (apparently), revenge is just a recursive metaphor for equalization.

Can you love him? Some say love is just an exchange of bodily fluids, and you suspect that Bauer is a man who has never been truly loved, quite possibly because of the schizoid nature of his profession... or perhaps he has his profession precisely because he is schizoid. His home life is dysfunctional (naturally) because love in the free market is a zero-sum game. Ironically, even though he keeps his wife and daughter close via cell phone, they, like everyone else in this drama, are always moving further apart.

Convergence and reconciliation are a false optic. Isolation & solipsism haunts every character. Terri Bauer [Leslie Hope] tries to re-engage, fails. Kim Bauer keeps trying to get back home, but when she does, there is no home. Sherry Palmer is expelled by her husband. Etc. The freneticism of the narrative is more than an action style prescribed by the producers to keep their itchy audience away from its remote control. The edit speed becomes a flag for a deeper seismology as it suggests a society disengaging from its social and moral axis. Behaviour is cyber-reactive rather than reasoned, although there's a lot of mathematical reasoning going on as the clock ticks. Dispute resolution is a 9 mm bullet.

Nina Meyers [Sarah Clarke]: a modo Lucrezia Borgia... or more likely a Gundrun Ensslin, (Baader-Mienhof gang a.k.a the RAF) who hung herself in a German prison, 1977. While Sherry Palmer is old school, Nina represents the death of the nuturing female, becomes a *de facto* feminist harridan of the post-gender world. There's no rhetoric, no ideology, only the transgender role. Sexual identity is merely a facade, a costume, like a nice paint-job on a Lexus. In fact, the only sex you see in *24* is Black Widow, a prelude to execution or political humiliation. Trap and kill, or trap and extort.

Operation Nightingale. Alexis, Andre & Victor Drazen emerge from the recent nightmare of the Balkans with unlimited monies (it seems) and a mythological desire for revenge. Typically, any war America becomes involved in is never finished, despite the score. Seems Jack was sent to Bosnia on a clandestine search and destroy mission by a Senate subcommittee chaired by Palmer... hence parallel lines converge.

Is this a good plot-line? Despite the unwieldy absurdity of it all, and that the "game" seems more important than the desired result, the revelations are cleverly advanced. Scripting by committee has its advantages, especially when blocking a 24 frame narrative. Cochrane and Surnow, the creators and producers of *24*, wrote scripts for the seminal *Miami Vice* series in the eighties, and certain characteristics follow through. Stylized violence is one, nihilism is another. *Vice* was the first television drama to embrace nihilism via the death-wish of its villains. Death is always the preferred exit of the existential criminal, and includes the mysterious psychology of "suicide by cop".

Quite often the art style of *24* looks as if it has been storyboarded for gamers. The industrial warehouse sequences during the abduction of Kim Bauer [Elisha Cuthbert] and her friend could be from *Hitman* or *Grand Theft Auto*. In the DOD secret prison—an underground bunker somewhere outside of L.A.—the action becomes a direct facsimile of a video game. Concrete tunnels, bare interrogation rooms, AV rooms, cells, blind corners and stairs descending into darkness... a chiaroscuro maze, shadow lit, CCTV wired, a dungeon for robots and insane marauding killers. The set becomes techno-medieval as the characters assume the grim body armour costumes and spastic homicidal combat pursuits familiar to those who play such virtuals.

It's here that Victor Drazen [Dennis Hopper], the crazy Balkan Don of an ethnic cleansing family, is delivered, and it's here that his son Andre Drazan mounts a break-out assault. Kevlar vests are de rigueur.

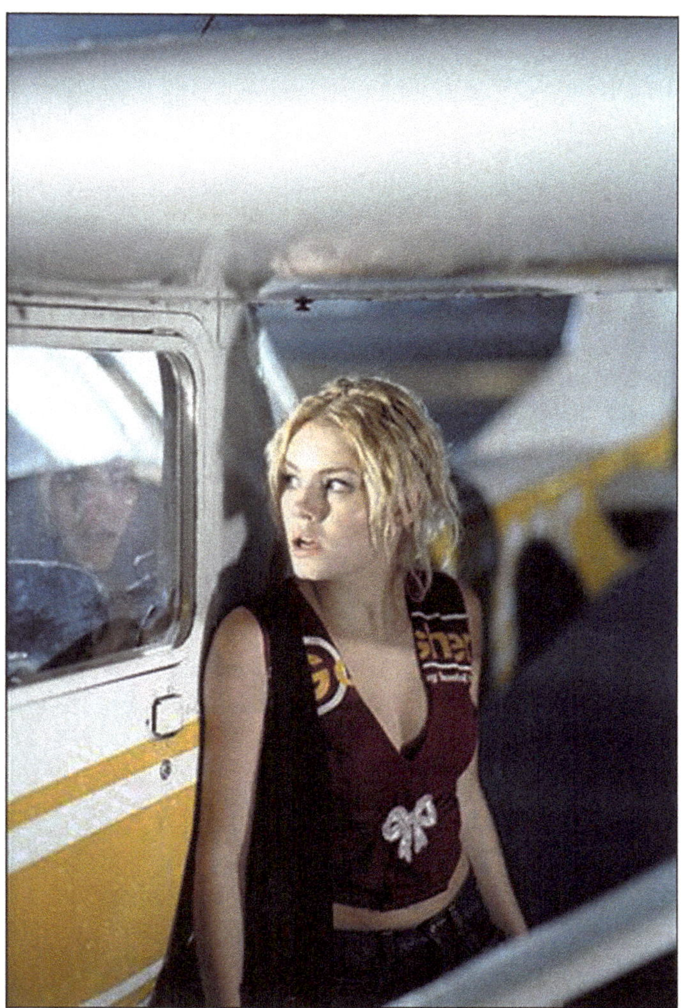

24: Season 2
Technique Of The *Coup D'etat*

Report comes that middle eastern terrorists have smuggled a nuke into Los Angeles, plan to detonate it sometime within a day. David Palmer, we quickly learn, is now President, and he believes Jack Bauer is the person who can find the bomb, even though Bauer has left active service with CTU, traumatized by the execution death of his wife Terri at the hand of Nina Meyers. Contacted by CTU and later by the President, Bauer declines involvement... but *en route* to his SUV has a change of heart when he sees an anonymous mother and child walking past. Once again the usual cast of sociopaths and technopaths drive the weaponized action in a series of brutal vignettes and Bauer responds with his characteristic whatever-it-takes-to-get-the-job-done intensity.

He starts by shooting a smug petty criminal and hacking his head off, then delivering the macabre artifact to a group of mechanics who have been contracted to make the nuke detonator in their grotty garage. Why? The victim had turned State's evidence, was going to testify against the leader of the group re another matter. Thus Bauer infiltrates the cell, and, although he is unable to stop them bombing the CTU building along the way, within the hour has shot them all... and moved closer to discovering the location of the nuke.

So it goes. As in Season I, the action rocks with unexpected gun battles and creative violence, including sabotage, torture and even domestic battery. In an unrelated story-line, Jack's daughter Kim runs afoul a psycho father during her Nanny job, ends up on the run trying escape her employer, the police and the nuke. President Palmer, suspicious of his crustacean Secretary of State, tortures him with electro-shock pads. A rogue para-military unit known as Coral Snake shoots down the helicopter carrying Bauer and Nina Meyers, somehow seems to be in control of the nuke.

What's going on? Muslim fundamentalists are involved to be sure, but as is typical of *24*, there are other faces below the paint. Could it be the good old American bogey, the military-industrial complex? Whether it's the producers exercising conscious or unconscious political correctness, or an opportunistic mirroring of the Bush-Cheney administration's Iraq fiasco... or simply relying on stock ideas provided by *Seven Days In May* or *The Manchurian Candidate* is difficult to say. Such measures, such actions, repeat within history. While this part of the plot is executed well, it views as propagandistic rather than aesthetic direction, even though some will argue that it reflects the increasing ambiguity of American political culture. In his famous treatise *Technique of the Coup d'Etat*, the Italian writer Curzio Malaparte says "a parliament that undertakes to legitimize a *coup d'Etat* is merely signing its own death warrant." For Jack Bauer, the verb is "attempts". Once again, as in Season One, many people plot, many people die.

The casting of Dennis Haysbert as Senator—later President—David Palmer was a great directive, not only because he owns the part completely, but because he looks big. In a world of sixes, he's a seven or an eight, literally "a giant of a man". Again, he is another isolated character, the condition reinforced by his color, height, and incorruptible spirit. What binds him to agent Jack Bauer is integrity, a quality which requires aloneness. A great leader may walk within a cadre, yet withal he walks alone, and the excoriating loneliness in this instance is scored by Palmer's separation from his wife Sherry, who has been reduced to the status of a ghetto hustler with a concealed grudge.

Penny Johnson's performance as Sherry is superb, and it must be noted that the scripting of her complex character must also be above average for a medium well-known for silhouettes. The tenacity of her ambition makes you cringe with its naked political opportunism and amoral real politic. Family, friends, country... all can used to serve the God of Power. If Jack Bauer is David Palmer's right hand, then Sherry is his left. As the left hand of darkness, her implication in the nuke and the *coup* against her husband certainly brings a new dimension to female penis envy... and when viewed in tandem with the killer-doll treachery of Nina Meyers, you wonder if the misogyny is Hollywood-traditional or American New Age.

Sherry is certainly a more traditional female character than Nina, as she follows the film noir tradition of the woman using a male patsy... and the history of drama is filled with such devious, manipulative women. Nina is something else... criminally fantastic, yet entirely possible in this day and age. Women as front-line killers has become a matter of human rights, not necessarily a societal ideal. A literary view of her execution killing of Terri Bauer would see the historical shift as feminine into masculine. Effective? Absolutely. This ugly, sordid act both demoralizes and actualizes the sleeping citizen voyeur. Not long ago such a scene would never have been allowed because the powerful documentary medium of film so easily legitimizes such criminal behaviour. Fiction becomes documentary, documentary becomes fiction. A look at the alternate ending [included with the Season 1 DVD set] in which Terri is rescued might appeal to sentimentalists, but in fact would be seen as the usual old school social engineering lie because *24* spares no sinners, no saints, no innocents.

By contrast, the ending of Season 2 might seem to fall back into the cuddly propaganda of prime-time TV. The forgiving David Palmer treats his cabinet like naughty school children, seemingly forgets the putsch in the name of some absurd pragmatism and falls back into the rhetoric of the rah rah placebo. But... is this script delinquency merely a dumbing down device to place the viewer in a happy stupor before the shock of the final sequences? You be the judge.

The timely story-line of *24* Season 2 has many excellent situations and dramatic moments, although it must be said that the overall dynamic is more uneven than that of Season 1 wherein Terri's convenient amnesia & aftermath might be considered the only false move... unless you see the casting of Dennis Hopper as the Balkan villain Victor Drazan as a mistake. Hopper's persona carries so much baggage now that he can only be viewed as funny, and as such his inclusion merely trades on cliché and comic relief... although, God knows, the homicidal rhythm of *24* might need "some" humour.

Season 2 includes a major counter-line with Kim Bauer, yet whatever its merits as drama, essentially has no bearing on the master story... and the sequences with the cougar in the woods belong to a Walt Disney production. No doubt the majority could care less as not only does Elisha Cuthbert look good, her acting is also good. The problem of why some villains take so long to shoot & kill, take care of business, etc, remains problematic... even when masked by the overall speed of the narrative. As usual, film cheats 24 times a second, even if presented as digi HD.

24: Season 3
You Can Spy On Them Too

You're up, you're down, you're all over town... and you've got a rig in your pocket. Seems Jack has picked up a big time habit in the last couple of years while taking down a Mexican drug lord called Salazar... and he's fighting the heebie jeebies as he tries to save L.A. from a biochem attack masterminded by Salazar's brother. Seems too that President David Palmer survived the attempt on his life... and that his choice in women still remains questionable, especially for someone who is in charge of the most powerful country on the planet.

The Daughters of Satan are at work once again, whispering their poisoned honey in the ears of their child men. Haciendas & prison breaks, closed-system gunbattles & existential moments. And once again the CTU has been infiltrated and compromised by the bad guys, which raises serious doubts about the sophistication of this agency... or has it? Just when you're thinking narrative decadence, the producers have gotten lazy, are winging it on the karma of the stars and their supporting cast, you realize you've been duped again. Reversals. Aristotle 101. Nothing is ever what it seems. Yet the sense of *deja vu* increases with this season's stories, and not only because of *24*'s own narrative formula. Brother Hector plotting within his Mexican hacienda with his sweet scheming vixen... a plague carrier a.w.o.l. in the streets... an ugly presidential candidates' debate... a game of Russian roulette for Jack... a prison break, etc. And... yet another mole within CTU?

It's amazing too how a drama can succeed on such industrial dialogue. No rhetorical poetry, no swearing, no *bon mots*, no sub-text. The jargon of compuverts and killers. In a sense, dialogue gets in the way of the dreadful choices many characters are forced to make. As in Ryan Chappelle's sacrificial execution, who needs talk? It just gets in the way, drags the action.

You're staring at a mosaic of flickering screens and flickering agendas... you, citizen voyeur, resisting hypnosis, refusing to be duped... as the direction and acting remains excellent.

But don't despair: you have a computer and you can spy on these characters as well. Nice flash sites for each season, complete with dossiers and other possibilities at *www.fox.com/24.*

Kiefer Sutherland has played plenty of punks before, bad-tempered volatiles who now provide the latent, dangerous element in his role as Jack Bauer. Now he's good cop/ bad cop/ feel alright all in one. Not only is his visual presence superb, but also his voice, cadenced and measured, free of any obvious regional handicap... pure radio in the night. Sometimes soothing, sometimes malevolent... like Richard Burton with a hangover. Anyone old enough to know will recognize the similarity to his old man, the fine Canadian actor Donald Sutherland, pedigreed in Stratford. When Jack Bauer uses his phone—and he uses it a lot—your eyes close instinctively as you listen. A great deal of this character's power is in the articulation, the rasp & the roar. Jack Bauer: civility is a discipline, forgetting is an art. The future is a flat line. As the series/seasons progress, a sense of humanity is regained... just a glimmer, a flash between the coffins.

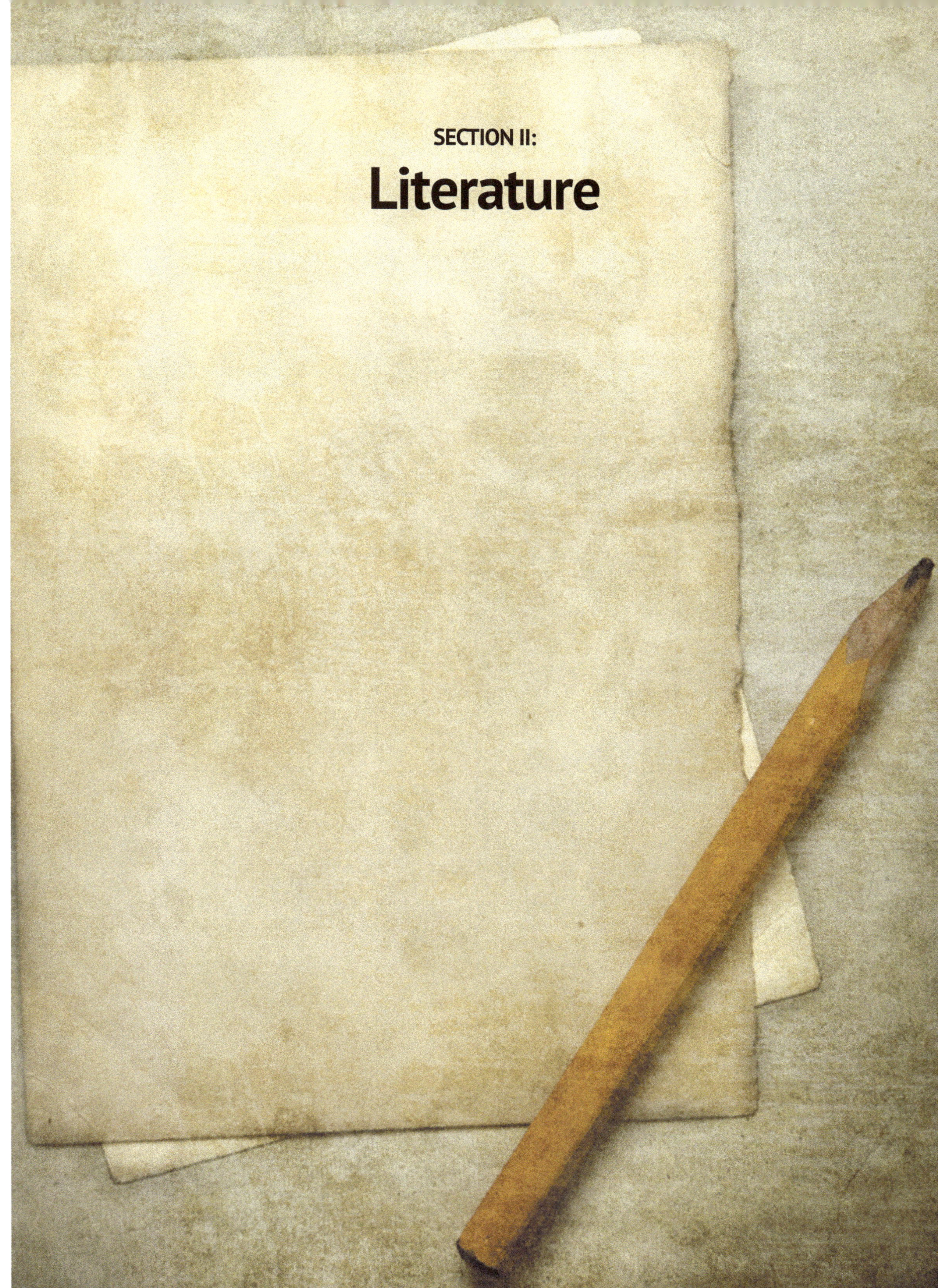

SECTION II:

Literature

PART ONE:

Writing And Me

The Voice

I was on the cinder path between the hedge and the potting shed when I heard the Voice. It wasn't my mother or my father or anyone I knew. It was a voice inside my head and it was the second time I'd heard it in this spot, me standing there looking up at the paned glass window of the shed.

It said, "Pick up that stone and throw it."

It was like someone on the radio, only it was in my head, like a memory of an instruction about what to do when seeing a window where it shouldn't be, high up, twice my height and more.

This time I obeyed. I picked up a stone and threw it, and as the glass broke, I ran off down the path that led to the sand dunes and the beach. I don't remember if I was a suspect or not, but I know the same thing happened two or three times more. If I saw the glass had been repaired, the Voice returned, commanded me to pick up a stone and throw it.

It was a big mystery, and I remember the adults discussing it. I felt pleased with myself, with my accomplishment, this act of crime, this self-assertion.

I was three or four years old, and of course I was receiving a lot of commands from adults in those days, do this, don't do that, and so on, yet the Voice was no one I knew. Was it me or was it someone who came with me when I was born?

It wasn't the sort of voice you later recognize as your own, the one you have conversations with to work out some problem, or complain to when you can't. What comes first—language or thought? Most people would say thought, but who knows, there might be a hidden instructor who actualizes our reasoning.

Remember being on the beach with my mother, and I was trotting along beside her, still learning to walk, I suppose, when I saw something protruding from the sand. It was metal with holes in the casing, and blades or fins on the end that was sticking up, like a little V-2 rocket or a *Fritz X* glide bomb, and I ran towards it eagerly as it looked like a toy, a treasure worth claiming. My mother cried out and grabbed me, and we steered wide towards the surf. Touch nothing on the beach, she said.

She was probably right, as the fields near the aerodrome were littered with war junk and not far away the beach was used as a decoy runway and once in a while the Germans did come around and drop a few bombs.

Why was I doing naughty or dangerous acts? Was it naivete or was it the Voice? My mother was crouched down on the lawn picking clovers and I thought I would surprise her, sneak up and thump her on the back. I threw everything I had into that blow and she fell forward with a scream and I can tell you there was no love for the rest of that afternoon. Was just expressing myself... although, again, it was the Voice. It was the Voice who told me to not just surprise her but to really hit her hard, show her what a strong little man I was.

Not long before I'd been standing in my crib and would cry until she came along, looked after me. Then one night I cried and she didn't come along, and I kept crying harder and louder and she still didn't show up and I realized she wasn't in the house... and I lay down angry and disappointed. This was my first lesson in aloneness.

It was after this that I first heard the Voice. Was there a connection? Don't know. One day I was standing outside the house and a column of soldiers came marching past, heading for the sand dunes. Americans, training for D-Day, I suppose. One of them dropped out and gave me a stick of chewing gum, just the way you see it in the movies, the *Red Ball Express* in Italy or somewhere, only this was Wales.

Chewing gum was new to me, so I hesitated.

He smiled, said, "Eat it."

Was he the Voice? I put the stick in my mouth, chewed... and he patted me on the head, then hurried off to rejoin his platoon.

I never heard the Voice after that, or at least not in a way that I would respond to without question. You talk to yourself now and then or you talk to somebody who never actually talks back, as you can fill in both sides of the conversation yourself. People who hear voices are generally regarded as lunatics, unless they're Joan of Arc or some religious type who is favored by a visit from God. Bereaved people often talk to a departed loved one, and many believe they've actually had a visitation, had a conversation, received instruction. But this is all dismissed as the babble of damaged goods by those whose hearts run so silent as to be forgotten, so they think they're normal or even worse, immortal.

I seldom think of my earliest days, the memories, the montage of aircraft and fear, the people I first knew, my mother and father, no longer in this room or any other room except memory, whatever memory is. Those days were reality, yet now they might as well be fantasy. Gaps exist, like nights without dream. If it wasn't for injury and pain, I wouldn't even know I exist.

When you come out of the universal coma, who knows if it's reincarnation or the trauma of re-entry that activates the Voice. Now that I'm old, I've started to hear the Voice again. It might be loneliness or senility but I've been hearing it, like the blind man hears the path rather than sees it, knows the way. For example, it was the Voice that told me to pick myself up and write this book.

I Just Like Modern

How did I get into writing as something beyond what you were made to do in school? My first writing assignment was in Sunday school, a scripting job. We were told to make a play about the infant Moses being found in a wicker basket among the bull rushes by the Pharaoh's daughter and how she explained the incident to her father and got to keep Moses as her own little prince.

Mine was the best apparently, so I was rewarded by getting

an illustrated war book at the annual prize ceremony. Might have been ten or eleven years old. Never thought about it much until years later when I read that the first thing the famous Scottish writer Robert Louis Stevenson wrote as a boy was a dramatization of the same thing. Great writer, much better than I, of course.

Wrote my first short stories as a class assignment in English the second year I was at Ballymena Technical. Would've been fifteen, I think. Usually we had to write one short essay per week in a notebook on a topic handed out by the teacher, George Tully. However, he started us off with a short story and when he handed them back, he said (quietly), "Very good, Russell, you can write another if you like." So every Saturday I sat down at the table in the library at home and wrote a story straight into my notebook.

These stories were all modified rip-offs from the comics or the pulps... except for the very last story, which was autobiographical social realism, something I realized was a bit risky considering the behavior of the characters, the young thugs I hung around with at night, prowled the byways getting up to mischief. But this was dull compared to the first story I wrote, which might've been a '50's B-movie or a sci fi comic channeling exercise.

Scientist working at the atomic test site in Nevada has a theory that if one remains at Ground Zero right beside the bomb, then he will survive the blast, and he tries this clandestinely during a test detonation. When samples from the test site are crated for shipment to a lab, a shadowy figure slips into the cargo hold of the aircraft.

During the flight an oozing luminous slime invades the aircraft cabin, killing all on board in a horrific ordeal of nightmare suffocation, and the plane crashes into a swamp. Investigators find a high level of radioactivity at the crash site and are left wondering about the missing scientist.

I didn't have time to include a female love interest as in, say, *The Fly* or *The Creature From the Black Lagoon*, although I was aware of these seminal works, and others like them. The action radio serial *Dick Barton Special Agent* was a big influence, and radio serials like Rider Haggard's *King Solomon's Gold Mines*... anything with action and the bizarre, for, growing up on a farm, I'd already learned how bizarre life can be.

Mr. Tully must've been a far more eclectic reader than I imagined, given that the course novels were Walter Scott's *Ivanhoe* and Charles Dickens' *Great Expectations*, the standard Anglican brainwash texts of the time. He was a short man, maybe five seven, a little plump but not fat, a middle age figure with thinning hair and rosy cheeks.

He wore bifocals that made him look like an eccentric scientist in *Rupert the Bear* and he wasn't a beast like a couple of the other male teachers who viewed the students as criminal deviants or idiots fresh from the asylum. I think he travelled down from Belfast every day on the train, with his umbrella and briefcase, and a paperback in his hand.

I sometimes saw him walking from the station with his eyes glued to an open paperback, reading as he came off the street into the yard and passed through the front door heading for the staff room.

Anyway, it was strange how he let me write nothing but fiction for the year, with just the odd syntax correction here and there, and an approval tick at the end. When he walked up and down the rows handing back the exercise books, he seldom said anything to the students beyond the odd cryptic remark, so most were able to keep their grading humiliations a secret. On my last story—the one about hooligan vandalism and gang warfare on the night roads between Ballymena and our village—he smiled at me, said, "You should try writing a paperback before you get killed."

Unfortunately there was no more Mr. Tully for me in English the next year, so I forgot about fiction writing. Anyway, I was more involved with my skiffle group, The Zombies, and dreaming about how I could get myself to America. Even one of my art teachers picked up on my interest in American culture, as the buildings I drew in my sketches were skyscrapers. He learned over my shoulder, said, "You want to go to the USA?" and I felt uncomfortable, as if I'd been caught out at something illegal, said, "I just like modern."

I just like modern. I certainly did, even if it included an atom bomb in Nevada.

The Library

It was a big sideboard bookcase made of walnut with glass doors and cupboards on the bottom, where you could hide books in darkness or a bottle of Bushmills, as my grandmother did, although she was no drinker. There were a lot of good books on those shelves, and I ended up reading a lot of them just to pass the time, including the Bible, cover to cover, *Genesis* to *Revelation*, one afternoon and evening, just to see what was going on outside of what the minister was reading out in church or what was going on in Sunday School. Gentlemen spilling their seed on the ground stuck with me more than the moralizing, although the story of Jesus was certainly interesting and I could see why the Church was obsessed with him.

But it was books like Coleridge's *The Ancient Mariner* (illustrated by Gustave Dore) and the H.G. Wells set that grabbed my imagination. *The Time Machine... the War of the Worlds... The First Men in the Moon...* this stuff was so out there, so mentally liberating from the cautious protestant middle class culture I knew in rural Ulster. Cavor and his anti-gravity cavorite capsule and his missionary work with the Selinites on the moon was a lot more sexy than the satiric *Alice In Wonderland* even if there were no women in sight.

Wells was so New Colonial, where the conquest of space brought the clash of civilizations into a whole new level of barbarism. The imperialism was scientific and secular, fraught with irony and prophecy, disease and death rays. The Martians with imperialist dreams? The Morlocks eating the Eloi? The industrial plebes feeding on the bourgeois art nouveau dreamers? I sensed the murderous humour and the real politik although I was still too young to take it seriously.

Anyway, I read books, lots of them, novels and encyclopedias, dozens of them, and they were all windows into the post-Victorian generations, the rise of industrialization... everything, including the rise of the railways, the first aircraft, shipyards and shipbuilding, airships and canals, everything... the Great War, incredible period photographs of everything, except for raw Death, although they did have the R-100 crash in France, the skeletal ruins of the airship, and everything you need to know about the Hindenburg, including its fiery end at Lakehurst, New Jersey.

I learned a lot from those encyclopedias.

My Aunt Nan and my father were the two educated ones in the family, although Nan was the only one who actually finished her degree. Her striped university tennis blazer hung for years in the harness room where my grandmother had a griddle and made potato bread and soda buns. The harnesses for the drays were still on the wall, even after their days were done and we were using tractors. Can still smell that room, the smoke and the leather.

It was in a stone building in the backyard, which was a quadrangle. I don't know why the jacket wasn't moved. It was like one of those you see in those illustrated romances from the thirties, when young women rode Raleighs with chain guards, gazed at young men in cricket jackets lounging against Rovers and Rileys and MGs.

Maybe my grandmother needed it there, needed to stop the clock.

I missed my first year in school because I contracted scarlet fever, and was in hospital for months somewhere in England. I was in a bed with others in the ward and just sat there quietly when I wasn't sleeping.

This is why I was taken back to Ireland and left to live with my grandmother (my father's mother) on the estate at Knockboy in the Braid Valley. The last time I was there, my grandfather died when he was out inspecting the cattle in one of the fields. They pulled a door off the Corn Room to stretcher him back to the house. This door was a dirty white with a set of tables painted on it in black paint. What these tables were for, I don't know, although they were mysterious and occult.

Biggles

Boy, I liked Biggles. He was in the bookcase, *The Camels Are Coming,* stories by W.E. Johns about a WW 1 "scout" pilot who starts out flying Sopwith Camel biplanes, learns aerial combat and goes on to lead his own squadron in the Royal Flying Corp. Biggles stories were authentic, and while tragedy was minimized, the mix of camaraderie, risky adventure, and male bonding was something any teenage boy could identify with. It was a world of machines and hidden adversaries in the clouds, and the action was like the combat of the gods in mythology. There was a beautiful loneliness in it too, the thing that later appealed to me in the poetic aviation books of the French author Antoine de Saint Exupery.

These two or three Biggles books were my father's and they were a substitute for him and by reading them repeatedly I suppose I thought they might bring him back to me, like a cargo cult. I asked for Biggles books as Christmas presents, so I was able to keep up with his lengthy career flying all sorts of exotic aircraft and conducting covert operations in the jungles and deserts of the world.

There were villains, although the arch-villain was a German intelligence flyer called Erich von Stalhein, and it's von Stalhein that Biggles thwarts in my favorite story, a WW 2 adventure in North Africa called *Biggles Sweeps the Desert.*

The story has historical validity. The Allies were using a south Atlantic route from the Brazilian island of Fernando de Noronha to the African "bulge" to ferry aircraft and men into the combat zone and the Germans, in order to intercept these flights, send in von Stalhein with a squadron of Messerschmitts,

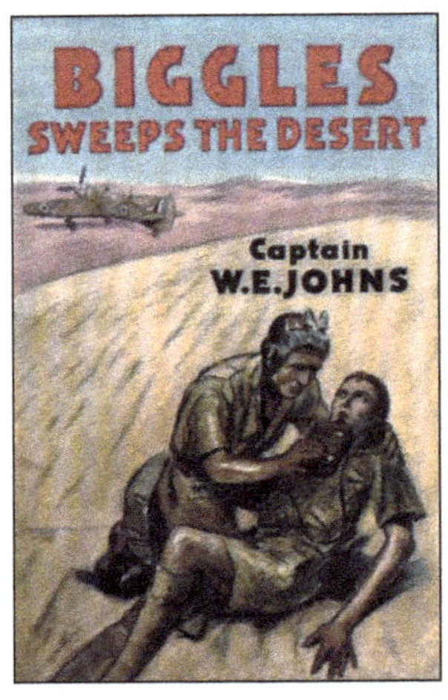

which starts to take a toll. The British, not absolutely certain the Germans are operating in that area of the desert, send in Biggles and his squadron of Spitfires to set up under some camouflage netting at an oasis.

Combat, crashes and intrigue dominate in the dunes and rock desert. Of course Biggles and the boys triumph in the end, although only just—von Stalhein, while a thoroughgoing German swine, is a competent swine, and a damn good pilot himself. As a character, he's somewhere between Hans-Joachim Marseille (the Star of Africa) the Luftwaffe ace who was killed in North Africa, and the Nazi Minister of Propaganda, Joseph Goebbels.

Biggles also had romantic skirmishes, nothing too detailed or lasting, except for the German spy, Marie Janis, who gets under his skin for life everlasting. Doomed, of course. His squadron mates can have dalliances wherever they go, but Biggles, the disciplined loner, flies with the ghosts.

The schoolyard racism so typical of war between nations, is now considered an aberration rather than a fact of history, so old Biggles is taking it in the neck for this, and is no longer deemed suitable for adolescent modelling. I dunno... I came across a *Biggles Omnibus* recently and reread some of the tales, and they took me right back into the romantic absurdity of it all, the first lunar phase of the twentieth century. Racist? You might as well call a Spitfire racist. These stories just made me more curious about the other side.

Just Saying, Crime Pays

What can you tell about a culture from its fiction? Is it a more accurate barometer of the domestic population's psychology than the objects they make, the buildings, the machines, the parks, the candies and the toys?

For example, crime fiction, which is a global obsession these days—does it tell us that America and Europe are sick, so afflicted that both cops and criminals are sick, the one blaming the other? Or is there a limit to "creative sickness", the genius for murder and torture, robbery and vandalism, politics and religion? And is the moral relativism that guides our legal systems in the western democracies the tacit admission of defeat, that there is no right and wrong, that we're all victims of an unknown author in a feckless, violent universe... well, this seems to be Henning Mankell's position, and that of his now famous alter-ego detective, the occasionally sentimental but always fastidious Kurt Wallander.

Mankell's despair is the square root of Ingmar Bergman, so you have to wonder about these Swedes, ABBA be damned. Did Bergman ever crack a smile? He tried, but he was never as funny as he was the authentic face of tragedy. Mankell understands humour, although it's never allowed to melt the snow below which evil hides.

Take what happens in *The Secret* (Hemligheten, 2006), the Kurt Wallander episode I watched recently (the *Yellow Bird*

Swedish language dramatization). Sub-titles... but you don't really need them. A cop is a crafty paedophile and serial killer who it turns out molested Wallander's capo, Inspector Stefan Lindman, as a child. Stefan has been losing it recently—in part because of his failed relationship with Wallander's daughter, Linda, also a cop with the Ystad detective squad—and gets suspended for beating up a wife beater, so is unable to take part in the investigation of the paedophile cop's latest killing... but of course Stefan goes vigilante, kills another pedophile involved in the murder, and, tragically, commits suicide shortly thereafter.

It's ugly. His body is found by Linda and, well, it's ugly. She finds a photograph of Stefan as a boy, realizes he was a victim of the pedophile "undercover" cop Rasmussen, goes hunting for revenge. When she discovers Rasmussen cleaning up after his latest murder, she's on the verge of shooting him in the head when her father shows up, sharply advises her to put her gun down.

"Don't shoot him, Linda," says Wallander. "Don't let him win again."

What secularized Lutheran nonsense is this? Sweden doesn't have the death penalty and you know all this monster is going to get is a warm room in a warm compound where he can reflect on his sins and jerk off until he either dies or is rehabilitated and rationalized back into to society like some bad toy that has been fixed. Tombstones and death are for others—forgiveness and cultural eugenics for everyone else, maybe a few pills, a few movies and any kind of therapy some genius with a grant gets to try. Recidivism? No problem. Just keeps everyone in a job. It's priced in.

Is this Sweden? Is this the western world? You wonder. You wonder if it's always been like this, back a hundred or two hundred years ago before the social sciences got involved in the process of crime and punishment. Today it's as if hideous murder is a career you can study like any profession, and if you can give it a sexual spin, you might even become a celebrity. As we move from fiction to documentary, we move from understudies to leading roles in the theatre of day to day living and dying. The criminal is he who says, "I create my own role."

Yes, I know, De Quincey laid it all out in *On Murder* considered as one of the Fine Arts in 1827. And when it comes to murder the only moral difference between the state and the individual is the blizzard of politics. When one of the pedophiles is found shot in *The Secret*, a uniformed cop says briskly, "Well, let's find the hero who did this" and you know he isn't being sarcastic. It was all done before in the comics, the animal traps with the sharpened row of sticks waiting to impale anything that falls into the pit (*The Fifth Woman*, 1996/2000)... scalping (*Sidetracked*, 1995/99)... and so on and so on. Sometimes it's just the verboten dross of what used to be called "para-literature", the sensational stuff that escaped the censor pre-1960 as being too ridiculous to be believed. *Cherchez la creep*. Still, Mankell knows a thing or two about imagery, wherever he culls it from—for example, the burning swans in desperate flight above the water in *Before the Frost*.

A large part of Mankell's appeal—and of crime fiction in general—is to the infantile sadism that's within all of us.

Great writer, almost poetry, makes you want to get drunk and suicidal... until you realize that he's thinking in a circle, trapped by the institution and the ghost morality it offers.

Linda doesn't shoot Rasmussen, although most of us have already put him below the snow. She turns away, hunched over in emotional agony, wails, "I loved him!"—meaning, of course, Stefan, her colleague and lover who now lies below a sheet in the autopsy lab where he himself had viewed so many victims in previous episodes. While his fate is tragic, you realize there was an inevitability to it, as if he was a doppelganger for the younger Wallander, and that Wallander could easily have had a short, fatal career as a cop. You recall some of the stories, the novels, the cases in the Wallander ethos... robbed of love and family, his drunkenness, his despair, his aloneness, as if every case was a puzzle about his own situation, and if he solved it, he might get better.

But back to the first question—does fiction reveal the psychology of a culture? While I read that Mankell was married four times, lastly to the daughter of Ingmar Bergman, I think, well, he had to get there sooner or later. But when I read that he quit writing the trilogy of novels with Linda Wallander as the protagonist after the actress Johanna Sallstrom—who played Linda in the Swedish series—committed suicide in 2007, I wonder about all those clichés concerning the Swedes, their famous depressions and suicides, their socialism and their neutrality... was this the price they paid for side-stepping WW 2? Is/was Henning Mankell just an exquisite testament to their deceptive daylight tranquility?

Mankell's view is that characters/people react, become monsters because of the societal situation they find themselves in. It's a familiar social scientist circle-of-victimhood view. Personally I think it's a lot more complicated than that. We don't have teeth for just smiling. Yet I'm impressed by Mankell's fluency and output, how he managed to write so much quality fiction in such a relatively short time. Even within the stock formula of crime fiction plotting via newspaper research, it's never as easy as just plugging in the characters and writing about the landscape you grew up in, just rolling with the disguised autobiography sublimated as dark fantasy. He was a natural.

Not bad for a guy who thought *Macbeth* and *Heart of Darkness* were the best crime stories ever told. And "Wallander" came out of a telephone book, like the names of so many fictional characters. It might be that Mankell is a blueprint for murder rather than a symptom, as the murder genre is now so proliferous that countries and authors seem to be competing for who has the best to offer in nastiness. He has said that he chooses a domestic (Swedish) issue to base his stories around, so he is/was an issues writer. Melodrama might be the frame, but it's not the whole picture. When you read about his off-stage politics, you might expect his fiction to be propaganda... yet it isn't. He might have a Jim Jones cultist type encouraging a group suicide, but the sociology is the lesson, not the crime.

It's all imported, isn't it, from the bad old US of A.

Sweden is a small, ancient country—big enough to be a modern state, yet small enough to be tribal. Around 10 million in 2015. Socialism can work in this context, when society is just an extended family. Current suicide rates are about 24 per 100,000—certainly nothing like Greenland or South Korea, and similar to the UK, Canada, and not as bad as the US or Russia, which is reputed to have one of the highest rates in the world. Crime? Twice as many rapes as the US, but the US murder rate is (apparently) currently more than a 143 times that of Sweden's. According to a recent report in *The Local* (Swedish News in English), there were 87 murders in 2013, with most being in the three major cities (Stockholm, Gothenburg and Malmo).

The annual rate is rising, although not fast enough to justify the despair projected by Wallander. Mankell said that he works his plots out beforehand, that it was "bullshit" the notion that writers just sit down and make it up as they go along. If this was his method I suspect he was not only a behaviorist but also an atheist. Poets don't work out their narratives. They don't have a clue. They just wait for the divine message to guide their hand and if they're lucky, it might make sense.

I always seem to be on the wrong side of the wall. Yes, it's wise to have a plan, some idea of organization... but if nothing is left to the unknown, what is there for the writer to discover?

You don't see Wallander's father in Season 1 of the TV series, but he's in a number of the novels, an old cuss who lives alone in the country painting the same picture over and over—a grouse, the sort of sentimental bird image that passes as kitchen furniture in the northern hemisphere.

While the joke is on the father, you might wonder what difference there is between painting the same thing over and over and solving the same crime over and over... or, dare I say it, writing the same detective novel over and over?

O'Flaherty

It's a strange thing that I had to leave Ireland before I discovered Irish literature. In the fall of 1958 I was a new arrival in Kitimat, B.C., a town which recently had been carved out of the coastal wilderness. One evening I took a walk to a small corner store in a loghouse in the Garfalcon crescent, above the main commercial district. It was snowing lightly, and occasional cars passed by, V-8 engines growling, snow chains clicking. It was all so new, so unfamiliar, so distant from the rolling overcasts of Atlantic Ireland. I went into the store, noticed a pocket book rotary display, checked out the books, looking for some sci fi or maybe a Leslie Charteris *Saint* novel. But instead my attention was drawn to this Signet paperback, *The Selected Stories of Liam O'Flaherty.*

A quick scan of the description was intriguing, reminded me of a John Millington Synge play I'd seen once, an Ireland way back when donkeys and carts were still on the road, gypsies and itinerant peddlers... Ireland before the partition, the Rebellion in the South, the Civil War, all the history I was denied back in Ballymena. Suddenly I realized I didn't know Ireland at all, any more than I knew Canada.

> "29 stories of passion, insight and strength... by one of the great writers of the twentieth century... edited by Devin A. Garrity".

I bought the book, took it back to my room, started reading. "The Mountain Tavern"... "The Tent"... "Red Barbara"... "The Sniper"... it was incredible how he could take a simple situation, give it complexity, or a complex situation, give it simplicity. Who else could make a story about a sea wave destroying a cliff or a young maiden having sex with the sun lying on the rocks beside a tidal pool? And irony? I'd never thought about irony. What was "The Sniper" but a master class in irony. Illusion and delusion like a bullet to the head.

O'Flaherty wrote with a poetic lucidity that was unfamiliar to me, these short stories that described in an objective way a raw pastoral life that was also unfamiliar, yet was a world that I could identify with. I'd grown up and worked on a farm, had some idea about the rhythm of Nature, and sort of folk who depended on it for a living. Of course the Aran Islands—where many of his stories were set—was a peasant society, and these were mostly fishermen who lived like a cargo cult on the shores of Time. There was a Biblical simplicity to their gruelling lives and frequent early deaths, and even the urban stories about gunmen and tramps and drunkards were lessons in survival. Images. O'Flaherty wrote in images, like a photographer capturing "the decisive moment". He knew how to start and he knew how to end and he knew how to make you forget that you'd ever left one to arrive at the other.

Mesmerized? Well, not quite... more bedazzled, say. Educated? Yes. Not only did I learn something about Ireland, but also that you didn't need to exaggerate an event or a character in order to be interesting. Authenticity trumped fantasy, especially if a story made you believe the impossible. O'Flaherty's eloquence was deceptive, of course—it seemed easy, but that sort of literacy just isn't, as I was later to learn for myself.

I suppose I was picking up the pagan, pre-Christian spirit, the ancient gaelic face of Ireland. O'Flaherty was an outlaw, as he knew there were forces out there stronger than any of the institutions of Man. He was a Romantic as well, wrote like one, wild and easy, and I would come back to him, as I was learning a thing or two.

The 3rd Face

When you look in the mirror there are two faces pushing back at you—your mother's and your father's, even if you don't know them, came off a doorstep or out of a tube. And there's a million faces behind theirs, all pushing history like a bulldozer blade... but you, you're always looking for you.

For a while I thought "you" was Robert Mitchum, so I got a trenchcoat and a box of cigarettes, sucked in my cheeks. Then I thought "you" was Elvis, got a flash jacket and a guitar, started dancing crazy. Then there was the undergraduate, the hooded dufflecoat and the fruit boots, the monk in the shadows and sleazy cafes. Girls had makeup for their reincarnations, but me, I was always watching the movies, the magazines and the street, as if I was already out there somewhere, and when I saw this person, I would forget about me.

Imagine a world without mirrors. "You" would only exist in the eyes of others, the death masks and statues they raised in your honor, if you rated honor.

A girl tried to make a mask of my face once. A younger sister of one of my pals... her and one of her giggling friends, no shape to them, just schoolgirls, and I was hanging around on the doorstep with her brother. First she suggested pushing my face into a soft patch in the lawn, then drying the mud with her mother's hairdryer, but this was just teasing. They would use paper maché—all I had to do was let them cover my face with damp newspaper clippings and wallpaper paste and presto, I'd be ready for Halloween.

I let them do it, as I'd always enjoyed soft hands cutting my hair or being used as a toy. I lay back, closed my eyes. The process was rougher than I anticipated and my pal was laughing, as if this was a plot he'd put his sister up to. My hair was pushed back, newspaper clippings stuck to my forehead, eyelids, nose, cheeks, mouth, chin and I couldn't move my jaw least the first layer came apart. Glue, then another layer... and so on, and I had to remain still for an hour or more until the layers bonded.

When she sealed my eyes, the last thing I saw was her serious expression, her freckles, just like her brother's, her eyes, just like her mother's, and she wasn't a girl, she was an artist. She wasn't fooling around, as she wanted to get this mask just right, all those old news reports locked and bonded.

They bonded a bit too well as the mask wouldn't come free, and they were laughing like hyenas, and I was too, because even if I couldn't see myself, I knew I was now something special, like the *Creature from the Black Lagoon* or some other freak from the comics.

My pal thought it would be great if we took a walk around this end of the village, indulge in a little theatre. So he led me around the side of the church towards the tennis courts where some kids were playing hopscotch. Could also hear the tennis balls popping, pants and curses. The kids emitted giddy shrieks, "Frankenstein! Frankenstein!", and I hammed it up, lurched stiff-armed and stiff-legged. Someone threw a stone... to be expected, I suppose.

I was a sensation in the village, even though we didn't venture too far, gave the old ladies in the doorways a laugh, although the dog-walker nearly lost control of his dogs as we crossed the street and they went berserk. Greyhounds, very skittish animals. My pal hustled me into Ronnie's shop where we usually fueled up on chocolate bars and other rubbish.

"Get out of here!" shouted Ronnie from behind the counter, as he knew we were bad for business, maybe nicked things now and then, Smarties, chewing gum, stuff.

"I need a couple of cigarettes," said my pal. "Have any loose ones? For my father."

Ronnie snickered, said, "Who's the clown?"

He was a young man, early twenties, wore bifocals, lived above the shop with his mother.

"*The Creature from the Black Lagoon.*"

"He's not old enough to smoke either."

My pal put his money on the counter. As he didn't smoke I expect he was telling the truth. Ronnie gave him the cigarettes as, well, he was in business and he wanted us out of the shop. We went back to the house, and I tried to get the mask off.

His sister was there and she said, "Don't take it off, I want a photo."

We agreed that might be good, something for the old album. I sat down on the step, and my pal offered to light a cigarette for me, stick it in my mouth.

"Mitchum," he said. "Fag in your mouth, you'll look fantastic, me boy!"

He stuck one of his cigarettes through the hole, and I was able to wiggle it with my tongue. His sister took a photo with the Brownie, and then they decided it would be nice if Mitchum was actually smoking the cigarette.

My pal had a lighter, not something I'd seen him with before, and he was a real amateur with it, kept hitting the trigger, misfiring, and then, when it did fire, the flame surprised him. Missed the cig, caught the mask, which ignited like creosote, that mache of news clippings, Juan Peron overthrown in Argentina, the Suez Canal Crisis, James Dean killed in a car crash... and Johnny Ray and Guy Mitchell top the charts. I stumbled onto the lawn trying to tear the damn mask off and I heard my pal shouting for his sister to get a bucket of water.

I ended up face down in the soggy patch, and I felt someone's hand on the back of my head pushing my face into the mud. That did it. Could hear the fire die with a hiss, and when I rolled over and sat up, the remains of the mask just slid off like dead skin from a snake. I was lucky. Sure, it took a month for my hair and eyebrows to grow back and my cheeks were red for longer than that but my mouth and eyes were o.k., so no damage there.

And when I looked in the mirror, I saw a better "you", better looking than either my mother or father—although I can't say that with certainty—and this face, the 3rd face, was the person I'd been searching for. He was older, more cynical, ready for the love and treachery that such a face would bring.

The Teacher

I had a teacher once who taught me a lot more outside the classroom than she ever did inside, and I doubt if she ever knew it. I'll call her Elaine X because I heard recently that she's still alive, sits in the solarium of a nursing home reading this and that. Amazing. She must be ninety, although this seems impossible to imagine as she's forever twenty-five and beautiful in my memory.

She was notoriously beautiful, actually. Elaine X, subjects French and English, and even the black academic gown all the teachers wore at the Academy couldn't conceal her statuesque elegance, that left the little eleven year old boys blushing when she spoke to them, or nervously twiddling their fingers in their hair. She was my English teacher that year, the year of the idiot, when I sat in my uniform with all the other idiots in uniforms, row on row of us, and me, especially me, full of fear and awe.

It made me sick and I missed a few classes and the headmaster said I was a barefaced liar when I presented my Grannie's sick note, that I was close to expulsion, even though I'd only been there a month, was just a humble farm boy eager to please.

Fear and intimidation were his weapons, as guilt was to be assumed and we were just cowards in the face of battle. Weird. Old school tyrant, Oxford graduate... or so he said. Although my hatred is a dim, distant star, it's a hatred that rekindles with the memory nonetheless and I cannot imagine this angry, bruising man as Elaine X's lover as some of the boys declared he was.

They were always speculating, this teacher or that, Big Bob who taught math or the hunchback who taught physics. Not me. Salacious speculation was an insult, as she was a neighbour. Her family had a modern house where the road passed through a beech tree grove a mile from the village on the way to the coast, and my Aunt K knew her, knew the family. Merchants. Bulk coal, flour, animal feed, hardware, two or three trucks, and the old boy drove a Rover, sat lurched towards the middle as he supported his weight on the arm rest, so you always knew it was him coming.

My aunt was cleaning eggs with my Grannie, sitting there with two buckets, the one wiping, the other polishing. I was at the table, short pants, bare legs, finishing some homework.

Aunt K said, "What's wrong with him?"

My Grannie said, "Must be his kidneys."

Aunt K said, "Did he wet the bed? He can't stay home forever... he'll fall behind and then what?"

My Grannie kept her eyes on the egg, kept rubbing. How

many times had I seen this? No wonder I was sick of eggs and farm food. Everything was fried.

Aunt K said, "How are you getting along with Miss X? She says you're not stupid."

I said, "I get nervous."

My Aunt grunted, said something about getting on in school, did I want to end up digging ditches for a living. No, I did not. I was already doing enough of that in the garden. Dig that potato row, son. Pick those daffodils... clean out that hen-house... help an old woman, show how useful you are.

Then she said, "Is that for Miss X? You should get on your bicycle, ride over there and drop it off, show her you're not lazy. You can't be falling behind."

Ride over to Miss X's house? It was a long way. It was a mile to the village from here, and it was a mile beyond the village to her house. Still, it was something to do.

I'd been past the house when my uncle took a drive down to the coast to have a look at the waves and have an ice cream but I'd never been on the property. It had a brick wall and a gate that was always open and the usual beach pebbles on the driveway and parking area. The house was merchant modern, probably had hot water radiators for heating.

Her car was there, the red Austin. And there was another one, a green Riley saloon, probably one of her brothers. No sign of the old man's Rover. It was a Sunday afternoon, I think. Must've been, otherwise she'd have been at school, although it might've been a week day, a public holiday or something. My idea was just to drop my composition book in the porch and bugger off quietly but then my curiosity got the better of me, wondered if there was a better door, one they used more frequently.

There was a sunroom and it had a door and it was open a few inches, as if someone had just gone in, or maybe it was too hot in there. Someone was talking. I took a look... the room was full of plants in fancy pots, hanging vines and stuff, a real jungle. I saw Miss X sitting in a lounge chair wearing a red bathrobe and a sunhat and there were regular books and student exercise books on the floor like the one I had in my hand. A man was talking but I couldn't see him because of a big urn.

I stiffened.

"That's the long and the short and the tall of it," he said. "Pregnant."

Sounded young, not country, educated perhaps. Had to be her brother—he was a doctor, wasn't he?

Miss X lit a cigarette, inhaled, then let the smoke roll out with her sigh. She was beautiful, alright. Just like a magazine.

She said something in French, finished with, "What can be done?"

I was always listening to adult conversation, overhearing stuff I shouldn't, because I was still young enough to be considered dumb, like a pet. But this time I just stole away, dropped my composition in the front porch and rode home. I felt feverish, drank a glass of water and then drank some more. My Grannie was sitting beside the fire, reading one of those Tuppenny Romances she favored, her knitting on the carpet. I didn't say anything. Pretty soon she was asleep, her head hanging to one side.

I went back to school. When Miss X handed back the homework, she said to me, "Did you drop this at the house?"

I lied, said, "My Aunt K did."

Her eyes were working me over, the way adults could. "Are you feeling better?"

"I don't know," I said. "Perhaps."

"Perhaps?"

"Well... I think so."

I could smell her scent, the stuff women use. Like my mother, who was also pretty, although I hadn't seen her in a while... long time, actually.

Then she said, "You have a problem with your auxiliary verbs, and the present continuous. Here, I will ride my bike, not I do ride my bike and, look, this should be we are here forever."

Blah blah... I didn't know what she was talking about. Couldn't concentrate, kept wondering if she was pregnant. I knew what that was.

Years later when I was visiting my Aunt K, now a widow and living in a bungalow on the coast, we got to talking about Elaine X and her family. K was sitting in her mother's chair, the one I remembered so well, my Grannie by the fire, knitting.

Now K was by the fire, and her knitting was on the floor.

I said, "Did Elaine X's brother drown while swimming near the White Rocks at Portrush?"

K said, "No, that was a friend of his."

I said, "Was this friend Elaine X's boyfriend?"

K said, "No... he had a girlfriend he got into trouble, and after he drowned, she went to the Isle of Man for an abortion."

"Who was the girl?"

"Nobody I know."

I knew the spot where the drowning took place. Long, lovely beach with sand dunes and white cliffs. But a dangerous undercurrent that rolled back from the beach and could send a body all the way to the Western Isles. I wondered if my Aunt had this right. I wondered if the girlfriend was really Elaine X.

"Elaine's brother got struck off the register," K said. "He did the abortion."

"So what happened to him?"

"He went to Australia and became a millionaire."

"What happened to Elaine? Did she ever marry?"

"No, she never married. She went and lived in France for a while."

"That's hard to believe. She was really good looking."

"She was fussy... and she had to look after her mother when her father died."

"I remember him. He drove a Rover."

K opened her hand, held it in front of the electric fire for a minute.

"Arthritis," she said. "My circulation is so bad, especially in my feet. Someone told me to put a bag of corks at the bottom of the bed, that it would help."

Corks. The Irish were full of these mystical solutions.

"Does it work?"

K grunted, smiled in a guilty way, said, "I think it does. Too soon to say."

I was still thinking about Elaine X. A few years earlier I'd written a story based on her, made her a fallen woman, as if I'd solved a riddle. Yet I hadn't included it in my collection, maybe because I knew I was wrong, that the plot was failing both the characters and the landscape, and the lie wasn't worth the price of admission. And now, after what K had revealed, I knew I'd made the right decision. K said, "I should visit Elaine... perhaps you could drive me there."

My Aunt was using a walker these days, didn't get around much. Neither did Elaine.

The next week we drove hither and yonder... Bushmills, Portrush, Coleraine... Ballymena, all the old favorites in Co. Antrim. We even parked near the beach where the drowning occurred all those years ago and few others since. It was raining one minute, sunny the next, just the way it did during my childhood. On the last trip we drove back through the village and I went slow as we passed Elaine X's place. K didn't say anything and I didn't stop. Didn't want to, didn't want to see a beauty in ruins or spoil the mystery.

Alice & The Other Nobels

The English Department offered a creative writing course, second year, all year, poetry, drama and fiction, and I was doing great in it writing about Ireland. Irish Lit was in vogue in those days, the early 60s, the "Celtic Twilight", people couldn't get enough of it, the natural poetry and the mysticism of the Bogmen. It seemed exotic, although that wasn't the way I remembered it. I wanted to write Beat, like Kerouac, get away from the old narratives, be hip, get the American cool, although I was stuck between two idioms, Irish English and North American English, and I just didn't have the North American down well enough, couldn't hit a sweet spot in the middle. It took years.

The instructor was an American novelist called George Cuomo, great guy, showed me the light. What was this? Simplify and minimize your writing, get rid of adjectives because if you used the right nouns and stuck to the observational facts, you didn't need them. In effect, you had to destroy your style in order to acquire a style.

Clichés? Bad. Similes? Only once in a while. Metaphors? Too many spoil the broth. And so on... what it was, really, was the "Protestant" style that emerged from American journalism in the days when the authors remained anonymous. It was a discipline, like the military. Just take "I" out of it, let the description speak for itself.

Point-of-view (POV) was another part of the architecture to learn about... and on and on. You'd be surprised at how much can be learned beyond what you're born with, comes naturally. In fact, you could almost say there's nothing natural about writing at all.

Towards the end of the course, George brought in a local writer who had just had her first short story published in *The Montrealer*, a Canadian glossy like the *Atlantic Monthly*. Alice Munro, who won the Nobel Prize in 2013. The story was about a fur farm and it's included in her first collection, *Dance of the Happy Shades*, which won the Governor General's Award in 1968, so she was launched and running right from the start.

Her story was called *Boys & Girls*, I think. I didn't like it and neither did the other guys in the class, although the two females seemed more comfortable with it. My objection was that it was too dull, who cares about these young people and their problems? I grew up on a farm, and I can tell you, these characters didn't know sweet bugger all about life and death and the inhumanity of it all.

But why O why did I open my big mouth? When the others demurred, said nothing or lied, and the females purred, I just let it go, this was bourgeois boring, no story here, move along.

Alice was sitting across the table. Must've been in her early thirties, not bad looking, sexy in the bitchy way that some guys like. Her eyes got bigger as I went on. Actually, I wasn't denouncing her, I was just denouncing the whole notion that you could write fiction about everyday life, no matter how routine, and be interesting. Harsh, naturally... too harsh, as that's part of the art, making something out of nothing.

But I was wasting my time, as the whole movement in literature from the mid-twentieth century had been towards the fiction of the quotidian. Sensitivity had nothing to do with the sensational, with war and adventure, it was to be found in the daily routine of the bourgeois as they drift through marriage and divorce, struggle to pay taxes, talk about literature, live like sheep, dream like criminals. But... this is what happens in societies where there are more writers than readers.

Anyway, I shouldn't have been so brutal, especially to a lady. I had manners, wasn't a young rock & roll thug. I was just trying to define my own position in the landscape. And as I later learned as a writing instructor myself, there's an art to face-to-face criticism when others are present, somewhere between Cicero and Caesar, the snake and the lizard. You move softly between the cracks.

A few years later when I was teaching writing at the University of Victoria I was walking across campus with Alice, escorting her to the room where she was to give a reading. I hadn't talked to her since her collection *Dance of the Happy Shades* had come out.

"I liked your book," I said.

She stopped, looked at me skeptically (not scornfully), said, "Don't give me that. You don't like what I write."

"No, no, those stories are good," I said. "They're well written."

Then I added, "There doesn't have to be murder to be art."

We continued walking. Then she said, "What are you writing?"

I was writing nasty little absurdist plays and while they loved them in Toronto, they weren't the sort of thing you got the Governor General's Award for. For the most part literature is by the bourgeois for the bourgeois, and while you can be an iconoclast, don't expect the institution to kiss your ass.

We had a lot of poets pass through on the reading circuit, and that's how I met Seamus Heaney in 1970, I think, when he was a visiting lecturer at the University of California in Berkeley. Anyway, at that time he was another rocking poet in the life-style-manner of Dylan Thomas, although he didn't write anything like that, was more in the agricultural theist mode, shades of Ted Hughes and Theodore Roethke. I hadn't heard of him before he showed up, although he was just a couple years older and a graduate of Queens University Belfast. His old man had been a cattle dealer, just like my Uncle Robin, whom I'd accompanied to various auctions in Co. Antrim, even down to Dublin for the moonlight auction, where all the dealing went down in the wee hours before dawn.

His family farm was near Lough Neagh, not far from Magherafelt, and not more than 25 miles from ours in the Braid Valley... although 25 miles in Ulster in those days could be as remote as the far side of the moon.

We knocked a few back after his reading, which was pretty good. Well, we knocked a lot back, talked the talk. "The Troubles" were just cranking up in Belfast, the Catholics going at the Protestants, and the IRA, once in remission, was blowing up buildings and machine gunning people left and right. The Provos (Provisional IRA), the Protestant paramilitaries like the UDA and the UVF, they were all out and about and up to bloody mischief.

Seamus was distressed about it, said to me, "We have to speak out against this... would you join this group of artists I'm organizing from both sides to speak out?"

Seamus was Catholic and I was supposedly Protestant. Remember, these were still the days when you had to state your religion on your passport.

But I wasn't interested. I had a Canadian wife and children and I had no interest in the misery of the old country. Self-inflicted by romantics and bigots, I felt. Neither my father nor my mother lived there and our Ulster family had evaporated.

I said, "Those people don't want to hear the likes of you and I telling them to desist."

That was that. A group of us were taken by the poet Robin Skelton to a cosy little restaurant downtown called Pablo's—my wife and I, Robin and his wife, somebody else and Seamus—and the booze flowed. Seamus got so hammered he ended up below the table crawling on all fours, bleating like a sheep.

He won the Nobel Prize in 1995. I was surprised because I thought he was dead, had either drank himself to death or had been shot by the paramilitaries. But no, Seamus Heaney had had a very productive career—Professor at Harvard, Professor at Oxford, and had been winning all the prizes poets can win. People were saying he was the greatest poet in the English language since W.B. Yeats. Maybe so, maybe so—I hadn't kept up. I knew he was good, but when I thought Irish, he wasn't on my go-to list. But was any poet on it? Not really. Why drink Jameson if you can drink Bushmills?

William Golding won the Nobel Prize in 1983, based largely on his famous novel *Lord of the Flies*. He spent a week or two as a guest of our department at UVic speaking to students and faculty around 1990... he was around eighty years old then and died three years later, so there was no carousing or late adventure. I had the chance to talk to him a number of times, mostly about cosmology. He was very interested in the science of the stars, and the implications of the latest discoveries.

I'd taught *Lord of the Flies*, and like nearly everyone else, thought it was a very clever reworking the desert island genre—you know, *The Coral Island, Swiss Family Robinson, Robinson Crusoe,* and so on—and reflected the nuclear paranoia that gripped the world after 1945. But the later books... *Pincher Martin?*

Tried it, liked the central image, but no, too cerebral. Same thing with *The Spire*. Etcetera. Anyway, this was all old news, even for him. He was long tired of people masticating on his brilliance. His hair was white, and he wore a cravat, looked like an old English Major furloughed on the Cote d'Azur. Several of us went for lunch with him at a restaurant located in what used to be the English artist Katherine Maltwood's Victoria home. Maltwood had bequeathed the house to the university as an art gallery to house her works, and the university promptly broke the codicil on the grounds that the house was uninsurable as an art gallery, and so it ended up as a restaurant-pub.

This is what happens to those who think they can buy the future, even to an astro-archaelogy artist like Maltwood, the discoverer of the Glastonbury Zodiac.

He ordered a salad. Others were talking at him, especially an annoying middle-aged groupie who sounded like someone from an Agatha Christie novel. When his salad was placed in front of him, his eyes were glazed from the noise, from the droning of the insects, the swarming predators of English Lit. I was sitting directly across from him, noticed there was Ladybug on his salad. Perfect symbolism, I thought. I watched. Did he see it? If so, what would the great author do? Would he eat the Ladybug as a show of power? He was a Nobel Laureate, after all. His eyes were definitely on the salad, although he hadn't picked up his knife and fork. Gee, what a fiasco for the restaurant! If the Pope had been the honored guest, could it have been any worse?

I knew the man who was running the restaurant obliquely, through the eyes of others that I knew. His name was Dominic. French. He arrived in town in a sports car one day and started throwing parties and pretty soon a lot of people wanted to be at them, as if he was some sort of cultural guru who attracted the elite from Paris, New York and Bangkok.

Of course he was just in the tradition of European restaurateurs who established a clientele by first throwing decadent parties, then going into business, something I hadn't quite figured out at the time. But now I was wondering if maybe, just maybe, this fellow Dominic had deliberately put the Ladybug in Golding's salad. Art, you know.

In his novel *The Inheritors* (1955) Golding has the Neanderthals being wiped out by some new arrivals, probably Homo sapiens. The Neanderthals were just too nice. Was Golding nice? Too nice to eat the decor?

Think it was his wife who noticed the bug, raised the alarm. Dominic appeared, whispering apologies in that mixture of amazement and solicitude that denies responsibility while leaving the victim on the list for the guillotine later. Yes, I dramatize. It was funny, although everyone was too polite to laugh.

Best Actor

I'm on stage at the Metro Theatre in Vancouver, in a one man play using tape recorded voices that come through a short-wave radio. Gives the play an avant-garde feel as well as being easy to produce. Full house. Crowd's into it. I'm feeling confident—the previous year I'd won Best Actor and Best Original Play here at the Festival.

Then suddenly there's a terrible pain in my abdomen, drains me like I've been shot, and I drop to my knees, barely able to say my lines. Gall bladder attack. Well, I didn't know that's what it was although the attacks had occurred now and then during the last two years and the doctors were still trying to figure it out.

The audience thinks I'm acting as I crawl across the stage under the barrage of voices and radio noise. Yes, they think I'm acting... the whispers, the moans, the crawl, it's all acting, fits in with the action as far as they're concerned.

The adjudicator—a respected female director from Kelowna—also thinks it's acting. Bad acting. After the show she convenes the casts and crews of the three plays for a quick workshop critique. We're last, and by then the pain is just a low ebb, although I'd rather be somewhere else. Well, my acting... started out well, sir, but then you became melodramatic and silly, and for goodness sake no one could understand what you were saying... you were talking to the stage, not the audience. I was in the front row and even I couldn't understand what you were muttering about. Thank you, lady.

No Best Actor for me this year, 1969. Too inauthentic.

The Lonely Voice

If you write plays, you have to have 'an ear' for dialogue unless your intention is to write in a non-natural way like, say, Beckett, where you seek a symbolic world that neutralizes the vernacular. But writing prose fiction seems to have forgotten that it comes from an oral tradition long before it became a print medium. This is what Frank O'Connor says in his study of the short story, *The Lonely Voice* (1962), that generations of skilful writers after Chekov have removed the sound of a man's voice telling the story.

This certainly made sense to me. You could learn a lot about self-control learning to write in plain language, but the omniscience of the journalistic method was visual rather than oral, mechanized rather than human. "Good writing" couldn't handle the inarticulate voice, the street voice, the rich lore of slang and the poetry of shifting fads and metaphors that slang provides. On the one hand the fiction writer was trying to use a universal voice, a groupthink voice that was institutional, legitimate, followed the laws of grammar while at the same time was supposed to capture the rhythm of character, region and time.

Very difficult. Of course some writers used slang, submerged themselves in regionality, or tried stream of consciousness, which abstracted the narrative. Both these methods limited the audience, just like the algebra of higher mathematics. While regionality is important for the authentication of "identity", it can ghettoize the story if the language is too vernacular. The writer is always, always searching for a balance, a voice that belongs somewhere and everywhere. In his interview with the *Paris Review* (The Art of Fiction, No. 19, 1957), O'Connor tosses off a couple of beautiful anecdotes as examples of his "bare bones" notion of the short story whereby action is reduced to fable:

> I remember a friend of mine who painted in water colors and he was rather shy. He was painting in the city, so he used to get up at six in the morning when there was nobody to observe him and go out and paint. And one day he was going in to work at nine o'clock and he saw a little girl sitting where he had sat, with a can of water and an old stick, pretending to paint a picture—she'd obviously been watching him from an upstairs window.

He uses this as an illustration of the imitative process of art, the Aristotelian method in the madness. Yet, cryptic as this summary is, it has a powerful symbolic aura that reveals much, much more than the simple action of one generation following the other.

His other anecdote might be a fantasy of his own death. A young American woman visits Ireland on the advice of her doctor, meets her husband's family and friends, rejuvenates, and it's only after she returns home that the family learns that the son, her husband, is dead.

Ergo, de te fabula narratur... the story applies to you.

[O'Connor married a young American woman, had a stroke in 1961 while teaching at Stanford]

One of the things I noticed in writing workshops was that even quite well-written stories just didn't hold people's attention, especially when read out loud. Why? Because the narrative was visual, meant for the scanning eye. Some readers would confess, "I just skipped the pages until something pulled me in" or "I just skipped until I found some dialogue". This was a helluva situation, as it suggested that words meant more than "story" and grammar more than reality.

The oral voice is less ambiguous than the written voice, can be more inferential, and for this reason alone can make the narrative much shorter. When I started recording stories, it wasn't long before I abandoned the written text except for notes... key lines, modulation cues, names, that sort of thing. Description disappeared, unless it was natural to the point-of-view. Everything became tighter, much tighter, like poetry. Then, by creating electronic soundscapes, the atmosphere was enhanced, and the art of the story became the art of the sound painting.

This is not to say the written word is a waste of time or anything like that. It's the technique of writing that became decadent and out of step with the electro-mechanical world. Art follows the dominant media of the times and writers were trying to imitate the documentary methods that abandoned the poetry of language in what amounted to the socialism of the soul. Newspapers, then movies. This modernism wasn't all bad in the sense that plain talk was preferable to endless folk clichés and religious poetic riddles. This secularization of the arts was necessary in the culture of rapid scientific advancement, where the eternal opera of the past had mangled all words into an unseemly emotion, regardless of intent.

As Artaud said in his essay *No More Masterpieces* (1938), "We must have done with this idea of masterpieces reserved for the self-styled elite and not understood by the general public; the mind has no such restricted districts as those so often used for clandestine sexual encounters."

Antonin Artaud was a French poet and dramatist who was in revolt against European "psychological" theatre, was essentially trying to find a new way forward in the arts. He was the stammering child of surrealism, and in many ways a proto-Beat, as he investigated magic and primitivism as a revitalizing source of uncontaminated imagery. Artaud wrote the script for Germaine Dulac's 1928 film *The Seashell & the Clergyman*, a work whose surrealist dream narrative influenced the Dali/Bunuel *Un Chien du Andalu* (1929) and later Jean Cocteau's *Orphee* (1950). Artaud's iconoclasm is fully evident as the clergyman crawls through a maze of streets and corridors maddened by his lust for a General's wife, and the deteriorated print versions of this film posted on the Internet in no way diminish the beautiful shadow masochism of the instinctual world as filmed by Germaine Dulac, one of the first female directors.

So perhaps you ask yourself, what is the function of fiction? A remodelling of events to suit your idea of symmetry in the universe? Or is it a means of capturing identity as you pass from childhood belief into adult disbelief? I can only speak for myself. My origin was an utter accident. I was born in Ireland, yet my first memories are of Wales, although Wales could've been anywhere, left no ethnicity in me. My formative years were in Northern Ireland, and certainly made an impression, yet I never believed I was Irish, even later when I was in North America, studied some Irish history and literature. Certainly these studies made me think I should go back, reengage, awaken the real me. But I wasn't convinced, as this was going backwards, and all I could see was forwards, as if I'd been launched into space.

Every time you drop into darkness, you return, file a report.

The Point Of Recognition

There's a theory that posits that dreaming was the first state of consciousness, way back when we were just cellular blobs in the ocean, and that waking consciousness came later when we entered the swamps and began hunting. When the hunter paints on the walls of his cave, is the narrative a record of his kills or a dream of the kills to come? Is fiction mnemonic or is it a guide for things to come?

Does the killer write his memoirs first, commit his crimes later? While this sounds like dyslexia, perhaps the prophetic instinct does drive the action. Consider the paradox of the completed sentence, i.e., if you can't foresee the future, how could you complete a sentence? Some will argue that language is just a chant in real time, the present tense, with no past and no future... yet the structure of the sentence implies all states.

Everyone knows that plots are determinist—what happens at the beginning determines what happens by the end, even if the end predates the beginning. The only thing that can't be predated is the "recognition"—if the reader arrives at the recognition before arriving at the end, then the plot is deemed a failure. Therefore the only thing that matters in narrative is the point of recognition. An outstanding example of this is found in Liam O'Flaherty's *The Sniper*, a story about the Irish Civil War. A gunman, who has been duelling it out with another gunman on the rooftops, eventually tricks his adversary, shoots him, watches him fall into the street... and then, overcome with curiousity, risks his life to find out who the other sniper is, if maybe they fought on the same side at one time. He descends to the street, and then, risking a hail of machine gun fire, runs over and drops beside the corpse.

Then the sniper turned over the dead body and looked into his brother's face.

There can be several points of recognition or the recognition can be submerged like a time-delay fuse, only occur to the reader later. One such narrative might be J.G. Ballard's surrealist story *The Garden of Time*, where the elegant aristocrats Count Axel (a nod here to the Villiers de l'Isle prose poem, *Axel*, 1890... and perhaps Edmund Wilson's famous critical work *Axel's Castle*, 1931) and his harpsichord playing wife live in the sublime beauty of a flower garden within a walled Palladian estate, vaguely European like an oil painting by some forgotten artist.

The peculiar thing is that the flowers are crystalline and when picked, their beauty seems to stall Time for a brief period, a day or two, before they wither and die as real flowers do. As the story unfolds, the garden season is nearly over, and the illusion of security and life everlasting dying with it... for, beyond the walls, a vast Napoleonic army is approaching, only stalled every time a "time flower" is plucked.

When the army finally arrives, the estate is already in ruins, and the horde swarms through the site oblivious to the two stone statues hidden in a thorn grove.

> "As the sun died away behind the house a single ray of light glanced through a shattered cornice and struck the rose, reflected off the whorl of petals on to the statues, lighting up the gray stone so that for a fleeting moment it was indistinguishable from the long-vanished flesh of the statues' originals."

Ballard's story *Thirteen To Centaurus* starts with a recognition by the sixteen year old protagonist but isn't shared with the reader, until later. In the bigger scheme of things, it's only a partial recognition, doesn't impair the ending. The pivot recognition comes when you learn that the starship—which has been journeying towards its interstellar destination for generations—is in fact a flight simulator and has never left Earth. But the final recognition is that the crew knows it and has been playing along with the charade.

Or, on the other side of the aesthetic plateau, there is Alice Munro's dense, meandering parable *Material* wherein a woman compares her first marriage to her second, the first to a philandering academic writer, the second to a placid Romanian engineer. There's a certain malevolent passion in the profile of Hugo the writer, who appears to be the quintessential bullshit Canadian small press hustler, yet the story goes into sidebars that don't seem to be relevant to the forward thrust of the reminiscence... until you realize the story within is the "material" for one of Hugo's and that the woman is still in love with him. Mind you, it's the hatred of love, the modern woman's sadomasochism, with its wild resentment within the infatuation that the reader finally comes to understand.

> I found a pen and got the paper in front of me,
> to write my letter, and my hand jumped. I began
> to write short jabbing sentences that I had never
> planned.
> 'This is not enough, Hugo. You think it is, but it
> isn't. You are mistaken, Hugo.'
> That is not an argument to send through the mail.
> I do blame them. I envy and despise.

No plot, just the narrative and the point of recognition. And the reader is left to gloat or feel ill.

A Hundred Poets And One Gentleman

> "We have to articulate ourselves... otherwise we would be cows in the field" (Werner Herzog, talking about the disaster of making his film *Fitzcarraldo*)

Writing poetry is like giving a blood sample—it doesn't make any sense when you first look at it, although it contains your secret code. A hundred years ago, after it went free verse and the rules were abandoned in favor of random thought in pursuit of prophecy, it was a revolt against the institutional narratives and the photography of the machine.

Speaking in tongues became fashionable again, was seen as a desirable alternative to news-speak. After all, what were the great religious texts of the world but messages delivered in dream? Therefore it was wise to seek incoherence, make the reader come to the poet rather than the poet coming to the reader.

Rhyme—who needs it? Rhyme was for memory and singers. The printed page made poetry visual, just like a monastic text or an engraved tombstone. Paper could fly. You could be cloned, appear in many places at once, be a shaman, wear a cloak... or simply be a book.

While money was necessary, disciples were more necessary—even Charles Manson knew that.

> It is my hope and dream
> To hook up through the satellites
> With everyone that's in the Family
> Red and Blue, Green, Gold and Yellow
> All the girls that are in jail with me
> That gave their lives, took their lives Gave their
> lives again
> This is on the other side of the noose
> That hangs in the sky
> Where the infinite consciousness
> Within all living things cry
> Sometimes you can just hang there and fly

(from *Rags, This is a Letter to You*—Charles Manson)

The shocking thing about Manson is that one writing workshop would either kill his talent or make him a professional. The question is, would anyone pay attention to any of his writing if he was just another teenager? He's like documentary photography—can you separate the art from the accident of history? We all know about his desire to be a pop star, and the demo recordings he did with the Beach Boys, so you have to wonder what the difference is between Manson and, say, Jim Morrison, another drifter who wrote poetry, and who was actually able to become a successful recording star. The irony is, fame killed him, whereas Manson's fame just allowed him to live longer than he should've.

Morrison was educated, intellectual, was mannered in his approach to poetry. Where Manson was a primitive, Morrison used the distempered stream-of-vomit method of the Beats, wrote like a movie, blinked like a camera shutter. The images are nuanced, scripted for effect, whereas Manson is just memory rolled out like blacktop, the good, the bad, the ugly, the cloven tongue of poverty and desire.

Perhaps the comparison is obscene, but then, isn't America full of just such exciting obscenity, churches and penitentiaries, and the highways that run between?

> Trade routes
> guidelines
> the Vikings & explorers
> discoverers
> the unconscious
> a map of the states
> the blue hiways
> beauty of a map
> hidden connections
> fast trampled forest
> madness in a whisper
> neon crackle
> the hiss of tires
> a city growls
> rich, vast & sullen
> like a slow monster
> come to fat
> & die

(from *LAMERICA*—Jim Morrison)

Nothing special here... could be any one of thousands of young poets doing Ferlinghetti or Ginsberg or Rimbaud. You could write a thesis on Morrison without even leaving the library. But with Manson, there is no obvious influence, except basic pop culture. It's raw trauma, direct to Rorschach metaphor:

> I was in the back of this horse-drawn wagon
> Some kids had a bucket over my head
> They were poundin' on this bucket
> The people drivin' the wagon (Uncle Jess)
> Looked over the seat, down at me
> And told me to "Shut up the racket"
> Then I was in a cabin once
> A ghost with no head came to me
> With a long butcher knife
> Scared my mother
> She put that fear off on me

(from *First Recollection*—Charles Manson)

Poor Charles, you think. That "bucket over the head" changed him forever, and when he had the visitation from the headless ghost with the "long butcher knife", well, he was just a sleeper for the Devil, ready to to activated when needed.

Morrison is a commercial for atrocity—he fantasizes about murder and incest (*The End*), pisses on carpets, exhibits his genital witchcraft to thousands, yet no one is absolutely certain whether he did any of this or not. Enough people say he did. He was like an ape on holiday who puts everything unlabeled in his mouth, gets sick, ends up making a mess any old place, somebody's bed, somebody's room, on-stage, off-stage... it's all a jungle. Shock theatre? Artaud? It was the style in those days, all that built-up repression from the old folks, and the need to break on through to the other side. If it wasn't that, then he was an anal expressive fuckup.

But Charles Manson went further. We know Manson and the Family committed the hideous Tate-LaBianca murders and wrote about it on the walls of the houses that became death chambers as if Manson was directing a "Happening" in some trendy L.A. art galley.

They say it was all part of a prophecy Manson divined from listening to the Beatles "Helter Skelter", although you'd be hard pressed to find anything about murder in those lyrics, except perhaps the emotion with which they are sung.

Interestingly, Jim Morrison later wrote this:

> When play dies it becomes the Game.
> When sex dies it becomes Climax.
> All games contain the idea of death.

This is from *The Lords and the New Creatures*, a collection he published in 1971. The Tate-LaBianca murders occurred August 8 and 9 in 1969. Morrison continues:

> It takes large murder to turn rocks in the shade
> and expose strange worms beneath. The lives
> of our discontented madmen are revealed.
>
> Camera, as all-seeing god, satisfies our long-
> ing for omniscience. To spy on others from this
> height and angle, pedestrians pass in and out of
> our lens like rare aquatic insects.

Life and death as a movie? Or the view from the pop star's stage? While Death is a common subject for all poets, it's the infantile response that Manson and Morrison share, the need for a grand exhibitionist statement. The poet is his own hero, madness his goal. The need to desecrate and shock is paramount and, if possible, dissemble the scaffolding of civilization. While Manson was a natural politician and manipulator, Morrison never fully evolved from childhood. He was a black soul, a drunk, and a bully when really drunk or hungover. His sense of theatre, once elegant, became violent and fascist. He was lazy, avoided work, embraced dream, and when the dream failed, he fell fast and hard. Manson was also violent and fascist, led a harem, called it a commune. He played at madness too but despite the murder and the ugly theatre, he was never mad, just a dangerous idiot with a cast of idiots.

Both poets were vandals in a psychosexual manner, and both went out big in the public eye. But without the Doors, without the rock & roll chorus, would anyone have paid any attention to Morrison's poetry? Doubtful. The Doors gave him a theatre. And Charles Manson... without murder, would he have any stature as a poet? No. Yet, such is the world, he probably has more readers these days than a Pulitzer Prize winner.

Writing is a mask. Even Mishima, who ended his life in a staged atrocity, knew this, made it the title of one of the more interesting "Beat" novels, *Confessions of A Mask*. Writing is a manipulation of the personality, a revision of the facts, an act of fiction even when you think it isn't. Memory plays a large part in this process, even when it's near-field, part of the existential *now*. Language is just a metaphor, whether it's a picture on the wall or some writing on a scroll. There's a gap between the world as we know it and the world as we express it. Even our documentary machines can't quite capture it without a sense of latency, a fractal deficiency in the calculus. We're forever trapped between the infinite and the finite like some particle in the lens of reality.

Big thoughts as I remember some of these poets, some of them swine, uptight, drunken Hydes besotted with their own vanity, and others, careless desperados just trying to get by, neither looking for nor demanding attention. Unfortunately the Hydes stick in the memory more than the others, regardless of talent, their special codes and grandiose perspectives. Some were comedians, although comedy tends to debase poetry, makes it doggerel. Some were politicians, mostly sneering moralists who used poetry as a call to judgment. But most were tragedians, diving into the darkness of the soul... or something. Alcohol had a lot to do with it, made them black... although they—well, all of us— said it was the blackness that made them alcoholic.

Some males used poetry as a life-style, as a means of picking up chicks. A typical English Department in a typical North American university or college always has a couple of poets on staff whether they teach writing or not because, hmm, it's a lot easier to write a little bit of free verse than it is to write a novel or that damn Ph.D. thesis, and poetry is always the buzz word for sensitive. Publication can be a bitch, but once you're in, cronyism takes over. It's like a cult—all temples are connected by ley-lines known to the itinerant preacher.

Females were often nervous about gender, saw the art as a preparation for suicide... although this might be the hidden web that captures all who write without rhyme or reason. A lot of men, young and old, go for these temple priestesses. I remember one instructor saying, "It's like having your own translator in bed with you." Sex and the occult, always a potent combo, and any woman who held a crystal ball in one hand and your ass in the other could go far.

Let's name some names.

Stanley. He was a Hyde. Met him at Robin Skelton's, possibly the night of the earthquake that passed below the house like a subway train, rumbled right through, twisted the pictures on the walls and left the huddled groups of intellectuals stone silent, clutching their glasses of wine and dead crackers and cheese, stone silent... until someone laughed uneasily. Stanley wore a Nehru jacket, *passé* by 1970, but that's what he wore. Black hair, black goatee and heavy black glasses. Don't remember anything he said or if I actually talked with him. He was there for the chicks, although I don't think any of them were there for him. He'd just given a reading from his new collection of poetry, a nice looking hardcover published by Sono Nis, who later published a collection of my plays.

The second time we met he lunged at me, took a swing, missed. Guess he didn't like the words that came out of my mouth.

Didn't know what to make of him at the time, but later when I was given his book to review, I knew what his game was. Tight little stanzas, haiku style, poetry for the page, not for the street. Images, often sexualized... and death, stylized. Almost like 'concrete poetry' but not that far detached from academic formalism. Not sure if he'd read the review, had me identified, took the swing, or whether I wrote the review later, took my swing. I was too harsh, wrote like an industrial stapler, had to take him out. Vietnam was still going on but I had no need to talk about Belsen and masturbation and so on, even if he was guilty. Punk academic.

A friend who graduated from Simon Fraser University back then says: "He had an intro for frosh that would get him fired today: he'd wander into the first lecture—big class: hundreds—and start off by noting that yes, he'd put his book on the course… he'd hold it up and say if you buy a copy and come to my office I'll sign it in ink… buy two copies and I'll sign in it blood… buy three and I'll sign it in semen."

George Hitchcock, the San Francisco poet who published the funky poetry quarterly *Kayak* was also a Hyde, went ugly after a few drinks... or a lot of drinks, who knows what it took. He started swearing and cursing at me one night, same venue, same reasons, I guess. Aesthetic discord. He didn't take a swing at me, just went Hyde, got ugly and personal, real schoolyard stuff. I hadn't insulted his poetry or his magazine or his woman, whoever she was. He just started swearing violently and there was still an inch left in the bottle. But these older men, always in a perpetual middle-age crisis, just couldn't keep their guns holstered after a few drinks.

The absolute worst I encountered was the Scottish bard W.S. Graham, someone I neither knew nor had read before he showed up at UVic for a week as a guest of the university—air-fare, accommodation, food and amusement paid for by the university with a generous honorarium to boot. I'd been recording a lot of these poets as they passed through, but I was advised to ask Graham for his permission first, as he was a bit touchy. Touchy? Hostile? Are you kidding? If you looked him in the eye, he went nuts, like a bear with a thyroid problem.

Sidney was at the faculty club, with five or six *literati*, and they were well into the whiskey when I arrived. I sat down, thinking, what am I doing here? I had no interest in playing court. He was another of the many. But the boss was entertaining the guest and one of my pals was there who thought Sidney was a neglected genius and he certainly thought Sid should be recorded on tape.

Some of these poets thought you were stealing their copyright, which was worth millions, sir, millions. Or others like Sidney Graham thought you were stealing their soul, like a jungle poet going voodoo over a photograph. Sir, you will not record me. I forbid it, absolutely, categorically. You may try and kiss my ass but my ass is not for kissing. Sir.

There was a lull as the insolent Club manager, who sometimes doubled behind the bar, refilled the drinks. The boss gave me a nod.

I said, "We would like to record your reading on behalf of our students."

Sidney was hunched over his drink like a pig at the trough, silver hair, pale skin tinted red with boozer fever. He sat up, fixed me with his hostile stare.

"There will be no recording. I forbid it."

"This is not for commercial distribution. You can have a copy."

"No."

Somebody said, "Come on, Sidney, they love you."

Sidney made a dismissive gesture as if to say, of course, but what difference does it make? There will be no electro-mechanical images.

I am Ossian/ I wander far and free/ speak words of pitiless wisdom/ if only to a fucking tree

Such were my thoughts.

"Come on, Sidney, don't be a zuh, zuh, zunt."

Who said that? Me? No, it was the Illustrated Man, a friend of the boss who could get a little strange after a few. These were the days before tattoos became a fad and he had them up and down his arms and legs. Welsh. No Dylan Thomas, just a hack journalist who played the local art scene.

Sidney squirmed, said, "I'm not being a—what did you call me? Whatever it was and it better not be what I think it was... I tell you, there's no value in this for me."

You'd think his recordings were being bootlegged in Russia to hear him go on... that he was Hit Parade material, gold record in outer space class. Anyway, the vulgarity seemed to break the freeze. The Illustrated Man was ganching, stuttering before he could get his sentences going. Loaded. Seems he and Sidney had been drinking together since late morning someplace. They were new buddies... at least for now.

When the boss finished cooling things down, he leaned over to me, said, "Don't worry. Just set up the tape recorder as usual...."

Readings were held in a lecture theatre in the Science Building in those days, a steep room which you could enter at the back on the upper level or down front on the lower. It held a hundred people and more if they sat on the steps or stood up back. It was pretty full. The powers that be had talked it up, did a bit of advertising, and the Illustrated Man did a profile in the newspaper.

I set up the ReVox and was sitting in the front row so I could keep an eye on it. Sid came in the side door with Skelton, had a coffee in one hand and one of his books in the other. A little bit of shake, not much. I wondered if he was straight or if the Glenmoragie was still telling him what to do. Skelton gave him a hyperbolic intro, then sat down. Sid looked around, saw me. No sooner had he set up his reading materials, when he said, "Shut it off."

I made no move.

He was staring at me and murmur passed through the crowd. He said it again, a little louder this time: "I said shut it off."

I thought, I should just shut it off and start it again, he'd be none the wiser, then I realized the audience would laugh, and he would know. Why had I agreed to do this? Why was the university paying this jerk a whole lot of money for this reading which would be forgotten by the next sunrise?

It wasn't much of a reading. What about the poetry? What about it—it made no impression on me, although obviously I wasn't in a receptive mood. He could've been Catullus for all I cared. He also picked up a few more bucks by selling some of his papers to Special Collections. No doubt he needed the money, but really, he could've been a little more generous with his talent if indeed he had as much talent as some said he did. Another poet, another zunt... whatever that is.

Robert Duncan, the Black Mountain poet, was a gentleman, and not just because he wore a cape like Sherlock Holmes. When he came into town—might've been 1971 or 72—the New Zealand poet Mike Doyle brought him around to the house one frosty morning and we sat and talked by the fire. Robert filled me in about the Black Mountain School of poets, which came out of an arts college in North Carolina and where he taught for a while in the fifties at the behest of Robert Creeley. I knew some of these names from my time in graduate school in California—Charles Olson, Robert Creeley, Ed Dorn, Francine du Plessix Gray, and I knew about "projective verse", where the line breaks followed the poet's breathing pattern rather than trying for a rigged metrical pattern.

Robert was from San Francisco and an out and out mystic, raised in the occult from birth, not just another born again New Age Zen Master. He was a very friendly cat, unlike most of the Toms who passed through, completely authentic and at ease with himself... at least, during this visit. His enthusiaism about the poetic method as he knew it was persuasive and by the time he left I was thinking, hell, I should bag drama and fiction, become a poet. Or at least I should incorporate some of these ideas into my own writing. There was no problem about recording his reading—he was only too happy to oblige, as he was fully hip to the importance of the spoken word. The reading was packed, and he delivered. His *My Mother Was A Falconness* was very good, and one of the few poems that left an impression on me for years thereafter (another would be Robin Skelton's *Vancouver Island Night Poem*—and Robin was no projective verse fan). He also read *Often I Am Permitted To Return To A Meadow*, which was a religious vision without seeming religious, an astral landscape that uses both traditional lyricism and a modernist sense of shadow and light.

> Often I am permitted to return to a meadow if it were a scene made-up by the mind, that is not mine, but is a made place, that is mine, it is so near to the heart, an eternal pasture folded in all thought so that there is a hall therein that is a made place, created by light wherefrom the shadows that are forms fall.

I suppose he was an old school American transcendentalist at heart, but he had that San Francisco vibe, like a Zen lighthouse, where you looked West to see the East.

Nixon's Nephew

My wife and I and our two kids camped for a couple of days and nights at the Grand Canyon in our small Boler trailer. February, 1976. Warm during the day, but chilly enough at night to ice up the windows and freeze the puddles in the campground. We weren't far from the edge of the canyon, south side, among the pines. Strange vibe. A mile deep and ten to twenty miles wide in places, and it wasn't easy to sleep, as vertigo kept coming at me like a dangerous Indian spirit.

Second night it was so bad I got up and drank some red wine, dialled through my multi-band radio, picked up a Canadian warship on the short-wave, HMCS *Athabaskan*, out on the Pacific somewhere. Reception was good because we were at 8,000 feet here on the Arizona part of the Colorado plateau. Anyway, it settled me down, hearing this ghost voice from home, even if it was further from home than we were.

The ship and the position "Latitude 41, Longitude 172" was all I could understand, as the operator repeated it several times. There was more but it was lost in the noise.

When I got up in the morning and stepped outside for a piss, shivering in the purple shadows, I saw a big ugly bird sitting on a rock near the canyon rim. A condor. It startled me as it looked like a human, an Indian in a black poncho, then I saw others circling overhead. That was it. We were out of there.

There was a hippy guy hitch-hiking, skinny, wearing beads and a tie-dye below a loose sports jacket and I thought what the hell, pulled over. We didn't have room in the Mustang really, as our son and daughter were sitting in the back, but I hadn't talked to a hip person in weeks, thought we might learn something cool about the area. What a mistake—this guy turned out to be damaged goods, too many drugs or quite possibly too much electro shock treatment. He squeezed in with our kids, who were staring straight ahead, as if they knew already this was a mistake, instant psychic uneasiness.

"Where you headed?" I said as we pulled away from the shoulder.

"Uh, where you going?" he said.

Now I could see his eyes were zombie.

"The next happy campsite," I said.

Left it vague as I was already hedging our bets.

"I need to get to Vegas," he said.

We were heading south, or maybe further east, New Mexico, check out the mystics in Santa Fe.

"I'm Diana," said my wife, trying to cool the tension.

"Carlos," he said.

I laughed, said, "Castenada?"

Castenada was the South American writer who was a big counter culture hit with his books about a Mexican Indian shaman called Don Juan, the first volume alledgedly written as his Master's thesis at UCLA. Fact or fiction, no one seemed to agree. *The Teachings of Don Juan*... I think I actually had the paperback with me.

This "Carlos" didn't laugh. He told us he'd been down in the canyon living in a cave with "a man" who could read minds and he was learning to read himself. His eyes locked onto mine in the rear-view mirror.

So he was doing a Don Juan Mateus trip. Figured.

I said, "An old Indian guy? Havasupai?"

Carlos said, "I project as well."

"Project? Project what?"

He tapped his head.

Now I'm wondering if he's serious or just trying to freak me out. Maybe this fellow is a Manson follower.

"I read somewhere the Havasupai have been living in the Grand Canyon since the Stone Age," I said. "They must have a lot of magic."

"They came from the south," Carlos said. "I could go south. Where you going?"

A shadow crossed the road... another Condor. Bad omen, I thought, as I saw it swoop away over the pines.

We rode in silence for a couple of miles. He reminded me of a store clerk who'd gone derelict, was still wearing some of the same clothes. One day he went out for lunch, dropped some acid, never went back.

We came to a junction where a couple of young Indian women had a table set up, selling beads and jewellry, the silver and turquoise stuff that was all the rage in those days. I knew Diana didn't care for turquoise but I pulled over anyway.

Carlos said, "I really need to get to Vegas, get some money. I'm Nixon's nephew."

I exchanged looks with my wife, said, "This is a good place to catch a ride to Vegas."

We all got out of the car and the kids eagerly followed Diana over to the roadside stall, started checking out the merchandise. Carlos was fidgeting with the sling bag he had over his shoulder and I'm thinking, does he have a gun?

Made some excuses, wished him well, tried to disengage, but he followed after me.

"Listen," he said. "I could pay you. I'm Nixon's nephew, understand?"

"President Nixon?"

"Yeah. That's why I got to get to Vegas."

"You'll get a ride, no problem."

Diana actually bought a blanket and we still have it to this day. Navajo zig zag. We got the kids back into the car and were just ready to drive off when Carlos came over, leaned down.

"I can read minds," he said. "Understand? When I get to Vegas, there's money waiting."

I eased the shift into "Drive", felt the transmission lock in.

It was a little slow, slipping a bit from pulling the trailer, even though we'd had it beefed up during a stopover in Frisco.

"Good luck," I said.

"I don't need luck, man," he said. "I got the numbers: 41... 172."

I smiled as we drove off and my wife sighed in relief. The kids were happy again. But I started thinking about the numbers he said, 41... 172 ... where had I heard those before? A bank account? A lottery ticket?

"Nixon's nephew," said Diana. "He's crazy. Why on earth did you stop for him?"

"I really don't know," I said. "I saw him and just hit the brakes. Maybe I thought I knew him. I don't know."

I kept juggling the numbers until I realized I could make my birthday out of them. My God... he was a mind reader! I was just his freakin' puppet!

Started laughing, and my wife said, "Are you o.k.? Want me to drive?"

Dream Weaver came on the car radio, our daughter's current favorite, and she sang along with the chorus. Seemed appropriate, so I sang too.

That night we camped in a sandy KOA site surrounded by big saguaro cacti. I poured myself a glass of wine and opened my notebook, and saw what I'd written at the Grand Canyon.

Latitude 41, Longitude 172... so that's where I'd heard the numbers before, heard them on the short wave last night, the warship on the Pacific. Mind reader? Was this why I stopped and picked him up? Were the numbers some sort of telepathic code? And who was this guy Carlos who claimed to be Nixon's nephew? "Carlos Nixon"? Nix had resigned in disgrace in 1974 following the Watergate Scandal, and he hated hippies, and the possibility that he had a mind reader hippy family member was too good to be true. Still, it was creepy. The thought came to me that this fellow had maybe spent the night below the Boler and had heard the numbers on the radio when I did. Bloody hell—the very thought gave me vertigo. For all of its natural beauty there's a strange vibe about that canyon, that abyss that's full of birds that look like men and men who look like birds.

Torremolinos

I was sitting in the early morning Costa del Sol sunshine drinking a San Miguel and reading the New York *Herald Tribune* when I learned about the American Airforce bomber crash the previous day in the Med somewhere off Alicante, just north of here.

January 17, 1966, a B-52G carrying four MK-28 hydrogen bombs collides with a refuelling tanker which explodes and both planes disintegrate. One of the nukes drops into the ocean, while three others hit the ground at a place called Palomares and the site is still contaminated from the radioactive impact leakage 50 years later.

I didn't know these details at the time, only that there was one or more nukes in the ocean not very far from where I was sitting. How far? 500 klicks? If there was an explosion, I'd probably survive the blast but the radiation would get me. God almighty, another Cold War fiasco. The atomic submarine the USS *Thresher* had imploded and sunk in the Atlantic not long ago and who knew if it had nukes on board? This was getting ridiculous, the chance of something truly ugly happening was increasing every day, either by accident or Strangelove malfeasance. As I walked back to my apartment, I saw a dead black cat on the road, recently flattened. Poured myself some vino tinto, lit a cigarette, let the ash fall into the wine, wrote a poem called *Alicante* which started *dear dead spanish cat* and went on to say something about B-52s and lost nukes and wondered if the Thresher was playing Bob Dylan on its jukebox went it went down.

Chick in the bar liked it... but I think she just wanted to get my cowboy boots for her boyfriend who was Dutch and didn't speak much English. We all got really drunk, because who knew if there was going to be a tomorrow. But there was and I was really hungover when I went down to the beach and sat on the sand looking at the waves, played some blues harmonica, wrote a postcard to a friend back home, played some more, finished the card: some come to Spain to watch the bullfights and read Hemingway, but *amigo* I came to play the mouth organ.

Tangier

Saw William Burroughs once or twice in Tangier but never talked with him. Both times he came out of an alley from the bathhouse that led into the Zoco Chico where I was sitting having a mint tea outside the Cafe Central. This is not to say he was in the bathhouse but this was the alley he came out of. I might've been sitting with Morris Lurie, the Australian writer, who drew my attention to the man in the suit and fedora, who crossed the square and disappeared into the throng heading for the European sector like a spy in an old movie. Burroughs, a Tangier legend. Certainly Lurie, an Aussie who'd been wintering over here, knew stuff about the old junky. But who knew what stories were true? Was he really into little boys, recruited them for his consciousness experiments? He went to the Amazon, didn't he, hung out with the head hunters, did some serious dope... Burroughs was more notorious than the old satanist, Aleister Crowley.

Lurie said, "Burroughs is a follower of Wilhelm Reich."

Oh yes, I knew a little bit about Reich: the family is the first cell of the fascist society. Came out of the Freud school. An outlaw thinker, no question.

I said, "He thought he was a communist, until they kicked him out."

Lurie chuckled, said, "I don't know much about him except he was into capturing orgone energy. The Yanks put him in jail, didn't believe a word of it. Burroughs is a disciple. Word is he has an Orgone Accumulator."

"Yeah? What does it do?"

"Captures bions, whatever they are. Supposed to cure various sorts of illness. Anyway, the story going around is that Burroughs has one of these chambers or boxes, and he picks up local kids here in the Medina, takes them back to his place in the European sector, makes them sit in the box, then threatens them with a revolver, fires off a shot or two... fear is supposed to release a lot of bions, so when they're going out of their minds, old Burroughs lets them go and jumps in the box, soaks up the lovely bions."

This was wild... but was it true? Burroughs was the infamous junky whose notorious novel *The Naked Lunch* was only recently taken off the banned books list in the UK and North America. Did he shoot his wife between the eyes in New Orleans while messing around with a pistol and trying to do a William Tell? Did he hang out with the headhunters in the Amazon jungle, go cannibal?

Feeding on paranoia—what an idea. Fear as a rejunvenation force. This legitimized all sorts of activity, including war and murder. Imagine fear as a black sun.

In those days I was drawn to all kinds of crazy imagery, thinking that figures of speech could reveal the unexplored regions of the mind. For example, I was writing a really dumb piece that started with the line I have fallen through the crust of the earth many times, etc. It was a hook, sure, but idiotic otherwise. It was the idiot Irish writers like Flann O'Brien and J.P. Donleavy who set me off in this direction. Waste of time but that's what you do when you're still learning. Messing around with words seems more important than the narrative, the nail more important than the hammer.

The line amused Lurie greatly but it wasn't a direction he thought was worth pursuing. He was meat and potatoes, just follow the old narrative, bugger trying to be a scientist with words. He was older than me, had already published a couple of professional stories, one in *Argosy* (I think) about a young fellow who tried to play trumpet, and ended with a great image of him struggling to play a note or even a sound, his face grotesquely inflated with impotence.

He'd worked in advertising, which is where he learned some chops. He introduced me to another Australian who was living in Tangier, a blond guy who was trying to write a novel about young love and homosexual awakening in the dunes in Australia... Jim Anderson, had a law degree and was later to earn some notoriety when he was in London, editing the underground magazine *Oz*. I read some of Jim's novel... it was rough, lots of ragged syntax and unnecessary description, although it did capture Australia for someone like myself who'd never been there. Since it was about sex, I said he should hit the reader right away, quit pussying around, and rewrote the opening scene for him, had the young hero masturbating in front of a vanity mirror. You know, just an example of how to get people's attention, cut to the chase stuff. Jim was scandalized, said you can't do that blah blah... but I knew he liked the possibility. As I said, he got into some trouble over *Oz*, got arrested with some others. What did they do? *Rupert the Bear* porno satire, I think... but I'm not sure.

Either way, Burroughs wouldn't have had a problem with any of this, *Rupert*, masturbation or Russian roulette. When it came to inner space, he was flexible. The artist explorer was entitled to use sensation and outrage, if outrage was sensation and sensation was one path to revelation.

Morris was a friendly guy and we often sat outside the Cafe Central talking about art and writing. He took me to see the Dancing Boy—literally a boy dressed as a girl who danced to live Moroccan music. It was hard core ethnic stuff, what we would call drag queen culture, although it felt sinister to me... at least at first, until the routines became boring. You find it throughout the Arab world, anywhere hashish is smoked. They call it *bacha bazi* in Afghanistan. These "boys for play" typically wear a skirt over loose pants, have bells in their sleeves and conceal their faces as part of the tease.

It was a dangerous place for us to be as Morris was Jewish and while Tangier was generally tolerant, there were some around who weren't. Once, a local hustler sat down beside us—black market dollars, hash, woman, boy, whatever—and in a friendly way asked us where we were from. Australia... Canada... easy.

Then he said, "Jewish?"

Morris laughed uneasily; at the time, I didn't know he was Jewish.

I said no way, I'd never even met a Jew. I was a modern man.

"Me too, mate," said Morris.

We kept in touch for a couple of years, and I read his novel *Rappaport* when it came out. Zany, funny like the *Beano* comic, absurd in the fashion of the times. I thought his story about the trumpet player was better, had more edge. While writing this, I checked the Net, saw that Morris had a successful career, published many novels and stories, even raised a family. Died in 2014.

Tangier was like a sci fi version of the Bible. The sci fi was us, the white Europeans and North Americans, and the Bible was the locals, the Moroccans who lived in the Medina, the women robed in black and the men wearing fez hats and prophet shawls, and even those who wore suits often wore a fez. It was like two thousand years of history at once, where nothing changed except the strangers who passed through like extraterrestrials. The solar wail of the morning and evening prayers passed over the city maze with the hypnotic familiarity of the incoming and the out-going tides. It was forever.

Yes, there was a European sector, like the other half of the bicameral mind. But who instructed whom?

At first it was a trip, later a nightmare. By March it was wet and miserable, and my face was too familiar. You want to be part of the scene? You sink slowly into its misery, unable to remain a watcher, a voyeur, an outsider who steals images, gives nothing back. You make friends, but these friends move along, answering the Draft Board or going to Turkey or deeper into the Magreb or back to England or Sweden or Paris... or just vanish, one day they're buying hash candy in the Medina or some souvenir, the next they're nowhere to seen, leave no message, create no rumour.

Paranoia starts to set in. The hustlers are no longer friendly, just demanding, even threatening. I see this little guy come into the cafe, the swarthy little mute who had his tongue cut out by someone for some unknown reason, maybe he blasphemed the Koran or bad-mouthed the King. He sits down at my table uninvited, grunts like a dog, signals for a glass of mint tea. Of course he has to want something and he does, pulls a comic book novel from his jacket pocket, war action shit, blazing machines guns and hate-filled faces, explosions and aircraft falling from the sky, raw pop art.

But he wasn't trying to sell me the novel or engage in a discussion about a serious graphic narrative; he grunted, flicked his eyes, and I saw a thin slice of *Black Atlas* hash between the pages like a book mark. He grunted, held up five fingers, then three. Eight dirham. I shook my head. He became agitated, thrust the book at me, jabbed free hand, and I noticed he was missing some fingers as well.

"No, man, I don't want it," I said, hoping he would just bugger off.

Looked around, not another hipster in sight. But the locals were picking up on the altercation on this chilly wet day in the Zoco Chico. I got up, headed outside but he followed me, waving a knife, grunting and hissing, all crazy eyes demanding justice. He was a little man but by Allah the knife made him bigger and I backed into the square holding my notebook up as a shield. He sliced at me once, twice, showed his teeth like a dog as the crowd closed in, all these men in jalabas, and I'm thinking if I drop kick the guy with my cowboy boots, will they set upon me or what. Fortunately a couple of men stepped in and led him away, as if he was known to them.

I saw another hustler in the crowd, the guy who wore the leather RAF flight jacket who worked both the European sector and the Medina, uptown and downtown, and he was smiling when he came over.

"What does he want?" he said. "Dollars?"

"Tried to sell me a book," I said.

We started walking towards the alley back to my cold, empty place.

"You read?" he said. "I get you all the books you want—English, French, what you want, I get it, man."

"You want to buy my boots?"

"No problem."

"What's your rate on the dollar?"

He held up some fingers... yep, definitely better than the official rate. Well, ride with the sun or fall fast. We agreed to meet here in the Chico in a couple of days after I made a quick trip to the bank in Gibraltar. There was a Yugoslav freighter leaving Casablanca in a couple of weeks and I meant to be on it.

I had a Penguin copy of Malcom Lowry's *Under the Volcano* (1947), the novel about an alcoholic British Consul drinking and behaving badly in a Mexican town near a couple of volcanos. It was perfect for my purposes. Somebody had divested himself of a kilo of kief, dropped it on the floor of my Medina room, more weed than he wanted or I could possibly smoke during my last couple of weeks in Tangier. The guy was getting out of town, was paranoid about somebody, so here you go, my man, free weed. It was in little packets, 5 dirham hits wrapped neatly in gray merchant paper, easy to slip into your hip pocket. I in turn gave most of it away, but I did save a fat lid and mailed it home inside *Under The Volcano*. How? Just cut out a rectangle, made it into a box, then sandwiched the book between two other paperbacks, bundled them, bought some stamps, mailed it home, Canadian Magazine Post.

Good novel, even if a bit fat. Photos show the mature Lowry as resembling Errol Flynn. He revised *Volcano* for publication in North Vancouver, where he lived during the WW 2 years, which is why some Canadians claim him as one of their own. His second wife says he tried to strangle her a couple of times before he died in England in 1955. Some say it was suicide, some say it was murder.

I knew none of this when I read the novel or even later when I enjoyed John Huston's film version. Lowry was a 'black soul' or what the Irish fondly call 'a desperate man'. In some ways the protagonist Geoffrey Firmin is pathetic, a drunk who revels in playing the victim, yet the portrait is devastating in its poetic honesty and spoke to many of his generation who had either lost faith and the novel confirmed it, or had lost faith and didn't know it until the novel revealed it.

So Lowry was a writer of self-inflicted isolation, a popular destination for writers in the twentieth century when suffering was cult, considered an essential rite of passage. The trauma of modern warfare obviously affected the European mind, although writers like Lowry were part of the Romantic tradition, where beauty killed just as effectively as ugliness.

Dreamless sleep and daylight amnesia seem to be the goal, although boozer fever can produce some crazy dreams, as the Consul's wild rampage on the *Day of the Dead* shows. This character, this cast, cannot be pulled from the imagination completely, so the novel is dressed autobiography, a metafiction (or metafaction) where hindsight instructs the journalist whose only audience is himself.

Interesting narrative, which probably owes something to the montage sequencing of film noir, which was popular in the 40s and 50s. Lowry spent a brief period in Hollywood trying to make a go of it as a screen writer and his second wife—who became his in-house editor—had experience both as an actress and a scriptwriter. I admit I found *Volcano* a bit wordy when I first read it, perhaps missed its clever irony. It's not a book for young men, but it's one young men should read if they live long enough.

In 1965-66, Tangier had a hip American bar called The Lion & Lizard, down on the waterfront near the docks, right on the edge of the Medina. When you stepped inside it could've been a bar in Boston, Chicago or San Francisco, with a tiled floor and a long polished wooden bar where you could stand and drink, look at yourself in the big mirror... or there were the usual rondal tables where you could sit and sip or shoot your Heineken or Jack Daniels. I'm not sure how this worked as alcohol was forbidden in the Koran but Tangier was like a city state, an international town with rules of its own... and I guess money talks.

They played the latest hip music in the Lion & Lizard. It was the first place I ever heard John Hammond, the young white blues singer. As I had a couple of Dylan records with me, they played those occasionally, so you really felt like you were on the Beatnik trail. They had a couple of tables outside on the street, and that was the first place I ever heard the word "hippy". Some guy with long hair and shades was sitting there drinking a beer and I stopped and asked him if he'd seen a guy I knew in Torremolinos, tried to describe him... you know, he's got long hair blah blah... and he laughed, said, "You mean, he's a hippy, man!"

That's exactly what I meant: a hippy.

He jerked his head, indicating a hotel across the street. "Check in there, man—that's where they all stay."

Never did find the guy I was looking for but I found lots of others, some just here for a couple of days before setting off on the Roman march around the Med... Tunisia, Carthage, Egypt, Israel, Palestine, Turkey... or some might swing east to Afghanistan, others south to Marrakesh or even further. Or others just hung around Tangier until the money ran out or the Draft Board called.

Some girls, not many. This was not girl country. Spain was safer, the Civil Guard packed sten guns, and they were everywhere. Here, nobody was a cop or eveyone was a cop, they were hidden and secret, part of the herd.

I'm looking in my notebook, see someone tried to sell me a French .32 Modele 1935 automatic in the Lion & Lizard. Maurice... although I called him Saigon Maurice as he'd supposedly been in the Foreign Legion. Wore a camouflage jacket and jeans. Big, tough, mean, but could pass for a hipster from the Left Bank.

Said, "If you're going east or south, you'll need this."

He popped the clip, which was full, then reloaded.

The only other note I have about this hombre is that he called me a fag when I said I wasn't planning any trips out of town. Guess he needed money fast.

Guess he could call me anything he liked.

Guess I thought I was Jack Kerouac or Jan Cremer, a hitcher on the road to Hell, which was a desirable destination in the 60s. It was a cheap way to get around and always full of possibilities for the young writer. The day after our secret wedding, Diana and I were hitching on the side of the road north of Victoria, intending to head up Island and break the news to the old folks, when a young guy in a shiny blue 1967 Mercury Cougar pulled over. He looked a bit mulatto, was very friendly. Joseph, he said. He was a type-setter for the local newspaper, had just done the graveyard shift, putting the morning edition out.

Later he said he'd just gotten divorced, and he'd pulled over because of Diana, not me. He was so forthright, what the hell could I say? I knew the way it was, as it was always easy to get a ride when accompanied by a young good looking gal. In those days the driver was often drinking, radio blasting, regardless of the time of day. Sometimes he might offer you a swig, even drive you to the door.

What Joe offered that day was to show us four acres he'd recently acquired on the Koksilah River just south of Duncan, less than an hour away. A four room shack, a chicken run, a horse corral, a tool shed, all in a recent clearing among the young alders and the mossy maples, now turning yellow and red in the clear Indian Summer weather. Primitive, but hell, we ended up staying a week, drinking beer and wine and skipping rocks on the river... and looking after his rabbit-cat, the most bizarre creature I'd ever clapped eyes on. It was a cross breed, with the face of a cat and the hind end of a rabbit, something I thought was impossible. Joe had just acquired it from some hillbilly Dr. Moreau somewhere in the neighbourhood, thought it was exotic, and left us with the task of feeding it when he was at work.

It was a pathetic thing really, didn't last long, was dead a week or two after we moved on. Otherwise our time at Joe's shack in the woods was an interesting honeymoon, as I spent the solitude writing some essays for $20 a shot, pass guaranteed. Must've written six or seven, history and literature topics, and you'd be surprised by how many of the clients bitched, even when they got an A or a B grade. I could've done better than this blah blah but I just didn't have the time. Let me tell you, it was no way for a writer to make a living, writing term papers and feeding a rabbit-cat.

Still, I used Joe for a character in something I wrote later, can't remember what. He had a couple of horses, rode the trail along the river and in the woods. He was after the simple life, but somehow it seemed messy, divorced so young, his pet doomed. He was an outsider, uneducated, a bit feral, just rolled with the seasons. We ran into him several times over the next few years, always with a new wife, a new property, a new horse... what happened to him? No idea. I suppose I could say he picked up a hitchhiker and they got into some heavy drinking along the way and the spectacular crash we all read about in the newspaper broke his back and he was forced to use a motorized wheelchair thereafter, yet was still able to pick up another wife out there on the highway. Fine. Just as long as she wasn't mine.

I'd been walking all day along the dry, dusty road and no one stopped. I sat down in the ditch in the shade of some eucalyptus trees that rattled in the warm air that came off the sparkling ocean just beyond the ruined casa below. I looked behind me, across the vega towards the hard jagged mountains a few miles distant, although of course in Spain they thought in kilometers, bagged the milia years ago. There was a mountain town, like something out of a children's book, gleaming white towers and walls bubbling in the haze, quite possibly a mirage. No, I wouldn't change course, try for it before nightfall. If I had to sleep under the stars, so be it.

It sounded like a lawn mower but it was one of those three wheeler Piaggio trike vans, the sort you saw all over Europe in those days, the poor man's delivery unit. It came around the corner, then pulled up and I saw the guy beckoning to me, a fat man with a pencil moustache, like somebody from a circus. There certainly wasn't much room, even when I put my bag in the back, as the handlebars extended across the tiny cab, making it easy for him to rub his elbow in my crotch.

At first I thought it was accidental, but the further we went, him panting and grunting, shifting gears and weaving back and forth across the road like a chimp in heat, I knew this couldn't be just the way you drove one of these absurd little vans. He was a beast, a wheezing, grunting sex beast with thick arms and fat hands, and even if my Spanish had been better, a normal conversation would've been impossible. Hitchhiking? This was getting to know the natives? I could've taken a bus, but no, I wanted to be "on the road", and I was very surprised that the road was like this in Spain, as not so long ago they were shooting guys like this... they shot Lorca, didn't they?

This was out and out assault, yet I knew it would be futile to report it, should I get out of this unscathed. The Guardia would just look at me and laugh. Young foreigners on the road were just riff-raff and the smell of onions and garlic proof of nothing at all. Cut your hair, muchacho. Go home.

We went on like this for a mile or two following the coast road until we came to a vineyard and Lorca made a drinking motion with his hand, bottoms up, let's party. We weren't going fast anyway but as he slowed to swing into a lane, I bailed, was able to stay on my feet when I hit the road. He pulled over a few yards further along, nearly tipped the van into the ditch, got out, made an appealing gesture with his hands and his swollen, lizard eyes. He opened the back, pulled out my bag, gestured. Gee, I'd misjudged him—he was just an over-weight gypsy, a lonely guy who worked in a vineyard. But as I lifted my bag, he grabbed me by the back of my neck, hissed, *pendecho*.

I knew what that meant. And I stomped down hard on his foot with my boot and he let go, collapsed backwards yelping. I considered tipping the Piaggio over but no, better to get the hell away, so I sprinted back to the main road, then resumed walking briskly, my kit bag swinging from my shoulder... hup two three four, hup two three four. The light was failing but I could see the Rock of Gibraltar in the red flowing sunset and knew I could reach Algeciras in maybe an hour if my blisters didn't get me or if El fucking Gordo didn't run me down.

Same thing happened in Canada, same sort of situation, standing on the side of the Trans-Canada highway on the British Columbia-Alberta border in the Rockies, beautiful scenery and long-shadow dusk approaching, me thinking am I going to have to sleep under the stars, only this time it won't be warm, could be zero or worse. It was Spring, but Spring at this elevation was still winter after sunset.

A guy in a big sedan pulled over. Tinted glasses, wiry

middle-age. He was going to the Okanagan, which was at least half-way to the coast, and I could always find a bus station to sit in, wait until dawn. Seemed friendly, if a bit weird, asked me where I'd been, where I was headed... the usual. Then he started talking about his "chum" and how his chum had died fighting a forest fire last year or the year before. "Chum"—I knew what chum was. Chum was code.

The thing about hitching is whenever you ride in the cab with a stranger who doesn't seem quite right you start to consider escape or assess your chances in a rumble. I had a small hunting knife but it was in my bag which was on the back seat and I wasn't really a knife guy anyway, never wanted to believe I'd be pushed to a point where I had to kill somebody. Naive? Guess so, especially in light of all the killing that was going on over the horizon in Vietnam, the blood fever that was spreading everywhere these days. But this gentleman, this lonely stranger in search of love, was he a shallow grave type?

It was a slow awakening for me, these biometric games where you realize you're being hunted, where men aren't interested in your conversation but your body. First it was amusing, these free beers that arrived at your table from so and so sitting back there—the waiter jerks his head—and you think who do I know? Sometimes you saw no one, just the crowd... others, a smiling man, an older man, a man who's been watching you, raises his glass, cheers young fella, why don't you join me? And you just look away, embarrassed maybe, or just cynical, free is free, thanks, man.

And when you're in a car, speeding down the highway at night, and the situation is ambiguous, when the undeclared game is underway—you both need something—you're wondering how far you can travel before the paranoia becomes insufferable. Who has the upper hand? How desperate is the driver? You?

So the conversation is classic drama, full of feints and retreats, banality and sub-text.

"You ever do any hunting?"

"Sure." (lie)

"Lots of game in the Monashees. You know the Monashees?"

"Heard of them." (lie)

"My chum and I liked to go up there, lots of game. Couple of lakes too. You fish?"

"No."

"Got a rifle?"

"Not anymore." (double lie)

After a while he says, "I should be turning off here, but it's not a good place to be stuck. Be difficult to get a ride this time of night."

He's right about that.

"Tell you what, I could go as far as Salmon Arm...."

So then you're thinking maybe he's not so bad. When he drops you off at the bus station, he makes one last pitch.

"Thinking of going up to the cabin. You interested?"

The moon is up, almost full, and a cortege of Canada geese fly over, honking, heading home to the wildnerness. You, you can almost feel it, the coast, the Island. Home.

There's resentment in his look, as if he's been taken for a ride, no *quid pro quo*, as if a point of honour has been broken, no *quid pro quo*. He pulls away from the kerb quickly, like an angry teenager. Christ, what's with these people? You look around. The town is quiet, it's around 10 pm and it's a stretch before dawn, and there are plenty of trucks out there on the highway hauling for the coast. But that's it, you think, no more damn hitch-hiking.

My wife and I ran out of gas in the Yucatan on our way to see some pyramids in the jungle. Because I was used to renting cars with a full tank, I assumed the gas needle was working in a Mexican reverse measurement... complete and utter idiocy on my part. So in other words the tank was almost empty when we started out, and when I realized my mistake, I didn't turn around, just kept going, assuming there'd be a gas station around the next bend. Stupid? Certainly was. I was a bit hungover from the previous evening, but really, my utter lack of preparation for this expedition was criminal.

He could see the white worm floating at the bottom, its corrugated body curved in a half-circle as if asleep. It was like sex, he found himself trembling as she pushed the bottle against his lips. One gulp, then another, and his face twisted as he groaned....

We had to hitch-hike a hundred klicks to get some gas, and it was quite an adventure, and five years later I used the experience to base a story on called *The Worm* (*Gusano*), published in the collection *Unauthorized Landings* (1996), now out-of-print (the story of my life). The true stuff was the two Maya twins or near-twins who picked us up in their rusting Chevy:

> "They watched him approach, the one lounging against the fender with his arms crossed while the other stood by, smoking a cigarette. They looked vaguely familiar, so maybe they were brothers. Short, black greased hair, definitely indigenous. Both wore black cowboy boots, the shanks concealed below the cuffs of their trousers, although the sharper one also had a black leather belt with silver diamond studs, a touch of machismo. The one leaning against the car touched the stems of his frameless glasses as if he was getting Reg into focus. He's the driver, Reg thought."

It seemed to take forever to get back to the outskirts of Cancun—the industrial, native periphery—as they kept stopping to pick up and drop off different Mexican workers along the way. Guess it was an illegal taxi service. I know it cost me. Some of the detours had sociological interest, sometimes funny, sometimes unnerving. The upshot was that we lost three hours, and by the time we got back to the Nissan rental and gassed up again, it was the afternoon and a hundred sweating degrees by the time we made the pyramids.

Strange and fascinating, I suppose. But there's a monotony to bright-light weather and equidistant days.

PART TWO:

The Trials

When I started my website *Culture Court* in 1998 one of its first inspirations was to use the "trial narrative" as a way of criticizing books, films, albums, art and so on. The first one to go on trial was the popular TV soap *The Young & the Restless.* The idea was to take some of the weight out of the high culture essay by dramatizing the narrative instead; quite possibly I fell into this template from my time writing stage and radio scripts.

Camille Paglia: Sex & Violence, or Nature & Art

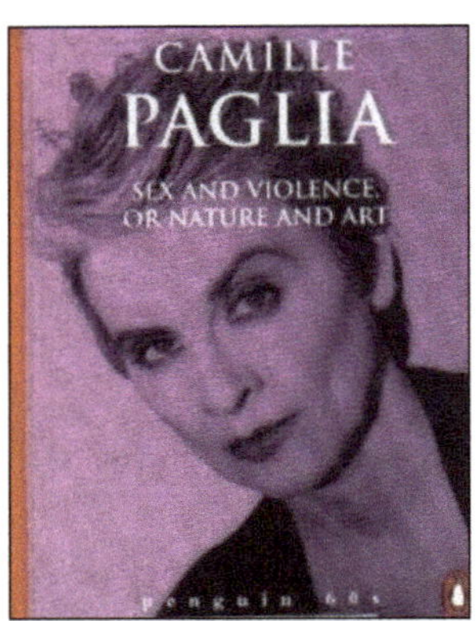

"I agree with Sade that we have the right to thwart nature's procreative compulsions, through sodomy or abortion."
"Nature is a Darwinian spectacle of the eaters and the eaten.... Man justifiably fears being devoured by woman, who is nature's proxy."
"...male homosexuals of every social class have preserved the cult of the masculine, which will never lose its aesthetic legitimacy."
"Man is a fetishist. Without his fetish, woman will just gobble him up."
"Men, bonding together, invented culture as a defense against female nature. Sky-cult was the most sophisticated step in this process, for its switch of the creative locus from earth to sky is a shift from belly-magic to head-magic. And from this defensive head-magic has come the spectacular glory of male civilization, which has lifted woman with it."
"I contend that the pre-menstrual woman incited to snappishness or rage is hearing signals from the reptilian brain."
"The femme fatale is one of the most mesmerizing of sexual personae."
"spiritual castration is the danger every man runs in intercourse with a woman."
"Woman is literally the occult, which means 'the hidden'."

"The Third Hand of Love"

Scene: a jetliner somewhere over the Gulf of Mexico. Cicero and Iago on their way to a convention in Cancun. Re: *Pornography & the Law.*

Cicero: Finished it?

Iago closes the small "Penguin 60s" paperback, stares blankly at the in-flight movie (*Armageddon*, star. Bruce Willis) in the overhead monitor.

Iago: My ears are popping.

Cicero: We're descending.

Iago: This woman Paglia is a speaker at the Convention? Think I'll stay in the bar.

Cicero: That bad, eh. Is it the writing... or the ideology?

Iago: Too many short sentences.

Cicero: Maybe. She writes in maxims, so...

Iago: Enough to make me take up smoking again. Poetry workshop cadet who took her astralizing too seriously, thought it had the deductive power of logical reasoning. Too many birth control pills, man.

Cicero: Camille Paglia is a self-professed lesbian.

Iago: What did I just say?

Cicero: Aahh... someone who takes too many birth control pills becomes a lesbian?

Iago: Her ideology is nonsense. It's all a transparent argument to justify deviant behaviour. Like the lady wants to make lesbianism orthodox.

Cicero: Well she states categorically that she takes the point-of-view of the Marquis de Sade.

Iago: And that is?

Cicero: Sex, violence, lust, sodomy, bondage, cruelty, whatever, is a revolution against Nature and the means by which Art is created.

Iago: So that makes homosexuality A-ok with her, right?

Both contemplate the overhead monitor but who can say if they are watching the movie or not.

Armageddon: Bruce Willis is chasing the young roughneck (who has been screwing his daughter) around a south seas oil rig, firing reckless rounds from a pump-action shotgun into the machinery....

Cicero: Ever make it with a lesbian, Iago?

Iago: (mutters) My first wife.

Cicero: I'm serious.

Iago: Hetero-defect or genetic?

Cicero: Genetic.

Iago: You see, there you go... this is the kind of shit she writes. "Women have no problem to solve by sex. Physically and psychologically, they are serenely self-contained." Are these the words of a lesbian chauvinist or what?

Cicero: My dear Iago, if you'd read this book with an open mind you'd have seen that Paglia is quite sympathetic to men, not at all like some of the little ideologues who are paralyzing bureaucracies everywhere these days.

Iago: You mean homosexual men, don't you? "Male homosexuality may be the most valorous of attempts to evade the femme fatale and to defeat nature," she proclaims. Take this statement at face value: homosexuality is a chosen life-style, not what the liberal leftists say, that is, a genetic *fait accompli.*

Cicero: I always knew you were a member of the Christian Right.

Iago: Her ideas are full of contradiction.

Cicero: No... I think she distinguishes between evolution and free will.

Iago: Whole argument's a rationalization for the Black and Decker boots and whips scene. She quotes Nietzsche the good old proto-Nazi for Christ's sake: "Almost everything we call 'higher culture' is based on the spiritualization of cruelty."

Cicero: Actually I think one of her big influences is Artaud's *Theatre & Its Double.*

Iago: Yeah, and Artaud was nuts.

Cicero: In the context of its time, *Theatre & Its Double* is a brilliant book. He pretended to be nuts in order to avoid the Nazi occupation of Paris.

Iago: He wasn't pretending.

Cicero: Well let's say he took too much dope. You do see the similarity in style? (no reply) The use of rhetorical maxim, metaphoric generalizations, emotion over logic, cruelty as poetry... her writing is poetry, pure poetry.

Iago: Linguistic noise. And Artaud never claimed Art was homosexual.

Cicero: I don't think Paglia does either.

Iago: Could've fooled me.

Cicero: Even if she does, a case can be made in support. I mean, take Drama: name a playwright who is/was straight... Oscar Wilde? No. Noel Coward? No. Edward Albee, Tennessee Williams, Genet—

Iago: Chekov wasn't queer... or Shaw.

Cicero: Shaw was eunuch, as was Beckett.

Iago: Oh? Who says?

Cicero chokes, has a coughing fit. The Flight Attendant swings past with a bottle of wine, fills their plastic cups. Cicero takes a greedy gulp, calms.

Iago: (to the FA) What is it?

F.A. *Cuvee Speciale*, sir.

She pours seconds. Both men sip.

Iago: Cheap French table wine.

Cicero: (sighs) Not bad, tho'. Cheap French is nearly always better than expensive-anything-else.

Iago: The only thing the French are good at is throwing rocks. Bastille complex.

Cicero: Not as good as the Arabs.

Iago: French think they invented Art.

Cicero: Sure, Iago... and we know Art is Greco-Italian.

Iago: Yeah. So what's an Italian chick like Camille Paglia doing playing at Lucretia Borgia?

Cicero: She's a dyke vamp, man. *Femme fatale.*

Iago: Right. (looking at the book cover) This a recent photo?

Cicero: Doubt it. Interesting woman, eh. (Iago hisses dismissively) You'll get to see her in the flesh at the Convention. (adds) Maybe you'd like to ask her a couple of questions....

Iago: Expert on porno, is she... I did notice, Cicero, that she conveniently passed over the issue of pedophilia. *Femme fatale, homme fatale*... but no *enfant fatale*.

Cicero: (frowns) She touches on it, but....

Iago: (reads) "I will speak at length of the beautiful boy, one of the west's most stunning sexual personae." She doesn't. She avoids it.

Cicero: Talks about the male hustler.

Iago: Kids, man. Kids. She avoids the subject. Why? 'cause it damages her quest for a homosexual respectability.

Cicero: As a disciple of the Marquis de Sade, I think we can assume pedophilia is part of her equation, part of the amorality of Art.

Iago: And you're cool with that?

Cicero: Just because I see merit in her book doesn't mean I put on a leather mask and prowl the parks at night.

Iago: It's the school yards I'm worried about. (nods towards the window) Still over the Gulf?

Cicero: (looks out) Solid cover. Beautiful... cloud cities.

Iago: Know what Orson Welles said about flying? "There are only two emotions: total boredom or total fear".

Cicero: Very good. Drink more wine.

Iago: I hear Mexican wines are lousy.

Cicero: Couple from the Baja that are alright... but hey, this is Cancun we're going to. It's an international resort. They have everything.

Iago sips his wine, watches the monitor.

Armageddon: Willis and his hand-picked roughnecks are undergoing training to be astronauts. As is usual in this sort of film, all is buffoonery and dumb wisecracks (if you have the headphones on to hear it). Etc.

Iago: (staring) What is this bullshit?

Cicero: Camille Paglia would say it's a mondo male driven by his mondo dick into realizing his mondo artistic self in a Sky-Cult.

Iago: Christ, you could be talking about Clinton.

Cicero: Think he'll be found guilty?

Iago: Only if Monica testifies.

Cicero: Know what Paglia said about Monica Lewinsky? Because of her "slack jaw and doe-eyes" she was perfect for giving head.

Iago: Where'd she say that?

Cicero: A column she has in *Salon*. I'm quoting from memory but that's more or less what she said.

Iago: Slack jaw, doe-eyes.

Cicero: You don't understand Clinton, do you....

Iago: What's to understand? He's a party boy who balled his way into the Presidency.

Cicero: The Clinton male figure has been a long time coming. It's like, say, Henry Miller becoming President. The sensualist hipster. The guy who didn't fight World War II.

Iago: Clinton skipped Nam.

Cicero: Exactly. Dresses like a Republican but carries on like a hippy.

Iago: The kid who killed Versace... where is he now that we need him?

Cicero: Very funny. So when are you going to put the *Star Report* on trial?

Iago: Isn't literature.

Cicero: It's bloody subversive is what it is. Far more dangerous than Paglia's little book.

Iago: I admit it is the major publication of 1998.

Cicero: But is it Art?

Iago: Might as well ask is *Hustler Magazine* art, Larry Flint an artist.

Cicero: You could ask Camille that very question. Her column for *Salon* is interactive.

Iago: Gotta be kidding.

Cicero: *www.salonmagazine.com*. Try it. She's the Dear Abby of the chic electro-surf crowd.

Iago: Tell me you're not one of them, Cicero.

Armageddon scene: Willis and his squad of clowns have landed on the rogue asteroid that is on a collision course with Earth. Visuals of the shuttle are reminiscent of an early Buck Rogers crash landing. Somebody dies but no one sexy. They commence drilling a shaft for the nuke that will disintegrate the asteroid and save human civilization.

The Asian passenger across the aisle is mesmerized.

Cicero: You must admit her analysis of the 'eye' and the role of the visual sensibility in western culture is pretty good.

Iago: All I remember is that she said a man's penis is like an eye.

Cicero: Or a third hand.

Iago: See? Masturbation. Pure queer methodology... a third hand.

Cicero: The third hand of love.

Iago: I sense a lack of orgasm here. Like D.H. Lawrence, there's a feeling of missed ecstacy behind the language.

Cicero: Really? I agree about Lawrence, but surely you will admit that the notion of a female orgasm is hypothetical at best.

Iago: Certainly isn't necessary for conception.

Cicero: (quotes) "The eye is the avenue of Eros...."

Iago: Crap. Smell, maybe. Paglia's generalizations about History, these, these sweeping metaphors and maxims as you call them have the facile transparency of images lifted from childrens' encylopaedias. Her notion of History is superficial, her sociology bogus, her anthropology baked. Does she support argument with fact? Does she?

Cicero: Instinct, Iago.

Iago: Instinct ballocks. Listen to this: "Lust and aggression are fused in male hormones. Anyone who doubts this has probably never spent much time around horses. Stallions are so dangerous they must be caged in barred stalls; once gelded, they are docile enough to serve as children's mounts...." What has a horse gotta do with a human being? Is this best she can do?

Cicero: Makes perfect sense to me.

Iago: She has tenure at a university?

Cicero: Not one I've ever heard of, must admit.

Iago: Only credentials you need today are a big mouth and a jar of vasoline.

Cicero: Hey, when we get back home, why don't you take it to the DA, see if you want to put it on trial.... Of course, you'd have to read the whole book....

Iago: This isn't the full Monty?

Cicero: Just Chapter 1. The big book is called *Sexual Personae: Art and Decadence from Nefertiti to Emily Dickinson.*

Iago: (groans) Emily Dickinson, epitaphs for tombstones.

Cicero: Yes, tombstones. Think about it—could be yours, Iago.

Iago: (reflects) I like little books.

Cicero: Yes. Ones that fit easily in a hip pocket.

Iago: This one's a pain in the ass.

Cicero: Pain in the ass is often a requisite for brilliance.

Iago: Bloody hell... what am I doing sitting on this plane next to you?

Cicero: Expanding your mind, dear public prosecutor.

Iago: Free trip, Cancun, not worth it.

Armageddon: Willis has decided to sacrifice himself and remain behind on the asteroid, detonate the nuke by hand. His daughter stands tearfully in the NASA command centre as the grizzled Willis says his goodbyes. One suspects there is more going on between this young nymph and Willis than meets the eye...

The Asian passenger is leaning forward in his seat.

Iago: Is Bruce Willis a *homme fatale?*

Cicero: They say his core fan club is gay.

Iago: Is this movie Art?

Cicero: Meets Paglia's criteria: marginal plot, dialogue, lots of spectacle.

The FAs are cruising the aisle, checking seat belts. The middle-aged Asian male has lit up a cigarette, presumably in anticipation of the big explosion and Willis' annihilation—or a crash landing on the Yucatan peninsula.

Iago: (to the Asian) See that sign, fella? "No Smoking".

Asian: You talk filth.

Iago: You nuts? This is a goddamn airplane, so no smoking!

FA arrives, intervenes.

FA: Sir, please put out that cigarette.

Asian: (jabbing his lit cig towards Iago) He and his buddy talk filth!

Iago and Cicero exchange looks, then fake innocence by watching the movie.

Armageddon: Willis hits the button. Montage of explosion: shrapnel hits the Earth, tidal waves, cities ex/imploding, debris spreading throughout the solar system, etc. But in all, it's a minor incident and the world survives. Meanwhile the shuttle lands with the surviving roughneck-astros to a heroes' welcome. Blow jobs all round.

The Asian man takes a final drag on his cigarette, pinches it out.

Asian: (to FA) Good movie.

FA: (coldly) Thank you, sir.

B. Traven is one of those writers whose own story is the equal or better than any of those he wrote. His best known novel is The Treasure of the Sierra Madre *(1927) which was made into the internationally successful film of the same name by John Huston in 1948, and is the Traven work that most people will know. Most of his writing is set in Mexico, and shows a deep knowledge of that country and its Indian culture. But who was Traven? German, most likely, but as he hid behind several aliases—Traven, Marut, Torsvan, Croves, Feige—his real identity remains moot. Like Shakespeare, he fictionalized himself into a cult.*

But is he really worthy? Iago and Cicero take him to court to find out.

B. Traven: *The Bridge In The Jungle*

Hill & Wang 1967 Knopf 1938

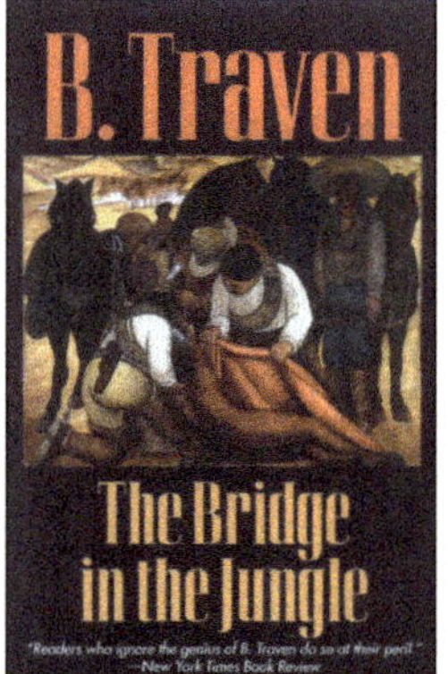

Charges: technical incompetence; gross sentimentality

Bench: Judge Reader presiding

Prosecution: Iago

Defense: Cicero

Synopsis: The action is probably somewhere in the jungle of the Aztec-Mayan triangle, in Mexico's Chiapas State, during the late twenties or early thirties, although the author leaves time and place largely generic. Gales—a recurrent Traven hero—is on an alligator hunting mission, although we never see any hunting or gators as he becomes distracted by a local tragedy when staying with a fellow American called Sleigh in a remote Indian village.

In the opening scene, Gales is ambushed by Sleigh at a water-hole, disarmed as a precaution, then abandoned only to encounter Sleigh sometime later in another part of the jungle. Sleigh has "gone native", taken a young Indian woman as a wife, and is living in a jacale in a small village beside a big bridge that an American oil company built to span the gorge near their drilling operations. He invites Gales to hang out with him, and together they will go hunting alligators.

The story can be reduced to a simple dialectic: a party which becomes a funeral which becomes a party again. The village pump-master has decided to throw a party, and the peasants roll in from the neighboring villages. With no electricity and few lamps, a bridge with no railings would be a dangerous crossing in the tropical darkness except for the agile moccasin-footed Indians... yet the bridge does bring tragedy.

The young son of the fiddler disappears early in the festivities and when his body is found in the river below, the cause of his accident is easily identified with his new shoes, a gift from his older brother Manuel, a visiting oil worker from Texas. The search is hampered by the darkness of a starless night until a consecrated candle is used in a peculiar, primitivistic ritual. Repeated dives by young men, even draggings by a hook suspended from the bridge, fail to realize the body until a "holy" candle is rigged to a board and floated into the pool below the pilings.

The triumph of superstition? Gales repeats the incident with controlled disbelief and later struggles to comprehend what has happened in a conversation with Sleigh. Sleigh, of course, has long ago blended with the supernatural predispositions of the Indians whose fatalistic view of life and death is still largely rooted in a pre-Christian mythology. The party finds a rebirth and new energy in the "wake" and subsequent funeral procession. As the long night gives way to the dawn, more people arrive, drawn by news of the tragedy. Women console the bereaved mother with flowers, paper crowns, weeping, while the men smoke and drink mescal. The procession to the cemetery at a neighboring village is like a carnival, replete with dancing, the latest music (*Ain't Gonna Rain No More*) and drunken revelry.

The school teacher is called upon to say the final words but, dazed and fearful, ludicrously falls into the grave. The dead boy's mother throws herself on the coffin while people stumble over the remains of the dead, their bones expelled from their shallow graves by the action of the merciless sun and the scavengers of the jungle. Gales, confused by the grotesquery, yet moved by the simple honesty of the emotion, reverts to his (by now) familiar philosophic pondering. "Man comes, man goes, the jungle stays on." In the end, a story that started with a stick-up closes with "yes we have no bananas today", Traven's bitter refrain on the folly of human government and the latest victims of civilization.

Prosecution: What we have here, your honour, is a short story padded into novel length by the strident beer hall rantings of *Herr* Traven, a.k.a. Marut, Torsvan, Croves, Feige, *et. al.* "How insignificant is man in the universe," he brays. "What is left of the great Caesar?" Etc etc.

It is said he concealed his true identity because he considered himself a revolutionary, and subject to harassment, arrest, even assassination. What vanity! The man was barely literate, wrote with the technical skill of an amateur. Admittedly there is an occasional flash of charm in his portraits of the Central American Indian, a rustic sense of authenticity even, but the writing is very confused. So what he was German.

He claimed to be an American. Just remember that he was writing at the same time as the great Ernest Hemingway. Mixed tenses, double negatives, authorial intrusions, expositional dialogue, confused narrative... the examples are endless. It's known, for example, that Harlan Ellison had to rewrite many of the stories for the collection *The Man Nobody Knows* because the English was so poor. But let me just draw attention to one early example of Traven's technical incompetence: in the first chapter Gales is ambushed and disarmed by an unnamed gringo, then later he encounters an American called Sleigh, whom he knows from elsewhere.

A hundred and thirty seven pages later Sleigh refers to the water-hole stick-up, and this is first time the reader has this important connection confirmed. Traven isn't good with names. Maybe he had a psychological problem with them as his own deck of aliases suggests, but this doesn't excuse his duty to the reader. He names characters as an afterthought. It's like he's talking about his own family, assumes we already know these people.

The second charge—that of gross sentimentality—is one that maybe fifty, sixty years of hindsight makes possible. We know utopianism is part of the human spirit, but the romantic excesses of this bush rat Traven are ridiculous. Like all the socialist misanthropes of his era, he blames the white industrialist for the corruption of the native, and here it's the almighty gringo with his oil rigs and his death-trap bridge and his lousy shiny shoes.

It's people like Traven who started this reactionary secular morality we call "political correctness", infecting the caucasian intellectual with this absurd global guilt. Did he really believe that the Aztecs and the Mayans lived in some sort of pastoral harmony devoid of political intrigue and murder before the Conquistadors arrived with Christianity? And the American gringo with his machines and exploitative labour practices?

For all his sneering about the insensitivity of the gringo, Traven chose to proselytize through an American protagonist. "What is left of the great Caesar..." Gales ruminates. He could easily have said Montezuma, but that wouldn't have fit the ideological thrust, would it? No. He rails against ethnocentricism with the fervor of an Old Wave Marxist. The kid drowns; he blames the bridge, the shoes, yet he might as well blame the party, the parents, the jungle night.

Judge: Is that it?

Prosecution: It is, your honor. I rest my case.

Defense: Now that my learned friend has finished jeering, let us reflect for a moment on the legacy of one of this century's more interesting authors, B. Traven. He wrote—what? Twelve novels, perhaps thirty stories, some non-fiction. Some of his fiction is very well-known—*The Night Visitor, Macario, The Treasure of the Sierra Madre*, for example. The fact that he chose to conceal his identity, and allow his work to speak for itself rather than be confused by the cult of personality is hardly a sign of sentimentality. And the fact that he used the natural cadence of the oral voice to tell his stories rather than the omniscient grammar of an academic robot is hardly a sign of technical incompetence.

The Bridge is very justly recognized as a masterpiece. Using the sympathetic voice of the American adventurer Gales is the perfect POV for describing the subtle but deadly encroachment of industrial imperialism on the simple, isolated world of the Mexican bush peasant. And unlike the older Sleigh, Gales is always forcing the threshold of his naivety, which is exactly what the average reader requires. In the beginning, Gales is shown as a relative innocent (which is why he was easily bushwhacked by the canny Sleigh), but by the end he is a man examining his conscience as a representative of an insensitive European culture driven by New World excess and capitalist predation.

"The more fatalistic I become, the closer I get to

understanding these people," Gales reflects. "They could not bear life were they not all fatalists." The symbolism of the bridge itself is excellent. That we experience it mostly in the concealment of night reinforces its ambiguous significance, brilliantly dramatized by the death of Carlosito, a young Indian boy who loses his balance because he is wearing a pair of unfamiliar shoes. We never see a truck, or a gringo boss, but we are aware that this bridge exists only to help extract oil from the jungle. On one side of the river is the village, on the other the capped wells. Yet this bridge spans not only space but also time, like a link between the pre-Christian past and the post-Christian future. While the body is recovered by a ritual of pagan intervention, the spot is marked by a cross hacked into the centre of bridge.

The prosecution claims weakness of narrative voice through gross sentimentality. Consider this description of the dead boy on display in his mother's hut: "The kid, who had been a very beautiful sight at night, was now an ordinary carcass—a carcass dressed up in a monkey suit. His mouth was green, and matter was running out of his smashed jaw."

Does this sound sentimental to you, your honor? I think not. Nowhere does Traven gloss a description of the unpleasant or disguise his cynicism when discussing the fundamentals of life and death. Nowhere does he spare the Indians from his unflinching observations. He could've romanticized the funeral but he didn't. He could've romanticized his alter-ego Gales but he didn't. And if he was a mere propagandist, he could've had the bridge destroyed... but he didn't.

The prosecution has some hostile remarks about Traven's technical skills as a writer. Mixed tenses, he claims. I see active and passive voices, not ungrammatical switching. Authorial intrusion, he claims. I see interior monologuing, not broken omniscience. I see a master of the oral narrative, regardless of what language he composed in, one who doesn't allow stylistics to get in the way of telling a good story. Ideology? What's an artist without ideology—you might as well say "personality". He wasn't writing anonymous bylines for the newspapers, after all. As in *The Night Visitor*, a jungle narrative by Traven is always a beginning or an end of a hallucination.

Judge: What was Traven—a drug writer?

Defense: (patiently) No, sir. It's a condition, a way of seeing.

Judge: Thank you, Cicero. Let me ask you, though: did you realize right away that the man who disarmed Gales at the water-hole was, in fact, Sleigh?

Defense: It was obvious.

Prosecution: Your honor, we ran a survey, and every reader we canvassed was confused.

Defense: (sotto) Too sophisticated for you, eh.

Judge: I found it to be unclear too, as a matter of fact. However, on the charge of technical incompetence I find there to be enough reasonable doubt to dismiss the charge. And now that our attention has been drawn to the plight of the Chiapas Indian by the masked pipe-smoking "terrorist" Commandante Marcos, maybe now is a good time to take another look at this novel by the enigmatic "B. Traven".

There's some very provocative stuff in there. (reads) "He is the white, who has not been invited to come here, but he has come nevertheless. He is the guilty one. By his blue eyes and by his skin of the pale dead he has brought the wrath of our gods upon us poor people. He is a gringo. He has brought us misfortune and sorrows...." (sighs)

The charge of gross sentimentality is also dismissed.

Prosecution: (stunned) Did we read the same book?

PART THREE:

Crime & The Mysterious

Are you as tired of "mainstream" fiction as I am? Fiction which exalts the routine victories and defeats of an average life in an average setting as being the true marker of culture and civilization?

Blame the Academy.

While this sort of writing isn't without its masterpieces, there's a dictatorship of the middle class at work here, a near religious narcissism that believes you can only be serious if you're cautious, keep your imagination well within the laws of reminiscence.

Of course the beauty of literature is that so many interesting authors are bypassed or ghettoized, limited by national boundaries, language and the law. Acceptable imagery is subject to cultural faddism or, as is often the case, institutional propaganda. Educators make lists, and these "classics" can remain classics for a generation or two while other fictions are lost to the mysticism of the neighbourhood thrift store or a box in the author's basement.

But these distant, orbiting masterpieces are out there, relics of the pulp fiction era when the story became a movie and someone else took the credit or the author wrote so much that his/her best work got lost in the numbers. The French writer Georges Simenon is like that, so famous for his Inspector Maigret crime novels that his *roman durs* (hard novels) almost slipped by unnoticed (he went into a rage when he heard that Albert Camus had won the Nobel in 1957, perhaps with good reason, for did not Gide say that *La veuvre Couderc* a.k.a *The Widow*, written in April 1940, was 'remarkably analogous with *L'Etranger*, published in 1942, about which everyone is talking, but that (*The Widow*) goes much further, without appearing to do so, which as we know, is the height of art') (as quoted in Patrick Marnham's biography of Simenon).

Well, it didn't matter, did it? Henry Miller thought Simenon was the best of all of them in those years, an interesting fact when you recognize that Miller's style had nothing in common with Simenon's, except perhaps for a shared view of raw human behaviour.

So who gets translated?

Who gets rediscovered?

Who gets her intellectual due even when making big sales and big money?

Woman on TV: "How do I deal with it? I cry, then I drink."

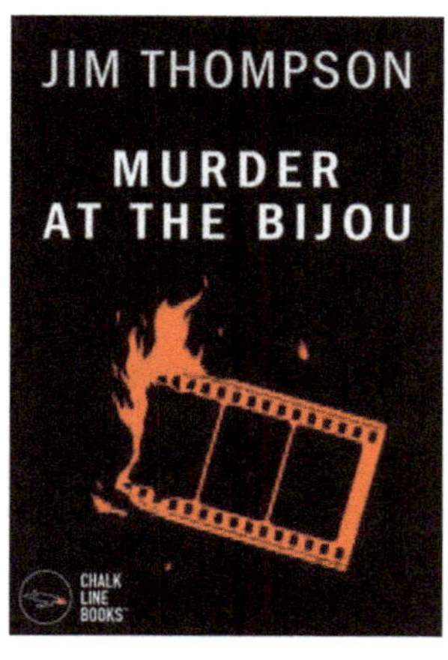

Jim Thompson: *Murder at the Bijou*

[a.k.a *Nothing More Than Murder*, 1949]
DeVault-Graves Agency eBooks

This is an easy read. Fast, minimalist pulp fiction with a superb plot and a completely authentic setting. Stoneville—could be Texas, could be anywhere south of the Mason-Dixon Line, sometime in the 1940s. Seedy, ruthless cut-throat characters, where murder is just an opportunity for blackmail and business is just business and sex the strangest business of all. Could be a movie, reads like a movie and indeed the author, Jim Thompson, was a screenwriter later in his career.

Worked with Stanley Kubrick, although one has to look hard to know it, as Kubrick claimed the premier writing credits, as directors are wont to do. Thompson wrote *The Killing* (1956), a semi avant-garde crime drama, and the better known WW 1 war film *Paths of Glory* (1957), both of which have gained in critical stature in recent years.

So Thompson has chops and it's no surprise that there's been a revival of interest in his work... or shall we say, an emancipation from the crime fiction ghetto. The crime in *Bijou* has some resemblance to the scam in James M. Cain's *Double Indemnity*, although Cain is a romantic compared to Thompson.

Here's the set-up: having eliminated the competition, Joe Wilmot runs the best and only movie house in Stoneville, The Barclay, which he owns with his older wife, the former Elizabeth Barclay, the daughter of a once important local family. Joe has worked his way up from being a film delivery boy, doing runs from a nearby unnamed city to the various small town theatres in the surrounding counties.

Crime is in his background—he came from an orphanage, did some time in a reform school for vagrancy—so his world-view is cynical and his low-level criminal pragmaticism just part of a businessman's modus operandi where every other businessman on Main Street is trying to screw him.

"You've got the most remarkable record for chiseling I've ever laid eyes on," says Sol Panzer, the predatory chain-theatre owner and business rival. Joe is laid up in bed suffering from nervous exhaustion (mistaken for grief) when Sol visits him... and of course it's a case of the kettle calling the pot black as just about everyone in this story is a needler and a chiseler.

Elizabeth recruits a young farmer's daughter, Carol, as a domestic helper, although it's obvious the childless Wilmots have no need of a domestic, and while she's no beauty, Carol's feral eroticism soon has her in the sack with Joe. Elizabeth catches them out, yet it seems she hired Carol for just this purpose. Joe needs sex, she needs money; in fact, they both need money because a cash crunch is looming, and the sharks are circling.

Everyone is putting the squeeze on Joe: his employees, the movie projectionists' union, the distributors, a large movie theatre chain, his fellow businessmen in Stoneville... even his damn wife, who wants to be gone, and will be gone if she can get her hands on the 25 thou, her part of the "double indemnity" insurance policy the couple hold on each other. And while murder is part of the plan, all three in this unholy *menage à trois* are collaborators, albeit uneasy ones. Harness this with the fact that a couple of people want to get their hands on the Bijou, and two or three more want revenge on Joe for past grievances, and that all of the spectators to the "tragedy" seem to be psychic (perhaps arson does that), the subsequent action is both heavy on the paranoia and the double dealing.

As a tap on the movie theatre business, the novel has a text-book accuracy, an insider's been-there-done-that view, so Joe Wilmot's fatal career reads like part of an autobiography. The sociology is classic noir, complete with casebook forensics and a protagonist with the expertise to pull off the crime.

Perhaps Elizabeth as a passive-aggressive femme fatale is a bit shadowy, especially later in the action, and the sexual dynamic of the menage à trois anti-erotic... although this adds realism, because, while certain couples often defy logic, trios always make sense.

> "The next thing I knew, I was back as far as my memory went..."

In noir, there are always at least two victims, the corpse and the patsy. There can be more, and here... well, the reader will have to find out. This is a tricky narrative, full of switcharama sub-plots and flashbacks, although the forward linearity is relentless. Joe's vernacular monologue is full of street savvy and casual fatalism. The dialogue moves the action and monologue stories are used as sideways illustrations (or parables). Symbolism? Yes, we get symbolism. Thompson even inserts himself for a brief, ironic cameo, the sort of post-modern conceit we've seen film-makers from Hitchcock to Fellini use.

Of course most people will miss this, the virtuosity masked by its own easy movement. Writers will marvel, aficionados sweat. If it wasn't for the brutality of it all, the venality and the desperate corruption, some might call the writing beautiful. Thompson isn't for everyone. He's masculine, like a poker game is masculine, with lots of psychic foreplay, bluffing, innuendo, and dangerous gambling. Lying, cheating, false conviviality... all this is routine, love and honor just words.

The ugly face of capitalism? No wonder Thompson joined the Communist Party briefly in the hungry thirties. Still, he could and did write lighter stuff, two of which were made into movies—*The Getaway* (1972 & 1994) and *The Grifters* (1994). Even the Steve McQueen-Ali McGraw version of *The Getaway* is almost a chick flick, is more style than substance despite being directed by the master of Hobbesian violence, Sam Peckinpah.

This is a nice reprint edition by the DeVault-Graves Agency under their Chalk Line Books imprint, which seems to be modelled on the Black Series crime paperbacks started by the French publishing house Gallimard in 1945. The black pen line drawings by Martha Kelly add an extra element of cool.

Bijou was first published in 1949 as *Nothing More Than Murder.* It might be the best of Thompson's work, although of course we haven't read it all. It's just possible that *Murder At the Bijou* rates as the definitive marker of the move by the American novel from document to schematic, book to scenario.

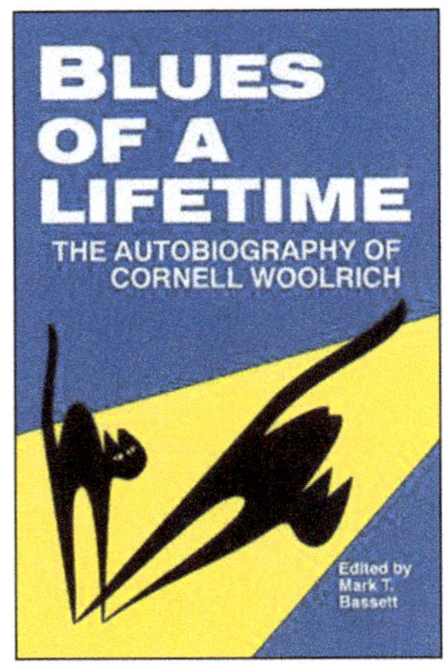

Blues of a Lifetime: the Autobiography of Cornell Woolrich

Edt. with fore/afterword by Mark T. Bassett [2011]

What a fascinating artist, this Woolrich. Lived in hotel rooms most of his life, starting in Mexico with his father during the Revolution, and then after his parents split, living with his mother hither and yonder, mostly in New York (Harlem) or any city that took their fancy... could be Paris, could be Seattle. He was like a Samuel Beckett character, always trapped in the same room where space is both finite and infinite, waiting for the end, and to amuse himself, messing around with a typewriter.

In fact, the first piece in *Blues* is about his typewriter, Remington Portable NC69411. So this isn't a conventional autobio by any means in the sense that we can take it as the whole truth and nothing but, etc. It's a series of five recollections written in the fiction narrative, so that they appear as short stories, only connected by 'I', whom we suppose is Cornell Woolrich.

The manuscript was left in his papers at Columbia University, written for his own edification and not for publication. Anyone who has taught creative writing for any length of time knows that fiction writers either can't or would rather not write essays; writing outside the first person is a struggle, although if we've read any Woolrich, we know he could write in the 3rd. To find narrative unity without fiction is a drag, although a straight-forward autobiography doesn't need much unity beyond the facts.

Here's the issue: Cornell Woolrich didn't consider his cloistered world all that interesting. "This sort of life would be fatal to a writer trying to write realistically," he said. So he wrote "entertainments", escapist fiction with a dark edge, where his doomed characters fall inevitably into the abyss that sits unmapped in the shadows of everyone's mind. Yet *Blues of a Lifetime* does contain some Fitzgeraldian flashes of loneliness and pain so that the five episodes do reveal the measure of the man, how he became a writer, and possibly why.

Woolrich: exotic settings (1880s Gold Coast, in his masterpiece *Waltz Into Darkness*, or Caribbean, as in *Papa Benjamin*), voyeurism (*Rear Window*), low life on the street (his stories for *Detective Fiction Weekly*, *Black Mask*, *Ellery Queen's Mystery Magazine*, and other pulps) demarcate his fictional terrain. His mastery of period jive talk is evident in many of these pulp stories, where the hard-boiled and the soft collide in criminal stitchups and bizarre blunders.

Innocents are victimized, criminals snake-eyed. In *The Dilemma of the Dead Lady* (1936), an American hustler kills a French shop girl, is forced to board an ocean liner at Cherbourg with her body in a trunk. In *Phantom Lady* (1942) a man accused of murdering his wife has only one alibi: a mysterious woman no one seems to remember even though they saw her with him.

A cyanide cigarette, a cyanide tooth filling, a thousand dollar bill cut in two as an invitation to murder... Black Widows, dope fiends, the falsely accused, good cops, bad cops... grifters, hoods, burlesque dancers... hotel clerks, doormen, managers... jazz musicians, voodoo priests, actors and movie queens... Woolrich has them all, sometimes cheap and sleazy, often homicidal, all willing to roll the dice for good or evil, even if it means jumping through a seventh storey window or putting on the mask and getting strapped into the electric chair.

Perhaps the most interesting metafiction in *Blues* is *II, Poor Girl* (*Vera*), Woolrich's cruelly poetic recollection of first love. Student falls for a poor girl down the street, dresses her up, takes her to a party above her social station where she becomes a hit, a glamour doll everyone wants to be or get. She then disappears from her boyfriend's life, and he becomes a tragic pariah to her family. In the end he discovers she's been siphoned into the underworld, the moll of a faceless hood in a faceless black sedan.

So much for Vera, so much for the early dream of Woolrich. The bare essence might remind us of Maugham's *Of Human Bondage* or any other student love story. The New York landscape is real, as are the characters; only the ending is suspect, a romantic masochism in sketchy relief. Women go to Hell in a black car, and boys are left to become artists.

IV, President Eisenhower's Speech, is also very good, not only as a story, but also for the insight it gives us about what life was like living in a Harlem hotel with his mother. There are two actions—Eisenhower's address to the Nation on the radio, and a fire that's coming up the ventilation shaft—which work as contrapuntal symbolisms. As a Cold War metaphor or a straight forward account of Woolrich's concern for his mother, it tells us a lot about the reclusive writer's psychology. He's a caring man, both for his mother and the colored lady who lives just down the hall... and perhaps he's a bit like Eisenhower, concealing the truth in order to sustain a sense of calm.

V, The Maid Who Played the Races is a late Woolrich tale, based on his days in the Roosevelt Hotel in Seattle. It's whimsical, uses the old sit-com bromide of the mistaken assumption or convenient misunderstanding. The room maid thinks he's a jockey, has inside tips to offer. He goes along with the charade, not wishing to offend the aged maid, gives her the name of a horse which—wouldn't you know it wins and brings a nice payout for the maid, who is facing retirement. The strength is in the telling, not the fairytale of a "writer" mistaken as a "rider".

We can say what we like about Cornell Woolrich: he's pulp, he's yesterday, he's a cheap thrill good only for B movie scenarios, a writer who always sounds like someone else, Poe or Fitzgerald or the comic book you used to read in the laundromat or the station waiting for the next bus to nowhere. "First you dream, then you die"—didn't he write that? Cheap, lurid fatalism.

And those plots where coincidence is as predictable as the entrances and exits in a stage play—it's all for convenience, an easy roll so the author doesn't have to "sweat the details", and luck drives the action and the word count fits the column. All of this is true, yet there's beauty in the rubble, some great phrases, scenes, characters and dialogue that jumps, hit me daddy eight to the bar.

Talking about film narrative, Jean Cocteau said, "Mistakes in continuity are part of the unconscious poetry." While we can't excuse all the lapses in Woolrich's fiction, there is a sense of hidden unity in his poetic style that allows us to view the action as fated rather than accidental, and the moral optimism as reasonable.

He was homosexual, although like many others in that period of history, i.e Somerset Maugham, tried to play it straight, and married the daughter of a film producer. The marriage lasted three months. Perhaps this sort of outlaw existence of moving freely between genders (in his head at least) fueled his ability to write convincingly not only about the low-life of the Jazz Age but also from the female point-of-view (*Angel Face, Phantom Lady, I Married A Dead Man*). In this sense he's a less nasty mock-up of Patricia Highsmith, lighter on the realism, sweeter on the poetry

Says Bassett: "We know almost as much about him from reading his fiction as we do from studying the evidence." This is how it should be. The world today is overloaded with documentary evidence, is far too light on poetry and mystery. In the near-field, imagination is killed, so we are left staring into space, waiting for signals, possibilities.

So, Woolrich is uneven. *I Married a Dead Man* is full of that internal air-brushing that some might think is poetry, others, verbose nonsense. There's a sort of delirium in the wind-up that frustrates the reader, makes him/her withdraw, lose the thread. Yet this novel still gets read, as the plot is good (the classic 'mistaken identity' gambit) and the Jamesian psychology provocative.

So *Blues of a Lifetime* is a great read for those who've read some Woolrich and/or seen some of the noir movies based on his stories, or for those who want to study his work in depth. Some might see Woolrich as the precursor of Jack Kerouac because of the stylistic appropriation of the jazz rhythms of their respective eras.

Bassett has done a good job here editing this "autobiography", filling in some of the gaps while leaving the episodes to speak for themselves. He has tracked several sources and/or analogues for some Woolrich *bon mots*, and explicates the soul of the man as a son, a lover, a writer and a loner extremely well within the short profile and addendum he adds to the autobiographical reconstruction. Bassett ends with a fragment from Woolrich's notes for *Blues*, "I was only trying to cheat death... a fool and his machine... yes, a fool and his machine." 'Machine' being his typewriter, we suppose. This melancholy metaphor is only surpassed by another Woolrich dagger, "First you dream, then you die."

We wish there was more. Recollections of Mexico, Hollywood, some confession... but, he is who he was: the unreliable narrator, a little bit bent, completely human, almost supernatural. He was buried with his mother in a double-sized crypt.

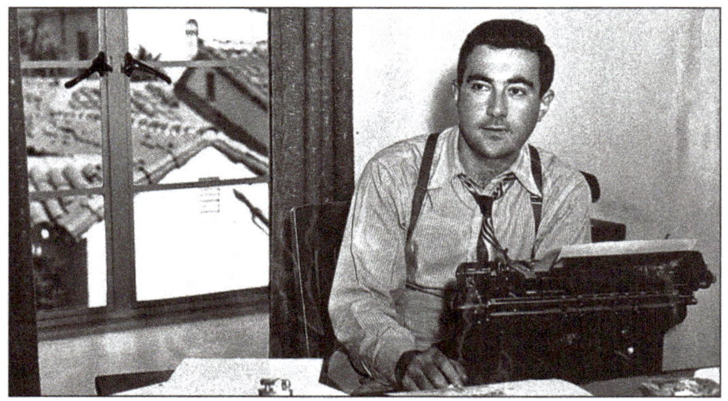

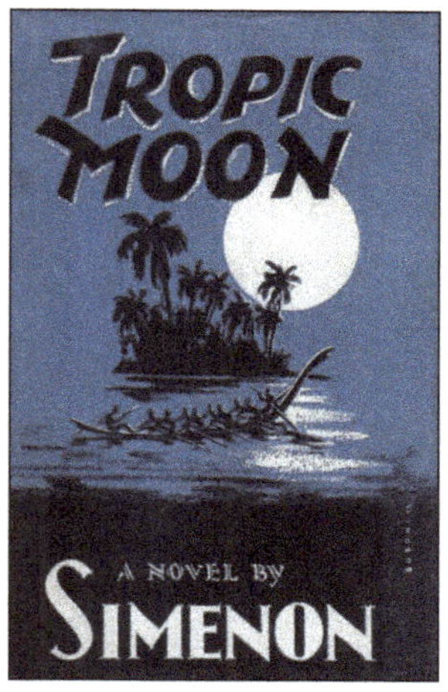

Georges Simenon: *Tropic Moon* [1932]

You don't read this because it's fiction, you read it because it's true. This isn't *Babar the Elephant*, although you can console yourself by saying all this was then, back in the inter-war years when colonialism was still considered a civilized thing, part of the white man's burden and all that. A young fellow by the name of Joe Timar is sent to French West Africa to work for a timber company, lands in Libreville, gets stuck in the local hotel because it seems the man he is to replace has said he'll shoot anyone who comes up river, tries to usurp him. So Timar turns his attention to the wife of the hotel owner, a thirty something *femme fatale* from Hell who has pussy-whipped all the local white males into submission because, well, she can... and this is how you survive in the jungle, it seems. Despite the blistering heat, she always dresses in black but wears no underclothes, in some sort of totemic adaptation of the black native identity. Her name? Adèle... Adèle Renaud.

> "He looked at her in alarm. And yet she was a woman with soft skin, a good figure, a yielding body."

While Adèle can be compared to other *femme fatales* such as Phyllis D. in *Double Indemnity* or any other James M. Cain female or even Kitty in Maugham's *The Painted Veil* (although the setting is more appropriate than the character, perhaps), her self-assured relentless amorality takes on a larger, more symbolic identity than that of a mere hot woman with nothing better to do. Going deep, the real comparison for Adèle is to Camus' Meursault—who came later—another French colonial who murders a native just to get rid of him, as you would swat a bug or step on an insect. Of course the usual comparison for *L'Etranger* is to *La Nausée* (1938), Sartre's classic novel of existential angst... and you know, in a very general way, *La Nausée* has some resemblance to *Tropic Moon*, which is saturated with physical and mental nausea. Who influenced who, exactly? Or is it rather that these three writers were drawing from the common pool of a maladjusted culture—not just French—that is, the modern secular sickness of rippling disbelief.

Certainly Camus—the Oran schoolteacher—admitted hijacking the "hardboiled" American style of Hemingway and James M. Cain, and if you look at Simenon, you have to say he was hardboiled right from the start, despite the softer Inspector Maigret series that made him rich. *Tropic Moon* annoyed a lot of French people when it came out, apparently. The face in the mirror was too ugly. The character of Adèle was beyond the pale, misogynist even. A classless French adventuress slapping the natives around, committing murder, stitching up a patsy... a bullet and a heartless shag her two main weapons, all this sordid stuff going down just over the horizon out-of-sight in Gabon, equatorial Africa. Dengue? Jungle fever? It certainly gets Timar, her latest love toy. In Herbert Lottman's massive 1979 biography of

Albert Camus, he says "a Finnish economic geographer" told him him that when Meursault pulled the trigger, "it was a textbook example of the effect of climate on the population." (244)

This pretty well syncs with Simenon's anti-colonial views: white people should stay out of Africa, let the Africans find their own way. As Joe Timar travels up river, he catches jungle fever and is certainly never the same thereafter... although the bug that bit him was a woman, first day in town. Later he succumbs to sunstroke, becomes a raving paranoid idiot... yet although his paranoia turns out to be justified, it's certainly not tolerated by the white clique in Libreville, and he's expelled from the colony, sent back to La Belle France to disappear into bourgeois conformity. So, zombies were once idealists too. As usual, some electric Simenonian detailing along the way, some outrageous incidents and superb characterizations all framed within the utter absurdity of cultures in collision. Who can forget the sordid, drunken wee hours orgy under the "tropic moon" involving the white patrons of the Libreville hotel and some native women they round up, then abandon 20 klicks from their village? "Moonstroke", for sure... and although Timar is just an uncomfortable witness, he eventually succumbs to the promiscuous lure of the jungle when he shags a village chief's nubile daughter somewhere down-river during his desperate pursuit of Adèle. Wearing a white suit doesn't remove a man from the cycle of bodily functions, it seems.

Then, in a stroke of genius, Simenon draws out his color symbolism by having Timar's white suits confiscated before he's put on the steamer for home; he failed as a colonial, as a white man, and now he exits wearing a black suit, like a mourner at his own funeral, an exoskeleton that signals his total corruption... or failure... or the disease his lover in black gave him.

> "They were standing, their bodies like two pale smudges in the room."

Simenon: a great writer? A match for Celine? Better than Maugham, perhaps? Because of the period, comparisons of their subjects and themes are inevitable, of course. For a long time Simenon's hard fiction drifted out-of-print in English—perhaps displaced by his popular Inspector Maigret stories—but now Penguin is busy bringing back many of these forgotten titles. You can get *Tropic Moon* as an eBook, or, if you're willing to pay the cult premium, find a used *New York Review Books Classics* paperback.

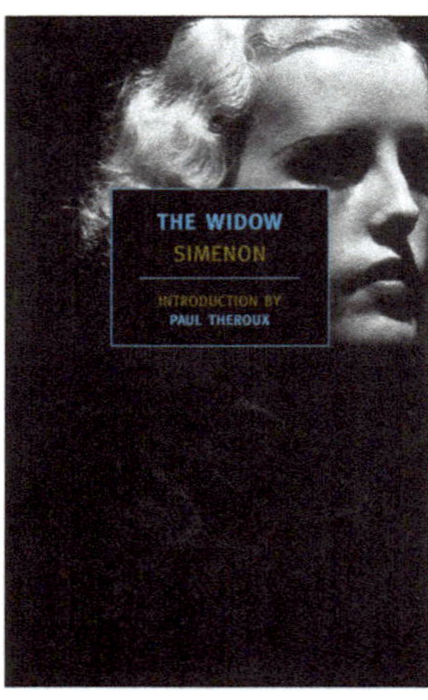

Georges Simenon: *The Widow* [1940]

"A man walking." With this simple phrase, Simenon starts one of his strangest novels, as if he's just struck a piano note, follows the sustain into the mystic. He describes the slanting shadows cast by the trees over the road, and the shorter shadow cast by the man as if he's a character in a film noir. Well he might be, as he's just been released from prison, is returning home, although in fact there really is no home, just the memory of a childhood and a personal disintegration. There's a symbolic intensity to the description, the man walking through a landscape where light rather than substance is the reality. Modernism. Mobility rather than reason, action rather than thought. The favorite word for this is 'existential', although as Paul Theroux says in his excellent introduction to this edition [*New York Reviews Classics*] of *The Widow*, Simenon would likely have had little use for the term.

The 1930s produced a lot of drifters in modern fiction... you see them in the short stories of Liam O'Flaherty (Ireland) and famously in James M. Cain's *The Postman Always Rings Twice* (1934), to which Georges Simenon's *The Widow* (1940) bears some resemblance... in the way, say, that an ugly sister can be seen in the face of the beautiful one. A French film version of *Postman* called *Le Dernier tournant* (*The Last Turning*) was released in 1939, so Simenon might have been stimulated by this to write his own grotesque, somewhat surreal, version. Certainly the widow Tati is no Cora; as a femme fatale, Tati is the ugly sister, a paranoid control freak whose sexual appetite is more Roman than Catholic, although both women share the same greedy business ambition. And Jean Passerat-Monnoyeur is no Frank Chambers, although both men play the roles Fate has set them up for.

Many people have noted the passivity of Simenon's Jean character, the desensitized Oedipus Rex type who can only take orders from a woman. He seems to be an inter-war cultural phenom, a man who carries a vague internal trauma, as if the 10 Commandments have been ripped from his soul, so that he goes through the motions of life like a machine. He doesn't care. He doesn't care for any bourgeois dream or appearance... which is why, after being released from five years incarceration for manslaughter, he drifts into the arms of a peasant widow, a 45 year old vixen who is the mistress of her drooling, cretinous father-in-law. A laughable Freudian nightmare? Certainly. Set by a canal deep in rural France, the bizarre politics of *The Widow* are both pagan and modern, animal, vegetable and mineral in no particular order. Welcome to Eden (*sur-le-Cher... mes amis*).

In a way the widow Tati is inhuman, more like a mythological creature who lives in a cave and accepts sacrifices as a natural right. Her son René, a petty criminal, is in the Foreign Legion, yet is still pathetically dependant, always writing for more money to be sent. Her father-in-law, Couderç, the old deaf 'tomcat' who really owns the house and garden, and a field near the brickyard, dependant... booze, food, sex. And now Jean, to become a surrogate son and lover, a catalytic part of this (un)holy *ménage à trois*. Thus the religious patina of this strange story sets it apart from similar works, delivered in such a matter-of-fact manner that the broken taboos slip past in the soft surrealism of it all.

Theroux draws attention to the similarity in attitude between Jean and Meursault, Albert Camus' celebrated existential killer in *L'Etranger*, which was published in 1942, a couple years after *The Widow*. Others have also noted the similarities, wondered if Camus was influenced by Simenon, and if so, what an injustice as Camus won the Nobel and Simenon never did. The thing is, if you look at any of the protagonists in Simenon's *romans durs*—before and after *The Widow*—you see the same uncaring mummy's boys doing their antisocial, unchristian acts. In a godless universe, murder or any other antisocial act is merely political, and as such has no meaning. This dead wire attitude is especially noticeable in fiction following the carnage of WW 1, an incubator for nihilism if ever there was one. Institutional discipline and logic fails, and the anti-romantic criminal triumphs.

Does a man feel guilty every time he ejaculates? Only if he leaves a mess. There's a helplessness in the action, a manipulation by the Unknown. Like the rabbits in Tati's garden, the multiplication is mechanical.

'His Face Was Reminiscent Of An Image Of Christ'

Certainly Jean has a more immediate motive for murder than Meursault, and both by no means commit motiveless murders. It's the lack of remorse that fascinates scholars of the genre and the period. Tati is a nagging mind-reader with a choke-harness on her pawn, so why shouldn't something bad happen? Simenon also provides a lot of history for Jean—too much perhaps. Dead mother, playboy father, greedy girlfriend ("she lied as she breathed"), gambling problem... knuckle dusters in his pocket, what the hell. Body in the river? Book 'im, Maigret. Another bad case of Oedipus Rex.

His inevitable love affair with Tati's niece Félicié—the teenage slut with the mysterious child—turns out to be another part of the Freudian politics. The patriarch is taken hostage—old Couderç, the grandfather, possibly the father of Félicie's child—by his eldest daughter Françoise and the slut is sent across the canal to entrap Tati's muscle, the hopeless Jean. It's an old story—a family civil war for possession of an estate (in this case, a house with no electricity, a garden, a field with two cows)—lit in Greek macabre. It has a modern absurdist feel due to the anthropomorphic imagery ('hills like breasts' etc) and the continuous flow of natural symbolism. There's so much symbolism, it's like hunting for faces in the foliage of the trees. One of the most important is Tati's incubator, central to her dream of farming chickens on an industrial scale. One hundred and two degrees for twenty one days... something has to give.

The hanging gourd of dripping cheese... the dressmaker's dummy torso... the taciturn lock-keeper with the wooden leg who fathers children seasonally... the canal that separates Tati from her sister-in-law... the shackled cattle... and so on. "The dung was warm beneath his feet" sums up the situation. The narrative is therefore modal, shifting easily between text and subtext.

Article 12 of the Penal Code: "Every person condemned to death shall be decapitated" recurs in Jean's consciousness like a flash frame when he sleeps, does chores, listens to the bullying, the pleading, the monologuing, the endless verbal noise that propels the widow Tati, on her feet or lying down... or watching through her window, her paranoid vision penetrating walls, shadow and bone and even Time itself, it seems.

Article 15: "Men condemned to forced labour shall be set to the hardest possible work; they shall wear an iron ball at their ankles and shall be joined in pairs by a chain." He's left prison, but what, really, has changed? The faces, the game... yet behind these things, the imagery remains the same.

Many writers aspire to write in code and Simenon did it without even thinking. Not every action is a symbolism, but the important ones are. Thus there are many ways to read this novel, which puts it in compliance with most religious texts, yet the message certainly isn't religious. Bizarrely, the widow attends church on Sundays, yet this is just a gesture towards her bourgeois dream, just as Jean is, as he is the son of a wealthy distiller, and a possible source of money. The pornography of her actions—this pagan stitching of sex, politics, murder and light industry—is secular.

A strange and powerful novel that captures a modern culture in the shadow of its pagan peasant past. When Jean's sister Billie comes to visit to find out what's going on, why hasn't he returned home, he says, "I'm saying I like living with Tati. She's my mistress. Besides me, there's the old goat, as she calls him. He's her father-in-law. From time to time she takes him to bed with her, like giving sweets to a child to keep it quiet. It's the only way of retaining the house...."

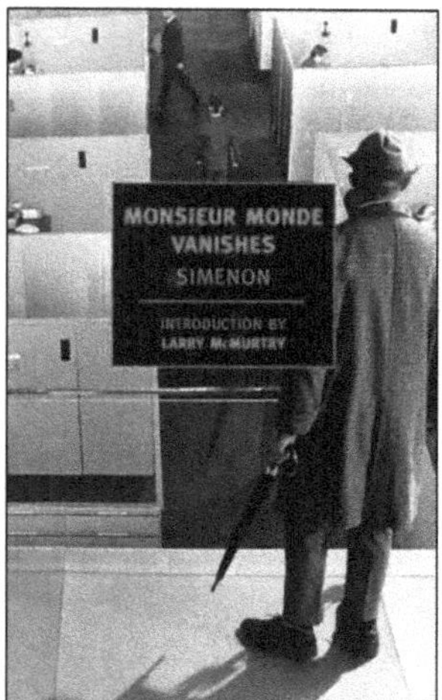

Georges Simenon: *Monsieur Monde Vanishes* [1945]

Affluent Parisian businessman in his late forties walks out of his office one summer day, exchanges his expensive suit for something a little more down-market, and with 300,000 francs wrapped in a newspaper, hops a train for Marseille where he checks into a cheap hotel with a view of the Port. With no warning, he has left behind a wife (his second), a son and daughter, and a successful family business. It's an adventure to be sure, a sudden rebellion against conformity, perhaps a classic middle-age reinvention of the Self, or a self-indulgent fling that conceals a manic depressive resignation from a life that will end as suicide.

Yet *Monsieur* Norbert Monde is anything but irresponsible, even if his initial actions suggest it. First night in his dingy hotel he overhears an ugly row between a pair of young lovers in the adjacent room. The man punches and kicks the woman, who grovels at his feet, protests innocence, begs him to stay. The scene is raw and electric, like something Monde himself might've participated in with his first wife but never did. When the man leaves, Monde checks to see if the young woman is alright; thus starts the strange relationship between Monde, the bourgeois runaway, and Julie, the nightclub dancer... and runaway.

Beautifully written in that slightly dysfunctional Georges Simenon way, with a subtle modal shifting between exterior and interior narrative, present and past, that gives the action a dreamy feel, whether Monde is in bed with Julie or sitting on a bench on the Promenade des Anglais in Nice, where this strange couple end up. There's a sense of *déjà vu* within the action, as if Monde is reenacting a past he has forgotten, or is now acting out a future that his past has fated.

Julie gets them both employment at a gambling club, the Monico—she as a dance hostess and sex bait, he as a hidden book-keeper and spy on both the customers and workers (there's a similarity here to Little Frank's brothel voyeurism in Simenon's roman noir *Dirty Snow*). Monde is over-qualified for his job, but here, in the gray borderland where crime and respectability can be one of a kind, no one asks questions. Because Monde saved

Julie's life, she repays him by enabling him to find his true self.

Both are sympathetic characters, and bond despite the disparity in age and class. Both are victim—Julie of a childish petty thief, and Monde of two marriages and two selfish wives. Somehow they make it easy for one another to move on from the past, yet the past isn't done with Monsieur Monde or the dopplegänger he assumes, Monsieur Désiré. Strangely, when the police do come looking, it isn't for Monde/Désiré, but rather for his first wife Thérèse who is a *habitué* of the Monico as the companion of a wealthy bloated American known as The Empress. Tragedy strikes when The Empress ODs and Monde/Désiré has to rescue his former wife, now an impoverished drug addict without a patron. No one would expect him to, yet he bears no ill will towards her (or wife 2 back in Paris) despite the fact that she walked out on him and the kids all those years ago to satisfy her pornographic fantasies. In a clever analogue to Julie's debasement with her lover, Thérèse ends up on the street grovelling at Monde's feet, begging him to get her another fix. Monde helps her out, and what thanks does he receive? A bite on the hand.

> "They had hardly been together a quarter of an hour, a half hour at most, and she had already degraded everything to the level of her own feminine mind."

However, Monde becomes a leader, takes care of business. 'He was a man who, for a long time, had endured the human condition without being conscious of it, as others endure an illness of which they are unaware.' So, like a spell in the Foreign Legion, his holiday in the gutter shakes him free of his cultural and psychological somnabulism. But how does it all end? Better read this novel and find out. Great characters, settings, scenes... and some powerful humanism despite the selfishness and venality. Hard fiction with a heart, and as relevant today as it was in 1945.

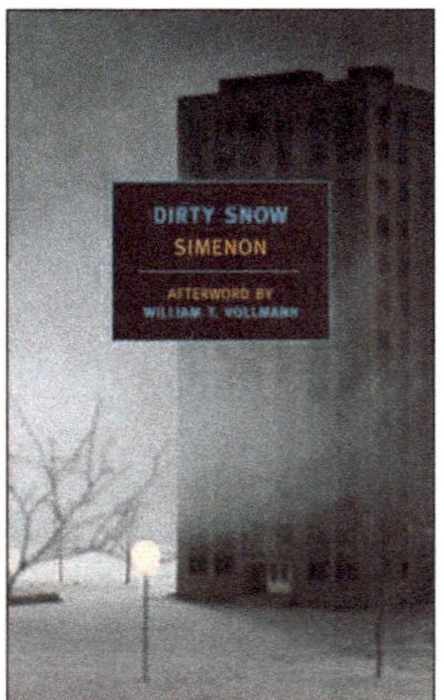

Georges Simenon: *Dirty Snow* [1948]

Despite the fact that Simenon's reptilian protagonist Little Frank has a similar psychology to Camus' desensitized secular anti-hero Meursault (*L'Etranger*, 1941), his slimy passage from his mother's Parisian brothel to a Nazi firing squad in *Dirty Snow* (1948) is a parable of genius, a naturalist masterwork of gritty detail and symbolist architectonics. Subtext? Symbolist looping? Modal landscape shifting? Characters so real, you look over your shoulder? You don't have to understand such things to feel their subliminal pull as you read this ugly story, but those who do can only marvel at Simenon's artistry and way of doing business.

Another distasteful existential lout, you say... why should I bother? Enough of these criminals and their prurient narcissism, you say... but of course the story is much bigger than the character through whose eyes we see it.

They say Georges Simenon had to clear out of France after WW 2 because some patriots considered him a collaborator. For a while he settled in Montreal, then later in Arizona, where he wrote *Dirty Snow* in 1948. Guess it must be his revenge. Although it's never spelled out categorically, the setting is France under German occupation, and as a biopsy of the cultural sickness, *Dirty Snow* is a damning portrait of the French character (or is it the German?), veiled like Kafka, exposed like Nuremberg. Women won't want to read this, as the women are whores, and men will cringe, as the men are corrupt and cruel. The hero is a pimp, a thief, a murderer, a child man incapable of love who has never seen the sea and fails to recognize who his father is even when it should be obvious. The sexual undertone of the title says it all.

"I Am Not A Fanatic, An Agitator, Or A Patriot. I Am A Piece Of Shit."

The protagonist is a spoiled eighteen year old son of an opportunistic brothel madame called Lotte who gives "refuge" to unfortunate women during the Occupation. The invading force is never named and the characters have German names, as if they've undergone some sort of rapid mystical acculturation, leaving their French identities buried in the snow. Frank watches the women with their clients (usually Occupation officers) through a circulation vent in the wall, and when he comes home drunk from his favorite local, avails himself of this one or that one as a house privilege due to the favored son of the Madame.

He ambushes a drunken client known as 'The Eunuch', knifes him in an alley for his revolver, leaves him to die in the dirty snow. Later he shoots and kills an old widow Madame Vilmos (perhaps Jewish) when he robs her of a watch collection, later sold for a handsome sum to a German General. He deceives a young neighbour girl called Sissy by using a subterfuge to sell her virginity to a drinking partner who has business contacts within the upper echelons of the Occupation forces, i.e. the General who collects watches. Frank's depravity progresses rapidly, and he knows it's only a matter of time before he's arrested. Will he be tortured? He doesn't care, as if his moral emptiness will somehow ensure he transcends pain, like all sadists who long to be masochists. In all, this journey through the squalid politics of the Occupation appears to be a rehearsal for 'suicide by firing squad'.

"The Snow Falls In Handfuls, Never Enough To Cover Up The Filth"

The plot is an amazing progression of incidents and characters which seem as chaotic as a dream, yet interact powerfully within the fated fluid of destiny. No incident, no image, no character is wasted... a wounded cat scales higher and higher in a linden tree, resisting all attempts at rescue, just as Sissy flees her rapist into the night, hides in the moonlit frozen wasteland of an abandoned school, her innocence the only moral light in the entire story... or the other school now used as a prison that has echoes of the infamous Cherche-Midi—once a nunnery—co-opted by the Germans to incarcerate and torture political prisoners... Sissy's key... the watches... the woman in the distant window... the stolen revolver... the snow... these images, these characters—at first senseless—keep recurring until the snow wants to quit. In the end, Frank quits; he "(can) almost taste the dawn". Who turned him in? Maybe his mother, maybe his not-so-secret father; we never know, and it doesn't matter, as the corruption is so total everyone would have motive for doing so... including Frank himself.

Criticisms? Perhaps Sissy and her father Holst—the art critic who is now a tram driver—are a bit false in their final appearance. The idea that anyone who had suffered as much as they, would or could, extend sympathy to "Little Frank" is stretching the idea of Christian charity a bit far... yet, in the end, such is the mysterious weaving within the fabric, you don't really know what was going on at the brothel, whether it was a nest of collaborators or a safe house for the resistance; at times you wonder if Frank is an unwitting dupe of both sides in this sad tale of human degradation. The right-and-wrong of it is like a paper aeroplane—it never lands where it should. Yet the mysticism allows you to make choices, avoid the obvious.

Some might criticize the translation, as sentence subjects are often ambiguous, and the flow a bit primitive. But otherwise you have to admit that *Dirty Snow* is a masterpiece, despite the fading politics of its time and space. At face value, a simple narrative about a pampered criminal princeling, yet a text loaded with code, like an encrypted message between spies.

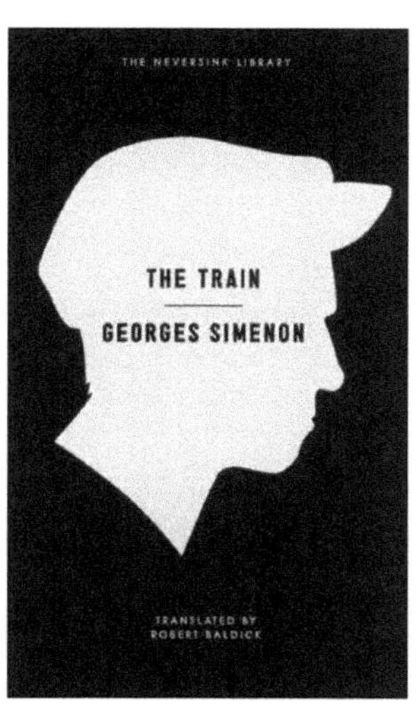

Georges Simenon: *The Train* [1961]

Georges Simenon knew how to tell a story, and *The Train* (1961) is among the very best by anyone about the Second World War. It concerns the invasion of France following the 'Phony War' (Sept '39-May '40) when German troops overran Holland and Belgium, then by-passed the Maginot Line by attacking through the forested hill region of the Ardennes. Marcel Féron, a radio repairman with a pregnant wife and daughter, is living in Fumay, a sleepy town right on the Belgian border and in the path of the advancing Panzers.

He's an unremarkable type, with an invalid's past (pleurisy as a child) whose family was wrecked by WW 1 (his mother was shorn as a German whore), so he grew up as a quasi-orphan and as such, has a detached way of viewing things. Whether you call it trauma or alienation or survivalist compartmentalization, it seems to be a European characteristic of the times. As such, it makes Marcel the ideal protagonist for this authentic and entirely credible story of just what happened to people as they fled the advance.

Marcel knows when to pack up and leave because he hears the military chatter and foreign broadcasts on his radio, but of course the 'bush telegraph' has it in the air, in the street, the alarm passing quickly through the neighborhood as military traffic passes by. Marcel takes his wife Jeanne and daughter Sophie to the station, where they become separated by the ancient dictum of "women and children" first; pregnant Jeanne and Sophie with her blue doll board a carriage near the front, while Marcel is lucky to get a cattle car at the back. He's not bothered by this, but rather exhilarated by the prospect of this adventure into the unknown. Besides, some Belgians arrive in another train, and one of them—a pretty young woman in a black dress—quickly crosses the tracks and jumps into his carriage.

On Top Of Her, The Both Of Us As Silent As Snakes

Sex in the boxcar, in a field, in a tent... sex on a fishing boat... and in the desperate hours of their flight, the sounds of sex everywhere in the darkness, as people console themselves in the shadow of death. It's not Sodom and Gomorrah. Somehow it's all a lark, a liberation from the normal world. It's cold in the boxcar at night, warmth is another body, and the only privacy is darkness. Marcel hears Julie—a buxom local cafe owner—get it on with another man he prefers to call 'The Horse Dealer' (even if he isn't). "I knew the exact moment of penetration," he notes, as the night grows more pornographic.

So, as usual, Simenon has a strong sexual undercurrent in his writing. It's not *Lady Chatterly* but raunchy for the times. Young readers might find this odd, as they have no idea about censorship in the English language world before the 1960s, would say the sex here is tastefully understated. Well it is, yet the truth of it would've made this book unpublishable in English before the sixties. The French, you know. Their continental liberalism was a barometer of decadence for the English world... 'French Letters'... liaison... *ménage à trois*, etc. No wonder Henry Miller was an admirer of Simenon's writing.

Simenon was for a long time involved in a *ménage à trois* with his wife and housekeeper, so he was familiar with the psychology of such an arrangement. Of course there's a seedy feel to such activities whereas affairs that happen during prolonged separation have a more romantic aura. Such is Simenon's skill as a scenarist that when he mixes the reprehensible with the excusable, he makes the cheating Marcel a sympathetic character—even a romantic hero—despite his rather dull c.v. A radio repairman who needs bifocals to see the world? A weakling who was never drafted and has little experience of the world beyond Fumay? Yet his childhood was tragic, although perhaps not an uncommon one for many French children scarred by WW 1. His alienation, his compartmentalization—which Anna remarks upon—aides him in his odd casting in this fated love story. It's a measure of Simenon's superb talent as a writer and explicator of the human condition that he makes us accept Marcel's commitment to a stranger refugee when all his emotional and physical energy should be devoted to reuniting with his pregnant wife and daughter.

And who is Anna? What is her secret? Is she really Belgian? Was she really just released from a women's prison in Nantes? She fears she will be mistaken for a German, perhaps a spy, because of her accent... so she could be Flemish, whose Dutch inflection could sound German, we think. We soon forget about this, as the young couple's quest for survival distracts us, and them. The train stops for the night on a siding somewhere in the country... troop trains pass... refugee trains... a 'lunatic's train' from an asylum... and sometime before dawn the cattle cars are decoupled from the rest of the train, and Marcel awakes to find his wife and child have disappeared, routed elsewhere in the confusion. A squadron of German planes appear, strafe the train. The engineer is killed, passengers too... many badly wounded. But Marcel's train continues, eventually arrives in La Rochelle in south western France. La Rochelle was certainly a place that the boat-loving Simenon was familiar with. We wonder, perhaps, if Simenon himself was anything like Marcel Féron. To some extent, yes. Simenon was misdiagnosed with a terminal heart condition in 1940... and his *ménage à trois* was exposed. During this period he and his family lived not far from La Rochelle so naturally he had a first hand feel for the area and this period in French history, and the authenticity of the story-line shows it.

"No past or future. Nothing but a fragile present, which we sipped and savored together." Although famous for his plain language, Simenon has moments of poetic beauty, the sort of sensitive inscaping that gets to the emotional reality of the situation... this affair, this moment in history.

"We feasted ourselves on little pleasures, on patterns of light and shade which we knew we should remember all our lives." The narrative is in the 1st person, not Simenon's usual 3rd. You learn by the end that it's in fact a journal or testament by Féron of what happened to him and his family during the German advance, between May and June 1940, when Marshal Petain signed the controversial armistice that ended hostilities. As a confession, it's by no means docile, as Féron is proud that he was capable of such a wild, other-worldly romance. It is, of course, ironic, as the true ending (when it comes) is a real choker. Again, that Simenon ambiguity, that romantic sadism that separates his work from the sentimentalists and liars.

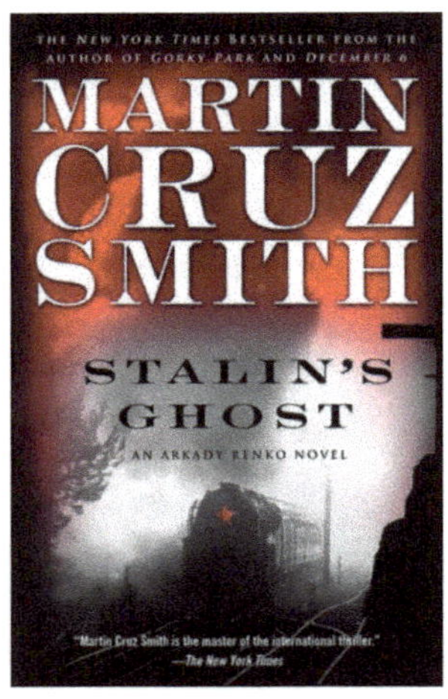

Martin Cruz Smith: *Stalin's Ghost* [2007]

Was coming back to the house with some supplies around noon, stopped at the lights to wait for the left-turn signal. In the rear view mirror I see a guy in a gold compact SUV behind me, got a book in one hand and something in the other... hand goes to the mouth and he puffs some smoke and I'm thinking what's this, one of those electronic cigarettes? He rolls down the window. Notice a couple of those pine scent danglers hanging above the dash, so I guess he does a lot of smoking and toaking. He sets down his book and it's a small pipe he's got, hash or crack or something. Lights a match, fires it up again. Young guy. Glasses. Looks professional, a bit like my son, but younger. Thirty-five maybe. The green arrow starts flashing and I make my turn. He pulls up beside me at the next light, and he's still multi-tasking, no hands on the wheel. He hangs his hand with book out the driver window, like he's shaking some ash from it. Holy Christ, it's *Stalin's Ghost* by Martin Cruz Smith—I just finished reading that!

What he's doing is what we call "distracted driving" hereabouts, you know, one hand on the wheel, the other holding a cellphone or a beer or whatever. Only this guy has no hands on the wheel, he's busy with the dope pipe and *Stalin's Ghost*.

Imagine him being pulled over by a cop. If I was the cop I'd say, "Is that a hash pipe you got there, son? I hope so because hash isn't a criminal offense if it's medical."

And he'd say, "Oh it's medical, officer... I can't function without it."

And I'd say, "Well be that as it may... but the book... you can't be driving and reading at the same time, that's Distracted Driving, son. $280."

He looks really choked. Maybe it's those thin-rim glasses. "I just picked the book up," he says. "While I was waiting fer the light, honest."

And I'd say, "Sure, kid. The book any good?"

And he'd say, "Don't give me a ticket, man. I'm kinda freaked out... going for a job interview."

"What do you think of the ending?"

"Haven't got that far. See? I'm shakin'...."

"So is it really Stalin's ghost they see at the railway station?"

"You've read it? I didn't like that... they explain it and I don't like that."

"It's a scam?"

"Yeah. These kind of books are always like that, eh... built around a scam. Ghosts are for real, man."

Ghosts are for real... must be the hash, I'm thinking. Superstitious, like half the characters in that book.

I say, "How do you do it... smoke and read and drive at the same time?"

He demonstrates by bringing his knees up on either side of the steering wheel, locks on. Peer inside, see he has no feet.

Amazed, I say, "You're handicapped!"

"Yeah," he says. "Like I say, I need my medicine."

"Don't you have blades or springs or something?"

"Blades? I don't need blades, officer. I can walk on my hands."

I don't ask what happened, how he got to be here in a shabby gold Kia SUV with no feet, driving through town reading Martin Cruz Smith. It's obvious, he's a victim, like all the ghosts Stalin left behind. I send him on his way, tell him to go home and finish the book, even though he's a hard-core distracted driver. He's not smoking hash—it's crack cocaine.

"Some cop that Renko."

"Yeah, I like him. He's fair."

"You think I'm fair?"

He doesn't seem surprised that I show mercy. He's cynical, steeped in tragedy and death; anyone who reads Martin Cruz Smith has to be. Sure, MCS's protagonist Renko is a utilitarian moralist, son of a predator killer (one of Stalin's generals) who doggedly survives from novel to novel like a Lada passed down through the generations. If you start at the beginning with Gorky Park and keep going through a few of them you get a lazy reader's guide to the collapse of the Soviet Union and its chaotic survival as a gangster state. Not only are they well-written, they are extremely well-researched with an impressive authenticity considering MCS is an American writing as an outsider. *Gorky Park, Polar Star, Red Square... Havana Bay... Wolves Eat Dogs... Stalin's Ghost* and one or two others. All of them have great setups, drop you into the action, no sweat. But the measure of a truly great writer is how he/she ends the story and MCS often falls back on bullshit to tie it all up. For all his realism, and excellent writing, he has a prime time affliction.

Polar Star is perhaps the most successful narrative in terms of symmetry (considering the asymmetric world Renko operates in). It's set on a Russian factory ship fishing off Alaska, where Renko has been banished following the inconvenient truth of Gorky Park. It's almost a dystopian science fiction setting, brilliantly conceived and executed, even if at heart it's a basic reinvention of an Agatha Christie country murder house. Red Square... well this one is a clever play on the painting by the Russian godfather of abstract impressionism, Kazimir Malvelich. The scam here concerns a substitute version of the Red Square painting which has a natural analogue to the confused state of affairs in the new Russia. Here, perhaps, Renko's tortured romance is more important than the mystery of the 'red square' (this might be true of all the Renko novels, with their reverse Byronic romanticism) (yes, you can connect Renko to Pushkin and Lermontov). Renko has more than a mild case of masochism, although his detached persistence is the classic 'silence, exile and cunning' approach to life as a Russian moralist, er, investigator. The same can be said about *Stalin's Ghost*, where once again Renko grinds out his daily existence like a fox in a fenced triangle. As usual, everyone is out to get him, including the people he works with... and maybe the woman he sleeps with. All is treachery in the red vodka dawn. Story starts with Renko and his partner Victor pretending to be corrupt investigators from the Moscow Prosecutor's Office who will not only kill an irksome husband of a business woman (Russian brides) but also investigate the murder, make sure it is never traced back to her. Renko receives a call on his cell from his boss, Prosecutor Zurin, telling him to go immediately to the Chistye Prudy Metro Station. Yeah, it's late, it's cold and it's snowing but... Joseph Stalin's ghost has been sighted on the platform.

Is this a good opening or what? As with any Renko story nothing is what it seems, and there are lots of powerful reversals en route to the ending. You want chess? You get chess. You want Chechens? You get Chechens. You want mass graves? Homicidal lunatics and bikers? A little touch of Lara (*Zhivago*) in the main woman? Maybe Renko even comes back from the dead... because, in truth, he's a sort of utilitarian ghost figure himself. It's a nasty world MCS draws, a bit like the TV news, but with the complete back story. Nastiness is like a good whiskey—nice, but it's gonna burn a little.

Nothing reveals the Soviet nightmare better than Stalin's purges and mass executions. Katyn Forest: the NKVD massacre in the Spring of 1940. Beria and the Soviet Politburo acting on Stalin's orders directed the secret police to execute 22,000 Polish officers and other citizens in order to make sure Poland would never again be a threat to the Soviet Union; ironically the massacre was discovered by the Germans. It's said that Churchill kept quiet about it for reasons of *realpolitik*. The event was horrible by any stretch of the imagination, a human cull of holocaust dimensions [and of course a subset of the Holocaust itself] and one which blurs the moral distinction between communism and fascism. Knowledge of this mega-atrocity has been a slow dawn in the west, more or less missed the entire generation who fought the war, and gives some ugly credence to Hitler's view that the Bolsheviks were the real enemy. If it wasn't for the fatal Polish President Lech Kaczynski plane crash near Smolensk (Russia) in 2010 en route to a commemoration ceremony at Katyn the western public would still be largely ignorant of this genocide; novels such as MCS's *Stalin's Ghost* (2007) and Philip Kerr's *A Man Without Breath* (2013) use the Katyn Forest Massacre as a macabre setting, and secular moral investigators to uncover the grim supernatural absurdity of it all. Smith's investigator Arkady Renko does some muddy grave excavation aided by a squad of bikers looking for body ID bounty and warrior (Nazi and Soviet) souvenirs, although his involvement is incidental to his homicide case; Kerr's Kripo/Gestapo detective Bernie Gunther is involved full-throttle under the direction of Joseph Goebbels, the opportunistic Nazi Minister of Propaganda. Kerr's novel is bleaker than Smith's, although his cop is every bit as brilliant as Arkady Renko... and, unlike Renko, isn't afraid to pack a gun and use it.

It's a nice way to get your history if you find the textbooks too dry and presumptuous. Western liberals would do well to study the modus operandi of Renko and Gunther; don't look to your government for your survival, look to yourself. Sure it's fiction, but is it anymore untrue than last week's news? The State is always a serial killer. Watch out, baby—the cop who pulls you over might not be your best friend when you're in need of some literary compassion. Well I'm driving through the forest on the back road thinking... sort of distracted... thinking... with these murder mysteries what you get is a life-style. Here it's Russian, although the most popular is British with murder. Now the form is global, a tourist itinerary for death and destruction some place you might like to go if you had the time and the money. Of course it's the job of these crime writers to draw the mysticism from an event, even if the truth can never be fully explained in social terms. Government, society, the human herd insists that the world be reduced to a binary reality. It's easier. The science of it suggests control. Where I live is remote, the forest pretty thick and lonely; guess it has a few shallow graves. Nothing like Katyn but the odd hooker has been dumped there, a dope dealer or two... a suicide. Nuthin' industrial like Stalin or Hitler. European normal is a lot different than normal around here... but then, who knows? In the mind there is no Time and Space, just a dream waiting to be terminated.

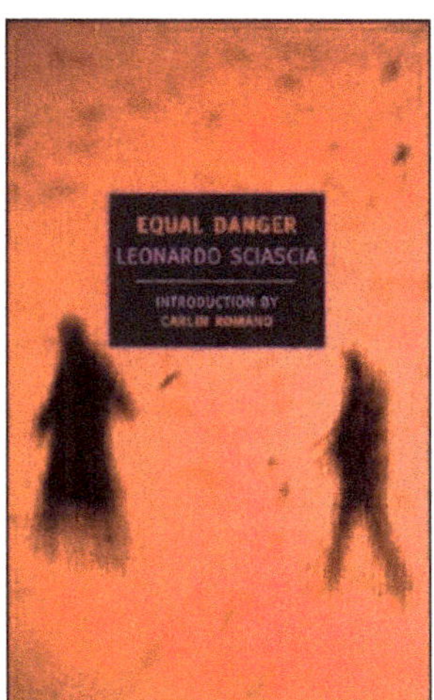

Leonardo Sciascia: *Equal Danger* [1971]

"All my books are the story of a series of historical delusions seen in the light of the present" Sciascia (1921-89).

Sicilian. Beautiful writer... and you wonder why he never won the Big One, as he's better than most. Might be the genre—crime—or the salon impressionism of his style, the old world rhetoric underlying the modernism. Borges comes to mind—acrostic plots that solve nothing, leave you out of words this side of the metaphysical horizon. This isn't Lee Child, isn't fiction for dummies. Early Sartre... Stendhal, certainly. The conversational voice, the aesthetic discoursing that moves between the essay narrative and the dramatized exchange.

Equal Danger: it's like a pyramid scheme, where each victim confides his situation to the next victim, and Death follows like a virus. A DA prosecutor called Varga is shot; the body is found, a flower in its hand. Inspector Rogas, a cultured *bon vivant*, is summoned, but barely is his investigation underway when a judge is shot in a nearby town. The same assassin is assumed. Rogas quickly fixes on revenge as the likely motive and a convicted pharmacist as the most likely suspect. More assassinations follow, always members of the judiciary. After seven, Rogas' superiors transfer him to the Political Crimes Department, even though he's convinced it's Cres, the pharmacist who's gone underground, may have assumed a new identity, even modest plastic surgery. "The way it happens in asylums, Rogas thought, where you always run into the man who stops you to confide about his Utopia, his Civitus Dei, his phalanstery."

Strangely, the "political" and "revenge" hypotheses converge. Rogas interviews a neurotic magazine editor called Galano—a guest of Nocosis, a Voltairian author—who is convinced his phone is tapped. Even when Rogas intrudes on a soiree at the Minister of Justice's apartment and finds Galano present with a number of revolutionaries, he raves against the police, claims he is a victim of a conspiracy. True enough, he is. It's funny stuff; one suspects Sciascia had specific targets in mind with a couple of these characters. In his afterword, Sciascia says, "I sketched the story of a man who goes about killing judges, and of a police officer who, at a certain point, becomes the man's alter-ego... but then I went off in a different direction...." No kidding. There's Nocio's free verse diatribe and a polemic about middle-class writers—which might be the point at which the story collapses for some readers, but for others, gets really interesting. There's a "phalanstery" of sorts in an urban forest where not only the Minister and the President of the Supreme Court have apartments, but also the suspect Cres who is now masquerading as a wealthy Portuguese businessman. Or so Inspector Rogas thinks.

In LS's brilliant novel *To Each His Own* (1968), the amateur investigator Professor Laurana ends up dead in a sulphur mine for his trouble. *In The Day of the Owl* (1961) Bellodi the Caribinieri Captain is shuffled off the case by the "Establishment" in Rome when he gets too close to a solution, but at least he retains his life. Rogas ends up in a museum gallery, mired in symbolism and... well, you'll have to read the novel to find out.

Great lines, old world cynicism, with a narrative that unfolds like a series of suspended chords. Not too long—maybe a novella, maybe a novel—like all of Sciascia's works.

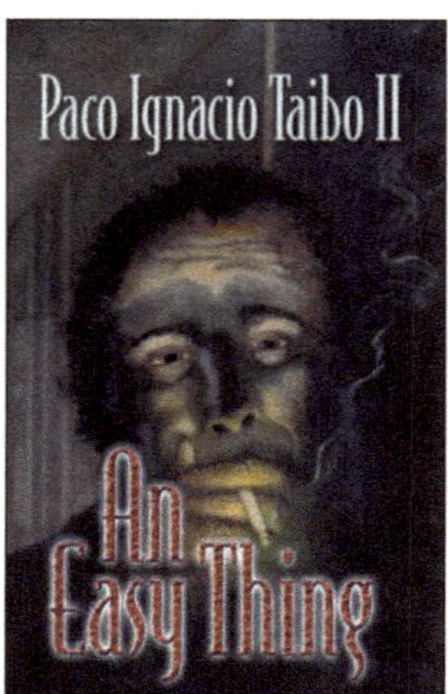

Paco Ignacio Taibo II: *An Easy Thing*

(A Hector Belascoaran Shayne Detective Novel Book I)

"It was up to him to defend himself against the myth of the super-detective, with its cosmopolitan and exotic delusions...."

Yes, you know: detective novels are a global pandemic and they're all the same, thank you very much... yawn. True, but this Mexican guy Taibo II (a.k.a. "PIT") can actually write outside the genre without the cliches killing your brain. It's fast food lit extremely well delivered, smoothly written with great figures of speech and a soft surrealist action driven by a likeable anti-hero called Hector Belascoaran Shayne (Spanish father, Irish mother) who perambulates around Mexico City at night (yes, he's an insomniac) listening to a DJ called El Cuervo (yes, he's an old school friend) on the radio as he goes about solving the crimes (or mysteries that could be crimes) with the dogged persistence of a Joycean Jackie Gleason. He shares an office with a plumber and a sewage engineer, so while satire is never far away, the action is more post-modern than farcical, and quite realistic unlike most post-modern narratives.

If Godard had written novels instead of making movies, this is the way they would've turned out. Taibo's/Belascoaran's crimes are mostly political, regardless of the motivation. Latin American society is a polarized society between top and bottom, and Belascoaran is a bottom feeder bringing down the top. An ex-engineer, he's a cop with a social conscience. Like a socialist priest, he's not in it for the money. He's not married, but he has a brother and sister, so he could be a Latin Mike Hammer with a family. Compulsive smoker and soda pop drinker, he hallucinates his way forward like an academic who works all night in his office and sleep-walks into trouble during the day. He packs a gun, dynamite, a notebook and an endless pack of Delicados ciggaros. Yes, he gets laid, he gets hammered, he gets injured (loses an eye), he works three cases at once (or four if you count the disposition of his mother & father's estate), all the while mining the soul of modern Mexico.

Not bad, and at the moment a real bargain in the Amazon KDP format. What's not to like about sentences such as, "It was a country where power was won and held at cock point" and "The lonely gloom of his cigarette...." Now, *senores*, that's noir.

PIT II: *Some Clouds*

Some Clouds is number #2. Here Hector Belascoaran Shayne plays the white knight for a friend of his sister, a redhead who gets thumped and raped by some nasties who are after her inheritance. The usual Mexican sociology and witticisms abound and the writer "Paco Ignacio" is integrated into the action. You might hiss or you might laugh and laugh.

PIT II: *Return To The Same City* (Poisoned Pen Press, 2005)

"If a detective orthodoxy happens to exist, a heterodoxy must also exist, a kind of heresy." If this guy Hector Belascoaran keeps adding sugar to his Coca Cola he'll be dead from diabetes and jaw rot long before a bullet takes him out. No matter. He's alive when he should be dead and like Lazarus keeps going down for the wrong woman... or the wrong book. He reads. He reads in his office armchair and he reads on the subway and he reads on a stake-out, all the usual suspects, Borges, Dos Passos, Carlos Fuentes, Graham Greene... and some gringo called Marc Behm, whoever he is (look him up) (in a genre full of cults, he's another).

Again, what saves PIT's writing from the sterile post-modern trap of the writer having no real subject other than writing itself are the real-time characterizations, the authentic insider view of Mexico City (the scape, the people, the institutions), the droll humor and aesthetic balance between his hero's working fantasies and the real world. But now he goes to the squid-pit of Acapulco, accompanied by a piss-tank Brit reporter for *Rolling Stone* (after all, you need someone to talk to) trailing a sleazy Cuban CIA mule who reputedly cut the hands off Che (for proof) when CG was captured and shot in Bolivia. This is number 4 in the Hector Belascoaran Shayne series and the story-line here is a bit of a sow's ear, so maybe PIT II should've left him face down in the pouring rain, dead and done (No Happy Ending). "The detectives before were good, these days they're worth pure dick," says the shrink. You got that right, pal.

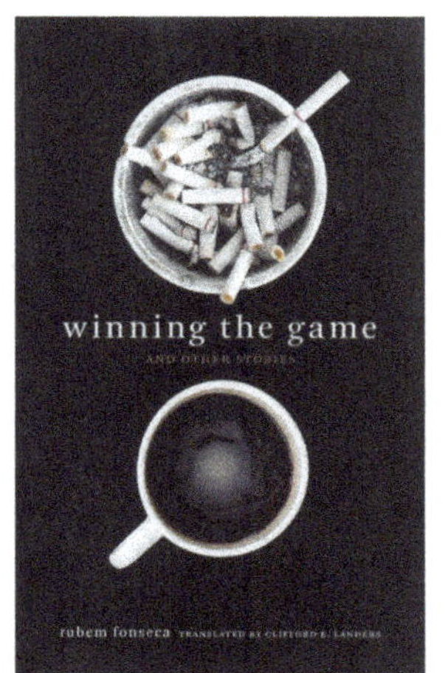

Rubem Fonseca: *The Taker & Other Stories, Winning the Game & Other Stories*

Very honest. Honesty and hypocrisy are perhaps his favorite themes. Line by line an excellent writer, strong oral voice (loves the 1st person confessional). Women are spared no mercy, and their men are often criminals, regardless of birth or place in society. His stories are frequently violent in a contemporaneous way without succumbing to ethnic conceit, even if the anthropological barbarism appears uniquely Brazilian. Rio is his landscape, yet his characters could be anywhere in the industrialized world. Behind the elegant *machismo*, there are often hints of sentimentality, pity, and moments of pure love. The humor is black, but never so black you can't share the criminal impulse, sympathize with the protagonists. Some are victims, some are opportunists, some are sociopaths, some are just plain mad. Sometimes Fonseca's tales wobble on the edge of fantasy, like the daydreams of passive males longing to be free of anger or boredom. Incorrigible womanizers, homicidal drifters, homicidal professionals, geriatric victims, hitmen, hookers, philanthropists, *nouveau riche, favelados*... uninitiated boys, poets, and women... women... women. Beautiful women, not-so-beautiful women, slags, society queens, sexual servants, murderess', artists... the whole *carioca* palette.

The stories? The soft cynicism of his narrative is relentless. Man visits the dentist to have a tooth pulled, considers the fee exorbitant, goes on a killing spree. Trio of geriatrics stage a revolt in an Orwellian hospice run by an Order of unnamed Brothers, take the Director hostage. Early morning commuter bus collides with a cow, plunges off a bridge, and as the rescuers deal with the dead and injured, hungry locals ignore the tragedy below, butcher the cow. A bored lawyer slips out in the evenings as his wife watches soap operas, uses his new car as a recreational killing machine. A Copacabana hit man becomes the hit. A man walks the old streets of Rio, maps the memory like Borges. A young boy comes of age in a ritual act of family cannibalism. A man cuddles his dying pet like a spouse in a final act of loneliness and love. A naive retiree volunteers to help the homeless, ends up as a organ donor. Etcetera. Sick of ghetto lit, fat novels than read like chocolate, leave you gorged and stupid? Try Rubem Fonseca. Exotic, hip, poetic, clean and swift, leaves you with enough room in your brain to fill in the dots yourself.

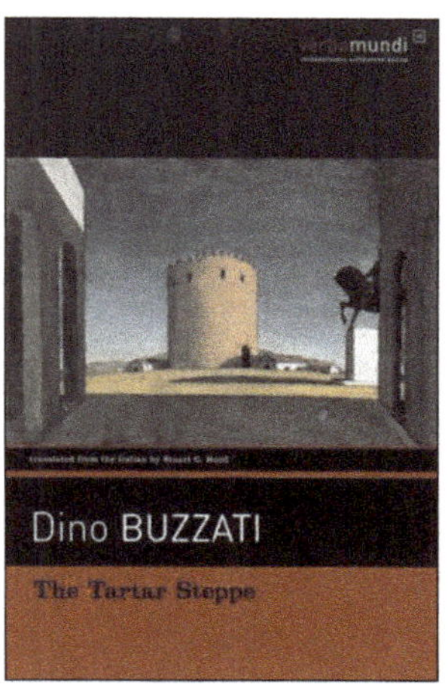

Dino Buzzati: *The Tartar Steppe* (1945)

"On the northern plain there was no longer anything suspicious to be seen on the fringe of the eternal mists"

For those who aren't wild about naturalist detail and prefer a more allegorical narrative, the Italian writer Dino Buzzati (1906-72) might be your man. Not widely known in the English-speaking world, he is gaining respect following the republication of his novel *The Tartar Steppe* in paperback. His style? Somewhere between the paranormal imagery of Stephen Crane (*Blue Hotel/Red Badge*) and the dream journey logic of Franz Kafka (*The Castle*). Some say *The Tartar Steppe* owes everything to the example set by Kafka, although this strange novel probably owes more to Lermontov (*A Hero of Our Time*, 1841) and the Tartar adventure-romance novels of the 1905 Nobel Prize winner Henryck Sienkiewicz, a Polish author who excelled at historical Tartar stories involving the Golden Horde. Quite possibly Buzzati read a lot of Sienkiewicz as a child. Certainly *The Tartar Steppe* often reads like a fairytale for adults, although there's nothing childish about its modernist metaphysical narrative. The 'first impression' sensibility, the anxious naivete of the protagonist Lieutenant Giovanni Drogo is like that of a child dispatched on a long journey. His destination? Fort Bastiani, a forgotten outpost in the mountains facing the mysterious desert known as the Tartar Steppe. Even though he arrives at the Fort, he never really reaches his destination as he longs to be somewhere else. He believes his posting is a mistake, so will be temporary. The Fort has stone walls, ramparts, battlements, courtyards, stables... redoubts—the details are generic, yet poetic like a painting. The soldiers have names, swords, guns, dream of being somewhere else, but who are they? What nationality? They could be toys or chess pieces, even though one or two die by misadventure. At first, reality is two-dimensional, then three-dimensional, with the fourth dimension—Time—barely understood, like the white desert and the Northern Kingdom somewhere beyond the horizon. In a sense, the characters are paralysed by Time. They hallucinate, they procrastinate, act out rituals, exchange passwords, respond to trumpets, play chess, play bridge, drink, long for another garrison, the city—but what city? What Time?

> "On the yellow courtyard they (the 7 guards) made a black pattern that was good to see"

The Tartar Steppe was written on the eve of WW II, so one is tempted to lock it into an Italian context. A garrison on the North Shore (Libya), perhaps, and the Tartars as a euphemism for the wild unknown of the Italian colonial adventure. The soldiers are waiting for a war that never seems to come. Yet it's elusive, like a dream that includes amnesia. As so much of the action is psychological and the landscape metaphysical, it could be anywhere, yet the author was Italian. The mystery of its being is the mystery of modern man. Even though we are preoccupied with the cliches of everyday living, we dream in mythologies as we wait on the edge of the great unknown. We put childhood behind us, but in fact we never leave it. We long for love—maternal, romantic, cosmic—but love is not for a soldier posted in the desolate regions of the Frontier. And yet we know this place, even if our passports deny it. Some might find the home stretch a bit preachy and predictable, therefore mildly disappointing. But the eloquent style remains consistent.

So, *The Tartar Steppe*—literary ephemera or masterpiece?

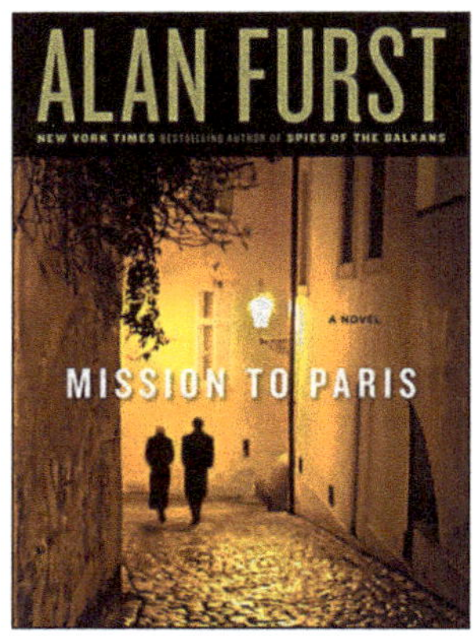

Alan Furst: *Mission To Paris*

Random House 2012

Ah, France... where communists and fascists compete to prove who is the most liberal. But what the heck—great wine, great women, ridiculous cars... and where every traffic cop looks like Charles de Gaulle. Too bad the Vichy crowd shot some Americans when the Allies landed in Morocco in 1942. A misunderstanding, obviously, just like Vichy. That France was largely Nazified following its occupation by the Germans in June 1940 is well known, but just how did this situation evolve? Was it really the rape and subjugation of one sovereign state by another... or was there a culture of compliance within the French government and public gestated by fear, ennui, and Nazi money? Was this collaborationist desire obvious and manifest in Paris in 1938-39, say? This pre-WW II Euro-schizo landscape is what Alan Furst chooses to explore in his latest spy novel, *Mission To Paris*.

It's interesting, now and then kicks with a little bit of gun play... but not much. Bit of sex, bit of travel, and money is never really a problem. If you like the old black and white movies of the 1930s and 40s with their *èmigrè* stars and European settings (like *Night Train To Munich*), you'll like this novel. Furst has enough of a feminine feel to his writing to capture the escapist romance of such dramas, yet is masculine enough to make the brute action fit the political realities of the time. And what was the time? The old class order in collapse, phony aristocrats and *nouveau riche* and fantasy artists of all persuasions everywhere filling the sidewalk cafes and salons of the old Parisian art mavens. In 1938 you could be anyone you wanted in Paris, especially as the cultural mood craved fantasy. Movies cut across all classes, all minds. French Foreign Legion films such as *Beau Geste, Le Grand Jeu*, or *La Bandera* formed a sub-genre within action-romance drama which exploited the cross-cultural milieu of multiple nationalities and exotic locations.

So there's a lot of old movie noise in Furst's head when writing this novel. It could be an expression or even a symptom of mass hypnosis therapy. Our sense of the past has become pure fiction. Movies today, the Bible yesterday: all is mythology.

parable of the good movie star. To some extent, *Mission to Paris* is a play-within-a-play in the sense that the protagonist Fredric Stahl has to go into acting mode both on stage and off. He arrives in Le Havre mid-September '38, disembarks the Ile de France, and is promptly chauffeured to the Hotel Claridge in Paris in a new Panhard Dynamic (steering wheel in the middle) laid on by the local Warner Brothers rep. As a Hollywood movie star, he's as politically important as, say, a Cardinal from Rome; as he soon comes to realize, Hollywood is like the Vatican, a state onto itself, quite possibly religious, certainly propaganda. Naively he believes he can avoid the post-Depression politics of the new Europe... but as the groupies start queuing up for a piece of his action—including the Ribbentropburo, the political propaganda service of the German Foreign Ministry—he quickly learns that there are many ways to get screwed. The Nazis, for example, have their local advocates and domestic spies everywhere.

Who is Stahl exactly? He's forty, originally from Vienna, has an Oscar nomination or two, yet his career is stagnating. Why else would he have been shipped to Europe to make a movie about the French Foreign Legion? The title is *sotto voce* ironic: *Après La Guerre*. Of course there's always a war somewhere—in this script it's Syria (a French possession), with Stahl's character Colonel Vadic trying to reach Turkey with a fake countess who he just might be in love with. Off stage, Stahl is hustling the costume designer, a sexy German *èmigrè* called Renate Steiner. In the end, their fate is very similar to that of the lovers in the movie, so it's a case of life imitates art when it's usually the other way around. Yet there's nothing phony about it, although at times the reader might wonder when the cameras are running and when they're not, especially in the Hungarian interlude. Sometimes the fiction overpowers the reality of the situation, the location, the suspension of disbelief. Yet—

There is danger, there is tension, always political, always moral. Stahl can always walk away, abandon the movie, return to the US... which might mean the end of his career, but at least he would be alive. He seeks advice from a consulate officer (Second Secretary) called J.J. Wilkinson and ends up as a spy almost by accident. The Nazis want him to come to Berlin, adjudicate a "mountain film" festival, will fly him in, give him 10,000 dollars and the Bismarck Suite at the famous Hotel Adlon... and a woman, should he need one. She turns out to be Olga Orlova, a Russian actress and established German star, a favorite of Hitler and Goebbels. Deep water film buffs/scholars will immediately recognize the character model: Olga Checkova, known on screen as Olga Tschechowa, who famously played a double-agent in *Asew* (1935) and, it seems, in real life.

And the protag Stahl? Some males might think he's a bit of a fop, like a guy who carries a tennis racket and no balls. As Cicero said about Caesar: "Methinks he wears his girdle too loose." Yet it would be unfair to dismiss Stahl as an American cultural mercenary invented in Hollywood by old Europe. He's very believable and Furst has certainly done his research on the type. Paul Muni is one Warner Brothers actor who hailed from the Austro-Hungarian Empire; other actors come to mind... Charles Boyer (French), Edward G. Robinson (Romanian)... even the writer-director Billy Wilder. When Wilder fled Nazi Berlin in 1933 he hung out in Paris for a period at the Hotel Ansonia, a haven for other proscribed German film figures such as Peter Lorre and Franz Waxman; in fact he directed his first film in Paris, *Mauvaise Graine* (*Bad Seed*) before heading for Mexico and crossing into Hollywood.

The action is full of movie types: Moppi, Stahl's old boss from their days in Barcelona, who could easily be Peter Lorre in *The Maltese Falcon* or Kiki, the rich ingenue art model and party girl who could be Jean Harlow or Danielle Darrieux in just about anything. Furst writes with a sense of elegance—fluid, baroque, yet always within the American tradition of verbal economy. He's good. He isn't one of these writers who goes into "performance voice", who just lets it all hang out like a comedian in full improv mode. He writes tight like a movie, scenes that advance the action without a lot of verbal impressionism (where poetry is substituted for action). Here, his voice tilts towards high culture, with just a hint of Henry James, say, laundered through Graham Greene. The language captures the time when Hollywood English was stage English, hit me daddy five to the bar iambics, where everyone sounds like a butler even if he's a count from Vienna or a bum on Sunset Blvd. The art of declamation is still part of the style, the microphone still in the distance. Warner Brothers made 51 films in 1938 and *Après La Guerre* wasn't one of them... but in this fictional world, perhaps you could call it a "lost film". *Mission To Paris*: strong, escapist fare, yet authentic within its historical context. The ending is perhaps better managed than *Spies of the Balkans*, Furst's previous novel, although both share a strong period atmosphere. If you like planes, boats and trains fiction, you might like this—

PART FOUR:

Miscellaneous

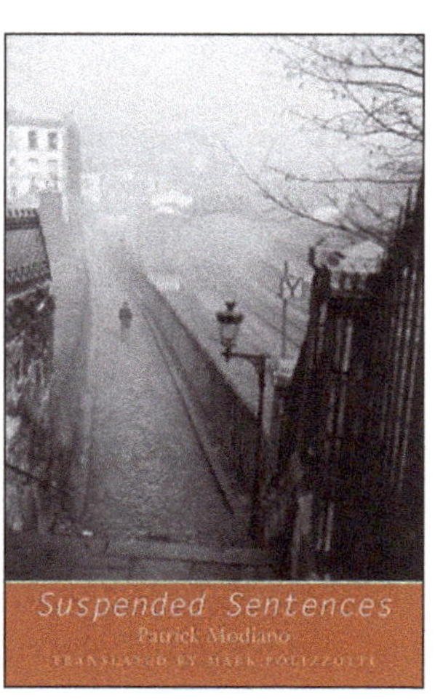

Patrick Modiano: *Suspended Sentences*

Three novellas translated from the French by Mark Polizzotti [2014] originally published as: *Chien de printemps* (1993), *Remise de peine* (1988), and *Fleurs de Ruine* (1991)

Patrick Modiano. French, won the Nobel. Writes for chicks, you might think, as his work lacks serious conflict and thrives on the adolescent sensibility, that is, nostalgia for the first impressions of life. Literary writing tends to be "I-remember-when"—indeed, the fading past is probably the most dynamic source of all art, except for near-field trauma such as war or love or illness. The relaxed feel to his writing has to be a large part of his appeal, the poetic placement of his imagery within the recollection.

He paints rather than reports; he photographs rather than judges; he smiles rather than frowns.

Novella I, *Afterimage*: "And I pictured him there alone, sitting at the far end of the sofa listening to the rings as they followed each other in the silence...." No , it's not Jay Gatsby ignoring the phone, although there's a similar sense of enigma about Modiano's character Jansen, the post-war photographer and protége of "Robert Capa" (Capa/Friedmann the famous war photographer); Jansen, who befriends the narrator (Modiano) when he's still a teenager living in Paris; Jansen, who gives "I" his Rolliflex camera, perhaps as a reward for organizing his portfolio, although he doesn't seem to put much worth in his own photos. He's heading for Mexico anyway.

The conflict, such as there is, comes from Jansen's relationship with Nicole, the young (actress) wife of a Left Bank performance artist called Gil the Mime. Gil isn't cool with this affair, despite the bohemian world they all live in, although the reader is never given any exact details.

They associate, maybe they copulate, sometimes they perambulate, have a meal, talk a little. At some point Modiano actually becomes Jansen. Meanwhile Gil takes on the menace of a symbolic carnival figure like Death in Marcel Camus' film *Black Orpheus* (1958)... and in fact there's an unreality about the narrator's perceptions that are not dissimilar to the sociopathic Meursault in *L'Etranger* by the other Camus, Albert. It's just a cultural tone, a stylistic, as Modiano's alter-ego is never put to a moral litmus test like Albert Camus' character Meursault.

The narrative follows a series of short scenes or chapters which can be considered verbal snapshots, and not a bad idea for a story about a photographer... or is this a story about a novelist who can't find a plot, even though he tries to organize a series of photographs into some sort of narrative? For those seeking a motivated sequence of beginning-middle-and-end, forget it.

Despite the slick writing, the last few chapters or snapshots do little to advance the action, for, by the time Jansen exits, the subsequent chapters/photos read like different versions of a conclusion. Is this good? Or is it merely the same photo from different angles? An "end" or "ending" probably isn't part of Modiano's way of doing business. The 'postponement of the arrival' is the game, as all resolution is left in the future.

"Some Day I'll Manage To Break Through That Layer Of Silence And Amnesia."

Bourgeois, evasive, elliptic, yet full of romanticism behind the nuanced alienation. Old selves dissolve into new selves. The final piece of wisdom seems a bit strained but in general Modiano is very good with resonating metaphors. Read it, try and remember what it's about. You'll be surprised by the space between memory and amnesia.

Novella II: *Suspended Sentences* has the naive charm of early Picasso when he was painting circus folk—acrobats, clowns, harlequins, dancers and animal props. It's a thespian world where everyone is acting even when the stage is in the imagination of a boy or a boy imagined by a man. Patroche (Modiano as a child) is a bit like a male Madeline and this meta-memoir is like a refit of the popular Ludwig Bemelman children's series about a young Parisian adventuress. So the imagery floats between children's lit and French film noir.

The narrator's mother is an actress, away from Paris with a theatre group in North Africa, leaving her two young sons in the care of four women at a house on the Rue du Docteur-Dordaine: Little Hélène, a former circus acrobat; Annie who wears tight pants, girlfriend of a gangster; Annie's mother, who claims to have a seeing eye in the bun on the back of her head; Snow White, the young girl they hire to mind the kids when they have other business to attend to.

The house turns out to be the former abode of Dr. Guillotine, the inventor of the execution machine, and his grave is in the garden. "Patoche" attends the Joan of Arc school nearby but is soon expelled by the principal for no apparent good reason other that he was dropped off one morning by a man (Roger Vincent) in a flashy American saloon... or because he wore an expensive wrist watch loaned to him and his brother by another shady associate of the caretaker women, John D. (a.k.a Buck Danny). The expulsion is baffling to the kid, although as the narrative advances and his mind matures, he has suspicions that eventually come true.

The writing has a liquid ease about it—literary but not crudely clever, clotted with pretty rhetoric or strained figures. There are lines, some of them very good i.e. "We glided on slack water." Or, describing Annie: "Her blond hair formed a stain on the thin light."

In its French version, SS was called *Remise de peine* (*Editions du Seuil*, 1988) and is admitted autobiography, that is, the author in his twenties recalls his boyhood back in 1952. The story never seems to develop beyond fantasy interludes at a chateau near an abandoned airfield (echoes of the French *Buck Danny* aviation comics) (like Biggles UK or Steve Canyon USA) and casual social visits by a man called Roger Vincent and another known as John D. who could be Buck Danny or an avatar.

As the memoir is occasionally hallucinatory, you just don't know what's legit and what's questionable. Patoche and his brother are treated to a ride on the bumper cars; later they decide to build a bumper car track with some boards in the back courtyard, and lo, one day a green bumper car materializes, a discard supposedly rescued by Roger Vincent. Fact or fantasy? Reliable or unreliable? You just don't know as the narrative allows mystery to shape make-believe into history.

The Memory Of A Memory—The Old Conundrum

Sometimes the narrative refocuses to the adult Patoche. Towards the end he accidentally encounters Vincent now driving a Jaguar and accompanied by another young silent woman. Patoche is now a struggling apprentice writer in an unheated dump somewhere in Paris. It's a difficult reunion, as Patoche knows from the newspapers that Vincent spent some time in prison for some sort of larceny. After they part, Patoche finds 2000 francs on his table.

Remission worthy? Could be, although the "good" in the Rue du Docteur-Dordain gang is quickly established simply by how well the two cast-off boys are treated by this surrogate family. They're *de facto* orphans, yet they are privileged to live a children's story-book adventure courtesy of some kindly crooks.

It should be noted that remission is an article of French law allowing an inmate to have his sentence reduced if he meets certain conditions. The French publication title *Remise de peine* obviously infers a moral clemency for Roger Vincent, Buck Danny, Annie & her mother and Little Hélène. In his articulate foreword translator Mark Polizzotti explains the difficulties presented by a literal translation of the original title; his choice of 'Suspended Sentences' certainly fits the moral of the story and describes Patrick Modiano's metaphysics exactly.

The title is a pun, referring both to the criminal back story and the "suspended" style where the author never cuts-to-the-chase if he can detour into some descriptive sidebar which may or may not help the reader understand just exactly what's going on. Perhaps it has appeal for those who love words for words' sake. Perhaps it supports the atmosphere, shares the love. Perhaps it's simply another way to tell a story without resorting to sex and violence.

If you need a clear through-line, you'll be disappointed. There's little or no conflict to drive the action, just a series of scenes and portraits that happen as they occur to the narrator. Unlike most literary writers who just change the names and post their journal as fiction, Modiano admits the memoir, and in typical Gallic fashion is greeted as *avant-garde*. Other writers have done it although the approach has gained momentum in the post-modern era.

The political necessity of hiding in fiction has diminished, and so has the need for 'plot' (unless one is writing about a conspiracy). Modiano is such a writer. Memory, nostalgia and fantasy are his weapons... and while he's a damn good writer line-by-line, the lack of conflict and the disorderly sense of *Time in Suspended Sentences* will cause a lot of readers to drop out fairly quickly. No wonder his work has been largely ignored in North America even though he's been publishing steadily in France for years.

This evasiveness, this piling on of place names and people —what to make of it? Art is the correction of a neurosis, says Freud. Modiano is a bit like a drunk who has a story to tell but who can never get to the point as he keeps vanishing into personalized asides, laced with nostalgia and sentimentality and irrelevant ghosts. You might marvel at the performance, yet grow impatient with the indulgence.

That's the brutal view. For those who persevere, the beauty of the writing might overcome the voyeur's hunger for forbidden thrills and easy space travel.

Novella III. *Flowers of Ruin*: here 'I' plays voyeur detective for no real reason other than geographic curiosity. Once again Modiano writes like a man serving time in prison who has nowhere to go but meander through his memories, especially those that form puzzles, hang in the mind like unresolved chords. People he encountered, then forgot—surely they were exotic criminals, impoverished aristocrats, funky artists etc etc?

Once again many will find the details foreign and frustrating, while others will no doubt luxuriate in the poetic impressionism. There are some killer lines, mystical descriptions, and an orchestral atmosphere that borders on pedantic madness. The passivity of the narrator is anti-dramatic, as he drifts through Time and Space like a camera, ducking the responsibility that goes with being a bonafide protagonist. What is he, you wonder—animal, vegetable or mineral? Well, it's like he studied some old tour guides to Paris, some news clippings, cannibalized them, then montaged them into the narrative.

Does Modiano use the cutup method of textural montage? Who knows... possibly he's a cultural archaeologist... but a novelist? If you try to reduce the action to the essentials, isolate the through-line, would *Flowers* even be a short story? Not really.

Causality is vague, characters are left hanging, and the narrative is occult; it's as if Modiano fell asleep with his head on a stack of paper, later awoke to find this perfectly imperfect story printed and ready to go.

It's maddening, these narratives where asides and transitions are as important—if not more so—to Modiano than the actual scenes that pass as action. He's a sadist, you think, and you must be a masochist for hanging in there.

And then, just when you're ready to jump, he hits you with a character or a scene that makes you purr like a sedated monkey.

> "Behind me, the jukebox was playing an Italian song. The stench of burned tires floated in the air. A girl was walking under the leaves of the trees along Boulevard Jourdan. Her blond bangs, cheek-bones, and green dress were the only note of freshness on that early August afternoon. Why bother chasing ghosts and trying to solve insoluble mysteries, when life was there, in all its simplicity, beneath the sun?"

The characters fleet... the philosopher in the ratty Shetland pullover... the New Wave starlet... Pacheco the Peruvian air steward (who might be the former German collaborator Philip de Bellune, maybe interned at Dachau) (aka Charles Lombard, waiter)... Jacqueline, the narrator's girlfriend who really has no character at all... Tony in the plaid shirt, the Danish girl who swears but likes the young wannabe writer... Claude Bernard, part of the old Rue Lauriston Gang along with the elusive Pagnon who ends up as a bouncer wearing shades outside a club ("a sentinel for all Eternity")... Simone, the former secretary of Modiano's father (probably his mistress)... the once famous goalie... *et al.* There are enough editions of noir characters to keep you going if you just forget about any resolution.

And in two of the stories Modiano inherits a suitcase from one of the characters... having assigned them to oblivion, the author is the only benefactor. Intriguing. Freud said, art is... well, you get it.

The narrator is sitting in the darkened apartment with "Jacqueline of the Avenue Rodin" as it rains steadily outside. Her old lover (literally old) the Marquis has followed them back, hammers on the door. She doesn't stir. The Marquis returns to the street, stands watching the window. "Little by little, that man melted into the wall."

'I' picks up a stray dog and he and Jacqueline take a train to Vienna. The dog business might remind some of the dog in Marcel Carne's 1938 film Port of Shadows. Just a thought; these post-modern writers do like movies; the 'memory of a memory', you know.

"Back then, the gates of Paris were all in vanishing perspective; the city gradually loosened its grip and faded into barren lots. And one could still believe that adventure lay right around every street corner...."

Great writer, no question... but a lousy story teller? You decide.

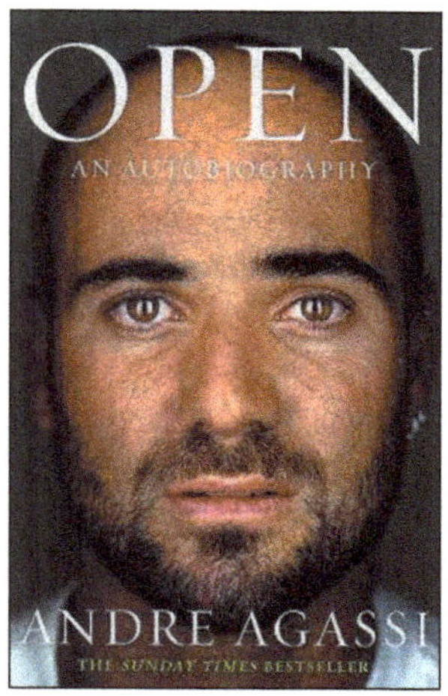

Andre Agassi: *Open, an Autobiography*

Vintage Books 2010

"Opponents are mere road cones"

This is a damn good read. In fact, when you pause for a sip of Primitivo, you think, how could Agassi have written this? It's fluid, literate, so hip and in the moment it could be a Beat novel, somewhere between *I Jan Cremer* and *The Subterraneans*... o.k. maybe it's a bit schmaltzy here and there, so let's say *On The Road*. How could a tennis player who says he dropped out in Grade IX have written this? Maybe Steffi Graf gave him a Vulcan mind meld. You have another sip of Primitivo, maybe a potato chip.

You think, this guy won all the slams and some, and when he was mere 10 years old whipped Jim Brown the NFL and Blaxploitation movie star *mano o mano* for five hundred bucks at some private Las Vegas club. Unreal... although he says he lied to the ATP panel about the circumstances that led to his failure of a routine drug test.

He says he deliberately tanked games, lied routinely during interviews. A ghost writer maybe? No such name on the jacket. An editor who does more than edit? Possibly. The street eloquence is stunning, the dramatizations and string dialogue ace copy... yet didn't Hemingway say anyone could write a novel in the 1st person?

Well, when you get to the end—and you will get to the end—you'll find a page of acknowledgments, and the secret is revealed: Agassi hired himself a writing coach (of course, of course) called J.R. Moehringer. What a team! Just get Andre on the couch with some Tequila, get him to spill it all into a recorder, and rachet it down from there. Brooke Shields... hmm, wasn't she the *Blue Lagoon* chick?

While their relationship wasn't exactly *The Attack of the Fifty Foot Woman*, Brooke is a big woman, so it was easy for her to mess with Andre's head, i.e. when he watches her lick "Joey's" hand during a guest spot shoot in the TV series *Friends*, flees the studio, drives like a madman to Vegas, trashes his pad, throws his Wimbledon and US Open trophies through the window. "It's just acting, Andre," says Brooke later. Sure, baby. You can understand the Champ's way of thinking when you realize tennis is 50% head games.

But forget the soap operas, forget Barbra Streisland and AA's questionable taste in music. There are some powerful psychological insights about what it's like to play championship tennis. "Tennis is just a form of pugilism," says Agassi.

You believe him, especially when it comes to Jimmy Connors, who never cracked a smile in his presence. As he was beating Connors in the US Open, a fan shouts, "He's just a punk, Jimmy—you're a champion!" Connors never gave up the rivalry graciously, and years later is still looking at Agassi with the cold homicidal stare of *The Rifleman*. Even Boris Becker—and he and Agassi had a big mutual hate—swallowed his bile and phoned his congratulations (via John McEnroe) when AA first won the French Open.

Well, he had to. Agassi had his number: Boris always stuck his tongue out in the direction he was going to serve. US Open, 1995. Grudge match against Becker. "The crowd is now wild. They seem to have figured it out, that this is personal, that those two guys don't like each other; that we're settling old scores.... Becker feeds on their energy. He blows more kisses at Brooke, smiling wolfishly. It worked once, why not do it again?" But Agassi outlasts Becker, wins the match, and when it comes to the final handshake at the net, "I leave him standing there like a Jehovah's Witness on my doorstep." Ugly... funny ugly.

We don't all play tennis, and if we do, we don't all play like champions. But most of us like to think we play life like champions, so there's a lot of common human insight in this autobio, a lot of truth. Agassi makes a great protagonist. Maybe you're driving along in your car and you hear him doing an interview on NPR. He's eloquent, speaks well and maybe you're surprised when you learn it's that punk Agassi and he's not only talking about the old days but today, his marriage to Steffi Graf and the charter school for disadvantaged kids he's started up in Vegas. He's pure rock and roll. You think, I'm gonna get this book... and maybe I'll get two or three because I know others who will dig it.

Andre Agassi: *Open*. Autobiography or novel?

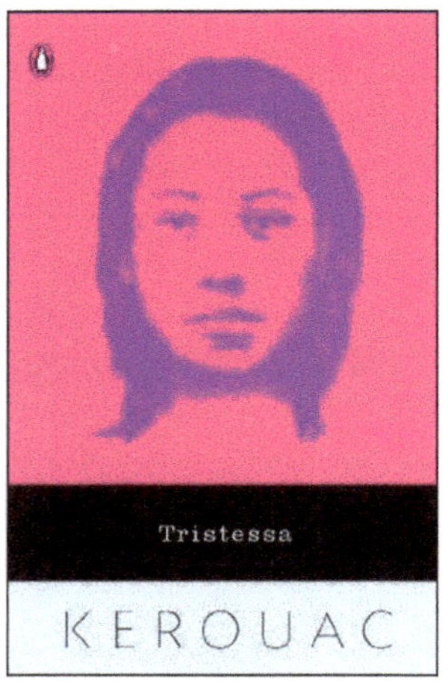

Jack Kerouac: *Tristessa*

afterword by Tom Graves
Devault-Graves Digital Editions eBooks

Maybe you're feeling nostalgic, remembering the days when guys just hit the road looking for adventure and something to write about, rather than tortured recollections of childhood or contempo 3rd person refits of the Bible. It's all TV scenarios posing as novels these days, isn't it? You want something raw, not ghost writers in the sky. You want something real, not university creative writing pretty, all dolled up and boring as hell.

How about some Jack Kerouac? "The first thought is always the best thought," he said, and just let the words spew forth in a metabolic vomit, achieving poetry as heady and real as the smell of leaded gasoline. Worked for W.B. Yeats... Francis Thompson... Alfred Jarry... all sorts of writers tried the "automatic" method... Henry Miller, James Joyce... all sorts, even Kerouac's good friend William Burroughs. You've read *On the Road, The Subterraneans, Big Sur* maybe—were they any good? You liked them at the time, the infectious Kerouac optimism, the New Age bullshit and the endless party he and his pals enjoyed, no matter what town or country they were in. Gentle outlaws. Free Birds. Jazz junkies. The Cold War? Nuclear annihilation? Fugg it, let's get high!

Did you read *Tristessa*, the one set in Mexico City? You can't remember, but think what the hell, Mexico City is a cool place to go nuts in, download the eBook, crack open a cider, turn off the sound on the TV. Well, you have to be loose to stay with this one, as the punctuation is experimental to say the least, and the grammar is often illogical (or, if you prefer, multi-dimensional). If you want raw, then this narrative is raw, as if scanned from Kerouac's notebook. In his afterword Tom Graves says Jack was too stoned and lazy to do the necessary rewriting, just winged it on the success of *On the Road*, which was knocked into shape by the editor Malcolm Cowley, a very influential figure in American letters in the 50s despite being monitored by J. Edgar Hoover. He might be right. Maybe fifteen good phrases, metaphors or insights per forty thousand words isn't worth a reader's time. Graves quotes Truman Capote on Kerouac: "That's not writing, that's typing". Yet there's something horribly magnetic about *Tristessa*, despite the chaos of the delivery and its squalid interior documentary of the madonna-whore morphine junky Kerouac chooses as his Muse. This isn't the sunny climes of Acapulco or San Miguel. Kerouac's Mexico City (circa 1955) is an endless barrio of night and chilling rain and living with animals in one room shacks. He sleeps with roosters, rats and cats, all in his desire to be near this woman who never really returns his love, as junk is the only thing she can love. But Jack "Duluoz" is smitten:

> 'The color of her face is really tan... but in the lights that shine her face keeps changing, sometimes it is jet-brown almost black-blue (beautiful) with outlines of sheening cheek and long sad mouth and the bump on her nose which is like Indian women in the morning in Nogales on a high, dry hill the women of the various guitar....'

You can see the picture, see what Jack sees, might even think the sluicing words are poetry. Others will find the syntax irritating, turn away after a page or two. Others will think Kerouac is just another sick traveller in a sick world. Despite everything, despite the graffiti narrative, the dismal sociology of it all is riveting at times. What lengths the author went to in order to express himself; the masochism, the degradation, the absurd humiliation of playing the junky's dog, crawling through the gutter, stoned and drunk, brazenly robbed of his money and poems by sinister Mexican drifters and poisoned by Mexico's open coffin of drugs: morphine, goofballs, pulque (cactus juice), mescal, beer, reefers, unknown caps of this and that. It's supposed to be romantic, but it doesn't take you long to see that this is the dark side of love, and that Kerouac just might be insane. Early photos show him to be a handsome guy and some of his women real beauties... yet no wonder he died in 1969 a broken alcoholic at the age of 47.

His contact friend in Mex City, the hard-core junky Bill Gaines, knows loving an addict is futile, puts it this way: "You put Grace Kelly in this chair, Muckymucks morphine on that chair, Jack, I take the morphine, I no take the Grace Kelly."

Kerouac knows this, of course. He's learned a thing or two about junk and love, despite his role as a Beatnik clown south of the border. 'But the sex when the morphine is loosened in your flesh, and slowly spreads, hot, and headies your brain, the sex recedes into the gut, most junkies are thin, Bull and Tristessa are both bags of bones....' So Dulouz/Kerouac comes to realize that if Tristessa loves any gringo, it's Bull, as Bull is Morphine. Jack might have money, he might have poetry, he might have devotion, but she recognizes he's too romantic to be a committed *heroinisto*. He thinks she's Mexico, a channel to the Aztec dream, another neglected goddess who can be rehabilitated through the love of a decent poet, and then, as his money runs low and his health lower, he realizes she's not a woman, rather, a place, a state of mind, a dream as desperate and unreal as the place that is Mexico City.

It might be the cider you're drinking but in the end you think, this works, the story of *Tristessa* works despite the messiness of the writing, the characters, the unwelcome confession of another drunken author who gets lucky with a publisher and starts a cult. He ends this sad tale of a sad woman with this: 'I'll go light candles to the Madonna, I'll paint the Madonna and eat ice cream... I'll write long sad tales about people in the legend of my life—This part is my part of the movie, let's hear your—-'

So it ends... he ends, and you're invited to pick it up, carry "the story" forward. This is exactly what America did, because when Kerouac was writing his main stuff—including *Tristessa* —in the fifties the country wasn't sympathetic to minorities, gays and junkies; later the Beat Generation subverted the conservative institutional culture, and today is as close to "anything goes" as it has been since the late Roman Empire.

Much has been said about Kerouac's Catholicism and you do see it in *Tristessa*: 'Her blood is on my pants like my conscience—' would be one fine example among many. Was he playing Christ here? It certainly would've been no surprise if he'd ended up nailed to a cross by the end of this short novel. But when you strip it all away, the existential journalism and the gladiator poetry, he's just a tourist with traveller's cheques and a passport. Great afterword by Tom Graves, *A Hard Look At The King of The Beats*, which is actually a review of *Jack Kerouac's Recordings and Other Matters*. It is a 'hard look', although a funny one. No academic devotee here glossing the King's failings, no homage in search of a study grant. Some good insight into the Kerouac method in general, although the real thrust of the piece is about his jazz poetry recordings. When you think of the success of rap in recent years, you realize that this idiom, this genre, this form of oral literature was never really explored fully in the bop era. Was Jack any good as a jazz rapper? Graves has mixed feelings about this. Maybe you're old enough to remember Kerouac with Steve Allen on piano doing some *On The Road*, thought it was o.k. (even if he was reading rather than rapping in the groove).

> "my poems stolen, my money stolen, my Tristessa
> dying, Mexican buses trying to run me down, grit in
> the sky, agh, I never dreamed it could be this bad"

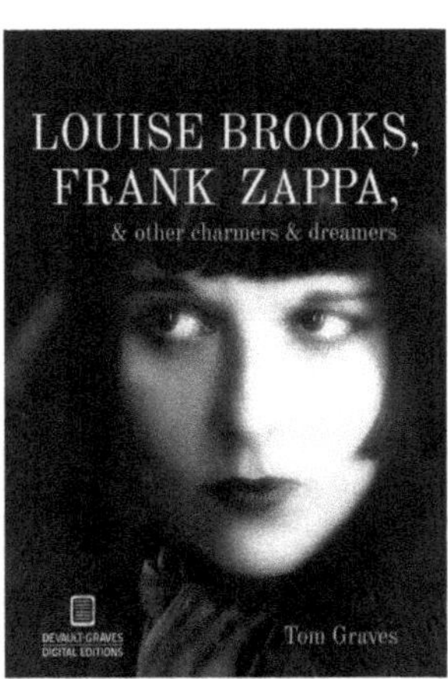

Tom Graves:
Louise Brooks, Frank Zappa, & Other Charmers & Dreamers
Tom Graves Devault-Graves Digital Editions eBooks

Have a Jack Daniel's, maybe a Colt on the side. Tom Graves is this kind of writer. Southern... Memphis, clear and personal, always courtly, with a sense of Southern Gothic ruling his tastes. A bit dangerous. He likes his *femme fatales* from the trailer park or the lost mansions of urban America; he likes his gunfights in the cinema; he likes his women for eyeshot ESP, and sitting close on the bench seat of a big Cadillac cruiser; he likes books for gonzo, barbecue ribs for a long life, gospel singers for religion, impersonators for Elvis... likes Roger Miller, Tennessee Ernie Ford, Cajun women, Cajun singers... biography assassins... and, believe it or not, Paul Revere and the Raiders.

How do you know? Just read *Louise Brooks, Frank Zappa & Other Charmers & Dreamers*, a compendium of his greatest hits as a journalist. It's all there, although sometimes you have to read below the lines.

Hemingway. The "Iceberg Effect"

Tom Graves... hmm. *Rock & Roll Disc Magazine*... and he wrote a book on Bluesman Robert Johnson, *Crossroads*. Your eyes move to the ceiling, remember the box set of the *Complete Robert Johnson Recordings* propped beside your vintage Bob Carver gear upstairs... have you listened to it recently? No. Got the *Crossroads* book in your music library? Don't know. Maybe. These days amnesia is just a nameless, familiar melody or a sleeping black guitar that's been below the couch for 15 years.

He writes about the movies like a fan, not a mechanic trying to pull the narrative apart. Picture of Louise Brooks, the silent screen star, on the cover of the book. Has the *fatale* look, the Surgeon General Warning, this chick is dangerous for your health. Interesting profile in the NJ style, the story-of-the-story, part biography (Louise), part autobiography (Tom). Was she Kenneth Tynan's lover? Suicide is part of the conversation. She's awfully interested in George Sanders... you remember when he checked out, 1972, Nice or Barcelona or someplace in between. "I'm bored with it all," his note said.

What's interesting about this cryptic biography by TG is not how Linda ends but rather how he ends.

A Lonely Woman With Many Bad Men In Her Past

So *cherchez la femme*, folks. Following the aborted Louise Brooks project, Graves uses the mystery narrative as an envelope to profile Linda Haynes, the seventies B-movie star that some might remember from the cult movie *Rolling Thunder* (1977). Where is she now? Why did she drop out of sight around 1980 after generating some heat with Paul Newman (*The Drowning Pool*, 1975) and a walk-in with Robert Redford (*Brubaker*, 1980)? Maybe the last shoot, *Guyana Tragedy*—about the horrific Jim Jones mass suicide—fried her head, so you're thinking, son-of-a, did she become a victim of one of her own parts as so many artists do... writers write their destiny, actors act their fate sort of thing... Mishima... Tony Scott... Hemingway... Virginia Woolf, Sylvia Plath... the Black Dahlia... Diana Dors... Pamela Moore... Diane Arbus, *et al.* Or is she just another Hollywood cliché, you know how they finish, rob a bank and end up on a warm beach or die before they get there.

As he paints the portrait, Graves develops the enigma while seeking aesthetic justice. She was "white trash beautiful" and "a woman who walked the edge between prostitution and respectability", says Graves, drawing the fantasy from her on-screen persona. Sounds like a Cornell Woolrich woman, available in dream, unavailable in life.

The film that throws the switch for Graves is Paul Schrader's *Rolling Thunder*, in which Linda Haynes plays a waitress working in a diner who drops everything to tag along with Major Charles Ranes, a Vietnam vet just repatriated back to Texas after several years of incarceration in the "Hanoi Hilton", and now looking for justice. His wife and son have been murdered by a gang of home invaders looking for his blood money, some silver dollars gifted by his home town during his return ceremony.

Yes, you've seen it, late night TV... the gunfight in the whorehouse. William Devane with a hook and a Winchester. Maybe you yawned, or maybe you thought, cool.

Devane—you know, the guy who sells gold and silver on TV. Appeals to survivalists in the Age of the Bullshit Derivative. He's good at it.

Rolling Thunder was eclipsed by *Rambo* as the more popular vet-returns-for-revenge movie of the era, even though the director Paul Schrader had established his killer credentials with *Taxi Driver. Rolling Thunder*... sounds familiar, right? Maybe you saw the Bob Dylan and friends tour of that name in 1976 but this isn't where the handle comes from... that's right, it was President Johnson's code for the B-52 carpet bombing campaign that was meant to take the Vietcong back to the Stone Age. So, fits good with this neo-western where Vietnam reverberates in the Homeland as a violent and bloody festival of repatriated violence.

Is/was Linda Haynes really worth getting hot and bothered about? Fantasy drives the submerged bicameral mind without regard to reality. While we supposedly left all this behind thousands of years ago, a case could be made that military training, for example, reintroduces the "command voice" so that the ability to kill without question is always latent, no self-awareness necessary. Seems to work for Tommy Lee Jones in *Thunder.* So maybe this is also true for film in general, which, as a form of sensory immersion and hypnosis, re-introduces the bicameral proto-consciousness.

A classic of this sort of schizophrenia would be *Sunset Boulevard*, where Norma Desmond appears to take instructions from the celluloid version of her former self.

Just thinking, just saying.

But Linda Haynes... would she drive a man mad? All it took for Tom Graves to lose his infatuation with Louise Brooks was to actually enter the hive, meet her and her drone friends. Linda was different.

Once again the Jack Daniels brushes your lips. You think, should I get myself a Ranes hook and a trigger bitch like Linda or should I make a piece of toast and continue reading? You make the toast.

"I played to the camera and no one else," says Linda.

There is a certain beauty in the Tom Graves method, an artifice that allows two appositions to mingle. He's a writer in search of a subject, not a voyeur in search of a lover. His extensive telephone trawling finally pays off and he finds Linda Haynes—neglected and forgotten—living in Florida. Well, not completely forgotten; it seems that the filmmaker Quentin Tarantino has recently phoned, suggesting she come to Los Angeles, test for a part. She declines to test, so it comes to nothing, yet reading her story you sense no lasting disappointment, no permanent defeat.

TG's portrait is sympathetic—perhaps overly so—downplays the drug abuse and so on, yet you have to admire a journalist who has some moral restraint in a world where neither morals nor restraint are common. Reading this story, you might be reminded of Max Cherry's gentlemanly crush on Jackie Brown in Tarantino's film of the Elmore Leonard novel *Rum Punch.*

Or you might think of Joe LaBrava when he gets involved with Jean Shaw... eh, when you enter a darkened cinema and look up, beware of the 50 foot woman!

I Know Who Ray Wylie Hubbard Is, So Why Don't I Know Who Harry Is?

Who is Harry Crews? Another New Journalist? A novelist? Name seems familiar, like a porno star or a fictional detective from the pulps. You missed this guy, you have to admit. Southern. Has written all kinds of well-received novels but you missed him. As you read TG's gritty interview with the gritty Crews, you realize what a multifarious ghetto the whole lit scene is, and truly, in the post-modern world there are more writers than readers.

But the Darwinian Crews is interesting, his character vivid even if you haven't read him. "Florida is not the South," he insists, and goes on to make some pithy remarks about Norman Mailer, Truman Capote... boxing, pit bull fighting, even the photog Diane Arbus. And Graves baits the hook, feeds him the verbal meat, has him going. The beauty of an interview like this is that the reader becomes a voyeur, the conversation, fiction.

Graves also writes on music, and has included several profiles, reviews and interviews. His extended essay on the white gospel group the Blackwood Brothers Quartet is educational. So much of rock journalism is a blurry impressionism where you can't separate the hype from the reality, the worship from the dream. Not these pieces.

A Kind Word For Albert

> "I have a confession to make: I like the work of Albert Goldman, rotting carcasses and all."

Rock music... and those who feed off it. Often you just end up writing info commercials, especially if you like the stuff. It's hard to get aesthetic distance; it's like booze, gets you drunk, mission accomplished, move on. But when you politicize and fictionalize the profile in order to create a sensation, as Albert Goldman did, then you wonder about the moral boundaries. Yeah, you know Goldman... you read his outrageous bio of Elvis, and you read the John Lennon assassination job. Good writer... but prurient. Fame and fortune got to him. Bad disco. He became a member of the Mile High Club, died from a heart attack on a transatlantic flight... like Paul Kossoff, the Free guitarist, although Albert was no guitarist, had a shitty Pioneer stereo setup.

So TG tells us. He did some research/editing work for Goldman, certainly has some reservations about him, his way of doing business... yet withal remains fond of the man, even after Goldman "grew tired" of him. Picked up some chops, realized the Lennon bio was slanderous... yet the brutal humour of the New York iconoclast tips the scales.

Do we all lie the minute we set pen to paper? The Cuban novelist Gabriel Infante has a good line about this sort of phenomena: "Everything you write is fiction, even the grocery list."

Re Elvis, some of those stories about the Memphis mafia had to be told, y'know. Maybe Goldman was like a sewer worker —somebody has to do it. "(He) came up with a morality tale and an American nightmare... no one explored the dark side of Elvis better than Albert Goldman," says Graves.

The Goldman piece is a good read, and all too brief. You wish there was more... because, well... because you know there is more. Well, you can always speculate, go meta. How about Albert ending up as a drug-crazed Elvis impersonator before he implodes? Just saying.

Pistols

The Sex Pistols... first of the Art Rock bands? Did they really burgle their amps and PA system from Keith Richards' Chelsea pad when he was away? Your mind wanders back to the time, the late sixties, early seventies when psychedelic rock was just about done. There were new oilers in the engine room, the "Punks". Everything about these jeering Morlock reactionaries who took music back to the Jurassic is apocryphal, although you can take it to the bank that TG's account in *When The Sex Pistols Played Memphis* in 1978 isn't.

In a town where an Elvis impersonator like Bill Haney can draw a full house, these guys should've been playing a local art gallery instead of a "former dilapidated ballroom (the Taliesyn) attached to the Twentieth Century Club on Union Avenue." $3:50 a ticket, 900 inside, 200 left standing outside in the freezing drizzle, according to TG who was there with his young wife and a friend. Imagine if they'd been a band of Brixton blacks, not cockney white trash, same act... what kind of crowd would they have pulled? You sigh. Didn't the singer, Johnny Rotten, say, "Gandhi is my life's inspiration" or something like that?

The idea of the Pistols playing Memphis stuns the imagination, like Woody Allen playing Mecca, say. Or *American Idol.*

> 'Sid Vicious, none of us knew at the time, could not play bass guitar at all. His sound was so thick and muddy, you could not distinguish the notes; all you could hear was a huge, earth-swallowing throb. Sid was shirtless and had red markings all over his torso that I originally thought had been made by a red felt-tip marker. I didn't know until much later that he had carved a message into his chest with a knife: "I need a fix."

Zappa

Anyone who has followed rock and jazz from the fifties probably knows about Les Paul's pioneer work in developing multi-track recording, but did you know that Frank Zappa had one of the first multi-track studios in Los Angeles in the early sixties?

This is something that you learn in TG's interview with Zappa. Killer stuff for those interested in early analogue recording and the start of the shift into digital (early eighties). For those seeking info on Zappa's fractured music narrative—face it, he used rock as a subterfuge—check out *In The Ocean* [a film about the classical avant-garde] which includes a clip of Zappa's *BeBop Tango*. Here he says, "Progress is not possible without deviation."

Sure... *Weasels Ripped My Flesh.*

Zappa: his name is like a cigarette lighter, and his approach to music just as incendiary. The man looked like a Sicilian bandit, and although he was pure L.A., he really came out of the fantastic Italian avant-garde tradition. Think of people like Luigi Russolo... even the over-exposed Ennio Morricone has done some off-the-wall, so Frank was no surprise inside the Academy even though he worked the street.

It was well-known that Zappa was anti-dope, and he reiterates this here. "Anything with a needle, give me a break," he says (although he didn't mind some nicotine).

> Graves: What kind of hate mail do you get?
> Zappa: Little or none. Well....
> [Zappa on the *Steve Allen Show* 1963]

Mick Taylor

Remember when he joined John Mayall, the English blues singer who sounded like a eunuch? Sure... *Bare Wires* and *Laurel Canyon*, best stuff Mayall ever did, some nice psychedelic blues going on in there, and Mick was perfecting his version of the "woman tone", roll back the treble and go sinal, that warm tube harmonics sound Clapton based his fortune on. Sure, you know him, admired that killer solo on the coda of the Stones' *Can't You Hear Me Knocking* (*Sticky Fingers* 1971). Yes, he was good, and he walked away from it all after six years.

The Graves interview is from 1988, originally published in *Rock & Roll Disc Magazine*. It's long, and very good. Taylor is quite forthcoming. His first rock concert? Bill Haley & the Comets, 1958. Check (you saw them at the Belfast Opera House, 1957). His first guitar? A Hofner President. Check. His first Blues album? *B.B. King Live at the Regal* (1965). Check. Why did he leave the Stones? Personal, not saying. Check (uh, you read too much coke blah blah). What do you think of Stevie Ray Vaughan... and so on.

Yes, it's mostly life-style evaluation, with some *Guitar Player* technical, but it's good stuff for those interested in the greatest rock period, that is, the British re-colonization of America... and the world.

So, you say, where can I get this book?

Do I have to go to Memphis?

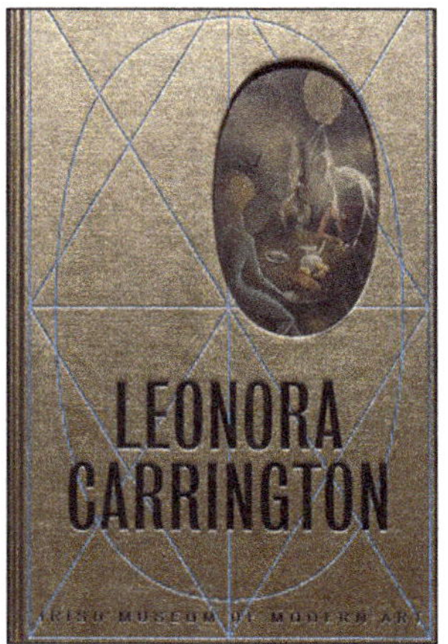

Leonora Carrington, painter, novelist and short story writer. Women like this artist, recently deceased at 94, and men should, although they might find her fantasies too close to the nursery, too much of a Freudian coffin.

A Mexico City recluse, the 'bad debutante' was born in England (affluent northern industrial family), did the Left Bank, fled the Nazis, was confined for a period to a Spanish asylum (love sickness and/or war fear), found refuge in Mexico. It was through art school in Paris and London that she gravitated to surrealism. Ran off with the cradle-robbing Max Ernst who was, perhaps, her biggest technical influence. You might think she's another forgotten treasure, but in fact she was written about quite a bit, and her own works were published internationally. Yet she remains relatively unknown except to a few travellers and female academics.

Like Remedios Varo, her close friend, she found refuge from WW II in Mexico City, came under the muralist spell of indigenous Indian mysticism which blended easily with her atavistic primitivism. And like Remedios Varo the uterine quality of her fantastic imagery is rendered with a soft feminine touch, highly detailed draughting, and a Bosch-like dark humour. Sometimes cluttered, sometimes simple, her compositions are like elegant autopsies... could be Alice (in Wonderland) or an alien from an unknown planet... or a bagpiper levitating a fish. Birds morph as humans, humans morph as animals, and the totems of ancient civilizations invade the dreamscapes.

Lots of women figures—always in "dress-up'—robed and veiled like priestesses guarding the holy egg of life, conducting witchcraft ceremonies. Birds, horses... birds, dogs, cats... LC is the Beatrix Potter of the spirit world. Her mysticism is a paranoid mysticism, as if flesh dies when exposed to light.

Fascinating.

Leonora Carrington is published by the Irish Museum of Modern Art, a way of claiming genetic provenance by way of LC's mother and grandmother who were Irish from the River Boyne hinterland. Beautiful book. Gold hardback with debossed title, oval graphics window, heavy paper in the 12 by 8 format, a bargain for collectors at the current price. Dozens of color plates, photos, childhood drawing facsimiles, and essays (of course) slanted towards sourcing the Celtic in LC's work.

Most of these essays have the academic slowhand touch, yet are closely researched and argued. Contributors include Alyce Mahon, Sean Kassine, Teresa Arcq, Giulia Ingarao, Dawn Ades, and there's an interview with LC by Hans-Ulrich Obrist. There's also a mildly bitchy opinion piece by one of her sons, Gabriel Weisz Carrington (people are always hijacking my mother's story for their own ends, etc), but no doubt he's had to endure a lot of dumb questions/intrusions.

Only one criticism: while the book design is great to look at, the vertical scaling leaves it with a short left-right throw, which in turn makes reading the essays a bit awkward. While it's not clear in the credits who edited or designed this book (Pony Ltd), it appears the Irish retrospective was curated by Sean Kassine, and this symposium followed. No matter: Leonora Carrington's time has come, and you need this book for your collection.

PART FIVE:

Brain Scan of a Dead Script Writer

Scripting J.G. Ballard

When the sixteenth century German explorer Hans Staden was blown onto the shores of Brazil, he was captured by the Tupi Indians and would've been eaten if he hadn't negotiated his way out of it. His account of his adventures, *True Story and Description of a Country of Wild, Naked, Grim, Man-eating People in the New World, America* (1557), was translated widely, became an international best-seller and inspired many follow-up books. Staden escaped the cannibal death but many others didn't, including J.G. Ballard's fictional character Colonel Francis Spender, the lunar astronaut in the short story *A Question of Re-Entry* whose capsule comes down in the 20th Century Amazon jungle.

Pure fantasy? Not really. There are still unacculturated tribes living secretly in the Amazon forest, sometimes photographed from the air, and reports of cannibalism persist. Why not? For every sweet flesh Namba in the green mansions of the Mato Grosso, there's a Jeffrey Dahmer or Albert Fish living near you. Cannibalism is part of the human instinct.

Re-Entry opens with a beautiful Conradian description of the UN Space Agency investigator Lieutenant Connolly travelling into the Amazon jungle by boat. The mission: to follow up on reports about a missing UN astronaut, Colonel Francis Spender. Lost in space? Forget it. How about lost on Planet Earth. The irony is elegant, sublime, and brutal. One part of our world is in the Space Age, another in the Stone Age. In Pierre Boulle's *Planet of the Apes* (1963) the astronauts return to Earth (after a long time-bending hiatus) to find their civilization in ruins, with the Apes in control; a crude, simple axiom that has since engendered several movies, making the original a classic, the spin-offs a cult.

In *A Question of Re-Entry* (also published in 1963), the astronaut returns to Earth to find himself deified and eaten, then become the rationale for a cargo cult. While Apes can be seen as a daring recast of Boulle's grim war classic *The Bridge (Over) The River Kwai* (1952), you have to look to the H.G. Wells short story *In The Abyss* (1896) for the *Re-Entry* mock-up. Wells has his hero Elstead descend into a 5 mile trench in a deep-sea bathysphere. He finds an aquatic civilization who consider him a god, and when he fails to return from the second descent, you're left wondering if he chose to remain with the aquatics (human fish) in their marine graveyard as an exalted being rather than return to the mundane world on the surface. Was Ballard familiar with this story? Almost certainly. No one of his generation could escape H.G. Wells.

> 'Sometimes sinking things would smite down and crush them, as if it were the judgment of some unseen power above, and sometimes would come things of utmost rarity or utility, or shapes of inspiring suggestion. One can understand, perhaps, something of their behavior at the descent of a living man, if one thinks what a barbaric people might do, to whom an enhaloed, shining creature came suddenly out of the sky.' [H.G. Wells, *In the Abyss*]

A Question of Re-Entry made a powerful impression when I first read it in the early seventies. An electronic composer called Phillip Werren passed along a copy of *The Terminal Beach*, a collection that included *Re-Entry*, after he heard one of my DNA tapes called *Geometry & Dream* (1971). Believe he directed me specifically to this story. Much later (1987) when Bill Lane, producer of the CBC's *Vanishing Point* radio drama series called, said he wanted to do some Ballards, I chose *Re-Entry*.

I chose it because it was conceptually brilliant, not because it was an easy dramatization, a xerox job, where you just photocopy the story, extract the dialogue, submit the script... 'money fer nuthin' and yer chicks fer free', you know? In fact, I chose it because it gave me a chance to re-conceptualize the narrative, invent new dialogue, reinvent a character, and extract the implied soundscapes from JGB's narrative, i.e., the launch travelling up the river, the jungle, the clock(s), a walkie talkie (added), etc. The major refit was the interior narrative of the witch doctor's son—who, as it turns out in my drama, is the incarnation of Colonel Spender, the astronaut—as the kid participated in the eating of the 'god from the stars' following the crash landing. I feel this got around the unfortunate exposition always involved when using an external, omniscient narrator, while at the same time retaining the integrity of JGB's story. Enchancing a minor character and using his interior monologues to frame the action not only establishes a contrapuntal point-of-view but also explicates the story's ironic theme, that is, the old occult versus the new occult, anthropomorphic spiritism versus scientific mysticism.

I don't know if JGB heard the dramas or not, and if he did, what he thought of them. Bill Lane says he forwarded copies but is otherwise vague. I thought—and still think—Bill's production was outstanding. The audio has a liquid depth and sense of montage that escapes the production clichés of your basic radio play. Ballard was probably pissed off. No author is ever happy with others messing around with his stuff. Radio... not enough money in it for anyone to be happy.

The Dead Astronaut... I dramatized that one too. That was also a challenge because, despite the great sonic possibilities inherent in the crashing satellites, the ending is murky, makes no real sense (at least in a conventional way). Believe that story first appeared in *Playboy* in 1971, which shows you how hip JGB was becoming by that time. Again, conceptually brilliant, which is his greatest chop other than his descriptive metaphors. Dialogue—forget it. Narrative—excellent, a true painter of the mind. The axiomatic symbolisms he dreams up for his best stories are text book lessons in how to rachet down a narrative to its essentials. Always visual, always extra-sensory, always promoting the back story which, like Kafka, is never fully revealed.

That's the thing about the *Dead Astronaut*—why, what, and how? It's madness, both American and human, an endgame born in Nazi Peenemunde ending at Cape Kennedy (nee, Canaveral). It's a science fiction film noir... remember the plutonium suitcase in *Kiss Me Deadly* (1955)? Yes, some people write stories about facing death in small towns, but Ballard? He was wired into the industrial estates of the mind, where space and time collapse, so the lab and the livingroom coexist. Contemporary life. You don't go down to the saloon and start shooting, you die in a car wreck *en route*, or your space capsule is punctured by a 9 millimeter meteor. Once upon a time you disappeared on a mountain like George Mallory. So you can die like Madame Curie or Valentin Bondarenko or any number of Soviet cosmonauts. The 3 man crew of Soyuz 11... there's a grim fascination about death in space. Well, exotic death. It's always a target in our minds.

In some regimes, a story like *The Dead Astronaut* would be banned for promoting defeatism. While the landscape is grim, and the moral even grimmer, there is a beauty in the telling. The imagery is superb, the heroic loneliness a metastasis of all human loneliness. The 20 year death orbit of astronaut Robert Hamilton is not unlike the ghost vigil of the French author and aviator Antoine de St. Exupery who crashed just off the coast of Marseille in 1944 and remained there 60 years before the wreckage of his P 4 Lightning was identified in 2004. If all Judith Groves got was a suitcase of some radioactive bones, the St. Exupery family got even less: a seaweed encrusted bracelet engraved with the name of his risque wife (Consuelo) and a fragment of a flying suit.

Suicide? Saint Exupery had plenty of reasons for suicide, and this is something I thought about as a possibility for Robert Hamilton when scripting *The Dead Astronaut*. Not that I had Exup's story to guide me back in '87. Suicide... or, maybe, should it be murder? Something to lock it down, ease the mysticism, massage the listener. With audio, you have to catch the action as it happens; you can't pause, flip back a page, reread, see if you missed something. There is no reverse gear in radio drama. Extreme poetics don't work. If there's a plot, you have to make it simple (even if it isn't), and if there isn't a plot, you have to have a great soundscape.

In North American pulp fiction, where every male suffers from gunshot trauma and every woman is a *femme fatale*, characters are on the long crawl from the saloon into the urban heartland of the twentieth century. JGB recognizes this, makes adjustments, plots the trajectories of citizen dissatisfaction as the criminally artistic urges of the counter-culture. So the new hipsters in Berlin will watch cockpit footage of Hamilton's death as they huddle in stoned rapture within their Cold War lofts and art gallery latrines. Voyeurism is the order of the day, sex and death the players. Forbidden tapes, forbidden texts—in this sense, *The Dead Astronaut* itself becomes one such forbidden artifact. Like Jim Morrison exposing himself on stage in Miami, you just never know how long you're going to get away with it.

Well, that was *Playboy* in its golden era. And of course another Ballard 'influenster', Ray Bradbury, had his Orwellian novel *Farenheit 451* serialized in *Playboy* in its early days. Robie Macauley, the fiction editor, was always looking for something with a forbidden feel, something to help drive Hefner's liberal snow-plow through the moral banks of the Establishment. Bad boy jeering and cynicism were commodities, not heresies.

(A Criminal Astronaut, You Say? Perfect.)

So the American astronaut with a nuke in his capsule dies, a fitting judgment for such a reckless act... even if he was just following orders. Impotency: a dead astronaut, a dead child, a dead world. There's no resurrection here, no tomorrow, just the pornography of despair.

Only the carrion profit. Quinton for one, a hustler who makes a living from thieving the military-industrial wreckage of the US and Soviet governments. Then Philip Grove—the dutiful husband whose Anglican loyalty seems too good to be true. That he also plays the part of undertaker in this New Age farce just makes the action seem like a forgotten play by Fernando Arrabal. Indeed, Arrabal's *The Automobile Graveyard* (1966) parodies the crucifixion, and Robert Hamilton's persona can be seen in this context, like a New Age Dali icon hanging in a drug dealer's crash pad.

You see traces of Arrabal in *Crash*, just as you see Beckett in *Concrete Island*. Theatre of the Absurd's method of shock therapy is Ballard's method in *The Dead Astronaut*, where he's a Futurist painter celebrating the violence of speed for the purposes of transfiguration. Some say the war is over; Ballard says no. We carry it like a gene worming its way through history.

The Cold War. As a figure of speech, it's more than just politics.

As the narrator Philip Groves says about Robert Hamilton: '...(his) albino skin, so like Judith's pale eyes and opal hair, the same cold gene that crossed them both with its artic pallor.' The poetry of it, the Ballardian word-stroke that sends us deep into the dream logic of its inferential imagery. Hamilton, the secular Jesus, with a hint of the Wagnerian godhood, the Aryan warrior hatched in the science of Peenemunde, nurtured in the service of NASA and the US military, now meets his Valkyrie maiden. And... when Judith Groves recovers the remains of her dead lover, is it love or is it guilt or is it just the absurd Anglican need to do the right thing? Like Mary Magdalene, she has seen the crucifixion, so now perhaps she is hoping to see the resurrection.

Hamilton is the victim here... like the criminal Time traveller in Chris Marker's photo-montage film *La Jetée* (1962). Hamilton's death orbit is the subject of a feminine obsession that prefigures his death, and while the roles are reversed, this is what happens in *La Jetée*.

While Marker's film seems rooted in the French trauma following the German occupation, its atmosphere of 'guilt-by-*deja-vu*' is similar to the crushing anxiety of *The Dead Astronaut*. JGB knew *La Jetée*, liked it, and the bleak monochromaticism of the airport observation deck in this influential film has a similar *Terrain Vague* feel to the abandoned spaceport in Astronaut.

So why did I want to make a radio drama out of this complex story? Well, the layered, polarizing imagery—always a feature of absurdist shock theatre—for one, and for another, the natural soundscape potential of the action. The low flying satellites as they transit the stereo field and crash in the dunes is no mere "sound effect" but implicit electronic music, an integral part of a true audio narrative that's as important in moving the action along as any of the words.

That's how I saw it, that's how Bill Lane saw it when he produced it, and that's how it was. Sounds as great today as it did in 1988. Tim Clark, a veteran of the Toronto Planetarium, did the synth.

My own father was a test pilot in the RAF, so Ballard's dreamscape fitted nicely with the sort of formative nightmares I experienced as a child during WW 2. Here was a story that was as macabre as anything Poe ever wrote, yet utterly contemporary and relentless in its prophecy. *Playboy*? Just what it was doing in the handbook of masturbation is beyond me. Especially as they had recently rejected a commissioned story by Burroughs about St. Louis. Again, like *A Question of Re-Entry*, the symbolism is outstanding: the dead astronaut in his capsule, circling, as if he really died in utero when his lover gave birth to their still-born child.

The foreground is simple enough, the background less so. An English couple, Philip and Judith Groves, arrive at the old Cape Kennedy launch site on a strange mission with an intimate agenda. The site is now a satellite graveyard, where homing beacons grab obsolete satellites as their orbits fail. The couple's particular interest is in Robert Hamilton, a NASA astronaut who has been dead in his capsule for twenty years and soon will be returning. First Valentina Prokovna, a dead Soviet cosmonaut known by the code name "Seagull" crashes.

The Groves watch the bounty hunters pillage the wreck for valuable metal, instruments and other tech. Of particular interest are the cans of film that recorded her death, which can be sold like snuff porno on the underground thrill market. The same fate awaits Hamilton when his capsule crashes. Behind all this a sex triangle exists with peculiar religious overtones.

It's a Cold War parable with a New Age ending.

The scripting was easy insofar as the narrative is in the lst person, unlike *A Question of Re-Entry* which is in the 3rd. So the narrative bridge between the scenes could be Philip's rap, retaining the POV of JGB's story. The real problem was the ending, for, while it seems categorical, is very ambiguous. Philip asks his wife Judith a question, which she doesn't answer, and he draws his own conclusion which, again, we're not privy to. Obviously part of the metaphysical back story.

So I decided to take a position in order to simplify the action for the listener, that is, far from being the docile masochist, the husband, being a Nasa programmer, knows more than he lets on.

As a parable, it comes close to being a definition of evil. The mysticism is both secular and religious.

Well, the production was great—the acting, the soundscape, the atmosphere—yet the exit remained uncertain. Philip's interrogation scenes—instead of being 'at the precinct' as I wrote it—became an internal argument Philip has with himself about his motives. No big deal, but maybe this tweak threw it all off. Remember at the time Bill Lane cast the character of Captain Pereira in *A Question of Re-Entry* as a drunk American rather than as a Brazilian which I thought would certainly displease Ballard should he listen.

Translating from one medium to another is poetic at best, ruthless at worst. Now, of course, years later it sounds perfectly o.k., and if you don't know the story, would you care what liberties had been taken? Maybe it's the same with Astronaut. The CBC certainly preferred it, used it as their submission for the *Prix Futura*, the big European radio award.

Didn't win. D.O.A.

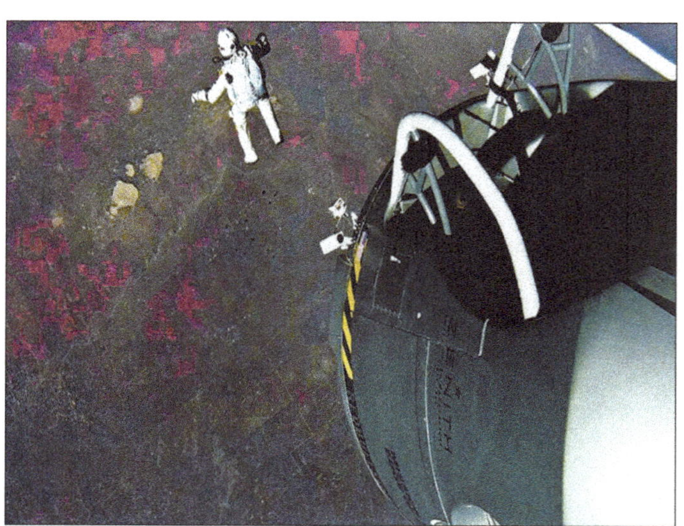

SECTION III:

Music & Media

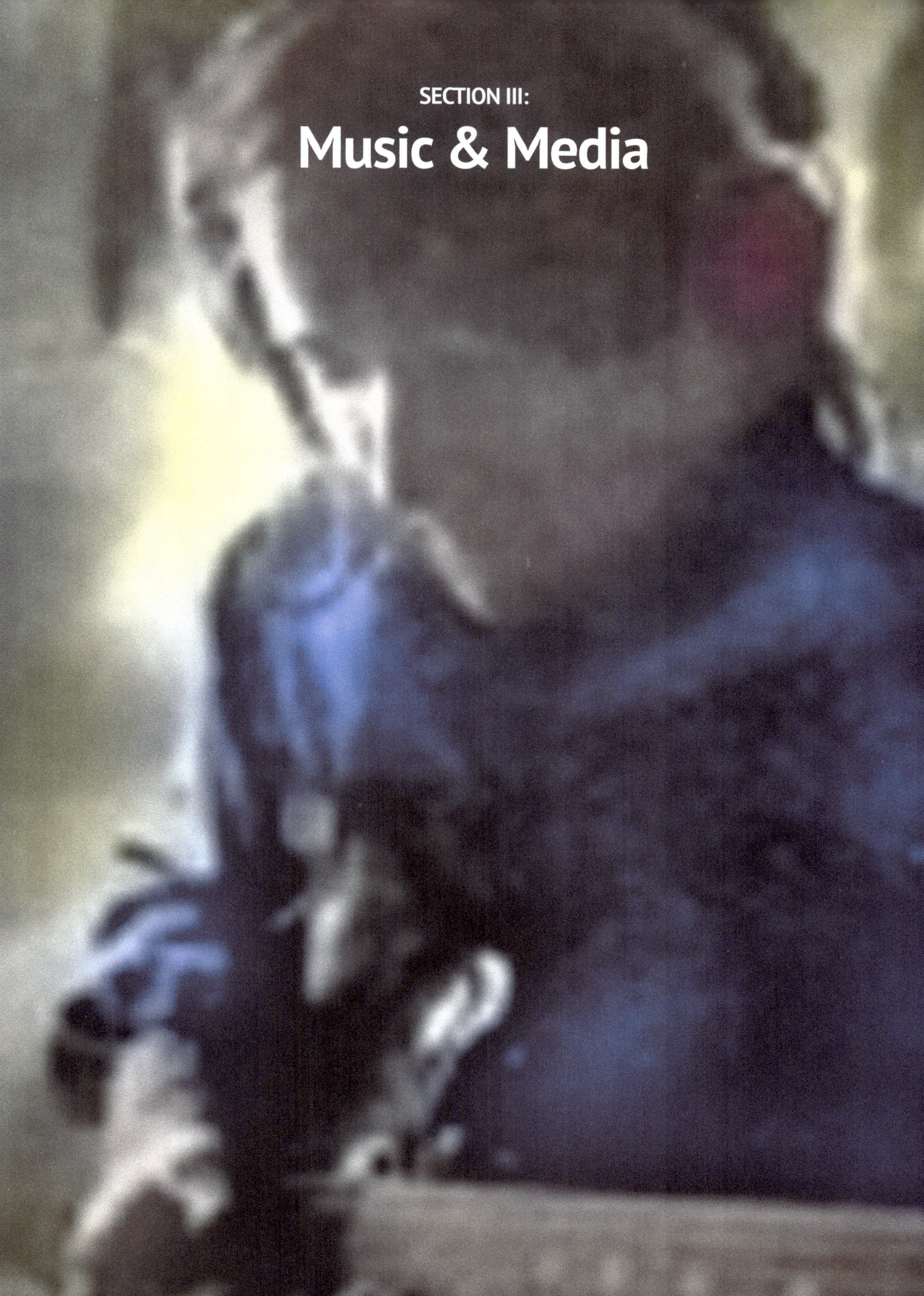

PART ONE:

Music And Me

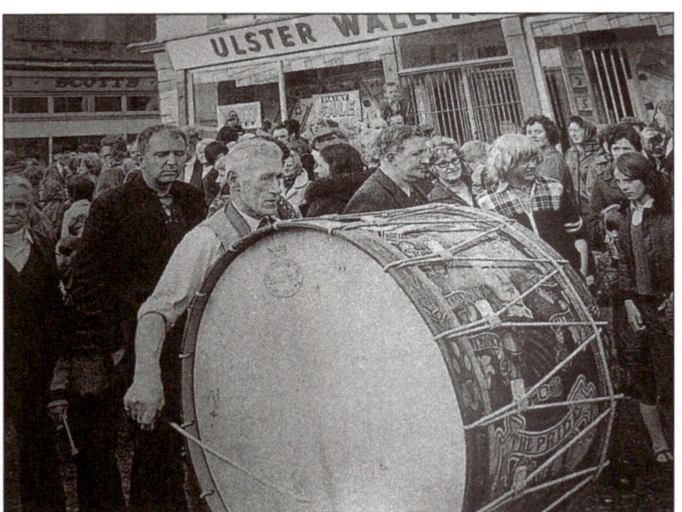

Lambeg

I could hear this hammering, like someone nailing the door shut, and I froze in my bed. It was still light out, although it was fading. July. Must've been six or seven years old, still couldn't measure the time or season properly. The hammering continued, growing to a crescendo, and I realized that I was hearing an echo, that the sound was coming from a distance, probably from one of the hill farms beyond the hazelnut grove... and that more than one person was at it, whatever it was.

It was primitive, like a team of plough horses stampeding this way, their nostrils flared and their teeth gleaming, eyes bulging like big marbles, hell bent on trampling every living thing that was in their way. I buried myself below the blankets, trying to shut it out, the hellish thunder that sounded as if you'd been buried alive and were hearing the first sods as they hit the coffin.

The Lambeg Drum. The loudest acoustic in the world, a hundred and twenty decibels and rising, depending on the beast who pounds it. A war drum, refined in Ulster, can be five or six feet in diameter, the perimeter made of oak, the drum heads animal skin—usually goat—stretched tight and thin. No screws, just a harness of linen ropes, maximum sadistic tension, the whole shebang ready to explode. The drummer uses malacca canes... you can imagine the whack, the thunderous roll, the reverberation, the blood lust. The Lambeg is the core instrument of the Protestant Orangeman Order, is used in parades, especially on the 12th of July, the annual celebration of the Protestant Victory over the Catholic Fenians at the Battle of the Boyne, 1690. Some folk call them Slashers. The Catholics have their version, the smaller Bodhran, played with skittle head sticks.

The purpose of these drums needs no explanation. Every summer before "the 12th" you can hear them pounding in hills and valleys of Co. Antrim, as if summoning the ghost army of King Billy. A farm yard or a parking lot or an Orange Hall, one or two drummers will start the wind up, and it can go on for hours. First time I witnessed it was in the yard outside the cottage the pig killer and his family rented from my Uncle up in the trees beyond the derelict flax mill. There were two of them, and they were drinking heavily, the ground covered with empty stout bottles. It was an unbelievable spectacle, every bit as brutal as the seasonal pig killing rituals. I was both frightened and fascinated... it was that time of my life, where every second day was a new experience, the shedding of the scales, an initiation.

At times you felt like dancing, when an evil rhythm would emerge from the chaos, and others you felt like throwing rocks. It reminded me of the big baler we used, the piston pounding the hay into compressed bales for storage as winter cattle feed. It was dangerous and violent, all the more so because everyone was drinking, and I was beginning to understand what drink could do to a man.

I never much cared for the Orangeman stuff yet somehow I ended up in the local Lodge for a brief period, two or three weeks max. How? How when I was never impressed by the parades and the Orangeman marching bands? A school mate convinced me, Tudor, a crafty young bugger whom I ended up shooting with my Luger pellet pistol when all was said and done. You like music, don't you, he said, join and they'll give you a free flute. He showed me his, and right enough it looked not bad. It's a laugh, he said, you get to go places, march with the men. So I joined, got the flute, but what the hell, after a few goes at trying to play *The Sash My Father Wore* I gave it up, sent the flute back.

Then Tudor told me the Lodge was angry, that there was a death threat on me.

"Why?" I said. "I sent the flute back."

"Because you put on the sash and took it off," he said. "That's why."

The sacred orange sash, the symbol of the Ulster Loyalist... Jesus Murphy, it was his fault, he'd gotten me into this mess. Was 12 years old, in the Cubs, was happy to be in training as a Boy Scout, never needed to be a bloody Orangeman, an Apprentice Boy, or whatever. For weeks I kept close to the wall whenever I was in the village, and when I was riding my bike to the Academy, I took the most obscure paths. There were hard men in the Lodge. I didn't know exactly who might be after me but I believed they were. It was Natch who set me straight. He was the older brother of the fellow who got me into this mess, and his uncle was in the Lodge, said they knew I would never last... and neither would his brother, who joined for the flute and was promised a drum if he got someone else to join. Lighten up, son. If anyone's going to get his melts kicked in, it's my brother.

Should've known. I got my revenge. The next time Tudor came for a visit with one of the other Cubs, I lay in ambush below the bank where the avenue passes over the millstream. He was sitting on the bar of the other guy's bike, schoolboy shorts, bare legs, easy target. I levelled the Luger, fired... the pellet nicked his leg and he yelped, they lost control of the bike, wobbled, then crashed... cries and curses, of course.

Now that's music.

Radio

In 1956 I carved the name "Elvis" on the back of a balcony pew at 1st Broughshane Presbyterian Church. It was the last time I attended church, actually. Why? Elvis Presley had arrived, had galvanized me with his shouter blues, *Heartbreak Hotel.* For many, it was anti-music, atonal nonsense, even if they didn't use the term "atonal'. I knew what it was, it was the next step from Johnny Ray's *Cry*, a wail of such powerful emotion that official music had neither the scale nor the measure to contain. I loved Johnny Ray, the way he broke with form and social normality, but this guy Presley, this song *Heartbreak Hotel*, this was something beyond *Cry*. It was my first introduction to the Sun Records Memphis slap-back echo, an interiorization that exposed the soul like a banshee cry in the distant night.

And it was really my first exposure to the Blues, although I didn't know that's what it was at the time. Elvis had four number 1 hits in the UK that year—*Hound Dog* and *All Shook Up*, and a couple of others. How do I know? Have a list written in the back of my *Biggles Omnibus,* a book my mother gave me in 1954 because she knew I liked Biggles, the daredevil pilot and his rogue squadron. The list contains a who's who of early rockers who scored big on the charts in '57... Gene Vincent, *Blue Jean Bop*... Little Richard, *The Girl Can't Help It*... Terry Dene, *White Sports Coat*... Chuck Berry, *School Days*... Fats Domino, *I'm Walking*... Jerry Lee Lewis, *A Whole Lotta Shaking Going On*... Bill Justis, *Raunchy*... I mean, these are seminal tracks in the early days of rock & roll.

There was a radio station on the Continent beaming English broadcast programs at the UK: Radio Luxembourg. When the state sponsered BBC was putting us all into a brainwash stupor with the light fantasy of Edmundo Ross & his Orchestra and the endless drear of European classical, a revolution was going on elsewhere, the blending of black American "race music" with white hillbilly "country music", a roadhouse combo beat genre they were calling "rock & roll" and Radio Luxembourg had it on their playlists. It was subversive from the start—new instrumentation (electric guitar), new recording ambience (tricked studio), new singing (raw), and outrageous couture. No more poker-up-the-ass opera, no more Anglican hymns, no more brass band marches, no more Jimmy flippin' Shand and His Scottish flippin' Dance Band, no more hate ballads and their sickening sentimentality, no more fife and drum, no more *Sweet Lass of Richmond Hill... Galway Bay... God Save the Queen*—let's rock!

This is the pre-TV world, the world of radio. Like my pellet pistol, like my slide projector, my crystal set radio was found through an ad in the back pages of a *Boy's Adventure Magazine*. It was small, a white bakelite resin box, with a tuner, a knob to tweak the crystal, and a pair of crude headphones—perfect for listening to *Dick Barton, Special Agent*, the 15 minute radio thriller that aired every week night. Also *Journey Into Space*, a serial that was popular with the kids. Was able to get Radio Luxembourg o.k. although the big set in the Library was better for that, had more kick, especially if I was doing some homework. The old Murphy lacquer wood model with the sound baffles... valves, of course (or tubes as we outlanders call them). All those European stations on the dial... Hilversum, Bonn, Stavanger, Brussels, Lisbon, Belgrade... Venus, Mars, Pluto, the universe.

Magic. Radio was incredible, like evesdropping on ghosts, their secret conversations, their bizarre ionospheric music. As a quasi orphan who was left alone much of the time, radio was an education, an uncensored access to the adult world. I loved the noise, the signal drift and the crosstalk as much as the clear channel, the accidental electronic music of the spheres that bridged the stations and even intruded on them. It was a code, the most secret of messages, the noise that hid the face, the alien beyond the forest and the stars... and while some complained about fried eggs in their radios, shitty antennae and low watt broadcasts, I revelled in it, and this spectral sound was influential in my later attraction to—and exploration of—electronic music.

The BBC 3rd always sounded better with the antenna removed, the Benjamin Britten or the Joseph Haydn doused with a flame thrower. I recommend it to this day, especially with a tequila and a beer. No antenna. The government makes better sense, sounds a whole lot more reasonable.

I started buying the records, 78s, when I was 14. My Aunt K. had an old HMV windup phonograph, one of those beauties with the big green metal horn. Listened to Frankie Lane's *Cool Water* on that and when we went to Portrush at Easter, I started squandering my money on the jukebox at Barrie's instead of plugging it into the slot machines. Peggy Lee, Pat Boone, Tennessee Ernie Ford, Gogi Grant etc. Was getting a lot of my information from a couple of music industry papers, *The Melody Maker* and *The New Musical Express*, who alerted us to who was hot and coming, and who was on the charts, and might be in your neighbourhood soon. The whole pop business was a life-style, a way of stepping into the future, a less insular thing, more international, more stardust sexy... and less Bogman.

As my record collection grew, I managed to buy a small electric gramophone, and wire it through the radio for a bigger sound. Now I was buying Elvis, Carl Perkins, Gene Vincent, Little Richard... you name it, I was on it. I was attending Ballymena Technical, which was right at the centre of town, a block away from the Town Hall, no uniforms, dress as you see fit, and I saw fit to buy my patch pocket hipster jackets from Sammy McQuigg's, a draper just up the street who catered to Teddy Boys and Flash Harrys. At lunch time I pumped my silver into a juke box at a nearby coffee bar... the Everly Brothers, Ricky Nelson... and the fabulous Buddy Holly & the Crickets.

The Zombies Of Broughshane

Things were moving fast. Had a commercial art class at the Tech, and it was taught by Ottilie Patterson, a young bohemian bird in a baggy sweater and a low hanging necklace. Half Russian, I think. Her mind didn't seem to be there... and it wasn't, as she disappeared after Christmas, got a full-time gig singing with Britain's premier Trad Jazz group, The Chris Barber Band. The university crowd was crazy about New Orleans jazz and groups were springing up all over the place, sometimes getting records on the charts... like Humphrey Littleton's *Bad Penny Blues*, some boogie piano with a snazzy snarly trumpet lead, very catchy, almost rock and roll.

The important thing here is that Lonnie Donegan's skiffle group emerged from the Chris Barber Jazz Band and this more than anything seeded the British rock group culture, as Donegan's version of Leadbelly's *Rock Island Line* inspired thousands of people to take up the guitar, start skiffle groups —

guitar, tea-chest bass, washboard—and copy early American folk blues. It threw the switch for me. Elvis was great, but hey, instead of buying records, why not start playing the music yourself? I talked it over with a couple of pals, then hopped the train to Belfast, went to a pawn shop and traded my record player against a Spanish acoustic that had been painted black by someone (this might explain why most of my later guitars were black). When I got it home, I immediately stripped the paint off and restored the original yellow wood look with some linseed oil.

It was a nothing guitar—the neck was thick, the action heavy—but at least I was started, especially after I sent away for a booklet wth some basic chord diagrams and another one with some skiffle tunes notated with the words. Within two or three months I had *Rock Island Line, Grand Coulee Dam, John Henry, Midnight Special* and *Worried Man* down pat... or pat enough to summon the band. My fingers were raw, but my confidence was high. We would rehearse at the farm, in one of the many old abandoned grain rooms above the pig dens. What was our name? Why, The Zombies. Great name, but many of the Bogmen around and about could never pronounce it properly.

But anyway we were the Zombies Skiffle Group from the village of Broughshane and it was in Broughshane that we made our first public appearance. It was a gutsy and outrageous act, as we were rough to say the least. The tea chest bass... what was that? A box with a broom shaft and a piece of wire for a string, just bend it, shift the pitch, produce a throbbing sound like hammering on a barbed wire fence. Washboard... what was that? Piece of corrugated zinc in a wooden frame and you strummed it with sewing thimbles jammed on the fingers, maybe went ratta tat tat now and then. The whole operation was primitive, very rudimentary, no tuning required except the voice and the guitar, and that was problematic. It was a sort of hooligan's chorus, just a raw mimicry of the Blues, a caveman's approach to art. You just let go with emotion and this infected the animals who came to watch. Nobody listened... really. It was spectacle, like the circus, and the crude rhythms did the rest. I mean, it was bloody close to bestiality, easily understood and respected for what it was.

Our first gig was in the village recreation hall, beside the local Police Barracks. The hall was small, had a high ceiling to capture the smoke from the ubiquitus cigarettes, was big enough for a couple of pool tables and a dart board... and a few tables and chairs. There was a bit of a stage, a raised area with an old upright piano, but none of us could play the piano. These blokes were bored, watched in disbelief as we set up. Skiffle? What the hell was that? Look at these idjits, who do they think they are haw haw. We had a banner with The Zombies painted on it. The bass player, ashamed to be part of the certain fiasco, faced the back wall, head down. *Worried Man* was the first tune we learned and as it actually sounded like a tune, we started with that. The guffaws and hoots subsided as the mob of twenty or thirty louts stood and listened with frozen grins. There weren`t any women or girls there that I recall but maybe there were some at the door, maybe as the word passed up and down the street.

When we finished, there were some hoots, but mostly an uncertain silence. *Midnight Special* brought a few claps and whistles, but it was the attempted rock and roll that broke the damn. Little Richard`s *Rip It Up*, with me doing a few Elvis shakes, had them roaring in happy disbelief, and knocking a few of the chairs and tables around. They didn`t want us to quit, made us repeat the four or five numbers we knew. *Worried Man*? Sure, they were all worried men, understood it now.

After the gig, we were approached by a couple of Orangemen about maybe rejoining the Lodge marching band. I demurred, said something like 'my manager wouldn't like it'. Who was the more deluded, them or us?

We were actually asked to play the next gig for some pop and chips at the recreation hall for the local linen mill at a place called Raceview. It was a dance, with music like Jimmy Shand records, and was for the mill workers, although anyone could wander in. We played a set, and they liked it well enough, the live action better than a bunch of accordians they'd heard a thousand times before. I think we played a second gig there, and then we were so famous we were contacted to play in a "battle of the skiffle groups" at the Ballymena Town Hall.

Fame Did, However, Bring Some Unwelcome Attention

"Hey Elvis!" came the coarse thick shout from the shadows.

There were a few anonymous laughs.

Me and Natch and another friend were standing across the road from the hall the Orange Lodge band was rehearsing in. It was dark, and we were just passing the time, perhaps looking for a fellow we knew who played the marching drums. The practice was over and some of the young louts were lurking outside on the porch. I knew what this was... an invitation to trouble. Mockery was a standard insult, an extension of the bullying that went on at school, usually an older youth practicing on a younger youth. Didn't know who it was, only that he was older, and sitting on a bicycle.

"Shut your hole," I said... just loud enough.

"Oh? Why don't you try and make us?"

Could see him more clearly now... not someone I knew. Definitely older, nineteen or twenty. Farmer's son or farm labourer, more than likely a sash wearing Orangeman. Coarse and faceless, a shape from another century.

"Bogman," I growled.

"What's that?" he said sharply, then glided out of the shadows to his side of the road. He glowered at me, said, "If you think you're man enough...."

"I'm minding own business," I said. "You should mind yours."

He spat on the road, muttered, "Elvis."

He didn't want to take me on because I was with Natch, who was older, and had a few moves, although who knew if he knew. He spun his bike around and glided back to the porch. We moved off towards the bridge that marked this end of the village. The Bogman wasn't done with me and I knew it.

A week later he and a couple of his associates nearly caught me in an ambush between the village and our place. I'd been in Ballymena doing the night patrol—Joe's Cafe and a laugh—when they jumped me on a lonely unlit road near the village. I was on my bike when they materialized from somebody's driveway like they were in a Western and riding horses instead of bikes and came after me. Fortunately I had a piece of lead pipe that I'd crimped into a cosh and kept swinging it until I connected, caused a pile up. I got away that time, humping the pedals like it was the *Tour de France* and the moon was racing through the clouds. He tried again, sort of. But I wasn't alone, so it was mission impossible and the whole business evaporated. It's a rough business, music.

You just never know who's out of key.

The Zombies played the Ballymena Town Hall twice and drove a couple of hundred people crazy and didn't win the competition either time even though we got the biggest applause. There was another group, wooden stage presence, but better musicians, harmonies and so on, so they deserved to win and did. Catholics. Two of them went to the Tech, so I knew them slightly. The singer was decent on the guitar too, although his band didn't do country blues, rather, Celtic folk.

You have to understand the divide between Catholics and Protestants back then. They lined us up in the school yard, then divided us into two squads for religious instruction. They followed the Priest inside, we followed the Minister. I didn't care for this; it gave me the creeps and I didn't see the need for "religious instruction" at all, as we weren't there to be priests, monks or missionaries. But Catholics were allowed to have separate schools, follow their own culture, and when it wasn't feasible i.e. for applied arts education, such as at the Tech, they were allowed separate religious instruction. Bad scene. Only perpetuated the divide... but of course I was already secular and couldn't see the benefit. Still don't, although today's political correctness is a lousy substitute for morality.

The Zombies were now using a snare drum instead of a washboard, and I'd made a standup bass with a "Z" cut in the plywood as an acoustic slot. Still had a piece of fence wire as a string but it looked damn good. We also had an electric guitar —probably the first skiffle group in Ulster to have one. Again, I did the work, upgraded my guitar, bought a pickup, borrowed a P.A. amp one of our school mates had made. We added another guitar player and he picked out a solo for *Midnight Special*.

But the end was nigh. The last gig we played was in the summer, 1957 I think, at the Ballymoney Town Hall which was about twenty miles to the north. I remember nothing about it except we went there in someone's van, behaved badly and after that, never practiced again. People had things to do, places to be, and the skiffle era was fading out.

Bill Haley

Saw Bill Haley and the Comets at the Belfast Opera House with Natch, who was in first year medicine at Queen's University. Terrific concert, just like the records, just like the movies. Haley had made his big breakthrough with his soundtrack for *Rock Around The Clock* (1955), a movie about young thugs in a New York school.

He was also in *Don't Knock the Rock* (1956) a piece of total rubbish except for the songs. Everywhere Haley played in the UK, riots broke out, and fire hoses followed. It wasn't quite that bad in Belfast, although people were dancing in the aisles. We were up in the Gods, and a Teddy Boy in full regalia danced by himself, his feet (blue suede shoes) moving in double time, a blur as he pedalled on the spot, right there on the stairs. If he'd lost his balance, he would've cartwheeled over the balcony and crashed into the mob below. It was that kind of anarchy, that kind of power.

Haley played all his hits, and he had a lot of hits for so

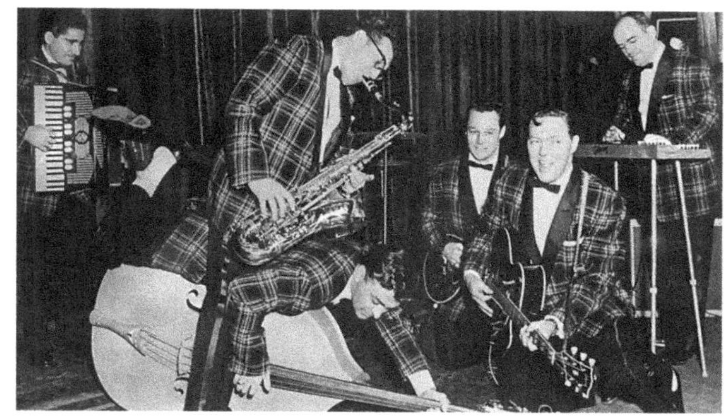

short a time on the scene. Until Elvis displaced him, and the Beatles displaced Elvis, no music act had dominated so completely. It was boogie rock, or rockabilly, or cowboy swing with a sledgehammer back beat. You could hear the chain gang behind it, hammering the railway ties, or smashing the rocks. There was a bit of Big Band jazz in it too, the tenor sax solos, the speed guitar solos, the dance hall imperative.

Shake, Rattle & Roll, Skinny Minnie, See You Later Alligator, Thirteen Women & Only One Man In Town—these beat tunes with their nonsense lyrics just swung like crazy and the Comets knew how to stick it to you, pump action shotgun all the way. The sax player dropped to his knees or onto his back, the bass player jumped onto his double bass, rode it like a horse, the guitar player hitched his axe behind his head, peeled off the licks in amazing speed runs. Christ, who could do this? It was a circus act, yet these guys knew how to play, knew the real animals were in the audience.

Haley himself wasn't dangerous, was just vaguely amusing with his kiss curl and happy face. He wasn't like Gene Vincent, who trembled like he was wired into the mains or caught in an alien tractor beam. There was nothing psychotic about Haley or vocally gritty like Big Joe Turner. He could be the school principal after a couple of drinks at the Christmas party. This might be why he faded so quickly when the others came along. Maybe he was too Big Band. Maybe he didn't use enough minor keys. No matter. He kicked the doors open and the others followed like barbarian raiders.

Kitimat

Late 1958 I was in Kitimat, was looking in the *Eaton's* catalogue, saw a nice combo for under a hundred bucks, a sunburst hollow body f-slot electric with case and a small tube amp with a 12 inch speaker. The guitar was a Harmony *Rocket* and when it arrived I discovered against all odds that it was the best instrument I'd owned to date... nice action, nice sound, and the chords sounded like chords, as this baby held its tune. Couldn't believe it really, and I made rapid progress picking up some new tunes. I could actually play rock on this guitar, do the Bill Doggett *Honky Tonk* line or lay down the power chords for Link Wray's *Rumble*, a number of such subversive simplicity, I couldn't believe I was playing it right.

First band I was in there was with the local high school Principal's son, who played the piano, a bit of guitar, and sang. The Rockin' Birds, because we had three high school beauties as a chorus line, not my idea, but one was Fat Ron the drummer's girlfriend and another was Ian's and so on... get the picture?

Ian was able to get gigs and we rehearsed at his house. It was an education, as I'd never really played as part of a group—before, with the Zombies, I was just the horse that pulled the plough. It was fun... parties at the Firehall, even though you had to be 21 in British Columbia to drink in those days... sockhops at the school, where we played in the gym, or sockhops at the Presbyterian Church, where we played in the basement.

It was no surprise that the minister was from Northern Ireland (Ulster). His son organized the sockhops, was a bit older, perhaps 20 and smoked and wore a black leather jacket, already looked a bit dissipated. He'd been in trouble for something, B & E and bootlegging, and it was certainly no secret that if you wanted a beer, talk to Austin. I thought we might have something to talk about seeing as we were both Bogmen but apparently not, he was too cool... or too hip to be cool. Chicks were his thing. Spinning records was just an entre, and the sockhop just something to assure the parole officer he had a job.

Well, the Rockin' Birds played here and there, even some private parties, but disbanded when the summer came and people were at the lake or drinking down by the river. Ian was getting ready to leave for university in Vancouver, Fat Ron too, and the girls were looking for husbands. There were laughs, there were fights, and I still sang some Lonnie Donegan, kept the old skiffle folk blues going between the Little Richard and the Elvis... but, as usual, things were moving fast.

A Radio, A Guitar And A Typewriter

Another great acquisition at this time was a Grundig portable transistor radio, which I kept beside the bed, listened to late at night when all the stations up and down the west coast came in on the ionosphere bounce. *Endless Sleep... Green Door... I Fought the Law... Peggy Sue* (the Rocking Birds did all these)... *The Happy Organ...* on and on the hits kept on hitting like cosmic rays and the unsettling news bulletins about the Cold War... what a radio, so compact, so portable. Good sound for the times, nice design, latte and green. Think I'm going on too much about this radio? It was a great comfort to me, like a talking teddy bear, one I'd had around since childhood... although of course this was my second radio, the crystal set being the first.

I also bought an Olivetti portable typewriter at this time, which became part of my essential triad: a radio, a guitar, and a typewriter. Think it was 1962 when the Grundig was stolen from the back seat of my car that I'd left parked on lower Johnson Street in Victoria. Forgot to lock the door, of course... I was vexed... nay, I was pissed off. My Grundig, my direct connection to the hits! Gone, gone, gone. How depressing... what's that song from back then? *The Fool* by Sanford Clark:

> gather around me buddies
> hold your glasses high
> and drink to a fool
> a crazy fool
> who told his baby goodbye...

Yeah, I'm that Fool, and my baby had gone goodbye. Was in such a hurry to vacate the auto, get to the movie or the bar, I didn't check if all four doors were locked. Yet the story doesn't end here. Twenty-five years later I was browsing in the big new (oxymoron) *Sally Anne* in Langford (*nuevo* Victoria) when I saw the Grundig sitting on a shelf. There was no doubt that it was the same one, as I'd never seen any others like it anywhere... and it was still working. Long Wave, Medium Wave, red merlot elongated station dial. Three bucks. Some jerk called "Rick" had scratched his name on the inside of the back cover... was he the thief? Or was he the guy who bought it from the thief? I didn't care. Easily buffed off. Three bucks. Cost eighty when I bought it, so what did I care? I had my baby back. Three bucks, shrapnel and amnesia, what the hell. Rick, whoever he was, was probably dead.

Mama Don't Allow

This was 1959 going '60 in Kitimat... the second band with some older guys, heavy drinkers, did dances at the Firehall and the Legion. We did *Green Door* and *St. Louis Blues...* I learned *St. Louis* from a young Scottish piano player (he worked for the Bank of Nova Scotia) who had picked up all his chops from Meade Lux Lewis... black hair, had a birth mark down one side of his face, skinny, good lookin' guy, wore a mustard yellow leather jacket, quintessential piano man... Alan Mac from Glasgow, and the boys called him Al of course.

The bass player, though, he was the real demon... about 23, had just finished two years in the navy... blond, with a ducktail... remember his name, Gary Lockhart... married but didn't act it, drank to the point of violence. The drummer was a fireman, could spin the sticks. Jerry. Might be still alive.

Al was the best musician. Told me he'd learned boogie piano in three months, had stayed in his mother's front parlour and just kept practicing. He could play *Bad Penny Blues*, which I just loved. It was like a Professor Longhair New Orleans number, left hand running bass, he explained. He showed me *St. Louis Blues*, the chords, the melody, the lazy feel... although we had to swing it as people had to dance.

Our feature number was *Mama Don't Allow*, something I showed them. When the lyric went, "Mama don't allow no bass playing here," the bass would solo for a few bars... and the same for the other instruments—piano, guitar, drums—when their turn came. Lockhart loved it, as it grooved to his idea of Beatnik jazz when he ran his hands over his stand-up bass like it was a woman.

One night after a practice at Lockhart's, he decided we needed to take a spin up the highway to Terrace, 40 miles away, in his '57 Mercury Monarch, V-8, ass low to the ground. Late winter, still lots of snow around, but the highway was plowed. Quite new, lots of straight stretches, lots of banked curves, nothing between us and Terrace, just forest all the way into the night. Case of beer, mickeys... Lockhart was driving, radio blasting, and we were all pissed.

Remember thinking we were never gonna come back from this ride. He had the pedal to the floor some places, and the needle was way over 100 mph and the other guys were cursing, laughing, telling him to slow down... and he just said fuck it, we're all gonna die anyway, get fried by them Russian nukes. I was in the back, just kept my head down. Just 19.

The agonized growl of the V-8, the halo of the headlights, the jive of the radio and a maniac at the wheel. Think about it. The last stretch was all gravel, and in those days Terrace had no paved streets, so there were potholes everywhere. We cruised a couple of streets looking for some woman Lockhart said he knew, then went to the beer parlour, which was in a old clapboard hotel like something out of a Western. I was underage [21 to drink in BC in those days] but I guess I didn't look it. We just got the table loaded with those dime glasses and kept drinking, the piano man plugging the jukebox, and everything was a blur. I was sitting beside a door and at one point I pushed it open, leaned out and vomited into the street. It was snowing and everything looked like Christmas. Yes indeed, a lot of laughing going on behind the Green Door.

I think we slept for a couple of hours in the car, sitting like dead men. Then we drove back to Kitimat, not talking much except when Lockhart told us about doing nuclear attack exercises with the Canadian and US Navies. And there was some talk about "going on the road" with the band. The dawn came up as we drew closer to town, and on one of the curves there was a '58 Edsel hanging in the trees. We slowed down for that. Nose in the air, like it had launched on the curve, which was ramped. There was a busted box of Lucky Lagers, the bottles scattered in the snow.

Some guy from the potlines where they boil the aluminum, apparently. Had happened after we passed through last night. Edsel, you know, one of those mothers with a horse collar for a radiator grill. Probably a Hungarian or a Greek or something, one of those DPs who didn't know how to drink and drive.

I resisted Bob Dylan at first—"the answer my friend is blowing in the wind", gimme a break. The mystery of life according to some bum hanging off a railroad car, looking for a cosmic payoff from the New Deal and not finding it. Throw away the cigarettes, man. Get off your squat. Buy a telescope, or at least a pair of binoculars. Learn some math, forget the commie hymns. The simplicity of the message was criminal, rubbed the undergraduate and budding writer the wrong way. To me, I'd been there, done that with the skiffle. Folk? *Passe.*

Trini Lopez was more my kind of guy, if we had to have folk. He played electric, the way I sort of played it, driving to the beat. Narrative songs, some folk, and even when it sounded rock & roll like *La Bamba*, it was Hispanic folk. The folk crowd were into revivals, the old church campfire thing... but you want revival? You want to raise up the brothers and sisters, have them singing, clapping on the beat, off the beat, polyrhythmic, get the old mystic pulse going? *Trini Lopez, Live At PJ's* (1963), one of the best live albums released on vinyl, maybe the first in the genre of "live" lps. Simple set up: guitar, bass and drums... no phony orchestrations, no church and state, just give me what you've got, man.

If I Had A Hammer—forget Pete Seeger, go Trini. The hammer was Lambeg, the hammer was ape. Anyone could understand it, even a kid trying to smash her way out of the crib. Monster hit all over the world, and they're still playing it.

Trini put out a lot of live ambience albums, although the first one remains the one that collectors want. He was a bridge to electric folk when it came, which is what The Byrds were... and Dylan when he woke up. The folk crowd were snobs, saw rock as kids' stuff, folk as serious. But the Beatles just put a stop to all that nonsense, as they were simply too damn good to be dismissed. They did covers and they also wrote their own stuff and what they wrote was extremely clever within the verse-chorus idiom and getting progressively more clever with every album they put out. Remember *Norwegian Wood*? That was folk without even trying. *Day Tripper*? Sure, everyone knows the lick now but in 1965 it was new and stunning. *I Saw Her Standing There*? The seventh chords and the raised fifth? The boogie pulse bass? Genius.

Apache

In 1963 I was working for the Department of Highways in Kamloops. Summer job. Stayed in the Plaza Hotel right on the main drag on a *per diem.* Met a guy in the engineering office who'd dropped out of university recently, a local, who, in the course of a conversation said he had a band called the Tritons. He seemed reasonable, even cool, although he turned out to be a real flunk, so let's call him Flunk... because it rhymes with, you know, well it rhymes.

Flunk played piano... not bad but not in the same league as my old friend Al Mac in Kitimat. Flunk just didn't have the funky pedigree, the Blues roots. The Tritons had a guitar player but as I soon found out, he was for visual effect, only knew the most elementary chords low on the neck, couldn't barre, had to capo. He had a very unusual guitar, though, and to this day I don't know if it was home made or some rare Fender prototype. It had a Fender neck and a violin body with a single coil pickup. Black, sort of... the paint job was so distressed and the frets so worn down it looked as if it was a survivor of a 1940's cowboy swing band. Great sound, though, considering.

When Flunk heard me play, he knew he needed me for the rock stuff. For example, I could play *Apache*, the great instrumental by the UK group who backed Cliff Richard, The Shadows. I could also play *Honky Tonk* and the Tritons had a saxophonist, a local garage mechanic, who liked to honk. *Rawhide*? *Tequila*? No problem.

But there was a problem... I had no electric guitar, hadn't been playing for a while. Ed had a guitar but he couldn't play. What was Flunk going to do? If you've ever been in a band, you know how the politics sometimes go... the rivalries, the jealousies, the double-dealing, the *prima donna* stuff, the drinking, the dames and the incompetence... in no particular order.

I'd drifted away from the guitar because my university studies had taken over. I was reading novels, short stories... nay, I was eating them, any and all. It was lonely in my hotel room after work, even though I was thinking like Jack Kerouac, that I was "on the road", maybe like those guys in Route 66, because I had an M.G. sports car and they had a Corvette. There was a nice young widow working behind the desk, a statuesque blonde whose cop husband had been shot to death in a gulley beside the Highways office where Flunk and I worked, and sometimes I'd sit in the lobby reading or talking to her and the bellboy when things were slow. Had to be a story there.

But I was lonely and the idea of a little social action in a rock band for a couple of months was appealing. Maybe I'd meet a woman, the love of my life or something, even though I suspected she was back home living next door.

Anyway, Flunk took advantage of me. Sob story? Well, no, Flunk was a pure flunk, a self-absorbed jealous bastard, a user and an abuser, a spoiled brat who lived with his parents in a house by the river. He used Ed for his guitar, and he used me for my car. And I was also old enough to buy booze and he wasn't and his old girl friend liked polite guys who played guitar and arrived in town clean. She was a reporter on the local small town newspaper. You can see where this is heading, right? Like a Jim Thompson story, pure pulp fiction. Anyway, I met the guys, rehearsed a couple of times, expanded their repertoire, played a couple of gigs... they even started calling me "Apache"... then Flunk decided he didn't need me. I was drawing attention away from him, even though I was just drinking my beer and playing my... er, Ed's, axe. It was Flunk's band, I was just a hired hand.

Then a gig came up and well, um, he did need me. He turned on the charm... even though he didn't invite me to his party a couple of weeks earlier, the one he had at his folk's place down by the river, and we'd nearly come to blows over an incident at work. Kamloops was semi-desert, cowboy country, so a trip down the Fraser Canyon was a desired field trip as you got to stay in the new motel at Shaw Springs, drink a few cool ones by the pool, nice *per diem*.

The boss sent me and a couple of other geo-techs instead of him. Boss's decision, nothing to do with me, but Flunk was pissed. Remember Lennon's song, *Jealous Guy*? As I said, Flunk was a real flunk. Sort of good looking, I suppose, in a Grade XII popular kind of way. But he was a Jekyll and Hyde, a control freak. Think his parents were from some outer system religious group... Pentecostal. The Minister of Highways, a local man, was Pentecostal.

How did Flunk get his job? Figure it out.

The *Louie Louie* is a basic 1-4-5 pattern—like a lot of rock tunes—although the 5 is a minor seven, which gives it a tonal signature, makes it sound a bit mental and maybe why the vocal line is so deranged and clinically dumbass. People loved it, still do. The Kingsmen had the hit version, although it originated with some guy called Richard Berry who vamped it off a Cuban number about a crazy drunk. The Rockin' Robin Roberts version was the first one I heard, but everyone was doing it as the people loved it as dancing had become more primitive, a primal stomp and booty shake, no fancy steps necessary.

Sure, there was *The Twist*, the *Hitchhiker*, and so on, but things had degenerated fast. Ballroom was done, porno was rising. In those days, if you didn't have the *Louie Louie* in your set, you might as well stay home.

The Tritons did it, probably botched the triad chord. The juicy summer gig was the High School graduation dance, and we played some classic rock numbers. We certainly messed up *Party Doll*—just before the ascending guitar solo, Flunk stepped back from the mike, barked "Take it, boy!", stamped down hard with his boot thereby ripping the cord from my instrument.

Silence.

The couples stopped dancing, as if they'd also been unplugged, and stared at the band. Flunk was bewildered, then my amp started to roar and shriek the second I picked up the jack. Well, that was a fiasco and we had to start the song over. Not my fault. Otherwise it wasn't a bad gig.

So you'd think my position in The Tritons would've been sealed in cement. They just weren't a rock & roll band without me. *Blue Moon*, *Birdland*, and other tired shuffles just didn't raise the barn... o.k. for the Legion or the Kiwanis maybe, but not for the young and the restless. But Flunk decided two guitarists was one too many to share the money with.

He was right but the way he went about it was wrong. He toasted Ed when he needed to, toasted me when he needed to. When a column in the newspaper drew attention to the great fun graduation dance, and how great the Tritons were, despite a small "hiccup", he laughed, tried to shrug it off.

But he was angry. "Hiccup"?

"She's a bitch," he said. "Good piece of ass, but a bitch."

He'd hinted at his deep relationship with the reporter gal before, but now he was grudge bragging. I never played another gig with the Tritons, and didn't care much as the summer was almost over. I'd saved up some money, read a lot of books, written a couple of essays in anticipation of some upcoming course work... had material for stories, what the hell. Kamloops was bush. Soon I'd be back in the Garden City, Victoria... Victoria by the sea.

But then he got bitten by a rattle snake, and decided it was my fault. Happened at Shaw Springs when he was down there doing the monthly survey of the slide. A few years back part of the Canyon wall came down, swept across the highway into the river. They cleared it, of course, but there was always a chance it could repeat, so the Highways Department put some pins across the boulder field so they could plot their movement, get a heads up if another rock avalanche was about to happen. It was hotter than hell in that part of the Canyon in August and the area was notorious for rattler dens. Seems there was one at the south hub pin, obvious to anyone with eyes, so why wasn't it noted as a hazard in the *Shaw Springs Slide* survey book? The tables the geo-techs recorded the survey angles in?

Who did the survey in July?

It was my fault, said Flunk. He said it as a joke but I knew damn well he wanted to believe it.

"Fuggin' Apache," he said. "You knew those rattlers were there."

They got the poison out of his leg and he spent a couple of days in hospital. Snake was just a young 'un, didn't have much venom. He was gimped, had to use a stick to hobble around, and couldn't drive. As I was leaving in a few days, he decided to be friendly, and invited me to a family cabin on the lake. Guess he was feeling vulnerable.

Anyway, he had his case of beer, and I had mine, and of course as it a was nice sunny day and we were driving with the top down and having a couple. We got caught in a road block that was set up on a blind curve near the lake, a Labour Day Weekend tax grab bullshit thing. I managed to drop mine into the ditch but Flunk was caught cold. I was over 21 but Flunk, well, he was a mere 20 year old and they might or might not charge him. They confiscated his case, told him to report at the barracks next week.

It was a bitchy afternoon and long day's evening into night and the following dawn. Some other people showed up and Flunk got into the hard stuff and went Hyde. Nasty. Cheap innuendo. I took off, left him there with the others, drove back to the Plaza Hotel. Never saw Flunk after that as he had a week off and I was done with the job. Mentioned the incident to the blonde widow on the desk, that I wasn't compeletly sure that I wouldn't be charged with something myself. The widow had friends in the cops, naturally, as they were looking out for her since her husband died.

Seems they did charge Flunk, minor in possession or something. Didn't charge me but they charged him. That's justice... and the flunk deserved it as he had big stupid feet and didn't play the Louie Louie right anyway.

> *I need some love, I need some affection/ gotta get me some psychotic reaction*—the Count Five, from San Jose.

Psychotic Reaction. Big hit in the Bay area when we arrived in the last quarter of 1966, so I could start my graduate program in literature and creative writing. Was married now and had more or less given up the guitar as there were many people out there who were far far better than I ever would be, and besides, I wanted to be a writer, not some loud clown in the circus.

Was still into music, though. Had recorded my Dylan albums onto some quarter inch reel-to-reel tape and picked up a small tape recorder from a music shop on Market Street in San Francisco so I could play it and any other music I might acquire. Like The Byrds. Loved Roger McGuinn's 12-string translations of *Mr. Tambourine Man* and *All I Really Want To Do*, although the one Byrds tune I played late (at) night when I was at the typewriter was *Eight Miles High*, something they wrote themselves and had the same psychedelic inscape as *Tambourine Man*, although you suspected it was pure LSD. It had that inner space quality, the search for a new level of consciousness. McGuinn's guitar lines had a free form jazz tone, a bit eastern, capable of triggering the sort of impressionist imagery that made physical painting or photography redundant. You didn't open your eyes, you closed them. *Eight Miles High* was a masterpiece in this regard. It was *deja vu*, reincarnation, astral projection, remote viewing, all those things you associate with the out-of-the-body experience and you didn't necessarily need to be high to get there. But of course, if you wanted to go ESP and be part of the cult, well, you know....

Far as I was concerned, this was the aesthetic test for any and all music—did it or did it not make you abandon the physical world? Of course this is "head" music as opposed to "body" music, the stuff you dance to. But sometimes, just once in a while. it could be both.

Dylan's *Tambourine Man* had another edge to it, a melancholy haunted forest kind of feel, the sort of sensation I experienced once driving a station wagon after midnight through thick drifting snow on a deserted highway north of Lake Superior. There was a strange exhilarating sense of isolation about it; with me were four sleeping McGill and Concordia students heading west to Alberta for summer work, and I was just the driver, was going to drop the vehicle off at a dealership in Calgary. It was a non-stop drive from Montreal, and I was the only one licensed to drive. Dylan grew up near Duluth (Hibbing), Minnesota, not really all that far from where I'm thinking of... *the haunted frightened trees...* yes, played that one a lot and had been playing it for two years, home and abroad, on the road, off the road... playing it, playing it, and it became more and more haunted as the grooves wore down, gave it up, surrendered their secret messages.

This was Dylan's hallucinatory period, where his lyrics peeled like poetry and prophecy, the twin bells of higher consciousness. But it was the combination— the words without the music would've been nothing. Great poets abound, but without music they're just fading tombstones in the graveyard.

It's Alright Ma (I'm Only Bleeding) is a stunning talking Blues that could well be his masterpiece when it comes to invective as art. The urgent ripping guitar, that seems to slash its way through major and minor like a machete, punctuates and propels the lyric which is a catalogue of human crimes against humanity and nature, seemingly political yet also mystical, and oddly cathartic even if much of it remains incomprehensible. Enter the gallery, close your eyes, choose your target... er, picture.

The Gates of Eden is like Edgar Cayce on acid. I listened to this one a lot too, and it made a lot more sense than Wallace Stevens and Ted Hughes and the other poets I was studying in one of my graduate seminars. Really, who were these dudes, how valid was their tortured messaging, their private codes? Exhibit 1: Sylvia Plath. Exhibit 2: Anne Sexton. Exhibit 3: the tomb of the unknown poet.

To get a good grade and pass the course, you really had to show how deep your sympathy ran. But then, as an accomplished poet and teacher I met later in life said, "It doesn't matter what you study, as long as you study it hard." Intellectual masochism as a form of enlightenment? Not an impossible argument, a bit like oranges and brussels sprouts—you prefer one, but you need the other as well. You are part of the syllogism.

But then, wasn't Jim Morrison a Rimbaud fan? Dylan too? If written text was for fundamentalists and comic books for idiots, then these urgent balladeers were just dysfunctional ciphers. Garbage in, genius out? It was a conundrum.

The thing about *The Gates of Eden* and Bob Dylan's lyrics in general is/was the inferential power, the two-way manipulation. You were being led, yet you could process and project your own imagery within the theatre of the mind. *Upon two-legged forest clouds/ the cowboy angel rides*—what exactly is this, Bob? A surrealist painting by one of your stoned out Village friends? You think, well, he's talking about Lyndon Johnson, making a mockery of his aggressive and foolhardy Vietnam policy. But of course it could mean anything; you could channel whatever you needed. Nuclear anxiety? Got it: *Upon two-legged forest clouds.* You could never fail an academic Rorshact Test with this stuff.

This was a lesson that repeated over and over again during the Hippy Era where the written word took a back seat to music and the visual arts as culture reverted to the McLuhanesque Ancient "cool" (as versus the prevailing "hot" of Modernity), so that even the most inane or disconnected lyrics took on incredible power when supported by a visceral sound track. Suddenly illiterates were being taken seriously for their "poetry", were giving interviews to *Rolling Stone* and others eager to divine just exactly what was on these artists' minds, the more personal the better. So much psycho babble, so much soap opera! Of course Dylan, Morrison, Lennon and many others weren't illiterate, but the majority of the rockers were or at least feigned to be. Cultivated stupidity was part of the game, a self-mockery that insulted the pliant listener, the easy sap who not only took it but paid for it. But when drugs became as important as sex, then the coding took on a new linguistic lore, and Papa found a brand new bag.

These artists, with their incomplete or zero university educations, had stepped away from institutional mind control and fearlessly embraced their own fantasies. What the hell was I doing, going for the framed diplomas? When the time came, Ronald Reagan would sign mine. Surely to God that was proof enough of the folly? There was always Zen Buddhism, which many people adopted because one of their icons did or because it went well with dope... or because they could actually go East and get lost.

"Tune In And Drop Out" Was The Siren Song

But I never believed it, even if I liked the pedigree of the movement, its Bohemian style, the raw personal expressionism of the counter-culture. The Beatles didn't drop out—they just did what they wanted to do and did it well. Same with Dylan, for all his revolutionary poetics and apprenticeship as a workers' rights balladeer. These people were disciplined even if their discipline seemed more like recreation, cigarettes and whiskey and wild wild women, bang on me drum, make cool sounds on me guitar, get me money in a brown paper bag.

Outrageous, wasn't it? And the press gangs wanted all these sweet boys to go to Vietnam... unless they were in college or gimped. I saw it everywhere I went in '65, '66, '67: London, Spain, North Africa... young Americans were like puppets, waiting for the string to be jerked, be called into action. At Hippy Central in Tangier—the Hotel Royal, which had communal rooms and army cot beds for one dirham a night —Americans received telegrams and disappeared as suddenly as if they'd already been shot and body bagged.

I was in London in 1965 when Dylan was there, started his tour of the UK, the one you see in Pennebaker's seminal documentary *Don't Look Back*. Read about him in the tabloids, but missed seeing him in concert as I was cutting out for Spain. Did buy *Highway 61*, however, as I was packing a portable Phillips record player (which I eventually sold along with my cowboy boots to some Arab merchant in Tangier), so I had my Dylan fix for my days of sun and wine on the Costa del Sol. The thing about *Don't Look Back* is how, against all logic, the raw exposition enhanced Dylan's mystique rather than condemning him as a spoiled contrarian brat. Why? Other than the performance clips of undeniable native talent and friendly fan accommodation, you sense he's playing for the camera, messing with the journalists and the local poets, who—rendered in charcoal monochrome—look undeniably like troglodytes. There's a deceptive simplicity about Dylan, as if he's just come from busking in the Tube station or outside a liquor store. It seems too easy, sounds too easy. Just listen to him sing *Baby Blue* in the hotel room when Donovan asks him to. Just like the record, you think. The fabulous Picasso tone, the hint of autobiography, the gentle blow to the head, a mercy killing or an invitation to suicide... it's all over now, Baby Blue.

There's no way anyone can cover the tune and capture the Dylan feel, even if he/she knows the low E string is dropped to C, and the brush strokes are crying like a fire in the sun. It's "blue period" Dylan, the haunted Beat apprentice, the first of the global *mariachis*.

Dylan was one of my greatest influences, no lie. Not that I ever covered him much, as his style was so elusive and sacred. His later compositions were more mainstream, more songbook, more for others. You could reel off *Serve Somebody* or *Broken* in a bar band but the early stuff was too verbal and detuned to be captured by fools. One exception would be *All Along the Watchtower*—a flamenco fragment—which was skilfully appropriated by Jimi Hendrix and exalted into a rock anthem. Hendrix, of course, had done some Dylan immersion in his first attempts at song writing; what is *The Wind Cries Mary* but Bob Dylan channel-jammed with some black gospel?

Often hear people say Dylan can't sing and/or can't play guitar. This is wrong. Watch and listen to him in *Don't Look Back*, and don't be fooled by the casual manner. His vocal accuracy is excellent, that walking-into-running way he moves from talk into song. Guitar? He uses a capo, you say? So does Clapton when he wants the sort of country arpeggio that certain triads and open strings provide. Lyle Lovett too. These guys know what they're doing. I saw him live now and then, acoustic and electric... and always liked his solo acoustic sets best. Last time he was playing electric piano. He knows what he's doing.

Flashback

I started coughing, and then there were lightning flashes over the nearby Atlas Mountains. My lungs felt like they were scorched, then scraped. Then my brain started to bubble and my limbs went elastic. The Moroccans laughed as I staggered back, collapsed into my seat. *Allah akbar!* somebody emoted and there were more laughs. The driver waved at me, then spun around in his seat, fired up the engine and we were on our way again, past the women with the baskets on their heads, past the white city walls and murky minarets, past the donkeys and the camels and the sinister sedans from another era, lurching in a dust halo until we hit the asphalt again. *Adios Fez.* The driver was putting the boot to it, like he was in the Dakar 500, clipping the gravel shoulders and cutting the corners. Adios reality. Dylan surged back into my head like *Snakes and Ladders*. *Highway 61*? Crazy. 61 was everywhere, the universal highway of madness.

> Well Abe said, Where you want this killing done?"/ God say, "Out on Highway 61

We'd stopped in Fez en route to Tangier from the port of Ceuta, a Spanish enclave on the Moroccan coast. Most of the people got off the bus and nobody else got on. We were there for twenty minutes and I broke out my portable record player, set it on a low wall and played Dylan's *Highway 61*, much to the amusement of some kids who were playing nearby. The bus driver and a couple of his mates were also amused and broke out the hash. Small clay pipe with a long wooden stem. They offered me a blast and I took it. I wasn't a professional smoker and this hashish was thermo-nuclear. I went paranoid in a flash, even though my fellow riders seemed unconcerned about dying on Highway 61. The driver got into a groove, made better gear shifts, got the feel of the curves. But you know after that I only took one other bus trip in Morocco, a Red Eye to Casablanca a few weeks later to catch a freighter to New York.

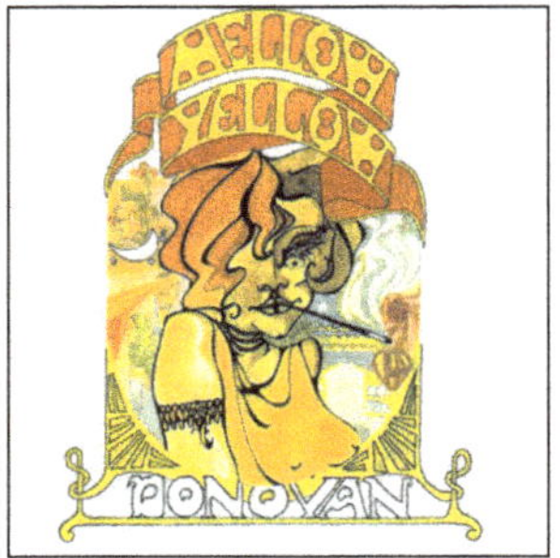

Electrical Banana

When Donovan's *Mellow Yellow* hit the Bay area charts in the Spring of 1967, the wildfire rumour spread that this was all about the recently discovered hallucinogenic power of banana skins. The word was whispered all over campus, Cal State Hayward, S.F. State, UC Berkeley, up and down Telegraph Avenue and in the stoner streets of San Francisco, throughout Haight Ashbury, Golden Gate Park, yes, children, believe it, *electrical banana/ is gonna be a sudden craze/ electrical banana/ is bound to be the very next phase.* I ran into a poet when I was cashing a cheque in San Mateo who said he tried it and he was high for hours, great visions, man, wrote 'em all down like Coleridge.

I commanded my wife to proceed... Donovan was even on the radio as she put the skins in the oven. Pretty soon the apartment smelled like a steaming volcanic banana split, so we opened the window and within minutes the sweet mystery fragrance was all over the motel quad, even down by the pool where the party heads were sipping beers and splashing around, SoCal modern. The skins went black fast, so we laid them out on the arborite table to cool. Frankly, the product didn't look too promising... but there was only one way to find out.

My wife was pregnant, so I couldn't make her test it, but we had visitors, a young guy I met in Tangier the previous year, a History major from UCLA, and his girl friend. They were eager, anything for a new buzz.

So I rolled up a couple of Donovans, passed one to Angst (his New Age handle), said, "Be my guest."

Fired him up and he took an experimental drag, started choking right away... a few coughs, a watering of the eyes.

His girl friend "Orchid" said, "He's hopeless, let me..."

Orchid was a hardened smoker, unfiltered nicotine since Junior High, and she sucked the electrical banana like a pro. Even she coughed a bit.

It was my turn but the joint was out. Definitely not a good sign. Anyway, Angst and Orchid were still alive, so I fired it up again, took a drag. No fun, no fun at all. Reminded me of when I was a kid, and some of us tried smoking dried reeds down by the river. Dizziness, followed by blackout, then zombie resurrection.

"It's... it's... it's a lie!" I spluttered.

"Did nothing for me," said Orchid.

We looked at Angst. "I might be sick," he said... and he did look grim.

My wife heaved a gallon jug of red wine onto the table, said, "Anyone want a drink?"

Bloody Donovan—it was a long time before I bought one of his records. Well, I did like *Season of the Witch*, and had to buy the *Sunshine Superman* lp as that was the only way I could get it. The manager of the motel came snooping around, trying to figure out what the smell was all about. He looked in the window, and my wife said (humbly), "I burned my banana cake." The man had that stressed weasel look, looked at us suspiciously, grunted, moved on. Guess a grunt was his idea of a laugh.

London Babylon

The Beatles: what can I say that hasn't been said? They're so institutionalized now that you forget that dirt lies below the asphalt of every highway. They were so innovative as they rose up out of the clichés of verse-chorus pop music you almost forgot there ever was an Elvis or even a thing called jazz. The date clock of music history was reset to BB (Before Beatles) and AB (After Beatles). Lennon said it: "We're more popular than Jesus Christ."

The UK was just crawling with rock groups back in those days as there were plently of gigs to be had in the dancehalls. I was back there in 1960, working at a vegetable canning factory in Lincolnshire. Ended up there by accident, as some of my old pals from Queen's University (Belfast) had summer jobs lined up at the factory, and at the last minute one of them couldn't go for some reason, so I pretended to be him. Young guys from all over rolled up... Glasgow, Newcastle, Belfast... couple of black guys from Nigeria, one of them a committed Marxist who was always threatening to "bury you imperialist puppets". Students. Wore Italian Mod suits with narrow trouser legs and bum-freezer jackets, and sharp-toed ankle boots with Cuban heels. The early Beatles wore these kind of outfits when they first appeared in North America three years later and some American jazzers where dressing that way, late fifties, early sixties.

The hit I remember from that summer was Johnny Kidd & the Pirates *Shakin' All Over*, a number that was destined to become a classic after it was covered by The Guess Who (Canada) and by The Who in their heavy metal incarnation, *Live At Leeds*. *Shakin'* was from the Gene Vincent school of shiver rock. It was all about sexual tension, not a visit to the chiropractor's. It's most obvious precursor in British rock was Cliff Richard's *Move It* (1958).

Saw one act then: Shane Fenton & the Fentones in Wisbech, an old town in "the Fens", a tidal region (or delta) on the North Sea. Fenton wore a tacky leopard skin Mod suit and his band played solid body Burns guitars, made by an English luthier, and now collect outrageous prices in the pawn shops. Period ephemera, bit like the US Mosrite. The dance was pretty good, as Fenton clowned it up, shook it for the ladies. They did *Shakin' All Over* and Johnny Tillotson's *Poetry in Motion* which the crowd called for over and over and Fenton obliged... over and over. What happened to him? Check the Internet.

1965. Had a friend who was a videotape engineer at the BBC, someone I went to school with in Ulster. Showed me around the "Bebe" and after inspecting the set for *Z Cars*, a cop drama serial they broadcast live (can you believe it), we went back to his place in North London, had a party. All sorts of rowdies showed up, and my man had a great sound system for the times. The Beatles had just released *Day Tripper* and *We Can Work It Out* as a single and it was played repeatedly throughout the evening. *Tripper* was stunning... and *We Can Work It Out* sounded progressively better every time it was played. Remember thinking how can the Beatles keep this up, this next-one-is-gonna-be-better output? The superb vocal harmonies, the urgent messaging, the powerful licks, these definitive generational signatures... how? Just remember they'd released *Rubber Soul* (1965) earlier that year.

That party... the Carnaby Street girls and the Mod guys who just carelessly dropped their cigarette butts on the carpet as they danced and drank and sang raucously along with John and Paul. Even saw people drinking wine from glasses that'd been used as ashtrays... deliberately or accidentally, I didn't know. Yeah, there was property damage, although my friend said you had to expect it, cost it in, this is London Babylon, mate. Sure. He could've blamed the Beatles, I guess.

Black Movie

I got into electronic music by accident. I was writing (and sometimes performing) short stage plays, one act absurdist pieces in the manner of early Pinter, Albee and Ionesco, stuff I considered surrealist. Kafka for a wet afternoon. These were dream dramas, maps of inner space. The actions were real, but the logic irrational. The psychology of the taboo and the lunatic predominated... because, after all, film could do realism/naturalism so much better. Theatre was always best as a figure of speech, a poetic expression because it came from poetry in the first place.

Symbolism and shock—these were my preferred methods.

The idea came to me for a voice play performed in total darkness, a sensory immersion experience in which the audience had no choice but to listen and absorb the message—whatever it was—as in dream. Psychedelic music was like that, wasn't it? What I was after was a sort of bicameral mind messaging, the mysterious command voices of early Man and his pre-rational motivation.

So I recorded a montage of monologues and conversations, plus some direct addresses to the listener. There was even a sequence of grunting (which was very popular with the audience when the drama was "performed"). It was called *Black Movie* (1969) and although it used no music *per se*, it was my first electronic tape piece. Some people called it *musique concrete.* Whatever it was, it was the foundation of all the recorded sound-text pieces I did thereafter, and I did a lot as the medium was new and the portability of tape too good not to explore.

But this is not all there was to it. There was a San Francisco artist called Jack living in a garret with a colleague of mine from the university who had an incredibly hip and extensive record collection. This is where I first heard such psychedelic classics as John Mayall's *Laurel Canyon,* The Allman Brothers first album... ah, all sorts of weird and wonderful stuff and Jack was into some of the raga inspired electronic music coming out of the academy... Steve Reich, La Monte Young, Philip Glass, those guys. One afternoon he played me Terry Riley's *In C* and *Rainbow In Curved Air*. The experience was, in the parlance of the times, mind blowing. The sheer hypnosis of the peeling runs and the polyrhythms was pure astral projection, a space elevator to the stars.

How did he do it? Tape loops, I supposed. Instrument? Wasn't sure, but some sort of early synth module (actually, a custom tuned organ). What struck me about the architectures of these two pieces was how a relentlessly linear progression of sound could develop into a multiplicity of acoustic avenues. Incredible. It was cosmic noise of the most visonary kind. Again, how did he do it? In a way, I didn't want to know, didn't want to remove the mystery in case the beauty went with it. One thing I knew: no more verse-chorus bollocks, no more vertical up-and-down narratives and change ups to keep people amused. Just get in the groove and keep it locked on infinity. It was like modal jazz improv... and if you could multi-track, you could do it all yourself too, no politics, no kindness to animals.

I bought a couple of modest reel-to-reel quarter inch tape recorders with sound-on-sound (monaural multi-tracking) and began to experiment. While the machines were an instrument onto themselves, they needed input, so I bought a cheap no-name electric guitar, plugged it straight in to the tape recorder. Cassettes had arrived, and the small portable recorders to play them. So I used various Sony portables to record "field sounds" —crowds, street traffic, waves, rivers, conversations... phone calls... anything that might hold dramatic or sonic interest.

A technique I used once or twice was to record a location sound and then impose a conversation on it. To get naturalism, there was no script. I did *Beer Parlour* (1970) like this. I recorded a conversation with an artist friend as we watched one of his video tapes which was a montage of magazine stills of various people, and when this was mixed into the stereo beer parlour recording, it sounded as if we were talking about various people sitting here and there in the bar with occasional asides into politics and art. However, to give it a more *avant-garde* ambience, I mixed in some short-wave radio noise, something the beer parlour babble gradually dissolves into, and thereby adds spectral mystery to the proceedings. The tape was about 12 to 15 minutes long, but could be faded anytime anywhere in the ionospheric roar at the end. It was played a number of times at the UVic Music Department's noon hour experimental music concerts organized by Prof Rudolph Komoros, the resident electronic composer at that time. While my colleagues in the Writing Department showed no interest in such stuff, some people in the Music and Art Departments were all ears.

Beer Parlour fitted nicely into the techno multi-media narrative that Gene Youngblood wrote about in *Expanded Cinema*. So while I'd started out in the theatre, I'd now moved into the art gallery—sculpture, sound sculpture, light shows, stroboscopic film looping, etcetera, were happening as artists moved away from the traditional arts and interacted with the new technologies. All of this was perfect for "conceptual" expression.

In the seventies, the art gallery was where it was at, because it was the medium of multi-media experimentation. It took in all of the arts—theatre, music, film, poetry, as well as its traditional expressions, painting and sculpture. The "happening"—usually some anti-social improvisation—became a gallery fad. Early video found a home there. Installations, kinetic sculpture, sound sculpture, video, stroboscopic film loops... artists were embracing the new technologies, interacting with the algorithms even if they didn't know what an algorithm was. Why the art gallery? Because it is the home of personal expression rather than group expression. Theatre and film are collaborations, whereas painting and writing are usually solo expressions.

This personalism certainly generated a lot of suspect art, if not outright fraud. Think it was in the early eighties when I interviewed Michael Snow who had just given a "concert" at Open Space, the local counter-culture gallery in Victoria. Snow and four others had a group called CCMC2 (Canadian Contemporary Music Collective Squared), played various instruments purely for noise and random effect. They were touring the galleries of Canada courtesy of the Canada Council, and after hearing their primitive set, I suspected none of them could actually play an instrument of any sort. It was like therapy for the asylum detainees stuff. This would've been irrelevant if the "sound" had had some sort of narrative possibility, no matter how oblique or simple.

Either scare me, or hypnotize me, man.

Snow got testy with me when I asked if some jazz improv might be useful here and there as a counterpoint to all this abstraction, this random personalism, if maybe they should kick into 4ths now and then (I was just trying to find out if they could play it straight) and blow like Coltrane. No fuggin' way, Jose. I was just a thick chump, a bottom feeder literalist who didn't know dick. But I did know—the act was fraud, although the frauds who funded it deserved all they got in return.

I know, I know... the ability to play *Louie Louie* isn't the only mark of a real musician but if Snow and the boys had tried it, they would've gotten a better review.

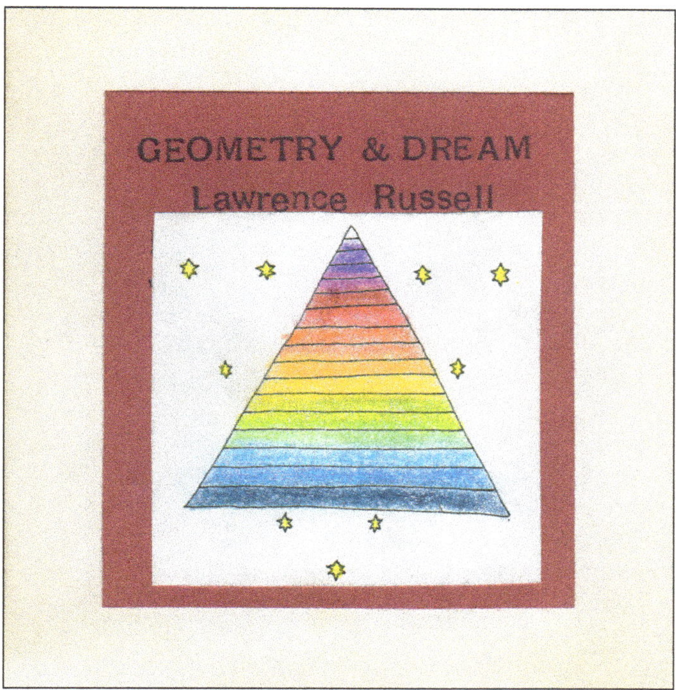

Geometry & Dream

Early synths didn't interest me at first, as they were mono, and you couldn't play chords on them. Good for sound effects... but music? They were mechanical, atonal, and soulless. And they cost a lot of money. I was used to writing for the stage, where the limitation of space and time forced you into creative solutions to make the narrative happen. To me, the misuse of the tape recorder and the musical instrument was the way forward. Take the wrong fork in the road... but keep the human touch *primo forte.*

Whatever sound you got, you had to make it a mystery. How did he do that? Scales were to be avoided as they were cliché, obvious chords likewise. You just wanted atmosphere, and you wanted hypnosis. It didn't matter if it was tonal or noise or anywhere in between, as it was all about noise in the first place, language or music or just the mysterious sound of gravity at work.

Noise. Find a new noise.

When I used the guitar, it didn't matter what way it was tuned or if all the strings were intact. I dialled the tuners and let the strings find an interesting chord, then sawed it with a steel bar to get a symphonic roar or jungle drummed the strings with screw drivers and let the drone paint the soundscape. The use of echo delay gave the soundscape an enhanced three dimensional depth—the sort of thing that's commonplace in today's polyphonic synthesizers but back then in the start of the seventies, less understood, often dismissed as gimmicky.

Camouflage (1971) was my break-through tape, the first recording that harnessed voice with a trance pattern soundscape created by playing straight into the recorder through the microphone jack and playing the guitar all wrong, like a street artist spraying illiterate graffiti... if it looks good, who cares if it reads stupid? It was cosmic noise, rhythmic and polyrhythmic, and the pulse blew the listeners away.

The sound helix patterns just kept spiralling through the jungles of the mind. The voice monolgue was like a helix itself, classic unreliable narrator stuff—a war vet recalls an incident in Italy when he comes across some dead Germans laid out in a circle, as if in some mystic rapport with another dimension.

A few years later there was a cult suicide in Quebec where the bodies were arranged in a circle facing the sky, and I always wondered if they'd listened to *Camouflage* and were inspired in a perverse way to attempt a transcendental exit. Besides being circulated widely by tape through the underground culture via *DNA Stereo Magazine* and played on FM radio throughout North America, *Camouflage* was also issued by Radio Canada International (Montreal) as a transcription LP (*Stereo Stories from Canada*) to various affiliates around the world.

Next was *Geometry & Dream* (1972), a recording I found hard to go beyond, and dithered around in its shadow for the next few years without getting serious. The vocal was a fragmented narrative constructed using cannabalized text from other sources and some fragments from my journal. The imagery was Jules Verne run through M.C. Escher, a sort of psychedelic guide book for sleepwalkers. The soundscape was direct input guitar, multi-tracked. The coda used a river recording looped through an equalizer and two reelers running at different speeds... and the result was quite spacey. The phasing was done by occasionally slowing one of the reels with a heavy hand. This recording was probably the most popular of all from my *DNA* period, and was played on many of the Listener Subscription FM stations of the Pacifica Network... Seattle, Portland, Berkeley, L.A., San Diego... WBAI in New York, even a station in Memphis, home of the slap-back echo that so influenced nearly everything I did in audio.

In those days the exploration of inner space led to an awful lot of talk about Death, and if life continued on. The Zen idea of "Oneness" was popular, and contributed to a lot of the carelessness about drugs, I think. Some people just didn't give a damn what they ingested, and others had a religious curiousity about the afterlife, as if it was the ultimate nightclub or the only place left to explore if you didn't have a rocket. Death was a big subject for a lot of artists and writers, always had been, and why not? It's ongoing, never as far away as you might like.

DNA got some local press but it was Rick McGrath or "McDog" who broke it big in the *Georgia Straight*, Vancouver's premier underground newspaper. McDog was the Big Game rock critic, interviewed all the big acts as they passed through Vancouver—Led Zeppelin, Van Morrisson, Fleetwood Mac, Mitch Ryder... even real off-the-wall guys like jazzer Al Neil and Captain Beefheart... and once in a while he wrote book reviews, so I sent him a couple of *DNA* tapes on the off-chance the concept of a free tape exchange and the sort of *avant-garde* electronic lit we were doing might appeal to him. It did. McDog responded with both barrels, firing off a big two page article with the headline, "Meet Doctor DNA" and things went nuts after that. For a while people had been showing up at my door with blank tapes and some were coming in by mail, but now requests for dubs appeared in the mail every day and strangers were knocking on the door like pilgrims seeking the Oracle of Delphi.

It was quite amazing the reach of the underground counter culture—not only up and down the west coast but also to other parts of the world. In North America the tapes came in from East to West and there were some from England and the Continent, although the strangest request came from a Royal Navy fellow whose warship was based in Gibraltar, a place I knew from my "On the Road" days as a Beat apprentice.

DNA was a tape magazine that worked on a free exchange principle, initially a conceptual art project as much as it was a means of distributing audio art via the counter-culture. The idea came to me after I was asked to contribute a "page" to Dana Atchley's *Space Atlas*, which was a loose leaf binder of 100 contributions by 100 contributors, who were "artists" if they said so. Nothing was rejected as long as it was no more than one page and could fit into the binder. A poet? Just xerox 200 copies of your poem. A visual artist? The same. Why 200 copies? Because you received two copies of the Atlas—one for yourself, one to pass along. So it had an exponential aspect, like a booze bottle pyramid scheme.

Tape was easy to copy, easy to bootleg. I was after distribution, not money, an audience, not alms. Print was dead, dying on the vine. Art follows the dominant media of the times. Gutenberg arrives, books follow. Fox-Talbot arrives, films follow. Edison arrives, records follow. Xerox arrives, everyone's a publisher... McLuhan said that, didn't he? Magnetophon arrives, tapes follow... and the story is obvious. Every advance in technology leads to a new form of art.

DNA was very successful as a distribution network for three to five years until it ran out of steam. Copying tapes in real time was a bit of a chore eventually, the novelty wearing off. It was fortunate that the *Village Voice* (New York) didn't write it up as promised. I'd met a young assistant editor on the train somewhere on the prairies—I'd been in Toronto where some of my plays were on at the Factory Theatre Lab—and he said *DNA* was definitely something the *Voice* would be interested in. I passed along a couple of tapes.

A short time later I was sitting in my office at the university when the phone rang and it was someone from the *Voice*—not the man I met on the train, probably the Arts editor. He said the notion of a tape magazine available as a "free tape exchange" was a great idea, but, umm, could I handle the thousands of tapes that were sure to arrive if the *Village Voice* wrote it up. Sure, sure, I said, no problem.

But of course it would've been a problem, even if Canadian Customs let the tapes flow in. But I was riding high in those days, '73. '74. as the Stratford Festival had performed several of my one act plays and had commissioned me to write a multi-media play for their main stage... and I had a book coming out shortly. It was all crazy, irresistable, like rock & roll, the babes at the door and free drinks in the bar.

The Art Of The Monologue

Is reading or listening the ultimate theatre of the mind? It quickly became obvious to me that while writing a story gave it organization, it also gave it a pretentious pallor, as the need to be verbally clever was in-built into the act of writing. Also, "reading" a written text into the microphone was the kiss of death, no matter how accomplished the vocalist was. Listening to visiting authors read their texts also exposed the critical difference between reading and listening, where the attention span of even the more friendly of listeners is quite brief. Ever read your carefully crafted story that you published in a literary magazine to a roomful of people? The exercise can be sobering. Imagine doing the same thing in a coffee shop or bar with a few friends... no way, Jose.

A novel... how artificial is that? Who listens to someone telling a story like that? Even a proto-human with a bicameral mind wouldn't listen to that voice in the head droning on, even in an eight hour sleep cycle.

"Print-consciousness" was my term for the affliction.

The art of the oral story is the ancient heart of narrative exposition. You can't mess around, and the more natural your voice, the more accepted it will be. The persona can have style, certainly, but it can't be phony unless phony is the objective. You can mimic and you can exaggerate, but you can't lose the listener. The listener doesn't skim the dead zones. The listener tunes out, either falls asleep or starts talking to someone else... even if it's himself.

It's true that the young will listen a lot longer than adults, and they will accept reading just as long as it has children's lit brevity. Remember bringing an Enid Blyton *Five* novel to school—must've been grade 3 or 4 back in Broughshane—and the teacher trying it out on us, and it was a big hit, and she ended up reading the entire novel in forty minute blocks over a couple of weeks. My classmates—boys and girls—sat obediently or rested their heads in their arms as if napping, and took it all in, enraptured. Enid Blyton. And who knew that the woman behind these family action adventure tales was such a bad girl, the bitchy hostess of loose drunken parties at her thatched roof house in Buckinghamshire?

Blyton was a classic trance writer, who just closed her eyes and let it all flow. Jack Kerouac, same thing.

How many words, how many sentences are uttered before a monologue becomes a story? Not many. This was something I learned from writing plays, learned from the rhythmic movement of dialogue into monologue and back. It was clear that on stage you couldn't monologue or soliloquize forever. No matter how dysfunctional the character, there was an art to it, a sense of purpose and sub-text that locked into the final architecture. If not, it was dead air. It wasn't long before I abandoned a written script altogether—except perhaps for a few notes—and just rapped the story over the soundscape, allowed the music to pace the delivery, inflect the tone, blend like a singer. You memorize the story, make it a lyric, make it a dialogue with the soundscape, which is a *de facto* character. Allow the sound to say what can remain unsaid. Intonation, implication. Ergo, sub-text is found in the harmonics of the mind. In other words keep it tight, keep the opera real.

All narrative is monologue, even if the persona remains hidden (as in, say, the 3rd person, the quintessential written voice) and it's the failure to recognize this that leads to stilted writing, and, for that matter, speaking.

All of this economy of form is known in film, which, despite synchronous sound, aspires to be silent, an omniscient eye on Nature. If you can show it, don't say it—this is the maxim that drives script writers and the directors they unfortunately serve. For the actor, body language is every much of an art as is speaking. The close-up and the facial expression move the message, dialogue passes the time.

Actions speak, language conceals.

The influence of late night radio listening on my approach to audio art is/was big. Or just the night itself, the random sounds, in the room, beyond the room, and the need to articulate them as an understandable narrative was essential to survival. One sound was an accident; two, a pattern; three, a plot. And radio, as a bridge to sleep, was also the engine of dream.

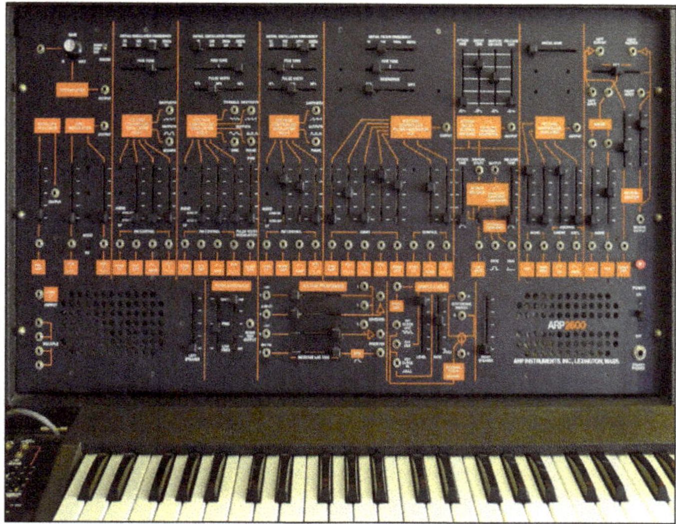

To Synth Or Not To Synth

An electronic composer called Phillip Werren who'd just bagged his teaching gig at Simon Fraser University (SFU) and gone Zen up on Quadra Island (just off Campbell River) had heard some *DNA* and was curious about my methods, which were as primitive as they were mystifying. He used an Arp *Odyssey* synthesizer to get his minimalist drones and helix swirls... I liked it well enough, although I preferred human oscillators. Synths were like sex toys—they could keep going forever, sure, but who wants forever?

PW gave me a list of recent avant-garde compositions he considered important—pieces by Berio, Boulez, Cage, Stockhausen... the usual suspects—and I pulled them from the university library, gave them a listen. I liked Stockhausen's name, be great for an electric guitar model, I thought... and I looked into him some more. All of these composers had something, and I could see the shift away from conventional symphonic orchestration happening, the modernist descent into minimalism and all, yet they seemed like prisoners of tradition and institutional thinking... a bit totalitarian in a way. Enough religious impressionism. I liked raw and I liked improvisation, less formalism and class consciousness, more bad boy, even if it meant not getting tenure and a pension.

As technology was developing quickly, the Mini Moog and the Arp *Odyssey* soon ended up in the closet or the junk store along with the Cray super computers. Collector's items today, of course, in the same way a first edition of Jules Verne's *Twenty Thousand Leagues Under the Sea* is: the crude fantasy of yesterday is today's sacred relic, and possession thrills to the bones.

Folk

Folk did hit my neighbourhood and I made a brief visit to it. There was a coffee house in Victoria called The Secret, a funky cellar that was below The Westholme beer parlour on Government Street, a bar some of us bohemian *literati* could afford. The beer parlour had large murals on the walls, Canadian forest and mountain scenes with the odd moose or bear fording a river or a loon on a sandbar, the majestic loneliness I certainly knew all about from my days in the North and doing wildnerness surveys for the Mica Dam Project. The murals were grimy with smoke and despair, like forgotten windows to a world from when most of the derelict patrons were young and the hunting was good. For us, drinking our glasses of 20 cent generic, it was all cool and only the hip could appreciate it.

So why would I go down below the street to The Secret, which didn't even have a license, check out these Ivy League clowns with acoustics who didn't even go to university, yet had so much to say about everything? Anyway I did and one night I thought I'd give it a go, as they had an open mic. I still had my Lonnie Donegan repertoire, the folk blues stuff, the Woody Guthrie and could even play a recent hit, *Walk Right In* by the Rooftop Singers, a number that was a bit beyond most of the hackers I'd seen on stage.

Actually, the Rooftop Singers had performed at the college recently, and I had to admit they were pretty good and maybe they were the reason I was willing to give Folk a look. Of course, as usual, I was out-of-step, didn't have the *de rigueur* acoustic dreadnaught or mandolin, but rather a solid body electric that looked like it was out of a science fiction movie. Italian, called an Eko. Black, with a silver sparkle face, four (4) pickups and a whammy bar that you could ride straight up 33 floors and, well, you might or might not still be in tune when you came back to the lobby.

Remember this local folkie called Murray McA—think he emerged from one of the local "boys schools" here on the southern Island—who had a mickey mouse little acoustic and was maybe o.k. for a campsite party, except that he wore the uniform, the Ivy League suit and a haircut like James Coburn, sorta military but these days, campus.

When he finished his set, I was coming on, and he gawked at my guitar in disbelief, said, "What the hell is that?"

I suppose, hmm, he had a point. He just hung at the back, watched, joked with his friends. But after I rolled through *Grand Coulee Dam, Frankie & Johnny, Midnight Special* and a couple of other tunes from my Zombies skiffle days, he slipped away. I wasn't great, was a bit rusty, but these tunes were out of the loop for a trendy choir boy like him. Me? I was wearing cords and an Irish tweed jacket with leather elbow patches and a sweat shirt, was somewhere between Varsity and Beat. I was in transition, and while I wasn't sure about Folk, I knew damn sure I wouldn't be wearing a Brooks Brothers suit or a fisherman's sweater anytime soon.

Saw Sonny Terry and Brownie McGhee, the black blues duo around this time. They came in annually to Victoria College (affiliated to UBC) when I was there. Very professional, never dropped a beat. They were the real deal, down South and muddy, yet urban slick. McGhee's guitar playing was great, and Terry's howling harmonica was my first exposure to a real down and dirty blues harp. Again, the economy of form was impressive—the voice, the stomp, the wail.

But in the end Folk was too church, too classroom, too nostalgic or too serious, hijacked by propagandists and killjoys. It couldn't last and it didn't, just like gaslight. I remember the Driftwood Singers, a Seattle group, coming to Victoria and hanging out with them at a party, and then a few months later they showed up as The Daily Flash, a rock group. This was typical of what was happening. They were taking their cue from Dylan: one side of *Bringing It All Back Home* was acoustic, the other electric.

In the end, university claimed me. Yes, I still carried a guitar in the back of my M.G., did a few rave ups at a party now and then... but essentially I was done as a musician, recreational or otherwise, at least for now. Got hammered one night drinking sake at a friend's house, went out into the starry night, hit some black ice, ploughed into a tree, was thrown clear, like the hand of God reached in and yanked me through the passenger door. This was on a lonely stretch of road, and before I crawled out of the ditch, I ate some dirt in case I had to have a conversation with the police. The car was wrecked, and my acoustic guitar had a hole in the ass end, but I was o.k.

Billie Holiday (or if you want, Etta Jones) sings, so mellow, so fine:

> love will make you drink and gamble
> make you stay out all night long
> love will make you do things
> that you know is wrong

Warning received and understood.

Notes For An Extended Conversation

The Doors | The Chambers Brothers | Jimi Hendrix | Jefferson Airplane | Grateful Dead | Country Joe | Sir Douglas Quintet | Quicksilver Messenger Service | Gabor Szabo | Tim Buckley | Moby Grape | Otis Redding | The Monterey Pop Festival | The Zodiac | Big Brother | Janis

In his recent autobiography (*The Universal Tone*, 2014) Carlos Santana says: "The Doors started what I call shaman music, or LSD music. Music that casts a spell and transports the listener to a place beyond time and gravity, beyond problems." (156) One can always quibble about who was "first" into the trip music style in the radio chart culture—the Beatles after they went Ravi Shankar on *Rubber Soul* or The Byrds or Country Joe or X, Y and Z—although Santana is thinking more in the Carlos Castaneda sense, the evocation of the Messenger, or the Guide in the North American Indian spirit world. *Light My Fire* was a massive hit in the summer of 1967.

It's a curious mixture of crude sexual innuendo and mystical revanchism, Paradise Regained, where sin and innocence interchange as easily as major and minor. It's a psychedelic flamenco with a spectacular astral coda, an instrumental groove lock that just puts your head in the 5th dimension, if there is such a place. At the time, Morrison's choral chant, *Come on baby light my fire!* annoyed me, nay, pissed me off, as it cheapened the whole experience, was bare-faced sexual harassment. I mean, does porno and spirituality coexist?

If they do, then they take turns sitting on each other's face.

And yet you ended up muttering or humming *come on baby light my fire* in the strangest places... as you translated some Maxim Gorky for your Russian language proficiency exam or listened to speculation about a killer in the Bay area they were calling the Zodiac.

The Zodiac was shape-shifter, alright, just like the angry, psychotic persona Morrison adopted in his Oedipal confession, *The End* (1967). Good stuff. It made the listener think rather than driving around gurgling baby talk, like *bimbo bimbo/ where you gonna go-e-oh* or *how much is that doggy in the window*. If it had to be psycho babble, let it be psycho.

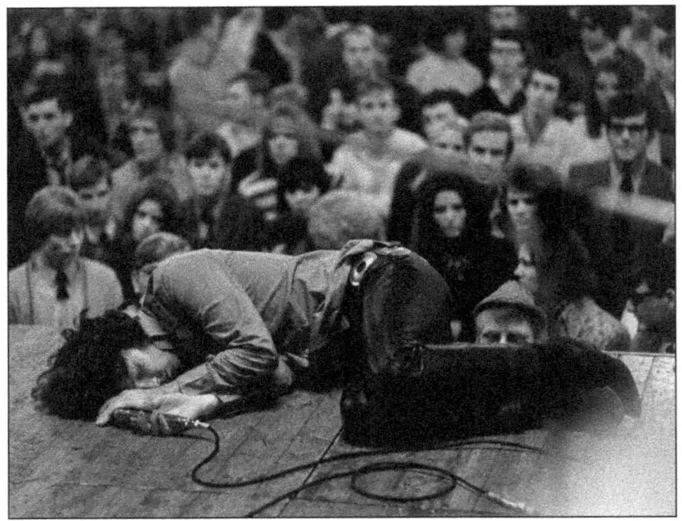

Morrison was another one of these guys who couldn't sing, but sang nevertheless as he had something to say. Real singers mouthed rubbish, used language as sound notation, the language of birds. These rock singers like Morrison were like Bluesmen, raw engines in the night.

Talk was part of the song and the song was part of the talk. Much of it was sex talk, the pleasure grind, the search for orgasm. *L.A Woman*—what was that? Mumbo rhyme in search of a Muse? Great lick, great muso facsimile of American big city madness. The lyric is classic Morrison primitivism, a Tourette Syndrome mojo grunt elevated by a beautiful personifcation:

> I see your hair is burning
> Hills are filled with fire
> if they say I never loved you
> you know they are a liar

You know the keyboard player Ray Manzarek was one half of the poetry, as his urgent Fender Rhodes sang in unison with guitarist Robby Krieger like a Triumph *Twin*. One of their best numbers, and it certainly didn't sound like a Brit Rock knockoff.

But... *Riders On the Storm*... what shite is this? I thought when I first heard it on the radio. It was like a lounge lizard narco version of *Ghost Riders In the Sky*. Sure, it had a sort Thelonius Monk Misterioso keyboard sound... the line wasn't that unusual within the Blues idiom, I mean, didn't Steppenwolf use it for *Pusher Man*?

Once again Morrison and The Doors had confounded me with that pop mash of radio and New Age elevator that —because it had a jazz and a movie soundtrack feel—seemed like a con job. Yet, as the years go by, the track has worn well, despite the fact it's a cheap suit, something to sacrifice to smoke damage in the street, the lounge and the office. It's not the worst piece they did. So Morrison got arrested for alleged indecent exposure in Miami. What was new? His lyrics were all about indecent exposure.

Jim Morrison was an accident of history. He didn't play an instrument and his singing was restricted to howling at the moon before Ray Manzerak found him on the beach with his notebook of poems. The self-loathing that led to his premature death was fed by the exhibitionism he resorted to as a frontman.

Theatre, you say. Satire, you say.

When Ed Sullivan objected to the line, *come on baby light my fire*, Morrison responded with *come on baby pull my wire*. Mind you, "bad boy" was part of the period style, especially in rock and roll. How could you not court death? It was part of the art, the heresy and the danger. Brian Jones was gone. Hendrix... Janis. Poets burned bright, left the party early. Apparently he liked Celine's *Journey To The End of Night*, which might explain why he went to Paris to die. As Celine says, "You have to choose: death or lies."

Stone's film *The Doors* is very good, and honestly, could you tell that Val Kilmer wasn't indeed Jim Morrison? Therefore it's fitting that as a graduate of the UCLA film school the Lizard King's life turned out to be a script.

Yuba River

I did the sound-installation act once or twice, although I always felt the visual aspect distracted from the audio dream experience. My friend Jack K, the old Frisco beatnik artist with the great record collection, wanted me to do some sound for a show he was doing at Open Space. He had some large black and white photo blowups of some rock debris on the Yuba River in Northern California which was like natural-born Alexander Calder or Henry Moore, big eggs and rock shelves shaped by the water through the generations.

Some artists thought this "art-in-nature" was bullshit, a sort of taking credit for something you had no hand in creating... but Jack's idea didn't end with just the photos. They would be arranged as a spiral enclosure, which the viewer would enter, and a looped soundscape would enhance the experience.

So I took a river recording, ran it through an equalizer, then into two tape recorders patched into one another as a loop, messed with the echo, the play and record speeds, the stereo field pan, had a friend and student of mine, Wayne S, improvise some piano into the cosmic cascades.

It was good stuff for 1974, and the installation was a big hit, some people sitting in the vortex for an hour or two. No money in it, of course. A review in the paper, CV stuff, some smiles, some hisses. The visual art scene is so visceral, staggering between furniture, ancestor worship, narcissism and mental illness, yet is always seeking approval. Art openings always made me feel ill, so many sensitive people gliding about, so much ectoplasmic voltage in the gallery air.

Show biz.

Music And Noise

Where and when does electronic music begin? Where does it end... or is it possible it can never end, as it's running through the universe in the endless radio roar of the stars?

Luigi Russolo (1883-1947), who has the same initials as me, but looks nothing like me, might be Mile 1 on the highway, if not zero. He wrote a great little Futurist manifesto in 1913 called *The Art of Noises* (*L'Arte dei rumori*) which starts with the premise that before machines, there was no sound except for those from occasional natural events. By the Middle Ages there were chants, then chords, and as the sound of machinery intensified, polyphony. This also occasions a move away from the Pythagorean sweet tone into dissonance, which would

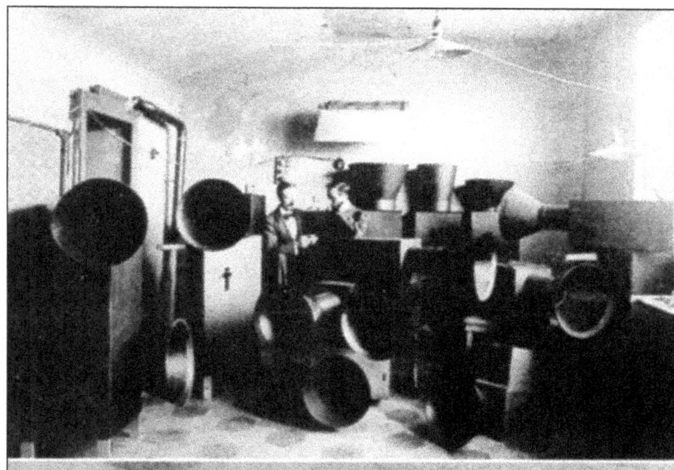

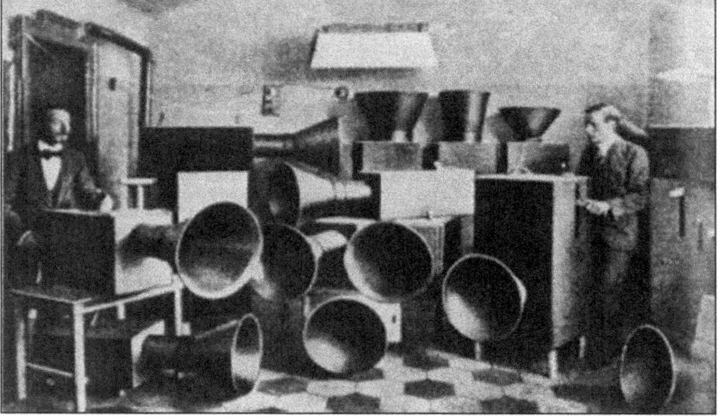

unravel the complexity of noise. Needless to say he advised "Futurist musicians" to ditch the traditional instruments by inventing new ones that would capture the diverse rhythms of noise.

This sounds like a command for the invention of the electric guitar and the polyphonic synthesizer to me. But while he was waiting, he teamed up with the Godfather of Futurism, Marinetti, constructed a few hand-cranked noise machines with horns with Ugo Piatti and staged the first *intonnarumori* concert in 1914 which apparently ended in a riot. Given the titles of the four "compositions" played, a riot would fit right in with Russolo's noise-music aesthetic and the Futurist declamation that "war is the only hygiene of the world".

Russolo was a reactionary, tired of the old orchestrations which sought to emulate the sound of the pastoral before the pastoral surrendered to industrialization. The Futurists liked the mathematical magic of machines, the geometry of the future, not the accident of the past. While his instruments were as crude as a miller's wheel, their primitivism was an atonal assertion of the fundamental laws of gravity.

Thus he thought in terms of noise networks: *Awakening of a City... Meeting of Cars and Aeroplanes... Dining on the Terrace of the Casino... Skirmish in the Oasis*, etc. If the tape recorder had been invented earlier, perhaps Russolo's simulations would've been unnecessary. Yet the fundamentalism of the exercise was a attempt at reeducation within the existing dialectic of stage, orchestra, and listener. Unfortunately the rise and fall of Fascism led to Futurism's partial disgrace due to the political aspirations of some of its proponents... yet when you think of the real-time films of Andy Warhol like *Sleep* (1963, 5hrs 20 mins) or *Empire* (1964, 8hrs 5 mins) where the visual "noise" is purged to its documentary essential, what is this but a Futurist reeducation exercise? In Warhol's case, voyeurism and narcissism replace

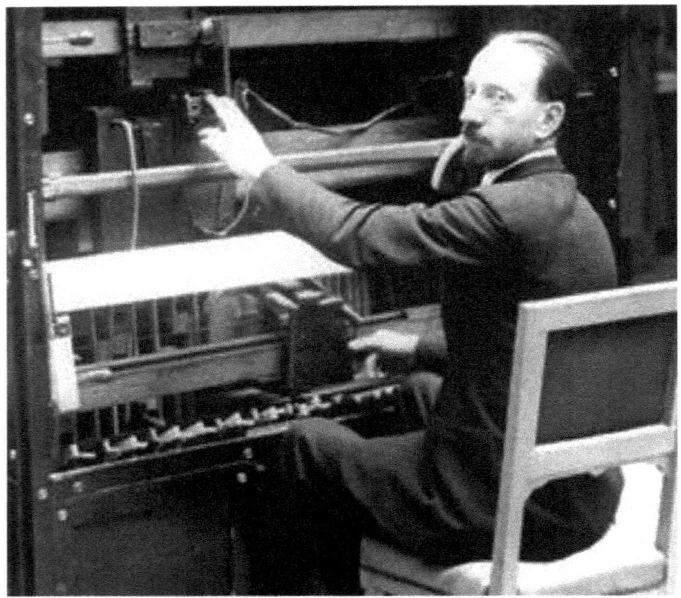

the politics, but as in Russolo's case, the "action" of the artist is the historical marker, not the art itself.

Another opponent of the twelve tone scale was the Russian composer Arseny Avraamov (1886-1944) who went big time symphonic with his *Symphony of Factory Sirens*—perhaps the first piece of environmental art outside of monumental sculpture—wherein he used not only factory sirens and automobile horns, but also the ship horns and artillery of the Russian Navy stationed at Baku on the Caspian Sea. This was orchestrated noise in real time, a political statement in honour of the Soviet as much as it was artistic.

But this was only one part of his devolution from the concert hall—"graphical music" was the other. Avraamov was part of a group working on an early synchronous sound film who noticed the visual pattern on the optical strip, wondered if "art" was rendered on the strip might it not produce a new form of music (it was even speculated that if they used Egyptian images these might reveal a lost language, the music of the ancients). This sort of ornamental pattern music was also being developed at the same time by a couple of Germans, Rudolpf Phenninger and Oskar Fischinger.

As with the invention of photography, technological invention appears independently in two or more places at once. Many people think electronic music started with the soundtrack for *Forbidden Planet* (1956), composed and recorded by Louis and Bebe Barron, although the film industry had been using Tesla's Theremin for a number of years for its spooky beyond-the-grave feel. But the Barrons went way beyond that. They overloaded a ring modulator circuit, and, using a two recorder loop feeding into a third, came up with the soundtrack. This technique of "misuse" and "accident" is the improvisational root of early electronic music.

Louis Barron built a number of oscillators—sawtooth, square and sine wave—which you'll find in all of today's synthesizers. It's interesting to note that the Barrons recorded a number of famous authors in their Greenwich Village studio, including Aldous Huxley, Henry Miller and Anais Nin, thus anticipating audio lit. These red vinyl pressings must be worth a fortune on the collectors' market today.

In actuality, it's the Barron's soundtrack for Ian Hugo's short film *The Bells of Atlantis* (1952) that might be the first applied electronic music. Hugo was Anais Nin's husband, and you can hear her as the "Queen of Atlantis" reciting her story against Hugo's expressionist montage, which predates anything done in the sixties by the "Expanded Cinema" crowd. You can find this short film on the internet.

John Cage was one of the first composers to use the Barrons' studio. In 1953 he created *Williams Mix*, which was for live performance using eight different tapes. The concept sounds very similar to Luigi Russolo's *intonnarumori* concert in its desire to simulate environmental noise in order to establish a pattern of proto-music. It's an eclectic montage of real sounds, tape flutter, tape speed manipulation, azimuthal jitter and so on... and is quite an impressive soundscape, because, while there's no beat pattern per se, it appears to be "cut to the beat"... and the use of eight playback machines achieves spacialization in the era of the monaural broadcast, albeit in a theatre setting.

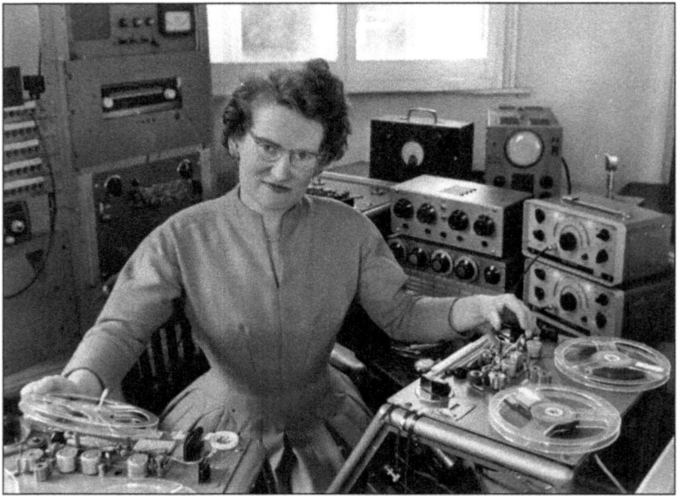

In parallel to the Barrons is Daphne Oram (1925-2003) who got into electronic composition while working as a junior recording engineer at the BBC in the 1940s. While she used the *musique concrete* approach—the manipulation of natural sounds—she also followed the Russian example of drawing on blank optical film, which was a way of translating pictures into sound. She built a composer which ran ten strips of 35 mm film that enabled quite a sophisticated level of control, and in some ways resembled the Russian ANS optical synthesizer developed by Evgeny Murzin.

Her *Oramics* compositions were used in UK television and film throughout the fifties and sixties, i.e. the 1957 BBC production of *Amphitryon 38* by the French dramatist Jean Giradoux, and Jack Clayton's horror film *The Innocents* (1961). She also used a sine wave oscillator and built her own studio in a cottage on the south coast of England, as she wasn't getting enough respect at the BBC. While her work was sublimated as commercial ephemera, she was in fact the Agatha Christie of audio art—persistent, prolific and more popular than you would suspect.

Another realization of the Russolo noise-music aesthetic was Pierre Schaeffer's *musique concrete* exploration of radiophonics and the electroacoustic possibilities of recording. He came up with the term *musique concrete*, initiated the revolt against notation as a form of scripting. Bag traditional instruments, collect sounds, mine time and space. You could say the only difference between Russolo and Schaeffer is a tape recorder. *Musique concrete* is/was the realization of the ideas first expressed in Russolo's *The Art of Noises*, and led to the electrification of European classical music, and the *de facto* dematerialization of the concert hall shell in order to include the sound of the world outside. It's a movement from fiction to documentary, and you see it in all the arts as recording replaces the mnemonic need for scripting.

Messiaen... Boulez... Barraque... Varese... Stockhausen... Xenakis... Honegger... all of these now well-known composers studied and hung out at Schaeffer's *Musique Concrete* Research Group in Paris in the 1950s. It doesn't take a genius to recognize that electronic music had arrived and all that remained was for the development of the polyphonic synthesizer to finalize the triumph of noise over tone.

Was this a good thing? Did the absence of technical limitations lead to a decline of compositional imagination? Is it an art anymore when a fist on the keyboard can produce the music of the spheres? Has culture been handed to the scientists, the people who write the algorithms, manufacture the machines?

There's certainly a lot of delusion when an artist stands between an accident and an oscillator and thinks he's sexy... and even more when the crowd thinks so too. It becomes more and more difficult to distinguish between the fiction of the player and the documentary of the machine.

The artist rises, opens the curtains and sunlight pours into the room, and by the time night returns it doesn't matter if he's alive or dead as the sun will return with or without him.

PART TWO:

Art of The Hipster

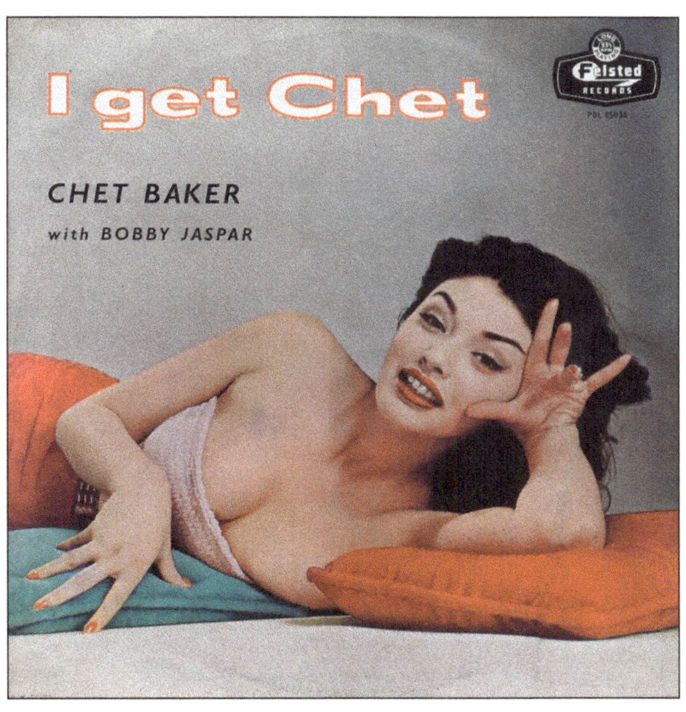

Art of the Hipster: Chet Baker
and introducing Chet Baker and his Trumpet

Chet Baker—what a paradox. Gentle, playful, loving, hard-working some of the time; cruel, self-centred, lazy and downright ugly a lot of the time. This could be anyone, of course, as moral frailty and creative expression are a wedded contradiction, and the occasionally-famous are seldom allowed private ugliness. Drugs, addiction, women and cars—his crimes were all secular, even though these things drove the omnivorous industrial dynamic of American free enterprize, and as a jazz hipster junkie longing to be free, his persecution was part of the corporate cultural lie. Perhaps. Perhaps true freedom always requires some sort of enslavement.

He had the Hollywood look that fitted his time—the 40s, the 50s, maybe the 60s—the sort of falsely innocent face that looked good on an album cover, the sweet white beauty of post-war American triumphalism. Indeed, Hollywood called, gave him a small part in the 1955 Korean war movie *Hell's Horizon*. In the credits he's listed as: "and introducing Chet Baker and his Trumpet", as if the trumpet personified a ventriloquist's dummy. He plays close to character, a B-29 airman called "Jockey" who lies around in the crew tent blowing pensive figures on his horn. Acting? Not really. A few jive talk lines and he gets to die. Following a fatal mission to the Manchurian border and a belly landing back in Okinawa, his skinny body is recovered from the burning wreck and laid out on the runway; one of the crew finds his trumpet mouthpiece, tucks it below his crossed hands... up violins as the crew walk away and that's it for Hollywood and Chet Baker. It was a 10 day shoot, fast even by B-movie standards, yet Chet says he "got really bored" hanging around waiting for his scenes. Truth is, his voice was all wrong, too high and androgynous for any male lead, so he could only be a bit player, a parody of himself.

But this didn't mean he couldn't live like a movie...

Los Angeles, summer of '57. Corner of Hollywood Boulevard and Western. The Hipster arrives late for a gig at the Peacock Lane Club, parks across the street, sees the cops under a streetlight checking for crucifixion marks. Two friends, users, their arms outstretched and gleaming. The Hipster slips into the club, recovers his trumpet, follows the shadows back to his car where his young wife is waiting. She's seven months pregnant, shows it, is anxious. The Hipster slips into first gear, pulls away softly, then spots a black unmarked Ford coming at him. He guns it, hangs a left, then another. He's driving kinetic, getting low yo-yo like the Red Baron, soon loses the eyeless narc, makes the freeway. He stops at the ramp, gives his wife some dough for a cab home. She gets out, and he breaks west for Newport Beach.

Cut To: the Hipster's 1955 XK 140 Jaguar sports slipping through the pre-dawn luminosity. The Hipster likes sports cars, will always like them, blew some savings that was owed to the taxman for this one. Well it's cool, flies like Bird, the great Charlie Parker who made him a bop disciple. Low deco streamlined chariot of the damned. He has a taste for the European, acquired during his US Army bugle-boy days in Germany. Jags go good in SoCal. Mike Hammer drives one in *Kiss Me Deadly*, and what's good for Hammer is good for Chet Baker, junkie hipster, winner of the 1954 *Downbeat* poll for Best Jazz Trumpet.

Check out his features: yes, he could be in the movies. He has the 50's chiselled jaw, cheek bumps, surfer wave hair, the SoCal cool. He could be Ralph Meeker playing Mike Hammer, although he's a ringer for Chuck Connors, *The Rifleman*... a handsome skull with eyes. Too bad he's an outlaw. Too bad he shoots it in his arm. Too bad 'cause he's white and Miles Davis is black and America still wants white. Cops don't care, though. They'll hunt anything, especially junkies, especially jazz junkies. They'll hunt the lizard and the lizard knows he's gotta head for the ocean.

Chet has a friend across the bridge in Balboa, where all the fishing boats hang up. Bobby's just heading out to harvest abalone in the Santa Barbara Channel, off San Miguel Island, so Chet decides "to cool it for a while, to clean up and let the sun work on my arms". After four days, he starts to feel better, get a little sleep.

Meanwhile his friend Bobby is doing the bottom crawl, a hundred feet down, bagging the abalone, sending it up top on the electric lag line. Ten, maybe twelve dozen primo pinks every dive. Easy. No great whites around and the sea lions are cooling it on the rocks. Time for the Hipster to solo. Sea birds are dropping from the sky like footballs, using their wings to propel themselves deep underwater to snatch some fish. California Murres, smarter than penguins, faster than humans, hip as D Dorian. Yep, time to drop from the ladder, break the surface, play a little below the centre of tonality.

Well, he's done lots of diving before, skin and Aqua-Lung, but never any air-line stuff. Suit, helmet, lead boots. Down he goes, feet first, following the bag line, down, down into the undulating sea-weed forest... he starts walking around, gets lost, and his feet are getting colder. The suit is leaking, the water is up to his chest... he's been going in the wrong direction, doubled back on his air-line, just like he's gotten lost during a horn solo, can't find the point of resolution, very uncool and something he never does unless way too stoned and then some. But down here, hiding from the Man, doing the lizard but not doing it right, he's in trouble.

Yeah, let's get lost.

It was a close call for Chet Baker, in a life with many close calls—on the street, maxing fast cars, surviving prison or diving underwater or shooting skanky dope—so you recognize that he was a natural risk-taker. Reckless cliff climbing at Palos Verdes or fights with football players, dealers... armed robbery, forgery... he took risks. He was California casual—T-shirt and jacket—the early hipster look that captured nearly everyone eventually, from lazy Joe College to the amped-up rock n roll cool of *Miami Vice*. West Coast Cool. It's not only a jazz sound, it's a life-style, and Baker becomes its icon, part of the young rebel chancer brigade that includes Brando, Dean... even Montgomery Cliff, sometimes Robert Wagner. They were always looking for a new sensation, a new high, a lost chord. Cars, women... women, cars. Brando was primal—he played bongos, rode a bike. Later he did drugs and did them bad but never as bad as Chet Baker.

Chet Baker was a nomad, became stateless, even though he carried an American passport. The only property he owned was his car and his trumpet, and sometimes he didn't even own those. He wasn't Zen, although sometimes he sounded Zen in interviews and when he played. He grew up in Oklahoma against a flat, empty horizon, so perhaps this ruled his thinking.

His father was a C & W alcoholic, Chet was a jazz urban addict. He spent time in jail, but time was always a jail. He was always on the move, even when he was locked up or locked out. He drove like a dog, his face to the wind. His emptiness was a pipe, a mouthpiece, a passage to shape his fear of judgement. He embraced nothingness as if his reflection revealed the beauty of his destination. He didn't read charts, yet he moved by the stars. He wanted to be a sailor, get a boat and get lost. He sang of love, yet he loved the poetry more than the woman. He was a toothless oral compulsive, his mouth always on his horn, a cigarette, a drink, or a tit. He could be had, was had, yet was never owned. He stole from others, even stole from himself. He disliked work, seldom practiced, remembered nothing, yet remembered all. He was a junky liar, even before he was a junky, lived in the fiction his respondents craved. In the end, he was death in a suit, desire in a coffin.

He was photographed often, poetically, fetishistically, yet the photographs reveal nothing. He was an idea, not a man, a stand-in for something. Possibly he was just an accidental instrument, like a sentient wind chime, but in his youth he was used as advertising, so he became part of a non-redactable American fantasy. He was a measuring stick for tomorrow, where art is a commodity for selling eternal youth. Hipness was supernatural, and whatever it was or how you got it didn't matter, as he had it. He had it before he turned to junk, and then he had it because he was junk. He was hip because he was in the mystic spiral, the junkie's needle like a phonograph needle tracking the groove... and everyone wanted to be in the groove... some of the time, maybe all of the time.

Can you compare Baker's drug abuse to athletes taking performance drugs? Art is a gray area, has no game boundaries like professional sports, is not a closed system. The thinking persists that art is divine messaging. When it's secular, it's just work, isn't really art. "You don't learn jazz," he said. "You're born into it." Certainly people like Chet Baker seem to be born tuned-up and ready to go. He didn't like charts, he was an ear player, someone who could read a song on hearing just a few notes, who could wander all over the theme in any sort of improvisation and still find the runway. Not for nothing did Bird summon him out of the darkness.

West Coast Cool

The story of how Chet Baker meets Charlie Parker (Bird) in 1952 has been told by him and repeated by others many times, many places. Perhaps it's fiction but this is how Chet says it went down: audition at the Tiffany Club, Chet gets there late, eyes burning in the darkness, every trumpet player in LA waiting his turn, Bird asks if Chet Baker is here yet, Chet gets up, plays a couple of tunes, gets the gig. "Bird was a flawless player," says CB in his memoir. "He treated me like a son, putting down any and all guys who tried to offer me some shit." Sound like Miles Davis and Bird? It certainly does. The high priest of bebop was a heavy user and abuser himself, a cat who could get lost for days, weeks, at end. Bird knew what heavy dope could do, its corruption of the soul; perhaps Bird needed innocence to play against, an idealized anima to sweeten his affliction. Chet describes how he would drive Bird down to the Palos Verdes-San Pedro coastline, and Bird would get out of the car, stare out to sea, watch the waves for an hour of natural hypnosis.

In his book *West Coast Jazz 1945-1960* Ted Gioia says the "west coast cool" style really came out of the relaxed atmosphere, the fun climate and the oceanic rhythm of the place... but surely this is only part of it, the advertising face of it. West coast cool jazz was more than sports shirts and wave haircuts and monosyllabic musicians; it had the same hidden author as New York cool, that is, heroin. Heroin slowed the action down, turned it inward. As an avatar, the *heroinista* was static, an impassive figure in still-life, a pose.

As Alexander Trocchi says in his heroin master-work, *Cain's Book* (Grove Press 1958): "The mind under heroin evades perception as it does ordinarily; one is aware only of contents... the perceiving turns inward, the eyelids droop, the blood is aware of itself, a slow phosphorescence in all the fabric of flesh and nerve and bone; it is that the organism has a sense of being intact and unbrittle, and, above all, inviolable. For the attitude born of this sense of inviolability some Americans have used the word cool."

Gerry Mulligan was a user, a driven anal-retentive addict with a brilliant compositional intuition. He'd been part of the Gil Evans-George Russell-Miles Davis modal clique in New York, and his move to Los Angeles in the early 50s was lucky chronicity for Chet Baker, even though they clashed big time at the start, at the end. Without swing, jazz was just cocktail lounge decor, yet Mulligan with his intellectual approach was able to compose and arrange modernist narratives that fitted nicely between post-war optimism and nuclear paranoia.

He got rid of the piano, as piano was cliché, softened the percussion, as percussion was cacophony, freed up space, as space was the fundamental. He played red low on baritone sax, and recruited Chet Baker on trumpet for the blue high. CB's early stuff with Gerry Mulligan for Pacific Records is sublime. It's a monophonic nirvana, where space is purely a mental dimension fixed by counter-point and tone. For example, the Quartet's recording of the Billie Holliday standard *Speak Low* might be a lover's code, but the walking bass suggests the easy flow of evening traffic somewhere near the beach. The four minute pop radio format, the soft porno of rent-a-dance, the narco sedation of cool. In 1953, music is still a 78 rpm format. Time is not a meter but a distance. The soft resolution of magnetic tape recording fixes the era as a mid-band memory. It's transformative, the decay and the noise, tube mics, iron oxide and the mystic vibration.

Chet Baker in Paris 1955 is really the story of the young pianist Dick Twardzik. Some accounts suggest Baker was more than just musically dazzled by Twardzik, who replaced Russ Freeman in the line-up for the European tour. Twardzik's teenage obsession with bebop included the complete lifestyle —a heroin habit and a black girlfriend. He was well-educated —perhaps to the self-destructive edge of nihilism—and his approach was bohemian, reminiscent of Mussogorsky, structured like Schoneberg, atonal and loose like Picasso with lots of bop and post-modern adventure in his avant approach to jazz.

The Quartet got off to a great start in Holland, and things looked promising in Paris, where they played the Sal Playel, then it all went to shit when Twardzik failed to show for a recording date at Blue Star Records. When someone goes looking, he's found in his hotel room "bright blue, the spike still in his arm". (*Memoir*, 71) Blame falls on his friend Peter Lippman, the Quartet's drummer, who immediately flees back to Boston, where he shifts the blame onto Baker. Commentators are divided on the issue of blame, but the facts seem to support that Twardzik and Lippman were established addicts long before they joined up with Chet Baker.

The October 25 Paris recordings—*Chet Baker Quartet Plays Standards*—is far better than you'd expect considering Dick Twardzik's death 4 days earlier, so CB is using a pickup pianist and percussionist. His trumpet tone is full, pitched for pleasure, with less melancholy than you'd expect. Perhaps the safe choice of a "standards" songbook was more than a commercial bet.

On October 23 he'd flown to London where he broke down four songs into the gig (absurdly, he wasn't allowed to play trumpet because of union rules), so his state of mind was fragile. Still, he managed to return to Paris and get on with it. Only Jimmy Bond on bass remained of the Quartet he started out in France with in September. *Summertime... You Go To My Head... Tenderly... Lover Man...* the usual covers known everywhere. *There's a Small Hotel*—fluid swing version with CB's trumpet uncharacteristically more out front.

He's followed by some Gerard Gustin splatter image piano which descends into a nice comp for the bass solo... Chet resumes with the melody, without improv, closes it. Best number is *I'll Remember April*, which has bomb-flash solos from Baker and Gustin, almost "free jazz" in their directionless direction. Yet, this is a conservative album. For medics seeking clues of Baker's disintegration, this isn't it.

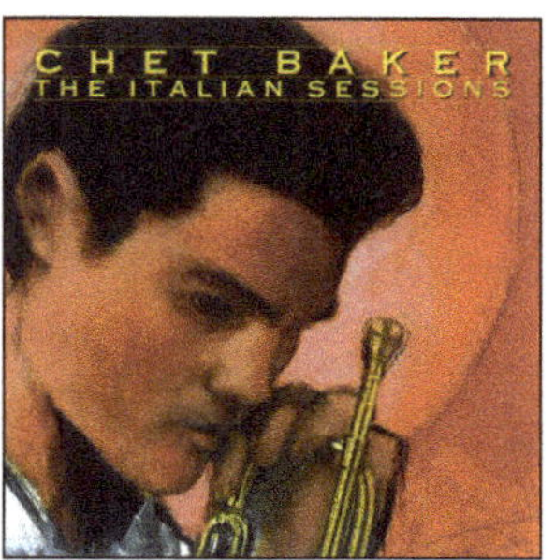

Il Silenzio

Late summer 1962. Dusk. The Penitenzianio San Giorgio (St. George Penitentiary), Lucca, Italy. The American Hipster is playing his horn, the melancholy sound falling like dust through the surrounding streets and courtyards, a requiem for a lost soul. He's serving a 19 month sentence for smuggling the synthetic drug Jetrium, a heroin substitute. He spends his time in the ancient prison playing chess in the book bindery, waiting for conjugal visits from his mistress who is living in Room 15 of the nearby Hotel Universo. His fans gather in the street, disciples of the 32 year old jazz god "Chettino", now an adopted "Lucchese" even if he was described as a viper during the trial.

Some gather on the walls that run adjacent to the prison, perhaps to hear better or even catch a glimpse of angel-face. He'd been busted in a gas-station washroom near Lucca, the needle still embedded, a pool of blood where he knelt, red like his Ferrari, its engine running where he left it.

His incarceration has become a cult, and his concerts seem like the cries of a ghost longing for rebirth, despite the fact that he is often heard playing the pop hit *Cherry Pink and Apple*

Blossom White at the behest of his fellow prisoners. He haunts, is haunted, the wandering Americano jazzman who played with Romano Mussolini, the old dictator's son, before this heartless injustice.

Does he resent Italy? No. Does he want to go back to America? No. He hates America.

While the Italian fans lamented Chettino's confinement and "Il Silenzio", he did draw perhaps on the experience when he recorded *Silence* with the bassist Charlie Haden in Rome, 1987. The Haden composition is a melancholy slow-step funeral march, based on the traditional military measure for fallen comrades. The jazz battlefield was littered with fallen Icari and of course the recording became an eerie forecast of Chet Baker's own death six months later.

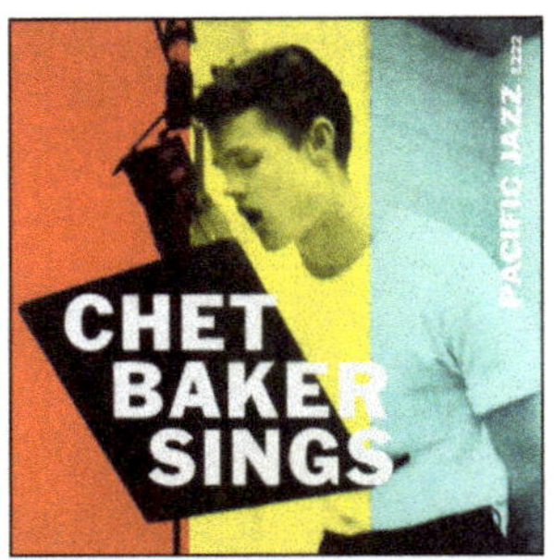

Jesus Satan

Can Chet Baker sing... could he ever sing? In the fifties, when he started, the critics were brutally hostile, offended by his effeminate impersonation. Impersonation? In his own words—when recalling his successful con of the army psychiatrist at the Presidio in 1952—he said, "I always gave the most effeminate answer." *My Funny Valentine... I Fall In Love Too Easily...* in the macho 1950s these torch standards were o.k. for chicks, not for men. Men sensed deceit, lies and manipulation... women and gays, loneliness and love.

Singing is like poetry—everyone can speak, but when is it poetry? Lots of people felt he was hopeless, always out-of-tune, drifting between clichés and lucky rhymes. Driving between gigs in the old days he'd sing in the car and jazz chicks would laugh at him. Yet at after-hours jazz parties in the Hollywood hills, he knocked them out. And if he couldn't sing, you have to consider that he couldn't play trumpet either as his singing was/ is very similar to his trumpet sound. The phrasing, the pursuit of the melodic thread, the dropped-below-centre line driving.

The complaints about his playing—and there were many, some of it legitimate racial envy—especially the perceived lack of dynamics and register range, seem to miss the fact that he plays into the group sound rather than over it. He says, "Most people are impressed with just three things: fast, high, loud... probably less than 2% of the public can really hear." (*Memoir*, 29)

The Thrill Is Gone (I can see it in your eyes/ love was grand when love was new). Poignant to the point of dreary, the lyric staggers between raw truth and love song cliché. Baker's vocal has the chanson quality, like a low-flying aircraft skimming between poetry and conversation. This dangerous aspect—where his voice threatens to break, go sideways flat or shrill, is perhaps the reason for his appeal.

So his vocal phrasing is his trumpet phrasing. The melody seeks the hidden resolution that he believes all songs and all melodies—whether written or improvised—contain. There is no such a thing as disunity. Balance is everything. Baker plays between truth and deceit like a falling knife. He's a perfect Jesus Satan whose musical introspection masks his amoral hustle and beautiful melodic loneliness.

But drugs, drugs... illegal and prescription, were dragging him down. The incredible grind of the road, the feral wandering through the oily pits of America and Europe, the constant projection into the callous souls of strangers. Who could do it? Who could do it without drugs... and even with drugs, who could do it forever....

The sad state of his degradation is all too evident in his 1964 Belgian TV set. The performance is dull, the leaden black and white broadcast showing a group of middle-aged men trying to keep the faith when the congregation was channeling elsewhere and these players knew it. Shabby to look at, boring to listen to, although the protocol holds a certain interest.

The French pianist Rene Urtreger—CB's go-to guy after the death of Dick Zwardzik—has a beer parked as the 89th key, and an ashtray with a smoldering cigarette on the rim of the sounding board. After a lurching intro solo, Baker sidles around to Urtreger's left, finds the pianist's box of fags, takes one, lights up, resumes his position centre stage, plays the rest of the set with the cigarette locked between his fingers and the valves as if he's up for a trick routine on Ed Sullivan. The players are clearly professionals, yet here they lumber through the old bromides like bums singing outside the soup kitchen.

Here and there you read what a great gig this was, but is this just the faithful grasping at rediscovered broadcast relics? The sax player/flautist Jacques Pelzer had a day job as a pharmacist, often accompanied American jazzers in Europe, was one of Baker's best Euro friends, and the only one not wearing a folk circuit sweater. Who's cool now, who's hip?

Fusion Or Confusion

It's reasonable to wonder if Chet Baker ever got into fusion jazz like Miles Davis and many of the young jazzers who grew up on early rock n roll. The answer is, not really. At times he backed into it, as this was the style his pick-up players knew. When pressed, he always said he didn't like country music and he didn't like rock, but he liked just about everything else.

The bootleg palette does reveal the occasional fusion gem, such as the live version of *Lovely Black Eyes*, recorded in Paris, 1980, at the Le Dreher Club. Some smooth *bossa nova* here, with Riccardo del Fra on bass, Nicolo Stilo on flute, and the Austrian jazz funk guitarist Karl Ratzer chopping a very nice 2-4 samba. No singing, all instrumental, with sunshine solos stretching this baby out to 20+ minutes. Mostly in fourths with a bridge and a turn-around. It sounds very similar to the Mike Sharpe (Shapiro) 1966 sax instrumental *Spooky*, which was later modified with words into a hit version by the Classics IV. The Classics IV became the Atlanta Rhythm Section in the seventies, issued a live version of *Spooky* that was very influential. Karl Ratzer lived in Atlanta at this time (playing with Chaka Khan), so no doubt he absorbed the *Spooky* groove.

Another interesting example is the instrumental *Five Years Ago* from a 1979 Norway Chet Baker Quartet performance. Written by Wolfgang Lacherschmid, a vibraphonist who played frequently with CB in his last years, the instrumental has a New Age trance feel far removed from the show tune casings of old school jazz. Lacherschmid uses a bow on the vibe plates to increase the ethereal sustain, and CB plays into the dream tremolo with a running lyricism that steps outside the cliché.

Throughout the years *Love For Sale* was part of his set list. This bluesy 1930 Cole Porter composition was made for fusion, and you can find many Chet Baker versions out there. The 1979 Monmartre Jazzhouse CB Trio version is also worth a listen. Here Baker follows Doug Raney's guitar solo by dropping into Miles Davis' *So What* for a few bars, gets funky with it, then drops back to the Delta. A highly dressed version can be found on the 1977 album *You Can't Go Home Again*, where he teams uneasily with Michael Brecker on tenor and some Miles Davis fusion alumni (John Scofield, Ron Carter, Tony Williams). Over-produced. Chet Baker just wasn't at ease with this sort of punch meter.

Could He Dance? Probably Not.

Ronnie Scott's 1986: Chet's trumpet has a husky morning-throat timbre, a little coarsening of the white bird's morning cry. Some, craving purity and death, might think he sounds off-the-mark, but really, he's just in his lizard persona. His timing is immaculate, his tone dangerous. In the first Costello interview clip, he's smiling, yet nervous, scratching himself with the junkie itch, his disarticulating hands crossing as they scratch one side, then the other. It's a strange gig—no drummer, which leaves lots of space between the bass and the piano. It's almost like a rehearsal without an audience. Even though CB sits on the stage apron, the performance is completely inward, as if space has been subtracted from time... he could be anywhere, as the song is its own space, and the material world is irrelevant. Perhaps, if you live on stage long enough, the only performance is when you leave it. Perhaps the junkie routine is his real performance, his real existence, the procuring and the fixing, the transmigration.

The rehearsal quality is sustained with both Elvis Costello's and Van Morrison's guest spots, as both use lyric sheets, the words written on pieces of paper, so they appear as poets reading hastily composed tomes in a bohemian cellar. Morrison sings *Send In The Clowns* raw like a busker at the entrance to the underworld, and Costello—another singer of ambiguous ability—talks his way through the old CB standard *I'm A Fool To Want You.* He gets away with it, although high altitude is not his thing. It's a *chanson*—which is in some ways the core of the Baker songbook—or an aria from an unknown yet familiar tragic opera. The poetry is modern, the lament ancient. Some might say, why didn't Chet sing it? And Chet might say, I have sung it, more times than I can remember.

The sound is near-field, close, as if you're a midget standing beside the lip of a giant horn. Piano is distant, bass less so. The gig is "featuring Chet" of course, and there's a bit of sound dialling going on at the beginning as the engineer tries to find the paradise level. Chet laments the decline of the jazz scene in the US: "The level of culture there is pitifully low." As you listen to him, you wonder, is jazz just another disposable American pop culture product, gone with the inter-war era, or does it indeed have classical possibilities as the Europeans seem to think?

Europe was late to rock n roll, as if the American occupation held it prisoner to the G.I. blues. Thinking about it, you see Chet Baker as a hangover from the *Red Ball Express*, a war groom left behind to colonize the survivors and the next generation. He started in '47 playing in the honour guard at Berlin's Templehof airport "where it was so cold... it would freeze your lips to the metal... the valves would freeze too" and then returned to the west coast for basic training in the post-bebop art of cool. So his return in the sixties as a cold war agent of American cool is just an unofficial part of the imperial plan; if Dave Brubeck could be sent abroad by the State Department to spread the good will, so could Baker. Brubeck was a marshal, Baker was an outlaw.

The boys do get funky here, especially on *Love For Sale*... the bass, the piano, but especially Riccardo del Fra on stand-up. Chet drops in below like a running stream, bumps and babbles, a poly-harmony that fits the group sound rather than challenges it. The three-piece setup allows lots of "strolling" free from orchestral clutter and bebop noise. It's SoCal cool reinvented as Euro cool. All in all, this is a very good performance documentary, coming two years before Chet's death. It's differs from the other concert documentaries out there because it's in-close and personal. The opening close-up shows CB's aging wizard face, eyes closed as he enters the trance, waits for the melody he will inhabit... perhaps die in.

And you're thinking, how far can a man go out without being obliterated?

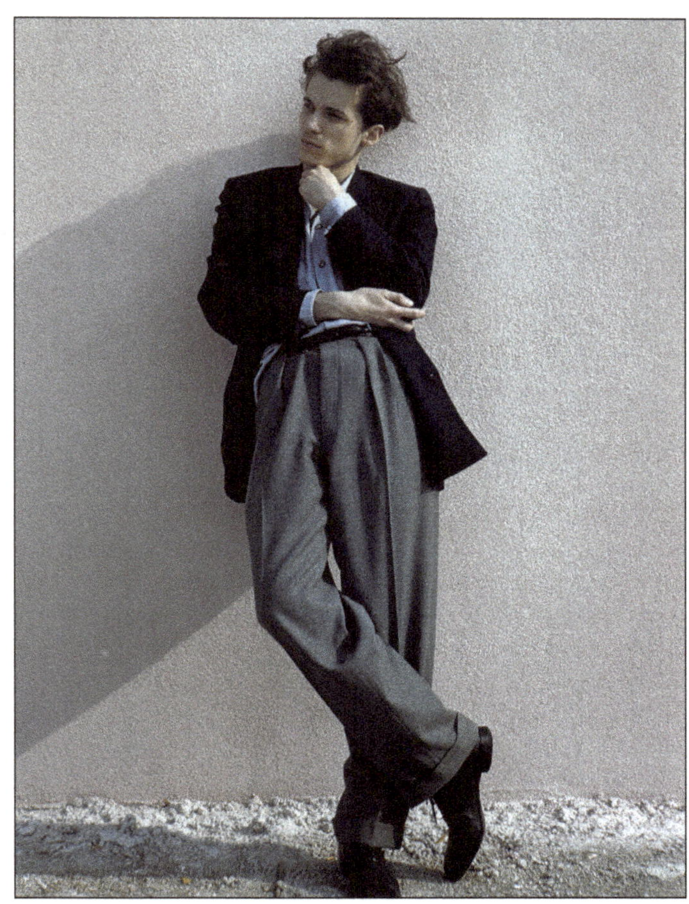

Glenn Gould

Visually, Glenn Gould was very interesting, as his Byronic pose fitted his artistic anachronism perfectly. The long overcoat, the gloves, the scarf, the cap, the dog, the lordly coach (Lincoln Continental, Chrysler 300, Chevy Impala), the lingering illness and the sense of exile no matter where he was—these things contributed to his image as the romantic desperado. He was a reincarnation of the nineteenth century artist, a neoclassical hipster seeking the perfect groove in the modern world, famous, idealized, doomed to loneliness and an early death. Fame came quickly, as he was in the right place at the right time. His first US concert was in Washington D.C. in 1955, the true centre of world power at that time. Within a few days he was offered a recording contract by Columbia Records in New York; he recorded Bach's *Goldberg Variations*, then—like Lord Byron—went to bed and woke up famous. He was 22 and had recorded the biggest selling classical album of the time. While it didn't go "gold" he did achieve that status in 1977 when his Bach recording was included on the gold disc launched into space with the Voyager satellite.

His playing was secular, because he personalized the scores of the masters to suit his own taste and emotional need rather than play to the communal, religious design. Hence he was considered a heretic by old school musicologists. But he was just part of the modern instinct, deconstructing the classics as would a painter—for, having copied the Masters, he must seek a new narrative landscape. Not as radical and obvious as Picasso, say, but towards the end of his short life he was moving in that direction by abandoning the concert hall recital in favor of the recording studio montage.

Even watching him today on some film clip, GG's technique is so good, it's heartless. He squats at the keyboard like an overgrown child playing with a toy, talks to it, babbles, sings, exhales the alien entity that controls him. The love whispers, the threats, all this emotive exposition as the alien leads him through the capricious corridors of godhood, the power and the glory. Has he ever turned on the instrument, attacked it, smashed it in an act of sadism or tragic therapy? If only. The piano was never his victim, rather he was a victim of the piano. Yet his genius is all technical, a worker within the mind of another. He talks about the architecture of music like a stone mason on the edge of a mystical revelation.

He dies at 50, too young to succeed, too old to fail.

A Duet With Yourself

The three DVD documentary set *Glenn Gould Plays Bach (1979-1981)* by Bruno Monsaingeon shows the pianist's physical decline in accelerated detail. Three years pass between the first and the third, yet the metamorphosis looks like thirty. The sessions are close, intimate, with Gould at the piano, and Monsaingeon nearby, leaning on the frame, or sitting *tete-a-tete*, the cultured interlocutor coaxing the mysteries of Bach from the more-than-cultured artist. In 1979, GG is still as handsome as Hollywood, his skin youthful, his hair full and sleek, his sensitive playing killing with its deadly accuracy.

In the next session his hair is thinner, less obedient, his skin moist as old stone... and in the third he looks old. Could be the movie lights or the crazy bifocals, of course, but with hindsight you know it isn't.

One year later, he is gone. As usual, the romantic poet arrives late, leaves early.

The Art Of Fugue

Evening, November 1979. The art deco auditorium on the 7th floor of the old Eaton's Department Store, College Street, Toronto, where Glenn Gould plays piano and records. As usual, GG's left hand conducts his entrance to the tomb, finds the tempo like a medium catching the vibe... his body draws in and out from the keyboard like a rower pulling across an invisible surface. This physical expression—an integrated one—seems like an illness at times, a leaching of the soul. Every time he plays, he pays a price, surrenders part of his being to the dead.

Imagine it as an archaeological dig, and Johann Sebastian Bach as a mummy with a heavy mojo.

It's been more than 200 years and Bach's need is powerful. He placed "the stranger maiden" in his choir (no women allowed), then married a cousin with whom he had seven children, and when she died, he married another woman with whom he had thirteen children. You could reason that "the art of the fugue" was the only thing he understood. He went blind, then died. Years later when the composer Schumann went looking for his grave, he was told "there are many Bachs". In 1894 a skeleton was found that was supposed to be J.S. Bach; it was taken to a museum, dressed up as the famous composer, put on display. This pagan travesty was an odd fate for the musician Glenn Gould calls "the greatest craftsman of his time"... but of course there were no photographers in 1750 when Bach died in Leipzig.

GG pursues his archaeological exhumation with impressive clairvoyance, as he rolls through Bach as easily as if he'd written the works himself. *Prelude in D major... Sonata in C minor...* the *Italian Concerto... The Well-Tempered Clavier...* etcetera. In his conversation with Bruno Monsaingeon, he doesn't really get into the pros and cons of harpsichord tuning or the mechanical problems of tuning at the time (circa 1700), but rather sees Bach as an intellectual and artistic advance, especially how he could create architectures in all the keys. There's a magic mirror here, and Glenn Gould is staring into it in selfless admiration. He sees himself as Bach—perhaps we do too—yet he realizes he's just a messenger, has been given "a tonal visa to pass through E sharp minor" into the future.

The music doesn't fill Time—it subtracts it. No wonder GG withdrew from concert performances. No wonder he died early. His face is flushed, fevered, and sweaty—no wonder Bruno Monsaingeon ends the biopic on a freeze-frame of the artist leaning close to the keys like a supplicant.

The Glenn Gould Bach heresy is overstated (he dared to play Bach on a modern piano). It's like saying Hitler's radio broadcasts should only be heard on a 1933 Volksemfaenger VE 301 or *Sparky's Magic Piano* on a 78. Bach is often referred to as the father of the modern piano, as he introduced the thumb and the little finger into the hand action. And before Bach, harpsichord players would find only two keys in tune, the rest out, so this "howling wolf" situation formed a default orthodoxy; Bach picked up the "well-tempered" circle of fifths tuning from an organist predecessor called Werckmeister, and, ripping-off the Italians, was able to compose *The Well-Tempered Clavier* and *The Goldberg Variations*. No more wolf fifths, no more two key lockdown.

The *Goldberg Variations* Redux

Evening, New York 1981. GG is rerecording *The Goldberg Variations*, this time for a Bruno Monsaingeon French TV documentary. His head rolls counter-clockwise as he stretches for the keyboard, back bowed like a hanging ape in brutal apposition to the beauty of the music.

Commissioned by Count Kaiserling—the Russian ambassador to the Saxony court—as a placebo for his insomnia, the *Variations* have become known as *The Goldberg Variations* as Goldberg was the name of Kaiserling's harpsichordist, and who had to stay awake to play them when needed. As GG says, the composition is thirty remarkable views of an unremarkable theme. In the context of today, this could be an algorithm for a synthesizer patch. Why has GG chosen to rerecord this Bach composition? The advance in recording technology. Stereo field, Dolby noise reduction and all the rest. "I thought I might find a harmonic thread," he said.

What he doesn't say is that the tape can be edited.

As lecture-recitals go, this is pretty good, and the playing is more than good. He grasps all of the polyphony, all of the voices. The music? Baroque to be sure, full of curls and shivers (trills and appoggiaturas), and that prancing meter that sent legions of brutes into war and women into pregnancy. Amazing. The groove is so far removed from the modern and post-modern vibe as to be ridiculous. It's life as a free-hand sketch, a doodling by candlelight as rodents run freely in the shadows and bats seek blood from the sleeping patient. Insomnia? Dream fever beauty? Sound wave narcosis? As music, it climbs all over itself in a tangle of crossing lines and hallucinatory hands. The diary of a madman, Bach, mad with religion and sex, and Gould, with neither score nor humility, channels it perfectly.

Baroque art is a pre-electric world where the sleeping and waking minds are drawn together in an easy occult mix of the natural and the supernatural. Lords and ladies cavort with demons as easily as with one another. The mathematics of superstition is the dance notation of the Minuet. Hop, hop, one two three four. You are reminded of jack rabbits gathering in the early sun. The groove might come from horse riding or a natural need to elevate in order to see above the crowd or simply telegraph the sexual impulse. The formality is a disguise for something, yet as music, the disguise is perfect. It's a windup, like a clock or a bucket from the well. If only life was as well-tempered.

In his eloquent introduction, Bruno Monsaingeon says that GG was trying "to reclaim the unity (composer-player-listener) shattered by the artistic concepts of the Romantic Age" and that his withdrawal from public performance was an attempt to "harness the undissipated intellectual power that only solitude can give". This is interesting, because the classicists were desperate to find a star who could stand between them and popular culture, revitalize the concert hall, bring it back from nostalgia and high-culture fatigue. Before Hitler (or Stalin), the songbook was always for the aristocracy; then, by his command, mass hypnosis for the industrial public. Glenn made nice records, and records were like books. Books are solitude in code. And then, solitude is just solitude, the solipsism that surrounds us all.

> "On the other hand, contrary to what has been written here and there, our dialogues were not scripted. They were improvised and completely spontaneous, all the while following a carefully thought-out dramatic sequence. Every take was to have a different verbal content. We would leave it up to the editing process to reconcile improvisation and preconception." [Bruno Monsaingeon]

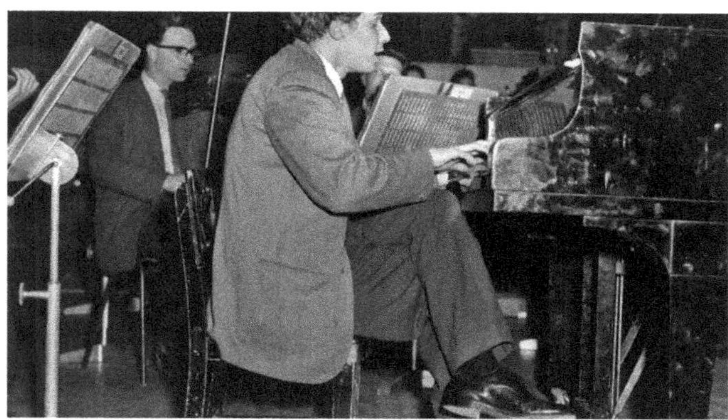

Madness In The Conditional

Much has been made of Glenn Gould's hypochondria, and given his swift decline, you have to wonder if his fear wasn't justified. His posture at the piano was simply preposterous. Anyone who plays an instrument knows what a toll it takes on the shoulders, the neck, the arms, the hands, the fingers —never mind the back, the hips, the legs all the way to the feet. The concentration, the tension required for balance and hand locomotion... these things wreck the muscles, damage the nerves. When he put himself in a body cast, he wasn't kidding. Peter Oswald, a San Francisco doctor and musician, who knew and treated GG for many years has a paper entitled *Glenn Gould As Patient* which sympathetically lays out the facts in professional detail. From the start, he was lazy about personal hygiene, as careless as a strung-out rock n roller like Keith Richards. "One of his worst habits, in my opinion, was of not informing his doctors about who else was treating him and prescribing medication, thus causing confusion and probably over-medication. He had little respect for the side-effects of drugs."

Gould lurched from crisis to crisis like a junkie trying to score in a strange town. His physical pain and social anxiety drove him deeper into prescription drugs in a game pattern not dissimilar to that of a heroin addict. He hid in his penthouse like Howard Hughes, feared pushy fans, refused to answer the door. Says Peter Oswald: "Glenn called me to say that disturbing things were happening in his apartment. Some neighbors were spying on him from the roof, shining lights into his windows, making strange noises, and sending him coded messages." Paranoia? He used TV as means of falling asleep, so no doubt he remained in the *Twilight Zone* even when he awakened. His condition was a celeb condition, especially when the celeb was an introvert. He had *bona fide* reasons for selective paranoia, yet the paranoia came to include nearly everything. Isolation had a lot to do with it, a bit like the goal-keeper's fear of the penalty shot. The audience? The parasites in the darkness sucking the splendour out of his music? The fear of failure drove him to say, ""I detest the audience... *en masse*... they're evil." The self-loathing here has a post-coital sense about it, the brief trauma that follows orgasm, as if every spasm subtracts from life, robs the future. Some artists know it as manic depression.

Neuropraxia... a facial tic... jawline asymmetry... fear of germs, fear of sunlight, fear of the cold, fear of people, fear of anywhere but Toronto... long midnight telephone calls to people he's never met except by mail or wire... the death of his mother, his first piano teacher (she was a Grieg, same family as Edvard Grieg, the Norwegian composer)... his valium intake out of control... the safety of a childhood forever receding, he becomes a monologist in search of a listener.

What sort of person does this? Alcoholics make midnight calls, junkies, burglars and bad girls, and somehow Glenn Gould slid into this desperado culture of off-road loneliness. He came to look the part, got stripped by the border guards, too many pills, man. While you couldn't exactly call him the Midnight Rambler, he was weird. He started out eccentric, ended up mad. The madness was conditional, but as his brain collapsed, it might have been clinical. "Electroencephalographic studies showed massive destruction of the right brain hemisphere, and other tests revealed death of the medulla oblongata, the brain's central controlling mechanism of bodily functions," is how Peter Oswald, MD, describes it. It was a stroke, the final chord of his strange, orchestral decline. Autism? Asperger Syndrome?

The doctors continue to debate.

First Of The Bourgeois Infiltrators

Yet before all this, before the fear and loathing, he had all the glamour that comes with youth and divine talent. He was born with perfect pitch and the monomania to exploit it. Flash fame in the US, flash fame in the Soviet Union. When he was in Moscow blowing them away with Bach and Beethoven... with the second Viennese School (Schoenberg, Webern, Berg), he met Sviatoslav Richter, the German-Ukrainian pianist who'd recently played at Stalin's funeral. What a contrast in playing styles and temperament—about the only thing they had in common was a fear of flying and an *ad hoc* education. Yes, both attended the conservatory, but Richter was a pounder, a player for large venues and large audiences, frozen churches and frozen squares. His style was preelectronic, declamatory and theatrical, whereas Gould was in love with the microphone, even before he saw its face. His touch, while *staccatissimo,* was light and personal, free of propaganda and false religion. As commentators have noted, the Russians responded to Gould's playing as if it was sunshine breaking through the gray overcast of state socialism. Because of the external repression, the average Russian could only turn inwards for freedom, so the phantasmic beauty of Gould's aural loneliness had great appeal. In 1957 there was no rock n roll in the Soviet Union but the coming of Glenn Gould was the nearest thing to it.

You could say he was a jazzman within a classical context. He liked to improvise... "in the manner of". He could drop into the style of any composer, any player—even George Gershwin. He went off-script eventually, yet the need for control eventually had him scripting interviews, seeking perfection through acting. He was a frontman, a bandleader without a band. He clashed with Leonard Bernstein, and in frustration quit the scene. Who is the boss? When you remember that Diaghilev challenged Ravel to a duel, things could've gone bad fast. It wasn't just Bernstein, of course, but the whole rigid musicological nightmare of evocation and necrophilia. The fundamentalism of the maestros was killing. So he went off-road, allowed the forest to swallow him.

Anxious Schoenberg Atonal Blues

Gould was completely smitten by the work of Arnold Schoenberg (1874-1951) (GG's first CBC radio documentary in 1962 was *Arnold Schoenberg: The Man Who Changed Music*). Schoenberg is associated with German expressionism, was a painter as well as a composer, could be considered a numbers mystic. His mature method is chromatic 12 tone serialism, which allows dissonance or "atonality" i.e. spirit world or blue note cries. He fled to the US in 1933 to escape the Nazi purge of art decadents and Jews, settled in Los Angeles where he composed and taught until 1951, when he died, aged 76. He anticipated his death as the number 7 + 6 equals thirteen, which he believed to be fatal ("triskaidekaphobia" or fear of the number 13).

Schoenberg didn't convince everyone with his aesthetic. The American jazz pianist Dave Brubeck clashed with him on the second day of class. Why did Brubeck use that note? "He wanted a reason for every note," said Brubeck. "I said, 'Because it sounds good, and he said 'That is not an adequate reason,' and we got into a huge argument in which he was screaming at me." Exit Dave, stage right.

Enter Glenn Gould... in his speed boat called *Arnold S* in homage to the great innovator. GG was introduced to Schoenberg's music by Alberto Guerrero, who taught the young Gould piano at the Toronto Conservatory. He included work by Schoenberg on one of his recitals in Russia, despite the disapproval of the Soviet authorities. Yet they never met, and by the time Gould ever played in Los Angeles, Schoenberg was dead [there's an oblique irony in the fact that Glenn Gould's last public concert was in 1964 at the Wilshire Ebell Theatre L.A. where Dave Brubeck recorded one of his famous live gigs (Live at the Wilshire Ebell, 1953).]

Trance, Sex, And Dimension

He appeared asexual in a vaguely protestant way, his seclusion masking his need for love. He wasn't a womanizer, even though one or two women have confessed. He stole another musician's wife and children, although perhaps the musician's wife stole him. It was a selfish interlude, stupid in that 60's way that excused folly if you called it love, pain if you called it art. In the excellent Hozer/Raymont 2009 DVD documentary, *Genius Within: the Inner Life of Glenn Gould*, Cornelia Foss inserts herself into the frame easily, then painlessly removes herself by saying "Glenn became someone else" i.e. a paranoid control freak strung-out on anti-depressants. Listening to her (and her son and daughter) there's a benevolent sense of nostalgia, that it was no bad thing, as if fame and history made it all right—like being the mistress of the King or some other essential sacrifice. Orpheus was needy, what the hell. Without the kids, of course, it would've been just another day at the beach. The romance with Roxy, the singer who liked the *Mary Hartman Show*, is just plain normal by comparison.

Classical music is trapped within history, within its religious exhortation, and always will be. Its function is communal and orchestral, and its acoustic instrumentation fits the baroque societies of the past. How can you be modern within this narrative? While this might not be the sole reason why GG failed to move persuasively into composition, it certainly had something to do with his move into media art. "Writing"—whether it's music notation or script—is less relevant when working with recorded sound. The plan, the script, the score, becomes a schematic at best, and the rest is in the mind of the creative artist. Extemporization/improvisation becomes the narrative, and linear exposition less important. GG's "scripts" were geometric sketches, describing stereo-fields and sound transits rather than plotted narratives. He was a prisoner of the piano, yet knew instinctively that the architecture of sound is bigger than any instrument.

Improvisation wasn't new, and it didn't even start with jazz. It was the root of Beethoven's compositional method. When he was in Vienna in the early 1800s, Beethoven lived in "the final years of public improvisation" (extempore playing). By 1817 when he was almost completely deaf (some blame lead poisoning, others, Napoleon's bombardment of Vienna) he battered his new Broadwood (London) insensible... and the Broadwood was the loudest, most powerful piano of its time. Is the piano the devil's instrument, a death machine that requires a fatal compact? Beethoven's withdrawal from public performance, his decline and death is similar to Glenn Gould's... ill-health and madness, fame and deification. Sometimes Beethoven is viewed as the greatest artist civilization has ever produced, and while a case can be made based on his piano sonatas and concerti, it would be difficult to extend this superlative to Gould. Essentially he was a performer—not a composer—and his fame was/is a modern media event, a fractal shiver in the electronic nervous system that determines culture globally. Like Elvis, he lived in someone else's song. Like Elvis, he became a cult. Every ten years there's a parade to commemorate "Saint Glenn" in Toronto. Children and teenagers march bearing icons of GG, others dress like Daleks wearing cones and packing shields in a mobile geometry of mass surrender like the robot dancers in a communist party tattoo. Yes, they're in it for the free donuts and pop, nothing to get alarmed about. It's perfectly normal, a simple celebration for a favorite native son. 1992, 2002, 2012... in 2013, Glenn Gould posthumously received a Lifetime Achievement honor from the US Recording Academy at the 2013 Grammy Awards. Thirty-one years after his death, he's still sexy.

> "As the performer's once sacrosanct privileges are merged with the responsibilities of the tape editor and the composer, the Van Meegeren syndrome can no longer be cited as an indictment but becomes rather an entirely appropriate description of the aesthetic condition in our time. The role of the forger, of the unknown maker of unauthenticated goods, is emblematic of electronic culture. And when the forger is done honor for his craft and no longer reviled for his acquisitiveness, the arts will have become a truly integral part of our civilization." [Glenn Gould, *The Prospects of Recording,* 1965]

> "the world of sound is essentially a unified field of instant relationships" (Marshall McLuhan)

In the mid sixties GG lived not far from the soon-to-be-famous media analyst Marshall McLuhan, the University of Toronto professor. Gould visited McLuhan often for long discussions in the philosopher's study, so you can assume there was nothing naive about Gould's move into media art. The recording studio as a means to performance perfection was already underway in the jazz industry, where tapes were being cut and spliced into new

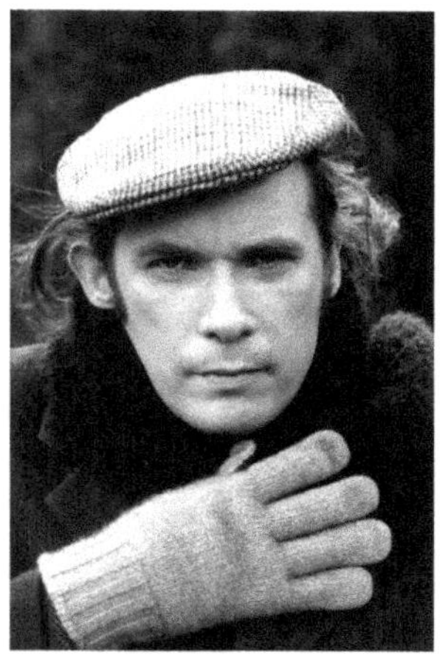

realities before being pressed to disc. Sometimes bungled parts were cut; sometimes better parts from several takes were assembled into a new take. With serial montage, the artist was no longer a victim of Time, but a co-conspirator.

Montage can be used to dramatize (or fictionalize, if desired) a narrative; it can also jazz it, or musicalize it, if metric montage is used. Eisenstein's famous treatise on montage in film editing examines the possibilities in terms of poetic configuration, the creation of a new image language by symbolism, Time-compression and psychology.

GG's first "sound-text" piece was a one hour documentary broadcast in late 1967 as part of the CBC *Ideas* series. It differs from orthodox radio documentaries in that it uses audio montage and contrapuntal voicings to develop the narrative, which is vaguely linear in the sense that an essay—rather than a drama—is yet the approach is soft drama. The interviewees or characters are not in conflict (except occasionally with themselves) but function as an ambient chorus of emerging and submerging voices. It starts with a female (a nurse) reading her poetic impressions of the northland as she flies over the lakes and forests; her voice is soon overridden by a discounting male with a less glamorous impression... then another male joins in like radio station drift, creating a babble which then submerges behind the female voice, which once again becomes the foreground. GG then appears as narrator, talking about "the North" and what it means to him, and then introduces the "characters" in the usual radio program set-up. Thereafter the action is basically on "the *Muskeg Express*"—the train that runs from Winnipeg to Churchill, Manitoba (on Hudson's Bay about 57 degrees north). The rail chatter is faint, the train horn less so. The monologues are intellectual, informed, abstract and moralistic, and listening to them 50 years later, you can discern the thinking that led to white guilt and political correctness. It's the chattering classes, the bourgeois, talking about the false romanticism of the Eskimo, "the articulate protest of alcoholism", aboriginal "stooges" and the aggravating "noise of civilization". Today, some will like it, some will yawn.

Basically, *The Idea of the North* is about solitude... what solitude does, and how to deal with it. Art for the artists? Might be. Obviously GG felt an affinity for the subject, growing up in Ontario, often in the summer solitude of Lake Simcoe where the wilderness extended northwards as a wall of sleeping mystery—forests, lakes, rocks, on and on into the frozen dead zone of the sub-arctic. As the sound of the wilderness on such a large scale is silence, it could be a subject for sound but not sound itself. The listener does have a choice: music or talk, or talk with music. GG uses his fugue music knowledge to construct a narrative that is as concerned about how it sounds as much as by what it says. Although technically not a tape loop, the fugue-ing voices act as transitions or dream passages from one monologue to the next. The babble fits nicely with the sound of the train, and over the course of the journey, you wish there was more of it. *Avant-garde* for CBC radio in 1967, but less so for other jurisdictions such as German radio which had a strong tradition of electronic music and concomitant editing techniques, and certain university music departments hip to *musique concrete*, tape loops, and ambient recording.

His move from the piano to the recording studio is that of producer (rather than auteur) as he used a technician to cut and splice the tape, move the dials, do the mix—a union issue, perhaps, although he was the "big ear" and the concept was all his. It was like the movies or playing with an orchestra: collaborate or stay home. Had he lived longer, he would have seen recording technology move from the corporate studio (with its division of labour) into the accessible domain of the individual. Certainly he had the dough to buy, say, a professional Ampex 2000 portable reeler or a Studer J37 and get into it himself... but he also had the fame that opened the CBC recording studios in Toronto when other artists could only dream.

The Latecomers (1969) is an aesthetically more successful "contrapuntal" documentary. A montage of voices talking about Newfoundland against the recordist art favorite, the restless sibilant hiss of big surf in stereo sweeps left and right. "This thing that has happened to us... robbed us of our solitude... the rush of civilization," begins the first male voice, setting up the familiar GG theme of lost romanticism, nostalgia for the wilderness and the beauty of nature. Laments, lap-dissolves, vocal fugues, clarity and abstraction... it's all coming at you like voices from the spirit world. It certainly works well as history, and as a social gestalt. It also has an authentic sonority, is more the way we actually hear life, which is not order or disorder, but rather a shifting mix of sounds. The mind focuses, the mind unfocuses, the relevant and the irrelevant blend and separate. As a narrative, perhaps its only weakness is Time—the action is conversation rather than drama, although the soundscape does dramatize. Without the conflict of real drama, exposition is always a failing narrative over time.

His 24 minute aural essay on Petula Clark (*In Search of Petula Clark*)—which really starts at 4:20 into his monologue—is not going to win him any fans outside of an alienated few in the music conservatories. He starts with a long discourse about life along Hwy 17 between Toronto and the "timber town" of Marathon on Lake Superior. Driving this route is where he probably listens to Petula Clark on the car radio, although you'd never know it by the way he falls smugly into the quotidian, kills his subject with deadening details about small towns, reservations, pulp mill smells and the "1984 prefab" mentality everywhere to be seen. No doubt meant to be pithy humour, yet it just comes across as tight-assed and patronizing.

And this attitude only gets worse when he gets to Petula Clark and the pop music scene. Petula is "pop music's most persuasive embodiment of the Gidget syndrome" which is no more or less than adolescent rebellion and conformity in its relentless diatonic expression. Yes, the man can be funny, but not hip and funny. He's a rebel in the conservatory or the concert hall or behind the wheel of his Lincoln, but otherwise he's as conservative as a school district superintendent. Armed with all the musicologist's architectural terms, the classical nazi holds forth on the "harmonic primitivism of the Beatles", "false tonic releases" and other sex crimes on or against classicism. "*Strawberry Fields* suggests a chance encounter between Claudio Monteverdi and a Jug band"—yes, that's a good knock—even an accurate one—yet it gets lost in the pontificating (you wonder if, in fact, it was the Beatles who finished him off as a recitalist). Well, the verbosity is a mask, isn't it? Everyone says he was obsessed with Petula Clark, wanted to collaborate with her. Perhaps he fancied himself as a Burt Bacharach doing a Dionne Warwick gig, knock old Tony Hatch off the Petula lectern. These catchy road songs—*Downtown, Do You Know the Way to San Jos*—and other pop radio hits would be a piece of cake for a savant such as him. Parody... could it be? You just don't know.

Requiem For An Alchemist

He rents a country estate, then walks away from the deal. He halts a concert in San Francisco because of a draft from an open door. He puts himself in a plaster cast to get real. He accuses a Steinway technician of assault and Steinway of crippling him with the heavy action of their keyboard, launches a lawsuit. He wears biker gloves, poses for fashion photos, makes home movies, plays on the beach, admires divas from near and far, monologues, monologues, his charming babble following him like locomotive smoke. He was real gone, as Elvis used to say. He was a classical rebel searching for a modern coma. He had the instinct of a hipster without knowing what hip was.

You don't have to be a witch-doctor to recognize that he wrecked his posture by using a kid's chair to sit at the keyboard. He did this, apparently, in order to expedite Alberto Guerrero's "pull-down" method for striking the keys. He squats or he clings like a child losing a grip on his mother. His performance is always a Freudian study of Oedipal isolation and the occult, as if the scales he follows are the pathways back to the origin of everything. He has an act—entirely natural and spontaneous—that is both infantile and intellectual, ecstatic and degrading. His loathing of the audience is the confused self-loathing of desire and expression, of being mad in public and being celebrated for it.

His obsessive drive for perfection suggests a fear of failure, as does his early retirement from concert performance. Fear of flying, fear of germs, fear of the public, fear of the wrong note—any one of these phobias by itself isn't irrational, yet as a combination, they are viral and lethal. Public adoration is a disease, eats at the soul, and he seeks seclusion. He hides in his penthouse, he hides in his car, he hides in his overcoat, he hides in his Chickering, he hides his Steinway, he hides in the night, he hides. Yet... we all hide. Civilization is a physical and psychic shell. We hide in clothes, houses, cars, aircraft... words, symbols, math and all the rest. How crazy was he?

Bottom line: people liked his work right from the start, and they still like it. While all things artistic are a matter of opinion and personal taste, his ability to play the piano with transcendental consequence is beyond question. Perhaps he didn't write a great original symphonic work or piano concerto, yet he was able to keep the faith, help others understand history. He was moving in an independently creative direction with his radio art—the sound-text montages he called documentaries — and had he lived, he would have explored synaesthesia (multi-media) as technology advanced. `He remained, as he started, incomplete. His private life is neither here nor there—it's a melancholy tale, not a shabby one. He was possessed, like a medium who receives instructions from another world. His tragic flaw was his belief in perfection. His success was—and still is—a metaphor, and his failure impossible to define.

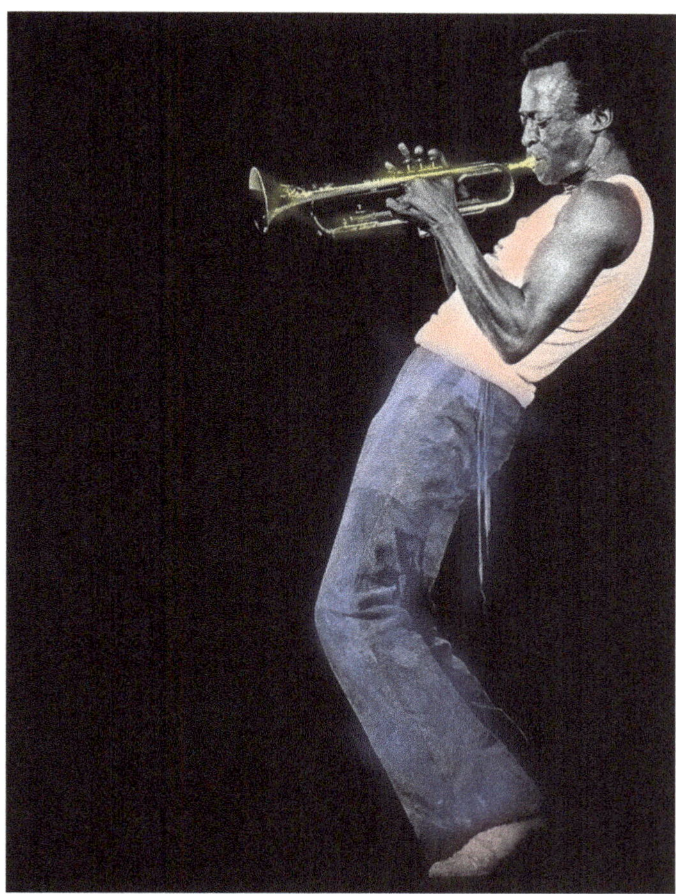

Miles Davis

In the 1985 Miami Vice episode *Junk Love* Miles Davis plays the aging pimp Ivory Keys. There is deliberate irony in this casting, for, as Davis says in his autobiography, "I started to get money from whores to feed and support my habit. I started to pimp them, even before I realized this was what I was doing." (p.136)

This was his New York 1950 *Birth of the Cool* period, when he became a serious junkie, master of the melancholy modernist blues. Hip? His modality was so hip he was a Dorian blur in the shadows of Harlem and 52nd Street, the jazz clubs, the flop hotels, grooving the dreamers and the schemers. The *Vice* episode isn't exactly great drama, although—like the whole series—it simplifies the idea of cool to a visual fantasy. Dialogue is minimal, epigrammatic at best, just something to pace the music. Essentially MD's part is two or three scenes more than a walk-in... a few growling lines in a sultanic costume. The baggy pants and the satin shawl jacket are a long way from the slim zoot suits of his New York bop days—well, the jumped shoulders remain, but here they sag as the hipster becomes androgynous in the rock n roll gestalt. "Stay loose" is now more than a figure of speech. The hipster shape-shifts to camouflage. He is Sky Man.

Ivory Keys dies off-stage, his Nigerian necklace a death trophy for Mr. Big, a dwarfed Latino hood called Silva, who is a killer drug dealer with a bad case of Oedipus Rex. But in real life, Davis ended up in Malibu, a hermit painter in an enclave of Hollywood stars, and his drug was no longer smack or coke, but the less than glamorous AZT. Whether his early hipster pimp career took him down or he wrecked his lungs blowing horn (pneumonia & a failed respiratory system took out a few of his fellow jazz horse traders, including Bird and Hawk), time caught up to him. He was 65—a decent age for his generation—and had accomplished more than most, considering the ladder he had to climb. The black hipster's story isn't always a success story but his is. More than anyone, he took jazz from cultural novelization into the core of modern art.

Miles Davis' verbal expression is deeply ethnic, a black underclass jive speak full of scorn and self-congratulation, fatalism and wounded pride. Just read his 1989 autobiography (brilliantly ciphered by Quincy Troupe), see if you can survive. He tries to be fair, and he is mostly fair, although the wound of the ghost slave runs deep. His flowing obscenities and double-negatives obey a counter-rhythm and a counter-logic that uses insult as praise. *Nigger* and *motherfucker* predominate. It's blues talk, a defiant parallel language born outside of church and state, a black hipster's cynical blunt-force humour. Obscenity as chant therapy is by no means just a black American thing—manual workers the world over massage their physical pain with rhythmic swearing, and anyone who has used a hammer knows it. This sado-masochism is convulsive, like the squeal and moan of heavy machinery doing its grind. Rage is the first note in the jazzer's scale of being. He blows or he dies.

So for a musician like MD, this way of talking is an exhalation, just like playing his horn. It's a shitting through the mouth, a modulation of a bodily function. Interestingly, Miles Davis cites his main musical influences as Dizzy Gillespie, Charlie Parker (Bird), Theolonius Monk and—believe it or not—Orson Welles.

Welles? For voicing, as MD saw the trumpet (or the sax, trombone, bassoon, whatever) as a modulation of the human voice. Tone, phrasing, pitch, intonation—all these things could be learned from a master of the spoken word. And in the Radio Age Orson Welles was a master of the spoken word. He was *Othello*, he was *Citizen Kane*, he was *The Shadow*, he was the "bad motherfucker" who duped millions of Americans into thinking they'd been invaded by the Martians.

He had tone, he had measure, he had the power to persuade, unlock the dreams of the sleeping listener. You can imagine MD driving between the great cities of the eastern seaboard in the Blue Demon—his 1948 Dodge—listening to Welles and the Mercury Players sandwiched between jazz casts and another fix before the gig. Or driving through Harlem or along 52nd Street or checking out Greenwich Village, slow cruisin' and schmoozin'. The traffic babble of the city, half-human, half-machine in the concrete jungle is the modal shell of consciousness. As MD says, and says often, he was a middle-register man, floated above the rumble, soared below the scream.

His trumpet speaks another language, one of melancholy, grace and beauty. There is no obscenity in the scale, no politics. He reaches into space, becomes free, so when he returns to life, it's a disappointment. Hangovers and manic-depression mark the boundaries, define the territory. He inhabits a night world, a spirit world. You don't dance to Miles Davis. You leave your body at the door and hope that it's there when you return. Despite his frequent barbs about dead white European music, the genre of bebop improvisation is jazz classical... and so is the MD post-modern "cool" style. It's all head, extra-sensory and personal. You lock minds, not bodies. It's theatre without the audience.

And so it came to pass that *The Birth of the Cool* (recorded

1949-50, released 1955) became the hipster's score to survival. The machine cities of America had been running hot for the war and bebop was war. It was fast, as nobody had time to be slow. Bebop was a blizzard of notes, like a creeping barrage of massed artillery, but now it was shutting down, would soon be an echo. MD didn't like the high-register—it might be o.k. for Dizzy and Bird, but it wasn't for him. He was going to cool things down. It would be heroin, pussy and space.

So MD was the classic "bad motherfucker" voodoo male, where "bad" is either hip code for "good" or just plain chauvinist nasty, depending on your point-of-view. Anyone who reads his autobio will know that he was not at heart a mean person, although he could be mean, was mean, as survival in the racist streets of America required the evil-eye look, the "don't mess with St. Louis" look. Yes, he idolized Sugar Ray, took boxing lessons, did some karate dance, but it was an off-stage pose.

Or it was heroin therapy, dressed cold turkey. His cool cat of the street persona was at odds with his notion of self, as he was bourgeois when it suited him. His old man was a St. Louis dentist, had dough, and Miles was—for the times—privileged. The gutter or the madhouse might claim others like Bud Powell or Monk, but MD could always go home to the farm.

His *machismo* was a vulgar attitude rather than a physical fact. He was of average height, skinny-assed, with a bad hip and elegant hands that couldn't be damaged or else. The only fight ring he performed in was a bitch's bed, although he did visit the gym. His power was all voodoo, spells and magic sounds. In 1969 when he was sitting in his parked Ferrari in Brooklyn with a girl and someone pulled up and fired a few rounds through door, he didn't go on a revenge quest, and if you believe him, he says he had no idea who was after him, although he was told it was some black promoters who didn't like the fact they weren't getting any of his action.

"Sometimes life is a bitch," he said, let it go at that.

The Smell Of France

In 1950 he goes to France, immediately hangs out with Jean Paul Sartre and Picasso, French artists who love jazz, recognize the expression (after all, France was an African colonizer). His romance with the chanteuse Juliette Greco is pivotal, mythical like Black Orpheus but without the death. Imagine it—it's a ballet on the walkways of the Seine.

Script by Cocteau, music by Davis.

"We had to communicate with each other through expressions and body language," says MD speaking of Juliette. The way he describes it, Juliette drops by the club when the band is rehearsing, and he doesn't know who she is, except that she looks good. He crooks his finger—she comes. Most of the time she's a faux lesbian ("I don't like men but I like you"), but for *Black Orpheus*, she's all woman, a creature unlike anything he's experienced previously. When she speaks, she's masculine; when she sings, she's feminine.

Quite possibly she isn't real, a bohemian fantasy, a character in a novel. And neither is he real, the American jazzman, a piece of skinny black nicotine in a funeral suit, a line sketch by Picasso or Cocteau, a transient spirit for the existentialist. Be hip or be mortal.

Juliette Greco recalls it like this: "And there I caught a glimpse of Miles, in profile: a real Giacometti, with a face of great beauty. I'm not even talking about the genius of the man: you didn't have to be a scholar or a specialist in jazz to be struck by him. There was such an unusual harmony between the man, the instrument and the sound—it was pretty shattering."

"I had been hypnotized, was in some kind of trance," says MD, reflecting on this period. "What I remember is the smell of France." Coffee, wine, Gitanes and women. The context is non-racist—at least insofar as the Left Bank art scene is concerned—although it would be naive to think that racism didn't exist in France outside the art ghetto.

The trance is personified by Juliette Greco—she played Aglaonike the sorceress in Jean Cocteau's *Orphee* (1950), a surrealist refit of the Orpheus-Eurydice legend. In a perverse way, they acted it out, Miles and Juliette. Years later, when she followed him into the underworld of America, booked into a suite at the Waldord-Astoria, he was cold to her, brutal... and like an uncultured pimp, demanded money. By his own admission, he was an asshole in love, couldn't handle the racial politics, the dope, the lack of control.

As American liberals say, it was a cringe-worthy situation, especially for anyone reading about it now. Juliette's view was—is—aesthetic: "Years later at the Waldorf in New York, where I had a very nice suite, I invited Miles to dinner. The face of the *maitre d'hotel* when he came in was indescribable. After two hours, the food was more or less thrown in our faces. The meal was long and painful, and then he left.

"At four o'clock in the morning I got a call from Miles, who was in tears. 'I couldn't come by myself,' he said. 'I don't ever want to see you again here, in a country where this kind of relationship is impossible.' I suddenly understood that I'd made a terrible mistake, from which came a strange feeling of humiliation that I'll never forget. In America his colour was made blatantly obvious to me, whereas in Paris I didn't even notice that he was black." [from the 2006 interview by Philippe Carles]

Today, super heroes in the comics wear exoskeletons, cyborg suits that make them invulnerable. The "pimp" persona was MD's exoskeleton, a defense mechanism in a rotten world where a black man could be standing under his own banner marquee outside Birdland and get beaten up by a white cop, or—for the cynical—it was nothing of the sort, was simply an attitude of jazz cool that plays well with the brothers. Sexism to the feminists, reality to the hipster noir.

Artists of all ethnicity are notorious for their fragile narcissism, for using art as a license to kill, and there is a certain greedy self-interest in MD's view of things that goes beyond fair play for the black artist. He's no worse than Picasso, maybe, yet sometimes he bitches too much. He criticizes Ornette Coleman for playing "free form" trumpet (occasionally) without having had any training on the instrument, yet later in life it's perfectly o.k. for him to take up painting without any formal training. He doesn't like the action white jazzers like Dave Brubeck and Chet Baker get, yet it's o.k. for him to use white musicians when history threatens to pass him by.

The Julliard School of Music was too white, too European, yet when the time comes, Ravel and Rachmaninoff are cool. He likes Kim Novak type blondes, yet white women have no fine ass, don't cut it. Alright, he's discriminating, not contradictory.

Malcolm X liked white chicks and zoot suits too.

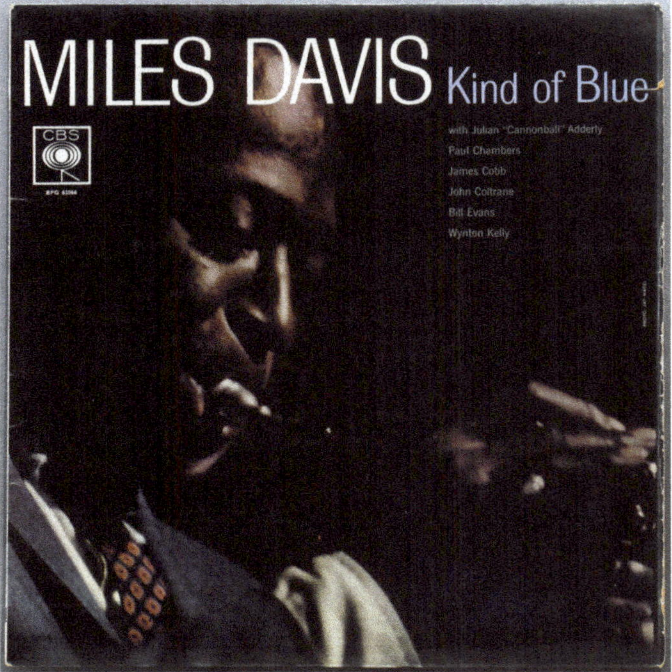

Kind Of Blue

Space. The big signature of MD's "cool" style is his use of space, narrative minimalism, ghosting. This style—the antithesis of bebop speed—is usually medium or slow tempo, and requires the piano to stay low, or even desist when the trumpet (or any lead) is playing, let the drums and bass "stroll". "Strolling" is the essence of the Davis hipster groove. Strolling and space. It's like Steve McQueen or the Buddha—it's not what he says, it's what you imagine he's thinking. Interestingly, MD arrives at this spatialization aesthetic right in step with the move from monaural to stereophonic recording. In 1959 the seminal *Kind of Blue* album was released in both mono and stereo versions.

Shortly after its release, Davis appears with his main men (*sans* Cannonball Adderly, who was sick) on a Studio 61 TV cast called the *Robert Herridge Theatre* [check out Miles playing *So What*]. Although MD didn't think much of the white corporate packaging, it is nevertheless a slick piece of work with a superb presentation. The camera point-of-view brings us onto the stage with the players, like privileged guests allowed to hang in the wings. The host, Robert Herridge, introduces the set as "a studio for a story told in jazz" as the Davis group plays some mood bars in the background. Herridge—veiled in smoke from a concealed cigarette—looks like he's hungover, has just pulled these guys in from Minton's. The camera swings away, closes on Davis dressed in an Italian chop suit, playing the riff to *So What* and from there on it's pure onomatopoeia. Lay the syllables on the beat. As the bass kicks into swing time, MD's trumpet scats "Bye... Be Bop", flows into his first solo, proclaims the future, buries the past. He's hot, although his expression is cool. When he finishes, he moves to one side (stage right) (the viewer's left), has a cigarette as Coltrane steps forward, testifies in a blaze of poetry and bullets. MD listens, watches, his passive horn pointing at the floor. A couple of idle trombone players stand with him, move gently to the groove, smile, smoke. Then, because Cannonball is missing, MD resumes the mic, takes another power solo. Wynton Kelly follows on piano. He takes us south, goes tropical. Miles comes in below and he and Trane comp the *So What* traffic signature. After a short bass solo, the Gil Evans orchestra joins in, fattens the chord, fuels the ending.

Because *So What* swings, you can dance to it, which is one important reason for its popularity. The modal architecture allows the improvisational expression to move away from Broadway Show tunes, swing in broader cultural sweeps, follow scales, not chords. It's a move away from orchestral expression into solo expression. The old way was communal, militaristic even—here, the Miles Davis way is personal, allowing the soloists to go deep.

But for the most part, bebop jazz or cool jazz, you couldn't dance to it, and this is the reason jazz went out of fashion in the sixties. MD doesn't see it that way, suggests that a conspiracy of the white critics—scared by the lyricism and beauty of *Kind of Blue*—pushed "Free Jazz" (i.e. Cecil Taylor, Eric Dolphy, Archie Shepp... even Coltrane at the end) which screwed jazz and lyric players like Miles Davis, so the public "turned to rock". His contempt for "white hillbilly music" (probably thinking of Elvis here) is an understandable intolerance due to the early politics of the situation, the ripoff of black blues artists and control of the recording industry. But by the end of the decade when he moves into fusion (or creates it as some think) it's not just a musical blend, it's also a racial blend. Moral: if you go modal, you go miscegenational.

He goes Spanish, investigates the *flamenco* mode. You can hear *Sketches of Spain* coming long before 1960—you hear it in *Blue*, you hear it in *Stones*. Dissed by some as a high-class *mariachi* plunder, it nevertheless has some beautiful Miles Davis flugelhorn in his familiar blues modernist saturations. It's the hipster going into exile, moving homeward to a home he has never known except in dream. It's a Daliesque underworld where Orpheus wanders, haunted by dream trauma and a cruel paranoid loneliness. The narrative labyrinth is European, yet the chambers extend into Africa. No groove, little hope, just psychic signals and a warrior's hunt shuffle as he moves further south into the racial memory. Once again, the feral sensitivity baffles the bourgeois mind.

The sixties is when the trumpet is replaced by the electric guitar as the hipster's instrument of choice. MD recognizes this, tries to adapt but has problems as the shift is a white generational shift. The guitar is more than just melody—it is rhythm and lead, and furthermore you can bend the notes, break the intervallic trap presented by fixed piano tunings, fully embrace the atonal possibilities of the blues. MD goes electric, as electric is dyna big, electric is dyna hip. He tries playing through a wah wah pedal—a frequency sweeper—a favorite of guitarists, especially Jimi Hendrix. He meets Jimi through his new young funkadelic wife Betty Mabry, and old hip confers with new hip. You could say that the Jimi Hendrix atonal power style, full of electronic abstraction and personal karma, is just "free jazz" pumped through rock n roll. It matches the direction MD thinks he's heading; he's been listening to Karl Heinz Stockhausen, recognizes the possibilities of poisoned noise.

Armed with a young wife (legally his second, technically his third) and a wah wah pedal, he channels Africa, "chases down the voodoo". The influence of Betty Mabry is significant. Hendrix, Sly Stone, funk. Her face doubles the mountain motif on the jacket of *Filles de Kilimanjaro* (1968), and includes a track that's named after her, *Madamemoiselle Mabry* (you wonder if the

French dressing is the ghosting of Juliette Greco). It's a short marriage—MD accuses her of playing Hendrix ("Betty was just a high-class groupie"). Whatever the case, "Backseat Betty" continues on with a career as a singer, her highly sexualized brand of funk a clear prototype for Madonna's later pop heresy. As the Second Quintet morphs into the Third, MD goes U.N., almost white. Joe Zawinul, Chick Corea, Dave Holland, John McLaughlin—it's a long way from Bird and Trane, but these guys can be led, be influenced. Yet....

1969. *In A Silent Way*... what a mistake... surely. At times there's so much space in these "compositions" it's like Miles Davis has amnesia. No wonder the jazz critic Stanley Crouch thinks *Kilimanjaro* is the last significant Miles Davis album. No wonder his drummer Tony Williams hid his wah wah pedal (just listen to some of those shrill live bootlegs from this period and you'll understand why), called for Miles to play his trumpet clean. Adios Ted Macero, the longtime Davis producer. Perhaps Macero's editing was poor, his sense of montage inadequate. Perhaps there was too much dope. Perhaps Miles leaned too much on Joe. Tuning up or tuning down, it's like cheap Christmas music for the infant Satan. There's a lot of searching, polite exchanges, should we fly or should we not, where is the runway, have mercy... well maybe tomorrow.

Let us reconsider. Perhaps there's a gentleness to the textures, these blue atonalities, electric skyscapes, a sense of mission possible in some of the tracks. Yes, some. McLaughlin goes Gabor Szabo gypsy and Wayne Shorter shows up, makes sense where no sense lurks. Compare this to *Bitches Brew*—which is the next album—and you can hear that this is a dry run. The major difference is the percussion. Here it's light and metronomic but in *Bitches Brew* it's a full-tilt jungle rumble.

Bitches is decisive: let's go to Africa.

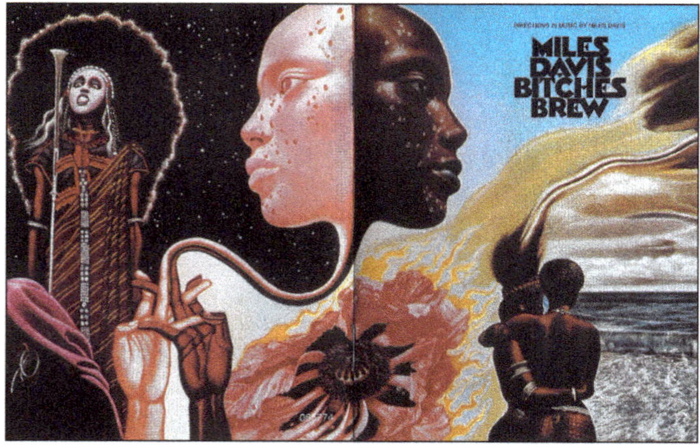

Bitches Brew

It's like he's playing through an elephant tusk, has found the primal groove. The echoplex trumpet blasts announce the arrival of Orpheus and his retinue of babes. It's a fantastic world, another planet, the birthing ground of the hipster. It's both the past and the future, a place where Sky Man learns the magic arts. It's beyond the lost cities of Igo-domi-godo, Jenne-jeno or any King Solomon Saharan fantasy. It's more like Rene Laloux's 1973 animation film *Fantastic Planet*, the place where a galactic civilization called The Drogs go for mating and reproduction. "Drog youth navigate to this rutting field of the demi-gods in glass spheres that float like spore bubbles and attach themselves to the shoulders of a statue of the appropriate gender. The statues then begin to dance in pairs, a ritual that allows these astral beings the necessary physicality for reproduction and the continuation of their species." Without question the late Mati Klarwein's famous album cover painting for *Bitches Brew* captures this sense of sexual ritualization and idealization.

The groove is modal funk, with everything submerged into the mix. The genius of it lies in the massed bebop instrumental attack style expressed within the polyphonic dynamism of contemporary electronic music. It's linear, yet complex... random, yet structured. It has mass, like a stream of heavy atoms from a black sun. The life-form is both human and animal, cyborg and divine. A stampede, a razzia, a disco elephant shuffle. The unwritten history of ancient Africa is accessed by metabolism and reincarnation.

Malibu, West Africa

Next to music, painting is the most primal and elemental of the hipster arts. Both became mathematical as societies built their temples higher in the sky, so it's no surprise that their narratives became institutionalized and decadent. Picasso showed the way, looked south, embraced primitivism, and of course Miles Davis knew Picasso. The style was in the air—let's go primary—as it cut out art school, allowed amateurs to indulge their infantile fantasies, get porno without consequence. But while MD had no formal training as a painter, he had all the mathematics of modern music, took jazz into the post-modern sensibility, so the notion of deconstruction and the return to root zero was already within his *modus operandi.*

The hipster was getting old, his body was a wreck, and the pressure of being an international celeb made a Malibu pad a welcome sanctuary for the final expression, painting. What you see is what you get. Skinny figures reminiscent of Dali, his favorite painter... swollen torsos and flattened heads... the usual scramble of West African totem art and furniture store deception. Oddly, for a man who claimed to have the second sight, his imagery is neither prophetic nor psychological. His genius is disguised, the expression comfortably bourgeois. Sure, you wouldn't mind owning one, especially with "Miles" on it. You would especially like a first press vinyl disc of *Star People* (1983), as he did the jacket, so you want the large format.

"Star People" is probably an allusion to the Dogon peoples of western Mali, some of whom believe they are descendents of amphibian extra-terrestials from the star system Sirius. The idea sits well with MD's New Age anthropomorphism and science fiction sound. He plays with his horses, goes on TV. His voice is low and bronchial, his familiar Sky Man nuke shades locked in place for the final count down. On the Arsenio Hall talk show the white lady who hunts parasite aliens on space ships and ugly planets sits nearby as the host dumbs down the questions. MD's responses are slow, as if he's in tape delay or drugged. He's hoarse, whispers, as if all the rage has been sucked out of him. He starts spitting, explains that this is how you learn to play trumpet without wrecking your cheeks, blowing the blood vessels... peas, rice, spit, spit... how you keep it cool, secret, so nobody knows if you're blowing or not. Yes, he's famous. Yuri Andropov loves him and he doesn't need a passport anywhere in Europe. It's all stretch limos and rock n roll now.

He is Star People.

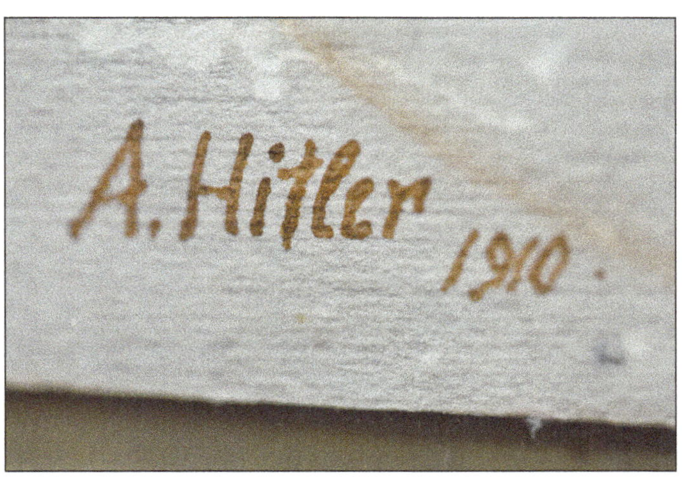

Adolf Hitler

Hitler—more popular by the day, by the hour. As artists go, his posthumous success has been phenomenal, although he destroyed more than he created. His political legend continues to grow, while his artistic expression is either forgotten or dismissed as amateur. In the 1930s, as his paintings were forged and bootlegged, he cynically dispatched agents to hunt down the copies and copyists. Is he another artist whose own story is far more interesting than any of the work he created, a homicidal lunatic who parlayed a failed career as a painter of sentimental Austrian landscapes into the leader of German defeat-outrage and the death-cult of *lebensraum*? He was a master of manipulation and revenge, but was he ever any good as an artist? And what was his "art" exactly: was it all show-biz uniforms and searchlight tattoos, radio monologues and neo-Roman salutes?

He always thought big, and that big statements were the best, so he wanted to be an architect. Speaking about a folio of a 125 drawings by Hitler that he had in his possession, Albert Speer said, "They were casually tossed off but accurate in perspective; he drew outlines, cross-sections, and renderings to scale. An architect could not have done better." [*Inside the Third Reich*, p.143] Albert Speer was Hitler's architect, a sort of benign doppelganger Hitler used to carry out his Wagnerian fantasies for the reconstruction of the new Germany as a mythic 1,000 year Reich. Speer certainly knew what he was talking about. He and Hitler designed their modernist, neo-classical public buildings according to an aesthetic they called "ruin value", that is, as a civilization and its culture is defined by the supernatural expression of its future ruined monuments, all building design should anticipate its archaeological fate.

While this "death as beauty" concept might seem radical, it is just the natural extension of Greco-Roman classicism and German Romanticism, which always loved madmen, ruined castles and forgotten tombs. A famous example of this would be Caspar David Friedrich's painting *The Cloister Graveyard in the Snow* (1810), which was destroyed by a bombing raid in 1945. The irony is obvious, of course, although Friedrich painted a number of variations of this setting and theme. [*Dolmen in the Snow, Giant Grave by the Sea, The Ruins of Eldena, et. al.*]

Hitler probably never read Madame de Stael's influential book *De l'Allemagne* (*Germany*) (1810), which drew a distinction between the "imitativeness" of classicism and the "spirituality" of romanticism. Hitler's failure as a painter and his success as a proto-architect is mirrored in this distinction. He was indifferent to religion and completely imitative in terms of architecture, although his obsessive knowledge of design minutiae reveals some intellectual depth. When he first went to Vienna in 1908, his application for admission to the Academy of Fine Arts was rejected on the basis that his painting wasn't good enough, but it was noted that he had a strong aptitude for architectural rendering. As he says in *Mein Kampf*, he was crushed by the rejection. Here he was, the best student in drawing back in his home town of Linz, but in Vienna he just wasn't good enough... and as a high school dropout he simply didn't have the mathematics to go on in architecture.

Yet the drawing obsession was rooted. At that time, Vienna was the capital of the Austro-Hungarian Empire, an uneasy multicultural coalition of eleven different states (or cultural groups) ruled by the absurd paternalism of the Hapsburg (dual) monarchy. No common language, no common law, and no common sense. It was Rome without Latin or common citizenship for the client states. It had the Emperor, it had the temples, it had the imperial illusion afforded by a combined population of 50 million. In 1910, Vienna was 2 million, of which 70, perhaps 100 thousand was a fluid multi-national underclass of unemployed coarselings. Crime, racism, prostitution, sweat shop slavery, demonstrations, riots and all the rest. Yet there was a lot of pomp and arrogance ingrained in the cityscape, especially in the large institutional buildings on the famous Ringstrasse, the road that encircles Vienna. The Ringstrasse followed the old medieval fortification wall, which was demolished in the mid 1800s, then became the access road to many elaborate buildings in the neo-gothic, renaissance, neo-classical and modernist styles by the time of Hitler's Viennese street education, 1908-1913. He mapped some of these buildings like a thief preparing a master heist, had a detailed knowledge of dimensions, materials, rooms, stairways and even doors unknown to the general public. For him, culture was a series of theatres, venues for mass hypnosis. His *weltanschauung* was secular, but its intent was religious. Intimidation and awe, glory and unconditional love. Speaking with the art critic Robert Hughes in 1979 about Nazi architecture, Albert Speer said simply, "Size matters."

Postcards From Vienna

After his mother died, Hitler left Linz, came to Vienna in 1908. He applied for admission to the art academy, was rejected twice. While his money lasted, he spent his time visiting the museums and the public buildings on the Ringstrasse, and going to the state opera to witness productions in the post-Mahler era. By 1909 he was broke. In *Mein Kampf* (*My Struggle*) he says he worked on a construction site but lost his job after a political argument with a Social Democrat got ugly. This appears to be fiction, as Brigitte Hamann says in her authoritative book *Hitler's Vienna* (1999) there is no documented evidence of this and no one has ever come forward to share his experience of doing manual labour with the Fuhrer at this time. Like the majority of autobiographies, *Mein Kampf* fictionalizes either by lying or by wilful omission of detail.

By late 1909 Hitler is so destitute he's sitting in all-night cafes or sleeping on park benches. Things weren't good in the capital, which was full of economic migrants from all parts of the Empire. Unemployment was running at an unhealthy 28%. People were sleeping in the sewers and canals, stables and workhouses, begging in the parks, the streets, the charity outlets. Because of his soft hands and petit bourgeois laziness, Hitler was begging in the streets and doing the soup-kitchen shuffle. His health was poor, his clothes were shabby, and to escape the freezing weather, he ended up in the Meidling (Meidlingerstrasse) homeless shelter (a.k.a. "the Asylum") in late 1909... which is where he met his first art agent, Reinhold Hanisch.

Like many hustlers, Hanisch existed under a number of aliases, moved around. As such, he was involved in petty crime, spent some time in prison in Berlin, which is how he acquired a Berlin accent and subsequently passed himself off as a Berliner. As Hitler was bedazzled by all things German, he quickly befriended Hanisch, who showed him how to hustle. It was Hanisch who suggested he draw postcards, and, after borrowing some money from an aunt to acquire the necessary paper, pencils, brushes and paints, Hitler settled down in the cheap cafes and started to work.

You cannot over-estimate Hitler's cunning as an artist. Was he any good? Crap, you might say, with swift moral ease. But the fact is, good or bad, he knew how to make money. There are hundreds of these drawings and paintings out there, some of which were seized by the US Army in 1945, and are still under curfew somewhere in the US government vaults. The commonality is the lack of human figures within the precise rendering of sentimental landmarks, usually buildings and scenes that appeal to the *volkisch* aspects of German culture.

For someone who later developed a dangerous psychopathology, you would expect these landscapes and buildings to have a van Gogh look, an electrified spacial muddling that betrays not only the amateur but also the madman. Not so. The perspectives are machine-like, free of ego, devoid of poetry. What about the subjects? Most are substitute photographs, suitable for the tourist industry, although some of the war time paintings do have the romance of "ruin value" i.e. "Ruins of a Cloister in Messines" (1914) and at least show some proof that Hitler actually was in the army and that his time at the front was not another *Mein Kampf* fiction. Yet there is little authenticity in the experience, either in the paintings or the account. If you compare Hitler's descriptions of the front in *Mein Kampf* to those of Ernst Junger in *Storm of Steel* (*Stahlgewitten,* 1920) you would think Hitler spent all his time painting well behind the front and was only accidentally involved in combat. Art for Adolph was strictly a fantasy of the present expressed as a sentimentalism of the past.

Feeling he was being ripped off, Hitler soon dumped Hanisch in favour of several other sellers, including Siegfried Loffner and a Jewish glazier called Samuel Morgenstern, who naturally had a lot of Jewish clients who became, ironically, major buyers of Hitler's art. Hitler himself said he liked Jewish dealers, as they were less judgemental, willing to take risks. Therefore it seems odd that Hitler later embraced the idea that the Viennese Jews were to blame for modernism and its corrupting influence on German culture. You would think that an architectural artist like Hitler would have been at ease with the anti-baroque stance of modernism, and the secular nature of its industrial straight-line economy of form. But no, he was too conservative; painting was furniture or souvenir illustration, never a means to enlightenment. While he would later say he was an artist first, a politician second, he nevertheless spent a lot of his time in the public gallery of the Austrian parliament, listening to anti-semitic politicians who followed Georg von Schonerer (German National Party) and the mayor of Vienna, Karl Lueger (Christian Democrat). Rhetoric comes from the mouth, not the hand.

Years later Hanisch and another artist called Leidenroth from the hostel days tried to blackmail Hitler by stating that he sold forgeries (copied from other drawings or photographs), that he claimed to have an art academy diploma, and inferred that he was in an unnatural relationship with a Jew, Joseph Neumann, with whom Hitler had become friendly. The Vienna Police files have only one entry about Adolf Hitler—that he was a "pervert". What this refers to remains a mystery. Neumann went to Germany and disappeared. Hanisch's relationship with Hitler was indeed odd, because, after the war when Hitler became famous as the leader of the National Socialists, Hanisch began painting and selling forgeries of "Hitler" watercolors. And he readily sold his recollections of Hitler to whatever magazine or biographer asked. Bizarre? It was certainly provocative and dangerous in the Nazi state and indeed he was arrested in 1936 and died mysteriously a short time later in prison. As Hitler's pictures had such a generic, anonymous look about them, they would be easy to fake, and it has to be recognized that forging them adds to the mystique of the Hitler cult.

The forgery of the forgery. Goering—a great collector of looted art—certainly didn't think much of the Fuhrer's art or his writing; he admitted he couldn't read *Mein Kampf* and that he saw "nothing" in Hitler's paintings. If art is the mirror of dysfunction, then the young Hitler was completely sane. There is no Rorschach confession, no symbolism, no sex, no death... no extra-sensory perception... no personality. If you compare him to one of his contemporaries like Giorgio de Chirico, the Greco-Italian painter who became famous for his metaphysical works (which were adopted by the surrealists), you might laugh, say the comparison is unfair. But De Chirico studied at the Academy of Fine Arts in Munich from 1906 to 1909 and came under some of the same influences as Adolph Hitler, albeit more formally. De Chirico was influenced by the great German symbolist painters Kasper David Friedrich (*The Wanderer Above the Sea of Fog*) and Arnold Bocklin (*The Isle of the Dead*), read Nietzsche and Schopenhauer. Hitler was fond of quoting these philosophers, although some have questioned whether or not he did actually read them (rather, he extemporized erroneously from newspaper summaries). As for Friedrich and Bocklin, they were everywhere to be seen. But of course Hitler had different preferences, such as the *Blut und Boden* (blood and soil) ethnic ideology... and he was poor. He was poor and his mother was dead. His idea of salvation was retrenchment, embrace all things German, including the old pagan religion. Paganism didn't show in his painting, but it was there later in his operatic politics and ruin-value architecture.

So as far as Hitler's "commercial" drawings and painting go, it appears to be a case of you can make a tombstone and sell it as art, but you can also do a painting of the same tombstone and never sell it as art.

Yet he did alright, got out of the homeless shelters, moved to Munich in 1913, continued painting, even after he joined the German Army in 1914. Later, when he became Reich Chancellor, he took a royalty payment from all stamps sold bearing his likeness, which, according to Albert Speer, was a lucrative source of extra income. What artists did he have in his personal collection? Arnold Bocklin for one, whose *Isle of the Dead* was so popular by the late 1800s that nearly every German household had a print of at least one version. Hitler also admired the ambiguous whimsy of Carl Spitzweg (1808-1885) whose corny portraits fitted well with the volk sensibility.

In a similar folk vein were the "happy drunk" paintings of Eduard Grutzner, which Hitler blindly adored (perhaps he recognized his brutal, alcoholic father). "This Grutzner will someday be worth as much as a Rembrandt," he told his court photographer Hoffman. Or there was Franz von Stuck, a graduate of the Munich Academy, whose raunchy mythological paintings extended Bocklin's classical symbolism, and owning a few von Stucks suggests that Hitler indeed had an erotic life, albeit a very camouflaged one.

Speer: "There was something fantastic about the absolute authority Hitler could assert over his closest associates of many years, even in matters of taste. Goebbels had simply groveled before Hitler. We were all in the same boat. I too, though altogether at home in modern art, tacitly accepted Hitler's pronouncement." (*Inside the Third Reich*, p.27)

Hitler As Wotan, Opera Artist

Look at Hitler's performance at the 1933 Nuremberg Rally as seen in Leni Riefenstahl's famous documentary *The Triumph of Will* and you will see his version of an operatic aria worthy of Richard Wagner. While his obsession with Wagner has been well-documented and accepted as an integral part of his megalomania, the actual stylistics of his appropriation are less discussed. These start with the redesign of the Nuremberg airship field into a vast Nazi Party venue with a wedge-shaped seating area on one end facing an elevated stage with a granite plaza or causeway between... consciously or unconsciously the entire make-over (with an adjacent stadium to hold 400,000) is like stretched modification of Wagner's personal opera house at Bayreuth in Bavaria.

Bayreuth was a radical move away from the ubiquitous horse-shoe design, anticipated the rectilinear feel of modernism by eliminating private boxes and using a seating slope facing the stage, thereby employing "the mystic gulf" concept of spaciality between the actors and the audience. At Nuremberg, "the mystic gulf" between Hitler and the audience is enormous, almost as if he playing from a projected castle rampart, a machicolation that seems to levitate in the "cathedral of light" tattoo. The effect at night is quite supernatural, like a god addressing a vast host of the living and the dead. Some call it agitprop theatre, some pure evil.

Here, under the giant Nazi eagle decal, Hitler's style is that of a declaiming tenor, sometimes roaming the misty forest of Valhalla, others the cobbled streets of old Germany. The money-lenders, the foreign socialists... weed the weak from the strong, be peace-loving but brave... *Deutschland uber alles... seig heil, seig heil.* The rap is call and response, Hitler and the crowd, Hitler spasmodically rising onto his toes like a giddy ballet dancer. His right hand scrolls, an invisible baton articulating the score. He clasps his hands to his breast, clenches his fists, barks, barks... wags his erotic finger, plays to the applause. *Seig heil! Seig heil!* they roar. Hail victory! He is singing *The Master*

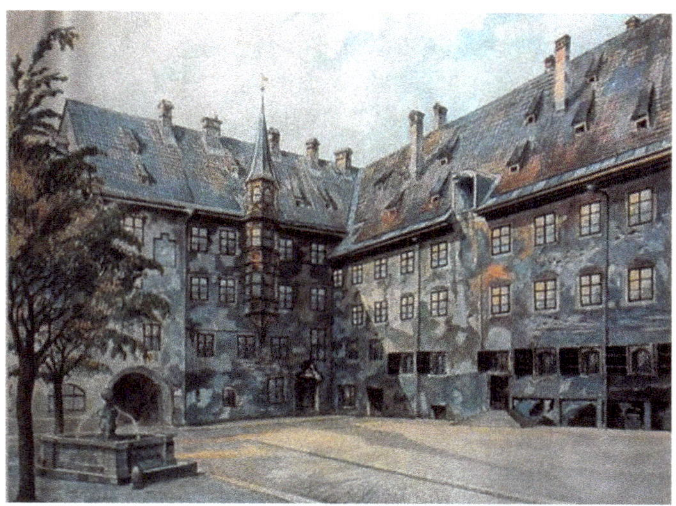

Singer's Song (*Die Meistersinger von Nurnberg*): never forget to honour all that is German, especially the fallen, never forget to defend the Fatherland from subversion within and without, *Deutschland uber alles.* And then he is Wotan, the god of gods, now before them as The Fuhrer, and while they don't know it yet, this is a rehearsal for Gotterdammerung. Soon, like Wotan, he will set fire to Valhalla.

Hitler's oratorical style is the rhythm of the Wagnerian suspended chord, a modulated sequence of suspension upon suspension, where he avoids settling on any clear key except madness. Speaking of Wagner, Yehudi Menuhin says "(the suspended tone) is part and parcel of the aesthetic stretching of sexual sensations, the prolongation of the ecstatic, the unreal, the mysteriously dark and visionary". Indeed. The calculated distance Hitler keeps between himself and the microphones is also an indicator of the power of his vocal delivery, the sense that his aria is ambient, is near and real, even though at the back of the field it will be a rolling echo. The symbolism of Wagner's folkloric operas is one thing, the theatrical delivery another. Hitler's imitation was a natural consequence of those pre WW I days standing at the back of the Vienna Opera House, later reading the volkisch romance novels of Guido von List (via AH's friendship with Dietrich Eckart, the "Nazi" poet). In fact, Hitler's debt to Wagner was so autodidactic that he became involved with Winifred Wagner, the English wife of Richard Wagner's homosexual son, Siegfried.

As Speer notes in *Inside the Third Reich*, when he and Hitler were driving to Nuremberg in the autumn of 1933 to survey the Zeppelin field, Hitler spent the night with Winifred at the Wagner house in Bayreuth where she managed the great composer's estate and the Bayreuth Opera Festival. While he makes no comment on the nature of this friendship, the duration of it suggests more than aesthetic companionship. Some say *Mein Kampf* was written on the paper wrapping of the food parcels that Winifred sent Hitler when he was incarcerated in Landsberg prison for his part in the failed Beer Hall Putsch (Munich, 1923). Some say it was the intellectual circle—now known as the Bayreuth Circle—that Winifred hosted that groomed Hitler into the committed xenophobe with a sense of historic destiny that allowed him to succeed. Male confidence is usually a feminine construction. Winifred Wagner remained incorrigible about Hitler to the end of her life, even resurrected a salon of the old fascists in Bayreuth, much to the disappointment of her children. Hitler was more than a one-night stand. Letters exist, jealously hidden and guarded by a granddaughter; one day, perhaps, they will be available to History.

When Hitler first visited Bayreuth in 1923, he was shown Wagner's grave, allowed to commune alone with the sacred vibe of the demi-god. On a return visit, he inspected the Wagner Opera theatre, abandoned since the outbreak of war in 1914 with the set of the *Flying Dutchman* still in place. Hitler reverently viewed this "dusty theatrical splendour from a bygone era... strangely transformed." (as quoted in Brigitte Hamann's 2002 bio of Winifred Wagner, p.61) This was the start of Hitler's immersion, where the Wagner Opera Festival became the Nazi Uppsala (*Ostra Aros*) in his atavistic quest for aryan pagan perfection.

Trophy Woman Art

Hitler's sex life was so undercover that many people felt he was either asexual or homosexual, and even today remains a subject of psychoanalysis and fantastic speculation. But it's obvious that he liked shapely young women, and had no problem reaching back through the generations to get them. Eva Braun, who had a swimmer's body, was 23 years younger than Hitler when they committed suicide together in the Reich Chancellery bunker in the spring of 1945, he 56, she 33. Everyone knows about her: daughter of a school teacher and the assistant of Hitler's personal photographer Heinrich Hoffmann, 17 when she met Hitler, soon to become his mistress. Eva, who attempted suicide on two occasions during their relationship, was a substitute-type for Geli Raubal, who committed suicide with Hitler's pistol in his Munich apartment in 1931. Geli was Hitler's half-niece from the family back in Linz, came into Hitler's orbit when he hired her mother as his housekeeper. Not only does Geli look like Hitler, she also looks like Eva Braun, and was also 17 when procured. Their "relationship" lasted six years. She tried to escape, wanted to be a singer, but Hitler held her under guard. It was, as they say, a Freudian nightmare.

It's easy to draw the conclusion that Hitler was a classic Bluebeard control freak, and a serial killer as a lover. Five of his women committed suicide; some say two were murdered, and suggest there were others, invisible to public knowledge. The movie actress Renate Muller who either jumped or was thrown from an upper floor window of a hospital in 1937 wasn't invisible, although the depth of her connection to Hitler remains ambiguous. Adopted by the Nazi Party as the "ideal aryan woman" after the defection of Marlene Dietrich to Hollywood, Renate—a beauty who was an artist as much as she was an object of art—was caught between a Jewish boyfriend and Hitler.

Mitzi Reiter tried to commit suicide soon after she met Hitler in 1927 when she was sixteen. Her story is complicated, perhaps opportunistic. Hitler was crazy for her, but his need was too complicated, too fixed with strings. She became depressed, tried to hang herself, but was saved. Four years later she had a one-nighter with the Fuhrer in Munich, and was then married off to a SS officer. Twenty five years later she sold her story to the German magazine *Stern*.

The story of Unity Valkyrie Mitford is the story of a groupie, the story of a young English aristocrat who first became infatuated with fascism, then with Hitler. She and her sister Diana—who was married to Oswald Mosley, the British fascist leader—travelled to the Nuremberg Rally, got caught up in the blood fever. Her contact really came through the Bayreuth (Wagner) Circle where she learned about the Fuhrer's routines, then moved to Munich and began to stalk him. It took a few months of parading in his favorite cafe before he invited her to join him; when he learned her middle name was "Valkyrie" and that her father had been a friend of the great composer Richard Wagner, then destiny took over. Hitler took her to the Olympics, even Austria during the *anschluss*.

He took her to his retreat at Obersalzberg, where Eva Braun, driven to despondency by the appearance of "the Valkyrie" with the "Valkyrie legs" attempted suicide. After war broke out between Great Britain and Germany in September 1939, Unity tried to kill herself in the "English Garden" in Munich using a pearl-handled gun Hitler had given her. He sent her to a hospital in Switzerland and then had her repatriated back to the UK on a tramp steamer. The bullet remained lodged in her brain, and was the eventual cause of her death in 1948. Her promiscuous career from London debutante to Nazi mistress was recently used as the model for the character of "Lady Persie" (Persephone) in the BBC period serial drama *Upstairs, Downstairs.*

The political fantasy became a sexual fantasy... or was it the other way around? Throughout the years of his Chancellorship, Hitler received thousands of letters from adoring women begging him to father their children. Once again, art is the sexual perception of an object.

Germania And Ruin-Value

Hitler's idea of "Germania" was a Palestine of the mind, a return to the pre-Roman pagan culture of northern Europe, the genesis of Aryan civilization according to Wagner's son-in-law Houston Stewart Chamberlain, the Germanophile author of the influential racialist book, *The Foundations of the Nineteenth Century* (1899). Then, of course, there was Guido von List, the fake aristocrat who wrote *The Secret of the Runes* and *Carnuntum*, a novel based on the pagan Roman city located on the Danube in lower Austria. It was from von List that Hitler obtained the swastika, the Nazi Party symbol, and the dominant symbol of the Third Reich.

Albert Speer includes a sketch of a triumphal arch that Hitler "tossed off" (and a photograph of the large model of this arch that was presented to Hitler on his 50th birthday in 1939) in his (seminal) book *Inside the Third Reich.* Of course it looks like the *Arc de Triomphe*, which is also a Roman rip (the Arch of Titus), yet just as obviously Hitler's design is a reinvention of the *Heidentor* (pagan gate) at Carnuntum. In keeping with "ruin value" Hitler worked from an archaeological model, just as Jean Chalgrin did for the Arc. So, as a search for grandeur in the monuments of the past, neoclassicism becomes a means of predicting the future. Size? *The Arc de Triomphe* is 164 feet high by 148 wide; Hitler's arch was to

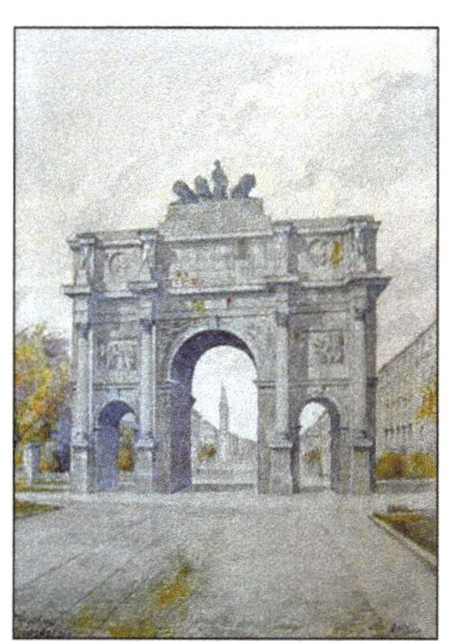

be bigger by far at 550 feet by 392. With a rooftop plaza of circa 200,000 sq feet, you could drill a small *Festung* (Fortress) Wehrmacht Division and watch Luftwaffe formations fly through the arch below. The scale was Babylonian, pure Fritz Lang. No wonder the Fuhrer often dismissed Speer's budgetary concerns with a soft hiss and a flutter of the hand.

When you think of large triumphalist "art" statements, what do you think of? Gutzon Borglum's *Mount Rushmore* (South Dakota) four Presidents sculpture that covers 1,200 acres... or the giant Soviet war memorials such as Yevgeny Vuchetich's 273 foot high female warrior *The Motherland Calls* in Volgograd... or the strange "monument to the Soviet Army" in Bulgaria... or the abandoned giant science fiction relics of the former Yugoslavia... yet none of these have the functionality of Hitler's arch. They are symbolism only, whereas Hitler's arch is a working fortress, a god window into Germania for those entering the *Welthauptstadt* (World Capital, as Speer called it) along the Avenue of Splendour (*Prachtallee*). The plan for the make-over of Berlin was statist theatre, a fashion code for fascists. Functionality, speed and indoctrination. All the old state games could be played—parades, rallies, drills, political operas all—with the thrilling efficiency of Hitlerian modernism. When Speer first showed Hitler the plan for the new Chancellery, he was worried that the hall—which was twice as long as the Hall of Mirrors at Versailles—was too long, and visitors would become fatigued. But Hitler approved, indeed, delighted in the distance foreign dignitaries would have to walk before reaching the inner sanctums of the Nazi leadership. Intimidation and awe were to be the order of the day. The symbolism of "space" was the secret of mind control. The visitor becomes metabolic and compliant, an insect within the Nazi Buddha.

Hitler's favorite architect was Paul Troost (1878-1934) whose shaven head bespoke of his baroque revolt and neo-classical modernism. Troost learned his method in part from the industrial restriction of designing ocean liner decor. Many architects were moving in step with human desire and the new building materials which allowed a new way, indeed, a new level of desire. Gropius... van der Rohe... Le Corbusier... and especially the Germano-Zen architect Bruno Taut who was forced into exile in Japan. This design evolution (or "Futurism") is all about movement and speed because, even if buildings are static, the world around them isn't. It's also a movement away from freehand doodling into the geometry of the set-square and the efficient mathematical description of time and space. Speer says anything Hitler knew about modern architecture came from Troost. When Troost died in 1934, Hitler allowed his widow Gerdy to become the art maven of Munich.

The mysticism that drove Hitler's idea of architecture is contained in his unrealized plan for an new planetarium in his hometown of Linz, which needed an ego makeover for his projected retirement sometime in the 1950s. It would have three levels dramatizing cosmological evolution: the ground floor would be the Ptolemic universe; the second, the Copernican; the third, the Horbiger *Welteislehre*. Who was Hans Horbiger? An Austrian engineer who came up with the *World Ice Theory* (*Welteislehre* or *WEL*) which Hitler became familiar with through Houston Stewart Chamberlain (Wagner's son-in-law) and began talking up at his discussion circles in the twenties, later incorporated as official Nazi doctrine. The *WEL* idea came to Horbiger as a "dream vision" which he eventually published as *Glazial-Kosmogenie* in 1912. *WEL* postulated that huge blocks of ice from a cold star fractured and fell into a large hot star, which in turn shattered and spread out in spirals, forming the universe and the Milky Way. Hitler was smitten with the concept, as it provided a nice aryan counter-challenge to Einstein's *Theory of Relativity*. Others ran with it, had the aryan races emerging from an ice field in the north. The idea was as crazy as it was convenient. It sounds suspiciously like Casper David Friedrich's painting *The Sea of Ice* viewed after ten schnapps, then dressed up as nightmare science. Yet its adherents were many and are still out there.

Brutalism Of The Flak Tower

Hitler had eight *flakturmes* built in various cities of the Reich, including Berlin (near the zoo), Hamburg and Vienna. These were massive anti-aircraft concrete towers, the ultimate expression of castle "keep" architecture, functional and impenetrable, outstanding examples of modern art as ideology. Today you could mistake them for grain elevators or low cost housing towers. During the war they were used as bomb shelters for thousands of Berliners, and were difficult to destroy by foe or friend, so that most remain standing. Some were solo towers, others were linked duals or quads, the walls 14 feet thick and seven stories high, and typically had several anti-aircraft batteries on the roof using the formidable twin-barreled Flakzwilling-40 5 inch guns.

When the Soviets invaded Berlin, their howitzers were useless against these neo-medieval keeps. Interestingly, their projected post-war function was envisioned as war memorials to the fallen German soldiers, the architectural brutalism to be disguised with marble, and so dressed for eternity. Who designed them? Friedrich Tamms, a Berlin protege of Hitler, and associate of Albert Speer.

Gotterdammerung

If you had to draw or paint a picture of Hitler, how would you represent him? As a hipster clown in lederhosen, or would you be more circumspect. He didn't smoke, he didn't drink, he had a fear of human touch. He was secretive and cunning to the point of anal retention. He had a shame of origin, yet he over-justified his origin in the cult of the *volk*. He had a sense of class inferiority, yet he despised Marxism because it was internationalist and Jewish. He was capable of compassion, although his compassion always seemed political. He seemed to be driven, yet he was often lazy, slept 'til noon, even when Reich Chancellor. He liked children, but didn't want any of his own. He liked war, never wanted it to end.

He liked getting his information from newspapers and museums, so he was like someone today who is educated by TV. He was visual, inclined to be pictographic (and yet he was quite literate as *Mein Kampf* reveals, political bore that it is).

How, then, would you draw him? As the Fuhrer in a leather great coat, seen from behind, anonymous, a figure staring into blank space... or as a child-man playing with his model buildings in the penthouse of the Chancellery... or perhaps you would steal from Fuseli's *The Dream*, show him as a demon monkey sitting beside a reclining unconscious neo-classical beauty as an insane war-horse stares through the curtains... or perhaps you would be a bit more modern, a block of Horbiger ice melting before an infernal sun (which could be mistaken for a furnace)... or you might go completely off the catalogue, go conceptual, because after all isn't that what Adolf Hitler was? A conceptual artist?

Gropius couldn't draw, and that didn't stop him from being a renowned and successful architect. It certainly didn't stop Hitler. He realized his fantasies through Speer and Gisseler and a number of other German architects, like a Master marshalling his students to assist in painting a giant mural (of the Apocalypse). He was, perhaps, one of the first media artists, anticipating the production-line methods of Picasso, Dali, and more obviously Andy Warhol. He started with postcards, did postage stamps, official photographs, marketed his own image and attitude. He did radio, he did theatre. He was a personality cult, the basis of any successful artist, be it Richard Wagner or John Lennon.

Albert Speer said it would be a mistake to look for a Hitlerian form of architecture, that he was merely a grandiose version of Troost neo-classicism. The art critic Robert Hughes didn't agree when he did his Third Reich architecture episode for the BBC documentary *Visions of Space* (2003). Hughes got quite moralistic about the bad vibes left by the Nazis in Berlin, Munich and Nuremberg: "It was about architecture as ideology: function, obedience, efficiency." This is the *de rigueur* response for the times, of course, and it might even be correct. Yet, when you look at the Hamburg flak tower in today's incarnation as a music school and nightclub, where is the evil? Removed from its original context, Hitler's *weltanshauung* is weak. Even Stonehenge requires imagination to see murder. Shape, by itself, is neutral. It requires the living to make it erotic.

Adolf Hitler: who was he? An artist, or just someone who existed—

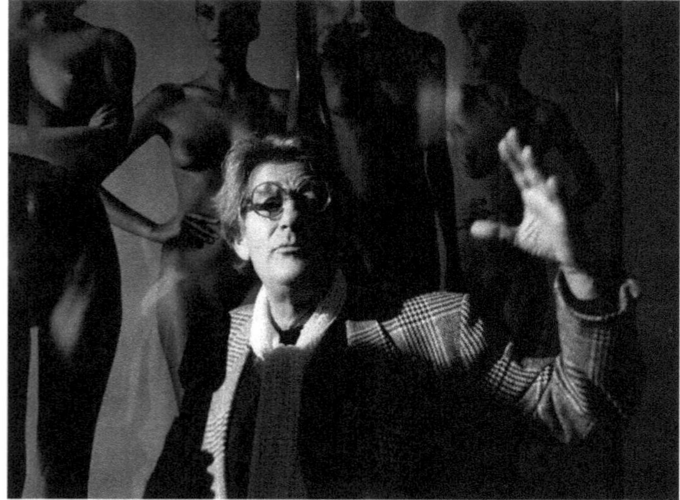

Helmut Newton: Death of a Voyeur

Deja Vu And The Chemical History

Art is the sexual perception of an object. Hence the obsession of the artist with the human form, especially that of young beautiful women. Passivity in the rendering is futile—there must be a flaw. Sometimes this manifests as a perverse form of eroticism, a dangerous mix of taboo and sexual ritual, innocence on the edge of corruption. As any artist knows, there are always two sides to a face... the shadow sphere of flaw and perfection... so the artist seeks to reveal the concealed, secret persona. And who understood and exploited this better than Helmut Newton, the great purveyor of chic porn who was killed recently when his Caddy SUV slammed into a wall as he exited his favorite L.A. hangout, the Chateau Marmont.

The Marmont is the famous replicate hotel of the stars, and therefore notorious for scandal. More often than not today's travel guides draw attention to the fact that John Belushi blew his mind here in 1982 with a speedball... that a drunken Jim Morrison dangled from a balcony, almost fell... that someone from Led Zeppelin rode a Harley through the lobby... and in the old days Jean Harlow, Robert Mitchum, Greta Garbo, Montgomery Clift, Carole Lombard and the likes had occasion to live here... or at least use it for romantic assignations.

A mixture of revivalist French medievalism and California deco, the Marmont sits above Sunset Boulevard like a bordello for the damned. No wonder Newton liked to winter over here, consort with the living famous and the famously dead. He actually used the hotel as a location for his 1992 series *Domestic Nudes* [naked women in various secluded moments by the gas range, the washer/dryer, etc, their sexual beings liberated by paradox]. "My favorite photos are often those which evoke a strong feeling of I have been here before," he says in his autobio, and certainly twenty six years of annual stopovers at the Marmont would enhance the *deja vu* and the chemical history left by yesterday's stars.

Given his obsession with grand hotels, grand cars and hot women, you have to wonder if his death was staged. Yes, he was 83 years old and had an on-going heart condition... and yes, he said not so long ago that he was tired of photographing nudes... he convulses, hits the gas pedal, plows into the wall, the air-bag deploys and he's smothered into silence... maybe. There's something sublimely symmetrical about his death that it makes it a pure extension of his work, like the *mise en scene* he would prepare in his notebook before going on a fashion shoot.

The sudden violence of it has the grim comedy of an incident from Ballard's auto/sex fetishist film *Crash* or the elegant death launch of Elizabeth Taylor in a Sunbeam Alpine at the end of *Butterfield 8*. The fact that he clips a UPA photographer just before hitting the wall adds symbolism, suggests predestination. Hence he joins the pantheon of auto-crash victims that includes such fashion luminaries as Grace Kelly, Jayne Mansfield and Princess Di... and James Dean, of course, who also visited the Chateau.

The recent publication of *Helmut Newton: Autobiography* suggests that the "summing up" has already occurred, his secrets revealed, his notoriety ensured. Certainly there will be more photographs to be seen, and judging by the brief journal clips included to close out his autobiography, the publication of his full working journal is inevitable. Bring it on. The journal will be the real testament of Helmut Newton.

Autobio Automatic/ Autobio Autofetish

The autobio appears to have been dictated for a ghost writer. The voice is conversational, anecdotal, often vulgar. You can imagine Helmut lying on his leather couch in his Monaco condo with a black sleep mask over his eyes, a silver Olympus micro recorder in hand. He will start with his childhood in Berlin, his mother and father, his older half-brother... his down-town secular bourgeois family ["more German than Jewish"] and the maid who gave him his first hard-on... or was it his mother... or that woman in the black evening dress in the resort hotel at Heringsdorf.

Maybe he mutters "I'm not a fighter, I'm a fucker" thinking this is a good theme for his life, but when the book comes to print, this insight gets pushed back to the Australian years when he's conscripted into the Aussie army straight from the enemy alien detention camp... no fighting, just some rural fruit picking and chauffeur detailing.

Yes, you've heard it/seen it before. The spoiled kid who is dressed to look like a girl by his doting mother, is hopeless in school and his only interest is his big brother's girlie magazines. The confessions are funny, tacky, at times almost fantastic... and certainly map out the sociology of the exhibitionism that is to later characterize his art.

While Newton is quick to lay claim on many women as lovers or objects of fantasy, this self-admitted apprentice bungler gives his photography mentor "Yva" [Else Simon] the measure of professional respect and affection this tragic figure deserves. Newton is in awe of her, learns the basic studio chops. Yet although he says he made many mistakes in the darkroom, he has the intuition and the backing to escape the Nazi roundup in 1938.

Yva refuses to leave Berlin, and consequently dies in the Auschwitz concentration camp. Later Newton will describe how he returns to Berlin in 1958, finds Yva's studio intact, unused and almost empty, save for some of her fashion prints, still on the wall... an inadvertent shrine that becomes symbolism and a marker for the Berlin of his youth.

> "Many of my fashion photographs have been taken in places that remind me of my childhood."

Sex at fourteen? Still wearing short pants and sporting a concealed erection behind a copy of *The Times*, the young Helmut rides the tram to the American School, encounters a 21 year old fashion model, and soon has her coming to the Neustaedter garden for clandestine encounters.

Shortly afterwards he joins a club and takes up some serious swimming, falls in love with a champion called Illa, and soon they are having heavy sex in his room with the approval of his mother. The body of the athlete defines one aspect of the future "Helmut Newton woman", as does the faux lesbian motif of the cross-dresser.

> "...there was a girl, a printer in the darkroom, who was an ex-Bauhaus student. She used to wear black velvet suits with a white shirt and collar. She also wore a monocle— that just drove me sexually insane."

Helmut reminisces erotically, geographically... youth and apprenticeship in Berlin, failed photographer and gigolo in Singapore, alien confinement and patriation in Australia, wedding photographer and marriage in Melbourne, breakout and fashion stringer in London, Paris, New York... jet-set famous in Monaco and L.A. ...with sidebars to Berlin, Rome, and places beyond. Politically, strategically, aesthetically Paris is the place that allows him to break the boundaries of conventional fashion illustration.

Skillfully using symbolism and anti-fashion accessories such as medical harnesses and equestrian riding gear, he pushes the envelope of erotic style and dramatization. Fashion takes on a dangerous edge as it reconciles objective ugliness with exotic beauty. How does he get away with it? Paris is the right place at the right time, a relaxed cultural oasis in which the new pornographers are already de-constructing the visual and literary arts. Maurice Gerodias of the Olympia Press publishes Pauline Reage's *The Story of O* about a beautiful though masochistic Parisian photographer who becomes the willing sex slave of a group of male libertines at a mysterious chateau... and Helmut, with a large supply of adventuress *Vogue* models and movie starlets at his disposal, takes his cue.

Deep Shadow Fever

His first photo, taken in the Berlin subway [untergrund] with a cheap box camera, fails to turn out. But despite this initial failure, it establishs his predilection for using available or indirect light. He says he was influenced by Brassai and other night photographers, although the obsession is clearly sociological, a condition of his early environment. It should also be noted that the photography of the period is almost exclusively black and white, so that the use of shadow is considered part of the art. This is evident in the nocturnal film noir cinematography of the era, developed from the expressionist lighting of live theatre, and the staged *mise en scene*.

Yet There Is Another Psychological Driver In The Registry....

The deep shadow fever of the Berlin homosexual underground provides Newton with the imagery of the impersonator. As a motif, cross-dressing is cyclical within the fashion industry and also within the tradition of the Theatre. As always, this specialty has economic largesse within the confusing culture of power and sexual fantasy. In his autobio, he describes how his brother Hans takes him into the red light district, points out the famous prostitute Red Erna, who wears red boots and carries a whip.

Overheard At The Bar Marmont

Behind the bamboo and the mohair walls, etc. Voices of men and women... some husky, like the nico hustlers of the movie industry... late Age Valley Girl... a bit player... screenwriter... a magazine photographer, a dope dealer, who knows. Pineapple vodkas, scotch, Coronas, etc.

The perspectives that he could achieve with a Rolli 80 mm lens and a 6x6 cm piece of film were simply amazing.

A Rolliflex? He never used a Rolliflex... he used a 35 mm Canon EOS.

The early stuff, my man. Twin reflex.

He's like Shakespeare... his work is so imitated now that he gets credit fer photos he never took.

If someone told me he was a Nazi, I'd believe it.

He's Jewish.

Stuff looks Nazi to me... same dark theatrical stuff. Nazis were into dress-up sex... Christ, Goebbels was banging everything he could get his hands on.

It always seemed to me that WWII took place in some mythological realm... Kennedy is like that too.

Reifenstahl—you can see that influence in Newton's work... well maybe not hers exactly but they both draw from the same *uberfraulein* image.

Berlin bondage, man. Ever see Marlene Dietrich? *Blue Angel?*

Is it on DVD?

I recommend you watch *Mephisto*... Klaus Maria Bander... if you wanna see that scene.

What scene?

Berlin in the 30s... Nazis, art, kink.

You guys are talkin bullshit... Newton is a great photographer. Edgy, he's edgy.

His photos were for men and made to express his concept of eroticism—not true portraits of the women he photographed.

Yeah? All the women I know like them.

Hookers and art sluts... right?

"Not true portraits..." Jeeze. So your idea of a true portrait is one that suits the vanity of the subject?

Hey, you're on it, man... Margaret Thatcher hated the photo he took of her.

He did Margaret Thatcher? This I gotta see—

Relax... it's a portrait.

You mean like Karsh?

Now there's a guy who played to vanity.

Was Newton homosexual? They always take the best photos of women.

Bull-sheet...

Bet he was.

His wife is a photographer... got a show biz name.

We know—"Koala Springs".

[laughter, hoots, expletives]

It's Alice Springs, you ass. Better than Helmut by a mile.

Listen to to yerself, would ya... better than the maestro.

I happen to know that Newton considered his work fake compared to hers.

Was she in the Cadillac when it crashed?

(heavy whisper) Look... there's Britney.

(low) Is that her? Is she in town?

That's not Britney.

Who's the old guy with her? Helmut Newton, isn't it?

No way... supposed to be dead, right?

The Making Of The Voyeur

> "I would stand on the balcony looking up at the sky to watch the zeppelin come in from America, and I would look down the street and watch the pitched battles between the cops and communists and Nazis."

Imagine this scene as a large photo mural. While it has the surreal logic of a dream, in fact it is a German reality, and neatly encapsulates the collapse of the Weimar Republic. Even though Newton was later forced into hiding and wandering the streets after his old man is taken away by the Nazis, there's never any sense of fear or bitterness. In fact, it was an opportunity for adventure, and he slid easily into the fantasy of romantic intrigue on the Italian ocean liner that took him to safety and exile in Singapore.

While he didn't have to be a Berliner to conceive of his burlesque dressup photo featuring his wife June as Adolph Hitler and the Texan model Jerry Hall as Eva Braun, the native view gives this work a certain insider cachet. The theatrical aspect of Nazism is part of the totalitarian desire for spectacle, like the large cast location theatre of Eisenstein or the unrealized fantasies of Antonin Artaud. Newton admired the work of Leni Reifenstahl, regardless of whether or not she was a Nazi whore. Sado-masochism demands a wide cast and a big shadow.

The Ideal Model

> "Men were completely capitvated by her, followed her immediately, sensed her sexuality. There seems no rhyme or reason to all this. I have no explanation why one girl seduces the camera and another one doesn't."

While Newton said that he liked all shapes and sizes of women—and indeed he used a wide physiological cast, as the perverse demands it—without question he liked the "Big Nude" best of all.

Art Pimp: Scene From A Journal

> "...the interest that the writer has in my model seems to increase. His wife seems not to mind, and they manage to stay near us whenever possible. As the (shoot) rather bores me, I decide to enter into the game with them. Every night, before dinner, I dress the model myself. I choose her clothes carefully, making her look more daring and *risque* as the week goes on; what I don't find among the clothes we have with us to photograph, I borrow from a nearby boutique. Her skirts are getting shorter, her necklines more revealing. The writer's excitement mounts, and I become more and more interested in my experiment in fashion; the model's attitude does not change, she stays cool but not uninterested."

As you can see, this incident during a shoot on the Atlantic island of Lanzorote [Canaries] in 1970 contains all the rationale of a classic Newton pictorial tease. Recorded in his journal, it sounds like something from Jerzy Kosinski's novel *Steps*. Game protocol and infantilism are sequential for both the exhibitionist and the voyeur.

Consider these images: chick kneels on the bed, a riding saddle on her back, a dadaist metaphor that begs the question: victim or perpetrator? A shapely woman in a business suit reclines against a balcony [and the city skyline], skirt raised just enough to expose her thighs and the lower harness of her garter belt... or woman in red lies on a black leather couch bound by a rope to a naked dummy wearing red pumps... who is her double. Etc.

A classic Newton is his 1987 *Vanity Fair* photo of Brigitte Nielsen at the Old Beach Hotel in Monte Carlo. Photographed from behind, the tall shapely Nielsen dominates the foreground like a giant robot chick from the Planet Bondo. Her swim suit is merely a harness, more like a holster belt for a ray gun than a piece of clothing. The earthlings sit in the pool, smiling like condemned idiots.

While Newton was never interested in making movies, he did create compressed scenarios. Like a young girl who grows tired of simple domestic games, then rearranges her dolls in pornographic positions, Newton's psychology seems completely female. He prefers dummies and cross-dressing women over male models.

His double-figures are narcissist, women posing before mirrors or with other women or dummies. Even if the camera is masculine as it approaches a hooker on an ancient shadowy street at night, the agenda is always the same: masturbation.

Photography & Witchcraft

There's nothing spiritual about Newton's art, although it does display a sense of the occult. Night photography and ritual sexuality often sets a Newton scene, so that many commentators have described him as a corrupt marquis like de Sade playing warlock in his chateau. Red eye flash, usually the dreaded mistake of the amateur, is exploited by HN in a 1971 "accident" in Rome when experimenting with a new shadow-guard called a Coffin Ring. "Devil eyes" or "zombie eyes" were a cliché in the movies even then, although, when applied to fashion, they were absolutely avant-garde.

A woman in an ethereal evening gown emerging from the shadowless darkness assumes a supernatural aura as her eyes gleam dangerously. Once again the maestro finds a way to draw attention to the subject, shake up the fashion *status quo*. Red Eye makes the non-figurative subject a figurative description which includes not only the physical but also the metaphysical.

Strangely, Newton is drawing from a tradition within photography that has sought to use the process as a means of extra-sensory perception. In 1891 the notorious Swedish playwright August Stringberg attempted a series of "psychological" portraits while living in—of all places—Berlin. These were done using a lensless camera [Strindberg believed the lens distorted reality] and long exposures.

Terrain Vague

Just what is a Helmut Newton worth? The sold-out edition of prints *Sie Kommen I & II* are reputedly worth more than $55,000. One panel features four naked models approaching the camera, the other the same models in the same stride but dressed in fashion couture. Curiously, this "image within an image" is neither erotic nor revelatory, as the women remain civilized and unreal in both photos. The idea is an inversion of the fashion dummy before and after clothing.

According to an article in *American Photo* [Feb 2000] the record price for a Newton was set in 1993 when his 45 print portfolio *Private Property* sold for $24,150. This consists of 75 numbered prints and 10 lettered artist's proofs. Apparently some of these images are now circulating at large prices, culled from broken collections. Currently a few used lst edition copies of his historic first US collection *White Women* [Stonehill 1976] are available from booksellers on the Internet for anything between $25 and $200... which seems like a bargain considering that dealers who specialize in Helmut Newton are selling single prints from $3,500 to $11,000. His last book—a giant 66 lb retrospective called *Sumo* that requires its own stand—was sold for $1500 when it was first published in 2000 by Taschen of Cologne... but is now worth $3000... if you can find a copy.

According to some dealers, more of Helmut Newton's work is sold to women than men.

White Women

Helmut Newton says this 1976 coffee table book was his wife's idea, so that his stuff would be taken seriously. And yes, its influence was phenomenal, as women in the art scene began to affect the Helmut Newton "look", a risque combo of punk deco and trash designer. For a while not only the Club scene but also Halloween was redefined by Helmut Newton.

The provocative title befits the provocative imagery. The transformation of high fashion tableauxs into pure voyeurism where elegant women are suspended in erotic moments within exotic settings that leave their target lovers off-camera. These shots are always a prelude for other shots that remain unpublished except in our imaginations. Sometimes the women are waiting, clearly positioned for sex, anonymous exhibitionists in a private dreamscape... the baroque decadence of a European luxury hotel, a walled garden, the swimming pool of a private villa, a yacht in the Mediterranean, etc... sometimes the women are in transit, as if fleeing some debacle or rushing to join an orgy.

The few men that are seen remain passive and anonymous, like crash-test dummies dressed for the occasion. For example, the rectilinear view of a woman lying with her lover beside a black Citroen. The man is concealed by the woman, whose back is to the camera. As usual, the woman is naked except for her red elevator shoes which gleam like lipstick. The ground is covered with dead leaves, an *ursatz* which heightens the romanticism of the image. The passive man, still wearing his suit, becomes a bi-gender surrogate for the photographer... who, by declension, becomes you, the viewer. While Newton says his work is all documentary and never fantasy, always based on experience, this can be discounted as political modesty. It must be noted that not all these photos are successful: some are merely weird, succumb to the infantilism of perverse sexual decorum. The documentary gestalt overrides the surrealism, challenges the notion of art. Hints of bi-sexual adventurism adds to the general vibe of old Euro decadence in a contemporary ethos.

Two years later [1978] he follows with *Sleepless Nights* which clearly shows his debt to the culture of bondage. Various models pose wearing various medical support gear... Paloma Picasso, Suzy Dyson, Jane Kirby, breasts exposed, wearing neck braces... or the famous *Saddle I* photo of the crouching model wearing a horse saddle.

Like all fashion illustrations, the poses are stagey, like window dressings with dummy models. The satire over-powers the sexual possibilities and draws into question the whole notion of high fashion. The imagery is caricature yet delivered in a documentary manner.

Women as animals, prisoners within a culture, like the decorative public statuettes in any major European city... or women serenely indifferent to the world and their roles as totemic sex icons.

Fashion advertising is always symbolism, as the target viewer must be able to interact and idealize the self.

The provocation in this collection is established immediately with the dust jacket, which is of a man in drag, an impersonator in full burlesque. The blackened eyes and red lipstick mouth are ambiguous enough... but not the heavy masculine shoulders. Surprise and revulsion give way to humour, although outrage will always be an option.

A risky way to make a first impression, and perhaps the reason *Sleepless Nights* is considered less successful than the ultra chic *White Women*. Throughout this period, Newton is publishing in *Vogue* (international), *Elle, Queen, Nova, Constanze, Playboy, Vanity Fair*, and others.

Waiting For Helmut

A famous Hollywood actress is waiting in her hilltop house for a famous European photographer. He was supposed to have been here an hour ago and she's still waiting, wondering if she really wants to go through with this anyway. Guy doesn't like makeup, thinks movie stars have no patience... and, well, he's notorious. What would he want her to do? Will he bring one of those plastic dummies, make her pose in a compromising position? No. It's a portrait shoot. He might make her look ugly, but he won't make her look dirty.

She knows he photographed Jody... not so bad. Jody didn't like them at first although now she thinks they're o.k., cool even. He photographed old Liz too, sitting in her pool. Well, she would have to sit in it at her age. Angelica... looks like a man... well, a nice man. Catherine Deneuve... god she's so beautiful, how could she not photograph well... that one he took of her in Paris, 1976... cigarette in her mouth, bra slightly dipped... so sexy, so cool, so nice. Could she pull something like that off? Available... but unavailable. Sure.

Charlotte Rampling... how the camera loved her... bet she wouldn't pose like that now.

TV is running, sound off. Breaking news, another smashup, somebody in a silver SUV. It barely registers... just more media noise. She gets up, looks at the clock, avoids the mirror. Where is this guy? She must have it wrong. Maybe the tranks are messin with her head... maybe her press agent screwed up. She picks up her cell, wanders to the sliding glass door, looks down the canyon at the city, already masked in a faint lead haze. Up here, though, the sunlight falls clear and clean on the turquoise pool. Pluto, her faithful German shepard, is sprawled beside the recliner, so still he could be dead.

The young gardener is working as usual in her neighbour's yard, just below the terrace. Blond hardbody. Another wannabe... uh, maybe not. Maybe he likes being a gardener.

She goes into the bedroom, tosses the cell on the gold thread duvet, goes into the walk-in closet... shoes, she must have a hundred pair of shoes... sandals, walkers, pumps, stilettos, elevators... yes, the elevators.

When she walks out to the pool, she's naked except for her gold high heels with the 5 inch risers... and her sunglasses, the Alfred Sungs she bought the other day in Century City. She steps carefully over the dog, starts a slow walk of the pool perimeter. The hell with *Vanity Fair* and that photographer... Helmut-wherever-you-are. This is the last time she'll walk naked, confident someone somewhere is watching.

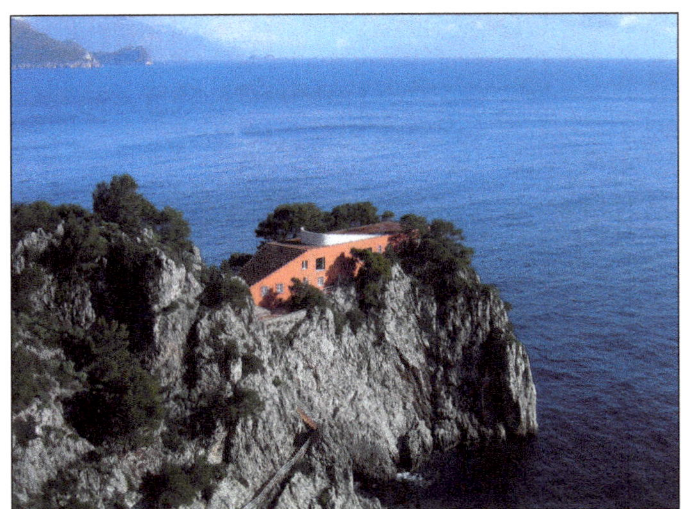

Malaparte: Portrait of an Italian Surrealist

Malaparte & Godard

"Every time I hear the word culture I bring out my cheque book," says Jack Palance in his role as a dominant ape in Godard's *Contempt* (*Le Mepris*, 1963). Actually he plays an American producer called Jerry Prokash who's in Italy to make a movie about Ulysses travelling hither and yonder in the Ancient World. The director? None other than the celebrated Fritz Lang, who plays himself. The Ulysses/Odyssey stuff is just a backdrop to a neurotic sex drama between the French chauvinist script writer Paul (Michel Piccoli) and his unhappy attractive wife Camille (Bridgett Bardot). It's familiar Godard territory, one he has explored more successfully in *Breathless, Pierrot Le Fou, Le Petit Soldat*... same principals, different actors.

Godard's male leads are usually just totems for himself, as they dress pretty much the same movie to movie: small fedoras and tight suits, which make them peculiar French parodies of American movie hoodlums of the film noir era. Godard's films are always improvisations, photo essays made on the fly... so repetition of theme is to be expected. Many people like *Contempt*, see it as a hip insider's view of the movie business, and a damning of the Hollywood method—that crass capitalistic credo that brutalizes old Europe and her prerogative in Art. Combine this with the usual Godard pop-art funkiness—that iconographic magazine ad style—wherein he collages an American star with a French star, has them directed by the maestro Fritz Lang, and what have you got? A post-modern multi-cultural classic?

Maybe. Others think this expensive in-joke (the slagging of producer Joseph E. Levine) is a tedious journey to Capri that's held up far too long in the writer's condo as he works out his neurosis about writing and women... and the only good parts are when Bardot removes her clothes. Real-time drama... an aesthetic ideal, sure, but the conversation better be good. Is it? Sometimes, but most surely repetitious. Are they going to accept Palance's invitation to the shoot on Capri? If so, is Paul pimping his wife? Ten thousand bucks for a script about Ulysses and Penelope is a lot more than he can get for writing a stage play in Paris. He slaps her around, screws her, has a glass of wine, a smoke... hmm, ten thousand bucks. At the core, you know he's a pimp, but there's a lot more talking and self-evaluation to go through before you're let out of this unfinished condo.

They go... finally, thank God. And it's on Capri that you see the real star of *Contempt*, the villa on the cliff known by architects and artists far and wide as the Casa Malaparte. The location is stunning: a rooftop patio high above the Mediterranean, near the rock of the sirens and the villa where the Roman Emperor Tiberius communed with the Gods. More or less the gateway to the mythological realm of the old Greco-Roman world. Bardot certainly looks good swimming naked in the warm blue water beneath the rugged limestone cliffs while the film crew goes about its business on the roof of the villa. The play-within-the-play... the script writer watches his wife from the boat landing below while the director watches his actors go through their moves on the patio above.

The curse of History, or the blessing of Modern Art? The setting here is brilliant insofar as the Casa Malaparte is a hybrid of ancient and modern architecture. In truth, the building looks quite shabby in 1962, its low squat profile, flaking stucco and rusting barred windows making it look like an abandoned artillery bunker from the Second World War. Could be German, could be Italian—just like its creator, the writer Curzio Malaparte. Despite the condition, the dualism of the concept dominates... the rectilinear modernism of the actual building acting as support for the 32 steps that fan upwards to the flat roof like an inverted pyramid, creating an open platform theatre. No walls, no railings, no parapets... nothing to impede the view or the communion. This temple minimalism with its straight-line modernism and curved-line paganism exists in contradiction, a terminus to nowhere and somewhere simultaneously.

Art gallery primitivisim and the existential moment? Palance could care less. His only real interest is the pursuit of Bardot, who finds herself drawn to his brute animal vitalism like an Ayn Rand woman who is always drawn to a man with balls and money. It certainly isn't a relationship based on conversation, as neither can speak the other's language.

They split together for Rome, driving a red sports car, another favorite prop of Godard's. And of course they crash and die in short order... the usual Godard fatalism. An easy moral about Europe and American capitalism? Or is Godard the Marxist tipping his hand towards the auratic violence of Futurist art and the cleansing fascism it extols? Or....

Malaparte & Kurt Erich Suckert

The surrealist duality of Curzio Malaparte a.k.a. Kurt Suckert (1898-1957) is rooted in his origin—German father, Italian mother. "I try to be Italian like all the rest and I can't succeed," he says somewhere. He fought for Italy in the WW I, was wounded in a mustard gas attack near Reims, an event which is blamed for his death in 1957 from lung cancer... although photographs show him smoking cigarettes like most of his contemporaries.

Photos also show him groomed in the style of Rudolph Valentino, fencing in Milan... or posing naked in the snow in Finland... talking with fellow writer Alberto Moravia [*Contempt* is based on Moravia's story *Il disprezzo* a.k.a. *A Ghost At Noon*]... looking unshaven and somber in a police mug shot... wearing a Captain's uniform of the Italian Alpine division... stripped-down and straddling a racing bike on the roof of the Casa Malaparte... or standing on the trapezoidal steps of a small church on the island of Lipari where he was exiled by Mussolini in 1933 (he taunted Il Duce for his poor choice of neckties). According to Moravia (in his *Life of Moravia*) "The arrest was a joke... Malaparte saw his friends, his women, strolled along the beach in a bathing suit, holding his Lipari greyhound on a leash." Mouthy, theatrical, a self-promoter... his whole life is a fiction, a dream metaphor just like surrealist rhetoricist Breton's blazing locomotive in a wild forest.

He embraces fascism, Futurism—indeed his writing gleams with the exalted poetic violence of a machine cult. He likes the idea of the fascist New Man, so in 1926 he adopts a new persona by changing his name to Curzio Malaparte (a crafty play on "Kurt" and "Bonaparte"), a manufactured Mediterranean handle that seems to sit well with the image of the fascist black shirt. Yet he's always in contradiction, a loose canon for whom propaganda is just another form of poetry. He visits Russia, writes a book on Lenin, has clear admiration for the machine-model of the Soviet. He visits Germany, calls Hitler a woman (*Une Femme Hitler*, 1932), has the SS talking to their opposites in Rome. He pisses off the Foreign Minister Italo Balbo, is arrested in 33 and exiled to the island of Lipari near Sicily. He is led in handcuffs through Naples, is followed by a dog called Frebo. Solitude now becomes his muse, and when he's repatriated he buys property on the eastern end of Capri, starts building a house on the dangerous cliffs of Punta Massullo.

"When I enter a grand hotel, my heart leaps with joy." (Malaparte, as quoted by Moravia)

Malaparte & Adalberto Libera

Many commentators see the Casa Malaparte as Malaparte's greatest work, surpassing even his superb writing. Certainly the project fits well with the Futurist idea of the Artist as Creator... a megalomaniacal notion also adopted by the French avant-gardist poet Antonin Artaud for his notion of a new theatre (Theatre of Cruelty). The stylistic contradiction— is it rationalist or anti-rationalist—fits perfectly with the surrealist dualism of conscious and unconscious expression. The rationalism comes from the original architect Libera (1903-63), who was published in an early issue of *Prospettive,* a.k.a *Perspective* (1937-52) "an international journal of culture and the arts" that Malaparte produced and edited following his release from confinement.

Libera was a favored architect with the fascist ruling elite, a hot item following the construction of his design for a new central post-office in Rome. The clean, simple arcade style of the post office's massed arches reconciled classicism with modernism, an integral precept of fascist aesthetic theory... and also seemed to play on the melancholy "Nietzche Autumn" atmosphere of the Italian surrealist/metaphysical painter Giorgio de Chirico, also published in *Prospettive* (strangely, de Chirico never mentions Malaparte in his elegantly paranoid *Memoir*). Libera's original design was so linear and rational it was institutional in the most basic sense, with nothing to distinguish it from a primitive Mediterranean stucco box, and could easily be mistaken for a prison or a military bunker. In this sense, it was merely a drawing in progress, a positioning of a shape in space. No matter—Libera and Malaparte fell out during the initial stages of construction, and Malaparte was left to continue building in whatever direction his contrarian mind led him. The dangerous siting and unregulated aesthetic—this is no house for kids—is viewed both as religious and classical, a sort of retro-pantheism worthy of the anthropomorphic world of the pre-Christian Romans. Close to the sun, close to the sea... close to Death. Casa Malaparte is a dream of flying, a dream of falling.

In his masterpiece, *The Volga Rises In Europe* (1943), Malaparte describes visiting a Finnish observation post during the brutal siege of Lenningrad. This "picket-post" is within 200 yards of the Russians, a simple bunker of stacked pines, mud and snow, manned by a single sentry—the *vartio*, the "dead man", he who walks the point. Malaparte's sympathy for the man assigned to this suicidal location is enormous, so he leaves a couple of packs of ciggies behind as consolation. The description of the visit is grim and clairvoyant. Malaparte concludes: "As we trudge in single file along the narrow path a stray bullet whistles past my ear and lodges with a ping in a tree trunk. But I scarcely notice it. I am haunted by the memory of that wrinkled, tear-stained face, I cannot forget that weeping man standing alone in the forest." Describing himself? Or the archetype of Man in a hostile universe? Casa Malaparte is a picket-post on the edge of Nowhere. As the architect Robert Venturi asks, "Do its steps lead to infinity?"

Malaparte And Fiction

Often quoted from Malaparte's bizarre non-fiction "novel" *The Skin* (*La Pelle*, 1952) is his description of a visit by the German General Erwin Rommel to the Casa Malaparte, en route to North Africa and a critical defeat by the British at el-Alamein. Some take it at face value, some as fiction. The "unreliable narrator"? Written as journalism, it reads as fiction. Written as fiction, it reads as poetry. Sound like the American "new journalism" of Wolfe, Mailer, Thompson, Didion, *et.al.*? It certainly does. A rejection of the fraudulent institutional 3rd person objectivity, the style is a return to the private, uninhibited view of the original 1st person singular journal writing. Cicero... Dafoe, Boswell, Byron... William Russell... Henry Miller, Jack Kerouac, Jean Genet, Anais Nin... Alexander Trocchi, William Burroughs... and of course Michael Herr. Herr's brilliant book about the Vietnam War, *Dispatches*, with its hallucinatory poeticism and transcendental values is clearly related to Malaparte's war journals/novels, especially *The Volga Rises In Europe* (1943) and *Kaputt* (44), even if Herr was unaware of Malaparte or his writing. Culture is an evolution, not a mimicry. Culture is extra-sensory, extends in sleep and dream.

Many resent Malaparte's insertion of himself into the central moments of 20th century history. Like some ancient prophet from the Bible, he's always there for the big moments and freely mixes fantasy with fact. Narcissism, *Dux Italiano*, the liar as artist and the nostalgia of the Mediterranean delusion. Sure... but the guy is a great writer.

Rommel asks Malaparte if he built this villa himself. No, he bought it as is... but he designed the scenery. The conceit is a joke, a surrealist pun. It pisses off the ideologue and the institutional maven. Truth is external event, not the chimera of the sleeping mind. Surrealism is a lie, a subversion of the secular being. Automism, the occult, dead classicism, dead gods, individualism and instinct. Bad. Malaparte. Bad. Poetry cannot coexist with the facts, for poetry is the mythologizing of the Big Lie. Yes... certainly accurate reportage is politically correct, and certainly only the sophisticated can follow such trans-dimensional narratives. The greedy, self-absorbed expression of the elitist? Possibly. But then, if art isn't elitist, is it art? He painted it red, then he painted it white... then red again. What's in a color? Plenty, some think. According to Guiseppe Pardini (in his fine essay on Malaparte included in Michael McDonough's symposium) red was the preferred color of the fascist elite for their villas... or red was the color of Russia. Construction went slow when Malaparte was assigned as an Axis correspondent to cover the German invasion of Russia. As seen in *The Volga Rises in Europe*, his impressions are heretical, as they show sympathy for the adversary, and seem to reconcile the social models of Nazi Germany and Soviet Russia as similar mechanized versions of the New Man. War, indeed, is the Sorelian action drama, and he describes it with the lyricism of an action painting. A burnt female corpse, fused into the cockpit of a Russian tank, the prairie panorama of the German tanks advancing below "a screaming arch of Stukas", the faces of the dead beneath the ice fresco of Lake Lagoda... or this description of a German convoy en route from Greece to the Ukraine:

> "Instinctively one knew that beneath the mask of the dust the soldiers' faces were scorched by the sun, pinched by the Greek wind. The men sat in strangely stiff attitudes; they had the appearance of statues. They were so white with dust that they looked as if they were made of marble. One of them had an owl, a live owl, perched on his fist... the bird undoubtedly came from the Acropolis, it was one of those owls who hoot at night among the marble columns of the Parthenon."

Yes, a beautiful snapshot... laced with Mediterranean revivalist nostalgia. No wonder the Casa Malaparte in some overhead b&w photos resembles a giant tank stranded on a cliff, a dream-fusion of classicist desire and Futurist war fantasy.

Quite possibly this imagery is romanticized too, as his friend Alberto Moravia used to take walks on Capri with an owl on his shoulder [this was in 1941 when Moravia, recently married to the writer Elsa Morante, hung out on the island].

The question must be asked: if no one knew Malaparte built this house, would it still draw the same religious attention? As a statement of autobiography, the fascination is obvious. "A house like me," is how the writer himself described it. Casa come me. In its decline following Malaparte's death in 1957 it has the shabby over-weighted ugliness of bad art deco... but now, in its recently restored splendor, it has the sleek lines of a metaphysical ship. The contradiction, the dualism, is as conflicted as Malaparte's death bed membership in the Chinese Communist Party and acceptance of the Catholic Last Rites.

We're All Poets

They're taking a break during the shooting of *Contempt*. Jean Luc and Fritz are having a smoke, chatting in French... Bridgett is sunbathing on the rocks like a basking mermaid. Palance? He's in the shade of the pines, reading. He's read Malaparte's *Kaputt* and now he's reading *The Skin*. Jack knows a thing or two about war, death and destruction... he was a bomber pilot, survived a fiery crash... played a plague carrier in *Panic in the Streets* (1950), a marine in *The Halls of Montezuma* and he can dig the way it was in Naples after the Americans came... the way Curzio Malaparte describes it in *The Skin*. Grotesque, he thinks. We look like idiots, talk like Hemingway, think like Presbyterians. They say this is a masterpiece? The Rommel scene is good... Colonel Dolman, the homosexual Nazi, yeah, funny... General Cork, the Prince of Candia, Consuelo, Mrs. Flat, whores and dwarf women... and the guy called Jack. No, he's not so funny. I dunno, think maybe *Kaputt* was better, less servile. He closes the book, thinks about the other art film he was in, few years back, *The Big Knife*, the *Odets* thing... a flop, no legs, fell like shit. Maybe this Godard is gonna do the same... Palance begins to pace, recite. "I'll give you poetry! Got a whole book in my head... *The Forest of Love*, yeah, one day I'll write it all down... people will know Jack is not just a pretty face, he's a poet!"

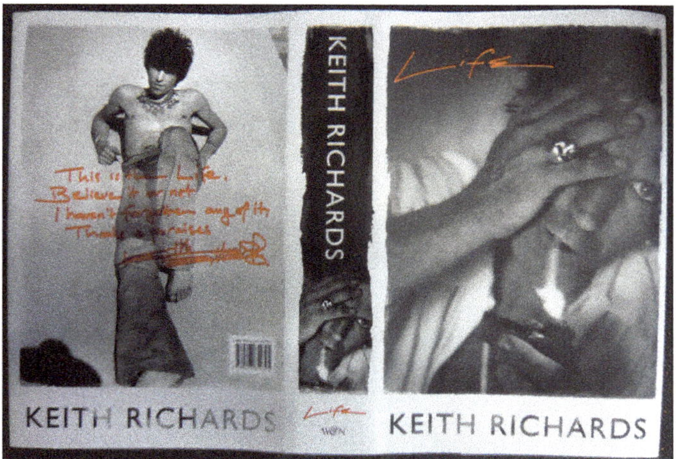

Life: Keith Richards

(with James Fox)

This book is quite an easy read, although not as raunchy as you might expect from a founding member of The Rolling Stones, and is often preoccupied with Richards' fractious relationship with Mick Jagger. It's similar to Andy Summers' *One Train Later* in this regard, where Summers' aching disappointment with Sting arcs through much of the action, and as such, is perhaps a recognizable guitarist-singer syndrome for rock and roll bands. Keith Richards certainly sees it as a syndrome, has a witty name for it, "LVS" (lead vocalist syndrome), although it could easily be designated PMS (Point Man Syndrome).

Symptoms include being a control freak, working sneaky deals behind the band's back, screwing your old lady and secretly plotting a solo career. For those who have read a lot of rock and roll gossip in *Rolling Stone* and elsewhere over the years, none of this will be news, and at times might sound like a bit of a chick "relationships" moan... and indeed, this book might be aimed at women more than men. Despite the casual obscenity, it's soft.

Even though he packs an unregistered 38 and a knife, Keith's *macho* nature is soft *macho*, the fugitive criminality of the junky pirate. When you spend so much of your life either sleeping (narced out) or performing on stage, there has to be a lot of acting going down. In this story of a rocker's transit from childhood to old age, you always see the boy in the man.

Possibly the ghost writer James Fox (acknowledged) has something to do with this persona, but for sure the editor did. This is prime-time reading, Walmart discount table stuff, 30% off and no bad dreams. No clinical sex, no true confession. Yes, the women and the groupies are mentioned, although you are left with about five or six who really mattered. For the most part, off-stage is off-stage. If you want more blow-by-blow, read the Tony Sanchez dope dealer view in *Up & Down With the Rolling Stones* (1980). Keith calls the Sanchez book tabloid but it's dramatic like a non-fiction novel, and is now a rock 'n' roll classic. These days Keith Richards has grandchildren, doesn't need that sort of notoriety, and probably isn't as interested in that old shit anyway. Other than dope, guitars and guitar playing is what he's all about, and there's plenty of that in Life... although, again, if you're a guitarist and have read the interviews over the years, you know this stuff already. In fact, you've read it in the official Stones coffee table book *According To The Rolling Stones* (2003), so you might be left thinking all the "co-writer" James Fox did was montage this existing material with a few updates by Keith on the tape recorder.

Linda Keith broke his heart, but you probably knew that. "That's the first time I felt the deep cut," says Keith, admitting that he stalked her a couple of times. Oddly, although Linda eventually became involved with Jimi Hendrix, she's still alive today. Then, of course, there's Ronnie Bennett, of the Ronettes, whom Keith met on a tour of England in the mid-sixties. Ronnie was the trophy girlfriend of the infamous American producer Phil Spector at the time, a man so jealous that when he and Ronnie were later married he had a gold coffin made for her, kept it in the basement "just in case".

Anita Pallenberg... you know about her. They had three children and would still have been together if she hadn't screwed up so badly under dope dereliction. In 1979 the toy-boy lover who shot himself playing Russian roulette was the last straw, probably, although she and Keith were no longer playing house. You might recall the particularly nasty description by some rock journalist back then that she was "now bloated beyond gender." Again, oddly, she survived this and is still alive today.

The others? You can read about them if you want. Keith likes models, especially German ones. There was Uschi Obermaier —"The best bad girl I know"—who reappeared unexpectedly in Cabo San Lucas when Keith spent a lost year there in 1982, and then vanished after her boyfriend was decapitated when he crashed his motor cycle outside of town.

This was just before he married Patti Hansen, an American model who is still his wife today. The Richards presence is still folkloric in Cabo, where many still point to a shack on the beach, say that's where he got married or got stoned, or claim to have drank Jack with him in Sammy Hagar's club Cabo Wabo. Even by then, Keith Richards was a legend, the subject of a collective hallucination. Many of you aspired to be him, just as he says "Mick was aspiring to be Mick Jagger, chasing his own phantom."

Keith mentions his friendship with John Lennon a number times, says Lennon was no good with dope, threw up easily. He admired Lennon's approach to music, the world, and indeed he had to have been affected by Lennon's assassination, although he doesn't go into it. If ever a rocker needed a reason to carry a concealed weapon, Lennon's death provided the rationale.

Lennon was an influence, no doubt about it, as he and McCartney provided the Stones with their first original song (*I Wanna Be Your Man*), which made it plain that Richards and Jagger should be writing their own material. And although Richards says he was introduced to "open tunings" on the guitar by Gram Parsons and Ry Cooder, it's possible that John Lennon may have shown the way as he started out using a banjo tuning under the tutelage of his aunt. Whatever way Keith Richards came upon the 5 string G tuning, there is no disputing its influence on the signature Stones sound, especially after *Honky Tonk Woman.* Discussing another Stones classic of the period, *Jumpin' Jack Flash,* Richards says he's heard many bands try to play it but just can't quite get it because you have to use the five string open G tuning to to get that chime. Would Johnny Winter and Rick Derringer agree? After all, they did a stunning live version of *Jumpin Jack Flash* on the 1971 album *Live Johnny Winter And* ... although you never know with Johnny, of course, as he often goes open E for his slide.

There is an interesting aside concerning the origin of this tune. Keith says it's a Richards-Jagger composition, implies the lick is all his, yet in his attractive 2002 coffee table book *Rolling With The Stones,* bassist Bill Wyman states categorically that the *Jumpin' Jack Flash* lick is his. Keith Richards describes quite clearly his song-writing method—the lick, the opening vocal phrase, with the Jag finishing off the words—and mentions nothing about Wyman when talking about *JJF.* In fact, more often than not he mocks "Bill Perks" (Wyman) for his pathological sexual gluttony and for bailing from the band back in 1992 supposedly because he'd developed a fear of flying. Could be so, and when you consider Wyman's age and his outsider status, there should be no surprise. By the early nineties, the Stones as a band were dysfunctional, and many considered them history.

Life: When is it sniping, or edgy fraternal humor, or plain brute innuendo? Mick's "tiny todger" or "Bill Perks" (Wyman), the thousand chick lothario with his own personal groupie spotter. When the Stones were living as tax exiles in France in the early seventies, Wyman started hanging out with the artist Marc Chagall; Keith Richards describes Wyman & Chagall as "one of the weirdest couples" out there. Maybe so, but the fact is Wyman's book *Rolling With The Stones* is a very good symposium of photos, art, artifacts and recollections about the Stones, tells you all you really need to know.

Keith often praises the drummer Charlie Watts, but doesn't move much charity Wyman's way (well, once, when Wyman came to see him in jail). Maybe this is why you never seem to hear the bass in the majority of the Stones recordings, especially in the pre-*Sticky Fingers* era—old Bill was only in there for the visuals.

Too much time, too much money; Keith Richards went straight from school into a rock band, never truly experienced the reality of ordinary work. He seems to have spent close to 40 years in a narco somnambulism, sleeping by day, partying by night. His anger at Jagger taking over the band seems misplaced; if Keith's going to spend most of his time doped up, hiding out like Norma Desmond in drag, missing appointments, gigs, sessions or taking an hour in the can to fix up between takes, what does he expect?

Still, it's all relative in a band of brothers, isn't it... with the appearance of Bianca, Jagger becomes insufferable, behaves with the worst case of *nouveau biche* a cat can have, hangs with the diplomats and the culture crowd. Disco was cocaine and Mick was cocaine. A betrayal of his Dartford street origin, Keith thinks. The movement from clown to pet to aristo is quite easy when you have money and all the flattery it can buy.

Keith is quite scornful about Mick's knighthood, and why not? It suggests that Mick really is the force behind the Stones, and that Mick is the person the Establishment prefers to negotiate with. Knighthood is like a gang tattoo, a snot inclusion zone, a perpetuation of that niggling class issue that the UK suffers from, that is, which side of town do you come from. These guys—the Glimmer Twins—are not from the middle exactly, they're from the hole in the middle.

Keith Richards' childhood... well, it's not *Rupert the Bear,* and it's not *Great Expectations* either, although the Dartford marsh is a bit like the bleak graveyard by the river where the boy Pip encounters the fugitive convict Abel Magwitch. Keith's mother and father split, he lives like a refugee. Yep, it's not ideal, but at least he doesn't whine about it, and you have to be impressed by how he stuck with his young son Marlon when his "marriage" to Anita Pallenberg became a thing in name only. But then again, even this isn't beyond criticism, as Marlon appears to have been looking after his dad rather than the other way around. If Keith didn't have minders, he'd be more than late. Despite his stated fastidiousness about measuring his smack intake, you recognize early on in the story that the man is a fatalist. Forget the eye shadow and the skull rings—anyone who wakes up and puts on his wife's clothes has to be.

Life is mostly the story of a junkie—the apprentice, the professional, the exhibit. The danger was that music would disappear, just as writing disappeared for the heroin author Alexander Trocchi, that the stupefaction becomes the art. The ritual and the trivia of finding and fixing... and the outsider culture of those who belong like persecuted Christians. And Williams Burroughs, the old bitch cadaver junkie, is floating around the edges of Keith Richards' recreational world, giving priestly advice about junk, i.e. apomorphine.

Did Burroughs really listen to the Stones?

Or did junkies read Burroughs?

You know the answers. Keith certainly absorbed the Burroughs-Gysin cut-up method, yet it certainly didn't make him a poet. It's a pity that he saw fit to print some of his lyrics towards the end of the book because they diminish the songs, reveal the banality within the sublime. When he went solo with the X-Pensive Winos, he proved he had a style, a dreamy nicotine sound reminiscent of Al Green, four shots of Jack and a concealed Bible. *Make No Mistake About It,* for example, is a funky fox trot with a Richards' vocal that hangs between inhalation and exhalation, pure suspension and astral detachment.

Yes, The Work Of A Maestro, Make No Mistake About It.

Gimme Shelter. The man has several houses... London, Sussex... Jamaica, France... Connecticut, British Virgin Islands and god know where else... rich enough that he never has to sell, yet withal he professes not to be materialist, even with a warehouse full of guitars, hundreds of them, not a materialist.

And you believe him.

When talking about the Klein rip-off—Alan Klein, the Stones' second manager, who swindled them by creating a mirror publishing company in the USA, sucked away the rights to such seminal songs as *Satisfaction, Angie, Wild Horses, et al*—he says: "I've made more money by giving up the publishing on *Satisfaction,* and my idea has never been to make money." And you believe him, because there's a simplicity behind the messiness of his life, a purity in his obsession with the guitar, and his place in its history. Well, some say, if he and his fellow Stones are so modest, how come they live as tax exiles? "(In the UK) the tax rate in the early 70s on the highest earners was 83%," says KR. No wonder they were forced to decamp to France (initially). Drugs aside, the move was good for them, as the double album *Exile On Main Street* followed, a basement classic from the Villa Nellcote. Now of course, no one thinks of it any other way; rock stars live wherever they want. Jagger, McCartney, Richards—you can run into one of them on a Caribbean beach anytime.

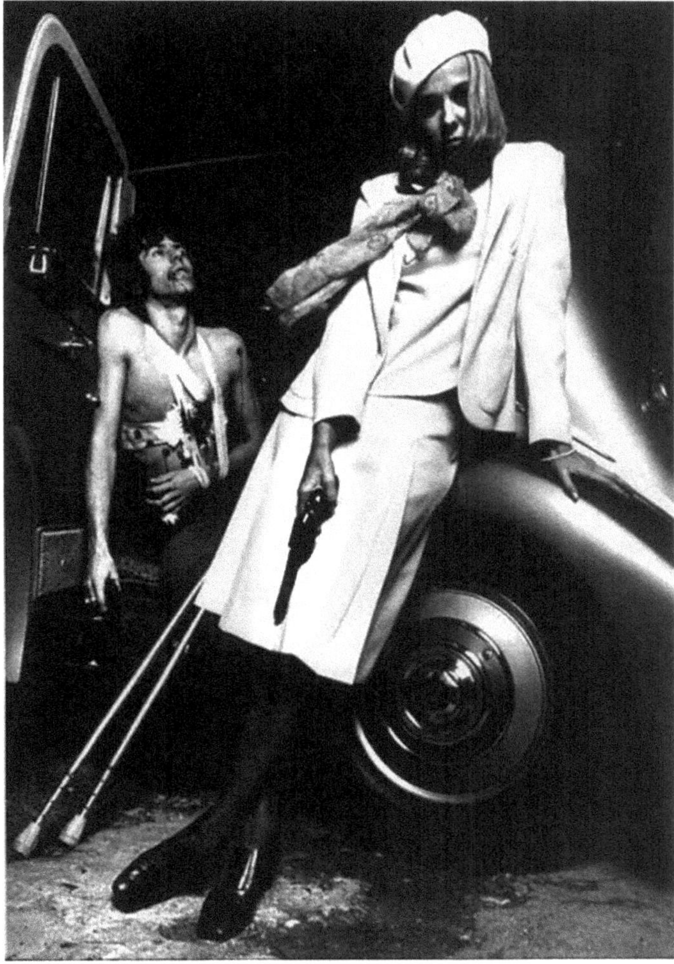

One of the more interesting episodes in the Richards legend is the *Blue Lena* story, when Keith and Anita go to Morocco, driving the famous blue Bentley across France and Spain. Brian Jones falls ill *en route*, is left by Anita in a hospital in France. "Anita, sexy fucking bitch," says Keith, obviously enjoying the memory.

And: "I have never put the make on a girl in my life... my instincts are always to leave it to the woman." Not a problem for Anita, the former German model and player in the Euro art scene. When they got to Tangier, it was all about art, wasn't it, lying around the pool being photographed by Cecil Beaton or doing hash candy in the Medina.

Tangier was a place where homoerotic artists such as Beaton and William Burroughs had easy access to young boys back in the 60s. The memoir reveals nothing new here, although the exoticism of the landscape, the decadence, the romance, in this illicit oasis at the Gates of Hercules captures the shifting morality of the times and the role that drugs played. By the time Altamont took place (Dec 6 1969), the idealism of the counter-culture movement was *passé*.

Altamont. The evil twin of Woodstock. A free concert in the bleak treeless hills south-east of San Francisco to celebrate freedom. Says Keith Richards: "In actual fact, if it hadn't been for the murder, we'd have thought it was a very smooth gig by the skin of its fucking teeth."

Is he kidding? Take another look at the film of the event, *Gimme Shelter* by the Maysles Brothers, see if you can watch it all the way. It's ugly, and shooting in color wouldn't have made it less ugly. The beautiful people stayed home, clearly, and the Stones played poorly. Once again, where is Bill Wyman in the mix? Wyman apparently missed his helicopter flight to the site, which delayed the Stones set, yet you have to wonder if he ever showed up at all as there is no bass in any of the live clips.

To a man, they were rattled. Perhaps after all these years old Keef is simply trying to finesse the memory.

He doesn't finesse his feelings about the 1970 film *Performance* which starred Anita Pallenberg and Mick Jagger, and what happened between them under the manipulative direction of Donald Cammell. Says Keith: "I really didn't like Donald Cammell, the director, a twister and a manipulator whose only real love in life was fucking other people up." Although he tries to refrain from gloating, Keith tells us that Cammell eventually shot himself as part of a videotaped suicide, no doubt his version of a Mishima exit.

Brian Jones dies, his replacement Mick Taylor stays a mere five or six years, suddenly quits, leaves Keith still wondering why. Ron Wood replaces him, and then Bill Wyman quits, and Keith wonders about this too. And then, for a while—this is the eighties—it looks as if Mick Jagger has gone his separate way and the Stones are finished as band.

But of course they're not, they acquire some new players, lumber on. It could be argued that the *Steel Wheels Tour* of 1989-90 was their best; certainly the Max concert at Wembley in 1990 is one of their best recorded concerts. How could they follow it? Bill Wyman felt they couldn't.

What is the appeal of these rock memoirs? The reliving of your own past through the celebs you considered friends? You played them at your parties, took road trips with them, got stoned with them in the darkness of your private past. Perhaps you even thought they were speaking to you in the hallucinatory way that song lyrics do. Hey, maybe you dressed like them at one time or even passed yourself off as the seventh member. "Friendship is a diminishing of distance," says Keith in one of his poetic moments.

Hmm. This makes you wonder about his statement that he hadn't visited another Stones dressing room in 20 years. Even in Rio, where they played to more than a million people on the beach in 2006.

And the final verdict?

What is, who is, Keith Richards?

"I need a jury that's at least half full of rock-and-roll players... a jury of my peers would be Jimmy Page (and the like)," he says, concerning one of his drug busts. No doubt it's been a stressful life, in no sense normal, and his survival is a thing of wonder.

When he fell out of a tree in Fiji, he concussed himself a blood clot on the brain, and that could have been it. He's a boogie man, a chemosynthetic man, a loyal man, but hey, is he a gold coffin man?

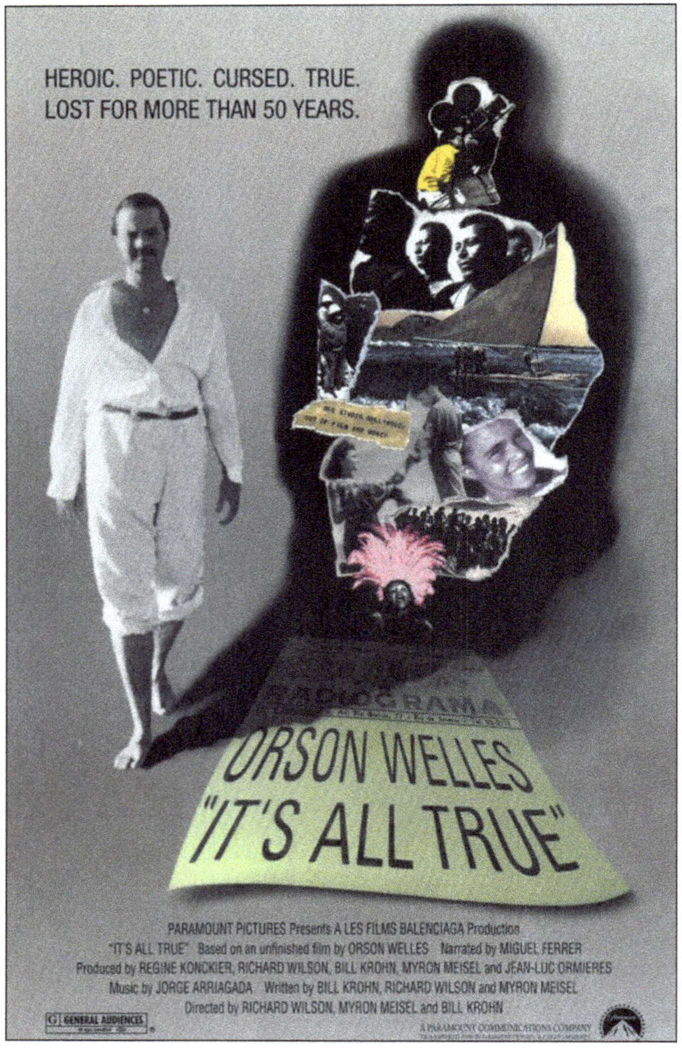

Orson Welles: *It's All True*

It's All True (1993) dir. Richard Wilson, Myron Meisel, Bill Krohn [based on salvaged footage from the 1942 Orson Welles docu-drama It's All True] | original cine by Floyd Crosby & Joe Noreigo [Bonito], Joseph Biroc, William Howard Greene, Harry J. Wild [Carnaval], George Fanto [4 Men On A Raft] | original score by Jorge Arriagada
Wilson-Meisel-Krohn docu narrator: Miguel Ferrer
editor: Ed Marx
cine: Gary Graver
sound design: Stephen Hunter Flick (Dean Beville, supervising edt)
Paramount Pictures/Les Films Balenciaga

The Shadow Flies South

Dec 7, 1941. The Japanese attack Pearl Harbour and America is at war. A couple of months later Nelson Rockefeller asks you to go to South America as a cultural ambassador. Well maybe you're strung out from your radio shows and movie projects... but hell, you're a patriot, so you pop another Dexedrine, head for Miami, catch the clipper for Rio, arrive just in time for the Carnival.

Actually, you have other reasons to fly south. For one, you've had second thoughts about marrying Dolores del Rio, despite her nifty bank account and thrillingly erotic underwear... and for two, you've been wanting to make this nice little art flick which seamlessly mixes documentary and fiction using two or three different stories set in Latin America. If the Feds will pick up some of the tab, then RKO studios will pick up the rest. Fraud? Hell, the concept is in the title: *It's All True.*

Who are you, exactly? You're Orson Welles, magician, the man who saws beautiful women in half... Orson Welles, radio actor, the man who plays *The Shadow*... Orson Welles, director, the man who made the greatest Hollywood movie ever, *Citizen Kane*... Orson Welles, world famous at 27.

The Mark Of The Voodoo

It's All True: a documentary about a documentary... or a documentary about a myth? The fascinating thing about the Wilson-Meisel-Krohn 1993 documentary about the infamous uncompleted Welles film is how it somehow becomes what Welles was aiming for all along. No script? He was the script. The man with the 16 mm Kodak in the middle of the dancing, perfumed mob of the Carnival is following the narrative instinct of the era: the lst person singular, where "I" is the unity. He could be Henry Miller, he could be Antonin Artaud... but in this case, he's Orson Welles, artist provocateur, a man well-schooled in the use of the new media to sell his personality.

In the 30s and 40s, the lst person narrative was a revolt against the institutionalized documentary narrative of the 3rd person... and the omniscience of the hidden persona. Like most artists, Welles was always at the centre of his work, whether he used a mask or not. His newspaper columns and radio spots were often unorganized improvs on political and cultural themes of the moment.

Today we see *It's All True* as a fragment made whole, a portrait of an auteur at work. Like the work of Sophocles or Homer or any number of ancients, the surviving sequences of Welles' Latin American film exist in myth, which in turn become the story, an interrupted history salvaged by legend. In a strange irony, there was never any need for Welles to complete *It's All True*, as the entire action is simply a background to his own story. Welles is a cult not because of his successes like *The War of the Worlds* or *Citizen Kane*, but because of his supposed failures, of which *It's All True* is the keystone.

It isn't surprising that politics eroded the cultural agenda of the Welles good-will mission. The authorities in both countries wanted something "pretty", a superficial view of Brazil that would encourage tourism rather than criticism and cries for social justice. Because the autocratic President Vargas had dismantled the Praza Onze—the boulevard the Carnival traditionally used as its route—and Welles decided to use the samba anthem *Farewell Praza Onze* as his soundtrack, his populist position was immediately anti-establishment. When he decided voodoo was the root of the carnival samba, and started filming in the favelas, the slum shanty towns on the hills of Rio, his cultural position was again anti-establishment.

Worse still, when the brass at RKO back in Hollywood viewed the rushes, they were unimpressed. "He's just shootin' a bunch of jigaboos jumpin' up and down, y'know?" is how Welles himself describes the studio reaction. So they cut off the money and *It's All True* was doomed.

But of course Welles has another more romantic explanation for the failure. The witch doctor who was contracted to lead the voodoo ceremonies sank a six inch steel needle through the "script" when told there was no more money. The needle had a piece of red thread, no doubt taken from the red suit that Welles wore as he filmed and danced in the Carnival procession.

All true... or just a Welles fiction?

My Friend Bonito

The Mexican story about a boy and his pet bull was already being filmed by a second unit under Norman Foster before Welles flew to Rio. Shot in black and white, the action details the strange ritual known as "the blessing of the animals", and has a child-like Antonin St. Exupery *Little Prince* feel to it. Legions of children and adults bring their pets and livestock to the village church to be blessed by the priest. Cats, dogs, chickens, mules, cattle, horses... creatures great and small. We don't really have time to consider the anthropology behind this charming fragment. The leaping sheep as seen through the church portal or the children running with their pets indicates a "peaceful kingdom" vibe in a world without brutality. The usual high and low-angle shots we associate with the Welles theatre style tantalize and leave us wondering about what might have been.

Bonito was based on a story by the acclaimed documentary filmmaker Robert Flaherty, who is surely a stylistic marker for Welles in the S.A. project. Flaherty's recurring elemental subject of Man and Nature, seen in his classic *Nanook of the North* (1922), and more obviously in *Man of Aran* (1934), is the template for Welles, especially for the third story, *Four Men On A Raft*.

And the samba story? That's all Dolores del Rio....

Carnaval

Most of the budget was spent—or squandered—during this story. Welles says he intended most of the 16 mm footage to be source material, to be restaged and refilmed in color on a soundstage later. By itself, the pandemonic dancing and "perfume wars" was insufficient, which is why Welles decided to shoot a voodoo ceremony in a favela, give drama to the action as well as trace the source of the samba.

The Wilson-Meisel-Krohn documentary uses the Carnival footage as a frame for their story of the Welles S.A. adventure. It opens with a sketched portrait of a witch doctor and Welles explaining his mission to Rio and his interest in the *samba*, closes with color footage of the Carnival, and a radio clip of Welles and Carmen Miranda explaining the various percussions used in the *samba*. Welles says he had in mind to actually intercut the third story about the voyage of the *jangadeiros* (*Four Men On A Raft*) with sequences from the Carnival.

We can see the possibilities here for dramatic contrast. The primitivism and poverty of the Fortaleza fishermen contrasted against the urban orgy of Rio in the throes of the Carnival would be one way of capturing the soul of modern Brazil. The cut-in method of the newsreel would be used, something Welles had done before in film and radio.

The Carnival as a subject was later brilliantly realized in Marcel Camus' 1958 film *Black Orpheus* (*Orfeu Negro*) wherein the Orpheus-Eurydice legend is used as a storyline, skillfully using the samba as a soundtrack and voodoo as a desperate resort by the distraught Orpheus—a Rio tramdriver, guitarist and samba leader—to reclaim his dead girlfriend Eurydice, murdered by an anonymous Carnival figure costumed as "Death". Did Camus get the idea for his film from Welles? No doubt, just as Welles himself was probably influenced by the lightweight musical *Flying Down To Rio* (1934) in which his then current paramour Dolores del Rio had a significant role, dancing the *samba* with Fred Astaire.

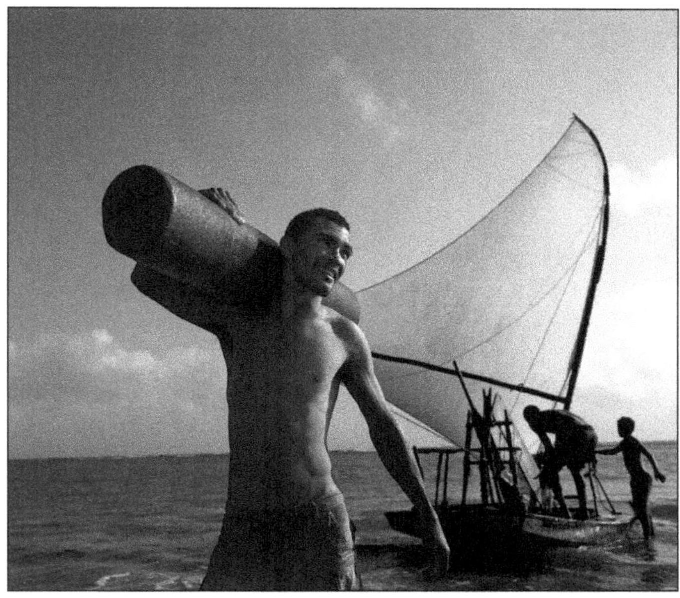

Four Men On A Raft

This story survives almost intact, although there are a few transitions that seem abrupt, as if footage is missing. This part of *It's All True* could be described as a work of love, a work of social commitment, as Welles had been abandoned by the studio with only minimal resources and a skeleton crew of devotees. "Minimal" means little money, a silent camera and black and white film stock.

How he came by the story of the four fishermen from Fortaleza has been well-documented. A feature in *Time Magazine*, the 1600 mile voyage was seen in Homeric terms, even if the adventure was relatively uneventful. Yet it gripped the imagination of the Brazilian public and gained the sympathy of President Vargas, who agreed to extend the social benefits the fishermen and their families had previously been denied.

The cinematic poetry of the big landscape of sky and sea is reminiscent of the classic silents of Eisenstein. No metric montaging to be sure, but we can see Eisenstein in the photographic grouping of the characters and the preference for large groupings seen in the long view, made small yet heroic in the face of an impersonal Nature. One of the most impressive sequences is when the body of the drowned fisherman is carried in a litter from the ocean to a primitive graveyard high on the dunes. We see the entire village strung along the ridges of the dunes, men, women and children, in a grim procession whose ultimate destination might be in the sky itself. The beauty is in the diagonal bisection of Time and Space. The shaping of the clouds is the shaping of the dunes, as if one is a reflection of the other.

Welles used his live theatre experience to good effect in this low budget re-enactment. The fishing community became his ensemble, eagerly participating in his fictional insert, namely, the romance and marriage of the young fisherman and a village girl (played by a then thirteen year old, Francisca Moreira da Silva, who is interviewed in the Wilson-Meisel-Krohn documentary, along with family members of the four *jangadeiros*). His premature death is the crisis which forces the village into action, and four volunteers decide to sail south and appeal for help. The journey is a journey through history, from a peasant feudal society to a bourgeois industrial society. Their arrival in Rio is remarkable for its juxtaposition of cultures. The crude raft with its white sail and simple crew materializes in the bay of a sophisticated city noted for its modernist tropical architecture and beautiful multi-cultural women. Women in swimsuits and shades loll on the sand as they and their playboy consorts look towards the commotion on the water. Fishing boats and pleasure craft swarm out to meet the smiling, triumphant *jangadeiros*. A military Stuka fighter plane makes a low pass....

What we don't see is the big "double wave" that capsizes the raft during the filming of the heroic *jangadeiros*' entry into Guanabara Bay, Rio. We don't see all four *jangadeiros* being tossed into the water and their leader Jacare disappearing below forever. The same day RKO cuts the funding and Welles, trapped by loyalty to his subject and the memory of Jacare, is forced to continue his film by whatever resources he can muster. Naturally, the irony of Jacare's death also becomes a point of political concern: he could survive the original 1600 mile voyage unscathed, yet drowns when performing a simple re-enactment at the behest of a party boy Hollywood director.

Thus Welles inserts the drowning of the newly married fisherman at the beginning, a symbolism for Jacare's Fortune denied.

The Ambassador Wears A Blue Silk Kimono

One, two... one two three four. Etc. Face it, all this dancing makes a man horny. You have your own samba, your own camera, and these aggressive ladies just love an American movie man who can dance. Besides, they know about you and Dolores, so they just have to have a piece of the action. Quickies before lunch, quickies after lunch... all arranged by your secretary who discreetly pretends to see it as business. President Vargas knows it isn't business, though... his spies are always watching, always reporting the erotic details. His spies, always watching... the names, the details... his spies, his movie.

Maybe one of them was the husband of that lovely creature, what's-her-name, was the person who took a shot at you as you lolled on your hotel bed in a blue silk kimono. Bullet tears a hole in the headboard and you swiftly drop to the floor, crawl out to the balcony and escape via the next room.

This is nothing, you already rehearsed this sorta action, last night you were in Hollywood, that movie you and Joe Cotton and Dolores made together, *Journey Into Fear*... only that time you fell from the parapet to your doom. This time you take the elevator, slip out into the throng on the Avenida Atlantica... take refuge in an art gallery where you mingle with some Brazilian acquaintances who insist you join them at a bordello for the evening.

No problem. You're already dressed for the occasion... and nothing like a close encounter with a bullet to stimulate a man's libido.

Ah, Rio! Takes a heavy toll on the body and the expense account. It's tough being a cultural ambassador when some people think you're a commie, others, a Nazi.

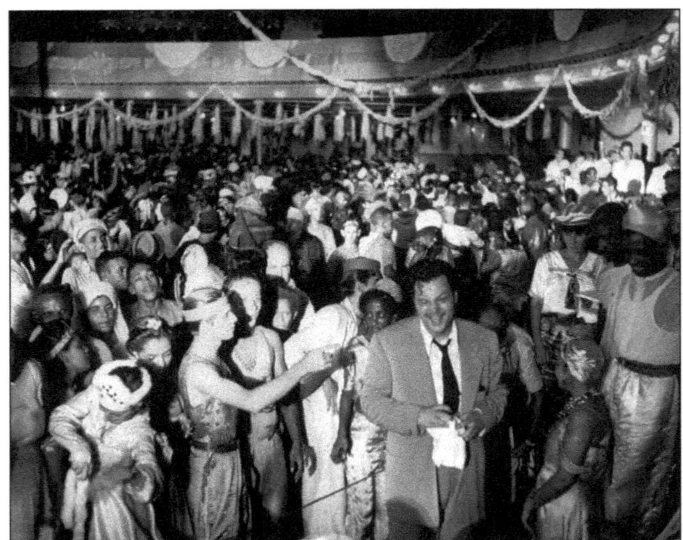

One, two... one two three four... you hate carnivals, actually. You hate all those lunatics spraying you with their atomizers as they dance around... it ain't perfume, buddy, it's ether... that's right, ether. They're all stoned outta their damn minds... so how can you avoid being stoned yourself?

Failure And Mysticism

"It began a pattern of trying to finish a film which has plagued me ever since," says the older Welles, indignantly recalling the fiasco of *It's All True*. Fact is, he did try to finish it.

He paid two hundred grand for the unprocessed footage of *Four Men On A Raft*, worked on it during lunch breaks and at night as he played Rochester in *Jane Eyre*. He had a deal to buy the rest of the film, predicated on the success of his theatre production of *Around The World In Eighty Days*... but the show was a financial flop, and so the fate of *It's All True* was a slow fade into failure and mysticism.

When Scott Fitzgerald died, he left *The Last Tycoon* unfinished, another work from the same Hollywood period. Like the Welles movie, the mystery of its interrupted narrative becomes mystical as the curious impose their fantasies on the design and create a mythology.

Coleridge's *Kubla Khan*, Byron's gothic novel.... The history of art is the blending of fragments and myth. Even work that appears to be finished exists as a extension of a mystery—if it's any good.

* Background info from Barbara Leaming's 1985 bio *Orson Welles* and Charles Higham's 1985 study *Orson Welles: The Rise And Fall Of An American Genius.*

www.ingramcontent.com/pod-product-compliance
Lightning Source LLC
LaVergne TN
LVHW060617110826
845147LV00019B/1040

9780994098245